CW00867463

Studies in Church History

53

(2017)

TRANSLATING CHRISTIANITY

TRANSLATING CHRISTIANITY

EDITED BY

SIMON DITCHFIELD

CHARLOTTE METHUEN

ANDREW SPICER

PUBLISHED FOR
THE ECCLESIASTICAL HISTORY SOCIETY
BY
CAMBRIDGE UNIVERSITY PRESS
2017

Published by Cambridge University Press
on behalf of the Ecclesiastical History Society
University Printing House, Cambridge CB2 8BS, United Kingdom

First published 2017

ISBN 978-1-108-41924-6

ISSN 0424–2084

Bible quotations are taken from the following versions:

The Authorized (King James) Version. Rights in the Authorized Version in the United Kingdom are vested in the Crown. Reproduced by permission of the Crown's patentee, Cambridge University Press.

SUBSCRIPTIONS: *Studies in Church History* is an annual subscription journal (ISSN 0424–2084). The 2017 subscription price (excluding VAT), which includes print and electronic access, is £100 (US $161 in the USA, Canada and Mexico) for institutions and £55 (US $88 in the USA, Canada and Mexico) for individuals ordering direct from the Press and certifying that the volume is for their personal use. An electronic-only subscription is also available to institutions at £78 (US $124 in the USA, Canada and Mexico). Special arrangements exist for members of the Ecclesiastical History Society.

Previous volumes are available online at www.journals.cambridge.org/StudCH

Printed in the United Kingdom by Bell & Bain Ltd
A catalogue record for this publication is available from the British Library

Contents

Preface

Studies in Church History 53 takes as its theme 'Translating Christianity'. It represents the product of the Ecclesiastical History Society's Summer Conference and Winter Meeting for 2015-16, held under the presidency of Simon Ditchfield at the University of York in July 2015 and the Institute for Historical Research, London, in January 2016.

As is clear from this rich collection of articles, which brings together the plenary lectures and a peer-reviewed selection of the communications offered at the Summer Conference and Winter Meeting, translation is fundamental to Christianity and to the spread of its ideas and practices. We would like to thank Professor Ditchfield for encouraging the Society to engage with this fruitful theme, and also for his leadership of the Society as President for 2015-16. Our thanks go too to all who presented papers at these two very stimulating and successful conferences; this was the first year that communications were offered at the Winter Meeting and we are pleased that this proved such a successful initiative. Those who attended these meetings, chaired sessions and participated in the discussions all contributed to the further development of our understanding of the multi-faceted and multi-layered translations of Christianity. The editors are also grateful to the peer reviewers for their time and their insights, and to authors for their willingness to offer their work for publication and to engage with the editorial process. Dr Tim Grass has once again provided unstinting help as Assistant Editor; we would like to thank him for his engagement and the Ecclesiastical History Society for funding his post.

The Summer Conference and Winter Meeting could not have taken place without the efforts of the Society's Conference Secretary, Professor Michael Walsh, the conference team at the University of York, the Society's Secretary, Dr Gareth Atkins, and the staff of the IHR. To them too thanks are also due.

Last, but by no means least, we would like to congratulate Miriam Adan Jones, this year's winner of the Kennedy Prize for the best article by a postgraduate student accepted for publication in Studies in

Church History. This was awarded for her article: 'The Language of Baptism in Early Anglo-Saxon England: The Case for Old English'. We are glad to announce that from 2016–17 the Ecclesiastical History Society will also be awarding an annual President's Prize for the best article by an early career scholar accepted for publication in Studies in Church History.

Charlotte Methuen
University of Glasgow

Andrew Spicer
Oxford Brookes University

Joel Cabrita
Lecturer in World Christianities, Faculty of Divinity, University of Cambridge

Marie Thérèse Champagne
Associate Professor of History, University of West Florida

Simon Ditchfield
Professor of Early Modern History, University of York

Alena A. Fidlerová
Deputy Director, Institute of Czech Language and Theory of Communication, Faculty of Arts, Charles University, Prague

Andrew J. Finch
Independent scholar, Ambleside

James H. Grayson
Emeritus Professor of Modern Korean Studies, School of East Asian Studies, University of Sheffield

Jennifer Hillman
British Academy Postdoctoral Fellow and Lecturer in Early Modern History, University of Chester

Margaret Wiedemann Hunt
Postgraduate student, University of Nottingham

Scott Fitzgerald Johnson
Assistant Professor of Classics and Letters, University of Oklahoma

Miriam Adan Jones
Postgraduate student, Vrije Universiteit Amsterdam

Kirsteen Kim
Professor of Theology and World Christianity, Leeds Trinity University

M. D. Laynesmith
Anglican Chaplain, University of Reading

Darin D. Lenz
Associate Professor of History, Fresno Pacific University

Anne E. Lester
Associate Professor, Department of History, University of Colorado-Boulder

Esther Ruth Liu
Postgraduate student, Cardiff University

Silvia Manzi
Postgraduate student, University of Teramo

Charlotte Methuen
Senior Lecturer in Church History, University of Glasgow

Aislinn Muller
Postgraduate student, University of Cambridge

Andrea Radošević
Senior assistant, Old Church Slavonic Institute

Morgan Ring
Postgraduate student, University of Cambridge

Joan-Pau Rubiés
Research Professor, ICREA (Catalan Institution for Research and Advanced Studies) and Universitat Pompeu Fabra, Barcelona

R. J. W. Shiner
Postgraduate student, Macquarie University

Michael A. L. Smith
Postgraduate student, University of Manchester

Jenny Wong
Postgraduate student, University of Glasgow

Lucy Wooding
Langford Fellow and Tutor in History, Lincoln College, Oxford

ActaSS	*Acta sanctorum*, ed. J. Bolland, G. Henschen et al., (Antwerp etc., 1643–)
AHR	*American Historical Review* (1895–)
AnBoll	*Analecta Bollandiana* (1882–)
ASE	*Anglo-Saxon England* (1972–)
AV	Authorized [King James] Version
BL	British Library
BnF	Bibliothèque nationale Française
CathHR	*Catholic Historical Review* (1915–)
CChr	Corpus Christianorum (Turnhout, 1953–)
CChr.CM	Corpus Christianorum, continuatio medievalis (1966–)
CChr.SL	Corpus Christianorum, series Latina (1953–)
CERS	Church of England Record Society
CHC	*Cambridge History of Christianity*, 9 vols (Cambridge, 2005–9)
ChH	*Church History* (1932–)
DBI	*Dizionario biografico degli italiani* (Rome, 1960–)
DOP	*Dumbarton Oaks Papers* (1941–)
EME	*Early Medieval Europe* (1992–)
ET	English translation
HistJ	*Historical Journal* (1958–)
IRM	*International Review of Missions*, vols 1–57; *International Review of Mission*, vol. 58 on (1912–)
JAH	*Journal of African History* (1960–)
JBS	*Journal of British Studies* (1961–)
JECS	*Journal of Early Christian Studies* (1993–)
JEH	*Journal of Ecclesiastical History* (1950–)
JHI	*Journal of the History of Ideas* (1940–)
JMH	*Journal of Modern History* (1929–)
JMedH	*Journal of Medieval History* (1975–)
JMRS	*Journal of Medieval and Renaissance Studies* (1971–)
JRA	*Journal of Religion in Africa* (1967–)
JRH	*Journal of Religious History* (1960–)
JThS	*Journal of Theological Studies* (1899–)
LPL	Lambeth Palace Library

LW	*Luther's Works*, ed. J. Pelikan and H. Lehmann, 55 vols (St Louis, MO, 1955–75)
MGH	Monumenta Germaniae Historica inde ab a. c. 500 usque ad a. 1500, ed. G. H. Pertz et al. (Hanover, Berlin, etc., 1826–)
MGH AA	Monumenta Germaniae Historica, Auctores antiquissimi, 15 vols (1877–1919)
MGH Epp. Sel.	Monumenta Germaniae Historica, Epistolae Selectae (1916–)
MGH SRG i.u.s.	Monumenta Germaniae Historica, Scriptores rerum Germanicarum in usum scholarum seperatum editi (1871–)
MGH SRM	Monumenta Germaniae Historica, Scriptores rerum Merovingicarum (1884–1951)
n.d.	no date
n.pl.	no place
NPNF I	*A Select Library of Nicene and Post-Nicene Fathers of the Christian Church*, Series I, ed. P. Schaff, 14 vols (New York, 1887–92 and subsequent edns)
n.s.	new series
ODNB	*Oxford Dictionary of National Biography*, ed. H. C. G. Matthew and Brian Harrison (Oxford, 2004)
OED	*Oxford English Dictionary*
OMT	Oxford Medieval Texts
P&P	*Past and Present* (1952–)
PBA	*Proceedings of the British Academy* (1904–)
PL	Patrologia Latina, ed. J.-P. Migne, 217 vols + 4 index vols (Paris, 1844–65)
RB	*Revue Bénédictine* (1890–)
RH	*Recusant History* (1951–2014)
RHE	*Revue d'histoire ecclésiastique* (1900–)
RQ	*Renaissance Quarterly* (1967–)
RTAM	*Recherches de théologie ancienne et médiévale* (1929–97)
s.a.	*sub anno* ('under the year')
SC	Sources Chrétiennes (Paris, 1941–)
SCH	Studies in Church History
SCH S	Studies in Church History: Subsidia
SCJ	*Sixteenth Century Journal* (1970–)
s.n.	*sub nomine* ('under the name')
Speculum	*Speculum: A Journal of Medieval Studies* (1925–)

s.v.	*sub verbo* ('under the word')
TNA	The National Archives (Kew)
TRHS	*Transactions of the Royal Historical Society* (1871–)
WA	*D. Martin Luthers Werke. Kritische Gesamtausgabe*, ed. J. K. F. Knaake, G. Kawerau et al. (Weimar, 1883–)
WA.DB	*D. Martin Luthers Werke. Deutsche Bibel*, 12 vols in 15 (Weimar, 1906–61)

Introduction

I

> All of them were filled with the Holy Spirit and began to speak in other languages, as the Spirit gave them ability.
>
> Now there were devout Jews from every nation under heaven living in Jerusalem. And at this sound the crowd gathered and was bewildered, because each one heard them speaking in the native language of each. Amazed and astonished, they asked, 'Are not all these who are speaking Galileans? And how is it that we hear, each one of us, in our own native language?'[1]

This archetypal depiction of the divine, Pentecostal solution to the challenge posed by linguistic diversity to the spread of Christianity lies at the heart of this volume. How was the curse placed on the citizens of monolingual Babel, who had the temerity to attempt to build a tower that reached heaven (Gen. 11: 1–9), so that God made their speech mutually incomprehensible and scattered them to the winds, to be exorcised, or at least best coped with?

It is well known that early translations of the Bible furnish evidence for the linguistic diversity of an expanding Christian world, involving the invention by missionaries of entirely new alphabets, such as the Armenian, Georgian and Cyrillic. Indeed, it has been observed that Christians were manifestly more 'open-minded' than their pagan (especially Greek and Roman) predecessors vis-à-vis their interest in foreign languages.[2] Tessa Rajak has gone so far as to argue that, at an earlier stage, translation of the Old Testament from Hebrew into Greek (mid-third to mid-second centuries BCE), in the form of the Septuagint, made the survival of the first Jewish diaspora possible (indeed, the very word 'diaspora' was coined by the translators) and thereby laid the foundations for the subsequent spread of the

[1] Acts 2: 4–8 NRSV.

[2] James Clackson, *Language and Society in the Greek and Roman Worlds* (Cambridge, 2015), ch. 6, to which the following account is indebted.

Jewish sect that became Christianity.[3] In this multilingual environment St Paul told his listeners to focus not on the medium but the message: 'My speech and my proclamation were not with plausible words of wisdom, but with a demonstration of the Spirit and of power' (1 Cor. 2: 4 NRSV). Moreover, no less a person than Augustine of Hippo (354–430) in a sermon assumed that his North African listeners would be familiar with a Punic proverb.[4] Nevertheless, to the best of our knowledge the Bible was never translated into a 'minority' language (such as Punic, Phrygian or Gaulish) within the boundaries of the Roman Empire. Coptic and Syriac (a Christian dialect of Aramaic), into which the Bible was translated, were both spoken on the margins of a linguistic zone that was dominated by Latin in the West and Greek in the East; both had their cultural epicentres outside it.[5] Greek was of course the written language of choice for the evangelists and other authors of the books of the New Testament, and even Christ himself, although primarily an Aramaic speaker, appears to have been able to speak Greek when necessary (as can be seen particularly in the Gospel according to Mark).[6] However, as Christianity came to establish itself amongst the elites of the Roman Empire, we can see evidence of a certain defensiveness on the part of writers such as Origen (d. *c.*254), though, as the father of modern biblical criticism, the Oratorian Richard Simon (1638–1712), noted, the early Christian commentator stressed that: 'in his preaching the Holy Apostle [Paul] made known the worth and excellence of the Gospel, not the sapience of human beings, so that the peoples' conversion would be seen as coming from the power of God and not from worldly wisdom'.[7] Further west, Peter Brown has even speculated that Latin, in becoming the marker of the universal Church, delivered the 'knock-out blow to the minority languages of the

[3] Tessa Rajak, *Translation and Survival: The Greek Bible of the Ancient Jewish Diaspora* (Oxford, 2009). For a compelling account of why the Septuagint subsequently lost out to the Hebrew Bible, which Jerome used as the basis for the Old Testament of his Latin (Vulgate) translation, see Timothy Law, *When God spoke Greek: The Septuagint and the Making of the Christian Bible* (Oxford, 2013).

[4] Clackson, *Language and Society*, 147. The sermon in question was no. 167: see John E. Rotelle, ed., *The Works of St Augustine: The Sermons, III/5 (148–183), on the New Testament*, transl. Edmund Hill (New York, 1992), 212 for the Punic proverb.

[5] Clackson, *Language and Society*, 148–9.

[6] Maurice Casey, *Aramaic Sources of Mark's Gospel* (Cambridge, 1998).

[7] Richard Simon, *Critical History of the Text of the New Testament wherein is established the Truth of the Acts on which it is based*, ed. and transl. Andrew Hunwick (Leiden, 2013), 264; cf. *The Philocalia of Origen*, ed. J. Armitage Robinson (Cambridge, 1893), 42.

Roman Empire' and that had the empire fallen in the second century CE rather than the fifth, 'Latin would have vanished along with the Empire in much of Western Europe'.[8]

II

The starting point for the idea of the conference theme lay with the work of the Gambian, Muslim-born Roman Catholic scholar, Lamin Sanneh (b. 1942) whose book *Translating the Message: The Missionary Impact on Culture* (1989) famously identified the distinctiveness of Christian Scripture, unlike that of Judaism or Islam, as lying in its translatability.[9] As Sanneh put it in a later work, 'Christianity is a translated religion without a revealed language. The issue is not whether Christians translated their Scripture well or willingly, but that without translation there would be no Christianity or Christians. Translation is the church's birthmark as well as its missionary benchmark.'[10] Accordingly, he argued, much scope has been given by Christianity to local agents who have indigenized their faith by translating it into their local idioms. This unique capacity of Christianity to particularize the universal has given rise not to 'global Christianity' – which Sanneh regards as a mere counterpart to Western, colonial hegemony – but to 'world Christianity': a 'laboratory of pluralism and diversity where instead of faith and trust being missing or compromised, they remain intrinsic'.[11] However, as Joel Cabrita points out in her contribution to this volume, such a focus 'runs the risk of neglecting the other side of the story: that local Christians across the world have prized highly contact with Christians in the so-called Global North, as well as sustained exchanges with believers in other parts of the southern hemisphere, choosing to stress not only their regional credentials, but also their universalist affiliations'.[12] Moreover, if Christianity's success as a world religion is to be so closely attributed to its linguistic

[8] Peter Brown, *The Rise of Western Christendom: Triumph and Diversity, AD 200–1000,* 10th anniversary rev. edn (Oxford, 2013), 232; Clackson, *Language and Society*, 168.

[9] Lamin Sanneh, *Translating the Message: The Missionary Impact on Culture*, 2nd edn (Maryknoll, NY, 2009).

[10] Lamin Sanneh, *Whose Religion is Christianity: The Gospel beyond the West* (Grand Rapids MI, and Cambridge, 2003), 97.

[11] Ibid. 75.

[12] Joel Cabrita, 'Empire of Healing: South Africa, the United States and the Transatlantic Zionist Movement', 448–75, at 453; cf. eadem, *Text and Authority in the South African Nazaretha Church* (Cambridge, 2014).

translatability, how do we explain the success of Islam, a religion whose holy book is written in the language of its revelation, classical Arabic, which is far from the demotic of Arab speakers? Richard Bulliet has calculated that more than half of the world Muslim community today is composed of descendants of people who converted to Islam between 1500 and 1900. By contrast, under 20 per cent of this planet's present-day Protestants and Catholics have ancestors who converted during the same time period.[13] Moreover, as I observe in my own contribution, after initial, unfortunate experiments, missionaries such as Francis Xavier and José de Acosta recognized the perils of mistranslation and came to insist on the 'untranslatability' of such key concepts as God and the Trinity. Such considerations of the limits of translatability, rather than its triumph, underlie the decision taken in this volume to understand 'translation' in its broader sense: incorporating not only linguistic translation but also the physical movement of sacred objects and even the mental, as well as material, reimagining of holy places and images.[14]

III

The limits of translation are central to Scott Johnson's contribution to this volume. As he puts it, 'the complexity of acculturation is primary, and the degree to which historical cultures are bound by modern preconceptions of their essentials should be made as transparent as possible. This is especially true given the incredible amount of cultural exchange and cross-pollination that went on in Late Antiquity.'[15] However, also core to his argument is the extraordinary resilience and resourcefulness which Christians, in his case Syriac Christians, displayed in the carvings on the so-called Nestorian stele, a 270-cm-high limestone block now on display in the north-western

[13] The lands which converted to Islam during the period included much of the territory covered by the modern-day states of Bangladesh, Malaysia and Indonesia, as well as large groups of sub-Saharan Africans and most of the Muslims of Pakistan, India and China. In addition, one should factor into calculations the substantial populations of south-east Europe and central Asia: Richard Bulliet, *The Case for Islamo-Christian Civilization* (New York, 2004), 40–1.

[14] For a stimulating recent discussion of the contextual significance of the visual dimension to Ignatian spirituality touched upon in this article, see David Morgan, *The Forge of Vision: A Visual History of Modern Christianity* (Oakland, CA, 2015), 35–41.

[15] Scott F. Johnson, 'Silk Road Christians and the Translation of Culture in Tang China', 15–38, at 16.

Chinese city of Xi'an, which was erected in 781 to record the first 150 years or so of Christian history in China. On it these Syriac-Chinese Christians displayed their Middle Eastern heritage through the use of several languages, including the Eastern Iranian language of Sogdian, which inflects several Syriac words carved onto the stele, including *zynst'n* for China (when the more usual Syriac alternative was *Beth Tsinaye*).

On the other side of the globe, in eighth-century Anglo-Saxon England, linguistic resilience of another kind was on display. By means of a careful reading of Bede and Boniface in conjunction with conciliar and liturgical sources, Miriam Adan Jones argues convincingly for the use of the vernacular Old English in baptismal ceremonies. This discovery shows the continued importance, in what was still a relatively young and 'Christianizing' Church, of the need to engage the understanding and compliance of new Christian converts. Translation of a different – physical – kind is the subject of Mark Laynesmith's account of the spread of the cult of St Alban, protomartyr of the English Church, to Merovingian Gaul, where veneration to him was far more widespread than in England itself. Eventually there came to be nearly a hundred churches dedicated to him in France, which may be found as far south as Provence and as far west as Brittany. A key figure in the spread of this cult – made possible also by the spread of Alban's relics – was Germanus, bishop of Auxerre (378–448). Marie-Thérèse Champagne takes us back to the Bible and its translation, specifically to the presence of Jewish scholars in twelfth-century Rome and their influence on translations such as Latin versions of the Book of Psalms.

Anne Lester's refreshingly radical retelling of the story of the translation and appropriation of the numerous relics from Constantinple which entered Western Europe in the aftermath of the sack of the capital of the Eastern Empire in 1204 is less of a stark contrast with Champagne's picture of a community of scholars who shared a common interest than might be expected. This is because Lester is able to demonstrate the degree to which there existed a communication network based on a community of interest in these sacred objects, which circulated openly as gifts, complete with certificates of authentification, over several decades, rather than furtively as booty stolen by the Crusaders and distributed randomly in the West. Arguing that the reason why we know so much about these relics was precisely because they were such 'demanding things', which 'needed to be enshrined, venerated, described and contextualized', she concludes that in the longer-term importation of so many holy objects which were directly associated with Christ had the effect of encouraging trends toward the *vita Apostolica* and *imitatio Christi* that were to shape late medieval devotion. Such approaches to devotion collapsed not only distance but also time, as was to happen again in late sixteenth-century Rome, when the catacombs, that mine of sanctity, came on stream as a seemingly inexhaustible source of relics and, in so doing, brought the early Church back to life for pilgrims to the Eternal City.[16]

Morgan Ring returns our attention to textual translation in her illuminating discussion of the English version of Jacopo de Voragine's thirteenth-century collection of saints' lives, the *Legenda aurea*, published by William Caxton with the collaboration of Wynken de Worde. Together they produced what was, in important respects, a 'new' work that made available in English both Bible stories and Bible paraphrase to priests and laity for whom the legacy of the Lollards had rendered the vernacular Scriptures out of bounds. Lucy Wooding continues the theme of translated language by looking at the various uses to which English translations of Erasmus were put in Henrician England. In short, Wooding shows how the Dutch humanist was 'good to think with': several English authors used their translations of his work to position themselves in relation to the early Reformation.[17] For example, the Bible translator William Tyndale's famous declaration that the 'boy that driveth the plough shall know more scripture than thou dost' was lifted from Erasmus's preface to his Latin translation of the Greek New Testament (based on the text of the fifteenth-century Italian humanist, Lorenzo Valla), the *Novum Instrumentum* of 1517. However, of far greater interest – and significance – for the influence of Christian humanism on the course of the English Reformation, were Erasmus's *Paraphrases* of the New Testament, which the Elizabethan Injunctions instructed must be placed in English parish churches next to the Bible. This article is

[16] See now an important survey of the circulation of catacomb relics throughout the Roman Catholic world from the late sixteenth to the nineteenth century: Stéphane Baciocchi and Christophe Duhamelle, eds, *Reliques romaines. Invention et circulation des corps saints des catacombes à l'époque moderne* (Rome, 2016).

[17] This quotation has its origins in the following anthropological context: 'We can understand, too, that natural species [animals] are chosen not because they are "good to eat" [*bonnes à manger*] but because they are "good to think" [*bonnes à penser*]': Claude Lévi-Strauss, *Totemism* (London, 1964), 89.

complemented by Charlotte Methuen's examination of Luther's *Open Letter on Translation*, as it related to his translation of such key passages as Romans 3: 28, which he saw as central to his doctrine of justification by faith alone. Methuen makes the important point that 'translation was not only a question of textual accuracy but also of defining orthodoxy and heresy'.[18] Luther's translation of this key passage from Romans, among others, was clearly designed to inspire new ways of reading and appreciating the source texts, to paraphrase the American translation theorist, Lawrence Venuti, whose campaign against the invisibility – or illusory transparency – of translation is helpful in reminding not only historians of the Reformation of the necessarily creative and interpretative role of such cultural work.[19]

My own article argues that the age of the Protestant and Catholic Reformations and the global spread of the latter brought with it the challenge that not only was it necessary to learn new languages in order to communicate the Christian message to non-European peoples encountered during the so-called 'Age of Discovery', but some kind of control had to be exercised over the new, global circulation of sacred images and relics. The latter facilitated the visual (and virtual) translation of such holy sites as Jerusalem and Rome and its specific holy treasures in the mental prayers of the faithful. The essay concludes that it was less Lamin Sanneh's 'triumph of [linguistic] translatability' and more the physical translatability of the sacred that made possible the emergence of Roman Catholicism as this planet's first world religion.

This creative dimension is also found in Silvia Manzi's case study of the translation into the vernacular of official instructions – either originally written or conceived in Latin – which were given by Roman Catholic bishops to their clergy and flock in the Italian peninsula. In view of the fierce hostility of the Counter-Reformation Church to the use of the vernacular in worship, this might seem counter-intuitive, but it demonstrates the value placed by post-Reformation Rome on the observance of papal instructions in the form of its official pronouncements – or bulls – as well as the decrees of the Council of Trent, which required the comprehension of those whom the directives were aimed at. However, as Manzi shows, individual bishops

[18] Charlotte Methuen, '"These four letters *s o l a* are not there": Language and Theology in Luther's Translation of the New Testament', 146–63, at 147.
[19] Lawrence Venuti, *The Translator's Invisibility: A History of Translation*, 2nd edn (London and New York, 2008).

used their discretion in how they translated the Latin directives from Rome to modify (and often moderate) this top-down pressure.

With Aislinn Muller's account of the distribution of the bull of excommunication directed at Queen Elizabeth I, *Regnans in excelsis*, we return to the world of things as well as words. Muller usefully reminds us that communication, including that of such dramatic acts to the intended parties, was far from straightforward even in the age of printing. The audience included not only the queen herself but also all those who had dealings with her, including those who traded with England. This explains why the earliest copies of the bull were distributed to the Spanish Netherlands and Poland, both of which were contiguous to regions or cities that had trade or diplomatic links, or both, with England. However, attempts were also made to distribute translations of the bull. Both Jesuits and seminary priests were involved in this dangerous task when the bull was renewed in 1580. Yet ironically it was Protestant reactions to the bull that contributed as much as any other factor to disseminating knowledge of its contents, as can be seen in the English translation of Heinrich Bullinger's reply, which summarized the original bull at some length.

Andrea Radošević makes a compelling case for the argument that translators of biblical passages from Latin performative texts into Croatian used archaisms derived from Croatian Church Slavonic in order to make their text more persuasive. This was because their audience would have been familiar with this kind of language from its place in the liturgy. In this way they adjusted the Latin text not only for lay people but also for priests with limited education. Alena Fidlerová, in her acute analysis of a translation into Czech of a late seventeenth-century German life of the Antichrist by the Capuchin preacher, Dionysius of Luxemburg, reminds us of the linguistic diversity of early modern Moravia and Bohemia; however, as a consequence of the re-Catholicization of the area after the defeat of Catholic forces at the Battle of White Mountain in 1620, Czech subsequently lost out to German. Nevertheless, in testimony to the enduring significance of the Czech language, despite its lesser prestige, there were at least three entirely separate Czech translations of this German work, which have remained largely invisible since they circulated in manuscript.

The demanding or 'needy' nature of relics described by Anne Lester is also encountered in Jennifer Hillman's article on the seventeenth-century fate of the finger of the third-century noble virgin martyr, St Pience. Here we see that by the early modern period the capacity of relics to generate a paper trail had in no way diminished, whether it be passages in visitation records that confirmed their legitimate translation to the private chapel of the duke and duchess of Liancourt at La Roche-Guyon or the 1628 *vita* authored by Nicolas Davanne. Hillman argues that such relics were evidence of the capacity of local post-Tridentine devotion to preserve such particular cults, but also that, in this particular case, the deployment of this cult in such a way confirmed the owners' 'deviant' form of rigorist, Jansenist sympathies.

In his wide-ranging and thought-provoking survey of the many ways in which missionaries attempted to understand non-European peoples in order better to convert them, Joan-Pau Rubiés makes an eloquent case for the need to consider not only their frequently impressive empiricism and systematic nature, but also their essential contribution to the early modern Republic of Letters. In particular, the evidence of cultural diversity that the missionaries brought back and disseminated in print came to be deployed as propaganda in favour of what were not only Christian but also colonial enterprises; moreover, it also offered evidence to use against the attempts of sceptical and atheist freethinkers to undermine the 'Christian project'. It would, however, be anachronistic to view the missionaries simply as 'proto-ethnographers', for, as Rubiés points out, we need to acknowledge fully the religious (specifically soteriological) purpose of their endeavours. We must also be aware of the role of local mediators in such cultural translation, whose contributions make it facile of us to insist on any sharp dichotomies between the Old and New Worlds, traditional and modern, or East and West. Rubiés leaves us with the provocative thought that perhaps an even greater act of translation was that carried out by those attempting to apply the implications of their discoveries to the religious challenges of the Old World.

Michael Smith takes the case study of uses of the Bible in post-Restoration England to argue that Holy Scripture was deployed to manage and foster feelings according to biblical precedent. By demonstrating how biblical citations were appropriated for their readers' own prayers and to frame their devotional activity, a practice which crossed lines of conformity, Smith takes issue with the commonly held view that the period saw both a cooling off in spiritual engagement and increasing religious division.

The next three articles, by Andrew Finch, James Grayson and Kirsteen Kim, all address the various ways in which Christianity was translated – both linguistically and culturally – by missions to east Asia. Finch focuses on the work of two missionaries to Burma – the Italian Barnabite, Vincenzo Sangermano (*fl.* 1783–1806), and the French vicar apostolic of the Missions étrangères de Paris, Paul Ambrose Bigandet (*fl.* 1838–94) – to show how the first stage in missionary translation was the challenge of understanding the dominant faith of the society being proselytized, in this particular case Theravāda Buddhism. Finch shows how the translation strategies adopted by Sangermano and Bigandet involved complex linguistic journeys: in the case of Bigandet, from Burmese or Pali to (probably) French, then English and then once more back into French. Moreover, for this French missionary, as for many of Rubiés's missionaries in a slightly earlier period, translations of texts from a non-European faith were informed not only by the desire to understand better 'the enemy' in order to defeat them in the missionary field, but also by the wish to demonstrate to those in Europe that such non-Christian texts were defective and 'wrong'. As Finch puts it at the close of his article: 'Implicit in Bigandet's interpretation of Burmese Buddhism is a defence of Christianity in Europe.'[20] For John Ross (1842–1915), the protagonist of Grayson's compelling account of the first translation of the New Testament into Korean, China remained the chief preoccupation of his career and energies as a missionary in north-east Asia. Indeed, because Korea was a 'closed' country, Ross was unable to penetrate the country in person (only briefly visiting it on a single occasion in 1887), and so his mission *was* his translation. Furthermore, it was one that also 'spread literacy [in Korea], promoted a sense of nationalism in difficult times [particularly under Japanese occupation], and left an important linguistic record of a regional dialect for use as a resource for scholars'.[21] In a contrasting approach to the Korean Christian Church in a later period, 1895–1910, that of its most rapid growth, Kirsteen Kim argues that in order to understand fully this phenomenon we need to move beyond Sanneh's translation theory, which Kim convincingly critiques, and consider instead the 'reinvention of the Church' in the sense inspired by John Parratt's

[20] Andrew J. Finch, 'Translating Christianity and Buddhism: Catholic Missionaries in Eighteenth- and Nineteenth-Century Burma', 324–37, at 337.

[21] James H. Grayson, 'John Ross and Cultural Encounter: Translating Christianity in an East Asian Context', 338–58, at 358.

work on Christian theology in Africa.[22] This alternative approach, she argues, gives more space to the agency of those on the receiving end of missionaries' efforts. Viewed from this perspective, as Kim concludes, 'Christianity was not so much *translated* into the Korean vernacular as it was *reinvented* to serve the need for the independence and modernization of the nation in its darkest hour.'[23]

Esther Liu looks at the work of the French Protestant missionary to Africa, François Coillard (1834–1904), to argue that such missionary-translators still have something to say to translation theory today. Echoing Venuti's preoccupation, cited above, that translators should keep their work 'visible' to the eyes (and ears) of their audiences, Coillard evidently believed that they should be both visible and invisible. On the one hand, he carefully presented his own (not inconsiderable) public profile as Christian missionary and translator, but on the other, he equally consciously tried to withdraw from centre stage in his own field work. As he put it in his account of his own work in Lesotho, echoing Christ's own sacrifice: 'It is [the] gospel and not the preacher which is the power of God'.[24] In addition, the entirely collaborative nature of Coillard's translation practice has a contribution to make to current translation theory, in which the translators' craft is still often (mis)understood as taking place in isolation.

Building on the idea of translation as rewriting and thus as reinterpretation in terms of the categories and values of the target language, as theorized by the Belgian André Lefevere (1945–96), Jenny Wong considers the translation and reception of Shakespeare in China in the nineteenth and twentieth centuries, and specifically at *The Merchant of Venice*. She notes how, traditionally, Chinese translations excised religious references in the play, but asks whether, with the economic and cultural 'opening' of China from the 1980s, such untranslatability might be overturned. The degree to which the very notion of enforced religious conversion is alien to Confucianism and Taoism, which champion social harmony and order, suggests otherwise.

[22] In a pioneering study, John Parratt, *Reinventing Christianity: African Theology Today* (Grand Rapids MI, 1995).

[23] Kirsteen Kim, 'The Evangelization of Korea, *c.*1895–1910: Translation of the Gospel or Reinvention of the Church?', 359–75, at 375 (emphasis added).

[24] Edouard Favre, *François Coillard. Missionnaire au Lessouto (1861–1882)* (Paris, 1912), 147; see Esther Ruth Liu, 'The Nineteenth-Century Missionary-Translator: Reflecting on Translation Theory through the Work of François Coillard (1834–1904)', 376–88, at 383.

Margaret Wiedemann Hunt considers the translation work undertaken in 1941 by Dorothy L. Sayers (1893–1957) from the Greek New Testament for her twelve-part radio dramatization of the life of Christ for the BBC, *The Man Born to be King*. Sayers is undoubtedly better known as the creator of the fictional protagonist of the popular series of detective novels, Lord Peter Wimsey, published in the 1920s and early 1930s, and then, at the end of her career, as the translator of the widely distributed Penguin edition of Dante's *Divina Commedia* (1949–62). Hunt places Sayers's radio adaptation of the life of Christ, which reached over two million listeners, in the wider context of her role as a lay Christian apologist. This included Sayers's idea for what she referred to as her 'Oecumenical Penguin', which was to be an accessible one-volume presentation of the ideas shared by the mainstream Christian denominations. Although this particular project never came to fruition, *The Man Born to be King* was clearly intended to fulfil a similar need for a translation of theology into terms that were comprehensible to the 'general reader'. How better to do this than to dramatize the life of Christ? As Hunt shows, although the words Sayers gave to Christ himself were close to the New Testament text, she did take imaginative liberties in the dialogue she wrote for other protagonists, including the apostles. Hunt concludes with a plea for more work to be done on Sayers's role as a leading practitioner of the literary arts in the name of Christianity in the middle decades of the twentieth century.

In what is in many ways a complementary article exploring the use of modern audio technology in translating Christianity to reach unprecedentedly numerous audiences, Darin Lenz looks at the work of the missionary Joy Ridderhof (1903–84). Unable to continue her work in the field owing to illness, Ridderhof sought to fulfil her ambitions to communicate the gospel to those who otherwise would not hear it by having recourse to the still-new technology of the phonograph, founding Gospel Recordings in 1939.[25] Ridderhof began by producing recordings in Spanish, but soon branched out into making recordings in many of the indigenous languages of central and south America, which facilitated access to 'primitive peoples' (for which read 'illiterate') who had not yet been exposed in any sustained

[25] Gospel Recordings is now referred to as Global Recordings Network and offers recordings in more than 6,000 languages: 'Global Recordings Network', <http://globalrecordings.net/en/>, accessed 22 October 2016.

fashion to stories from the gospels. After first using non-native speakers to record the stories and prayers, Ridderhof later took great care to employ indigenous speakers of the tongues being recorded so that her project has, inadvertently, become something of an archive of minority languages which have subsequently died out. Finally, Lenz leaves us with the subversive possibility that many of those who heard these recordings were actually 'converted' to the medium – which by the 1960s included ingenious hand-cranked phonographs made cheaply of cardboard – rather than to the gospel message itself.

R. J. W. Shiner also addresses the matching of medium to message in his illuminating article on how Donald Robinson rose to the challenge of translating the faith in Australia and helping Australians 'speak to God' by bringing sensitivity and principle to the drafting of the 1978 *Australian Prayer Book*. Shiner makes the important point that Robinson's failure to reverse the tide of secularism should not be conflated with a failure in either the conception or implementation of the prayer book, but must rather be viewed in the wider context of the 'death of Christian Australia' (at least the white Western mainstream), which arguably reached its high watermark precisely in the 1970s.[26]

The volume closes with Joel Cabrita's thoughtful and richly satisfying discussion of the nineteenth-century religious movement founded by a Scottish immigrant to Illinois, the Edinburgh-born John Alexander Dowie (1847–1907), who founded the city of Zion as part of a Protestant divine healing movement. This first took root in Illinois before being exported to South Africa where it was reimagined by Isaiah Shembe (1870–1935). In 1910 Shembe in turn founded the Nazareth Baptist Church in a very different context of Southern African territorial dispossession and racial segregation. Despite its transatlantic origins, this Church has been viewed by scholars, including the missionary historian Bengt Sundkler and the anthropologist Jean Comaroff, as an expression of Afro-Christian indigeneity.[27] By

[26] For an example of this explanatory paradigm as applied to Britain, see Callum Brown, *The Death of Christian Britain: Secularisation 1800–2000* (London and New York, 2001). However, the near-contemporary publication of Grace Davie, *Europe: The Exceptional Case. Parameters of Faith in the Modern World* (London, 2002) is a reminder that the secularization paradigm was – and remains – only of limited application.

[27] See Jacob Olupona, *African Religions: A Very Short Introduction* (Oxford, 2014), 101, where there is a photograph with the following caption: 'A Shembe Church ceremony on Palm Sunday, near Durban, South Africa. The Shembe Church, also known as the Nazareth Baptist Church, is an indigenous African Church that borrows from both indigenous Zulu traditions and Christianity.'

contrast, Cabrita argues compellingly that both Churches should be understood as responses to the common challenges of the demand for cheap labour by industrialization and of its impact on health, whether these be located in the railroad and commodity hub that was Chicago or in the consequences of the actions of the gold-hungry mine owners of the Transvaal. This has implications, she argues, for how we should go about understanding the ways in which Christianity was 'translated' to sub-Saharan Africa. In contrast to the still widely influential paradigm framed by Sanneh with which I opened this introduction, Cabrita highlights the potential dangers of African essentialism and the need to be open to the ways in which localization of Christian belief was achieved by means of transnational reception and reinterpretation.

Such a picture of cosmopolitan localism is an appropriate point at which to bring to a close this introduction to a volume devoted to the translation of Christianity and circulation of the sacred. If, as has been recently restated by Charles Taylor, language does not merely describe but constitutes meaning and shapes human experience, and linguistic capacity is not something that we innately possess, then it follows that we first learn our language from others, so that our separate selves emerge out of the conversation.[28] We ourselves come into being through a process of translation. These articles are intended to be contributions to that ongoing conversation: long may it continue.

Simon Ditchfield

[28] Charles Taylor, *The Language Animal: The Full Shape of the Human Linguistic Capacity* (Cambridge, MA, 2016).

Silk Road Christians and the Translation of Culture in Tang China

Scott Fitzgerald Johnson*
University of Oklahoma

This article attempts to analyse the famous 'Nestorian Monument' from Xi'an, set up in 781 by Syriac Christians, as a document of cultural translation and integration. Previous scholarship on the monument has tended to privilege either the Syriac or the Chinese sections of the inscription. By combining the two, and by making use of recent advances in the study of Syriac Christians along the Silk Road, this article argues that the Syriac Christians who set up the monument were using their long history, extending from Persia to China, as a means of establishing their community publicly in new political circumstances of China in the 780s. The role of Syriac on this monument was twofold: it signalled to the local Syriac-speaking community their fundamental ties to the world of Persian and central Asian Christianity, while it also allowed, through ideological and linguistic interaction with Chinese, the maintenance of a Syriac Christian identity through the process of translation. The language of Syriac therefore provides the background of a community looking both backward and forward in a foreign, changing cultural environment.

Introduction

In an article entitled 'Ways to Go and Not Go in the Contextualisation of the Jingjiao Documents of the Tang Period', historian of premodern China Max Deeg makes a provocative statement that may not seem so provocative on the surface: 'No Chinese Jingjiao text [i.e. text in Chinese written by Christians] … has a direct parallel in Syriac or another relevant – let us say Central Asian – language in which

* University of Oklahoma, Department of Classics and Letters, Carnegie Hall, Norman, OK 73019, USA. E-mail: sfj@ou.edu.

I would like to thank Peter Brown, Averil Cameron, Simon Ditchfield and Geoffrey Goble for their assistance in improving this article. The scholarly audience of the Ecclesiastical History Society's Winter 2016 Meeting was highly engaging and provided many excellent suggestions for improvement which found their way into the article.

Studies in Church History 53 (2017) 15–38
doi: 10.1017/stc.2016.3

Nestorian texts are preserved.'[1] I would like to take this quotation as a starting point. Deeg here is talking about Jingjiao, the so-called 'Luminous Religion' in Chinese, the name that East Syriac Christians adopted in trying to communicate their beliefs within a culture very foreign to their own. There is, however, no single word expressing 'religion' in Chinese, and the word *jiao* is often translated simply as 'teaching'. When coupled with *jing* ('the luminous') the translation of this key term is perhaps better rendered as 'the teaching of/about the luminous', in parallel to *daojiao*, 'the teaching of/about the Dao', or *fojiao*, 'the teaching of/about the Buddha'.[2] The question then becomes: what is 'the luminous' and how does it relate to Christianity? To put it more theoretically, almost immediately in this discussion the issue of transmission and intercultural exchange can be seen as a problem of definitions and essentials, and equally a problem of self-definition and self-expression in non-native environments.

Each of the proper names in Deeg's statement – Chinese, Jingjiao, Christian, Syriac, central Asian, Nestorian – will be discussed in what follows, although it should be emphasized that each is a world unto itself and cannot be fully debated here.[3] Nevertheless, I hope that by focusing on definitions and the debates surrounding them the question of the limits of cultural transmission can come to the fore. In a volume devoted to translation as an activity of the Church writ large, the complexity of acculturation is primary, and the degree to which historical cultures are bound by modern preconceptions of their essentials should be made as transparent as possible. This is especially true given the incredible amount of cultural exchange and cross-pollination that went on in Late Antiquity. I would argue that it is imperative for historians to find ways for the cultures of the Silk Road and China to maintain their ability to self-define in new and creative ways. The East Syriac Christians crossed so many seemingly unbridgeable boundaries (at least from the historian's perspective), and so much emphasis has been placed on their arrival in Chang'an

[1] Max Deeg, 'Ways to Go and Not Go in the Contextualisation of the Jingjiao Documents of the Tang Period', in Dietmar W. Winkler and Li Tang, eds, *Hidden Treasures and Intercultural Encounters: Studies on East Syriac Christianity in China and Central Asia*, Orientalia-Patristica-Oecumenica 1 (Vienna, 2009), 139–52.

[2] I am grateful to my Sinologist colleague Geoffrey Goble for his assistance with the Chinese nomenclature throughout this article.

[3] Many of the basic problems with the terminology are discussed in Samuel N. C. Lieu, 'Epigraphica Nestoriana Serica', in *Exegisti Monumenta: Festschrift in Honour of Nicholas Sims-Williams*, ed. W. Sundermann, A. Hintze and F. de Blois (Wiesbaden, 2009), 227–46.

in the seventh century, that it will be valuable to reconsider our foundational definitions of the people-groups involved, with special attention to the language and ideas they used to define themselves.

The example I will use to discuss these themes is that of Syriac Christianity. This subject is, of course, topical: a significant number of the refugees from Syria and Iraq presently seeking refuge in Europe and elsewhere are Christians. Of the Christians amongst these refugees, nearly all can claim, in one way or another, the language of Syriac as part of their inheritance, even if today their liturgies are celebrated in Arabic. My goal in this article is to discuss one episode from the heritage of Syriac Christianity. In particular, I will consider the arrival of Syriac Christians in Tang China. I am especially interested in how the Christians themselves thought of that arrival and how they translated their cultural and religious world into a Chinese milieu. What did they retain from where they had been before? Were they integrated into the culture? What role did linguistic translation play in that integration? I shall consider Syriac as a 'cultural actor' in its own right or as having a 'social presence' in the cultures in which it was used and spoken, particularly in its role as the medium of translation. Some necessary background will be given at the beginning to situate the Syriac language and the significance of Syriac Christians' presence in China. It is hoped that, despite the specificity of the evidence presented below, the example of Christianity in Tang China will offer avenues for the exploration of the role of translation in the history of the Church in other times and places.

Syriac, Empire and Translation

Syriac is a dialect of Aramaic, which was the imperial language of ancient Assyria in the first millennium BCE and which, during the Roman Empire, was the main language spoken by Jews in the provinces of Judea and Palestine, including Jesus himself. Syriac was originally simply the version of Aramaic spoken in the city of Edessa (modern Urfa in south-eastern Turkey). Edessa had been founded by the successors of Alexander the Great in the region, the Seleucids. From the second century BCE to the third century CE, Edessa remained an independent city-state ruled primarily by the Abgarid dynasty. Only in 213 CE did it come under direct Roman rule, having been made a colony by Septimius Severus. Coincident with becoming a Roman colony, Edessa was also Christianized, though via a different vector because the Roman Empire was not Christian at this point. One early legend, known to the earliest Church historian, Eusebius of Caesarea, recounted that Edessa's king Abgar had corresponded with Jesus and been healed by his disciples.[4] For these reasons, both legendary and not, Syriac claims an early and venerable Christian tradition in northern Mesopotamia and Roman Syria.

It is all the more surprising, therefore, that, despite its deep roots in the Hellenistic, Near Eastern and Roman cultural spheres, Syriac never became either an imperial language or a language of power and law (*Rechtssprache*). During the period during when Edessa was under the Roman Empire (later the Byzantine Empire, ruled from Constantinople), Syriac was a subaltern language distinctive of a group on the margins of imperial power and influence. Nonetheless, it was a vibrant and valuable language for many groups. In linguistic terms it was both a 'vehicular' language, in the sense that Syriac was used as a translation language via which texts were mediated from Greek into Semitic and other languages (e.g. Armenian and Georgian), and also a 'prestige' language, in the sense that texts which had originally been produced in Syriac were sought after by speakers of Greek and other languages and consequently translated into those languages.[5] Culturally speaking, from Late Antiquity to today Syriac has been known as the language of specific Christian groups with distinctive theologies and liturgies.[6]

[4] This reported correspondence appears at the end of Book 1 of Eusebius's *Ecclesiastical History*. However, Eusebius seems to have known less about the Syriac Church than he suggests: Sebastian P. Brock, 'Eusebius and Syriac Christianity', in Harold W. Attridge and Gohei Hata, eds, *Eusebius, Christianity, and Judaism* (Detroit, MI, 1992), 212–34. Elsewhere, Brock argues that the Syriac Churches constitute 'a third lung' for early Christianity, in addition to its more familiar Greek and Latin traditions: Sebastian P. Brock, 'The Syriac Orient: A Third "Lung" for the Church?', *Orientalia Christiana Periodica* 71 (2005), 5–20.

[5] The vehicular and prestige aspects of late antique multilingualism have been explored by J. N. Adams, *Bilingualism and the Latin Language* (Cambridge, 2003), for Latin, empire-wide; Roger S. Bagnall, *Early Christian Books in Egypt* (Princeton, NJ, 2009), for Greek, in Egypt; and Arietta Papaconstantinou, '"They shall speak the Arabic Language and take Pride in it": Reconsidering the Fate of Coptic after the Arab Conquest', *Le Muséon* 120 (2007), 273–99; eadem, ed., *The Multilingual Experience in Egypt, from the Ptolemies to the Abbasids* (Farnham, 2010), for Coptic and Arabic in Egypt. I have attempted to place Greek in the same sociolinguistic landscape across the eastern Mediterranean in Late Antiquity: Scott Fitzgerald Johnson, 'The Social Presence of Greek in Eastern Christianity, 200–1200 CE', in idem, ed., *Languages and Cultures of Eastern Christianity: Greek*, The Worlds of Eastern Christianity 300–1500 6 (Farnham 2015), 1–122.

[6] During the fifth and sixth centuries, Syriac Christians split into three different groups: East Syrian (formerly 'Nestorians'), West Syrian ('Monophysites') and

After the Arab conquests of the 630s and 640s, the majority of Syriac-speaking Christians, regardless of their ecclesiastical affiliation, were under the imperial rule of the Islamic Caliph. It is in this context that Syriac became a crucial vehicular language in Abbasid Baghdad where, around 800, Syriac Christians were employed by the caliph to translate a host of Greek philosophical texts into Arabic. They did so by translating first from Greek to Syriac, and then from Syriac to Arabic.[7] This 'translation movement' produced, in particular, Arabic translations of Aristotle that eventually found their way into medieval Spain (*al-Andalus*) and were translated there into Latin. It was through these translations that medieval theologians like Thomas Aquinas became acquainted with a much broader range of Aristotelian thought. The translation movement in Baghdad included scholars such as Hunayn ibn Ishaq, whose translation practices have been carefully studied by, among others, the Syriacist Sebastian Brock.[8] Brock emphasizes that Hunayn was working within a long intra-Syriac tradition of translation. Indeed, Hunayn and his fellow translators very often signalled that they were making use of earlier Syriac translations of

Chalcedonian ('Melkites'). The basic outlines of these theological differences can be found in Sebastian P. Brock, 'The Christology of the Church of the East in the Synods of the Fifth to Early Seventh Centuries: Preliminary Considerations and Materials', in idem, *Fire from Heaven: Studies in Syriac Theology and Liturgy* (Aldershot, 2006), 125–42. The labels 'Nestorian' and 'Monophysite' are considered derogatory and are not used by scholars out of respect for the modern-day adherents of these groups. In the Syriac world, these labels correspond to the living traditions of the Church of the East and the Syrian Orthodox respectively. The term 'Melkites' (Greek *melchitai*) – a late eighth-century coinage – comes ultimately from the Aramaic *malkā*, 'king', translating the Greek *basileus*, 'emperor'; they were, we might say, theological royalists (*basilikoi*). In the period, though not today, 'Melkite' was a derogatory label applied to them by their non-Chalcedonian co-religionists in the East. The term today signifies ecclesiastically the Christians under the Eastern Rite Catholic Patriarchate of Antioch. The ancient Melkites are today called Rūm Orthodox, from the Arabic term for the Byzantine Greeks.

[7] The scholarly touchstone for this movement has long been Dimitri Gutas, *Greek Thought, Arabic Culture: The Graeco-Arabic Translation Movement in Baghdad and Early 'Abbāsid Society (2nd–4th / 8th–10th Centuries)* (London, 1998), although his work has been strongly criticized for downplaying Syriac's role in this process. Garth Fowden, *Before and after Muhammad: The First Millennium Refocused* (Princeton, NJ, 2014), redresses the balance to some degree.

[8] Sebastian P. Brock, 'The Syriac Background to Hunayn's Translation Techniques', *Aram* 3 (1991), 139–62; idem, 'Changing Fashions in Syriac Translation Technique: The Background to Syriac Translations under the Abbasids', *Journal of the Canadian Society for Syriac Studies* 4 (2004), 3–14.

Greek works, and they critiqued and refined those Syriac translations even as they prepared their Arabic ones for the caliph.

Hunayn and his fellow Christian scholars who translated this literature were East Syrian (pejoratively 'Nestorian') Christians. I will refrain, however, from using the adjective 'East Syrian' because it conjures origins for this group in the geographical area of eastern Syria, which was the case only while the Syriac churches were unified and shared a common heritage, that is, prior to the fifth century. By contrast, 'East Syriac' refers to a distinctive variety of Syriac, especially in terms of literary and theological tradition, but also at the level of script and pronunciation. These were in reality the 'Persian Christians' who, since the Council of Ephesus in 431, had been ecclesiastically separate from Christians in the Roman Empire.[9] This was partly due to geopolitical factors – they were indeed in a different empire, that of Sasanian Persia, until the Islamic conquests – but also because the Western Churches had deemed them heretical in their Christology. The East Syriac or Persian Christians were associated in the West with Nestorius, the patriarch of Constantinople who had been anathematized and exiled as a heretic after the Council of Ephesus. Until that point (and for a while afterwards too, as the dust settled), the Persian Christians were affiliated with the patriarchate of Antioch and claimed two Antiochene exegetes, Diodore of Tarsus and Theodore of Mopsuestia, as their founding fathers. Regardless of these ties, however, the Persian Christians always faced East, and their formal disassociation from the Roman Empire only put into law what had been logistically the case already. Language was one key determinant in this regard. Unlike the Chalcedonian and Miaphysite (also known as 'Monophysite') branches of Syriac Christianity, the Church of the East never used Greek as a liturgical or literary language, and, as we shall see, the significance of Syriac in this unique tradition was carried everywhere they went.

East Syriac Christians were a part of a wide-ranging ecclesiastical body, one which was in constant and direct contact with Islam after the Arab conquests. However, the most eastward branch of East Syriac Christianity seems to have been less concerned with

[9] For the history of the Church of the East, see Wilhelm Baum and Dietmar W. Winkler, *The Church of the East: A Concise History* (London 2003); Joel Walker, 'From Nisibis to Xi'an: The Church of the East across Sasanian Persia', in Scott F. Johnson, ed., *The Oxford Handbook of Late Antiquity* (Oxford, 2012), 994–1052.

Islam and Arabic than it was with local indigenous cultures and languages along the silk routes. In this cultural matrix, it resembled much more the Manichaeism of Iran and central Asia than it did its own co-religionists in the Levant and Mesopotamia. It was through this eastward branch that much Syriac literature was translated into Middle Persian and especially Sogdian, and through Sogdian into Uighur, a Turkic language of western China.[10] It was also through this branch that Syriac literature and ideas found their way into Chinese and, consequently, that the first formal relationship developed between an eastern Mediterranean culture and the imperial court of China. The Syriac Christians in China were in origin central Asian Christians who, in the course of the fifth, sixth and seventh centuries had already translated their literature, and indeed their cultural outlook, from Syriac into Iranian languages, notably the east Iranian language of Sogdian, used by a major trading society covering the whole of central Asia.

However, what I hope to emphasize in this article is that, to tell the story of this eastward movement across the silk routes, it is imperative to begin at the end, with Christianity in China. This is because the evidence from China offers the best clues to the identity, culture and self-understanding of the East Syriac Christians across central Asia at the end of Late Antiquity. It is also because Christians in China produced the most significant, self-reflective and ultimately perplexing surviving artefact that speaks to the continuity of Syriac tradition across central Asia and especially to its willingness to adopt new foreign cultures and to integrate itself into them.

[10] We know of these translations and Christian literature in these languages largely through the discoveries at Turfan (western China) in the early twentieth century. Ideally that literature would be read in conjunction with the texts surviving in Chinese. See the articles in the following collected volumes for collaborative attempts at doing just that: Roman Malek, ed., *Jingjiao: The Church of the East in China and Central Asia*, Collectanea Serica (Sankt Augustin, 2006); Li Tang and Dietmar W. Winkler, eds, *From the Oxus River to the Chinese Shores: Studies on East Syriac Christianity in China and Central Asia*, Orientalia-Patristica-Oecumenica 5 (Vienna, 2013); Winkler and Tang, eds, *Hidden Treasures and Intercultural Encounters*; and now (unpublished at the time of the writing of this article) Li Tang and Dietmar W. Winkler, eds, *Winds of Jingjiao: Studies on Syriac Christianity in China and Central Asia* (Zürich, 2016). I have discussed the Turfan materials as evidence for Syriac along the silk routes in 'The Languages of Christianity on the Silk Roads and the Transmission of Mediterranean Culture into Central Asia', in Nicola di Cosmo and Michael Maas, eds, *Empires and Exchanges in Eurasian Late Antiquity: Rome, China, Iran, and the Steppes* (Cambridge, forthcoming).

The Nestorian Stele of Chang'an

The designation Jingjiao, introduced above, appears on the famous Nestorian Stele that was set up in Chang'an in 781 to commemorate the history and beliefs of Christians in China.[11] The stele opens, strikingly, with a short summary of Christian doctrine, one which is remarkably complete. It includes the following elements, listed in their order of appearance (§§3–10): a singular, all-powerful triune God; the creation, including the creation of humankind; Satan and the fall; the incarnation; the virgin birth; the ascension; twenty-seven books (*jiao*, 'teachings') left by the Messiah (i.e. the New Testament); baptism as initiation; the cross as an emblem ('the figure of ten'); monks as the Messiah's followers; a weekly discipline of repentance; and an emphasis on holiness. Notable in their absence are the New Testament events or doctrines of the crucifixion and resurrection. At the end of their recounting these are labelled collectively as the Jingjiao, the 'Luminous Teaching'. The stele goes on to tell the story that in the year 635 the first Christian missionary, Alopen, was received at the court of the Emperor Taizong (626–49). It then incorporates verbatim the edict from 638 granting permission for Christianity to be practised in China. This new appellation of Jingjiao in the Chinese context seems partly to coincide with the imperial view of the religion: as Taizong proclaimed in this edict: 'The way does not have a constant name, and the holy does not have a constant form. Teachings are established according to the locality, and their mysteries aid mankind' (§12). The edict also includes the official commissioning of a monastery in Chang'an with twenty-one monks to be ordained there.[12] It then offers a short dynastic history of the

[11] For the Nestorian Stele, I use throughout this article the edition, translation and commentary produced by L. Eccles and S. N. C. Lieu: '大秦景教流行中國碑, Stele on the Diffusion of the Luminous Religion of Da Qin (Rome) in the Middle Kingdom', 27 July 2016, online at: <http://www.mq.edu.au/__data/assets/pdf_file/0007/55987/Xian-Nestorian-Monument-27-07-2016.pdf>, accessed 4 November 2016. The editors have divided the inscription into verses, the Chinese verses marked by brackets and numbered, and the Syriac verses marked by brackets with 'S' prefacing the number. While Paul Pelliot, *L'Inscription nestorienne de Si-Ngan-Fou*, ed. Antonino Forte (Kyoto, 1996), remains the standard edition and commentary for the stele, he does not edit or comment on the Syriac text, which makes reading the monument as a whole through his edition more difficult.

[12] On this edict and other sources for it in Chinese literature, see Forte's comments, in Pelliot, *L'Inscription nestorienne*, 49–373.

bishops and emperors of China and their relations, up to the date of its installation.[13]

The stele, discovered in 1623, stands today in the Forest of Stelae Museum in Xi'an.[14] It is 270 cm high, 105 cm wide and 30 cm thick. It is inscribed with classical Chinese and Syriac inscriptions. An elegantly carved Chinese inscription – 1,756 characters over 32 lines – occupies the majority of the front face, and the Syriac inscription, in reality a colophon, occupies a small section of the front face at the bottom. The sides of the stele list names of clergy in both Syriac and Chinese. All told, there are three hundred Syriac words and names on the stele. In the introductory quotation above, Deeg is attempting to reset modern expectations of what we might find on this monument and in other exempla of Chinese Christianity, including twelve important texts written by this community that were found at Dunhuang early in the twentieth century.[15]

I would like to argue that the Nestorian Stele should be read as a piece of historiography. That is, the stele organizes knowledge about the past and publishes it in a systematic (albeit in part propagandistic) manner.[16] Moreover, the stele is the single piece of sustained

[13] The dynastic history (§§13–22) is too long to summarize here, but notable events that could be explored in more detail include the requirement to display the emperor's portrait in churches or monasteries ('temples'), the persecution of Christians in Chang'an in 713 and their restoration under the Emperor Xuanzong, the celebration of Christian liturgy in the Xinqing palace in 744, and the rebuilding and embellishment of churches or monasteries ('temples') by the Emperor Suzong. No mention is made of any emperor converting to Christianity, but several of the Tang emperors are described as highly favourable to the religion.

[14] See Lieu, 'Epigraphica Nestoriana Serica', for a physical description of the stele; and Michael Keevak, *The Story of a Stele: China's Nestorian Monument and its Reception in the West, 1625–1916* (Hong Kong, 2008), for a history of its reception in the West.

[15] See the translation and contextualization of these documents by Li Tang, *A Study of the History of Nestorian Christianity in China and its Literature in Chinese: Together with a new English Translation of the Dunhuang Nestorian Documents* (Frankfurt am Main, 2004), 103–204; see also her study of the Chinese Christian inscription discovered at Luoyang: Li Tang, 'A Preliminary Study on the *Jingjiao* Inscription of Luoyang: Text Analysis, Commentary, and English Translation', in Winkler and Tang, eds, *Hidden Treasures and Intercultural Encounters*, 109–33.

[16] Indeed, the noted Syriacists Muriel Debié and David Taylor included the Nestorian Stele in a notable article surveying Syriac historiography and chronicle-writing: Muriel Debié and David G. K. Taylor, 'Syriac and Syro-Arabic Historical Writing, *c.*500–*c.*1400', in Sarah Foot and Chase Robinson, eds, *The Oxford History of Historical Writing*, 2: *400–1400* (Oxford, 2012), 155–79. However, in her recent magisterial monograph on the writing of history in Syriac, Debié concludes that the stele is not a piece of Syriac historiography but rather a public document seeking to explain each culture to the other, arising from a

self-reflection on the movement of Christians across the Silk Routes to China and as such has an evidentiary value that is unparalleled. This is where Deeg's provocative statement on the content of the stele comes into play. For Deeg, the Nestorian Stele is 'linguistically and culturally Chinese' and it shares more with contemporaneous Chinese literature than with anything else, including the Christian manuscripts found at Dunhuang.[17] Moreover, when taken as a whole – that is, the stele and the Dunhuang manuscripts together – there is only one text that can be verbally identified with a known Syriac text, the *Gloria in excelsis Deo.*[18] Thus we are thrown immediately into the problem of cultural 'loans' and the adaptation of the essentials of Syriac Christianity to autochthonous Chinese norms.[19] Essentialization of religions, languages and cultural systems does not help the historian gain purchase on the inscription or the people who made it. For instance, does the use of Daoist or Tantric Buddhist concepts and language in the Nestorian Stele mean that some type of syncretism is happening, or at least that contemporary Daoism or Buddhism had an impact on the Jingjiao?[20] Deeg concludes by suggesting that scholars of Far Eastern Christianity during Late Antiquity need to think across disciplinary lines and create a dialogue between scholars of China (Daoism, Buddhism), Oriental Christianity and Iran.[21]

It is this conjunction that is most interesting and which provides an opportunity to consider the character of Christianity across central Asia. A close reading of the Nestorian Stele is unavoidable if one hopes to understand what was transmitted by Christians to central Asia and beyond in the fifth to eighth centuries. At the same time, the stele cannot be understood on its own terms without reference to the cultures from which Christianity came and, indeed, through which it

---

purely multicultural environment where genre disappears, perhaps, in the process of the document's construction: Muriel Debié, *L'Écriture de l'histoire en Syriaque. Transmissions interculturelles et constructions identitaires entre hellénisme et islam*, Late Antique History and Religion 12 (Leuven, 2015), 126–7.

17 Deeg, 'Ways to Go and Not Go', 139–40.

18 Ibid. This is also known in a Sogdian version from Turfan: Nicholas Sims-Williams, 'A Sogdian Version of the "Gloria in excelsis Deo"', in *Au Carrefour des religions. Mélanges offerts à Philippe Gignoux; textes réunis*, ed. R. Gyselen, Res orientales 7 (Bures-sur-Yvette, 1995), 257–62.

19 Deeg, 'Ways to Go and Not Go', 141.

20 Ibid. 149; Huaiyu Chen, 'The Encounter of Nestorian Christianity with Tantric Buddhism in Medieval China', in Winkler and Tang, eds, *Hidden Treasures and Intercultural Encounters*, 195–213.

21 Deeg, 'Ways to Go and Not Go', 149.

passed en route to Chang'an and the construction of the stele itself. Deeg comes close to the very essentialization he is trying to avoid when he assumes there are stable categories of Syriac, Christian and central Asian with which he can compare Chinese literature from the period. The stele provides, as noted, the only sustained self-reflection on these categories for the regions and period and so requires the most sophisticated investigation we can muster.

The colophon at the bottom of the front face of the stele is worth quoting here in full. I include here the prologue of the inscription (the uppermost portion, reading top to bottom), the final section of the main Chinese inscription on the front face (reading top to bottom, right to left), and the Syriac section on the front face (top to bottom, left to right):

> §1. [1] [Tit.] Stele (commemorating) the diffusion of the 'Luminous' Religion in the Middle Kingdom (China) –
> [2] an eulogy and preface composed by the monk Jingjing of the Da Qin (Roman) [i.e. Syrian] Monastery. {Syr.} [S1] Adam Priest and Chorepiscopos and Priest (*fapshi*) of China (*Chin(i)stan*).
> [The main Chinese section comes here.]
> [31] §24. This (monument) was erected in the second year of Jianzhong (period), of the Great Tang (Dynasty) (781 CE), astronomically the year being Zuō'è, in the 1st month, being the Great *Yàoseēnwén* (Pth. *ʿywšmbt* /eēwšambat) Day and (i.e. namely) on the 7th day, while the Patriarch Ningshu (i.e. Henanišoʿ) had the charge of the Church (lit. 'luminous congregations') of the East.
> {Syr.} [S2] In the time of the Father of Fathers, Mar Henanišoʿ, the Universal (*Catholicos*) Patriarch.
> [32] §24a. Written by Lu Xiuyan, Secretary to Council, formerly Military Superintendent for Taizhou.
> {Syr.} [S3] In the year One Thousand and Ninety and Two [S4] of the Greeks (1092 Sel. = 781 CE) My Lord Yazdbuzid priest [S5] and Chorepiscopos of Kumdān [S6] the metropolis, son of the [S7] late Milis priest, from [S8] Balkh a city of Tahuristan (i.e. Tocharistan), [S9] set up that tablet of stone. [S10] The things which are written on it [S11] [are] the law of him (who is) our Saviour and the preaching [S12] of them (who are) our fathers to the kings [S13] of Zinaye (i.e. China).
> {Chin.} [33] *Monk Lingbao* {Syr.} [S14] Adam minister [S15] son of Yazdbuzid Chorepiscopus.
> [S16] Mar Sargis priest and Chorepiscopos.

> {Chin.} [34] Supervisor of the erection of the tablet the monk [35] Xingtong. {Syr.} [S17] The priest Sabranīšōʿ.
> {Syr.} [S18] Gabriel Priest and an Archdeacon [S19] and Abbot of Kumdān (i.e. Chang'an) [S20] and of Sarag (i.e. Luoyang).
> {Chin.} [36] Assistant Supervisor: the High Statesman of the Sacred rites, [37] the Imperially-conferred-purple-gown [38] Chief Monk Yeli [i.e. Gabriel].[22]

These sections of the inscription move fluidly in and out of Syriac and Chinese characters, and in that regard they resemble more the left and right sides of the stele where the names of clergy are listed in both languages.[23] The seventy names of clergy on the bottom and sides in Syriac script are written vertically, following patterns present in Sogdian texts and gravestones from central Asia and western China.[24]

The Syriac sections all seem to have a technical character to them, signalling the fact that the author of the inscription, Adam in Syriac and Jingjing in Chinese, was working, as expected, from a Syriac template.[25] The narrative section in Chinese, occupying the main part of the front face, was also presumably written by 'Adam' (*'d'm* in §S1), but retains a theological and rhetorical unity that may be attributed to the carver of the Chinese, named as 'Lu Xiuyan, Secretary to Council, formerly Military Superintendent for Taizhou' in §32. In the Syriac part of the prologue, Adam is given the title 'Fapshy', 'Papshy' or 'Fapsh'' (*p'pšy*), translated above as 'priest' (§S1). This word has generated considerable debate, which I will not attempt to resolve here. Suffice it to say that 'priest' in the quoted translation is certainly incorrect since the standard Syriac word for priest, *qšyš'*, appears just prior in his titulature. The two main solutions proposed by scholars are: *fa-shih* ('teacher/master of the law'), a transliteration of a commonly encountered Chinese religious title, and *papas* ('pope'), a Syriac word

[22] Eccles and Lieu, 'Stele on the Diffusion of the Luminous Religion'.
[23] See the lists of these clergy in both languages: ibid. 9–14. On the names of the clergy and the habits of transliteration, see Erica C. D. Hunter, 'The Persian Contribution to Christianity in China: Reflections in the Xian Fu Syriac Inscriptions', in Winkler and Tang, eds, *Hidden Treasures and Intercultural Encounters*, 71–86, at 78–80; Hidemi Takahashi, 'Transcribed Proper Names in Chinese Syriac Christian Documents', in *Malphono w-Rabo d-Malphone: Studies in Honor of Sebastian P. Brock*, ed. G. A. Kiraz (Piscataway, NJ, 2008), 631–62; idem, 'On some Transcriptions of Syriac Names in Chinese-Language *Jingjiao* Documents', in Tang and Winkler, eds, *From the Oxus River*, 13–24.
[24] Hunter, 'Persian Contribution', 72.
[25] Compare, however, the suggestion that the 'Dhūta Monastery Inscription' served as a model for Adam: Forte, in Pelliot, *L'Inscription nestorienne*, 473–87.

misspelled here from the correct *pp'* (from Latin *papa*) or *p'pws* (from Greek πάππος), due possibly to linguistic interference of Persian or Chinese.[26]

Among these technical sections, the stele claims in two places, in both Chinese and Syriac separately, to have been erected in the year 781: the Chinese dating is made according to Tang customs, and the Syriac dating is made according to the Seleucid dating, completely foreign in China but standard in the Syriac Churches of Mesopotamia, Iran and central Asia. It also states, again separately in both Chinese and Syriac, that the Church was at that time under the rule of the 'Patriarch Ningshu (Henanišo')' (§31) and 'Mar Henanišo', universal katholikos' (*mry ḥnnyšw' qtwlyq' pṭryrkys*) (§S2).[27]

The author of the inscription, Adam, attributes the erection of the monument to 'My Lord Yazdbuzid, priest and Chorepiscopos of Kumdān [i.e. Chang'an] the metropolis, son of the late Milis priest, from Balkh a city of … Tocharistan' (*mry yzdbwzyd qšyš' wkwr'pysqwp' dkwmd'n mdynt' mlkwt' br nyḥ npš' mylys qšyš' dmn blḥ mdynt' dṭḥwrstn*) (§§S4–S8). He also gives credit to several other figures who assisted in the erection of the stele: first, another Adam, called a minister or deacon (*mšmšn'*) and son of Yazdbuzid Chorepiscopos;[28] Mar Sargis (i.e. Sergius), priest and Chorepiscopos; the monk Xingtong; the priest

26 For a detailed exploration of these options, see Eccles and Lieu, 'Stele on the Diffusion of the Luminous Religion', 19–22; Paul Pelliot, 'Deux titres bouddhiques portés par des religieux nestoriens', *T'oung-pao* 12 (1911), 664–70, cited by Hunter, 'Persian Contribution', 73 n. 10; Lieu, 'Epigraphica Nestoriana Serica', 236–41; idem, 'The "Romanitas" of the Xi'an Inscription', in Tang and Winkler, eds, *From the Oxus River*, 123–40; and, generally, Hunter, 'Persian Contribution'.

27 As an aside, we know that Timothy I was elected catholicos of the Church of the East in February 780, suggesting to most scholars that the news of his election had not travelled to Chang'an by time the stele was erected. However, Timothy I's election occasioned some controversy in the Church of the East in Iraq. He was opposed by Ephrem of Gundeshapur (Iran) and by Joseph of Merv (Turkmenistan): Hunter, 'Persian Contribution', 73. Joseph of Merv tried to get Timothy's election annulled through Caliph al-Mahdi in Baghdad and when that failed he converted to Islam: ibid. 73, citing *The Book of Governors: The* Historia Monastica *of Thomas, Bishop of Marga, A.D. 840*, ed. E. A. Wallis Budge, 2 vols (London 1893), 2: 383 n. 3; in turn citing Barhebraeus, *Chronicon Ecclesiasticum*, ed. Jean Baptiste Abbeloos and Thomas Joseph Lamy, *Gregorii Barhebraei Chronicon Ecclesiasticum: quod e codice Musei Britannici cescriptum conjuncta opera ediderunt, latinitate donarunt annotationibusque*, 3 vols (Leuven, 1872–7), 3: col. 171.

28 It is sometimes presumed that, because he is given a different clerical office, this is not the same Adam who authored the inscriptions. Yet it is nevertheless intriguing that they share a name and that the son of Yazdbuzid is mentioned so prominently: Hunter, 'Persian Contribution', 77.

Sabranišoʿ; the High Statesman of the Sacred Rites, the Imperially-conferred-purple-gown Chief Monk Yeli, (that is) the priest, archdeacon and abbot of Kumdān (Chang'an) and Sarag (Luoyang), Gabriel (§§34–8; S14–S20).

Taken together these names, titles and locales give the sense that two separate cultures invested in this monument in 781: Persian Christians in China, who traced their lineage to specific bishoprics in Iran; and local Chinese figures, both monks and laymen, who participated in its erection. As noted above, standing at the head of all these individuals, in both Chinese and Syriac, is the name Mar Henanišoʿ, the catholicos of the Church of the East, resident in Seleucia-Ctesiphon.[29] The two separate cultures thus signal their allegiance to a centre of Church order and unity far removed from the monument itself, even as they express that allegiance, in the details of nomenclature and dating habits, in terms consistent with the two separate cultures.

The Iranian element of East Syriac Christianity has become more and more important to scholars as a filter for understanding the stele and its implications. Despite the fact that there is clear bifurcation of culture on the stele into Chinese and Syriac components – without any overt Iranian linguistic strand (e.g. Persian or Sogdian) – the Persian character of the stele is clear. Important to note as well is that the Persian element is recognizable regardless of whether it reflects specific surviving Syriac texts. In an important study Erica Hunter has emphasized the Persian substratum of the language and organization of the colophon.[30] The Syriac term for 'China' is here *zynst'n*, which is not the standard word for China found in contemporary Syriac texts, *Beth Tsinaye*, but is instead the Sogdian term for the geographical location of China, known from numerous documents found in central Asia and western China.[31] The word *tsinaye* on its own is found

[29] Seleucia-Ctesiphon, the traditional capital of Parthian and Sasanian Persia, had long been the ecclesiastical seat of the Church of the East but was no longer a centre of political and intellectual discourse under the Abbasids. Catholicos Timothy I moved the capital to Baghdad upon his election in 780.

[30] Hunter, 'Persian Contribution'.

[31] Ibid. 74; Paul Pelliot, 'Christianity in Central Asia in the Middle Ages', *Journal of the Canadian Asian Society* 17 (1930), 301–12, at 310–12. For instance, Thomas of Marga states in his ninth-century *Book of Governors*: 'David was elected to be Metropolitan of *Beth Tsinaye* [China] – now I have learned concerning this man from the Epistles of Mar Timothy [I] – together with Peter his disciple who was alive and held the office of bishop of the country of *Yaman* [Yemen] and of *Tsan'a* [Sana]': *Book of Governors*, ed. Wallis Budge,

in §S13, but without the expected *beth* preceding it. Moreover, for *zynst'n* the consonants themselves, and not just the vocalization, are different from *tsinaye*.[32] Indeed, the substitution of consonants here follows known patterns for the adoption of Syriac words into a Sogdian environment: notably, the *-t'n* ending is a geographical locator, related to '-stan' in modern Iranian languages. In a similar manner, the names Kumdān and Sarag, for Chang'an and Luoyang (the western and eastern capitals of Tang China, respectively), while not found in surviving Syriac texts, are frequently used in contemporary Sanskrit and Persian texts.[33] The use of *chorepiscopa* and *qashisha* for clergy is very common on Christian gravestones from Semirechye (south-eastern Kazakhstan and north-eastern Kyrgyzstan) and Quanzhou (in China), where there was a strong Sogdian presence.[34] These titles

---

1: 238, 2: 448, translation adjusted. On this passage and the knowledge of Thomas of Marga about the Eastern missions of the Church of the East, see Scott F. Johnson, *Literary Territories: Cartographical Thinking in Late Antiquity* (Oxford, 2016), 115–32. Hunter notes that the use of *Beth Tuptaye* in Timothy's letters could possibly refer to the bishopric of Tibet: O. Braun, 'Ein Brief des Katholikos Timotheos I. über biblischen Studien des 9. Jahrhunderts', *Oriens Christianus* 1 (1901), 299–313, at 308–9, with other references in Hunter, 'Persian Contribution', 74 n. 14. See also Mark Dickens, 'Patriarch Timothy I and the Metropolitan of the Turks', *Journal of the Royal Asiatic Society* 3rd ser. 20 (2010), 117–39, on Timothy I and the Church of the East among the Turks.

[32] Lieu has argued that the consonantal orthography of *zynst'n* is replicated by the Greek word τζίνιστα which appears in the *Christian Topography* of Cosmas Indicopleustes: Lieu, 'Epigraphica Nestoriana Serica', 229 and n. 12. However, the τζ- cluster would seem to me to resemble more the Syriac *tsinaye* than the Persian/Sogdian *z*, even though all are distantly related. Given Cosmas's East Syriac connections and the fact that he mentions Church of the East monasteries in Taprobane (Sri Lanka) in the same passage in which he uses τζίνιστα, I would suggest that he is mimicking Syriac orthography and should not be taken as evidence of the widespread use of *zynst'n* outside Persian/Sogdian circles. The point here is that the stele is using a very unusual spelling for the Syriac term for China which is influenced by its trajectory across central Asia.

[33] See Hunter, 'Persian Contribution', 77–8 n. 30. On the Luoyang Christian inscription, see Tang, 'Preliminary Study on the Jingjiao Inscription of Luoyang'; Matteo Nicolini-Zani, 'The Tang Christian Pillar from Luoyang and its *Jingjiao* Inscription: A Preliminary Study', *Monumenta Serica* 57 (2009), 99–140; idem, 'Luminous Ministers of the Da Qin Monastery: A Study of the Christian Clergy mentioned in the *Jingjiao* Pillar from Luoyang', in Tang and Winkler, eds, *From the Oxus River*, 141–60.

[34] Hunter, 'Persian Contribution', 81. Many of the Semirechye inscriptions were edited by D. A. Chwolson: *Syrische Grabinschriften aus Semirjetschie*, Mémoires de l'Académie impériale des sciences de St-Pétersbourg VIIe série 34/4 (St Petersburg, 1886); *Syrisch-nestorianische Grabinschriften aus Semirjetschie*, Mémoires de l'Académie impériale des sciences de St-Pétersbourg VIIe série 37/8 (St Petersburg, 1890); *Syrische Grabinschriften aus Semirjetschie* (St Petersburg, 1897 edn). On the material remains in Quanzhou, see Samuel N. C. Lieu, *Medieval Christian and Manichaean Remains from Quanzhou (Zayton)*, Corpus Fontium Manichaeorum, Series Archaeologica et Iconographica 2 (Turnhout, 2012).

were common across the Syriac world, but in Syriac texts of the period one finds much more variety in clerical nomenclature, so that it seems that by this time these offices had fossilized among the central Asian churches. It has been further suggested that the name 'Alopen' (the first missionary to China), long interpreted as a transliteration of 'Abraham', is more probably an Iranian name, possibly Ardaban.[35]

In more general terms, even the preference for *Daqin Jiao* ('Roman /Western Teaching') over *Bosi Jiao* ('Persian Teaching') could be significant.[36] Paul Pelliot argued that this might signal an awareness of the final collapse of the Sasanian dynasty, in the sense that affiliation to the West (whether Rome or Syria) was preferable to the Chinese thinking the Persian Christians were in league with the caliph.[37] The last descendant of the Sasanian dynasty died in Chang'an in 707.[38] Between that date and the erection of the stele came both the battle of Talas in 751, in which the Chinese defeated the Islamic armies, and the Abbasid establishment of Baghdad as their new capital in 762. The Chinese imperial court was thus keenly aware of the Islamic threat on their western border, and the fact that the Abbasids claimed the Persian heritage for themselves complicated any claim to Persian (*Bosi*) origins the Christians in China might make. More recently, however, Barrett has argued convincingly that *Daqin Jiao* refers to a 'utopian' spiritual home of the Persian Christians, and not to a Roman connection.[39] Even more boldly, Todd Godwin has suggested

[35] Deeg, 'Ways to Go and Not Go', 146–8. On the confusion surrounding the names Abraham, Aluohan and Alopen in scholarship on Christianity in China in this period, see Forte, in Pelliot, *L'Inscription nestorienne*, 375–428.

[36] By 781, the term *Daqin* had become an archaic designation for the Roman Empire, the more common term under the Tang being *Fulin*. The word *Qin* was the name of an infamous dynasty in Chinese history (221–207 BCE) which ultimately gave China its name (*Qin* = *Ch'in* in Wade-Giles transliteration). The geographical significance of the *Daqin* in the context of the stele is still debated, but under the Han dynasty (206 BCE–220 CE) the Chinese interpreted the name Daqin ('the great/greater Qin') as deriving from themselves, because the Roman Empire resembled that of China: Lieu, 'Epigraphica Nestoriana Serica', 236–41; and now idem, 'Da Qin and Fulin: The Chinese Names for Rome', in idem and Gunther B. Mikkelsen, eds, *Between Rome and China: History, Religions, and Material Culture of the Silk Road* (Turnhout, 2016), 123–45.

[37] Pelliot, *L'Inscription nestorienne*, 364; cf. Lieu, 'The "Romanitas" of the Xi'an Inscription'.

[38] Interestingly, the last seated emperor of Sasanian Persia, Yazdgerd III, having been defeated by the Arab armies in the battle of Nihavand in 642, was buried by the Church of the East's bishop of Merv in 651: see Lieu, 'Epigraphica Nestoriana Serica', 235.

[39] T. Barrett, 'Buddhism, Taoism, and the Eighth-Century Chinese Term for Christianity: A Response to Recent Work by A. Forte and Others', *Bulletin of the School of Oriental and African Studies* 63 (2002), 555–60.

an etymology of *Daqin* from the name Tajik, signifying the central Asian network which planted the Chinese Church to begin with.[40]

It is obvious that Adam feels comfortable affiliating himself with a central Asian lineage, advertising that the donor of the stele, Mar Yazdbuzid, a priest and chorepiscopos of the church in Kumdān (Chang'an), was in turn the son of a priest from Balkh, the capital of Bactria in Tocharistan. The name Yazdbuzid is a Pahlavi name meaning 'saved by God'. His father's name, Milis, was common among East Syriac clergy and appears in Syriac as early as the fourth century.[41] Yazdbuzid's royal connection is made clear from the language of the erecting (Syriac *aqym*) of the stele in a mode of commemorating a formal relationship to the Chinese emperor: 'The things which are written on it [S11] [are] the law of him (who is) our Saviour and the preaching [S12] of them (who are) our fathers to the kings [S13] of Zinaye (i.e. China).' In this rhetoric the Nestorian Stele mimics numerous other steles from the Tang period set up by Buddhist and Manichaean communities attempting to curry favour or emphasize pre-existent and longstanding relationships with the court.[42]

Mar Yazdbuzid, in addition to being the impetus for the erection of the stele according to the Syriac section, has an even more elevated role in the main Chinese inscription on the front face. The final prose section in Chinese offers a mini-biography of this central figure.

> The great Lord of Donations, the 'Great Lord of Radiant Bliss, [Bearer] of the Golden [Seal] and of the Purple [Gown]', simultaneously the Vice Military Commissioner of Shuofang, the Director of the Palace Administration, Receiver of the Purple Kāṣāya (i.e. gown/robe), the

[40] Todd Godwin, 'Persian Christians at the Chinese Court: The Xi'an Stele and the Church of the East, 410–845' (PhD thesis, School of Oriental and African Studies, 2015), 84; see also W. Sundermann, 'An Early Attestation of the Name of the Tajiks', in *Medioiranica: Proceedings of the International Colloquium organized by the Katholieke Universiteit Leuven from 21st to 23rd May, 1990*, ed. W. Skalmowski and A. van Tongerloo, Orientalia Lovaniensia Analecta 48 (Leuven, 1993), 163–71.

[41] Hunter, 'Persian Contribution', 75. Pelliot posited that Yazdbuzid was an Armenian: 'Christianity in Central Asia', 303. While there was a substantial exile Armenian community in Balkh, here the East Syrian context seems more likely, especially given that Yazdbuzid's father's name was Milis.

[42] On contemporary Buddhist steles, see Dorothy C. Wong, *Chinese Steles: Pre-Buddhist and Buddhist Use of a Symbolic Form* (Honolulu, HI, 2004). This special relationship is signalled throughout the Chinese sections of the stele and through various epithets and honours attributed to individuals, such as, in the colophon: '[36] Assistant Supervisor: the High Statesman of the Sacred rites, [37] the Imperially-conferred-purple-gown [38] Chief Monk Yeli' (i.e. Gabriel).

> monk Yisi, was friendly and loved, had learned about the Dao and strived to practice it; [he] came from far away to China from the 'City of the Royal Residence'; his skill was higher [developed than those of] the three dynasties, his arts more comprehensive [than] the ten perfections [of the art of healing]. After he had served obediently in the cinnabar palace he was inscribed in the princely tent (i.e. the military roll). The secretary [and] prince of Fenyang, the venerable Guo Ziyi, for the first time undertook a military mission in Shuofang. [Emperor] Suzong ordered that [Yisi] should accompany [him]. Although he had frequently visited the [imperial] inner court (*nei*) he did not claim a different [treatment while] being with the troops. He was the claws and teeth of the venerable [Guo Ziyi], he was the ears and eyes of the army. He could distribute his revenues and token of honours and did not accumulate them in [his] house. He donated the glasses of the received favour and spread the golden brocade [of his] retirement, in order to extend their (i.e. the Church's) old monasteries or to enlarge the halls of the law (*fa*); he adorned the halls of the corridor until they resembled the plumage of a pheasant in full flight. He caused the 'Brilliant Gate' to prosper even more and gave [his] riches away, based on humanitarian [grounds]. Every year he summoned the monks of the four monasteries and gave them, with respect, spiritual donations. When hungry people came, he fed them; when freezing people came, he gave them clothes; he alleviated the invalids of their suffering diseases and raised them; he buried the dead and gave peace to them. The excellent *dasuo* (i.e. the Christian clergy) had not yet learned about such excellence, [and] the white-clad 'Masters of the Brilliant [Teaching]' [for the first time] saw a man like this. [He] wished to have a great stele-inscription to be carved [in stone] to demonstrate the glorious deeds.[43]

This narrative says that Mar Yazdbuzid – called here by his Chinese name Yisi – was 'the claws and teeth' of the Tang generalissimo Guo Ziyi (696–781) during the An Lushan rebellion (755–7) and had been assigned that position by the Tang Emperor Suzong (756–62).

Deeg has elucidated how the titulature and history surrounding Yisi is crucial to understanding the significance of the stele and the

[43] Translation by Max Deeg, 'A Belligerent Priest: Yisi and His Political Context', in Tang and Winkler, eds, *From the Oxus River*, 109–10 (with typographical corrections and with slight modifications based on Eccles and Lieu, 'Stele on the Diffusion of the Luminous Religion'); text and punctuation follows Pelliot, *L'Inscription nestorienne.*

role of the Church in China and central Asia.[44] The stele was set up under Suzong's grandson, Emperor Dezong (779–805), as a way of connecting his contested reign to the high water mark of the Tang dynasty. Recalling Guo Ziyi, who had died in the year the stele was erected, meant, in the context of the stele, recalling and celebrating his military adjutant Yisi, who was now a Christian monk. However, the reverse is also true, that in the early years of the new emperor, Yisi was using the story of his relationship with the Chinese imperial house to reiterate the long-standing intimacy of the Christian Church in China with the emperor himself. The earlier section of the Chinese inscription, which narrates the history of the Church under successive emperors from the time of Alopen to the present day, thus becomes even more significant.[45] Furthermore, Yisi claims a personal relationship with Suzong, even apart from his role in the An Lushan rebellion, saying that he had visited the inner chamber of the imperial palace and had received the emperor's own honours for his service. Yet, as Deeg notes several times, it is curious – though perhaps not surprising given the stele's propagandistic tone – that Yisi himself does not appear in any secular accounts of Chinese history from the period. By contrast, Guo Ziyi's campaigns and role in the administration, especially as 'a Tang loyalist', are very well documented in the near-contemporary *Old History of the Tang* (941–5) and the *New History of the Tang* (1044–60), as well as in later Chinese imperial histories.[46] Nevertheless, the secular titles attributed to Yisi here are known from other sources, including other steles: in particular, the purple Kāṣāya was traditionally given to high-ranking Buddhist monks who entered imperial service.[47]

Yisi (Mar Yazdbuzid) is thus much more important to the history of the later Tang Christian Church than the Syriac colophon admits. But even here, there are important parallels to draw between the two sections which can illuminate the Church's view of itself in China and how it was presenting its role vis-à-vis its roots in central Asia. Yisi was a northern central Asian immigrant from Balkh (called in the Chinese section *wangshe*, the 'City of the Royal Residence'). To have a monk achieve such a high-ranking place in China was clearly

[44] Deeg, 'Belligerent Priest'.

[45] Ibid. 111–12.

[46] Ibid. 110–12.

[47] For this and an explanation of all the Chinese titles granted Yisi, see ibid. 112–14. On the significance of the Kāṣāya, see Forte, in Pelliot, *L'Inscription nestorienne*, 494–5.

significant to the legitimization of the expatriate Church. However, when taking the whole stele into account, it is important to recognize that Yisi's role is rhetorically situated within a much longer historiography of Christians in China and, indeed, across central Asia. Presumably his son, the chorepiscopos Adam/Jingjing and author of the inscription, was Chinese from birth, brought up in a fully bilingual and bicultural community of Syriac Christians in Chang'an. It is known that Adam/Jingjing participated in a common translation project of the *Liu-boluomi-jing/Ṣaṭpāramitāsūtra* with the Buddhist monk Prajña/Banruo in 786, meaning that he probably had some acquaintance with Sanskrit, in addition to Chinese and Syriac.[48] The immigration of Yisi into that bicultural world, even after the Church had existed in, and been favoured by, the Tang dynasty for a century, shows at the very least ongoing cultural interactions between central Asia and the Tang capital. However, it also shows that Chinese Christians conceived of the Church in central Asia as their mother Church or, to put it better, that Yisi's origins in central Asia were compatible with the message that Chinese Christians were conveying about their own identity within the Chinese social matrix.

An irresolvable knot of questions surrounds the precise dating of Yisi's conversion. Was he a Christian already in Balkh? If so, did his participation in missionary activity lead him to China? More likely, it would seem, is that he converted in China once he was there, after or in the midst of his imperial service. However, that does not rule out ongoing Syriac missionary activity between central Asia and China, and, regardless, the Chinese Christians were eager to claim his central Asian heritage. Did Yisi marry and have a child after he converted and was tonsured, or before? Why are his secular titles, here celebrated, so much more elaborate than his clerical titles and accomplishments? If he married after he became a monk, Yisi would have followed certain allowances made for Buddhist monks in the same situation, even as the Syriac Churches of the Middle East were in the same era insisting more strongly on celibacy among their clergy.

[48] See Junjirō Takakusu, 'The Name of "Messiah" found in a Buddhist Book: The Nestorian Missionary Adam, Presbyter, Papas of China, Translating a Buddhist Sūtra', *T'oung Pao* 7 (1896), 589–91; Huaiyu Chen, 'The Connection between *Jingjiao* and Buddhist Texts in Late Tang China', in Malek, ed., *Jingjiao*, 93–113; Deeg, 'Ways to Go and Not Go'. On the Chongfu-si Buddhist monastery in Chang'an as a site for this intercultural and multilingual translation work, see Forte, in Pelliot, *L'Inscription nestorienne*, 429–54.

Regardless of the answers to these questions, the rhetorical parallelism between the first missionary Alopen and Yisi is evident, and the impression conveyed is that Yisi was a Christian from central Asia who, like Alopen, found favour with the Tang emperor. In this sense the stele is both historiography and a *speculum principis*, teaching that the current emperor, Dezong, should respect the Christian Church and its long history with the Tang emperors. The stele both colludes with Dezong's own rhetoric about re-establishing the Tang line of his grandfather, Suzong, and calls him to honour the dynasty in full by protecting the Christians.[49] It achieves this through pointing out the favour Alopen – and, by implication, all subsequent Syriac bishops in China – had received from the emperor, beginning with the second Tang emperor, Taizong (626–49), and extending to the present day.

Conclusion

In his recent study, *The Making of the Abrahamic Religions in Late Antiquity*, Guy Stroumsa states: 'the idea of translation, from an archaic to a common language, understood by all and sundry, was of the essence of [the Christians'] religion'.[50] He is here speaking about the fundamental role that the Septuagint, the Greek translation of the Hebrew Bible (made originally by Jews, for Jews), played in the early Christian world. The 'archaic' language here is Hebrew and the 'common' language Greek (these are contestable labels and translation did not always proceed from archaic to common in any case), but leaving aside the terminology, his main point, that translations were a part of Christian identity from the beginning, is irrefutable. The Septuagint was the Bible of the earliest Christians, and the writers of books making up the New Testament cited the Septuagint nine times out of ten and did not feel the need (or in certain cases were not able) to return to the original Hebrew.

[49] This argument can be extended further by tracing the activities of Suzong's early reign in reforming the tax system and curtailing the building of Buddhist monasteries. The stele was in this sense a 'self-promoting and self-protecting' mechanism of public identity-formation to which Suzong was apparently receptive, as evidenced by Buddhist and Manichaean petitions from the same period. See Deeg, 'Belligerent Priest', 115–18, especially 118: 'I think it cannot be completely ruled out that some of the issues addressed in these petitions, although the emperor's reaction was not completely foreseeable, are reflected in some passages of the inscription.'

[50] Guy Stroumsa, *The Making of the Abrahamic Religions in Late Antiquity* (Oxford, 2015), 33.

Further down the road, and continuing to the present, it should be emphasized that Christians have never considered translations of their holy scriptures to be defective in principle. Even though the original manuscripts of the New Testament were lost from an early point – or perhaps partly *because* the original manuscripts were lost – translations became a part of the fabric of Christian history, literature and worship. From the second century on, translations have been conceived of as missional and therefore fundamental not just to the descriptive reality of Christianity but also to its prescriptive nature. Stroumsa's point is even more significant in the context of his comparison with later Judaism and Islam. These were, in Islamic terms, 'religions of the book', that is, religions taking their impetus from divinely received and inspired scriptures, and all three – Judaism, Christianity and Islam – saw the revelation to Abraham, Moses and the Israelites as beginning that ongoing revelatory experience. On the other hand, Islam and Judaism (at least rabbinic and medieval Judaism) considered translations of their scriptures to be defective in principle. Translations existed in Late Antiquity – such as the Aramaic *Targumim*, which were read out alongside the Hebrew so that the Jewish congregation could understand – but they never took the place of the original texts in their original languages.[51] That is clearly not the case in Christian literary history, which used many translated texts, including translations of Scripture.[52]

The Nestorian Stele is a preeminent example of the value of translation in late antique Christian history. The East Syriac Christians were attempting to communicate natively in a foreign environment, which required linguistic and cultural flexibility. In this context, the stele also gives us a sense of the continued value of Syriac as a language and of the central Asian institutions of the Church of the East. It also shows us that as late as the last quarter of the eighth century the Christians of China were continuing to hark back to the

[51] Subsequent to the Hellenistic period, during which Jews throughout the Mediterranean diaspora used Greek translations for their scriptures, not least the Septuagint, Hebrew began to take on a more preeminent role in self-definition of Jewish worship and community: Tessa Rajak, *Translation and Survival: The Greek Bible of the Ancient Jewish Diaspora* (Oxford, 2009); Willem F. Smelik, *Rabbis, Language, and Translation in Late Antiquity* (Cambridge, 2013).

[52] As a counterpoint, one might cite the role of the Latin in the medieval West as the definitive scriptural language, in opposition to regional vernaculars. However, it was never claimed that Latin was the original language of the Old or New Testaments. Latin was a sacred and authoritative language, but the Latin Vulgate was still known to be a translation.

central Asian heritage of their Churches and presenting themselves as the heirs of this heritage to the literate public in China as a means of maintaining their favoured status under the Tang emperors. Crucial to this picture is the assertion that they used Iranian/Persian/Sogdian language and nomenclature, and that important individuals in their community, such as Yisi (Mar Yazdbuzid), continued to arrive in China and advocate for the Christians, even long after the Christian Churches had first been established in the 630s.

The question remains, however, what was their Christianity? What of the Mediterranean and Mesopotamian worlds had they brought with them? One vector for addressing this question is to look at the theological sections of the stele and at the handful of surviving Jingjiao texts and try to draw parallels between them and East Syriac theological concepts and language. However, this is not what I have attempted to do here, partly because that work has been done already, and partly because scholars have come to radically different conclusions about the amount of syncretism or borrowing between Jingjiao and Daoism, Buddhism and Manichaeism evidenced by those documents.[53] As asserted by Deeg in the quotation at the beginning of this article, very few direct parallels can be drawn between any of these texts, and, as a result, the training and emphasis of any individual scholar tends to skew the interpretation towards his or her scholarly matrix. Not that such treatments are not valuable, but there is simply too little common ground in individual texts, and too many texts, to do adequate justice to the cultures and religions involved on their own terms.

Ultimately, as suggested by Deeg's provocative statement, we are dealing with a question of essentials: what is Syriac about Christian texts in Chinese or Sogdian and, further, what is Christian about them? As noted, the summary of doctrine that stands at the beginning of the front face of the stele is remarkably complete, though certain Chinese words and concepts had to be used in order to communicate those doctrines to the Chinese public. The challenge is to understand how Chinese Christians, in narrating their own faith and beliefs before the Tang emperor, chose to use Chinese terminology – and even at the most basic level, the Chinese language – to communicate their history and identity in China in direct relation to the Syriac Christians in Persia and central Asia. There is no doubt that this

[53] For a survey of the issues involved, see Tang, *Nestorian Christianity in China*, 103–44.

relationship between Syriac, Mesopotamia, central Asia and China is complex. It is a very difficult problem fraught with lacunary evidence and, ultimately, it transcends any one scholar's competence. Deeg is correct in asserting that it must be a collaborative effort.[54] However, we must also be aware that very different interpretations of the trajectories of central Asian Christianity will emerge over time as the evidence continues to be sifted and as historical models require revision. I have tried to emphasize that the 'Nestorian Stele' of 781 is the most important example of Christian self-reflexivity surviving from Tang China or medieval central Asia. It deserves to be read carefully as a piece of Christian historiography. Only by continuing to put it in conversation with the Syriac, Iranian and Chinese historiography of the period will its nuances and the complex relationships engendered by Syriac, over such a wide geographical area and over several centuries, become clearer.

[54] Another sign of this collaborative effort, which appeared too late for incorporation into this article, is Pier Giorgio Borbone and Pierre Marsone, eds, *Le Christianisme syriaque en Asie centrale et en Chine*, Études syriaques 12 (Paris, 2015).

The Language of Baptism in Early Anglo-Saxon England: The Case for Old English

Miriam Adan Jones*
Vrije Universiteit Amsterdam

This article explores the possibility that the vernacular (Old English) may have been used in the baptismal rite in Anglo-Saxon England before the middle of the eighth century. Statements made by Bede (d. 735) and Boniface (d. 754), provisions in the Canons of the Council of Clofesho *(747) and the probable existence of a lost Old English exemplar for the 'Old Saxon' or 'Utrecht' baptismal promise (Palatinus latinus 755, fols 6*^{v}*–7*^{r}*), all suggest that it was. The use of the vernacular was most attractive in a context of ongoing Christianization, where the faith commitment of the baptizand was foregrounded and his or her understanding of the rite correspondingly highly valued. Later, the shift of focus towards the correct pronunciation of the Trinitarian formula and the increase of general knowledge about the baptismal rite reduced the impetus for translation, and Latin became the standard language of baptism. The translation and non-translation of the baptismal rite reflect broader concerns about the place of the Church of the English and its ethnic and cultural particularity within the universal Church, and particularly its relationship with Rome.*

In his *Ecclesiastical History of the English People*, completed in 731, Bede (d. 735) describes the conversion of the South Saxons as follows:

> Wilfrid taught them the faith and administered the baptism of salvation. … So the bishop, with the king's consent and indeed to his great joy, cleansed his ealdormen and his *gesiths* in the holy fount of baptism; the priests Eappa and Padda, Burghelm, and Eddi baptized the rest of the common people …[1]

* Faculty of Theology, Vrije Universiteit Amsterdam, De Boelelaan 1105, 1081 HV Amsterdam, The Netherlands. E-mail: m.a.adan@vu.nl.

[1] '[Uilfrid] huic uerbum fidei et lauacrum salutis ministrabat … Itaque episcopus concedente, immo multum gaudente rege primos prouinciae duces ac milites sacrosancto fonte abluebat; uerum presbyteri Eappa et Padda et Burghelm et Oiddi ceteram plebem … baptizabant': Bede, Historia ecclesiastica [hereafter: HE] 4.13 (*Bede's Ecclesiastical History of the English People*, ed. and transl. Bertram Colgrave and R. A. B. Mynors, OMT [Oxford, 1969], 372, transl. 373).

Studies in Church History 53 (2017) 39–50
doi: 10.1017/stc.2016.4

Although this story underlines the importance of baptism as the moment of transition from paganism to Christianity, it tells us very little about the rite itself. In this regard it is typical: many narrative sources from early Anglo-Saxon England make reference to baptisms, few indicate how baptisms were conducted.[2] This article highlights one particular aspect of the Anglo-Saxon baptismal rite which is here (and elsewhere) passed over in silence but which nevertheless carries significant theological weight: in what language was the rite performed?

Studies of the development of the medieval rite of baptism have tended to overlook this question, quietly assuming Latin as the universal liturgical language of the early medieval West.[3] Yet Anna Maria Luiselli Fadda has underlined the importance of a shared language of communication to the conversion of the Anglo-Saxons, and argued convincingly that the vernacular played a vital role in the dissemination of Christianity in Anglo-Saxon England.[4] Others have recently shown that, even among educated religious, Latin need not have always been the language of communication.[5] Helen Foxhall Forbes writes that '[t]he majority of the [Anglo-Saxon baptismal] liturgy itself took place in Latin', but leaves open the question of what parts, if any, may have taken place in another language.[6] And although Joseph

[2] Sarah Foot, '"By Water in the Spirit": The Administration of Baptism in Early Anglo-Saxon England', in John Blair and Richard Sharpe, eds, *Pastoral Care before the Parish* (Leicester and New York, 1992), 171–92, at 172.

[3] Studies of medieval baptism include John Douglas Close Fisher, *Christian Initiation: Baptism in the Medieval West: A Study in the Disintegration of the Primitive Rite of Initiation*, Alcuin Club Collections 47 (London, 1965); Peter John Cramer, *Baptism and Change in the Early Middle Ages, c.200–c.1150* (Cambridge and New York, 1993); Susan A. Keefe, *Water and the Word: Baptism and the Education of the Clergy in the Carolingian Empire*, 2 vols, Publications in Medieval Studies (Notre Dame, IN, 2002); Bryan D. Spinks, *Early and Medieval Rituals and Theologies of Baptism: From the New Testament to the Council of Trent* (Aldershot and Burlington, VT, 2006). For Anglo-Saxon England, see Joseph H. Lynch, *Christianizing Kinship: Ritual Sponsorship in Anglo-Saxon England* (Ithaca, NY, and London, 1998); M. Bradford Bedingfield, *The Dramatic Liturgy of Anglo-Saxon England* (Woodbridge 2002), 171–90; Foot, '"By Water in the Spirit"'.

[4] Anna Maria Luiselli Fadda, 'The Vernacular and the Propagation of the Faith in Anglo-Saxon Missionary Activity', in Pieter N. Holtrop and Hugh McLeod, eds, *Missions and Missionaries*, SCH S 13 (Woodbridge, 2000), 1–15.

[5] Alaric Hall, 'Interlinguistic Communication in Bede's *Historia Ecclesiastica Gentis Anglorum*', in *Interfaces between Language and Culture in Medieval England: A Festschrift for Matti Kilpiö*, ed. Alaric Hall et al. (Leiden 2012), 37–80; Anton Scharer, 'The Role of Language in Bede's Ecclesiastical History', in idem, *Changing Perspectives on England and the Continent in the Early Middle Ages* (Farnham and Burlington, VT, 2014), art. II, at 1–8.

[6] Helen Foxhall Forbes, *Heaven and Earth in Anglo-Saxon England: Theology and Society in an Age of Faith*, Studies in Early Medieval Britain (Farnham, 2013), 103–11, quotation at 104.

Lynch suggests that parts of the baptismal rite may have been spoken in the vernacular, he does not further explore that suggestion or its implications.[7]

This article argues that the vernacular was used in the rite of baptism in the early Anglo-Saxon Church. In addition to presenting the admittedly scarce and often indirect evidence that (parts of) the baptismal liturgy were translated from Latin into Old English, it examines the cultural, theological and institutional contexts in which translation made sense. It further suggests that in seeking the balance between acculturation and catholicity, vernacular baptism demonstrates how the Anglo-Saxon Church navigated the tension between asserting the local and universal aspects of its identity.

That the vernacular may have been used at baptism is suggested by the practical difficulties of using Latin, the language in which the baptismal rite would have been received from the Roman missionaries who brought Christianity to the Anglo-Saxon kingdoms, at a time when many Anglo-Saxons would have been unable to speak or understand it.[8] Although some scholars have suggested that the descendants of the Romano-British may have continued to use Latin well into the Anglo-Saxon period, there must also have been native speakers of Old English who never learned another language, or never learned it well.[9] Bede certainly treats fluency in Latin as something exceptional when he notes that it was only under the tutelage of Theodore and Hadrian that some Anglo-Saxon clergy had come to 'know Latin … just as well as their native tongue'.[10]

Explaining the duties of pastors towards their flocks in a letter of 734, Bede writes that preachers and priests should 'zealously preach in each hamlet the word of God and offer the heavenly mysteries and above all perform the sacrament of baptism'. The laity should learn the faith as expressed in the Lord's Prayer, the Creed and the gospel.

[7] Lynch, *Christianizing Kinship*, 176–7.

[8] This does not, however, mean that there were no multilingual Anglo-Saxons, or that all Old English texts were meant for a monolingual audience: Helen Gittos, 'The Audience for Old English Texts: Ælfric, Rhetoric and "the Edification of the Simple"', *Anglo-Saxon England* 43 (2014), 231–66.

[9] Anthony Harvey, 'Cambro-Romance? Celtic Britain's Counterpart to Hiberno-Latin', in *Early Medieval Ireland and Europe: Chronology, Contacts, Scholarship. Festschrift for Dáibhí Ó Cróinin*, ed. Pádraic Moran and Immo Warntjes, Studia Traditionis Theologiae 14 (Turnhout, 2015), 179–202; Hall, 'Interlinguistic Communication'.

[10] 'Latinam … linguam aeque ut propriam in qua nati sunt norunt': *HE* 4.2 (Bede, *Ecclesiastical History*, ed. and transl. Colgrave and Mynors, 334, transl. 335).

'[A]s for the unlearned, that is, who know their own language only, make these learn the texts in their own tongue … I have frequently offered translations of both the Creed and the Lord's Prayer into English to many unlearned priests.'[11] Although Bede's comments here say nothing about the language of baptism, they do make some things clear: first, baptism was considered a key element of pastoral ministry; second, most lay people and many priests did not speak or understand Latin; third, Bede approved of, even actively encouraged, the translation of religious or liturgical texts into Old English for the benefit of those who could not otherwise understand. All this suggests that Bede may have been open to using the vernacular in the baptismal rite. The canons of the council of *Clofesho* (747) make the connection between vernacular instruction and baptism more explicit. Among the requirements for priests is that they must learn to translate and explain the words used in the mass and at baptism.[12] The canon that immediately follows indicates that those who bring children to be baptized are to be taught those parts of the baptismal liturgy in which they play an active role: the renunciation of the devil and the confession of faith.[13] Here we have a clear indication that translation and explanation, obviously also in the vernacular, are taking place in the broader baptismal context.[14]

In addition to guidelines aimed at the priests providing pastoral care, we have evidence of the laity's desire to receive pastoral care in their own language. According to Bede, linguistic ability was an important consideration in King Egbert of Kent's selection of Wigheard (d. 664×667) for the episcopal see of Canterbury:

[11] '[I]n singulis uiculis praedicando Dei uerbo et consecrandis mysteriis caelestibus, ac maxime peragendis sacri baptismatis officiis, ubi opportunitas ingruerit … sed idiotas, hoc est eos qui propriae tantum linguae notitiam habent, haec ipsa sua lingua discere … et ipse multiae saepe sacerdotibus idiotis haec utraque, et symbolum uidelicet et dominicam orationem, in linguam Anglorum translatam optuli': Bede, *Letter to Ecgbert*, in C. Grocock and I. N. Wood, *The Abbots of Wearmouth and Jarrow*, OMT (Oxford, 2013), 130–2 (D. H. Farmer, *Bede: Ecclesiastical History of the English People* [London and New York, 1990], 339–40).

[12] Arthur West Haddan and William Stubbs, eds, *Councils and Ecclesiastical Documents relating to Great Britain and Ireland*, 3: *English Churches during the Anglo-Saxon period: A.D. 595–1066* (Oxford, 1871), 366.

[13] Ibid.

[14] Lynch, *Christianizing Kinship*, 175–6; but see Catherine Cubitt, 'Pastoral Care and Conciliar Canons: The Provisions of the 747 Council of Clofesho', in Blair and Sharpe, eds, *Pastoral Care before the Parish*, 193–211, at 196, for an alternative explanation.

> Egbert was eager to have him consecrated … reckoning that, if he had a bishop of his own race and language, he and his people would be able to enter all the more deeply into the teachings and mysteries of their faith, since they would receive them at the hands of someone of their own kin and [tribe] and hear them not through an interpreter but in their own native tongue.[15]

Wigheard's ability to communicate the *verbi fidei* and *mysteria* in his native English was a valuable skill that set him apart from earlier bishops of Canterbury, who had until recently all been Roman (although his immediate predecessor was a West Saxon). In this context, surely the 'words' and 'mysteries' which the Kentish hoped to receive in their native language represent the dual pastoral tasks of preaching and administering the sacraments, including baptism.[16]

What might a vernacular baptismal rite have been like? Unfortunately, we have no liturgical texts for the baptismal rite in the Anglo-Saxon kingdoms before the tenth century.[17] However, we do have a text which arguably derives from an English exemplar, but one which due to its continental provenance has not been given due consideration as evidence for English practice: the so-called Old Saxon or Utrecht baptismal promise.[18] The language of the words to be spoken is Old Saxon; directions are given in Latin. The candidate is asked *forsàchistu diabolae?* ('do you renounce the devil?') and prompted to respond (*et respondeat*): *ec forsacho diabolae* ('I renounce the devil'). In the same way the candidate renounces all *diobolgeldae* ('pagan sacrifices') and 'all the devil's works and words; Thunar and Woden and Saxnot and all the demons that are their companions' before making confession of faith in God the Father, Son and Holy Spirit.[19]

[15] '[C]upiens eum … ordinari episcopum, quatinus suae gentis et linguae habens antistitem, tanto prefectius cum subiectis sibi populis uel uerbis imburetur fide uel mysteriis, quanto haec non per interpretem, sed per cognati et contribulis uiri linguam simul manumque susciperet': Bede, in Grocock and Wood, *Abbots of Wearmouth and Jarrow*, 26–8 (D. H. Farmer, *The Age of Bede* [London, 1998], 189).

[16] D. R. Howlett, ed., *Dictionary of Medieval Latin from British Sources* (Oxford, 2001), *s.vv.* 'Mysterium, Misterium'.

[17] Foot, '"By Water in the Spirit"', 172; Spinks, *Early and Medieval Rituals*, 127.

[18] Vatican City, Biblioteca Apostolica Vaticana, Palatinus Latinus, MS 577, fols 6^{v}–7^{r}.

[19] '*6v^{o}*: Forsachistu diobolae. & respondeat. ec forsacho diabolae. end allum diobolgeldę respondeat. end ec forsacho allum diobolgeldae. end allum dioboles uuercum. respondeat. end ec forsacho allum dioboles uuercum and uuordum thunaer ende uuoden ende saxnote ende allvm them unholdum the hira genotas sint. *7r^{o}*: gelobistu in got alamehtigan fadaer. ec gelobo in got alamehtigan fadaer. gelobistu in crist godes suno. ec gelobo in

Although the language of this promise is Old Saxon, the text has long been recognized to show Old English influences, leading scholars to posit an Old English, possibly Northumbrian, exemplar for the extant text.[20] There are also strong historical arguments for associating the document and the collection in which it is found with the Anglo-Saxon missions to the continent, either that of the Northumbrian Willibrord (d. 739) and his circle to Frisia and later Saxony, with its base in Utrecht, or that of the West Saxon Wynfrith, later Boniface (d. 754), to Hesse and Thuringia.[21] This text therefore shows us that the vernacular was being used by Anglo-Saxon priests in the baptismal liturgy – certainly abroad, and, if the Old Saxon version was indeed derived from an Old English one, probably also at home, whence the now-lost exemplar came. Even without the linguistic evidence, it seems plausible that the idea of a translated baptismal rite could have originated in England, to which the missionaries often looked for their liturgical inspiration.[22] If nothing else, the baptismal promise shows that early eighth-century Anglo-Saxon clergy did not object to using the vernacular in the baptismal rite, but considered it perfectly acceptable and indeed preferable when called for by the circumstances. These circumstances may have been quite similar in some parts of England to the areas on the continent where Anglo-Saxon missionaries worked: among a largely unlatinate population, recently and perhaps incompletely Christianized, being served by a relatively small number of clergy, who may themselves not have been particularly familiar or comfortable with the Latin tongue.

It can hardly be a coincidence that of all the elements of the baptismal liturgy, it is the renunciation of the devil and profession of faith that exist in a vernacular translation. This reflects an ancient tradition in which the interrogation formed the heart of the baptismal liturgy,

---

crist gotes suno. gelobistu in halogan gast. ec gelobo in halogan gast': Maurits Gysseling, *Corpus van Middelnederlandse teksten (tot en met het jaar 1300)*, II.1: *Fragmenten* (The Hague, 1980), 26. I have substituted punctuation where Gysseling has line-breaks.

20 Agathe Lasch, 'Das altsächsische Taufgelöbnis', *Neuphilologische Mitteilungen* 36 (1935), 92–133; William Foerste, *Untersuchungen zur westfälischen Sprache des 9. Jahrhunderts.*, Münstersche Forschungen 2 (Marburg, 1950), 92–8, esp. 93; D. L. Machielsen, 'De angelsaksische herkomst van de zogenaamde Oudsaksische Doopbelofte. Een bijdrage tot de externe taalgeschiedenis', *Leuvense Bijdragen* 50 (1961), 97–124; Gysseling, *Corpus*, 22–6.

21 Marco Mostert, 'Communicating the Faith: The Circle of Boniface, Germanic Vernaculars, and Frisian and Saxon Converts', *Amsterdamer Beiträge zur älteren Germanistik* 70 (2013), 87–130.

22 Yitzhak Hen, 'The Liturgy of St Willibrord', *Anglo-Saxon England* 26 (1997), 41–62.

and the threefold immersion of the candidate was interspersed with the threefold confession of belief in Father, Son and Holy Spirit.[23] In this tradition, intelligibility was not just a practical but also a theological concern: baptism could only be administered if the baptizand understood and believed.[24] Old English is used sparingly in liturgical and other formal texts from Anglo-Saxon England, but it does occur 'in circumstances in which it is critical that [the person addressed] understands what is happening'.[25] Examples of such circumstances in late Anglo-Saxon England included trials, excommunications and coronations.[26] The evidence of the baptismal promise, and other indirect references such as those discussed above, suggests that in the early Anglo-Saxon Church the baptismal interrogation was among those instances when it was thought critical that the words exchanged should be fully understood. That understanding was ensured by translating the renunciation of the devil and profession of faith into the vernacular.[27]

Translation aided understanding not only by allowing the participants to understand the specific words spoken and thus the content of the promises made, but also to comprehend the structure and nature of the rite as a whole. Andreas Wagner, taking the Germanic oath of fealty as an analogue, has argued that in early medieval Germany, baptism would have been understood as a *Herrschaftswechsel* ('change of lordship') and the baptismal promise as a declarative speech-act that transformed the baptismal candidate through the transfer of allegiance from the devil to Christ.[28] There is evidence that the Anglo-Saxons, too, thought of baptism as a change in allegiance. For instance, Bede remarked that the baptized were 'changed from sons of

[23] Fisher, *Christian Initiation*, 16–17.

[24] Cramer, *Baptism and Change*, 186; Owen M. Phelan, 'Forging Traditional Liturgy: Exegesis, Mission, and Medieval Baptism', *RHE* 107 (2012), 833–9.

[25] Helen Gittos, 'Is there any Evidence for the Liturgy of Parish Churches in Late Anglo-Saxon England? The Red Book of Darley and the Status of Old English', in Francesca Tinti, ed., *Pastoral Care in Late Anglo-Saxon England*, Anglo-Saxon Studies 6 (Woodbridge, 2005), 63–82, at 80.

[26] Ibid. 78–80.

[27] Compare canon 27 of the Statuta Bonifatii: 'Nullus sit presbiter, qui in ipsa lingua, qua nati sunt, baptizandos abrenuntiationes vel confessiones aperte interrogare non studeat, ut intellegant, quae abrenuntiant vel quae confitentur; et qui taliter agere dedignantur, secedat in parrochia': MGH Capitula Episcoporum 3, 364.

[28] Andreas Wagner, 'Taufe als Willensakt? Zum Verständnis der frühmittelalterlichen Taufgelöbnisse und zur Begründung ihrer volkssprachigen Übersetzung', *Zeitschrift für deutsches Altertum und deutsche Literatur* 125 (1996), 297–321.

the devil into sons of God'.[29] The words spoken at baptism may well have been viewed as operating in the same way as legal oaths, for in Anglo-Saxon England the boundaries between liturgy and legal procedures were often not clearly defined.[30] Certainly in the early Anglo-Saxon church it seems likely that the new rite of baptism would have been understood by analogy to existing local customs, like the oath of fealty sworn by a man to his lord.[31] The similarities between these procedures would have been underscored by the use of the same language for both.

Baptism was, however, not only a sign of the faith commitment made by the candidate, but also of the grace poured out by God. The first aspect had been emphasized in the early Church and continued to be emphasized in missionary contexts in the early Middle Ages, while the second aspect became more prominent where Christianity was the established religion.[32] With the shift in focus from the action of the candidate to the action of God came a new preoccupation with form, and quickly the validity of the baptism came to hinge on the correct use of the Trinitarian formula: 'I baptize you in the name of the Father and of the Son and of the Holy Spirit'.[33] Boniface was so perturbed to encounter individuals who had been, on account of the priest's deficient Latin, baptized 'in the name of the fatherland and the daughter and the Holy Spirit' that he ordered their rebaptism.[34] But a generation earlier Bede had adopted a more flexible attitude: he argued that, while baptism in the name of the Trinity was the norm, the sacrament could be administered by naming only one Person of the Trinity, for to express faith in one was to express faith in all.[35] The shift in emphasis from the confession of the baptizand (or his or her representatives) to the correct use of the Trinitarian formula thus seems still to have been in process during this period.

[29] Cited in Spinks, *Early and Medieval Rituals*, 129.
[30] Janet L. Nelson, 'Liturgy or Law: Misconceived Alternatives', in *Early Medieval Studies in Memory of Patrick Wormald*, ed. Stephen David Baxter et al., Studies in Early Medieval Britain (Farnham, 2009), 433–47.
[31] Ibid. 444–6; Gittos, 'Liturgy of Parish Churches', 80 n. 101.
[32] Cramer, *Baptism and Change*, 130–40.
[33] Foot, '"By Water in the Spirit"', 178.
[34] MGH Epp. Sel. 1, 141 (letter 68). For this he was reprimanded by Pope Zacharias (741–52): it was the priest's Trinitarian intentions that counted, and the baptisms were to be considered valid. On later medieval philosophical debates regarding intentional versus conventional meaning, see I. Rosier-Catach, 'Speech Act and Intentional Meaning in the Medieval Philosophy of Language', *Bulletin de philosophie médiévale* 52 (2010), 55–80.
[35] Bede, *Expositio actuum apostolorum* 10 (CChr.SL 121, 3–99).

The new emphasis on form undermined the motivation for translation of the baptismal rite into the vernacular: no longer was the rite to be understood as analogous to a legal oath, nor were the understanding and faith of the baptizand a primary concern. Indeed, the new stress on correct formula potentially restricted the possibility of translation. Would baptisms conducted in another language be valid? Boniface apparently voiced just such a concern to Pope Gregory III (731–41), inquiring what to do about 'those who were baptized according to the varieties and the inflections of the heathen dialects'.[36] Boniface's original letter is lost, and the exact nature of his concern is not clear from Gregory's response. The latter makes clear, however, that any concerns Boniface may have had about the theological status of 'heathen' vernaculars were unfounded: those who were baptized in the name of the Trinity, regardless of the language, were to be confirmed in the usual manner.[37]

Pope Gregory's comments underline the point that Latin was not considered a sacred language. In Anglo-Saxon England, the influence of Archbishop Theodore of Canterbury (d. 690), originally from the Greek East, would have challenged the theological importance of Latin by exposing his students to another, and older, language of Christian worship and thought.[38] Anglo-Saxon theologians greatly respected the three languages used in the study of Scripture, Hebrew, Greek and Latin, but did not object to translation of biblical texts.[39] Bede's commentary on Acts made clear that he believed there was room within the Church for all languages: this was the message of the events of Pentecost.[40] Indeed, 'there was a sacrality in the use of the

[36] 'Illi … qui baptizati sunt per diversitate et declinatione linguarum gentilitatis': MGH Epp. Sel. 1, 73 (letter 45); ET *The Letters of Saint Boniface*, intro. Thomas F. X. Noble, transl. Ephraim Emerton (New York, 2000), 73.

[37] MGH Epp. Sel. 1, 73 (letter 45).

[38] On Theodore, see Michael Lapidge, ed., *Archbishop Theodore: Commemorative Studies on his Life and Influence*, Cambridge Studies in Anglo-Saxon England 11 (Cambridge, 1995). On the knowledge of Greek in Anglo-Saxon England, see Mary Catherine Bodden, 'Evidence for Knowledge of Greek in Anglo-Saxon England', *Anglo-Saxon England* 17 (1988), 217–46.

[39] Tristan Major, 'Rebuilding the Tower of Babel: Ælfric and Bible Translation', *Florilegium* 23/2 (2006), 47–60, at 50–1.

[40] Kees Dekker, 'Pentecost and Linguistic Self-Consciousness in Anglo-Saxon England: Bede and Ælfric', *Journal of English and Germanic Philology* 104 (2005), 345–72. On the status of Old English for Bede, see also Gittos, 'Audience for Old English Texts', 260.

individual language of each people', and this emphatically included Old English.[41]

Nevertheless, Latin had become the language of the study of the Scriptures in the medieval West, and so bound together the speakers of different languages.[42] In baptism, the candidate was understood to be entering into the Church universal, and to clergy desiring to emphasize the Church's catholicity it may have seemed appropriate to baptize in the language shared by all the Christian West. Latin was also the language of the Roman Church, and to Anglo-Saxon ecclesiastics, Rome stood for apostolicity and orthodoxy, making unity with Rome paramount.[43] The desire for *Romanitas* is reflected throughout the canons of *Clofesho*, which insist again and again that things be done 'after the model of the Roman church'.[44] Using Latin, even though unnecessary from a theological perspective, could be attractive if it was thought to lend the ritual, the priest and the Church as institution the legitimacy and credibility that came from being associated with the Roman Church.

Coupled with the Anglo-Saxon Church's association with Rome was a dissociation from the churches of the Britons. If Rome signified catholicity and orthodoxy, the Britons stood under permanent suspicion of heretical and schismatic tendencies.[45] They also used a different baptismal rite from the Romans, one which from the Roman – and Anglo-Saxon – perspective was deficient.[46] The difference between the two rites became enshrined in the Old English word for baptism, *fullwiht*, which derives from a root meaning 'complete hallowing' and contrasts the rite received by the Anglo-Saxon Church from Rome with the 'incomplete' version performed by the British.[47] The term captures something of what must have been a widespread

[41] Robert Stanton, *The Culture of Translation in Anglo-Saxon England* (Cambridge and Rochester, NY, 2002), 70.

[42] *HE* 1.1 (Bede, *Ecclesiastical History*, ed. and transl. Colgrave and Mynors, 16).

[43] Nicholas Howe, 'Rome: Capital of Anglo-Saxon England', *Journal of Medieval and Early Modern Studies* 34 (2004), 147–72; Nicholas Brooks, 'Canterbury, Rome and the Construction of English Identity', in *Early Medieval Rome and the Christian West: Essays in Honour of Donald A. Bullough*, ed. Julia M. H. Smith, Medieval Mediterranean 28 (Leiden and Boston, 2000), 221–46. Cf, in this volume, Simon Ditchfield, 'Translating Christianity in an Age of Reformations', 164–95, at 178.

[44] Richard William Pfaff, *The Liturgy in Medieval England: A History* (Cambridge, 2009), 45.

[45] E.g. *HE* 5.23 (Bede, *Ecclesiastical History*, ed. and transl. Colgrave and Mynors, 523).

[46] Ibid. 2.2 (Bede, *Ecclesiastical History*, ed. and transl. Colgrave and Mynors, 138).

[47] Carla Falluomini, '*Fullwiht* and the Baptismal Rite in Anglo-Saxon England', *Anglia – Zeitschrift für englische Philologie* 128 (2011), 391–405.

controversy about baptismal validity in conversion-age England. Adhering strictly to the Roman baptismal rite may thus have been one way for the English Church to distinguish itself from the British Church and distance itself from any perceived insularity. In addition to being an institutional identity-marker, baptismal completeness was a pastoral concern. The possibility that the baptism offered was lacking in some respect may have occupied not only theologians but also laypeople concerned about the fates of their friends and relatives.[48] Emphasizing the fullness of the Roman rite could have helped to assuage such concerns, at the same time leveraging them to bolster the position of Rome and discredit the British tradition.[49]

Although the Anglo-Saxons liked to think of themselves as allies and perhaps even heirs of Rome, they were also aware of their distinctive identity as the 'church of the English'.[50] One of the things that bound these 'English' together was a shared mother tongue, and this could be used for spiritual as well as secular matters. I have noted already that Bede translated the Lord's Prayer and the creed into Old English; Bede's pupil Cuthbert tells us that Bede was engaged at the end of his life with translating the Gospel of John, and that he composed or recited a vernacular verse about his approaching death.[51] Later generations would compose Old English heroic verse on themes inspired by scriptural and apocryphal texts. Cramer reads one such poem, which narrates the adventures of the apostle Andrew, as 'baptism put into a vernacular story, and so made accessible in both language and form'.[52] Such literary efforts testify to the ongoing project of the Anglo-Saxon Church to integrate the texts, teachings and practices inherited from the early Church into its own

[48] Such concerns are well documented in relation to the unbaptized. Consider, for instance, the woman who, fearing for her unbaptized child, sought the help of St Wilfrid: Eddius Stephanus, *The Life of Bishop Wilfrid*, ed. and transl. Bertram Colgrave (Cambridge and New York, 1985), ch. 18; Foot, '"By Water in the Spirit"', 190.

[49] Perhaps the use of Old English was one way in which the Anglo-Saxon baptismal rite could be distinguished from the British, especially if the Britons were seen by the Anglo-Saxons 'to be characterized not by their Celtic speech, but by their living use of Latin', as Harvey has suggested: Harvey, 'Cambro-Romance', 201.

[50] Patrick Wormald, 'The Venerable Bede and the 'Church of the English', in Stephen David Baxter, ed., *The Times of Bede: Studies in Early English Christian Society and Its Historian* (Malden, MA, 2006), 207–28; Sarah Foot, *Bede's Church*, Jarrow Lecture (Jarrow, 2012), 1–18.

[51] Cuthbert, *Cuthbert's Letter on the Death of Bede*, in Bede, *Ecclesiastical History*, ed. and transl. Colgrave and Mynors, 579–87, at 580–2.

[52] Cramer, *Baptism and Change*, 202.

context. They also show that direct translation of the liturgy was not the only way that the rite of baptism might be reinterpreted for an Anglo-Saxon audience.

In later Anglo-Saxon England, clergy came to rely on general Christian (vernacular) education to ensure understanding of the baptismal rite, rather than translation of the liturgy.[53] In earlier times, however, the situation was different. In the context of a semi-Christianized Anglo-Saxon landscape, the necessity of helping both priest and people understand what was transpiring in the waters of baptism – both practically and theologically desirable – encouraged the translation of the baptismal rite into Old English. Using the vernacular in the liturgy of baptism would have emphasized the conversion aspect of baptism; evoking associations with vernacular traditions of oath-taking, it would have placed the baptismal candidate's faith and commitment in the foreground, while the aspects of baptism that are done to and for the baptizand were correspondingly de-emphasized. Accordingly, this approach would have been most attractive in a context where adults were converting to Christianity and being baptized by choice: throughout the seventh century and perhaps the early eighth in some places.[54] The urge to translate would have ebbed as more and more people came to have a general knowledge of what baptism entailed, infant baptism became the norm and the emphasis in baptismal theology came to lie increasingly on form rather than faith.

The questions surrounding the language of baptism thus mirror broader concerns within the newly formed Church of the English, searching for balance between making the faith accessible and ensuring its correctness and completeness. The Anglo-Saxon translation (and later non-translation) of the baptismal rite sheds light on how the Anglo-Saxon Church sought to carve out an identity for itself between the local and the universal. It also illustrates changes in early medieval baptismal theology and how these were bound up with changing cultural contexts. Even though Latin won out in the end, what evidence we have for the baptismal rite in early Anglo-Saxon England shows that we should not assume that it was always self-evident to the Anglo-Saxons that the business of Christian initiation should be conducted in Latin: the vernacular could, given the right circumstances, be a viable and attractive option.

[53] Forbes, *Heaven and Earth*, 104–8; Spinks, *Early and Medieval Rituals*, 132–3.

[54] John Blair, *The Church in Anglo-Saxon Society* (Oxford, 2005), 168.

Translating St Alban: Romano-British, Merovingian and Anglo-Saxon Cults

M. D. Laynesmith*
University of Reading

This article treats the early medieval cult of St Alban of Verulamium. It explores how, and how far, the cult extended in Britain, France and Germany. As well as crossing geographical boundaries, Alban's relics were also shared among different cultures: British, Anglo-Saxon and Merovingian. The article argues that this resulted in differing appreciations, interpretations and applications of Alban's cult, and that the Gallic contribution to the cult's survival was particularly important.

This article treats one aspect of the burgeoning study of the cult of saints: the ubiquitous medieval phenomenon known as 'translation'. In this saints' relics were removed from their original context, typically the grave or execution site, and re-deposited in more elaborate shrines or buildings on-site, or shared across a wider area, often placed in churches newly dedicated to the saint.[1] Here I discuss where, when and (to some extent) how and why the relics of St Alban of Verulamium (St Albans, Hertfordshire) came to be translated and re-deposited in churches dedicated to him in the early medieval period. Aspects of Alban's cult – its antiquity, literary deposits and specific regional manifestations – have previously been examined, but this study represents the first attempt to treat the cult systematically as it spread across western Europe. Alongside this a second meaning of 'translation' emerges through examining how Alban's cult

* Chaplaincy Centre, University of Reading, Reading, RG6 6AH. E-mail: marklaynesmith@gmail.com.
This article is based on ongoing doctoral research into 'The Cult of St Alban of Verulamium, *c.*400–*c.*750' (Archbishop's Examination in Theology, Lambeth Palace). A gazetteer of medieval Alban churches is online at: <https://www.academia.edu/24430468/A_Provisional_Gazetteer_of_Alban_Churches_in_Medieval_North-western_Europe>, accessed 15 April 2016.

[1] Peter Brown's *The Cult of Saints: Its Rise and Function in Latin Christianity* (Chicago, IL, 1971) remains seminal. On the phenomenon of translation, see John Crook, 'The Enshrinement of Local Saints in Francia and England', in Alan Thacker and Richard Sharpe, eds, *Local Saints and Local Churches in the Early Medieval West* (Oxford, 2002), 189–224.

Studies in Church History 53 (2017) 51–70
doi: 10.1017/stc.2016.5

and story were reinterpreted as the relics of this British martyr were accommodated in fresh contexts.

Alban is in effect Britain's original patron, perhaps even the personification of Albion.[2] Believed to have been executed and buried on the site of the abbey of St Albans, to the east of Roman Verulamium across the river Ver, his dates are elusive, with suggestions ranging from the early third to the early fourth centuries.[3] Alban's earliest *passio* is of no help in settling the issue.[4] This narrates only his arrest, trial and (on the way to his hilltop execution) his Moses-like crossing of the Ver and the creation of a spring. The text concludes with an account of Germanus of Auxerre removing soil from the execution site, probably in 429.[5] Archaeological investigation at the abbey suggests that the cult began to flourish only in the 390s.[6] Thereafter graves of a 'distinctively "late Roman" rather than "early or mid Saxon"' nature continued to be cut.[7] These were interrupted by a four-century period of abandonment before resumption of building activity in the tenth century.

[2] Ian N. Wood, 'Levison and St Alban', in Matthias Becher and Yitzhak Hen, eds, *Wilhelm Levison (1876–1947). Ein jüdisches Forscherleben zwischen wissenschaftlicher Anerkennung und politischem Exil* (Siegburg, 2010), 171–85, at 178–9. On the classical background of this name, see Albert L. F. Rivet and Colin Smith, *The Place-Names of Roman Britain* (London, 1979), 39, 247–8. 'Alba' was the Old Irish name for Britain. On 'Albion' during the Anglo-Saxon and Norman periods, see Amanda Jane Hingst, *The Written World: Past and Place in the Work of Orderic Vitalis* (Notre Dame IN, 2009), 51–69. On Albion in Æthelred's charters, see Paul Antony Hayward, 'The Cult of St Alban, *Anglorum Protomartyr*, in Anglo-Saxon and Anglo-Norman England', in Johan Leemans, ed., *More than a Memory: The Discourse of Martyrdom and the Construction of Christian Identity in the History of Christianity* (Leuven, 2005), 169–99, at 183.

[3] Charles Thomas, *Christianity in Roman Britain to AD 500* (London, 1981), 46–50. The Severan date no longer holds: Richard Sharpe, 'The Late Antique Passion of St Alban', in Martin Henig and Phillip Lindley, eds, *Alban and St Albans: Roman and Medieval Architecture, Art and Archaeology* (Leeds, 2001), 30–7.

[4] For the *passio* text, see Wilhelm Meyer, 'Die Legende des h. Albanus des Protomartyr Angliae in Texten vor Beda', *Abhandlungen der Königlichen Gesellschaft der Wissenschaften zu Göttingen, Philogisch-historische Klasse* n.s. 8 (1904), 36–47. The text is erroneously labelled 'Excerpt', reflecting Meyer's (mis)interpretation: see Sharpe, 'Late Antique Passion', 32–4.

[5] Prosper of Aquitaine, *Epitoma chronicon*, *s.a.* 429 (in *Chronica Minora saec. IV. V. VI. VII*, MGH AA 9, 341–499, at 472).

[6] Martin Biddle and Birthe Kjølbye-Biddle, 'The Origins of St Albans Abbey: Romano-British Cemetery and Anglo-Saxon Monastery', in Henig and Lindley, eds, *Alban and St Albans*, 45–77, at 62. I am not persuaded by Ian Wood's claim that Germanus founded the cult: 'Germanus, Alban and Auxerre', *Bulletin du Centre d'Études Médievales d'Auxerre* 13 (2009), 123–9.

[7] Biddle and Kjølbye-Biddle, 'Origins', 62.

Victricius of Rouen's *De laude sanctorum* of 397 provides the first probable literary reference to Alban, referring to a martyr who, *inter manus carnificum, nequa mora fieret properanti, iussit redire fluminibus* ('in the executioners' hands, hurrying lest the journey be delayed, ordered the rivers to fall back').[8] This replicates details in Alban's *passio* and has been taken by most modern historians to refer to Alban. Thereafter, references to Alban's cult recur consistently: in Constantius of Lyon's *Vita sancti Germani* (*c.*480s), Gildas and Venantius Fortunatus in the mid-sixth century, Bede in the eighth, and in charters through to the Norman period.[9] This rich textual history led Wilhelm Levison to compare St Albans favourably with Bonn and Xanten, two other Roman-era Christian sites that survived through the Germanic invasions into the medieval period.[10] Yet, as the archaeology of the abbey site suggests, the literary impression of uninterrupted continuity within the British Isles is deceptive. Paradoxically the cult seems to have found its most extensive and consistent welcome in Gaul and neighbouring regions, though even here Anglo-Saxon influence may have been detrimental, resulting in a 're-translation' of the cult for reasons of cultural bias.

Alban's Insular Dedications

Surprisingly, there are records of only a dozen medieval churches dedicated to Alban within the British Isles (Fig. 1).[11] Admittedly dedications may have been lost and Alban's translated relics may also have been housed in side altars within other churches. For comparison, there are records of 27 churches dedicated to Augustine of Canterbury, 65 to Cuthbert, 151 to Martin of Tours, and 220 to Laurence.[12] Alban's cult never achieved such popularity.

[8] Victricius of Rouen, *De laude sanctorum* 12 (CChr.SL 64, 69–93, at 92; my translation).

[9] *Vita Germani episcopi Autissiodorensis autore Constantio* 16, 18 (in *Passiones Vitaeque Sanctorum aevi Merovingici*, MGH SRM 7, 225–83, at 262, 265); Gildas, *De excidio Britonum* 1 (Michael Winterbottom, ed., *Gildas: The Ruin of Britain and Other Works* [London, 1978], 19, 92); Venantius Fortunatus, *De virginitate* (Carmina 8.3) 155 (in *Opera Poetica*, MGH AA 4/1, 181–91, at 185); Bede, *Historia ecclesiastica gentis Anglorum* [hereafter: *HE*] 1.7, 18, 20 (*Bede's Ecclesiastical History of the English People*, ed. and transl. Bertram Colgrave and R. A. B. Mynors [Oxford, 1969], 28–35, 58–61, 64–5); Julia Crick, ed., *Charters of St Albans* (Oxford, 2007).

[10] Wilhelm Levison, 'St Alban and St Alban's', *Antiquity* 15 (1941), 337–59, at 338–9, 358.

[11] Frances E. Arnold-Forster, *Studies in Church Dedications: or, England's Patron Saints*, 3 vols (London, 1899), 2: 293–9.

[12] Ibid. 3: 1–26.

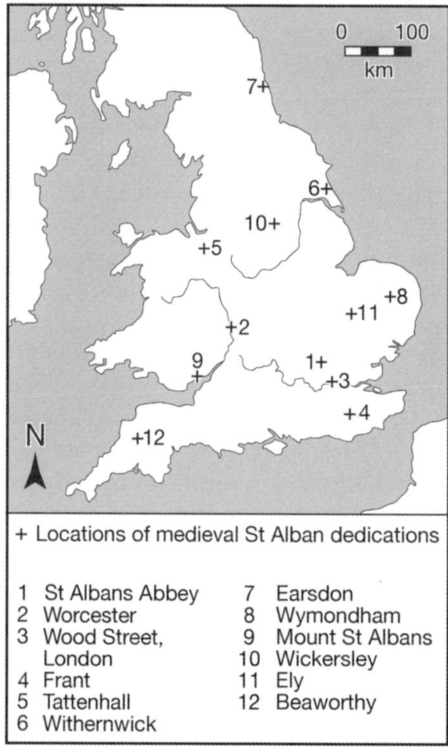

Figure 1. Medieval Alban dedications in the British Isles.

Dating Alban's churches is not simple. After St Albans Abbey (fig. 1, no. 1) the earliest are probably later Saxon, in Worcester (2) and London (3). The thirteenth-century chronicle of Evesham Abbey claimed Æthelbald had given Worcester's Alban church to it in 721, though no charter survives.[13] The building does survive and once occupied a prime riverfront location with an adjacent spring. It follows the line of, or possibly surmounts, the original Roman defensive rampart. Bassett has argued that, since the neighbouring parish of St Helen may have been a British (i.e. pre-680) episcopal see, the Alban church could have been an early dependent chapel.[14] Baker

[13] *Chronicon abbatiæ de Evesham ad annum 1418*, ed. William D. Macray (London, 1863), 73.
[14] Steven Bassett, 'Churches in Worcester before and after the Conversion of the Anglo-Saxons', *Antiquaries Journal* 69 (1989), 225–56, at 243–5.

and Holt, however, favour an eighth-century date, suggesting an association with an as-yet-unlocated Mercian palace.[15] Evidence for this date, too, is sparse and archaeological study is inconclusive.[16] London's Alban church in Wood Street (3) was also once considered to be of eighth- or ninth-century date and related to a mid-Saxon palace at Cripplegate.[17] However, the existence of an early Mercian palace and the antiquity of the church are both now disputed. An early to mid-eleventh century date is currently thought more likely.[18] Worcester remains the only plausible mid-Saxon, or just possibly British, Alban church outside Hertfordshire.

Much hangs on Offa's contested involvement in the cult. Even what form his supposed interest took is unclear: Matthew Paris claimed that in 793 he discovered Alban's body, but a translation would seem more logical.[19] Although the earliest St Albans charters naming Offa are late tenth- or eleventh-century forgeries, Crick has argued that the abbey's endowments are difficult to associate with other early royal donors, leaving Offa the most promising candidate.[20] Offa's supposed interest in Alban is surprising, though, as Anglo-Saxon Christians rarely displayed reverence for the British Church.[21] Indeed, Hayward has shown that there is scant evidence of Alban's cult among Saxons before the tenth century, noting in particular Alban's absence from the earliest continental Anglo-Saxon calendars.[22] Willibrord's calendar includes Irish saints (Brigit, Patrick and

[15] Nigel Baker and Richard Holt, *Urban Growth and the Medieval Church: Gloucester and Worcester* (Aldershot, 2004), 139, 197–203.

[16] Mike Naptham, 'Archaeological Evaluation at St Alban's Church, Deansway, Worcester, WCM 101278 (2006)', Unpublished report SWR18691, held at the Worcester Archive and Archaeology Service, 7.6.2, 8.6, 9.1–2.

[17] William F. Grimes, *The Excavation of Roman and Mediaeval London* (London, 1968), 203–7.

[18] Natalie Cohen, 'St Alban's, Wood Street', in Gustav Milne, ed., *Excavations at Medieval Cripplegate, London: Archaeology after the Blitz, 1946–1968* (Swindon, 2001), 86–100, at 94.

[19] *Gesta abbatum monasterii sancti Albani, s.a.* 793, ed. Robert Niblett, in 'Appendix 2: Sources for the Archaeology of St Albans', in Rosalind Niblett and Isobel Thompson, *Alban's Buried Towns: An Assessment of St Albans' Archaeology up to AD 1600* (Oxford, 2005), 359–88, at 360.

[20] Julia Crick, 'Offa, Ælfric and the Refoundation of St Albans', in Henig and Lindley, eds, *Alban and St Albans*, 78–84; see also Pamela Taylor, 'The Early St Alban's Endowment and its Chroniclers', *HR* 68 (1995), 119–242.

[21] Thomas M. Charles-Edwards, *Wales and the Britons, 350–1064* (Cambridge, 2013), 397–410.

[22] Hayward, 'Cult', 181.

Columba), but Alban is missing.[23] Might it be that Alban required cultural 'translation'?

A subtle downplaying of Alban's British origins seems already present in Bede's *Historia ecclesiastica.* There, when the judge asks: *cuius ... familiae uel generis es*? ('what is your family and race?'), Alban replies: *quid ad te pertinet, qua sim stirpe genitus? Sed si ueritatem religionis audire desideras, Christianum iam me esse* ('What does it matter to you what stock I come from? But if you desire to hear the truth of my religion: I am now a Christian').[24] A further bar to Offa's interest may have been removed fifteen years before when the Welsh Britons adjusted their paschal system. It is conceivable that these changes enabled Offa to promote Alban as a specifically Mercian patron, perhaps (alongside the creation of a third archbishopric at Lichfield) as part of an attempt to relativize Canterbury and its saintly patron, Augustine.[25] Intriguingly, the traditional date of Offa's involvement also almost coincides with that of Charlemagne's burial of his wife Fastrada in the church of St Alban of Mainz.[26] Is it possible that Offa was inspired by Charlemagne?

Of the remaining insular dedications three others do not pre-date the late Saxon period: Frant (4), Tattenhall (5) and Withernwick (6).[27] These, and perhaps London's Alban church, were all presumably founded using relics sourced from St Albans Abbey after its refoundation in the 970s.[28] They date to a period in which, as Hayward has shown, Alban began to be promoted as an English saint, the

[23] H. A. Wilson, ed., *The Calendar of St Willibrord from MS Paris. Lat. 10837* (London, 1918). Another Briton, Gildas, appears to be a later addition: ibid. 3, 20.

[24] *HE* 1.7 (my translation).

[25] For other speculations regarding Offa's motives, see Richard Martin, '*The Lives of the Offas*: the Posthumous Reputation of Offa, King of the Mercians', in David Hill and Margaret Worthington, eds, *Æthelbald and Offa: Two Eighth-Century Kings of Mercia*, British Archaeological Reports, British Series 383 (Oxford, 2005), 49–54, at 50–1.

[26] *Annales regni Francorum, s.a.* 794 (MGH SRG i.u.s. 6, 3–115, at 95).

[27] Tattenhall predates its acquisition by St Werburgh Abbey, 1096x1101: *The Chartulary or Register of the Abbey of St. Werburgh, Chester*, ed. James Tait, 2 vols (Manchester, 1920–3), 1: 13–37 (charter 3). Frant first appears in a 1093x1103 charter: Henry S. Eeles, *Frant: A Parish History* (Tunbridge Wells, 1947), 18–9, 46–9. Withernwick predates its acquisition by Aumale Priory in 1115: Keith J. Allison and G. H. R. Kent, 'North Division: Withernwick', *A History of the County of York, East Riding*, 12 vols, Victoria History of the Counties of England (London, 1969–2012), 7: 405–15.

[28] See Biddle and Kjølbye-Biddle, 'Origins', 66–9; Crick, 'Offa', 80–3.

'protomartyr Anglorum'.[29] The remaining six insular Alban dedications appear to be Norman.[30]

Three observations can be made. First, aside from Verulamium, British (i.e. pre-Saxon) interest in the cult, at least in terms of relic translation and church dedication, seems extremely limited. Levison showed that the only Welsh dedication, Mount St Albans (9) near Caerleon, was probably the result of relics gleaned during the translation of the martyr's body into the new Norman abbey church in 1129.[31] Alban's relics do not appear to have been translated into Wales before this period and whether Alban's church in Worcester was British remains unclear. Gildas's lament that the Saxon advent rendered Verulamium, and consequently the cult itself, inaccessible does not therefore seem to be hyperbole.[32]

Second, although Bede described miracles still occurring at the site of Alban's execution, he did not describe any functioning buildings or officiating clergy, observing only that a church 'of wonderful workmanship had been built' (*mirandi operis … exstructa*).[33] Bede's description of the miracles is similar to other accounts in which agents acting alone and on their own initiative remove dust from holy sites either without churches or from where a church has been ruined.[34] Verulamium may well have been part of a British enclave, possibly surviving until the late sixth century, but when and under what circumstances the town passed into Saxon control, and the fate of the cult site, is unknown.[35] Excavation at the Abbey has so far found little firm evidence of early and middle Saxon activity, most particularly an

[29] Hayward, 'Cult', 182–6.

[30] Earsdon (7), founded *c.*1097; Wymondham (8), 1107: Arnold-Forster, *Studies*, 2: 298. Wickersley (10), probably twelfth-century, is first mentioned *c.*1230: *Fasti Parochiales*, ed. A. Hamilton Thompson and S. T. Clay, 5 vols (Wakefield, 1933–85), 2/2: 118. Alban's body was briefly moved to Ely (11) during the Conquest (whence relics were translated to Denmark): *Liber Eliensis: A History of the Isle of Ely from the Seventh Century to the Twelfth*, transl. Janet Fairweather (Woodbridge, 2005), 207–8. Beaworthy (12) may be a confusion with John the Baptist: Nicholas Orme, *English Church Dedications: With a Survey of Cornwall and Devon* (Exeter, 1996), 131.

[31] Levison, 'St Alban', 340–3.

[32] Gildas, *De excidio* 10 (Winterbottom, ed., *Gildas*, 19, 92). On the interpretation of this passage, see Michael Garcia, 'Gildas and the "grievous divorce from the barbarians"', *EME* 21 (2013), 243–53.

[33] *HE* 1.7.

[34] *HE* 2.16; 3.9, 10; 5.18.

[35] Kenneth Rutherford Davis, *Britons and Saxons: The Chiltern Region 400–700* (Chichester, 1982), 118–20.

absence of burials.[36] Moreover, there is no evidence that Alban's cult was promoted elsewhere within England before the eighth century (again with the possible exception of Worcester). All this then might add credence to Matthew Paris's claim that Offa's involvement represented a significant new moment in the cult's history, perhaps indeed the creation of the first functioning Saxon church on the site.

Finally, it was ultimately late Saxon and thereafter Norman influence that was to have the greatest impact. Half of Alban's insular churches postdate the Conquest, and most can be directly related to promotion by the abbey's new Norman management. Ironically this was not a new departure for, aside from Gildas, all three pre-eighth-century versions of Alban's passion, including Bede's main source, were produced in Gaul.[37] It was Gaul that acted as a reservoir for the cult and perhaps primed the incoming Norman ecclesiastical elite to take an interest in St Alban.[38]

Alban Church Dedications in France

There have been previous studies of Alban's cult in France and neighbouring areas.[39] To date however there has not been a systematic examination of Alban dedications. By combining recent topographical surveys, online map-searching for Saint-Alban/Auban place-names, and searches in charters and other historical sources, it has become possible to construct the first map of western continental Europe

[36] Biddle and Kjølbye-Biddle, 'Origins', 65–6, 72–3.

[37] The 'excerpts' (*BHL* 211a), and the 'P' (*BHL* 211) and 'T' (*BHL* 210d) versions: Meyer, 'Die Legende', 35–47. *BHL* numbers refer to the Bollandist catalogue *Bibliotheca hagiographica latina antiquae et mediae aetatis*, 4 vols, Subsidia Hagiographica 6, 12, 70 (Brussels, 1898–1986).

[38] On Norman support, see Hayward, 'Cult', 186–98, though note the dispute with Ely: S. J. Ridyard, '*Condigna Veneratio*: Post-Conquest Attitudes to the Saints of the Anglo-Saxons', in *Anglo-Norman Studies 9: Proceedings of the Battle Conference 1986,* ed. R. Allen Brown (Woodbridge, 1987), 179–206, at 190.

[39] William R. L. Lowe, 'History of the Legend of St Alban', *Proceedings of the Society of Antiquaries of London* 27 (1914–15), 58–67; Eric P. Baker, 'The Cult of St Alban at Cologne', *Archaeological Journal* 94 (1938), 207–56; Marcel Beck, 'St Alban in Uri. Ein Zeuge spätantiken Christentums', *Zeitschrift für Schweizerische Geschichte* 28 (1948), 273–309; Heinrich Büttner, 'Zur Albanverehrung im frühen Mittelalter', *Zeitschrift für schweizerische Geschichte* 29 (1949), 1–16; Martin Dolch, 'Die Heiligennamen Albin und Alban. Zur Verehrung westfränkischer Heiliger im 8. Jahrhundert', *Archiv für mittelrheinische Kirchengeschichte* 39 (1987), 43–66. On Gallic cults generally, see Ian Wood, 'Constructing Cults in Early Medieval France: Local Saints and Churches in Burgundy and the Auvergne 400–1000', in Thacker and Sharpe, eds, *Local Saints and Local Churches*, 155–87.

showing the likely extent of Alban's cult in terms of church dedications.[40] Naturally caution is required, particularly in distinguishing churches dedicated to Alban of Verulamium, Alban of Mainz and the Merovingian bishop Albinus of Angers. Where they survive, festal dates help. Name slippage is also useful (Albinus typically produces 'Aubin' rather than 'Auban' place-names).[41] Moreover, the overall pattern can be confirmed from a previous study of medieval calendars by Martin Dolch. This demonstrated that, though overlapping, the three cults tended to concentrate in different regions.[42] Taking all this into account the resulting survey can claim that whilst there were a mere dozen or so insular medieval Alban churches, in France alone there were nearly a hundred (Fig. 2).

Fewer than half of France's dioceses had Alban churches. Of these, most possessed only one or two. However there are significant concentrations in the dioceses of Lyon, Vienne, Viviers and Trier. Three-quarters of Alban dedications appear in Provence and Burgundy, and a further fifth are in north-eastern France. If the cult had been propagated by British clerics one might have expected more in Brittany. However, whilst there was an explosion of later Welsh saints in Brittany (over a hundred churches are dedicated to Gildas alone), only one of Brittany's three Alban churches (Elven, Morbihan), can be dated with certainty to the first millennium.[43]

If British clerics were not responsible for translating Alban's cult to France, who was? The simplest answer is Germanus of Auxerre, whom Alban's *passio* describes as translating relics of blood-soaked earth from the site of Alban's execution. Ninth-century sources claim Germanus deposited these in Auxerre's former cathedral and rededicated it to Alban.[44] This would explain how Alban's cult reached central France, but why did it spread further south so spectacularly?

[40] The principal topographical source is Albert Dauzat and Charles Rostaing, *Dictionnaire étymologique des noms de lieux en France*, 2nd edn (Paris, 1978), 583–4, though this is far from complete. Brigitte Beaujard lists various sixth-century Gallic cults but not Alban's: *Le Culte des Saints en Gaul* (Paris, 2000), 524–31.

[41] Ernest Nègre, *Toponymie générale de la France*, 4 vols (Geneva, 1990–8), 3: 1530–1.

[42] Dolch, 'Die Heiligennamen Albin und Alban'.

[43] First mentioned in 910: Aurelien de Courson, ed., *Cartulaire de l'Abbaye de Redon en Bretagne* (Paris, 1863), 226. For Gildas, see René Largillière, 'La Topographie du culte de Saint Gildas', *Mémoire de la Société d'histoire et d'archéologie de Bretagne* 5 (1924), 1–25.

[44] Jean-Charles Picard, 'Auxerre', in Nancy Gauthier and Jean-Charles Picard, eds, *Topographie chrétienne des cites de la Gaule des origines au milieu du VIIIe siècle*, 16 vols in 17 (Paris, 1986–2014), 8: 47–65, at 56.

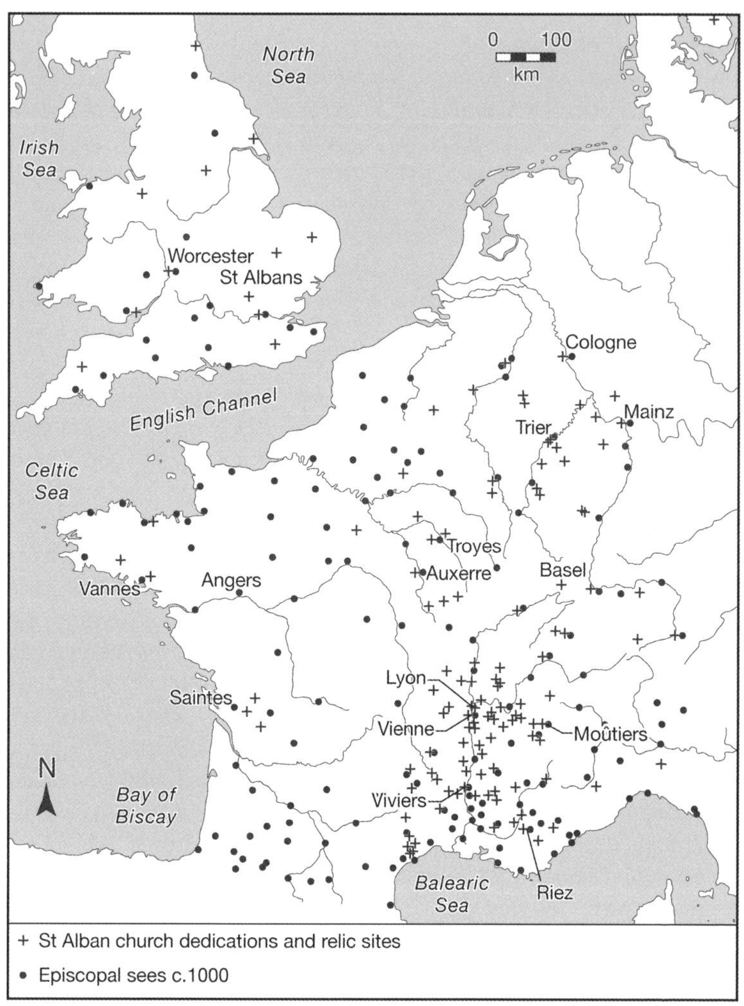

Figure 2. North-western European medieval Alban dedications.

Although Prosper of Aquitaine emphasized that Germanus's mission was papally instigated, Ralph Mathisen has argued that Germanus was acting under the more proximate orders of Hilary, metropolitan of Arles, and with the backing of the Provençal bishops.[45] This may

[45] Ralph W. Mathisen, *Ecclesiastical Factionalism and Religious Controversy in Fifth-Century Gaul* (Washington DC, 1989), 101–2.

explain why Provence and Burgundy provide the earliest and most extensive evidence for Alban churches.

The first of these to appear in the historical record is at Riez, where a sixth-century *vita* of Bishop Maximus of Riez claims that he dedicated a church to Alban.[46] If true, this foundation must have taken place before Maximus's death in 460, within thirty years of Germanus's return to France. Germanus's hagiographer claimed he travelled to Arles during this period.[47] Therefore Germanus himself could have been responsible for introducing Alban's relics to his Provençal episcopal colleagues (many of whom shared a Lérinian monastic heritage), who in turn deployed them in founding churches within their own dioceses.[48]

Early Christian Riez is well studied and sheds light on some of the possible motives for the spread of Alban's cult. The first half of the fifth century saw the city's bishops undertake a major process of Christianization, including the conversion of its baths, a former site of Asclepian cult, into a grand baptistery.[49] It was during this period that Maximus founded the Alban church on a hilltop adjacent to Riez, separated from it by the river Colostre. This topography closely mirrors Verulamium, suggesting a knowledge of Alban's *passio* with its description of Alban's execution.[50] The dedication was also toponymically appropriate, since the church occupied Riez's former citadel, originally named 'Alebaece'.[51] All this suggests that Maximus found Alban's cult helpful in reshaping his see. These three features – topographical mirroring, the crossing or channelling of water and pre-Christian 'Alp-' or 'Alb-' place-names – occur at numerous other Alban church sites in France, although rarely clustered so obviously.

Whether or not Germanus personally donated Alban's relics to Maximus, elsewhere there are suggestions of Germanus's direct

[46] Dynamius, *Vita sancti Maximi episcopi Reiensis* 8 (Pascal Boulhol et al., *Maxime de Riez entre l'histoire et la légende* [Valensole, 2014], 112, cf. 58–9); Alban's church was later rededicated to Maximus: 72–3. Philippe Borgard and Marc Heijmans, 'Riez', in Françoise Prévot, Michèle Gaillard and Nancy Gauthier, eds, *Topographie chrétienne*, 16/1: 240.

[47] *Vita Germani* 19–24 (MGH SRM 7, 265–9). Germanus died before November 450: Andrew Gillett, *Envoys and Political Communication in the Late Antique West, 411–533* (Cambridge 2003), 278–82.

[48] Cf. Mathisen, *Ecclesiastical Factionalism*, 69–173.

[49] James Bromwich, *The Roman Remains of Southern France: A Guidebook* (London, 1993), 286–8.

[50] Meyer, 'Die Legende', 41, 43.

[51] Albert L. F. Rivet, *Gallia Narbonensis: Southern France in Roman Times* (London, 1988), 243–6.

involvement. A possibly eighth-century *vita* of the mid-fifth-century Severus of Vienne describes this missionary founding an Alban church at Vienne.[52] The narrative is highly fictionalized but includes an account of a visit by Germanus. We might conclude that it was Germanus, rather than Severus, who brought the cult to Vienne. The church survives at Saint-Alban-du-Rhône (Isère) beside a major late Roman cemetery, another feature replicated at other Alban sites.[53]

An Alban church existed also at Lyon. This too could conceivably have been founded with relics given by Germanus to its bishop, Eucherius. The church was located beside the entrance to Lyon's episcopal complex. Destroyed in the eighteenth century, it has never been subject to archaeological study. Secondary literature has dated it to 1138 when it first appears in the historical record.[54] However this merely recounts its donation to the monastery of Saint-Claude (Condat, Ain), rather than its foundation. Devotion to Alban in Lyon certainly dates to the first millennium, as his *passio* features in a ninth-century *passionale* used in Lyon's cathedral.[55] There was a second Alban church, at a roadside Roman cemetery in Montchat, five kilometres east of Lyons. Now also demolished, its antiquity is suggested by its surviving, apparently eighth-century, font.[56] Similarly two Alban churches in the diocese of Troyes may have been founded using relics shared by Germanus. Troyes's bishop, Lupus, reputedly accompanied Germanus to Britain in 429.[57] Both buildings are situated at sources of rivers, perhaps indicating an attempt to Christianize pagan

52 *Vita sancti Severi Viennensis presbytreri et confessoris* 3, 8 (*AnBoll* 5 [1886], 416–24, at 417, 421). The *vita* mentions the relics of Desiderius of Vienne (d. 607), but was itself used by Florus of Lyon (d. *c.*860), so must have been composed between these dates.

53 Françoise Descombes, 'Vienne', in Gauthier and Picard, eds, *Topographie chrétienne*, 3: 31.

54 René Locatelli and Gérard Moyse, 'Une Pierre d'attente du volume de Gallia Pontificia en chantier pour le diocèse de Lyon. L'Abbaye de Saint-Claude', *Revue Mabillon* 79 (2007), 253–73, at 268–9 (charters 14, 16).

55 Autun, Séminaire, MS S38 (34), fols 70^{r}–70^{v}; Guy Lanoë, 'S 38 (34) Passiones martyrum', *Catalogue des manuscrits d'Autun, Bibliothèque municipale et Société Éduenne*, ed. Claire Maître (Turnhout, 2004), 128–33.

56 Coralie Belleville and Julie Régnier, 'Fonts baptismaux, actuellement bénitier', Inventaire général du patrimoine culturel, Région Rhône-Alpes, Dossier IM69000851 (2002), online at: <http://patrimoine.rhonealpes.fr/dossier/fonts-baptismaux-actuellement-benitier/e5df5d64-841b-436b-8b98-00f76e6b56a6>, accessed 14 December 2015. Gilbert Gardes, *Lyon. L'Art et la ville* (Paris, 1988), 129, considers the church to be sixth-century.

57 *Vita Germani* 12 (MGH SRM 7, 259). Bede indicates his diocese: *HE* 1.17.

water cults, an activity most likely to have taken place early in the diocese's history, possibly at Lupus's instigation.[58] Lastly, the previously mentioned single early Alban church in Brittany at Elven could also witness Germanus's involvement. Constantius records that after he returned from Britain Germanus travelled to Armorica.[59] It is conceivable that while there Germanus deposited relics with the bishop of Vannes that were later translated to Elven.

Of course, Germanus's personal involvement cannot explain the majority of France's foundations. An Alban church near Viviers almost certainly post-dates Germanus's death, since the see was not established until 475. This building features in the episcopal *res gesta* among a group of six other extramural churches.[60] Modern studies have dated each of these to between the fifth and seventh centuries.[61] Alban's church has never received detailed study but may well date from the same period.[62] It may even reflect the continuing significance of the older regional capital's name, 'Alba' (*civitas Albensium*).[63] Another extramural Alban church existed in Moûtiers (formerly Tarentaise).[64] Its graveyard contained a Merovingian-period, possibly episcopal, sarcophagus.[65] Both of these (sixth-century?) churches were presumably built by local bishops, using relics sourced through an extended episcopal network or perhaps from the metropolitans of Vienne, to hallow existing extramural cemeteries.

[58] Fontvannes (Aube), first mentioned in 1019: Laurent Denajar, *L'Aube* (Paris, 2005), 345–6; and Fontaine Luyères (Aube), near the source of the Barbuise.

[59] *Vita Germani* 28 (MGH SRM 7, 271–2).

[60] Johannes Columbus, *De rebus gestis episcoporum vivariensium*, 4 vols (Lyon, 1651), 1: 17.

[61] 'Inventaire général du Patrimoine Culturel de Rhône Alpes Canton de Viviers – Commune de Viviers – Saint-Ostian. Réf. Mérimée ia00048156', online at: <http://www.culture.gouv.fr/documentation/memoire/HTML/IVR82/ia00048156/>; from the same site: 'Saint-Michel', <… /ia00048151/>; 'Saint-Julien', <… /ia00048150/>; 'Saint-Victor', <… /ia00048149/>; 'Saint-Aule', <… /ia00048153/>, all accessed 14 December 2015; Paul-Albert Fevrier, 'Alba-Viviers', in Gauthier and Picard, eds, *Topographie chrétienne*, 3: 55–61; Marc Heijmans, 'Viviers', in Prévot, Gaillard and Gauthier, eds, *Topographie chrétienne*, 16/1: 326–8.

[62] 'Saint-Alban', online at: <http://www.culture.gouv.fr/documentation/memoire/HTML/IVR82/ia00048155/>, accessed 14 December 2015. The church is listed as twelfth-century.

[63] Fevrier, 'Alba-Viviers', 58.

[64] Paul-Albert Fevrier, 'Aime et Moutiers (Tarentaise)', in Gauthier and Picard, eds, *Topographie chrétienne*, 3: 141–4, at 144.

[65] Michel Jaulmes and Marius Hudry, 'L'Archéologie en Tarentaise, 1940–1980', *Mémoires de l'Académie des sciences, belles-lettres et arts de Savoie* 12 (1981), 57–72, at 66.

In the diocese of Saintes, a cluster of three Alban churches makes an odd outlier. Here a more detailed interpretation of how Alban's relics arrived can be advanced. The first to be built was probably at Merpins (Charente), where the surviving tenth-century church lies adjacent to a Merovingian-period fortification and near a Roman settlement and necropolis.[66] When the church was founded is unknown. Early knowledge of Alban's *passio* in the diocese, however, seems to be demonstrated from an apparent verbal borrowing from it in the *Vita Viviani*, an account of Saintes's late fifth-century bishop.[67] The *vita*'s age is contested: it seems also to borrow from the *Vita Germani* and a date in the 520s has been advanced.[68] The *vita* describes Vivianus sending envoys to Rome in search of relics.[69] Since they would have journeyed through Provence, they could have encountered the cults of Alban and Germanus en route. It may thus be that Alban's relics and *passio* came to Saintes, somewhat fortuitously, as a result of an episcopal commission in the late fifth or very early sixth century. When these relics came to Merpins is unknown, though it need not have been long afterwards, but the evidence of the *Vita Viviani* suggests that the *passiones* of Alban and Germanus rapidly became influential in the diocese.

As the *Vita Viviani* hints, what may have assisted the spread of Alban's cult was a symbiosis between the martyr and his 'host', Germanus, who himself features as a saint in the early versions of Alban's passion. This conjoined veneration seems to have resulted in a number of adjacent Alban and Germanus churches. At Vienne a now lost and undated Germanus church lay at one end of the city's Circus Maximus, whilst two kilometres to the south, near a

[66] 'Région Poitou-Charentes, Inventaire général du patrimoine culturel. Cognac Périphérie (Charente). Réf. Mérimée: IA00059251', online at: <http://www.culture.gouv.fr/documentation/memoire/HTML/IVR54/IA00059251/>, accessed 14 December 2015.

[67] '*De loco ubi sanguis* eius in*fluxerat*, sustulit ex terra *pulver*em cum *cru*ore et fideliter domi referens', *Vita Bibiani vel Viviani episcopi Santonensis* 8 (in *Passiones Vitaeque Sanctorum aeui Merovingici*, MGH SRM 3, 92–100, at 99). This seems to copy '*de loco* ipso *ubi* martyris *sanguis* ex*fluxerat* massam *cru*enti *pulue*ris rapuit' from Alban's *passio* (common words shown in italics): Meyer, 'Die Legende', 45.

[68] Krusch thought it dated from the eighth century: MGH SRM 3, 92–3. Ferdinand Lot thought it was earlier: 'La *Vita Viviani* et la domination Wisigothique en Aquitaine', *Mélanges Paul Fournier* (Paris, 1929), 467–77. On the possibility of borrowing, see Gillett, *Envoys*, 143–8.

[69] *Vita Bibiani* 9 (MGH SRM 3, 100).

Roman-period necropolis, there is an Alban church.[70] Similarly, thirty-five kilometres south-east of Lyon, Alban and Germanus churches straddle the River Bourbre, two and a half kilometres apart. The Germanus church is certainly Merovingian and built on the site of an earlier temple, whilst the Alban church has been claimed to date from the fifth century.[71] In total there are at least four French examples of this combination.[72]

Once shared by Germanus among the network of bishops closest to him in Provence and north-eastern France, Alban's relics were thence variously deployed within their dioceses. That there are relatively few dedications around Auxerre suggests that it was this secondary phase of translations that was most influential. Paradoxically, in Auxerre, once established by Germanus, Alban's cult seems to have received far less promotion. Why this should be is not clear, although there is an increasing awareness that many cults were regionally defined.[73] The southern Burgundian interest in Alban may be related to the fact that Germanus's own cult seems initially to have been promoted in Lyon rather than Auxerre. Constantius's *Vita Germani* was commissioned by Patiens, bishop of Lyon, and according to the author only later sent to bishop Censurius of Auxerre.[74] By contrast Gregory of Tours mentions neither Germanus nor Alban, and their cults seem not to have flourished within the diocese of Tours in this early period.

How quickly Alban's cult spread in France is hard to determine. Nevertheless, late antique Gallic bishops would most likely have sought first to Christianize those locations closest and easiest to reach, those that already possessed settlement infrastructure, and those that were of existing pagan religious importance.[75]

[70] In the suburbs of Saint-Germain and Saint-Alban-des-Vignes (Isère): André Pelletier, *Vienna, Vienne* (Lyon, 2001), 113. For context, St Vincent's church, at the north end of the Circus, is from the late fifth or early sixth century: Descombes, 'Vienne', 33.

[71] Saint-Alban-de-Roche and Saint-Germain d'Abeau, Isère: Michelle Berger et al., *Histoire des communes de l'Isère*, 4 vols (Saint-Étienne, 1987), 2: 432–3, 443–4.

[72] St Alban, Elven, and the hamlet of Saint-Germain (Morbihan); St Alban, Albens, and St Germain-la-Chambotte (Savoie). Dual dedications are also present in Auxerre and St Albans.

[73] See Wood, 'Constructing Cults'.

[74] *Vita Germani*, epistola ad Censurium (MGH SRM 7, 248–9).

[75] For Lyon, see J. F. Reynaud, 'Lyon du IVe au VIIIe siècle. Édifices religieux, nécropoles et topographie urbaine', Stephen Walker, ed., *Récentes recherches en archéologie gallo-romaine et paléochrétienne sur Lyon et sa région*, British Archaeological Records, International Series 108 (Oxford, 1981), 126–33.

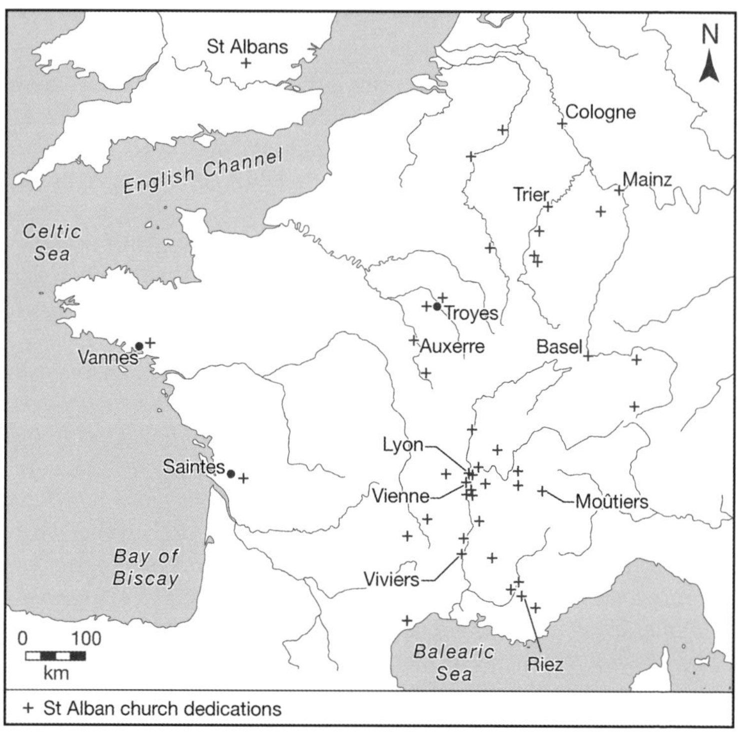

Figure 3. Conjectured Alban dedications before *c.*750.

A significant number of Alban's churches occur in precisely these locations: close to major cities, on or very close to France's major Roman roads, on the sites of former villas, at late antique Roman cemeteries or near the sources of rivers. Based on these factors and (as we have seen) in some cases more explicit evidence, it may be suggested that perhaps a third of France's nearly one hundred Alban churches may have been in existence by around 750 (Fig. 3), whilst in Britain there may have been only one. Nor should this necessarily surprise: by the end of the sixth century Venantius Fortunatus was already lauding Alban as one of Europe's most significant martyrs.[76] Moreover, there is no evidence that this success was due to British exiles or Columbanian mission; rather it was due to Gallic bishops, in

[76] Venantius Fortunatus, *De virginitate* 155 (MGH AA 4/1, 185).

particular Burgundian ones, using Alban's cult in the furtherance of their pastoral outreach.

Alban Dedications in Germany

Alban churches have long been known of in Basel, Mainz and Cologne but a major problem has been disentangling the cults of Alban of Verulamium (22 June) and Alban of Mainz (21 June). Levison considered they were the same saint, although domestic German scholarship has tended to preserve Alban of Mainz's independence.[77] Mainz's Alban church was constructed outside the city on a hilltop. Archaeology has revealed fifth- and sixth-century Christian grave inscriptions and a church possibly from the same period.[78] The earliest biographical details of this martyr are given by Rabanus Maurus, whose ninth-century account is creatively extracted from a possibly eighth-century *Passio Theonesti*, a bricolage of Italian, Gallic and Mainz traditions in which Alban plays a minor role.[79] Rabanus depicts Alban of Mainz as a martyred foreign missionary, very much in the manner of an idealized Boniface.[80] From none of this can we deduce anything other than that one of Mainz's early churches was dedicated to a saint named Alban. Levison's explanation of duplication remains the most economical.

Alban of Mainz's distinctive feast day first appears in additions to martyrologies of the late eighth century.[81] It is tempting to suggest that he may have been the product of the reinterpretation – translation, as it were – of the original British martyr by the Anglo-Saxon missionaries Boniface and Lull. Here the Wessex background of these figures could be significant. Yorke, amongst others, has noted that Aldhelm seems to have treated older Irish and British

[77] Levison, 'St Alban', 338. Hans Werner Nopper, *Die vorbonifatianischen Mainzer Bischöfe. Eine kritische Untersuchung der Quellen zu den Anfängen des Bistums Mainz und zur Zuverlässigkeit der Bischofslisten* (Norderstedt, 2001), 45–56, 124–33.

[78] Marie-Pierre Terrien, *La Christianisation de la région rhénane. Du IVe au milieu du VIIIe siècle*, 2 vols (Besançon, 2007), 1: 68–9, 78, 84, 94; 2: 141.

[79] Rabanus Maurus, *Martyrologium* (CChr.CM 46, 1–161, at 60); *Passio S. Theonesti*, *ActaSS* Oct. 13, 335–48 (*BHL* 8110); Eugan Ewig, 'Die ältesten Mainzer Bischofsgräber, die Bischofsliste und die Theonestlegende', in Ludwig Lenhart, ed., *Universitas. Dienst an Wahrheit und Leben*, 2 vols (Mainz, 1960), 2: 19–27.

[80] James T. Palmer, 'The Frankish Cult of Martyrs and the Case of the Two Saints Boniface', *Revue Bénédictine* 114 (2004), 326–48, at 338–43.

[81] Alban of Mainz figures as an addition by a second hand in the Berne and Wissembourg MSS: *Martyrologium Hieronymianum*, *ActaSS* Nov. 2, 1–156, at 80.

dedications in Wessex differently. The survival of the name 'Malmesbury' and its retention as an ecclesiastical centre suggests a respect for its saintly Irish founder Maíldub. By contrast, the British church centre at Lanprobus, 'the community of Probus', was apparently bypassed in favour of a new episcopal centre nearby at Sherborne.[82] This difference may reflect Anglo-Saxon antipathy to the British Church. The next generation of Wessex clergy, encountering in Mainz the pre-existing cult of Alban (perhaps, indeed, with little surviving evidence as to the saint's identity), may have decided on the basis of a similar anti-British bias to forge a new identity for this 'Alban'.

The Mainz cult ultimately came to dominate its hinterland, no doubt assisted by the patronage of Charlemagne, who in 794 buried his wife Fastrada in Mainz's new abbey. Indeed the rival cult seems to have caused a shift in the name of the British martyr to 'Albinus' throughout Austrasia. An eleventh-century tradition explained that Mainz and Cologne, which both possessed a church dedicated to the British martyr, had agreed to the name-change in order to avoid confusion. Cologne's 'Albanus' became 'Albinus'.[83] However, this shift appears much earlier. The British martyr is consistently named 'Alban' in all the copies of his passion but one. This, probably created in Soissons in the late eighth or early ninth century, changed his name in the title to 'Albinus', while retaining the older name in the body of the text.[84] Something similar is found in the Namur edition of Bede's *Historia ecclesiastica*, copied in the monastery of St Hubert in the Ardennes also in the eighth or ninth century. There the scribe altered Alban's name to 'Albinus' at the start of the account of his passion and at the final notice of his obit, but retained the original name 'Albanus' throughout the rest of the chapter.[85] Alongside this one can add Martin Dolch's note that the martyr appears as 'Albinus' in the Wissembourg and Berne recensions of *Martyrologium Hieronymianum* that also date from the latter part of the eighth

[82] Barbara Yorke, 'Aldhelm's Irish and British Connections', in Katherine Barker and Nicholas Brooks, eds, *Aldhelm and Sherborne: Essays to Celebrate the Founding of the Bishopric* (Oxford, 2010), 164–80, at 164–9.

[83] Baker, 'Cult', 217–18.

[84] Turin, Biblioteca Nazionale, MS D.V.3, fol. 254^{r}; David Ganz and Monique Goullet, 'Le Légendier du Turin et L'écriture *AB*', in Monique Goullet, ed., *Le Légendier de Turin. Ms. D.V.3 de la Bibliotheque Nationale Universitaire* (Firenze, 2014), 75–9.

[85] Charles Plummer, ed., *Venerabilis Baedae Opera Historica*, 2 vols (Oxford, 1896), 1: lxxxvi–viii, 18–21; 2: 18.

century.[86] Lapses in orthography cannot explain this phenomenon, since Alban of Mainz's name is never subject to such alteration. This suggests that in the second half of the eighth century in north-east France, Belgium and the Rhineland Alban of Verulamium underwent a name-change. The explanation might well be the Anglo-Saxon promotion of the new cult of Alban of Mainz and the desire to distinguish it from the older British cult.

It has long been thought that Mainz's Alban cult eclipsed other older (possibly British) Alban cults in the region, including Basel (Fig. 3).[87] However, an Alban church (now lost) in Trier has hitherto been considered a late eighth-century translation from Mainz, but several details suggest the church may be older and originally related to the British saint.[88] Trier's Alban church was extramural and located within a Roman-period cemetery suggesting some antiquity. It was situated in proximity to a pre-Christian 'Alb-' location name: the Roman 'Porta Alba'. A kilometre to the south lies another church dedicated to Germanus, thought to be of early Merovingian date and situated also in a late antique cemetery.[89] Taken together, there is a case to be argued that Trier's Alban church may have been a fifth- or sixth-century dedication to the British martyr, later eclipsed by the Mainz traditions, and the fifth case of a conjoined Alban-Germanus veneration identified so far.[90] According to Bede one of Trier's bishops, Severus, accompanied Germanus on his second visit to Britain, and it could be that Alban's relics came to Trier through a connection with Auxerre's bishop.[91]

Conclusion

Alban of Verulamium's cult underwent both physical and cultural translation in the early medieval period. British promotion appears to have been limited, perhaps by the Saxon *adventus*, and there is

86 Dolch, 'Die Heiligennamen Albin und Alban', 54–5.

87 Beck, 'St Alban in Uri', 281–3.

88 Petrus Becker, *Die Benediktinerabtei St Eucharius-St. Matthias vor Trier* (Berlin, 1996), 564.

89 Joachim Hupe, 'Ein römisches Gräberfeld bei Trier-Feyen und die Anfänge der Kapelle St Germanus ad undas', *Funde und Ausgrabungen im Bezirk Trier* 40 (2008), 95–106.

90 Space does not permit similar speculation as to the origin of the cathedral of Saint-Aubain in Namur.

91 *Vita Germani* 25 (MGH SRM 7, 269); *HE* 1.21. René Borius thought Severus was instead from Vence: *Vie de Saint Germain d'Auxerre*, SC 112, 89; cf. Nicholas J. Higham, 'Constantius, St Germanus and Fifth-Century Britain', *EME* 22 (2014), 113–37.

no evidence that relics were translated within Wales or Brittany. Anglo-Saxon interest at home appears initially to have been equivocal and probably dependent on a degree of cultural translation that began with Bede. The extent and nature of Offa's involvement remains unclear but, if it did exist, seems not to have reached further than the abbey site. Insular interest, on the whole, dates mainly from the late tenth century onwards. Abroad, a more drastic form of 'translation' may have occurred at Mainz, where Anglo-Saxon missionaries possibly created an entirely new identity for their local martyr. Gallic uptake of the cult, stemming from a translation undertaken by Germanus of Auxerre in 429, was by contrast highly energetic, particularly in south-eastern France. The subsequent translation of relics between and within dioceses seems to have provided Gallic bishops with a useful tool by means of which a further kind of 'translation' could occur, as pagan sites and extramural burial grounds were transformed by the construction of Alban churches into places of Christian worship. Paradoxical though it may appear, in the early Middle Ages it was France that saved Albion's foremost martyr.

Christian Hebraism in Twelfth-Century Rome: A Philologist's Correction of the Latin Bible through Dialogue with Jewish Scholars and their Hebrew Texts

Marie Thérèse Champagne*
University of West Florida

In mid-twelfth-century Rome, one clerical scholar, Nicolaus Maniacutius, honed his philological skills as he endeavoured to return the text of the Psalter to the original. Maniacutius met the challenge of editing Scripture in an unusual manner as a Christian Hebraist, consulting with Jewish scholars to compare the Vulgate Book of Psalms with the Jews' Hebrew text. In doing so, he followed the example set by his scholarly predecessor, St Jerome, centuries earlier, as well as his contemporary, Hugh of St Victor. While scholars have acknowledged that Maniacutius consulted with Jews and learned Hebrew, the identity of the one or more Jewish scholar(s) remains obscure. The Sephardic scholar Abraham ibn Ezra lived in Rome c.*1140–1143, and while there wrote a commentary on the Psalms. Nicolaus also revised the Psalter and wrote of a 'learned Spanish Jew'. This article explores the phenomenon of Christian Hebraism in mid-twelfth-century Rome through the life and work of Maniacutius, and presents evidence that supports Cornelia Linde's suggestion that Abraham ibn Ezra was the 'learned Spanish Jew' with whom Maniacutius worked. In addition, textual evidence supports Maniacutius's work within an informal, cross-confessional discourse community of Jewish and Christian scholars.*

Near the middle of the twelfth century, a Roman deacon wrote about his efforts to return biblical texts to their original form, while serving at the church of San Lorenzo in Damaso. He followed a practice, highly unusual in that era, of consulting Jewish scholars and comparing their sacred Hebrew texts with the Latin translations used by Christians, particularly the Book of Psalms, to determine the original wording and eliminate errors. Referring to one such encounter, he wrote of a 'certain Spanish Jew learned in the writings of several

* Department of History, University of West Florida, 11000 University Parkway, Pensacola, FL 32514, USA. E-mail: mchampagne@uwf.edu.
I wish to thank Michael Aaron Champagne and Steve Schoenig for their generous assistance with Latin translations.

Studies in Church History 53 (2017) 71–87
doi: 10.1017/stc.2016.6

languages'.[1] Nicolaus Maniacutius (Maniacoria)[2] who served as a deacon, Lateran canon and Cistercian monk (*fl. c.*1130s–1160s), filled a unique role in Rome as a Christian Hebraist.[3] This article explores the historical phenomenon of Christian Hebraism in mid-twelfth-century Rome through the lens of Nicolaus Maniacutius's life and work, as revealed in his own words.[4] Passages in his extant texts suggest that his Jewish contact in Rome was Rabbi Abraham ben Meir ibn Ezra (d. 1167), a Sephardic scholar who lived in Rome during the early 1140s. Linde first proposed that ibn Ezra may have been the 'Spanish Jew' that Maniacutius consulted, although she acknowledged that this cannot be conclusively proved.[5] Ibn Ezra holds an important position among the medieval Jewish scholars from Muslim Spain (Al-Andalus): 'He stands at a crossroads: behind him the

[1] 'Hebraeus quidam Hispanus diversarum linguarum litteris eruditus': CChr.CM 262, 141; Linde's introduction to this volume, which is entitled *Nicolai Maniacoria: Suffraganeus bibliothece*, was extremely helpful to this study, and I am grateful for her generous communications with me. See also Cornelia Linde, 'Basic Instruction and Hebrew Learning: Nicolaus Maniacoria's *Suffraganeus bibliothece*', *RTAM* 80 (2013), 1–16, at 11–12; eadem, 'Some Observations on Nicola Maniacutia's *Suffraganeus Bibliothece*', in Lucie Dolezalova and Tamas Visi, eds, *Retelling the Bible: Literary, Historical, and Social Contexts* (Frankfurt am Main, 2011), 159–68; eadem, *How to Correct the* Sacra Scriptura? *Textual Criticism of the Latin Bible between the Twelfth and Fifteenth Century,* Medium Ævum Monographs 29 (Oxford, 2012). Michael Signer, in 'Polemic and Exegesis: the Varieties of Twelfth-Century Hebraism', in Allison P. Coudert and Jeffrey S. Shoulson, eds, *Hebraica Veritas? Christian Hebraists and the Study of Judaism in Early Modern Europe* (Philadelphia, PA, 2004), 21–32, at 24, also notes that Maniacutius had mentioned a 'Spanish Jew' in his *Libellus de corruptione et de correptione psalmorum et aliarum quarundam scripturarum*, the text of which is found in only one codex: Montpellier, Bibliothèque de l'École de Médecine, MS H294, fols 144^{r}–159^{v}; Vittorio Peri published a transcription in 'Correctores immo corruptores. Un saggio di critica testuale nella Roma del XII secolo', *Italia medioevale e umanistica* 20 (1977), 19–125, at 88–125.

[2] Over the centuries, his surname has been recorded in at least twenty-eight different spellings. In this article, Maniacoria and Maniacutius denote the same individual.

[3] The sequence in which Maniacutius moved between these three roles is not certain. Most scholars have claimed that Maniacutius had joined the Cistercians by early 1145; however, I firmly support a position first proposed by Linde, that he probably joined that order in his later years (*c.*1160s), after having served as a deacon and then as an Augustinian canon regular. For a thorough discussion of the problems inherent in determining Maniacutius's chronology, see CChr.CM 262, vii–xv.

[4] Maniacutius's works have been extensively studied from Heinrich Denifle in the late nineteenth century onwards. For a recent study, see Rossana Guglielmetti, 'Nicola Maniacutia, "Corruzione e correzione dei testi"', *Ecdotica* 5 (2008), 267–98.

[5] CChr.CM 262, xxxiv; Linde, 'Basic Instruction', 10–12; see also Shlomo Sela, *Abraham Ibn Ezra and the Rise of Medieval Hebrew Science* (Leiden, 2003), 10; Michael Signer, 'Rabbi and *Magister*: Overlapping Intellectual Models of the Twelfth-Century Renaissance', *Jewish History* 22 (2008), 115–37, at 127.

flourishing era of Andalusian linguistics … before him, with his move to Italy, his transfer [of] the linguistic heritage of his Spanish ancestors to central Europe.'[6] Among the many texts ibn Ezra composed in different genres was a commentary on the Psalms, written while he was in Rome (*c.*1140–1143) or Lucca (*c.*1143–1145).[7] Maniacutius also undertook a revision of the Latin Psalter that had been translated by Jerome (d. 420) from the Hebrew text, apparently within the same time-frame as ibn Ezra.[8]

This article will delve more deeply into the evidence for Jewish scholars in Rome, and particularly Abraham ibn Ezra's presence and work, presenting additional correlations between the approaches to language skills, accuracy and concern for the sacred texts taken by Maniacutius and ibn Ezra, which further substantiate the possible relationship suggested by Linde.[9] In addition, it will argue that the evidence indicates the existence of a discourse community of Christian and Jewish scholars in mid-twelfth-century Rome, which extended to Monte Cassino; scholars from both religions circulated copies of scriptural texts and discussed them. Such cross-religious cooperation and consultation, which has been demonstrated among Parisian and northern French Christian and Jewish scholars from the early twelfth century, has not hitherto been noted in Rome.[10]

There is substantial overlap in the scriptural texts regarded by Christians and Jews as authoritative: the books known to Christians as the Old Testament and to Jews as the *Tanakh*, which Jews divide into the *Torah* or Pentateuch, the *Nevi'im* or Prophets and the *Ketuvim* or Writings.[11] Since all Western texts before the mid-fifteenth

[6] Luba R. Charlap, 'Abraham Ibn Ezra's Viewpoint regarding the Hebrew Language and the Biblical Text in the Context of the Medieval Environment', *Folia linguistica historica* 26 (2006–7), 1–11, at 1.

[7] Shlomo Sela and Gad Freudenthal, 'Abraham Ibn Ezra's Scholarly Writings: A Chronological Listing', *Aleph* 6 (2006), 13–55, at 18, 26–7. Sela and Freudenthal point out that in 1156 ibn Ezra wrote another commentary on the Psalms while in Rouen: ibid. 21.

[8] Robert Weber, 'Un Nouveau manuscrit de la révision du psautier «Iuxta Hebraeos» due à Nicolas Maniacoria', *RB* 85 (1975), 402–4; Linde, 'Observations', 160–1. Aryeh Grabois claims that Maniacutius was the first Christian scholar to focus on the Psalms in that century: 'The Hebraica Veritas and Jewish-Christian Intellectual Relations in the Twelfth Century', *Speculum* 50 (1975), 613–34, at 628–9.

[9] CChr.CM 262, xxxiv; Linde, 'Basic Instruction', 10–12.

[10] See Linde, 'Basic Instruction', 13–15, for Maniacutius's place among known Christian Hebraists of that century.

[11] David E. Sulomm Stein, 'Preface', *The JPS Hebrew-English Tanakh*, 2nd edn (Philadelphia, PA, 1999), xv–xxi.

century were handwritten, scribal errors, omissions and additions gradually altered the texts over centuries of copying. For Christians, the steady circulation of manuscripts between abbots, bishops, monasteries, churches and cathedrals added to the complexity by producing many copies of the same text, with slight variations between them. Even though the version of the Scriptures that Jerome had produced in the late fourth and early fifth centuries was the authoritative Latin text in the Christian West, hand-copying and the resultant numerous copies in circulation introduced variations in that text.[12]

In the era in which Maniacutius and ibn Ezra lived, the authoritative Hebrew text of the *Tanakh* was the Masoretic Text. In addition to it, another body of texts used by both men, although not considered sacred, were the Targums, paraphrased Aramaic translations of the books of the *Tanakh* with accompanying exegesis.[13] The Targums were known among the Jewish scholarly community in Rome; an early twelfth-century Roman scholar, Rabbi Natan ben Yehi'el (*c.*1101) referred to Targum Job in his influential Talmudic encyclopedia, the *'Arukh*.[14]

In both Christian and Jewish communities, a profound reverence for the Word of God underlay exegesis; within a renewed interest in the liberal arts, exegesis flourished during the High Middle Ages in Al-Andalus and Christendom among Jewish and Christian scholars alike.[15] As Signer has shown, from the eleventh century an increased emphasis on education prevailed among both Jewish and Christian students.[16] From the 1130s to the 1160s, the city of Rome was the setting for Maniacutius's endeavours to correct the Old Testament

[12] Linde, 'Observations', 159.

[13] CChr.CM 262, xxxiii–xxxv, 178; Charlap, 'Abraham Ibn Ezra's Viewpoint', 8; Abraham ibn Ezra, *Commentary on the Pentateuch: Genesis (Bereshit)*, ed. and transl. H. Norman Strickman and Arthur M. Silver (New York, 1985), 17–18; Signer, 'Rabbi and *magister*', 131. Étan Levine, 'The Biography of the Aramaic Bible', *Zeitschrift für die alttestamentliche Wissenschaft* 94 (1982), 353–79, at 374, explains: 'despite its didactic importance and element of sanctity, the *Targum* was not regarded as "sacred", and the distinction was zealously maintained'.

[14] Martin McNamara, *Targum and Testament Revisited: Aramaic Paraphrases of the Hebrew Bible* (Grand Rapids, MI, 2010), 318. For a discussion of the *'Arukh*, see Luisa Ferretti Cuomo, 'Le Glosse Volgari nell'Arukh di R. Natan ben Yehi'el da Roma', *Medioevo Romanzo* 22 (1998), 232–83.

[15] Beryl Smalley, *The Study of the Bible in the Middle Ages*, 3rd edn (Notre Dame, IN, 1978), xxxii; eadem, 'Andrew of St Victor, Abbot of Wigmore: A Twelfth-Century Hebraist', *RTAM* 10 (1938), 358–73.

[16] Signer, 'Rabbi and *magister*', 116–17.

texts in order to arrive at the original texts and understand them more accurately. From the early fifth century to the early twelfth, Christian scholars rarely followed the methodology that Jerome had used in his translation, correction and exegesis of the Old Testament; Jerome had learned Hebrew as well as Aramaic, consulted Jewish scholars and compared the Latin text with the Hebrew.[17] Jerome also knew and used the Aramaic Targums in his exegesis.[18]

Jerome's approach did, however, find some followers in the early twelfth century in northern France, where two Christian Hebraists, Stephen Harding (d. 1134),[19] third abbot of the Cistercian abbey of Cîteaux, and Hugh (d. 1141), abbot of St Victor in Paris, used elements of his method: each met with Jewish scholars and compared the Latin text with the Hebrew Bible.[20] Maniacutius and Hugh of St Victor were contemporaries, but while ample evidence exists for Hugh's Hebraism in Paris, the evidence suggests that Maniacutius was unique in pursuing Hebraism in Rome.[21] By the later 1160s, after Maniacutius's active scholarly period, the practices of consulting Jews, learning Hebrew and comparing the Hebrew and Latin texts became more common, as seen in the work of scholars such as Andrew of St. Victor (d. 1175) and Herbert of Bosham (d. *c.*1194). Stephen Harding, Hugh of St Victor, Andrew of St Victor and Herbert of Bosham all consulted Jewish scholars in northern France or England, where

[17] See Dennis Brown, *Vir Trilinguis: A Study on the Biblical Exegesis of Saint Jerome* (Kampen, 1992); J. N. D. Kelly, *Jerome: His Life, Writings, and Controversies*, 2nd edn (Peabody, MA, 1998); Matthew Kraus, 'Hebraisms in the Old Latin Version of the Bible', *Vetus Testamentum* 53 (2003), 487–513. Robert Hayward, in *Targums and the Transmission of Scripture into Judaism and Christianity* (Leiden, 2010), 281–2, determined that Jerome was skilled in Aramaic and Syriac as well as Hebrew.

[18] Hayward, *Targums*, 301–4, 315–17.

[19] G. Fiesoli, 'La "lectio divina" Cisterciense da Stefano Harding a Nicolò Maniacutia', *Medioevo e Rinascimento. Annuario del Dipartimento di studi sul Medioevo e il Rinascimento dell'Università di Firenze* 25 (2011), 161–97. Harding's complete Bible is in Dijon, Bibliothèque municipale, MSS 12–15. He also wrote of his work with Jewish scholars in the *Monitum* (*c.*1109): PL 166, 1373–6.

[20] Rainer Berndt, 'The School of St. Victor in Paris', in Magne Sæbø, ed., *Hebrew Bible, Old Testament: The History of its Interpretation*, 2 vols (Göttingen, 2000), 1/ii, 486–9; Smalley, *Study*, 83–106.

[21] See Smalley, *Study,* 77–82, 97–111, for a discussion of Hugh's predecessors and followers who also consulted learned Jews in Paris and elsewhere from as early as *c.*1070. This article presents the current state of knowledge regarding Christian Hebraism in mid-twelfth-century Rome; at this point there is only evidence for Maniacutius working as a Christian Hebraist in the city at that time.

a rich tradition of contemporary Jewish exegesis continued.[22] They perceived their Jewish counterparts as valuable resources; as Smalley suggested, 'the Jew appealed to [the medieval scholar] as a kind of telephone to the Old Testament'.[23] To that end, some medieval scholars also learned Hebrew and participated in a 'discourse community' that crossed confessional lines.[24]

While unique and significant for his time and place, Maniacutius's Hebraism is only part of his intriguing life story and oeuvre. Ten of his texts are still extant. They include hagiographic works, adulations (of the papacy), methodological treatises and revisions of the Psalter.[25] In these works Maniacutius demonstrated his familiarity, not only with a broad range of Christian texts, but also with the works of ibn Ezra and Rabbi Solomon bar Isaac, commonly known as Rashi (d. 1105).[26]

[22] Smalley, *Study*, 112–95; Deborah Goodwin, *'Take Hold of the Robe of a Jew:' Herbert of Bosham's Christian Hebraism* (Leiden, 2006), 73–94.

[23] Smalley, *Study*, 362.

[24] On the concept of the 'discourse community', see Erik Borg, 'Discourse Community', *ELT Journal* 57 (2003), 398–400; James E. Porter, 'Intertextuality and the Discourse Community', *Rhetoric Review* 5 (1986), 34–47. In the setting of mid-twelfth-century Rome, this informal group of scholars discussed common texts, and also circulated texts among themselves. The number of participants is uncertain; however, Maniacutius's *Libellus* clearly indicates communication and sharing of texts between Jewish and Christian scholars: see the excerpt from it at n. 48 below.

[25] *Vita beatae Constantidae virginis*; *Vita beatarum Praxedis et Pudentianae*; *Vita Sancti Hieronymi*; *Ad incorrupta pontificum nomina conservanda*; *Tractatus Nicolai Maniacutii de imagine SS. Salvatoris in Lateranensi palatio* (also known as *Historia imaginis Salvatoris* and *De sacra imagine*); *Libellus de corruptione et de correptione psalmorum et aliarum quarundam scripturarum*; *Suffraganeus bibliothece*; revisions of the *Psalter ad Romanum* and *Psalter iuxta Hebraeos* (Jerome's Gallican Psalter), and a third revised Psalter that apparently has elements of all three versions; in addition, each revised Psalter has a preface.

[26] CChr.CM 262, xxxii, 147–207. Linde notes numerous instances in Maniacutius's *Suffraganeus bibliothece* in which he used the works of Jewish scholars such as Abraham ibn Ezra and Rashi, but also Church Fathers and Christian scholars, including Jerome, Augustine of Hippo, Hugh of St Victor and Gregory the Great. Maniacutius's other texts also indicate his familiarity with specifically Roman ecclesiastical texts, e.g. *Descriptio Lateranensis ecclesiae* (*c.*1073–1105): see Gerhard Wolf, '*Laetare filia sion. Ecce ego venio et habitabo in medio tui*: Images of Christ transferred to Rome from Jerusalem', *Jewish Art* 23–24 (1997–8), 419–29, at 422–3. For further information on Rashi and his position within Jewish and Christian exegesis, see Jason Kalman, 'Medieval Jewish Biblical Commentaries and the State of *Parshanut* Studies', *Religion Compass* 2/5 (2008), 1–25; Herman Hailperin, 'Christian Acquaintance with the Works of Rashi, 1125–1300', in idem, *Rashi and the Christian Scholars* (Pittsburgh, PA, 1963), 103–34; Deborah Schoenfeld, *Isaac on Jewish and Christian Altars: Polemic and Exegesis in Rashi and the* Glossa Ordinaria (New York, 2013); David

In his revisions of the Psalter, Maniacutius followed Jerome's example, correcting different versions of the Psalter that had originated with him. Over seven centuries earlier, Jerome had produced three different Latin translations. The *Psalterium Romanum* or 'Roman Psalter' was Jerome's earliest revision of the Old Latin text, translated from the Septuagint into Latin *c.*383.[27] He produced a second version, the *Psalterium Gallicanum* or 'Gallican Psalter' (*c.*387) by using Origen's *Hexapla* to assist in translating the Septuagint into Latin.[28] Between 391 and 405, Jerome then translated the Old Testament directly from the Hebrew text, thus producing a third version of the Psalter, the *Psalterium iuxta Hebraeos*.[29]

Maniacutius knew of Jerome's three different versions of the Psalter. He revised the *Psalterium Romanum* and the *Psalterium iuxta Hebraeos*, to which he gained access through the efforts of a Jewish scholar who knew of a copy at Monte Cassino.[30] He also revised a third version, the only other variation of the Psalter by Maniacutius that is still extant, which has been described as an intermediate text between the Hebrew, Gallican and Roman.[31] As a Roman cleric, he

Stern, 'The Hebrew Bible in Europe in the Middle Ages', *Jewish Studies, an Internet Journal* 11 (2012), 235–322, at 301.

27 For a brief history of the Septuagint, see John Eaton, *The Psalms: A Historical and Spiritual Commentary, with an Introduction and New Translation* (London, 2005), 43–4.

28 Kelly, *Jerome,* 12–18. The *Hexapla*, compiled by Origen in the 230s, was a comparison of six different versions of the Christian Old Testament: the Hebrew text, the 'Greek transliteration of the Hebrew', the ancient Septuagint, and three Jewish revisions of the Septuagint then in circulation, by Aquila, Symmachus and Theodotion: T. M. Law, 'Origen's Parallel Bible: Textual Criticism, Apologetics, or exegesis?' *JThS* 59 (2008), 3–9.

29 The Gallican version of the Psalms, which Jerome had translated earlier from the Septuagint with the help of the Hexapla, was more familiar in most of Christian Europe, and was generally inserted into the Old Testament instead of a translation from the Hebrew. In the sixteenth century, the authoritative text became known as the Vulgate Bible: see Eaton, *Psalms*, 44. For a summary of these different translations and historical issues, see Kelly, *Jerome,* 89, 158, 283–6.

30 Maniacutius, *Libellus*, fol. 145r, col. B (Peri, 'Correctores immo corruptores', 91). His revision of the *Psalterium Romanum* is found today in only one manuscript: Rome, Archivio Capitolare Lateranense, S.M. in Trastevere, Arm. I, litt. A, num. 2, in capsa ferrea. The manuscript was examined in the archive of Santa Maria in Trastevere in 1953, but was moved to the archive in the Lateran basilica complex at a later date: Robert Weber, 'Deux Préfaces au psautier dues à Nicolas Maniacoria', *RB* 63 (1953), 3–17, at 4–5 n. 4.

31 The 'intermediate version' is referenced in the online catalogue entry for London, BL, MS Egerton 2908, fols 169r–185v, at: http://searcharchives.bl.uk/IAMS_VU2:IAMS032-002249251, accessed 27 August 2016. Linde noted Maniacutius's revisions of the *Psalterium Romanum* and *the Psalterium iuxta Hebraeos*: CChr.CM 262, xv–xvii, xxii–xxiv.

was familiar with the *Psalterium Romanum* in common use in the city; he also knew the *Psalterium Gallicanum* from its wider circulation in Europe at that time.[32] Differences between the Psalters based on the Septuagint (*Psalterium Romanum*), the Hexapla (*Psalterium Gallicanum*) and the Hebrew text (*Psalterium iuxta Hebraeos*) appear in the division of individual psalms and in the wording.[33] Translating the Psalms through multiple languages, such as Jerome's translation into Latin from the Septuagint, which itself was translated from the Hebrew original, had changed the text. Comparing the result of that process with a more direct translation from Hebrew to Latin, as Jerome later did, demonstrated variations in the wording.[34]

Maniacutius's motivation for following Jerome's example derived from a deeper reason than methodology. In his *vita* of Jerome, Maniacutius expressed his personal devotion to the saint, which was probably influenced by his mother's own devotion to Jerome. Maniacutius explained that when pregnant with him, his mother had prayed for Jerome's intercession for the safe delivery of her baby.[35] Undoubtedly Maniacutius was also influenced by scholarly motives, but where and when he received his education, learned of Jerome's approach, and decided to follow it, is unclear.

In another text, *Libellus de corruptione et de correptione psalmorum et aliarum quarundam scripturarum*, Maniacutius discussed his work in correcting the biblical text. He began by addressing his patron, Abbot Dominic, and in so doing revealed that he had acquired a scholarly reputation amongst the Roman clergy.

> Wishing to emend your psalter as you had asked, Abbot Dominic, according to our version, that is, that of the Cistercian Order, I discovered this one to be more corrupted than yours. What shall I do? For if I carry it out, I have not lessened corruptions, but rather increased them; if not, however, I shall perhaps incur suspicion of laziness, while you can suppose that what I claim is false. So that I can avoid this suspicion, therefore, I shall undertake a labour greater than that which you are demanding and no less useful to us ourselves than to you, unless perhaps

[32] Brown, *Vir Trilinguis*, 101–2.

[33] William L. Holladay, *The Psalms through Three Thousand Years: Prayerbook of a Cloud of Witnesses* (Minneapolis, MN, 1993), 4.

[34] Eugene F. Rice Jr, *Saint Jerome in the Renaissance* (Baltimore, MD, 1985), 15–18.

[35] Weber, 'Deux Préfaces', 3–17; CChr.CM 262, xv–xxv; see also PL 22, cols 183–202, at 185.

> it should fall into the hands of those despisers who, embracing custom alone, prefer naked lies to the truth.[36]

As Maniacutius gained expertise with exegesis and the mechanics of the Latin language, and recited the psalms day after day, he grew increasingly concerned about out-of-place words and phrases, and the differences between copies of what were supposedly the same version of the Psalter.[37] His words also indicate his frustration with others who did not value an accurate translation as much as he did.[38]

Maniacutius's texts also reveal a greater degree of familiarity, not only with Jewish texts but also with Jewish practices and traditions, than would be expected in Christian clergy at that time, suggesting that he had first-hand knowledge of rabbinic and scribal practices. His decades-long activity within the Roman clergy in different roles also indicates familiarity with the city and its people, including its Jews.[39] As Maniacutius wrote in his *Libellus*, again to Abbot Dominic:

> You will answer, 'And from what [source] will I distinguish a lie from the truth?' I will say, 'From the Hebrew source.' … Therefore, when you discover clashing versions, have recourse to the language from which they were translated and, from the volumes varying among themselves, believe that one which you will find to harmonize with the language from which it was taken. … You will say, however, 'Perhaps the codices of the Jews have been falsified.' I will answer, 'I will not neglect the counsel of wise men for the sake of that doubt of yours.'

[36] 'Volens psalterium tuum sicut petieras, abba Dominice, ad exemplar nostrum, id est Cisterciensis Ordinis, emendare, amplius hoc quam tuum deprehendi corruptum. Quid faciam? Si enim hoc egero, non diminui corruptiones, quin potius augmentavi; sin autem, suspicionem pigritiae forsan incurram, dum putare potes falsum esse quod assero. Ut igitur hanc suspicionem valeam evitare, laborem aggrediar eo grandiorem quem exigis et nobis ipsis non minus quam tibi utilem, nisi forte in eorum manus incidat contemptorum, qui solam consuetudinem amplectentes nuda mendacia praeferunt veritati': Maniacutius, *Libellus*, fol. 144^{r}, col. A (Peri, 'Correctores immo corruptores', 88).

[37] *Lectio divina* had been prescribed for the entire clergy by Augustine of Hippo (d. 430) and for monastics by Benedict of Nursia (d. 547): C. H. Lawrence, *Medieval Monasticism*, 3rd edn (Harlow, 2001), 30–4, 111–14, 142; Augustine, *On Christian Doctrine (De doctrina Christiana)*, NPNF I 2, 476–7; Benedict, *The Rule of St. Benedict*, ed. Bruce L. Benarde, Dumbarton Oaks Medieval Library 6 (Harvard, MA, 2011).

[38] On Maniacutius's attention to accuracy, see Leonard Boyle, 'Tonic Accent, Codicology, and Literacy', in *The Centre and its Compass: Studies in Medieval Literature in Honor of Professor John Leyerle*, ed. Robert A. Taylor et al. (Kalamazoo, MI, 1993), 1–10, at 3.

[39] A definitive chronology of Maniacutius's life is still not established, therefore any correlation of his works with each clerical role he undertook remains insecure.

> Still you will add, 'I myself believe that they have been falsified.' … Nevertheless, incline your ear and hear how they cannot easily be violated. Their whole zeal is given to the Old Testament, and among them it has not been altered by any translators (so that one translation can be mixed up with another). Furthermore, an old copy, written out with the utmost zeal, is guarded with great diligence in the reliquary of the synagogue.[40]

Somewhat surprisingly, this passage suggests that Maniacutius had personal knowledge of Jewish scribal practices, particularly within the synagogue. He also knew of the 'niche' in which the Torah scroll was kept in the synagogue.[41] In the middle decades of the twelfth century, Christian clergy who had personal knowledge of Jewish practices and traditions were usually converts from Judaism. There is no evidence, however, that Maniacutius was a convert. His confident statement reveals very specific knowledge, gained either first-hand or from his Jewish counterparts, that supported his belief in the accuracy of the Hebrew text.

[40] 'Respondebis: et unde mendacium a veritate discernam? Ex Hebraico, inquam, fonte. … Cum ergo discordantia repereris exemplaria, ad linguam recurre unde translata sunt et de variantibus inter se voluminibus illi crede quem linguae de qua sumptum est invenies concordare. … Dices autem: forsan falsati sunt codices Iudaeorum. Respondebo: pro dubitatione ista tua non negligam sapientium consilium. Adhuc subiunges: Ego eos credo falsatos esse. … Et tamen aurem accommoda et audi quomodo nequeant facile violari. Penes Vetus Testamentum est totum eorum studium et hoc apud eos nullis est translatoribus variatum, ut una translatio possit cum alia commisceri. Praeterea vetus exemplar summo studio exaratum in synagogae loculo magna diligentia custoditur': Maniacutius, *Libellus*, fol. 146r, cols A–B (Peri, 'Correctores immo corruptores', 92). Linde explains why Maniacutius turned to the *Psalterium iuxta Hebraeos* to correct the Latin Psalter versions, and why he believed the Hebrew was actually a more reliable guide to the original text: CChr.CM 262, xxxvii.

[41] The translation of *loculo* is rather uncertain. According to J. F. Niermeyer and C. Van de Kieft, *Mediae Latinitatis Lexicon Minus*, 2 vols (Leiden, 2002), 1: 808, *loculus* could mean a coffin, reliquary or grave. It is unclear how the Torah scroll would have been stored in a twelfth-century Roman synagogue, as compared to the Ashkenazic or Sephardic traditions, but it definitely would have been in a reverent and secure location within the synagogue; therefore 'reliquary' seems appropriate. In addition, that meaning would have been a familiar concept to Maniacutius: see also Kenneth R. Stow, *Alienated Minority: The Jews of Medieval Latin Europe* (Cambridge, MA, 1992), 69. This reference by Maniacutius to a *loculus* will be studied further in the context of the Roman Italo-Ashkenazic synagogue traditions. For an explanation of how the Torah was covered and protected in the synagogues of Rome in the early modern and modern eras, see Daniela Castro, ed., *Treasures of the Jewish Museum of Rome: Guide to the Museum and Its Collection*, transl. Lenore Rosenberg (Rome, 2010).

In the *Libellus* Maniacutius also referred directly to his personal study of Hebrew:

> For indeed I have decided to carefully mark all the passages corrupted either by the carelessness of scribes or by the presumption of any others, and to uncover the cause of each corruption with as much care as I can, having employed aids for this purpose from all sides, and especially the source of Hebrew truth, from which you know that I have tasted (even if only a little), but also the new translation of blessed Jerome and the Roman translation, and also other translations, when I can, so that from the collection of many considerations the truth may more easily begin to shine.[42]

Although he wrote that he had only 'tasted (… a little)' of the *Hebraica veritas*, Maniacutius's texts indicate otherwise.[43] The numerous correlations between his corrections to the Old Testament in his *Suffraganeus bibliothece* and works by Rashi and Abraham ibn Ezra stand as evidence.[44] In addition, Maniacutius occasionally wrote Hebrew letters within his Latin texts to demonstrate a particular point in his translation.[45] In the *Suffraganeus*, he only commented on corrections to the books of Christian Scripture that were in the Hebrew Bible, and not in contention between Jewish and Christian scholars. It is clearly apparent that Maniacutius valued the Hebrew source as the most accurate.[46] Again, from the *Libellus*:

> Meanwhile, I do not cease to wonder that this translation of Jerome according to Hebrew truth is not obliged to be included in his Bibles.

[42] 'Decrevi nanque cuncta loca, vel scriptorum incuria vel quorumlibet aliorum praesumptione corrupta, curiose notare et occasiones singularum corruptionum quanta possum cura detegere, adhibitis michi [*sic*] ad hoc undecunque suffragiis et maxime fonte veritatis Hebraicae, de quo me scis etsi modicum degustasse, sed et nova beati Ieronimi ac Romana translatione, aliis quoque, si possum, probationibus, ut ex multarum rationum collegio veritas facilius elucescat': Maniacutius, *Libellus*, fol. 144^{r}, col. A (Peri, 'Correctores immo corruptores', 88). Maniacutius's phrase *fonte veritatis Hebraicae* refers, apparently, to the Hebrew text.

[43] Linde posits that Maniacutius's statement near the beginning of the *Libellus* regarding the 'Hebrew truth, from which you know that I have tasted (even if a little)', reflects a 'humility-topos': CChr.CM 262, xl.

[44] See CChr.CM 262, 178, 206–7, for a listing of twenty-six instances identified by Linde in Maniacutius's *Suffraganeus bibliothece* that correlate with Abraham ibn Ezra's commentaries, and twenty-seven correlations with Rashi's texts.

[45] CChr.CM 262, xvii n. 34; Weber, 'Deux Préfaces', 6–8.

[46] Linde, 'Basic Instruction', 4.

> For even if, at the request of Pope Damasus, it is read that he first translated it [the Old Testament] from the Greek and afterwards corrected it again and again, as he says to Paula and her daughter Julia Eustochium in a certain prologue, nevertheless none of those editions so expresses the truth as this one does. I suppose, however, that, annoyed now by so many revisions, the Church made provision neither to include this one (though truer than all) in Bibles nor to chant it in churches. Thus, up to these times, his [*juxta Hebraicum*] version could scarcely be discovered.[47]

While recent scholarship, particularly within Cistercian studies, has continued to acknowledge Maniacutius's Hebraism, scholars have not focused specifically or extensively on his communications with Jews or his use of their sacred texts. Nor have they discussed his personal goal of learning Hebrew, also expressed in his *Libellus*:

> For even I would perhaps not have it unless a certain Hebrew, arguing with me and claiming that almost everything that I was objecting to him from the Psalms was otherwise, had indicated that it had been brought from Monte Cassino in the possession of a certain priest. It was then that I first aspired to the knowledge of the Hebrew language.[48]

The information provided by the 'certain Hebrew' indicates communication between that individual and a priest, and particular knowledge of the origin of 'it' (the Psalms text), the Benedictine abbey of Monte Cassino. These intriguing points indicate that in this case, Jewish and Christian scholars were comparing texts and discussing the meaning of the Psalms in Rome; however, they also indicate that

[47] 'Interim mirari non desino quod haec Ieronimi iuxta Hebraicam veritatem translatio bibliothecis eius non habeatur inserta. Nam et si petente papa Damaso de Graeco prius transtulisse legatur et postea iterum atque iterum correxisse, ut ad Paulam et filiam eius Iuliam Eustochium in quodam prologo loquitur, nulla tamen earum editionum ita exprimit veritatem ut ista. Puto autem quod tam multis renovationibus iam ecclesia fastidita hanc, licet omnibus veriorem, nec bibliothecis inserere nec cantare in ecclesiis procuravit. Unde usque ad haec tempora exemplar eius reperiri vix poterat': Maniacutius, *Libellus*, fol. 145^{r}, col. B (Peri, 'Correctores immo corruptores', 90–1).

[48] 'Nam et ego illud forsitan non haberem, nisi quidam Hebraeus, mecum disputans et paene singula quae ei opponebam de psalmis aliter habere se asserens, hoc de Monte Cassino allatum esse penes quendam praesbyterum indicasset. Tunc primum ad Hebraeae linguae scientiam aspiravi': Maniacutius, *Libellus*, fol. 145^{r}, col. B (Peri, 'Correctores immo corruptores', 91).

communication within this 'discourse community' extended to the circulation of texts beyond Rome to Monte Cassino, if not further.[49]

The significance of Maniacutius's Roman origin, long service in the local church, and communication with Jewish scholars is especially notable in light of the make-up of the Roman Jewish community, whose roots extended back to at least the second century BCE.[50] It had a long-standing relationship with the bishop of Rome, and at times had acted as intermediary between Jews elsewhere in Christendom and the papacy.[51] In twelfth-century Rome, an active and vibrant community of Jews continued to practise their faith and traditions. Despite separation from Christians in many aspects of their lives, these Jews thought of the city of Rome as their home. They interacted with Christians in the marketplace and participated, along with the Christian population, in the acclamation of a newly elected pope as one of the seventeen Roman *scholae*, civic groups of craftsmen.[52] One prominent Jew seems to have served Pope Alexander III as his papal steward. According to Benjamin of Tudela, 'R. Yehiel, a minister of the Pope … is a handsome young man, intelligent and wise, and has access to the residence of the pope, serving as the steward of his household and all of his property. He is a grandson of R. Nathan, who composed the *Sefer ha-'arukh* and its commentaries.'[53] These Jews participated in the discourse about the history of their city, holding many of the same beliefs in ancient legends, but also the same misconceptions about local sites and historic objects. For

[49] Both Weber ('Deux Préfaces', 14–15) and Linde (CChr.CM 262, xv–xvii) indicate that copies of Maniacutius's *Psalter iuxta Hebraeos* are bound in two other codices: Montecassino MSS 434, 467.

[50] Marie Thérèse Champagne and Ra'anan Boustan, 'Walking in the Shadows of the Past: The Jewish Experience of Rome in the Twelfth Century', *Medieval Encounters* 17 (2011), 464–94.

[51] Shlomo Simonsohn, ed., *The Apostolic See and the Jews, Documents: 490–1404* (Toronto, ON, 1988), 15 (no. 19).

[52] Susan Twyman, *Papal Ceremonial at Rome in the Twelfth Century* (London, 2002), 201–6; Cencius, *Liber Censuum*, in Paul Fabre and Louis Duchesne, eds, *Le* Liber Censuum *de l'église romaine*, 3 vols (Paris, 1889–1952), 1:304–6, paragraphs [42]–[56]). For a discussion of medieval Ashkenazic Jewish life in northern European societies, see Elisheva Baumgarten, 'Daily Commodities and Religious Identity in the Medieval Jewish Communities of Northern Europe', in John Doran, Charlotte Methuen and Alexandra Walsham, eds, *Religion and the Household*, SCH 50 (Woodbridge, 2014), 97–121.

[53] Benjamin of Tudela, *The Itinerary of Benjamin of Tudela: Travels in the Middle Ages*, ed. and transl. Marcus Nathan Adler (Malibu, CA, 1983), 63; Champagne and Boustan, 'Walking', 468–70.

Jews as well as Christians, Rome was a dense landscape of cultural memories.[54]

A respected tradition of Rabbinic studies continued within the Roman Jewish community through the Middle Ages; from the tenth century, that community supplied legal advice in response to the needs of Ashkenazic communities in northern Europe. Roman Jewish scholars, particularly the Qualonymos family, served as the main channel for Jewish thought and ritual to Jewish communities elsewhere, at first in Lucca, and later to others in northern cities such as Mainz.[55] This scholarly role of the Roman Jewish community meant that rabbinic scholars were present and active in Rome during the era in which Maniacutius was consulting Jews. The existence of such a learned element in the Jewish community could explain why Abraham ibn Ezra, after leaving Al-Andalus *c.*1140, first travelled to Rome and resided with that community for several years.[56] As Linde has argued, his expertise added to the collective skills of that community, and communications with him would have benefitted Maniacutius.[57] Perhaps Maniacutius's motivation for consulting the Spanish scholar lay also in the reputation for accuracy that Spanish Hebrew Bibles had within Christendom.[58] Maniacutius's respect for the highest scholarly standards, evident in his texts and in his standing within the Roman community, make the respected Sephardic scholar ibn Ezra a likely consultant.[59]

Abraham ibn Ezra was clearly one of the most influential medieval Jewish scholars.[60] After leaving his homeland, he spent the rest of his life as a wandering scholar. He lived in Rome from *c.*1140 until *c.*1143, when he journeyed to Lucca where he remained until *c.*1145. He then moved to France and thence to England; when he died *c.*1167, ibn Ezra probably was residing in London.[61] His written works included

[54] Champagne and Boustan, 'Walking', 487.

[55] Ibid. 472; Cuomo, 'Le Glosse Volgari', 232–83; see also Linde, 'Basic Instruction', 14; Aryeh Grabois, 'Écoles et structures sociales des communautés juives dans l'Occident aux IXe–XIIe siècles', *Gli Ebrei nell'alto Medioevo* 2 (1980), 937–62, at 952.

[56] Sela, *Rise of Medieval Hebrew Science*, 6–7.

[57] CChr.CM 262, xxxiii. Linde states that ibn Ezra 'brought the local Jewish community to intellectual flowering'.

[58] Stern, 'Hebrew Bible', 248 n. 23; Nahum M. Sarna, 'Ibn Ezra as an Exegete', in Isadore Twersky and Jay M. Harris, eds, *Rabbi Abraham Ibn Ezra: Studies in the Writings of a Twelfth-Century Jewish Polymath* (Cambridge, MA, 1993), 1–21, at 7–8.

[59] CChr.CM 262, xxvii–xxx.

[60] Grabois, 'Écoles et structures', 954–5.

[61] Sela, *Rise of Medieval Hebrew Science*, 2.

biblical commentaries, grammatical analyses, poetry, theological treatises, scientific texts and a comprehensive collection of astrological textbooks.[62]

Ibn Ezra revered Hebrew as the first language and the language of God, but he also believed it could be used successfully to express contemporary concepts, even if they would have been unknown to ancient writers.[63] In many cases he found that terms within the biblical text already carried a scientific meaning; in other treatises, as he translated from Arabic into Hebrew, he introduced a new use for a Hebrew term.[64] The reverence in which later Jews held ibn Ezra is apparent in references to him in the works of Maimonides (1135–1204) and Nachmanides (1194–1270), both highly influential Sephardic exegetes and philosophers, as well as their successors.[65]

While ibn Ezra studied and wrote in a range of fields, his work on Hebrew grammar significantly influenced his writings in other areas. Thus in his commentaries he stressed the importance of grammatical analysis in discerning the meaning of words.[66] He advocated an exegetical method which began with close examination of the grammar of each word, before moving on to discerning its meaning.[67] In his *Commentary on the Pentateuch*, ibn Ezra explained his preference for this particular method: 'It appears to me to be correct in the presence of God whom alone I fear. I will not show favouritism to anyone when it comes to interpreting the Torah. I will, to the utmost of my ability, try to understand grammatically every word, and then do my best to explain it.'[68]

Of the sixty-two extant texts by Ibn Ezra, five focus on Hebrew grammar.[69] It is known that he studied the grammar of biblical Hebrew, rather than the spoken Hebrew of his day, holding that the

[62] Shlomo Sela, *Abraham Ibn Ezra on Nativities and a Continuous Horoscopy*, Études sur le judaïsme médiéval 59 (Leiden, 2013), 4; Sela and Freudenthal, 'Abraham Ibn Ezra's Scholarly Writings', 18–48.

[63] Sela, *Rise of Medieval Hebrew Science*, 106.

[64] Ibid. 104–43.

[65] Silver, Preface to ibn Ezra, *Commentary on Genesis*, ed. and transl. Strickman and Silver, vii.

[66] Mariano Gómez Aranda, 'Grammatical Remarks in *The Commentary of Abraham Ibn Ezra on Qohelet*', *Sefarad* 56 (1996), 61–82, at 61, 80.

[67] Signer, 'Rabbi and *magister*', 131.

[68] Ibn Ezra, *Commentary on Genesis*, ed. and transl. Strickman and Silver, 17.

[69] Sela and Freudenthal, 'Abraham Ibn Ezra's Scholarly Writings', 18–22; Frederick E. Greenspahn, 'Abraham Ibn Ezra and the Origin of some Medieval Grammatical Terms', *Jewish Quarterly Review* 76 (1986), 217–27.

diaspora and consequent adoption of different languages by Jews living in many cultures had corrupted their spoken Hebrew.[70] It is also known that Maniacutius communicated with the 'Spanish Jew' about the Hebrew Scriptures.[71] His perspective makes ibn Ezra the perfect Jewish biblical scholar for Maniacutius to consult.

Other correlations between Maniacutius's methods and skills and those of ibn Ezra make consultations between the two even more likely.[72] In his commentaries, ibn Ezra used the *Targum*, the paraphrased Aramaic translation of the Tanakh and associated commentary.[73] Maniacutius also made use of the *Targum*.[74] Ibn Ezra apparently knew some Latin and may have assisted in producing the Latin translation of some of his texts; Maniacutius knew both Latin and Hebrew.[75] While much is circumstantial, the evidence increasingly supports Linde's theory that Abraham ibn Ezra was indeed the 'Spanish Jew' of whom Maniacutius wrote.

Similarities also exist between the views on textual correction held by ibn Ezra and those of Maniacutius, and specifically in their caustic reactions to incorrect methods. In the *Libellus*, Maniacutius complained of a reckless scribe he had encountered in the scriptorium of San Martino in Monte, who was incorrectly combining all variants from different copies of the Psalter into his new version.[76] Ibn Ezra

[70] Charlap, 'Abraham Ibn Ezra's Viewpoint', 4.

[71] Ibid. 6; Stern, 'Hebrew Bible', 235–322.

[72] CChr.CM 262, xxxiii–xxxv.

[73] Charlap, 'Abraham Ibn Ezra's Viewpoint', 8; Ibn Ezra, *Commentary on Genesis*, ed. and transl. Strickman and Silver, 17–18; Signer, 'Rabbi and *magister*', 131; cf. CChr.CM 262, 178. While the *Targum* was used by several notable Jewish scholars of this era, including Rashi, it was not always consulted. Some eleventh-century Jewish scholars had advised that study of it be stopped, but this was not generally implemented except in the northern provinces of Spain under Christian rule: see n. 14 above, and Alberdina Houtman, 'The Role of the Targum in Jewish Education in Medieval Europe', in eadem, Eveline von Staalduine-Sulman and Hans-Martin Kirn, eds, *A Jewish Targum in a Christian World* (Leiden, 2014), 81–98, at 88, 91–2.

[74] This raises the question of whether Maniacutius knew Aramaic too. In addition to numerous instances in which he utilized the texts of Rashi and ibn Ezra in his *Suffraganeus bibliothece*, Maniacutius also used the *Targum*: CChr.CM 262, 207.

[75] Sela, *Rise of Medieval Hebrew Science*, 23; Maniacutius, *Libellus*, fol 145^{r}, col. B (Peri, 'Correctores immo corruptores', 91). The question of Maniacutius's actual fluency in Hebrew is still unanswered; however, on the basis of evidence in the *Suffraganeus bibliothece*, Linde suggested that his skill was 'between cultural and lexical Hebraism' (CChr.CM 262, xli), terms that Michael Signer introduced in 'Polemic and Exegesis', 21–32. In other words, Maniacutius could not read Hebrew completely independently, but he was able to deal with Hebrew texts with the help of his Hebrew consultants.

[76] Maniacutius, *Libellus*, fol 158^{r}, col. A (Peri, 'Correctores immo corruptores', 121).

similarly criticized the Masoretes for the way they explained inconsistencies in spellings within the Hebrew Bible: 'Since the Massorites claim to be able to explain the reasons for full and defective spellings, let them tell us what spelling the scribes should have used in writing Scripture. … Actually, the reason[s] given by the Massorites for the different spellings of the same word are for children.'[77]

Circumstantial evidence supports Linde's thesis that Maniacutius and Abraham ibn Ezra consulted each other about their methods of analysis and correction of Scripture.[78] Both men had tremendous respect and reverence for sacred Scripture; their interests intersected in the value they both placed on the original Hebrew text. Both men worked on the text of the Book of Psalms, and analysed the grammar and meaning of the 'biblical Hebrew' words. Maniacutius's work focused on grammatical dissection and he urged careful analysis. In his treatises, not only those that focused on grammatical theory and analysis, ibn Ezra promoted the careful study of grammar.[79] Both men lived and worked in Rome at the same time, and could have met in consultation over the Hebrew texts. Maniacutius's linguistic skills included Hebrew; he conducted his work within an inter-confessional discourse community of scholars in Rome and outside it; he reported receiving a text from a Jew; and he also referred to a 'learned Spanish Jew', indicating that he was acquainted with the Jewish community. Moreover, Maniacutius's detailed knowledge of Jewish scribal traditions also indicates direct familiarity with those traditions. Whether or not ibn Ezra can be proved definitively to be the 'Spanish Jew' that Maniacutius consulted, at this point he is, as Linde has argued, the most likely candidate. Perhaps most importantly, the intersection of Jewish and Christian scholars in Rome made possible Maniacutius's innovative methodology, which still intrigues us today.

[77] Ibn Ezra, *Commentary on Genesis*, ed. and transl. Strickman and Silver, 18.

[78] CChr.CM 262, xxxiii–xxxv.

[79] Sela, *Rise of Medieval Hebrew Science*, 328–9.

Translation and Appropriation: Greek Relics in the Latin West in the Aftermath of the Fourth Crusade

Anne E. Lester*
University of Colorado-Boulder

Following the fall of Constantinople to French, Flemish and Venetian forces at the conclusion of the Fourth Crusade, an unprecedented number of relics and other holy objects poured into the West between 1204 and c.*1240. Sent as personal and diplomatic gifts, most holy objects moved in the open, with letters of authentication and identification, and not (as has often been suggested) as sacred theft. This article traces the work of translation, carried out by clerics, chaplains, monks, and laymen and women, and the mechanisms of appropriation that gave meaning to these objects in their new devotional contexts. Relics were demanding things; they needed to be enshrined, venerated, described and contextualized, and their movements needed to be accounted for and included within a broader Christian narrative that served to anchor the crusade movement to the apostolic past and to Christ's material presence in the West. Moreover, the materiality of the relics that moved from Constantinople was an important part of their significance and shaped devotional practices and connections, bridging differences between Greek and Latin culture and fostering conceptions of the material that facilitated other acts of Christian translation in the centuries to come.*

At some point in the spring of 1206, but possibly as late as 1213, Robert of Clari, a poor knight, returned from Greece to northern France, to his native Picardy not far from the Flemish border. He had travelled to the east with his lord, Peter of Amiens, in 1202, fought alongside the contingents of French, Flemish and Venetian crusaders, and in April 1204 he was among the knights, foot soldiers

* Department of History, University of Colorado-Boulder, 234 UCB Boulder, CO 80309-0234, USA. E-mail: alester@colorado.edu.

Research and writing of this article was conducted while I was a Derek Brewer Fellow at Emmanuel College, University of Cambridge and before that during the time I held a Charles L. Ryskamp Fellowship from the American Council of Learned Societies. I am grateful to both institutions for their support. I wish to thank Liesbeth Van Houts, Julie Barrau, Cecilia Gaposchkin, Julia M. H. Smith and Scott Bruce for their generous support and comments. I would also like to thank Simon Ditchfield for the invitation to speak at the EHS summer conference in York.

Studies in Church History 53 (2017) 88–117
doi: 10.1017/stc.2016.7

and 'pilgrims' who breached the walls of Constantinople and took possession of the Byzantine capital: a Latin triumph that marked the end of the Fourth Crusade.[1] Returning to the west, Robert carried with him stories, or in his words 'truths' about what had happened in the east. He also carried things: a great trove – a *theka*, or box – of relics from the treasuries of Constantinople.[2] Both – the knowledge, experience and, dare we say, traumas of an ill-fated crusade, and the holy materials he carried from the East – were burdens that needed to be preserved, explained and accounted for. As I hope to show, close attention to the translations of objects can offer a different understanding of the role of relics in the aftermath of the Fourth Crusade where once the umbrella category of crusader 'loot' or 'booty' sufficed. When given space to present their own narratives, the relics translated after 1204 served to communicate multiple ideas, including an affirmation of Latin legitimacy in the Byzantine East and the Levant, divine assent for the crusade movement and the crusaders' victory in 1204, and the complexity of Christian conceptions of holy matter.

In the years after his return Robert dictated two texts. The first is well known to most students of medieval history as it is one of the earliest French vernacular accounts attributed to a layman – that is, not a cleric – of a crusade expedition. This text has come to be known as *The Conquest of Constantinople*, echoing its opening lines: 'Here begins the history of those who conquered Constantinople (*Chi commenche li estoires de chiaus qui conquisent Coustantinople*).'[3] Therein Robert

[1] For Robert's travels and participation in the entourage of Peter of Amiens, see Jean Longnon, *Les Compagnons de Villehardouin. Recherches sur les croisés de la quatrième croisade* (Geneva, 1978), 202–4. Longnon suggests that Robert returned to Picardy with his brother, Aleaume, possibly as early as April 1205.

[2] See Hyacinthe Dusevel, *Histoire abrégée du trésor de l'abbaye royale de Saint-Pierre de Corbie* (Amiens, 1861), 45–86, for the treasure inventory; Robert's role in transporting relics is noted throughout, especially ibid. 21, 46. Dusevel states (ibid. 79 n. 1) that Corbie preserved in its treasury the bourses or scrips given to crusaders as part of the ritual of departure and which many used to translate relics from the East. We cannot know whether one of the bourses kept by the abbey can be associated with Robert, but crusader bourses and their preservation within treasuries was not uncommon: see Anne E. Lester, 'The Casket of Jean of Montmirail: The Sacred Politics of Reuse in Thirteenth-Century France', *Peregrinations: Journal of Medieval Art & Architecture* 4 (2015), 50–86. On the rituals of departure and the blessing of crusader scrips, see M. Cecilia Gaposchkin, 'From Pilgrimage to Crusade: The Liturgy of Departure, 1095–1300', *Speculum* 88 (2013), 44–91.

[3] Robert de Clari, *La Conquête de Constantinople*, ed. Jean Dufournet (Paris, 2004), 44. For the English I have used Robert of Clari, *The Conquest of Constantinople*, transl. Edgar

related the call to crusade in 1199, the mustering of troops from northern France and Flanders, the journey across the Mediterranean, the conquest of the city and the splendour of its palaces and chapels. In the conclusion, Robert implores his reader/listener to take his story as truth: 'now you have heard the truth how Constantinople was conquered … as he bears witness, who was there and saw it and heard it, Robert of Clari, knight. And he made the truth to be put in writing, how it was conquered.'[4]

Truth and its spoken and written form were palpably important to Robert as to many who took part on the Fourth Crusade.[5] Robert's pursuit of a historical truth and a translated narrative of the events he witnessed was shored up by the other text he dictated: an impressive list of the relics he carried from Constantinople. Robert's list was copied neatly, some time between 1281 and 1283, at the end of a *Rotulus* recording the inventory of the relics of the abbey of Corbie and rubricated as 'The shrine that Robert, knight of Clari, brought from Constantinople (*Sanctuarium quod Robertus miles de Clari attulit Constantinopoli*)'.[6] The text enumerated the fifty-four relics Robert translated,

---

Holmes McNeal (Toronto, ON, 1996; first publ. 1936), 31. Robert's text is preserved in only one manuscript copy now in Copenhagen, Royal Library, MS GKS 487, fols 100v–128r. It is the last of five texts copied together in two narrow columns in a book of 128 vellum leaves dated to *c.*1300. The volume brought together several popular and related works translated into vernacular French, including the *Recits d'un minstrel de Reims*; John of Flixecourt's translation of Dares the Phrygian, *De excidio Troiae*; the *Chronicle of Turpin*; and a treatise by Petrus Alphonsus, *Disciplina clericalis.* The manuscript is briefly described by McNeal in Clari, *Conquest*, 7–10. On the context of Robert's composition, generally dated to *c.*1216, see Jeanette Beer, *In their own Words: Practices of Quotation in Early Medieval History-Writing* (Toronto, ON, 2014), 57–68. For an important critical reading, see Sharon Kinoshita, *Medieval Boundaries: Rethinking Difference in Old French Literature* (Philadelphia, PA, 2006), 139–75. On similar crusade collections, see Richard H. and Mary A. Rouse, 'Context and Reception: A Crusading Collection for Charles IV of France', repr. in eidem, *Bound Fast with Letters: Medieval Writers, Readers, and Texts* (Notre Dame, IN, 2013), 215–79.

[4] 'Ore avés oï le verité, confaitement Coustantinople fu conquise, … que chis qui i fu et qui le vit et qui l'oï le tesmongne, Robers de Clari, li chevaliers, et a fait metre en escrit le verité, si comme ele fu conquise': Clari, *La Conquête*, 212.

[5] On the truth-claims of vernacular prose histories at this time and in this region, see Gabrielle M. Spiegel, *Romancing the Past: The Rise of Vernacular Prose Historiography in Thirteenth-Century France* (Berkeley, CA, 1993), although Spiegel does not deal with the crusader histories. For crusade narratives, see Nicholas Paul, *To Follow in their Footsteps: The Crusades and Family Memory in the High Middle Ages* (Ithaca, NY, 2012), especially 55–89.

[6] Amiens, Bibliothèque municipale, MS 527, Rotulus; Robert's relics are listed on the verso. The list had been copied by Benedicto Cocquelin, *Historiae regalis abbatiae Corbeiensis compendium*, which he compiled between 1672 and 1678. Cocquelin's text was edited by J. Garnier in *Mémoires de la Société des Antiquaires de Picardie* 8 (1845), 377–534; Robert's

in some cases describing the containers and their materials and in one instance noting the presence of a Greek inscription.[7] It is a familiar list of holy fragments and included several large crosses made from wood of the Lord, that is, fragments of the true cross; cloth and other garments associated with Christ and Mary; thorns from the crown of thorns; stones from the Holy Sepulchre; and many relics of the apostles, martyrs and virgin saints. In its fullness (see the Appendix at the end of this article), Robert's list of relics demonstrates the varieties of objects translated from Byzantium to Latin Christendom in the period following the Fourth Crusade, between *c.*1204 and *c.*1240.[8] His list also emphasizes the material quality of objects venerated as relics, both in the Greek East and Latin West.

The translation of these relics and the attendant strategies of appropriation that followed were part of and informed the broader processes of 'translating Christianity' that occupied Christians during the High Middle Ages and beyond. In using the term 'translation', I am deliberately indulging its double meaning: first, in the literal sense of *translatio*, from the Latin verb *transfero*, meaning to bear across, carry over, transport, transfer, copy, and even display in procession; and in this case to do with a sacred thing or sets of things.[9] This is the meaning at the root of concepts like *translatio imperii et studii*, the

list is at 506–8. It was subsequently published in Paul Riant's magisterial *Exuviae sacrae Constantinopolitanae*, 2 vols (Geneva, 1877–8), 2: 197–9. The relics are also enumerated in the back-matter of a missal-breviary from Corbie: Paris, BnF, MS Lat. 13222, fols 114v–121v. I am grateful to Cecilia Gaposchkin for calling this manuscript to my attention.

[7] Jannic Durand is probably correct that what is here described and enumerated are fragments of relics set within larger gold and crystal reliquaries. It is not clear, however, whether these reliquaries were made after the reception of the relic fragments (the most likely scenario, to my mind) or whether they travelled as complete Byzantine reliquaries. It is possible that the Latin *texto* is a rendering of the Greek *theke*, a box or container. Robert may have transported several Byzantine *theke* as well as other fragments, which were reassembled into new Gothic containers: Jannic Durand, 'Une Prétendue Relique de Constantinople. La "Véronique" de Corbie', in Anthony Cutler and Arietta Papaconstantinou, eds, *The Material and the Ideal* (Leiden, 2007), 205–18, at 210–12.

[8] These dates cover the period from the end of the crusade to the reception of relics in Paris following Louis IX's acquisition of the Passion relics from his cousin Baldwin II, Latin emperor of Constantinople, and the construction of the Sainte-Chapelle in Paris to house and honour them. After 1241 the translation of Byzantine relics into the West slowed markedly. In 1261 the Greeks retook the imperial city and translations effectively ceased. On the reception of relics by Louis IX and the royal court, see Karen Gould, 'The Sequences *De sanctis reliquiis* as Saint-Chapelle Inventories', *Mediaeval Studies* 43 (1981), 315–41.

[9] J. F. Niermeyer, *Mediae Latinitatis Lexicon Minus* (Leiden, 1997), 1039, *s.vv.* 'translatio', 'translatare'.

translation or transfer of imperial authority and learning in the sense of the Roman inheritance of the Carolingian period and early medieval concepts of the antiquity of imperial rule.[10] From the early Middle Ages *translatio* came to refer specifically to the movement of relics from one location to another, often during times of war when such translations were necessary. But it also described liturgical ceremonies, specifically when relics were moved from one church or city to another. The accompanying stories of their movement came to be known as narratives of translation.[11]

The second and now more common meaning of translation bears on Robert's activities as well, that is, in the context of a linguistic relationship: the transfer of meaning from one language to another or from one sense to another. This is an endeavour that often has at its core the relation of the essence of meaning, the trace of a perceivable truth or true form; an essential ontology.[12] Both senses of translation involve a taking up, and even taking in or over, that is, an appropriation of things and ideas, things and their meaning.[13] I will return to this sense of translation at the close of this article. Moving

[10] See, for example, Matthew Gabriele, *An Empire of Memory: The Legend of Charlemagne, the Franks, and Jerusalem before the First Crusade* (Oxford, 2011); Anne Latowsky, *Emperor of the World: Charlemagne and the Construction of Imperial Authority, 800–1229* (Ithaca, NY, 2013); also Sharon Kinoshita, 'Translatio/n, Empire, and the Worlding of Medieval Literature', *Postcolonial Studies* 11 (2008), 371–85.

[11] On *translatio* as a source type, see Martin Heinzelmann, *Translationsberichte und andere Quellen des Reliquienkultes*, Typologie des sources du moyen âge occidental 33 (Turnhout, 1979). See also Patrick Geary, Furta Sacra*: Thefts of Relics in the Central Middle Ages* (Princeton, NJ, 1990; first publ. 1978), esp. 9–15; Paul Antony Hayward, 'Translation-Narratives in Post-Conquest Hagiography and English Resistance to the Norman Conquest', *Anglo-Norman Studies* 21 (1998), 67–93.

[12] On the specific role of objects and images in translating ideas of the divine, see Glenn Peers, 'Object Relations: Theorizing the Late Antique Viewer', in Scott Fitzgerald Johnson, ed., *The Oxford Handbook of Late Antiquity* (Oxford, 2012), 970–93; Aden Kumler, *Translating Truth: Ambitious Images and Religious Knowledge in Late Medieval France and England* (New Haven, CT, 2011), esp. 1–13, 239–41. See also Emma Campbell and Robert Mills, eds, *Rethinking Medieval Translation: Ethics, Politics, Theory* (Woodbridge, 2012). For a broader conceptualization of translation as an undertaking, see Emily Apter, *The Translation Zone: A New Comparative Literature* (Princeton, NJ, 2006).

[13] My thinking about the enterprise of translation is much indebted to Walter Benjamin. First published in German in Heidelberg in 1921, his essay offers a fundamental point of departure: 'The Task of the Translator', in Hannah Arendt, ed., *Illuminations: Essays and Reflections*, transl. Harry Zohn (New York, 1968), 69–82. On Benjamin and translation, see also Barbara Johnson, *Mother Tongues: Sexuality, Trails, Motherhood, Translation* (Cambridge, MA, 2003), 40–64, 94–119. For ideas of appropriation, see Robert S. Nelson, 'Appropriation', in idem and Richard Shiff, eds, *Critical Terms for Art History* (Chicago, IL, 1995), 117–27; and the issue of the *Journal of Medieval and Early Modern Studies* 32 (2002) dedicated

objects and ideas, specifically relics and their rituals, from the Byzantine context into the Latin West depended on both senses of *translatio* and involved a physical transfer as well as a linguistic and intellectual relationship and refined perception.[14] In the second sense of translation, however, meanings are not fixed and often need assurances for belief to adhere. The armature of accompanying texts, histories, rituals and witnesses helped assure and affirm the material truths the relics professed.

* * *

As scholars from many different fields have begun to acknowledge, attending to objects and things as they were used and moved among and between people, especially in moments of contestation and colonization, can yield different perspectives on the past. Historians such as Michael McCormick, Robin Fleming and Julia Smith have shown persuasively how an analysis of material relationships can clarify interactions and 'communications' in instances when textual sources are either silent or do not describe and detail such encounters.[15] Indeed, a reliance on texts as our main sources, and in the context of crusading history very specific types of texts, often generated solely by monastic or clerical authors, many of whom were not present in the East or on the campaigns they report, often offers an incomplete view of relations among groups, especially concerning the meaning of religious actions.[16] With increased attention to materiality and its

to the topic, especially Kathleen Ashley and Véronique Plesch, 'The Cultural Processes of "Appropriation"', ibid. 1–15. For the concept more broadly conceived, see Daniel Rogers, Bhavani Raman and Helmut Reimitz, eds, *Cultures in Motion* (Princeton, NJ, 2014), 1–19. Bridging the translation of relics and narratives, see also Michael Wintroub, 'Translations: Words, Things, Going Native, and Staying True', *AHR* 120 (2015), 1185–1217.

[14] On this latter idea, I find the insights of Shirin A. Khanmohamadi, *In Light of Another's World: European Ethnography in the Middle Ages* (Philadelphia, PA, 2014), extremely useful, especially for the ideas about how Europeans perceived themselves. See also Kinoshita, *Medieval Boundaries*; Maria Marvoudi, 'Translating from Greek into Latin and Arabic during the Middle Ages: Searching for the Classical Tradition', *Speculum* 90 (2015), 28–59.

[15] Michael McCormick, *Origins of the European Economy: Communications and Commerce, AD 300–900* (Cambridge, 2001); Robin Fleming, 'Recycling in Britain after the Fall of Rome's Metal Economy', *P&P* 217 (2012), 3–45; Julia M. H. Smith, 'Portable Christianity: Relics in the Medieval West (*c.*700–1200)', *PBA* 181 (2012), 143–67.

[16] Standard histories of the Fourth Crusade rely almost solely on chronicles and diplomatic sources rather than material and visual evidence. See, for example, Donald E. Queller and Thomas F. Madden, *The Fourth Crusade: The Conquest of Constantinople*, 2nd edn (Philadelphia, PA, 1997); Michael Angold, *The Fourth Crusade: Event and Context* (Har-

methods, it is clear that people as subjects – both in the present and in the past – inhabit a world in which objects mediate and participate in the process of identity formation implicit in the creation of differences, boundaries, narratives and meanings.[17] As Glenn Peers has observed, 'because things can tell a different story than texts, … they can reveal a world informed and forming identities [and ideas] not expressible through words, but only through experience, action, contact'.[18] Consequently, objects and things need to be attended to in much greater detail than has hitherto been the case.

What follows addresses the translation and appropriation of relics from Byzantium to the Latin West, moving both chronologically and conceptually. I offer first an overview of the Fourth Crusade and its historiography with respect to the role of relics. I then turn to the acts of translation and those individuals – like Robert of Clari – who functioned as translators, that is, who carried sacred matter – bones, stones, wood, oil and the like in boxes, bourses and other containers – from Constantinople across the Mediterranean, up the Rhône or through central France to be deposited into the treasuries and chapels of northern France, Flanders and Germany. Christianity very often required trained translators: technicians of the holy who were trusted to authenticate, arbitrate, control and deploy sacred

low, 2003); Jonathan Phillips, *The Fourth Crusade and the Sack of Constantinople* (New York, 2004). On the sources for the crusade, see Alfred J. Andrea, 'Bibliography: Essay on Primary Source', in Queller and Madden, eds, *Fourth Crusade*, 299–313; see also Michel Balard, 'L'Historiographie occidentale de la quatrième croisade', in Angeliki E. Laiou, ed., *Urbs Capta: The Fourth Crusade and its Consequences / Le IVe croisade et ses conséquences* (Paris, 2005), 161–74; Fanny Caroff, 'La Narration des croisades dans l'iconographie française et flamande du Moyen Âge. Place et spécificité de l'expédition de 1204', in Laiou, ed., *Urbs Capta*, 175–92. For a corrective to this that incorporates visual evidence, see Thomas F. Madden, 'The Venetian Version of the Fourth Crusade: Memory and the Conquest of Constantinople in Medieval Venice', *Speculum* 87 (2012), 311–44.

17 On materiality and its methods, see Leora Auslander et al., 'AHR Conversation: Historians and the Study of Material Culture', *AHR* 114 (2009), 1354–1404; Caroline Walker Bynum, 'Perspectives, Connections & Objects: What's Happening in History Now?', *Daedalus* 138 (2009), 71–86; eadem, *Christian Materiality: An Essay on Religion in Late Medieval Europe* (New York, 2011); Finbarr Barry Flood, *Objects of Translation: Material Culture and Medieval 'Hindu-Muslim' Encounter* (Princeton, NJ, 2009), 1–14; Andrew Cole, 'The Call of Things: A Critique of Object-Oriented Ontologies', *Minnesota Review* 80 (2013), 106–18.

18 Glenn Peers, 'Translating Edges in Art of the Medieval Middle East: On the Resafa Hoard and a Painted Bottle from Liechtenstein', in Zaza Skhirtladze, ed., *On the Edge: Time and Space* (Tbilisi, forthcoming). I thank Glenn Peers for sharing this piece with me before its publication.

matter. Their role in this process, although often overlooked in crusade scholarship, was a crucial one.[19] I then consider several of the ways in which relics were appropriated into their new contexts. Many strategies were employed for making sense of Byzantine relics, which drew upon older traditions regarding the portability of Christian sacred matter. But these objects also offered new potential for nuancing historical conceptions of Christian time as expressed in the liturgical texts written in their honour and used to illustrate their meaning in the West. Finally, I address the specific material nature and meaning of the relics that moved westwards after 1204. For their material quality – their *materiality* – was part of their translatability: as fragments of cloth, stone, thorn, bone and wood – objects that were familiar, yet exotic, mundane yet sacred – their materiality was part of what gave them resonance and allowed them to be translated. Relics of this type offered an opportunity for thirteenth-century clerics, as well as the laypeople who visited new chapels and shrines, listened to sermons and liturgies, and viewed the objects through new or renewed containers and reliquaries, to consider the meaning of material charged by its relation to Christ. The notion that Christ's presence and the sacred qualities of Jerusalem were not specific to place, but rather could be translated – both moved and reinterpreted – into another physical context without diminution would be fundamental for future claims about the translation of Christianity beyond the bounds of charted Christendom.[20]

Framing the Fourth Crusade: History and Historiography

By almost any measure the Fourth Crusade was a decidedly unusual event. In 1198, as one of the first initiatives of his papacy, Innocent III renewed the call to crusade. By 1199 he had commissioned preachers – principally Cistercian abbots and charismatic priests such as Fulk of Neuilly – to recruit nobles and knights for the expedition.[21]

[19] For a correction of this oversight, see Paul, *To Follow in their Footsteps*, 90–133.

[20] See, in this volume, Simon Ditchfield, 'Translating Christianity in an Age of Reformations', 164–95.

[21] One of the best short accounts of the preparation for the crusade is Jonathan Riley-Smith, 'Toward an Understanding of the Fourth Crusade as an Institution', in Laiou, ed., *Urbs Capta*, 71–87; see also Alfred J. Andrea, 'Innocent III and the Byzantine Rite, 1198–1216', ibid. 111–22. For translations of Innocent's bulls and events leading up to the

The intention was to succeed where the previous campaign, the Third Crusade, had failed: to reclaim Jerusalem after its fall to the Muslims under Saladin in October 1187 and to recover one of the major relics of the true cross which had been captured in the battle of Hattin in July of that year. Indeed, almost all *historiae* as well as memoirs of the Fourth Crusade begin with the events of 1187. But, as many crusade historians have elaborated at great length, the expedition became sidetracked.[22] The French contingents, who had anticipated recruiting a great force, failed to gather the numbers of men and the amount of *matériel* originally planned. In 1201 they contracted with the Venetian doge, who had built a new fleet to transport them to the East, but falling short of men and supplies, the northerners found themselves greatly in debt to the Venetians. To make up for this disparity, a contingent of the French and Flemish crusaders agreed to aid the Venetians against their rival city of Zara. Following that victory and after a series of unsuccessful negotiations with the Byzantine rulers, still in debt and in desperate need of food and supplies, the crusaders and pilgrims agreed to attack Constantinople.[23] Their victory on 12 April 1204 was unprecedented and unplanned. It took some time to negotiate a settlement for the division and governance of the city, and to elect Count Baldwin IX of Flanders as the first Latin emperor of Constantinople.[24]

Historians have been divided in their interpretations of these events. Because the expedition 'deviated' to Constantinople, scholars have alternately characterized the crusade – much as some contemporaries did – as either a perversion of the original crusade ideals, or as a misunderstood manifestation of the changing nature of crusading by the turn of the thirteenth century.[25] Much of what has been written

crusade, see Jessalynn Bird, Edward Peters and James M. Powell, eds, *Crusade and Christendom: Annotated Documents in Translation from Innocent III to the Fall of Acre* (Philadelphia, PA, 2015), 24–66.

[22] This is the narrative recounted in most modern histories, see n. 16 above.

[23] On the important role of vows and agreements, see Thomas F. Madden, 'Vows and Contracts in the Fourth Crusade: The Treaty of Zara and the Attack on Constantinople in 1204', *International History Review* 15 (1993), 441–68. On the role of food and supplies, see idem, 'Food and the Fourth Crusade: A New Approach to the "Diversion Question"', in John H. Pryor, ed., *Logistics of Warfare in the Age of the Crusades* (Aldershot, 2006), 209–28.

[24] Filip Van Tricht, *The Latin* Renovatio *of Byzantium: The Empire of Constantinople (1204–1228)* (Leiden, 2011).

[25] For an early characterization of the latter perspective, see Paul Alphandéry and Alphonse Dupront, *La Chrétienté et l'idée de croisade*, 2 vols (Paris, 1954–9); most recently,

about the crusade largely concerns a detailed, even day-by-day, narrative of the military expedition followed by a general description of the sack of Constantinople.[26] Although this is beginning to change, most modern narratives stop at this point: the crusaders are condemned for their atrocities, principally for the fires that raged through the city and the looting of churches, chapels and monastic houses; they are mocked for their deviation to Greece; and derided for their failure to reach Jerusalem and thus fulfil their crusade vows. What happened thereafter, which pertains more to cultural and religious history than to military history, has largely been ignored.[27]

What is more, for modern scholars, understanding the crusade in religious terms has been complicated by its decidedly material and, as some have noted, 'colonial' outcome: the creation of a new crusade principality known as the Latin Empire in Constantinople along with further crusader principalities in the Morea (now southern Greece), and the outpouring of objects to the West after the capture of the city.[28] Moreover, the conception of the looting of Constantinople has for the most part been informed by those objects displayed in Venice. However, after the city's capture, the Latin forces divided Constantinople among themselves. The Venetians took spoils from Hagia Sophia, many of which the doge placed in his chapel at San Marco, where they are still (at times in replica) visible today: one thinks of the bronze horses that crown the façade, and the porphyry emperors along the passage connecting the palace to its chapel, or the many opulent treasures within.[29] This is not, however, how most relics passed into the West.

---

see Madden, 'Venetian Version'. As Madden points out, the 'internal dynamics of the Fourth Crusade could have allowed for the development of two different narratives within the same host': ibid. 326.

[26] The overviews of the Fourth Crusade by Queller and Madden, Angold and Phillips cited in n. 16 are all laudable examples of this approach; see also Thomas F. Madden, 'The Fires of the Fourth Crusade in Constantinople, 1203–1204: A Damage Assessment', *Byzantinische Zeitschrift* 84–85 (1992), 72–93.

[27] An exception is the Byzantine and Christian Museum, Athens, which has addressed the religio-cultural impact of the crusade. I thank one of the reviewers for this insight.

[28] For the crusader principalities and cultural production in Greece, see Peter Lock, *The Franks in the Aegean 1204–1500* (Harlow, 1995); Van Tricht, *Latin Renovatio*; Teresa Shawcross, *The Chronicle of Morea: Historiography in Crusader Greece* (Oxford, 2009); Heather Grossman, *Architecture and Interaction in the Thirteenth-Century Mediterranean: Building Identity in the Medieval Morea* (London, 2017).

[29] On the looting of the city, see, for example, the letter from Innocent III to Thomas Maurocenus, patriarch of Constantinople, in which the pope condemns the taking of icons and other holy objects: Riant, *Exuviae*, 2: 76–8 (no. 26); cf. Henry Maguire and

Finally, the Fourth Crusade also came at a fulcrum point in the longer history of the crusade movement, which destabilized Latin Christendom's confidence in crusading's goals and execution.[30] As Shirin Khanmohamadi has recently summarized:

> … excepting the First Crusade victory in 1099, … [w]ith successive crusades, ending in military losses or the inability to secure Jerusalem, we also see a coming apart of the grand, epic narrative that justified itself by God's will. Lack of success was, of course, already a sign of divine disfavor, but events such as those of the chaotic Fourth Crusade, in which Christians sacked Constantinople, an Eastern Christian capital, muddied the clarity of the crusading mission still further.[31]

And yet we must not lose sight of how medieval Christians understood these events, or of their interpretations of the diversion to Constantinople and its role in the longer unfolding of Christian history. For them, the confusion and the attendant anxieties about the legitimacy of the conquest and the meaning of the new Latin Empire made the material effects – and principally the movement of relics as Latin imperial gifts – all the more important. The relics' translations, their 'agreement' to move and be moved, connoted divine assent for the crusade's outcome.[32]

The Translations: Scope and Practice

From the surviving documentation, principally charters, letters patent, inventories and relic lists, it is clear that two waves of

---

Robert S. Nelson, eds, *San Marco, Byzantium, and the Myths of Venice* (Washington DC, 2010); David M. Perry, *Sacred Plunder: Venice and the Aftermath of the Fourth Crusade* (University Park, PA, 2015).

[30] The fact that contingents of the Fourth Crusade divided before they reached the East, with nearly half the French and Flemish crusaders continuing on to Syria, while the rest remained with the Venetians bound for Constantinople, is indicative of this shift and needs further study: see Donald E. Queller, Thomas K. Compton and Donald A. Campbell, 'The Fourth Crusade: The Neglected Majority', *Speculum* 49 (1974), 441–65; Benjamin Z. Kedar, 'The Fourth Crusade's Second Front', in Laiou, ed., *Urbs Capta*, 89–110. These divisions are also noted throughout Longnon, *Les Compagnons.* On the general shift in crusading during the thirteenth century, see Christopher Tyerman, *The Invention of the Crusades* (Houndmills, 1998).

[31] Khanmohamadi, *In Light of Another's World*, 88–9.

[32] The early letters the crusaders sent to the pope and to kin in the West speak of the confusion of the conquest and military engagement, but also of their understanding of God's role in assuring their victory. Many of these have been assembled and translated in Alfred J. Andrea, ed., *Contemporary Sources for the Fourth Crusade* (Leiden, 2000).

translation occurred.[33] The first began shortly after the fall of Constantinople, in late 1204 and early 1205. These were personal and diplomatic gifts that served initially to announce the success of the city's capture. They emanated from the new emperor as well as from the leading prelates on the expedition, who sent relics to their dioceses in the West. The second wave of relics came following Emperor Baldwin's death in 1205, during the reign of his brother, Henry, count of Hainaut (r.1205–16). Emperor Henry I and Peter Capuano, the newly appointed papal legate, monitored these gifts closely, personally assenting to many of the charters that accompanied and authenticated the objects.[34] These gifts were not spirited away in pockets or the folds of garments, but travelled in the open, often in Byzantine reliquaries, or in bourses or cloth bags sewn for this purpose and bearing inscriptions or relic tags written in Greek.[35]

Moreover, they moved in overwhelming numbers. Scholars have estimated that following the Fourth Crusade hundreds of relic fragments and holy objects pertaining to Eastern saints and the objects associated with Christ's passion migrated into the West.[36] To be sure,

[33] On patterns of relic translation, see Malcolm Barber, 'The Impact of the Fourth Crusade in the West: The Distribution of Relics after 1204', in Laiou, ed., *Urbs Capta*, 325–32; Perry, *Sacred Plunder*, 13–45. These practices are also discernible in the correspondence amassed by Riant, *Exuviae*, vol. 2. For his synthesis of this, see Paul Riant, *Des Dépouilles religieuses enlevées à Constantinople au XIIIe siècle et des documents historiques nés de leurs transport en occident*, Société nationale des antiquaires de France, Mémoires 36 (Paris, 1987); see also Anatole Frolow, *Recherches sur la déviation de la IVe croisade vers Constantinople* (Paris, 1955).

[34] See Riant, *Exuviae*, 2: 74 (no. 23), 78 (no. 27), 81 (no. 30), 82–3 (no. 32); cf. Barber, 'Impact of the Fourth Crusade'. Concerning this period in the Latin Empire's history, see Van Tricht, *Latin* Renovatio; idem, 'Robert of Courtenay (1221–1227): An Idiot on the Throne of Constantinople?', *Speculum* 88 (2013), 996–1034.

[35] By contrast, Gunthar of Pairis's *Hystoria Constantinopolitana* relates how his abbot, Martin of Pairis, stole relics by hiding them in the folds of his garments to bring to his abbey: Alfred J. Andrea, ed. and transl., *The Capture of Constantinople: The* Hystoria Constantinopolitana *of Gunther of Pairis* (Philadelphia, PA, 1997), 109–31. The Cleveland true cross reliquary also bears an inscription describing its theft from Byzantium. These examples, however, are rare. For the example of imperial gifts sent to the West, see Holger A. Klein, 'Eastern Objects and Western Desires: Relics and Reliquaries between Byzantium and the West', *DOP* 58 (1994), 283–314. Such pious thefts have attracted a disproportionate amount of attention in part because they make for scandalous stories. But their notoriety obscures the more common and routine gifts of relics highlighted here.

[36] See the literature cited in n. 33 above. Scholars such as Riant and Frolow have attempted to enumerate the relics that moved West, but as Jannic Durand has noted, such attempts remain imprecise as it is very hard to know from the written sources how many fragments were included in every reference to relics or how many fine pieces could have been kept within each reliquary, bourse or *stavrotheke*. Moreover, new discoveries of relics

many objects and relics had been translated during the earlier crusade period, some deposited in churches and monastic houses, others kept in personal chapels as souvenirs or mementos of a noble family's crusading past.[37] But after 1204 the scale of relic translations from the crusader East was far greater than ever before, so large as to be transformative. What is more, from the sources we have, both textual and material, little else appears to have been sent back to northern Europe, whether coin, credit, vestments (with rare exceptions), cloth or quantities of moveable wealth. What coinage the French crusaders were able to amass was owed to the Venetians, and the northern French and Flemish contingents did not benefit financially from this expedition.[38]

The first relics sent from Constantinople travelled as imperial gifts. In the weeks following his election and coronation as emperor, Baldwin I dispatched relics from the imperial collection of the Boukoleon palace to Innocent III, the king of France, Philip Augustus, and his brother Philip, count of Namur.[39] Not surprisingly, many of these early gifts correlate to relics sent from the Pharos Chapel of the Boukeleon Palace.[40] In 1205, gifts followed from several men of the upper aristocracy who sent relics to their spouses and kin, which were in turn donated to French cathedrals, monastic houses and local chapels.[41] Louis, count of Blois and one of the leaders of the crusade,

have since been made: Jannic Durand, 'La quatrième croisade, les reliques et les reliquaries de Constantinople', in Inès Villela-Petit, ed., *Quatrième Croisade: de Blois à Constantinople et éclats d'empires*, Revue Française d'héraldique et de sigillographie 73–75 (Paris, 2005), 55–78.

[37] See Jonathan Riley-Smith, *The First Crusaders, 1095–1131* (Cambridge, 1997), 144–5, 181–2; Paul, *To Follow in their Footsteps*, 90–133.

[38] For the precarious financial situation throughout the period of Latin rule, see Alan M. Stahl, 'Coinage and Money in the Latin Empire of Constantinople', *DOP* 55 (2001), 197–206.

[39] Riant, *Exuviae*, 2: 56–7 (no. 2), 61–2 (nos 7–8), 64–5 (no. 14), 74 (no. 23), 79–80 (no. 28). Both Baldwin I and Henry I commissioned a host of lesser lords and knights to transport relics to the West: Jean Longnon, *Les Compagnons*, 137–93.

[40] Holger A. Klein, 'Sacred Relics and Imperial Ceremonies at the Great Palace of Constantinople', in Franz Alto Bauer, ed., *Visualisierungen von Herrschaft. Frühmittelalterliche Residenzen, Gestalt und Zeremoniell*, BYZAS 5 (Istanbul, 2006), 79–99; Michele Bacci, 'Relics of the Pharos Chapel: A View from the Latin West', in Alexei Lidov, ed., *Eastern Christian Relics* (Moscow, 2003), 235–46; Alexei Lidov, 'A Byzantine Jerusalem: The Imperial Pharos Chapel as the Holy Sepulchre', in Annette Hoffmann and Gerhard Wolf, eds, *Jerusalem as Narrative Space / Erzählraum Jerusalem* (Leiden, 2012), 63–103.

[41] Anne E. Lester, 'What Remains: Women, Relics and Remembrance in the Aftermath of the Fourth Crusade', *JMedH* 40 (2014), 311–28.

probably employed one of his three chaplains to carry the relics of Sts Anne, Peter and Andrew to his wife Catherine, who then bestowed them on Chartres and Beauvais cathedrals in return for the communities' commemorations.[42] Louis also sent a tablet reliquary to the monks of Clairvaux, the great Cistercian abbey from which many crusaders had departed. This object, the monks noted, was made in the 'Greek style' with Greek inscriptions and may have resembled the true cross reliquary or *staurotheke* in the cathedral treasury of Limburg an der Lahn (Figs 1–2). Louis's gift was ferried with a larger cache of relics intended for Clairvaux and carried there by the Templar Artaud before he became a monk at the abbey.[43]

The arrival of Louis's relics in the West coincided with the reception of relics at the collegial foundation of Longpré-les-Corps-Saints, not far from Abbeville, in the Beauvaisie. Shortly before he died in 1205, Aléaume de Fontaine, like Louis of Blois, sent a collection of relics to his wife, Laurette of Saint-Valéry, which she gave to Longpré.[44] It was Aléaume's chaplain, Wilbert, who carried the relics that became the focus of devotion at Longpré.[45] Two charters attest to this story, but most of what we know of Wilbert and this translation comes from the lections written for the community to be read on the feast of the reception of the relics.[46] When Wilbert arrived at Longpré he offered up the precious relics as well as Aléaume's

[42] Riant, *Exuviae*, 2: 73 (no. 22), 183 (no. 2), 184–5 (no. 4); cf. Lester, 'What Remains', 317–21. In 1203 the household which Louis of Blois took with him to the East consisted of 'five knights, two of whom were accompanied by their own sergeants, and two churchmen, one of them the count's chancellor': Riley-Smith, 'Toward an Understanding', 82.

[43] The object is described in successive inventories drawn up by the monks of Clairvaux between 1405 and 1741. Parts of the inventories have been edited in Charles Lalore, *Le Trésor de Clairvaux du XIIe au XVIIIe siècle* (Paris, 1875), 25–6 (no. 49). On the Limburg *staurotheke*, see Nancy Sevçenko, 'The Limburg Staurothek and Its Relics', in Rena Andreade et al., eds, *Thymiama ste mneme tes Laskarinas Boura* (Athens, 1994), 289–94.

[44] Lester, 'What Remains', 321–2. On Aléaume and Laurette, see Riant, *Exuviae*, 1: cxxxiii; 2: 13–14; Susan B. Edgington, 'A Female Physician on the Fourth Crusade? Laurette de Saint-Valéry', in *Knighthoods of Christ: Essays on the History of the Crusades and the Knights Templar, Presented to Malcolm Barber*, ed. Norman Housley (Aldershot, 2007), 77–85. On the objects transported, see H. Dusevel, 'Notes sur divers objets provenant de l'anncienne abbaye du Paraclet, près de Amiens, et de l'église de Longpré-les-Corps-Saints', *Bulletin du Comité historique des arts et monuments. Archéologie, Beaux-arts* 4 (1853), 82–5. They had founded the community together in 1199, shortly before Aléaume took the cross, probably in the company of John of Ponthieu.

[45] On Wilbert, see Riant, *Exuviae*, 2: 17; Longnon, *Les Compagnons*, 179–80.

[46] For the charters, see Riant, *Exuviae*, 2: 69–70 (nos. 19–20); for the lections, ibid. 2: 10–22; cf. Riant's comments about this text: ibid. 1: cxxvii–cxxxv.

Figure 1. (Colour online) Limburg *staurotheke*, Byzantine true cross reliquary, *c*.968–85 (top cover closed). Donated by Henry of Ulmen *c*.1208 to the convent of Stuben, where his sister, Irmgard, was the prioress. Dom und Diözesanmuseum, Limburg an der Lahn, Germany. Illustration: Wikimedia Commons, online at: <https://commons.wikimedia.org/wiki/Category:Limburger_Staurothek#/media/File:Couvercle_de_Limbourg.jpg>, last accessed 5 December 2016.

armour and the letters patent that Aléaume had written to his wife and his son Hugh.[47] Here we catch a glimpse of the traffic between

[47] Ibid. 2: 16–17.

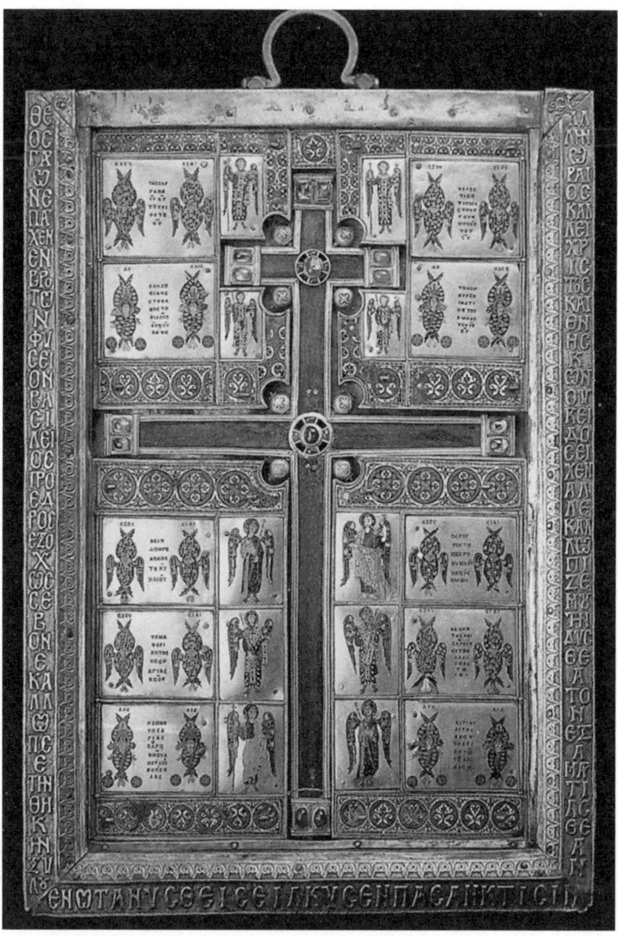

Figure 2. (Colour online) Limburg *staurotheke* (top cover removed, small doors visible). Illustration: Wikimedia Commons, online at: <https://commons.wikimedia.org/wiki/Category:Limburger_Staurothek#/media/File:Intérieur_de_Limbourg.jpg>, last accessed 5 December 2016.

Constantinople and northern Europe during the first years of the thirteenth century.

Such patterns of translation became more frequent and carefully defined in the years immediately following the disaster of the battle of Adrianople in 1205, during which campaign many of the leading nobles and knights from northern France, and especially the region of the Chartrain, were killed. Baldwin I was taken prisoner and died in captivity, his body never recovered.[48] His brother, Henry of Hainaut, initially ruled as regent during his absence and then, from 1206 to 1216, as emperor. Henry initiated a more deliberate policy of sending relics to the West in the hopes of inspiring a military response to the pressing needs of the Latin Empire.[49] Thus when Wallon of Dampierre sought to return to his native Langres with the head relics of St Mammas, believed to be the third-century bishop of Caesarea venerated in the city, he had to wait for the approval of both the papal legate and the emperor before proceeding.[50] The emperor also appears to have partially sponsored the dissemination of relics by Garnier of Trainel, bishop of Troyes (r.1193–1205) and by Nivelon de Chérisy, bishop of Soissons (r.1176–1207), both of whom gave numerous relics to the religious communities within their dioceses.[51]

It is principally from lectionary evidence – a source type to which I will return shortly – that the translation work of Wallon de Sarton, a cleric in the diocese of Amiens and a canon of Picquigny, can be reconstructed. Wallon travelled East with Hugh, count of St-Pol and other nobles and knights from the region of Amiens.[52] After the Latin victory of 1204 he became a canon attached to the community of St George of Mangana in Constantinople.[53] By 1206, he sought to return home. Before his departure, however, he had occasion to be alone in the church of St George, where behind the altar he found several relics, including two silver discs with inscriptions: one bore

[48] Robert Lee Wolff, 'Baldwin of Flanders and Hainaut, First Latin Emperor of Constantinople: His Life, Death, and Resurrection, 1172–1225', *Speculum* 27 (1952), 281–322.

[49] See, for example, Riant, *Exuviae*, 2: 102–4 (no. 42); see also Van Tricht, *Latin* Renovatio, 61–101.

[50] The lections (that is, the readings for this office) are reproduced in Riant, *Exuviae*, 2: 36–7; they follow closely the *Historia translationum reliquiarum S. Mamantis*: ibid. 1: cxxxviii–cxl, 22–34. The *historia* dates the receipt of the relics to 1209. On Wallon, see Longnon, *Les Compagnons*, 219.

[51] For the role of these two bishops, see Barber, 'Impact of the Fourth Crusade'.

[52] Longnon, *Les Compagnons*, 205–7.

[53] Riant includes two versions of this text, the longer *historia* attributed to Richard de Gerberoy, bishop of Amiens (d. 14 May 1211) (*Exuviae*, 1: lxiii–lxvii, cxxxvii, 35–44) and the lections drawn from the *historia* (ibid. 2: 26–30). The lections can be found in a fourteenth-century breviary: Amiens, Bibliothèque municipale, MS lat. 113, fols 221–2. On Richard's compositions, see Georges Durand, 'Richard de Gerberoy, évêque d'Amiens. Ce qu'on peut savoir de son oeuvre littéraire', *Bibliothèque de l'école des chartes* 99 (1938), 268–96; L. C. Brook, 'La translation de la relique de Saint-Jean-Baptiste à la cathédrale d'Amiens. Récits latin et français', *Neuphilologische Mitteilungen* 91 (1990), 93–106.

the relic of the head of St George and the other the face relic of John the Baptist. Taking both, he departed for the West at the end of September in 1206. According to the relevant *historia*, Wallon joined Wilbert, Aléaume de Fontaine's chaplain, and both reached northern France in December 1206, having shared the same travails as they passed through Venice and across the Alps.[54] Wallon then bestowed his relics liberally, giving the head of St George to the abbey of Maresmontier near Mondidier; the arm of the same saint to the church of Picquigny; and a finger relic to Sarton, where he was born.[55] The face relic of the Baptist he gave to the cathedral of Amiens, where its reception was celebrated on 17 December 1206. He then became a canon of the cathedral community, where he founded a chapel in honour of the two saints whose relics he had translated.[56]

Two other translators come to view as part of this second wave of relic translations: Hugh, former abbot of St-Ghislain in Hainaut, and the Templar Artaud, mentioned above. Both travelled at Emperor Henry's behest, translating relics along with the knowledge to explain and authenticate them. Hugh had accompanied Baldwin of Flanders when he departed on crusade in 1202, serving as one of his chaplains.[57] After Baldwin's death in 1205, Henry elevated Hugh first to the position of *clavicularius* (guardian of the relics) in the imperial treasury, and then to that of chancellor of the Latin Empire.[58] In 1207, Hugh authored a short charter confirming the authenticity of the relics sent from the imperial palace to Simon of Beaumont.[59] Not long after, probably around 1216, he 'retired' to France and took the habit as a monk of Clairvaux. At that point Henry sent a number of relics with Hugh as gifts for the abbey,

54 Riant, *Exuviae*, 2: 26–30.

55 Ibid.

56 On the face relics of John the Baptist, see Charles du Fresne du Cange, *Traité historique du chef de S. Jean Baptiste* (Paris, 1665); Annemaire Weyl Carr, 'The Face Relics of John the Baptist in Byzantium and the West', *Gesta* 46 (2007), 159–77.

57 For Hugh, see Lalore, *Le Trésor*, 18, 27, 31, 44–5, 60–4, 124–6, 156; Archdale King, *Cîteaux and her Elder Daughters* (London, 1954), 265–6, 306–7; Longnon, *Les Compagnons*, 193; Van Tricht, *Latin* Renovatio, 256–8, 262, 265–6. Van Tricht explains that Hugh is also referred to as a *clericus* and *magister*, implying that he had been educated outside the monastic context: ibid. 266.

58 Van Tricht, *Latin* Renovatio, 132; Riant, *Exuviae*, 2: 99–100 (no. 44). The position of *clavicularius* corresponded to that of the Byzantine imperial *skeuophylax*, who was responsible for the relics and religious treasures of the Great Palace.

59 Riant, *Exuviae*, 2: 78 (no. 27, Constantinople, July 1207).

including a significant fragment of the true cross.[60] Hugh's name appears throughout the Clairvaux treasury inventories, from which it is clear that he was responsible for ferrying hundreds of relic fragments. The Templar Artaud is harder to trace, except that like Hugh he is referenced throughout the Clairvaux inventories, credited with translating hundreds of relics to the abbey as well as several complete Byzantine *staurotheke* reliquaries.[61]

One could multiply such examples, assembled from the charters and letters accompanying objects or from the *historiae* composed for the relics once they arrived in the West.[62] There are two points, however, to be emphasized. First, as is clear from the texts, the great majority of relics moved out of Constantinople as gifts, and not as plunder, as has commonly been believed. They moved publicly, ceremoniously and between persons. Gifts are very different from looted wealth. Gifts mediate, confer, speak and need to be translated: to be offered up and carried forth. Gifts contain within them the trace of their donors and their provenance and there was a part of these translations that retained their Byzantine associations, which in turn gave them a different spiritual force that rendered them moveable if never completely culturally assimilated. Second, the vast majority of relics were borne by a cadre of translators, individuals who in the Christian tradition were adept at moving between cultures and peoples: the little known and scarcely studied clerics and chaplains highlighted here. The work of explaining, historicizing and appropriating fell to them and their texts, which provided the basis for a second level of translation.

Appropriations: Things in Place and Time

Relics were demanding objects. Once present in the Latin West they needed to be dealt with. The mechanisms of appropriation unfold in the ways that relics were adopted into the rhythms of sacred

[60] Ibid. 2: 99–100 (no. 40, Clairvaux, 3 June 1215). This was either the fragment of the cross that was incorporated into the reliquary made during the abbacy of Matthew, *c.*1319 (Lalore, *Le Trésor*, 16–18) or (more probably) a relic of the cross set into a gold reliquary made when Dreux was sacristan, thus before 1233, which is carefully described in the 1504 inventory (Henri D'Arbois de Jubainville, 'Trésor de Clairvaux', *Revue des Sociéte de la France et de l'étranger* 5th ser. 5 [1873], 490–508, at 497–8).

[61] Lalore, *Le Trésor,* 14, 19, 20–1, 24, 26, 38, 51–3, 64, 124–5.

[62] Many more such chaplains and clerics are identified in my forthcoming book, *Fragments of Devotion: Relics and Remembrance in the Aftermath of the Fourth Crusade.*

time in the liturgical calendar; into sacred history, which was in turn integrated into new liturgical offices; into ritual use and display; and within ways of seeing the holy. Appropriation conceived in this way also demonstrates how these objects were taken up and reused for specific sacred, historical and eschatological ends in the West. In this sense too, the use and reuse of relics offered a safe means of indulging in a process of 'replication' that was itself part of the dynamics of translation from one context into another. As with translation, appropriation contains a host of interlocking meanings that we should engage when thinking about these practices.

The appropriation of relics from Byzantium drew upon the specific knowledge and witness of the men I have labelled 'translators', who were called upon to work with bishops and abbots in the West to respond to the demands relics made. Fragments of Christ's presence on earth, the wood of the cross, vials of Christ's blood, fragments of cloth, his crib, the nails, thorns, all required proper treatment and veneration. Churchmen and donors, no doubt working in cooperation with communities, thought carefully about which relics to send to which location. Typically, the connections were associative and we can see an attempt at reassembling or gathering like to like.[63] The correspondence of Nivelon de Chérisy, bishop of Soissons, for example, demonstrates that he had a programmatic view of how to distribute and venerate the relics he acquired in Greece. He offered to his own cathedral church of Sts Gervais and Protais relics of the proto-martyr St Stephen, the apostle Thomas and the evangelist Mark, as well as many relics associated with Mary and Christ. To the nuns of Notre-Dame-de-Soissons he gave a relic of the Virgin's belt to complement the relic of her slipper that they already possessed, and to the canons of St-Jean-des-Vignes he offered relics of the arm of John the Baptist, 'the same John' as he put it, thus matching saints to their consecrated churches.[64] The same coordination was at work elsewhere: relics of St Mammas's arm and head were sent to Langres where the bishop had long been venerated; Louis of Blois sent a relic of St Anne's head to Chartres to join the relics of her daughter, the Virgin Mary, whose holy chemise had protected the diocese for nearly three

[63] On ideas of reassembly, see Caroline Walker Bynum, *The Resurrection of the Body in Western Christianity, 200–1226* (New York, 1995).
[64] Riant, *Exuviae*, 2: 58–60 (no. 4, March 1205), 65–6 (no. 15, October 1205), 67 (no. 16, 13 October 1205), 75 (no. 24, March 1206).

centuries;[65] and relics of the Baptist's face came to Amiens, whose cathedral abutted the hospital dedicated to Christ's Precursor, a building that was torn down to make room for the expanded gothic structure begun in 1218.[66] In some cases surviving evidence suggests that formal *adventus* ceremonies were planned to welcome the new relics and to process them with great ceremony into the receiving church or cathedral. Such moments, often restaged and repeated within the annual cycle of the liturgy, announced, as the Soissons sequence made clear, that the cities of the West were understood as the new Rome, the new Greece, the new Holy Land.[67]

The integration of the new relics into local liturgical calendars worked as a means of appropriation. Within the first decade of the thirteenth century new liturgies had been composed to honour the relics on the date of their reception, as well as amplifying the celebration of feast days already in place, thus further elaborating, for example, the liturgies for Mary, Thomas or the Exaltation and Invention of the Cross. The most detailed and immediate example of this kind of liturgical insertion is associated with Nivelon de Chérisy. Shortly before his departure for the East in 1202, the bishop had a new liturgical manual created as part of a general reform and rebuilding campaign. Part ordinal, part processional, part breviary, the text, known as a *Rituale*, detailed the rituals of the liturgical year.[68] After 1205 the text was augmented in remarkably explicit ways to reflect the accommodations made for the new relics Nivelon carried

[65] For Langres, see ibid. 2: 70–3 (no. 21, 1205); for St Anne, ibid. 2: 73 (no. 22, 1205).

[66] Ibid. 2: 97–8 (no. 38, May 1210).

[67] The scripting of prayers, praise and adoration are noted in the charters listed in nn. 64–6 above. For the Sequence of Soissions, see Riant, *Exuviae*, 2: 43–5.

[68] The 'Ordinarius et processionale ad usum episcopi Suessionensis', is now in BnF, MS Lat. 8898. Unusual in shape and size, it measures 365 mm x 165 mm and is written on parchment. It can be viewed on Gallica, online at: <http://gallica.bnf.fr/ark:/12148/btv1b8432463d.r=ms+8898>. An edition of the text was first produced by Alexander Poquet, ed., *Rituale seu mandatum insignis ecclesiae Suessionensis* (Paris, 1856); the section pertaining to the celebration of Nivelon's relics from Constantinople (ibid. 265–90) was reprinted by Riant with minor changes: *Exuviae*, 1: 3–9. Andrea has produced a new edition of these same folios: Alfred J. Andrea and Paul I. Rachlin, 'Holy War, Holy Relics, Holy Theft: The Anonymous of Soissons's *De terra Iherosolimitana*: An Analysis, Edition, and Translation', *Historical Reflections / Reflexions historiques* 18 (1992), 147–56. On this form of liturgical book, see Sarah Hamilton, 'The *Rituale*: The Evolution of a New Liturgical Book', in R. N. Swanson, ed., *The Church and the Book*, SCH 38 (Woodbridge, 2004), 74–86. Cecilia Gaposchkin is currently writing an article on this text, provisionally entitled 'Nivelon of Soissons's 1205 Relics in their Liturgical Contexts'; I thank her for sharing this piece with me and for subsequent discussion of the manuscript and genre.

back from Constantinople. The revised manuscript contains a short history of the events of the crusade and a list of the relics Nivelon bestowed across his diocese. It also elaborates a new feast in celebration of the reception of the relics from Constantinople, which drew on extant offices for several different saints, reflecting the variety of relics the bishops gave to the cathedral.[69] Nivelon's text also incorporated a newly composed sequence extolling the joy of the city of Soissons and the delight of its people at the reception of such holy objects.[70] In addition, the feasts celebrating St Stephen, the apostle Thomas, John the Baptist and the Exaltation of the Cross were expanded, incorporating the prayers sung in the reception feast. As Cecilia Gaposchkin has noted, the entire cycle of the annual liturgy was amplified as a consequence of Nivelon's donations.[71] Moreover, Nivelon instructed other churches in his diocese to sing the same sequence when celebrating 'those blessed martyrs whose relics we carried from Constantinople'.[72] Thus he used the acquisition of new relics as a means of liturgical renewal and reform.

The kinds of programmatic liturgical rewriting that occurred in Soissons found parallels in the other major episcopal centres of France that received relics. Although the evidence is not as elaborate or eloquent, it is clear that the clergy of Amiens, Beauvais, Chartres, Langres, Troyes, and Paris all amplified their liturgies to account for the advent of new Greek relics in the decades after 1204.[73] Moreover, all these new offices lay stress on the role of the people (that is, the community) in receiving and venerating the new relics.[74] They also stress the transformation of the place of reception: by means of these sacred fragments, the cities of the West were renewed as another Constantinople, a new Jerusalem.

The explanation of this transfer was elaborated in the liturgical *historiae*, the historical narratives that would be broken into nine or

[69] BnF, MS Lat. 8898, fols 211^{r}–224^{v}; Poquet, *Rituale*, 265–90.

[70] Riant, *Exuviae*, 2:43–5.

[71] For the details, see Poquet, *Rituale*, 265–90. This point is made by Gaposchkin, 'Nivelon of Soissons's 1205 Relics'.

[72] '[C]ontulimus ecclesie beati Petri Suessionensis, ob reverentiam beatorum martyrum quorum reliquias de Constantinopolitanis partibus Suessionem nuper attulimus': Riant, *Exuviae*, 2: 75 (no. 24).

[73] This is clear from the many feasts Riant amassed and the liturgical texts he excerpted. A study of the surviving manuscripts forms a chapter of my forthcoming *Fragments of Devotion*.

[74] This rhetoric appears in the liturgical evidence Riant gathered: *Exuviae*, 1: 3–50.

twelve units depending on the nature of the office and read aloud as part of the liturgy throughout the night preceding, and during the day of, the relic's celebration. Strikingly, among the relics translated after 1204, the *historiae* often focused on the relic as an object in its own right, narrating 'object biographies', which described the finding of the relic in the East and its donation and translation to the West, often highlighting the role of the clerics who served as translators, thus writing them into the sacred narrative.[75]

In the *historiae*, but also in other texts of commemoration, the translators – clerics, chaplains, Templars – played a critical role, for they stood as the witnesses to the authentic movement of relics from Constantinople. Their stories – the more detailed the better – worked to authenticate the relics they had translated.[76] Their memories became part of the readings made sacred by their incorporation in the liturgy and used for the celebration of the expanded liturgical offices. Sometimes these texts were appended to the reliquaries themselves, suggesting an interplay of text and object within the liturgy or on procession.[77] When personal knowledge of a particular saint or relic was lacking, as in the case of St Helen of Athyra, whose bones were among the relics Garnier of Traînel had sent in a large *châsse* to the cathedral of Troyes, clerics were dispatched to Constantinople to 'research' the details of their new Greek saint and to translate her *vita* (in the linguistic sense of the term) from Greek into Latin.[78] The creation of such new historical narratives also served to knit a history of the Byzantine East into that of the West.

Bishops and the clergy tasked with composing new offices also thought explicitly about how and when to integrate the relics into the rituals of devotion – the venerations and processions – they scripted. Nivelon's text, for example, instructed that at vespers on the evening before each new or modified feast the canons should move the relics

[75] On this concept, see Chris Gosden and Yvonne Marshall, 'The Cultural Biography of Objects', *World Archaeology* 31 (1999), 169–78.

[76] See Perry, *Sacred Plunder*, 77–134, who addresses the multiple uses of narrative.

[77] This was the case with the charter that Hugh of St-Ghislain drew up authenticating the relics he brought to Clairvaux: Lalore, *Le Trésor*, 124–6.

[78] Riant, *Exuviae*, 2: 105–6 (no. 44); cf. Giles Constable, 'Troyes, Constantinople, and the Relics of St Helen in the Thirteenth Century', in *Mélange offerts à René Crozet, à l'occasion de son 70e anniversaire*, ed. Pierre Gallais and Yves Jean Rion, 2 vols (Poitiers, 1966), 2: 1035–42; Patrick J. Geary, 'Saint Helen of Athyra and the Cathedral of Troyes in the Thirteenth Century', *Journal of Medieval and Renaissance Studies* 7 (1977), 149–68; repr. in idem, *Living with the Dead in the Middle Ages* (Ithaca, NY, 1994), 221–42.

from the sacristy to the high altar or to the relics' own altar, where they would remain for veneration and in public view for the remainder of the office, that is, over the course of the following day.[79] Thus for the feast of the apostle Thomas, for example, his relics alone were moved and displayed, whereas for the feast of the reception of the relics, all of the relics Nivelon carried from Greece were first set on the high altar and then, during the day of the feast, publicly processed throughout the city.[80] They were displayed and venerated as a collection of appropriated objects, displaced but integrated, and thus made Soissons's own saints.

Engaging the sense of vision, that is, seeing the material objects on display, was another means of appropriation. Not only was it important to display the relics on their altars on feast days and in processions, but after 1215 the canons of the Fourth Lateran Council also addressed the proper veneration of relics. Canon 62 instructed 'that henceforth ancient relics shall not be displayed outside of a reliquary or be put up for sale. As for newly discovered relics, let no one presume to venerate them publically unless they have been approved by the authority of the Roman pontiff.'[81] According to ecclesiastical authorities, proper veneration was to be mediated by papal authority. Moreover, seeing what one venerated was part of this renewed practice of devotion. As many of the inventories make clear, the reliquaries that contained the new relics were often made of crystal that rendered the substance of the relic visible. When Nivelon gave a relic of St Stephen's elbow to the church of Châlons, he sent it in a crystal container that was to be set upon the altar and remain there for the veneration of clerics and the people.[82] Although the use of crystal in reliquaries was not new, greater emphasis was accorded to visual access which concentrated the gaze on each holy fragment. Some reliquaries were made to display relics – especially of Christ and the Passion – behind small crystal doors.[83] By the 1260s in some cases

[79] Poquet, *Rituale*, 270–90; idem, *Notre-Dame de Soissons, son histoire, ses églises, ses tombeaux, ses abbesses, ses reliques* (Paris, 1855).

[80] BnF, MS Lat. 8898, fols 214^{r}–224^{v}, treats the augmentation of the liturgies; cf. Poquet, *Rituale*, 270–90.

[81] 'Fourth Lateran Council – 1215', in Norman P. Tanner, ed., *Decrees of the Ecumenical Councils*, 2 vols (Washington DC, 1990), 1: 263–4 (Canon 62).

[82] Riant, *Exuviae*, 2: 65–7 (no. 15).

[83] Klein, 'Eastern Objects, Western Desires', 299–305; Cynthia Hahn, *Strange Beauty: Issues in the Making and Meaning of Reliquaries, 400–circa 1204* (University Park, PA, 2012); Martina Bagnoli, 'The Stuff of Heaven: Materials and Craftsmanship in Medieval Reliquaries', in

the metal and enamel armature of the traditional reliquary had given way almost completely to the total display of a single fragment or piece of cloth or bone.[84] Such strategies of appropriation were in part about the truth-claims of the relics: their material nature was visible, made clear and transparent. At its root such visual access also made an argument for the shared substance of Christian devotion across East and West.

TRANSLATED MATTER: THE PORTABILITY OF CHRISTIANITY

What made the acts of translation and appropriation that I have described here possible? To answer this, I return to Robert of Clari's list. His relics, like so many others from this time, were decidedly Passion-focused and resonated with ideas about the life of Christ and the experience of Jerusalem in the first century. The qualities of these objects, the wood, bread, cloth, crystal – things of foreign, strange and yet mundane materials – made the apostolic context palpably, physically present for believers. Only in Constantinople could one find such curated collections of objects, and up to this point only in the Byzantine context had small fragments from such a variety of materials associated with Christ, Mary and the apostles been collected and 'boxed' together.[85]

As Julia Smith has begun to show, such collections of relics began during late antiquity. As collections of material fragments that retained the holy charge of the individuals associated with them, pieces of wood, shards of stones, vials of water were all indicative of an acceptance of 'holy stuff which was far more heterogeneous – far fuzzier – than the formulations of theologians, canonists, or liturgists

eadem et al., eds, *Treasures of Heaven: Saints, Relics, and Devotion in Medieval Europe* (New Haven, CT, 2010), 137–47. On enshrinement, see Seeta Chaganti, *The Medieval Poetics of the Reliquary: Enshrinement, Inscription, Performance* (New York, 2008).

[84] An example of such crystal reliquaries is that made for Louis IX and given to the canons of St Maurice d'Agaune: see Anne E. Lester, 'Confessor King, Martyr Saint: Praying to Saint Maurice in Senlis', in *Center and Periphery: Studies on Power in the Medieval World in Honor of William Chester Jordan*, ed. Guy Keltner, Katherine L. Jansen and Anne E. Lester (Leiden, 2013), 195–210.

[85] See, for example, Julia M. H. Smith, 'Care of Relics in Medieval Rome', *Rome and Religion in the Early Middle Ages: Studies in Honor of Thomas F. X. Noble*, ed. Valerie L. Garver and Owen M. Phelam (Farnham, 2014), 179–205.

would recognize'.[86] It was also all 'stuff' that emphasized Christianity's portability.[87] The very notion that pieces of places and people were portable made Christianity an expandable, translatable religion. The same divine charge or holy essence could appear in many objects and often in materials found in the natural world. Unlike language, which could be misused and misunderstood, objects and materials could communicate something of the ontological properties of their origin. The language of things had the potential to convey the essence if not the meaning of holy words and sacred concepts; words made flesh, flesh that touched bone, wood and water in which the divine was still present.

When relics from the treasuries of Constantinople began to appear in the West after 1204, Latin Christians encountered late antique collections and ways of thinking about holy matter that had not been in circulation in the West for centuries. This contact carried with it a renewed introduction to the vibrancy of things. In this case the translations were possible because they resonated with ideas and texts that spanned Byzantium and the Latin West. These objects were the very things referenced in the Gospels, the Acts of the Apostles, and even the Old Testament, particularly those texts that prefigured Christ's immanence. They spoke the common language of things rooted in the commonality of the apostolic past. In this sense these objects had the effect of collapsing time, bringing Christ's birth, passion and resurrection into the tangible, visible thirteenth-century present, adding to and deepening trends toward the *vita Apostolica* and the *imitatio Christi.* The presence of these objects in the West also meant that even if the terrestrial Jerusalem was no longer in Latin hands, its material remains offered an opportunity to the devout to live and experience a heavenly Jerusalem of the spirit. This was also part of a longer process of coming to terms with the realities of thirteenth-century crusading and its practical failures. As Aden Kumler notes, the 'translation of religious truth ... was a process, one that began in the making [we might say, taking up] of visible forms and continued in the perceptual and hermeneutical space between the visible object

[86] Julia M. H. Smith, 'Relics: An Evolving Tradition in Latin Christianity', in Cynthia Hahn and Holger A. Klein, eds, *Saints and Sacred Matter: The Cult of Relics in Byzantium and Beyond* (Cambridge, MA, 2015), 41–60, at 57.
[87] Smith, 'Portable Christianity'.

Figure 3. (Colour online) Wampum belt (6.5–7 x 143 cm), made of 3,546 wampum or shell beads, in the Mission of Lorette, near Québec, *c.*1678. Sent to Chartres and relics sent in return, *c.*1680. Trésor de la cathédrale de Chartres, Ministère de la Culture, France. Illustration copyright MBA Chartres, France.

and its beholder.'[88] This perceptual and intellectual process was the intended effect of a translation.

CODA: MARY'S WAMPUM IN THE LATIN WEST

There is a coda to this history. In the archives – that meeting place and middle ground of so much historical work and so many encounters – in Chartres, among the records that tell of the relic translations from *Nova Francia*, as the Latin rulers of Constantinople called their domains in the East, there are records of another object sent from another New France. Supplementing relics of Mary's chemise, her milk and her mother St Anne, was the gift of a belt, or *colier* as the French named it, donated to the Virgin, made of what are described as small purple and white 'porcelain beads'. Running across its length is an inscription: VIRGINI PARITURAE + VOTUM HURONUM ('vow of the Hurons to the virgin who will bear a son').[89] This wampum belt (Fig. 3), one of two given to the Virgin of Chartres and the cathedral canons in the late seventeenth century, joined its medieval precursors in the cathedral's treasury collection. It was translated to Chartres as an offering of thanks and recognition for the Virgin's special role as the progenitor of Christ – the first material embodiment of the divine made flesh. The wampum belt travelled with one of those true masters of translation work, a Jesuit, Martin Bouvart, who sent it to his native Chartres along with a record that he set down in French and in Iroquois of the vow the Hurons had made to bind themselves to the Virgin of Chartres in thanks for her favour.[90] In

[88] Kumler, *Translating Truth*, 241.

[89] For an early general history of the objects, see William Curtis Farabee, 'Recent Discovery of Ancient Wampum Belts', *Expedition Magazine* [Penn Museum] 8, no. 81 (March 1922), unpaginated, online at: <http://www.penn.museum/sites/expedition/?p=17237>.

[90] See the materials in Chartres, Archives départementales Eure-et-Loir (Fonds du chapitre de Notre-Dame de Chartres), G 340, 347, 351, 445 (1674–1702). For selections

return, several years later, the canons answered in the language of objects. They sent to New France a small slim silver reliquary depicting the Virgin of Chartres's chemise and containing several small relics. Where the wampum belt spoke the Huron diplomatic language of peace and commemoration, translated into Latin on the object itself, the gift of fragments of the Virgin's relics answered in the European Christian language of salvation. It spoke into a hermeneutical space that we continue to explore as we work to frame the long history of translating Christianity, listening as the wood, cloth, dust, bones and shell-beads speak a shared language of things.

APPENDIX:

Sanctuarium quod Robertus miles de Clari attulit Constantinopoli[91]
The shrine that Robert, knight of Clari, brought from Constantinople

In majori texto crux integra de ligno d[omi]ni – In texto cristallino crux magna de ligno d[omi]ni – In cruce magna de ligno d[omi]ni – Aurea crux per se dupplex plena de ligno d[omi]ni – Imago beate Marie virginis facta de ligno d[omi]ni in capsula per se. – In vase cristallino pannus lineus tinctus sanguine d[omi]ni – De … – De panno quem d[omin]us habuit circa renes – Vas cristalli per se habens de spinis corone domini – De corona d[omi]ni in duobus locis – De spongia d[omi]ni in tribus locis – De pallio et de vestimentis d[omi]ni – De soleis calciamentorum d[omi]ni – De calamo d[omi]ni – De sudario d[omi]ni in duobus locis – De sepulchro d[omi]ni – Dimidium zone beate Marie matris d[omi]ni – De panno quo beata virgo habuit caput involutum – In ampulla magna cristalli de camisia beate Marie v[irginis] – Item in alio loco de camisia beate Marie – De sudario beate Marie. – De guinpla capitis beate Marie. Brachium s[anct]i Marci evangeliste – De capite s[ancti]. Johannis Baptiste et de digito eius – De veste s[ancti] Johannis evangeliste – De s[anct]o Andrea ap[osto]lo – De s[anct]o Thoma apost[olo] – De s[anc]to. … – De s[anc]to Jacobo ap[osto]lo – De s[anc]to Barnaba

of this material, see Jules Doublet de Bois Thibault, *Les voeux des Hurons et des Abnaquis à Notre-Dame de Chartres* (Chartres, 1857). On the communicative role of wampum, see Marshall Joseph Becker, 'Small Wampum Bands used by Native Americans in the Northeast: Functions and Recycling', *Material Culture* 40 (2008), 1–17; Angela M. Haas, 'Wampum as Hypertext: An American Indian Intellectual Tradition of Multimedia Theory and Practice', *Studies in American Indian Literatures* 19 (2007), 77–100.

[91] Amiens, Bibliothèque municipale, MS 527. I have reedited the text here and the translation is my own.

ap[osto]lo – De s[anc]to Bartholomeo ap[osto]lo – De Innocentibus – De s[anc]to Stephano martyre – De s[anc]to Georgio m[arty]re – Dens s[an]cti [Christ]ofori m[arty]ris – De s[anc]to Blasio martyre – De s[anc]to Marcello m[arty]re – De s[anc]to Grisogono m[arty]re – De s[anc]to Legerio m[arty]re – D s[anc]to Silvestro – De s[anc]to Virgilio m[arty]re – In vase cristalli dens s[anc]ti Nicholai et de capillis eius – Item de s[anc]to Nicholao – De s[anc]to Honesto – De veste s[anc]te Marie Magdalene – De cilicio beate Marthe – Digitus s[anc]te Helene – De s[anc]ta Katerina – De sancta Anastasia – In texto quodam lapis jaspis celatus et litteris grecis notatus – Item de ossibus s[anc]ti Philippi apostoli – De s[anc]to Lito m[arty]re – De ossibus s[anc]ti Mauricii sociorumque eius m[arty]rum – De ossibus s[anc]ti Juliani m[arty]re – De columpna ubi d[omin]us ligat[us] fuit – De petra sup[er] quem fuit corp[us] d[omi]ni depositum de cruce.

In a great box, a complete cross [made] from the wood of the Lord. – In a box of crystal, a large cross [made] from the wood of the Lord. – In a great cross [made] of wood of the Lord. – A gold duplex cross containing some wood of the Lord. – An image of the Blessed Virgin Mary with wood of the Lord in a capsule within it. – In a container of crystal [some] linen cloth dipped in blood of the Lord. – Some cloth which the Lord had around his loins. – A container of crystal which has some of the thorns of the Lord's crown. – Some of the crown of the Lord in two places. – Some of the sponge of the Lord in three places. – Some of the mantle and vestments of the Lord. – Some of the sole of the Lord's shoes. – Some of the reed (sceptre) of the Lord. – Some of the handkerchief of the Lord in two places. – Some of the sepulchre of the Lord. – Half of the belt of the Blessed Mary, mother of the Lord. – Some cloth which the Blessed Virgin had covering her head.[92] – In a great container of crystal some of the chemise of the Blessed Virgin Mary. – Likewise, in another place, some of the chemise of the Blessed Mary. – Some of the handkerchief of the Blessed Mary. – Some of the wimple head-covering of the Blessed Mary. – The arm of St Mark the Evangelist. – Part of the head of St John the Baptist and some of his finger. – Some of the clothes of St John the Evangelist. – Some of the apostle St Andrew. – Some of the apostle St Thomas. – Some … – Some of the apostle St James. – Some of the apostle St Barnabas. – Some of the apostle St Bartholomew. – Some of the Innocents. –

[92] All of the fragments listed are set off by '*de*', possibly implying that that are all together in the crystal container with the thorns from the crown of thorns.

Some of the martyr St Stephen. – Some of the martyr St George. – A tooth from the martyr St Christopher. – Some of the martyr St Blaise. – Some of the martyr St Marcellus. – Some of the martyr St Grisogono. – Some of the martyr St Leger. – Some of St Sylvester. – Some of the martyr St Vigilius. – In a crystal container, a tooth from St Nicholas and some of his hair, likewise [other] relics of St Nicholas. – From St Honestus. – Some from the clothes of Mary Magdalene. – Some from the cloak of blessed Martha. – A finger from St Helen. – Some of St Katherine and St Anastasia. – In a box is concealed certain [stones of] lapis lazuli [and] jasper and inscribed with Greek letters. – Likewise bones from the apostle St Philip – from the martyr St Litus – Some bones of St Maurice and his companion martyrs – Some bones from the martyr St Julian. – [And fragments] from the column where the Lord was flagellated. – from the stone on which the body of the Lord was laid [after he was taken down] from the cross.

Translating the *Legenda aurea* in Early Modern England

Morgan Ring*
Gonville and Caius College, University of Cambridge

To its admirers, the Legenda aurea *is a powerful expression of medieval belief. To the evangelical pamphleteers of early modern England, it was a symbol of all the failings of unreformed religion. For historians, it is a convenient shorthand for popular hagiography before the Reformation. These readings, however, understate the* Legenda's *often ambiguous place in early modern devotional life. This article seeks to complicate the* Legenda's *history in late medieval and early modern England. It argues that the concept and the act of translation rendered Jacobus's text more complex than the historiographical shorthand allows. Translation contributed to the* Legenda's *power as a devotional work, was a means by which it found its use, impact and wide audience, and was central to how reformers remembered both the text itself and its author. The translated* Legenda *was not the exception to the narrative of the long Reformation, but an emblem of it.*

In 1582, Barnaby Rich declared that '[t]he Pope is very unwilling that the Scripture should be in a known language amongst us'. Rather than the Bible, '[the Pope] hath bequeathed us *Legenda Aurea* … with suche other stuffe. These we maie reade in English, you maie easily gesse why, but the Scriptures we must not heare but in Latin, because thei saie it is daungerous that we should reade the Scripture in a knowne language'.[1]

In fact, the man responsible for the best-known English translation of the *Legenda aurea* had not been paid by the pope. William Caxton began the expensive, time-consuming project on his own and finished it with support from William Fitzalan, sixteenth earl of Arundel. In his prologue to the first printed English edition, published in 1483, Caxton wrote that he undertook the translation

> by cause me semeth to be a souerayn wele to Incyte & exhorte men and wymmen to kepe them from slouthe and ydlenesse / and to lete

* Gonville and Caius College, Trinity St, Cambridge, CB2 1TA. E-mail: memr2@cam.ac.uk. I gratefully acknowledge the support of the Gonville Research Fund, the Archbishop Cranmer Fund, the Huntington Library, and the Bibliographical Society.

[1] Barnaby Rich, *The true report of a late practise enterprised by a Papist, with a yong Maiden in Wales* (London, 1582), sig. C3[r].

Studies in Church History 53 (2017) 118–131
doi: 10.1017/stc.2016.8

> to be understonden to suche peple as been not letterd / the natyuytees / the lyues / the passions / the miracles / and the dethe of the holy sayntes … I haue submysed my self to translate in to englysshe the legende of sayntes … & I shal praye for them unto almyghty god … that it prouffyte to alle them that shal rede or here it rede / and may encreace in theme virtue / and expelle vyce and synne / that by the ensaumple of the holy sayntes amende theyr shorte lyf / that by their merytes / they and I may come to euerlastynge lyf & blysse in heuen amen[.][2]

Caxton's translation furthered a goal: bringing the stories and examples of the saints to a wide array of English people, to the spiritual benefit of reader and translator alike.

Nonetheless, by the turn of the seventeenth century, the contrast between the ubiquitous English *Legend* and the banned English Bible had become a commonplace of Protestant polemic.[3] Rich and his fellow Protestant pamphleteers made the *Legenda* a symbol of the late medieval Church, full of fabulous stories read by incompetent preachers to ignorant parishioners.[4] Although their verdict has proved remarkably lasting, recent work has added nuance to this narrative. As Helen Parish, Martha Driver and Alison Chapman have shown, the *Legenda* and other works of hagiography continued to be read and remembered after the break with Rome, often – though not inevitably – being turned to polemical ends.[5] This article will explore the relationship between the *Legenda* and the vernacular Bible. It seeks to complicate not only the *Legenda* itself, but also the real and imagined histories of Bible translation in early modern England.

[2] William Caxton, *Legenda aurea* (London, 1483), Preface.

[3] See John Bridges, 'The Translatour to the Christian *Reader*', in Rudolf Gwalther, *An hundred, threescore and fiftene Homeleyes or Sermons, vppon the Actes of the Apostles* (London, 1572), sigs A4^{v}–C2^{r}; Richard Finch, *The Epiphanie of the Church* (London, 1590), sig. C2^{r}; Edward Bulkeley, *An Apologie for Religion* (London, 1602), 7.

[4] See William Charke, *An Answeare for the time* (London, 1583), fol. 41^{r}; Thomas Beard, *A Retractive from the Romish Religion* (London, 1616), 390; George Hakewill, *An Answere to a Treatise Written by Dr. Carier* (London, 1616), 117–18.

[5] Eamon Duffy, *The Stripping of the Altars* (New Haven, CT, 2005), 593; Robert Bartlett, *Why Can the Dead do Such Great Things?* (Princeton, NJ, 2013), 91; Helen L. Parish, *Monks, Miracles and Magic: Reformation Representations of the Medieval Church* (London, 2005), 71–91; Martha W. Driver, *The Image in Print: Book Illustration in Late Medieval England and its Sources* (London, 2004), 194–201; Alison A. Chapman, *Patrons and Patron Saints in Early Modern English Literature* (London, 2013), 11–13.

From *Legenda aurea* to *Golden Legend*

The Dominican Jacobus de Voragine was archbishop of Genoa from 1292–8. A prolific writer, his most famous work was the *Legenda aurea,* a collection of saints' lives and stories from the life of Christ. Although he included a handful of medieval figures, saints of the early Church predominated.[6]

In writing the *Legenda*, Jacobus used the concepts of physical and linguistic translation to connect his saints to his readers and listeners. Stories of relic translations allowed Jacobus to tie one saint to several places and audiences. The relics of Mark, for instance, were associated with miracles in Alexandria and Venice, and those of Mary Magdalene with both Aix and Vézelay.[7] Jacobus also used translation in its literary sense, starting many *vitae* with explanations of the saints' names. Different languages came together in these etymologies to reveal different aspects of a saint's character: Agnes could be derived from the Latin *agna* – lamb; the Greek *agnos* – pious, or the Latin *agnoscendo* – knowing. Jacobus presented each possibility as equally valid, with each one evoking a new resonance or insight.[8] These translations, physical and literal, made his saints more vivid and complex.

Jacobus's early translators rendered the text into vernacular languages and added local saints to his canon. The text was read in different formats and contexts, both public and private, and inspired works in other genres. England was a case in point. Between the thirteenth and fifteenth centuries, the *Legenda* was available in Latin and later in French and English. Lay people owned copies, with the best documented of these manuscripts being those that belonged to elite families.[9] Medieval book catalogues suggest that the work was a

[6] Alain Boureau, *La Légende dorée. Le Système narratif de Jacques de Voragine* (Paris, 1984), 33–8; André Vauchez, *Sainthood in the Later Middle Ages*, transl. Jean Birrell (Cambridge, 2005), 413–22.

[7] Jacobus de Voragine, *The Golden Legend: Readings on the Saints*, ed. and transl. William Granger Ryan (Princeton, NJ, 2012), 245–6, 381–2.

[8] Ibid. 101.

[9] See H. Leith Spencer, *English Preaching in the Late Middle Ages* (Oxford, 1993), 374, n. 71. The Beaufort family copy is London, BL, Royal MS 19.BXVII, which Carley suggests may have been the copy of *La Légende dorée* found in the 1535 inventory of books at Richmond Palace: James P. Carley, ed., *The Libraries of King Henry VIII*, Corpus of British Medieval Library Catalogues [hereafter: CBMLC] 7 (London, 2000), 199. For an analysis of surviving manuscript copies, see Barbara Fleith, *Studien zur Überlieferungsgeschichte der lateinischen Legenda aurea* (Brussels, 1991), 55–331.

standard holding of monastic and university libraries, and copies were also found in parish churches.[10]

An anonymous fifteenth-century translator produced an English version, known as the *Gilte Legende.* This survives in several manuscript copies, with some textual variation.[11] These differences suggest that the *Legenda* was a flexible text: English copies include British saints like Swithin and Winifred, and many have at least one Old Testament story, such as the life of Adam.[12] The scribe of one copy of the *South English Legendary*, now in Lambeth Palace Library, described his work as a version of the *Legenda*: '*Her endeth legenda aurea wrten by R. W. of this toun.*' The two are separate texts – the *South English Legendary* is entirely in rhyme and includes Old Testament lives – but the annotation suggests that the translated *Legenda* could serve as a concept as well as a book, encompassing works with both obvious and tenuous ties to the original.[13]

In preparing his translation of the *Legenda*, William Caxton acknowledged a debt to three sources, 'a legende in frensshe / another in latyn / & the thyrd in englysshe'. These were the French translation made by Jean de Vignay in the early fourteenth century and printed in Flanders between 1475 and 1477, Jacobus's Latin original, and a copy of the *Gilte Legende.*[14] Caxton began his work with an adapted translation of Vignay's preface to the *Legenda,* reproducing Vignay's ideas closely – notably that the *Legenda* was a means of allowing 'such peple as been not letterd' access to the saints' stories – but substituting an account of his own work and patrons.[15] Of course, he was clear that 'this sayd werke was grete & ouer chargeable' and would have to find

[10] For monastic and university libraries, see K. W. Humphreys, ed., *The Friars' Libraries*, CBMLC 1 (London, 1990), 165–6, 172–3; William P. Stoneman, ed., *Dover Priory*, CBMLC 5 (London, 1999), 97–8; M. T. J. Webber and A. G. Watson, ed., *The Libraries of the Augustinian Canons*, CBMLC 6 (London, 1998), 238–9; Peter D. Clarke, ed., *The University and College Libraries of Cambridge*, CBMLC 10 (London, 2002), 43–5, 333. For a Latin manuscript copy given to a parish church, see BL, Stowe MS 49, fol. 2^r.

[11] See Anon., *Gilte Legende*, ed. Richard Hamer and Vida Russell, 3 vols (Oxford, 2006–12). For discussion of the translation and manuscripts, see Hamer, 'Introduction', ibid. 3: 1–56.

[12] BL, Add. MS 11565, fols 55^r–^{v}; Add. MS 35298, Calendar and fol. 162^r.

[13] London, LPL, MS 223, fol. 297^r.

[14] Caxton, *Legenda aurea* (1483), Preface; Brenda Dunn-Lardeau, 'Introduction', in *La Légende dorée: Edition critique, dans la révision de 1476 par Jean Batallier* (Paris, 1997), 9–83.

[15] Paris, Bibliothèque Mazarine, MS 1729, fol. 1^r; Caxton, *Legenda aurea* (1483), fol. 1^v.

buyers, but translation was a pious act both for Caxton, who carried it out, and for Arundel, who paid for it.[16]

Like his predecessors, Caxton departed from Jacobus in several instances. In addition to shortening many of Jacobus's careful source citations, he connected the text more strongly to his readers by including lives of medieval French and British saints and adding interpolations of his own to some of the stories. Jacobus's life of George, for instance, concluded with an account of the saint assisting the Crusaders in their siege of Jerusalem, while the medieval English version ended with stories of the healing miracles performed by his relics. Caxton, in contrast, wrote that George was 'patrone of this royame of englond / and the crye of men of warre', and that both the Order of the Garter and St George's Chapel in Windsor Castle were dedicated to him. He also noted that George's heart, head and other relics had all been translated to England.[17] In translating this story, Caxton made a universally acknowledged saint particular to England.

Caxton also restructured the *Legenda.* While both he and Jacobus began with Advent, Caxton separated the New Testament stories from the rest of the text and grouped them together at the start of the book. After the Dedication of the Church, the final feast in this New Testament section and the last story in the Latin *Legenda,* Caxton added a series of Old Testament stories to be read over the course of the year, beginning with Adam and concluding with Judith on the last Sunday in October. Only then did he start the saints' lives.

Norman Blake has suggested that the restructured and expanded *Legend* did not make 'a structurally satisfying whole', and the added stories do differ markedly in length and tone from those of the *Legenda* proper.[18] Wynkyn De Worde's editorial decisions arguably made more sense of them. The 1493 edition, the first printed by de Worde, did not include the Old Testament stories, but the 1498 edition reinstated them and placed them before the stories of Christ's ministry. From 1498 onwards, the work was structured chronologically and typologically, with the stories of the Old Testament prefiguring the revelation of the New. The saints were part of the cycle of the Christian

[16] Caxton, *Legenda aurea* (1483), Preface.

[17] Jacobus de Voragine, *The Golden Legend*, ed. and transl. Ryan, 242; BL, Add. MS 35298, fol. 35^{r}; Caxton, *Legenda aurea* (1483), fol. 158^{v}.

[18] N. F. Blake, 'The Biblical Additions in Caxton's "Golden Legend"', *Traditio* 25 (1969), 231–47.

year, but they were also positioned within a historical framework, beginning with Adam and continuing to the saints of the recent past.[19]

Introducing the Old Testament section, Caxton wrote 'here folowen the storyes of the byble', and he began each one by noting when in the Church year it would be read.[20] As Sarah Horrall shows, he drew on the Vulgate as well as a number of Biblical paraphrases, principally Comestor's *Historia Scholastica*, but also Lorens's *Somme le roi* and the anonymous *Cursor Mundi*.[21] The closeness between Caxton's stories and the Bible varies.[22] He condensed the twenty-four chapters of Joshua into one folio-length column of text but translated Tobit in its entirety, apart from missing out 6: 9 and leaving the phrase 'in saecula saeculorum' in Latin.[23] Other stories fell within these extremes. The life of Abraham includes both paraphrase and translation from Genesis as well as additional details probably drawn from Josephus via the *Historia Scholastica*, like Lot's wife becoming a pillar of salt 'whiche abideth so in to this day', while the history of Job is a direct translation of Job 1–2 and 42: 7–17, linked by three sentences summarizing Job's conversation with his friends and referring readers to Gregory's *Moralia in Job*.[24]

Caxton's life of David, drawn from 1 and 2 Samuel and 1 Kings, illustrates many elements of his adaptation technique. He described it as 'shortly taken out of the bible the most historyal maters and but litil towched'. The story recounts some episodes at length: David's meetings with Saul's Amalekite killer and with Nathan are direct translations of more than ten verses at a time. Other scriptural text appears with cuts or in the context of a paraphrase. For instance, Caxton paraphrased the first nine verses of 2 Samuel 24 before providing the full text of the tenth verse:

> After this dauid callid Ioab & bad hym nombre the people of Israhel / And so Ioab walked thurgh alle the tribus of Israhel from dan

[19] For time in Jacobus's original Latin text, see Jacques le Goff, *In Search of Sacred Time: Jacobus de Voragine and the* Golden Legend (Princeton, NJ, 2014).

[20] Caxton, *Legenda aurea* (1483), fol. 36^{v}.

[21] Sarah M. Horrall, 'William Caxton's Biblical Translation', *Medium Aevum* 53 (1984), 91–8.

[22] These relationships are outlined in Blake, 'Biblical Additions', 231–7.

[23] Caxton, *Legenda aurea* (1483), fols 63^{r}, 75^{v}–80^{r}. For the missing verse, see fol. 77^{v}; for variations on *in saecula saeculorum*, see fols 78^{v}, 79^{v}.

[24] Caxton, *Legenda aurea* (1483), fols 42^{v}, 74^{v}–75^{r}; see also *The Historye of the Patriarks, with parallel Texts of the* Historia Scholastica *and the* Bible Historiale, ed. Mayumi Taguchi (Heidelberg, 2010), 102.

> to bersabee / And ouer Iordan and all the contre / And ther were founden in Israhel viii CM. strong men that were able to fight and to drawe swerd / And of the tribe of Iuda fyfty thousand fyghtyng men / And after that the peple was nombred / the herte of dauid was smeton by our lord and was heuy & said / I haue synned gretly in this dede / but I praye the lord to take away the wickednes of thy seruaunt for I haue don folyly[.][25]

There are also additions to the text, notably an account of David's penance, which Caxton claimed to have heard from a knight named John Capons while riding between Ghent and Brussels: '[T]his said noble man told me that he had redde that dauid dyde this penaunce folowyng for thyse said synnes / that he dalf hym in the ground standyng nakyd unto the heed so longe that the wormes began to crepe in his flesshe / and made a verse of this psalme Miserere / and thenne cam out'.[26] While Caxton cited this uncritically, he mentioned elsewhere that some stories attached to Old Testament figures were extra-scriptural. In his life of Solomon, for instance, he wrote: 'It is sayd but I fynde it not in the bible / that Salamon repentyd hym moche of this synne of ydolatrye / & dyd moche penaunce therfor'.[27] Caxton also added a summary to the end of his life of David. Over the course of the narrative, he paraphrased, translated, added and cut.

The significance of these Old Testament stories is twofold. First, they raise questions about how Caxton's *Legend* was used. The readers' notes in the margins of surviving copies suggest that these Bible stories were read aloud, and they may have been used in preaching. Many readers marked up the text for oral reading, summarizing the adjacent material and adding marginal marks akin to paragraph breaks. A copy in the British Library, for instance, is extensively annotated in this way: 'Howe Sara conceyued ysaac … Sara said to Abraham cast forth Agar & hyr sone … Howe Abraham sent forth Agar & hyr son'.[28] A John Rylands copy has extensive underlinings and manicules as well as many of the names and ages of characters written

[25] Caxton, *Legenda aurea* (1483), fol. 71^{r}. In the AV, the verse reads: 'And David's heart smote him after that he had numbered the people. And David said unto the LORD, I have sinned greatly in that I have done: and now, I beseech thee, O LORD, take away the iniquity of thy servant; for I have done very foolishly.'

[26] Caxton, *Legenda aurea* (1483), fol. 70^{r}.

[27] Ibid., fol. 73^{v}.

[28] BL, C.1.22.h.7, fols 9^{r}–16^{r}. For further examples, see BL, C.11.c.16, fols 3^{r}–52^{r}.

out in different hands.[29] Still another copy has marginal summaries in both Latin and English and occasional synonyms for, or corrections to, words in the text: Samuel was 'ruddy & fayre of vysage' rather than Caxton's 'rough'.[30] Such annotations are particularly frequent in the Old Testament sections of surviving copies, although they are sometimes present in all three sections of the text.[31] Some notes to the saints' lives also suggest use in preaching. A copy in the Thomas Fisher Rare Book Library survives with many marginal lines, underlinings and a hand-drawn box around a prayer to the Virgin Mary with the word 'omit' added.[32] While inconclusive, these give some credence to the Protestant charge that the *Legend* was 'alledged in Sermons and read in the churche openly'.[33]

Second, the Old Testament stories raise the issue of how the *Legend* fits into the historiography of Bible reading and devotional literature in the fifteenth century. In 1409, Arundel's *Constitutions* banned translations of Scripture made without a licence, although it became a Protestant byword that the medieval Church had banned the English Bible outright.[34] Nicholas Watson argues that the *Constitutions* created a climate of repression in which any written translation, even of very brief texts, could be dangerous.[35] The historiography

[29] Manchester, John Rylands Library, MS 54577, fols 2^{r}–54^{v}. Some of these are also present in the New Testament section.

[30] BL, C.11.c.16, fol. 33^{v}. Whether or not this annotator was trying to align the *Legenda* more closely with a particular translation is unclear. Both the Wycliffe Bible and the Bishops' Bible use 'ruddy' in translating 1 Samuel 17: 42. Elsewhere, the annotator substituted 'dreames' for Caxton's 'sweuenes' in 1 Samuel 28: 6. 'Sweuenes' is used in the early Wycliffe Bible, while 'dreames' is present in the later Wycliffe translation and in Coverdale. In Judith 5: 11, Caxton refers to 'claye tyles', which the annotator amended to 'bryke': Wycliffe's translation has 'clay', while Coverdale and subsequent versions have 'brick' and 'clay': see C.11.c.16, fols 36^{r}, 50^{r}.

[31] See, for instance, summary annotations to the life of Saul in San Marino, Huntington Library, MS 69796, fols 63^{v}–65^{v}; and to the lives of Adam and Moses in New York, Pierpont Morgan Library, MS 00767, fols 3^{r-v}, 17^{v}–20^{v}. For annotations throughout the text, see, for instance, Cambridge, Corpus Christi Parker Library, EP.H.7, fols 2^{r}–8^{r}, 14^{r}, 17^{r}, 20^{r}–21^{r}, 42^{r}, 45^{r-v}, 47^{r}, 70^{r}, 71^{r}, 83^{r}; BL, C.11.c.16, fols 3^{r}–52^{r}; John Rylands Library, MS 13418, fols 1^{r}–54^{v}.

[32] Toronto, ON, Thomas Fisher Rare Book Library, MS 97, fols 4^{v}, 95^{r}, 104^{v}, 105^{v}, 237^{r}, and fol. 47^{r}.

[33] Finch, *Epiphanie*, sig. $C2^{r}$.

[34] William Lyndwood, *Constitutions prouincialles* (London, 1534), 78–9.

[35] Nicholas Watson, 'Censorship and Cultural Change in Late Medieval England: Vernacular Theology, the Oxford Translation Debate, and Arundel's Constitutions of 1409', *Speculum* 70 (1995), 822–64. For a surge in devotional English writing coexisting with anxiety over the vernacular, see Susan Powell, 'Evidence for the Licensing of Books from

concerning Caxton and the Bible is divided. Susan Powell notes that saints' lives and sermon collections were comparatively rare in the first fifty years of English printing, perhaps indicating an apprehensiveness fostered by the *Constitutions*. Butterworth and Horrall suggest, respectively, that Caxton wanted to translate the Bible and that he wanted to write a complete biblical paraphrase but feared being taken for a Lollard. In contrast, Blake suggests that Caxton had no desire to translate the Bible and that he betrayed no anxiety that his paraphrases might be mistaken for an illegal, unlicensed translation.[36]

Caxton described his work as 'storyes of the byble', indicating that they were paraphrased rather than translated, and de Worde also wrote that they were 'shortly taken out of the byble', that is, adapted.[37] At the same time, Caxton stressed the closeness of his story to the Bible, writing that his life of David was 'but litil towched', and the Old Testament stories include scriptural extracts ranging in length from single verses to an entire book.[38] Moreover, the Old Testament stories survive in separate printed quartos, suggesting they had an audience independent of the rest of the book.[39] The English *Legend* was not a Bible, a Bible paraphrase or a hagiography, although it contained elements of all three. Instead, it was a book that made many Bible stories and extracts from Scripture available to clergy and laity, along with stories of the saints. Its popularity suggests that there was both toleration of, and demand for, vernacular works that allowed access to biblical stories and text without being complete Bible translations.[40]

Arundel to Cromwell', in Simon Horobin and Linne R. Mooney, eds, *Middle English Texts in Transition* (Woodbridge, 2014), 134–58; Shannon McSheffrey, 'Heresy, Orthodoxy, and English Vernacular Religion, 1480–1525', *P&P* 186 (2005), 47–80.

[36] Susan Powell, 'After Arundel but before Luther: The First Half-Century of Print', in Vincent Gillespie and Kantik Ghosh, eds, *After Arundel: Religious Writing in Fifteenth-Century England* (Turnhout, 2011), 523–41; Charles C. Butterworth, *The Literary Lineage of the King James Bible 1340–1611* (Philadelphia, PA, 1941), 53–5; Horrall, 'Caxton's Biblical Translation', 91–8; Blake, 'Biblical Additions', 238–47.

[37] Caxton, *Legenda aurea* (1483), fol. 36^{v}; ibid. (1527), fol. 2^{r}.

[38] Ibid. (1483), fol. 68^{v}.

[39] See BL, C.53.b.22.

[40] See also Alexandra Walsham, 'Unclasping the Book? Post-Reformation English Catholicism and the Vernacular Bible', *JBS* 42 (2003), 141–66.

THE *LEGEND*, THE BIBLE AND THE REFORMATION

Wynkyn de Worde printed the final edition of the *Legend* in 1527. Eleven years later, the work became subject to Henrician censorship. The 1538 Injunctions declaring Thomas Becket a false saint and ordering that his services be removed from service books seem to have been extended to the *Legend*, which included chapters commemorating both Becket's martyrdom and the translation of his relics.[41] Virtually all of the surviving copies have had one or both of the Becket feasts defaced as well as references to the pope removed, sometimes perfunctorily, sometimes with vituperative annotations from readers: 'thomas was a knaue' or 'a Rancke treytor'.[42] This suggests that the *Legend* was being held to the standards demanded of liturgical books. The work had become politically and spiritually suspect.

Its afterlife, however, was more than a protracted rejection: its complicated relationship to the Bible remained a matter for readers and writers to debate. As Helen Parish has observed, Protestant writers turned the *Legend* against the Catholic Church by repeating and mocking the book's most fantastic miracle stories.[43] Such mocking also took place in the pages of the book itself, as annotators added jokes into the margins. There were, however, less expected techniques: identifying saints whose behaviour supported Protestant ideals and undermined Catholic doctrine. For instance, the *Legend* noted that St Paula the Widow – Pauline in Caxton's translation – spoke 'parfyghtly hebrewe grece latyn and frenshe and redde … the scriptures in this foure langages'. A prolific annotator of a copy now in the Yale Center for British Art directed future readers to 'note howe sainte paulyne spent her time in redinge of scripture & that the frenshe tonge was one'.[44] Under the pen of this annotator, the *Legend* could be turned against the Catholic Church not only because its inaccuracies were so glaring but also because its ancient saints made the late medieval Church appear distant from the foundations of the Christian faith.

[41] John Foxe, *Acts and Monuments* (London, 1570), 1334.

[42] Pierpont Morgan Library, MS ChL1788a, fol. 212ʳ; Oxford, Trinity College Library, MS I.16.15, fol. 53ʳ. There are some copies in which both feasts are intact, such as the 1493 copy now in Lincoln, Lincoln Cathedral Library, MS B3/2; the 1503/4 copy now in Cambridge, St John's College Upper Library, A.1.9; and the 1527 copy now in the Huntington Library, MS 69790.

[43] Parish, *Monks, Miracles and Magic*, 85–91.

[44] New Haven, CT, Yale Center for British Art, MS BX4654.J32, fol. 84ʳ.

The Latin *Legenda* was also connected, although indirectly, to early modern histories of Bible translation. This fluid, contentious text provoked reinterpretations of its author and his relationship to Scripture. Just as Jacobus himself had used etymology to reveal character, English Protestant writers explored the meanings of his name. Voragine is the ablative form of *vorago*, meaning chasm, a point not lost on William Patten, who dubbed Jacobus 'Iames of the synkhole' – a hole filled with unclean water.[45] The play on words resurfaced in various forms well into the seventeenth century.[46] Others, however, found a more positive resonance. Edmund Porter and John Trapp both wrote that Jacobus had been a 'devourer' of the Bible, with Porter writing approvingly that he took his name 'not for gormondizing of meat, but because of [a] multitude of Bookes … devoured and digested'.[47]

Jacobus was recast as Bible translator as well as reader. Sixtus Senensis, a sixteenth-century Jewish convert to Catholicism, authored the *Bibliotheca Sancta*, first published in Venice in 1566 and dedicated to Pius V. The fourth book of the *Bibliotheca* consists of a long list of Catholic authors, including Jacobus, referred to as 'Iacobus, Archiepiscopus Genuensis'. Sixtus wrote that Jacobus was 'not to be condemned as a writer of stories, and learned in the works of Augustine … and was the first of all that translated the divine writings into the Italian language with great faith and diligence'.[48]

The Dutch Reformed theologian and classicist Gerardus Johannus Vossius repeated this claim in his *De Historicis Latinis*, published in 1627 and dedicated to George Villiers, citing Sixtus Senensis and noting that Jacobus 'is praiseworthy, because he was the first of all to translate the Holy Bible into the Italian language, as Sixtus Senesis witnesses'. Vossius was critical of Jacobus: he also repeated Juan Luis Vives's metallurgical pun that 'that golden legend … was written

[45] See *OED*.

[46] William Patten, *The Expedicion into Scotlande of the most woorthely fortunate prince Edward, Duke of Soomerset* (London, 1548), sig. D7^{v}. See also Daniel Featley, *The Romish Fisher Caught and Held In His Owne Net* (London, 1624), 10.

[47] Edmund Porter, *Christophagia* (London, 1680), 18; John Trapp, *A Commentary or Exposition upon These Following Books of holy Scripture* (London, 1660), 97.

[48] '[H]istoriarum quoque non contemnendus scriptor, & Augustini uoluminum ita studiosus … utriusque instrumenti diuina uolumnia primus omnium in Italicam linguam summa fide ac diligentia transfudit': Sixtus Senensis, *Bibliotheca Sancta* (Venice, 1566), 397. The Scottish Jesuit John Hay published a new edition of the work at Lyon in 1593, dedicating it to William Chisholm: Sixtus Senensis, *Bibliotheca Sancta*, ed. John Hay (Lyon, 1593), sigs ✝✝1^{r}–2^{r}, with the story of Jacobus at p. 251.

by a man of an iron mouth and a leaden heart'.[49] Nonetheless, the claim that Jacobus was an early Bible translator quickly found its way into English Protestant writing via both Sixtus and Vossius, with the latter's addition of Vives's wordplay usually cut.[50]

From the early seventeenth century onwards, Protestant writers used this claim as part of an effort to show that Bible translation had a history within the Catholic Church. In his 1614 *Enquiries touching the diuersity of languages*, Edward Brerewood, professor of astronomy at Gresham College, London, observed that there had been several medieval translations of the Scriptures, including those 'made by Iohn Archbishop of *Siuill* into the *Arabique*, about An. 717 … into the *Saxon* or *Englise* by *Beda*, about the same time: Into the *Slauonique* by *Methodius* about An. 860. &c. Into the *Italian* by *Iacobus de Voragine* about An. 1290, &c.'[51] Similarly, Richard Capel wrote: 'I look on it as a special providence of God, that there were translations, and those exact too in the heart of Popery'.[52] The idea of Jacobus as translator was used to construct a providential history of Scripture translation within the Catholic Church: translation became not merely Protestant ideal but Christian tradition.

While Brerewood and Capel did not mention Jacobus's authorship of the *Legenda*, Peter Heylyn came closer to reconciling the

[49] 'Hujus laus est, quod primus omnium sacra biblia in Italicam transfuderit linguam: ut Sixtus Senensis testatur ... Legendam illam auream … scriptam esse ab homine oris ferrei, cordis plumbei': Gerardus Johannus Vossius, *De Historicis Latinis* (Lyon, 1627), sig.):(1r, pp. 457–8.

[50] For citations based on Sixtus, see Edward Brerewood, *Enquiries Touching the Diversity of Languages, and Religions through the chiefe parts of the world* (London, 1614), 192; Richard Field, *Of the Church Five Bookes* (Oxford, 1628), 239; Richard Capel, *Capel's Remains* (London, 1658), 67–8; Thomas Pierce, *The Primitive Rule of Reformation* (Oxford, 1663), 26. For citations drawing on Vossius, see notes provided by Thomas Fuller, *The Appeal of Iniured Innocence* (London, 1659), 47–8; and Peter Heylyn, *Examen Historicum* (London, 1659), 74. Heylyn also quoted the story in *The History of That most famous Saynt and Souldier of Christ Iesus S. George of Cappadocia* (London, 1631), 16–17, and did repeat the pun, though only in reference to the *Legenda* and drawn from Vives himself rather than from Vossius. Thomas Tenison quoted the story with no source in *A Discourse Concerning a Guide in Matters of Faith* (London, 1683), 36–7.

[51] Brerewood, *Enquiries*, 192. Several authors made the same point regarding the embarrassment of 'learned Papists' over the *Legenda*, including John Rainolds and John Gee, both converts to Protestantism: John Rainolds, *The Summe of the Conference Betwene Iohn Rainolds and Iohn Hart Touching the Head and the Faith of the Church* (London, 1584), 495–6; John Gee, *The Foot out of the Snare* (London, 1624), sig. A2r [*vere* A4r]. See also Sherry L. Reames, *The Legenda Aurea: A Reexamination of its Paradoxical History* (Madison, WI, 1985), 28–42.

[52] Capel, *Capel's Remains*, 67–8.

hagiographer with the Bible translator. As Anthony Milton has shown, Heylyn's attitudes to Roman Catholicism and to the late medieval Church varied over the course of his career. His characterization of Jacobus, however, remained constant. In his *Historie of St George*, he sought to establish the saint's historicity and orthodoxy, making medieval hagiography an important, if treacherous, source of material.[53] He was critical of the *Legenda* and observed that 'now the learned Papists haue rejected it with shame inough', but he also noted that Jacobus was known for his 'Eloquence and Learning' and that Vossius called him 'the first Translatour of the Bible into the *Italian* language'.[54] Heylyn reiterated this characterization when debating with Thomas Fuller three decades later. The *Legenda* contained 'many idle and unwarrantable fictions', but Jacobus was 'learned for the times in which he lived', as well as being 'most eminent for his translation of the Bible into the *Italian* tongue (as we read in *Vossius*) a work of great both difficulty and danger as the times then were, sufficient (were there nothing else) to free him from the ignominious name of *a worthlesse Author*'.[55] The credulity of the *Legenda* was excusable in an author responsible for such a daring act of Bible translation.

The history of the relationship between the *Legenda* and the vernacular Bible was rewritten. Rather than crediting the English *Legend* with its imperfect mix of paraphrase, Bible translation and hagiography, these authors sought to write a providential history of the rise of vernacular scripture and of courage in the face of persecution, complicating the *Legenda*'s author but simplifying the text itself.

Conclusion

The translation from *Legenda aurea* to *Golden Legend* served to complicate an already rich, unwieldy book. William Caxton's *Golden Legend* was a new work. Together, he and de Worde reshaped the text, situating the saints within the Christian year and within a typological framework extending from Genesis to the Middle Ages. Much of the Reformation-era criticism of the *Legend* focused on its place as translated text: its vernacular language was an affront at a time when, according to Protestant writers, the English Bible had been banned.

[53] Discussed by Anthony Milton, *Laudian and Royalist Polemic in Seventeenth-Century England: The Career and Writings of Peter Heylyn* (Manchester, 2007), 29–31.

[54] Heylyn, *St. George of Cappadocia*, 16–17.

[55] Heylyn, *Examen Historicum*, 74.

But the fact that it was in the vernacular also allowed readers to engage with the book, finding details that supported Protestant ideas and stories with spiritual value. Jacobus de Voragine was doubly reinvented, both as 'James of the Sinkhole' and as an early translator of the Bible.

There were complex relationships, real and imagined, between the *Legenda* and the vernacular Bible in early modern England. Seeking a long history of Bible translation, reformers turned to the *Legenda*'s author, omitting or excusing his work as a hagiographer. Ironically, in doing so they ignored the book itself and its English translator, who had used the genre of biblical paraphrase to make both Bible stories and Bible extracts in English available to clergy and laity in late medieval England.

Erasmus and the Politics of Translation in Tudor England

Lucy Wooding*
Lincoln College, Oxford

Desiderius Erasmus was a significant figure in early sixteenth-century England, and many of his works were translated into English during the reign of Henry VIII. In the process of translation the original intention of these works was subverted as Erasmus's reputation was appropriated by his translators and their patrons for their own purposes. His works were recast in English form to serve a variety of different agendas, from those of Henrician conservatives to Protestants pushing for more radical religious reform. This article looks at some of these translations, showing how they illustrate the variations in religious attitudes during these volatile years and the competing claims for validation. In particular, Erasmus's pronouncements on the importance of Scripture translation were annexed and deployed in the debate over the English Bible, demonstrating how his views about translation were in themselves translated to reflect the political and religious needs of the English situation.

Desiderius Erasmus, the famous Dutch humanist scholar, achieved an uncommonly glowing reputation in the early years of England's Reformation. His customary diligent efforts to craft his own image were met with particular enthusiasm from English scholars.[1] The author responsible for the first English translation of a work by Erasmus, Gentian Hervet, thought it important that 'folke may knowe how noble is the autor of this warke / and how moche we be bounde to hym for it'.[2] In his preface to this translation, which was of the sermon *De immensa dei misericordia,* Hervet described Erasmus as 'the man / to whom in lernynge no lyvyng man may hym selfe compare', who not only exceeded all his contemporaries, but older authors too,

* Lincoln College, Oxford, OX1 3DR. E-mail: lucy.wooding@history.ox.ac.uk.

[1] Stephen Ryle, ed., *Erasmus and the Renaissance Republic of Letters* (Turnhout, 2014); Lisa Jardine, *Erasmus, Man of Letters: The Construction of Charisma* (Princeton, NJ, 1993); James K. McConica, *English Humanists and Reformation Politics* (Oxford, 1965).

[2] Desiderius Erasmus, *De immensa dei misericordia: A sermon of the excedynge great mercy of god*, transl. Gentian Hervet (London, 1526), sig. Aij^{r}.

Studies in Church History 53 (2017) 132–145
doi: 10.1017/stc.2016.9

including the Christian doctors of the Church.[3] On the continent he may have been a more contentious figure, but in England there was a rare level of agreement on the revered status of 'the moost famous doctour mayster Erasmus Roterodamus'.[4] This in part reflected his significance in the royal schoolroom, since Henry VIII as a prince and all his immediate descendants were educated in accordance with Erasmian precepts and using his works.[5] Yet it was more than just a question of royal patronage. This complex, unpredictable and ambiguous figure was to hold a place close to the hearts of a variegated array of English scholars and writers.

Erasmus made three lengthy visits to England, although he was often quite rude about it. 'I do not know how I can contrive to live in England any longer', he wrote to a friend in 1511, 'I am quite out of sympathy with this nation's dirty habits'.[6] He was unhappy with the climate and despondent at the poor quality of the wine. He was, however, genuinely excited about the friends he made there, who were the leading scholars and churchmen of the day and included among their number John Colet, Thomas More, John Fisher, Cuthbert Tunstall, William Warham, John Longland, William Grocyn, William Lily, William Latimer and Thomas Linacre.[7] It was Grocyn, Lily, Linacre and More who encouraged Erasmus in his study of Greek, which was to have such momentous consequences.[8] When in 1527 he drew up his will and arranged for bequests of his complete works, the first six beneficiaries in his list were English, namely Warham, Tunstall, More, Longland, Fisher and Queens' College Cambridge.[9] In turn, these friends connived in his energetic self-aggrandizement and encouraged and defended his publications. It is therefore unsurprising that many of Erasmus's works were translated into English from the 1520s onwards.

[3] Ibid., sig. Aij^{v}.

[4] Erasmus, *A devoute treatise upon the Pater noster*, transl. Margaret Roper (London, 1526?), title page.

[5] Aysha Pollnitz, *Princely Education in Early Modern Britain* (Cambridge, 2015), 9–12.

[6] *The Correspondence of Erasmus*, 2: *Letters 142 to 297*, transl. R. A. B. Mynors and D. F. S. Thomson, ed. Wallace K. Ferguson, Complete Works of Erasmus (Toronto, ON, 1975), 182 (to Andrea Ammonio, 1511).

[7] *ODNB*, *s.n.* 'Desiderius Erasmus'; McConica, *English Humanists and Reformation Politics*, 2–9.

[8] Pollnitz, *Princely Education*, 39.

[9] Léon-E. Halkin, *Erasmus: A Critical Biography*, transl. John Tonkin (Oxford, 1993), 215.

Erasmus himself had in part built his career upon his work as a translator.[10] He translated an astonishing range of works by the Greek Fathers into Latin, as well as pagan authors such as Lucian or Isocrates. Most famously of all, in 1516 he published an edition of the New Testament in Greek with his own Latin translation, and the association between Erasmus and the translation of Scripture soon became a recurrent trope in the books and letters of the time.[11] This article will suggest that in the process of translation into English, more than just words were translated. In the febrile intellectual environment of Henry VIII's England, a variety of different scholars and churchmen sought to validate their own religious agendas by association with Erasmus. The works of his which they translated show how his ideas were appropriated and reconfigured to reflect the circumstances of the early English Reformation as it slowly, painfully emerged.

It could be said that one of the earliest voices calling for the Bible to be translated into English was that of Erasmus, since William Tyndale's famous determination that the 'boy that driveth the plough shall know more scripture than thou dost' was lifted from Erasmus's preface to his 1516 *Novum Instrumentum*.[12] Yet Tyndale's utterance was in itself a kind of translation, or appropriation, of what Erasmus had originally written in that preface.[13] Like many humanists, Erasmus wrote enthusiastically in favour of the Scriptures being translated into the vernacular. It should be remembered, however, that this enthusiasm was invariably expressed in Latin. The conflation of these two quite separate utterances has obscured the distinctly different set of

[10] Paul Botley, *Latin Translation in the Renaissance: The Theory and Practice of Leonardo Bruni, Giannozzo Manetti and Desiderius Erasmus* (Cambridge, 2001); Jan Den Boeft, 'Erasmus and the Church Fathers', in Irena Backus, ed., *The Reception of the Church Fathers in the West*, 2 vols (Leiden, 1997), 2: 537–72; John C. Olin, 'Erasmus and the Church Fathers', in idem, *Six Essays on Erasmus* (New York, 1979), 33–47.

[11] Lisa Jardine notes how Erasmus was complicit in his own representation as St Jerome: see her *Erasmus, Man of Letters* (Princeton, NJ, 1993), 55–82. See also Erika Rummel, *Erasmus' Annotations on the New Testament: From Philologist to Theologian* (Toronto, ON, 1986).

[12] S. L. Greenslade, *The Cambridge History of the Bible*, 3: *The West from the Reformation to the Present Day* (Cambridge, 1963), 141–2. Ian Green has pointed out that Tyndale was also echoing Luther: see his *Print and Protestantism in Early Modern England* (Oxford, 2000), 42.

[13] Erasmus in his preface to the New Testament translation wrote that he wanted vernacular Scripture to become readily available, hoping to see 'the farmer sing some portion of them at the plow': J. C. Olin, ed., *Christian Humanism and the Reformation: Selected Writings of Erasmus* (New York, 1987), 101.

objectives held by their respective authors.[14] When Tyndale translated the Bible into English, it was with an evangelical aim in view, quite separate from anything envisaged by the humanists, for all that he was making a tacit appeal for Erasmus's sanction.[15] His invocation of Erasmus's words about the ploughboy, meanwhile, comes down to us through the rarely impartial conduit of Foxe's *Acts and Monuments*, in a carefully staged description of Tyndale's confrontation with a small-minded conservative.[16] There is an appeal here to a consensus about Scripture which never quite existed.

The apparently straightforward connection between Erasmus and Tyndale, who are so often linked in the historical record, is an early and influential example of the misappropriation of Erasmus's work. Tyndale did of course acknowledge his debt to Erasmus, and in many ways started out as an 'English Erasmian'.[17] The fluidity of religious identities in the early years of the Reformation stemmed in part from the complex and ambiguous relationship between humanism and reform, which almost always featured a shared enthusiasm for biblical revival.[18] Yet Erasmus's own views on the translation of the Bible were arguably much closer to those of his humanist friends in England, particularly Thomas More, than they were to Tyndale's more uncompromising stance. Later Catholics were uneasy about the friendship between Erasmus and More, and tried to play it down; but particularly when it came to their approach to Scripture the two expressed very similar opinions.[19] They were happy to countenance vernacular Scripture as long as the work of translation was done carefully and charitably. In early works they voiced their enthusiasm; in later works their caution. In Erasmus's case this emerged in the furore after the publication of *Novum Instrumentum* in 1516. Attacked by Henry Standish for his heretical tendencies, Erasmus responded by illustrating

[14] Stephen Greenblatt, *Renaissance Self-Fashioning: From More to Shakespeare* (Chicago, IL, 1980), 106.

[15] David Daniell, *William Tyndale: A Biography* (New Haven, CT, 1994); J. T. Day, E. Lund and A. M. O'Donnell, eds, *Word, Church, and State: Tyndale Quincentenary Essays* (Washington DC, 1998); Alan Stewart, 'The Trouble with English Humanism: Tyndale, More and Darling Erasmus', in Jonathan Woolfson, ed., *Reassessing Tudor Humanism* (Basingstoke and New York, 2002), 78–98, at 78.

[16] John Foxe, *Acts and Monuments* (London, 1563), book 3, 570.

[17] Anne Richardson, 'Tyndale's Quarrel with Erasmus', *Fides et Historia* 25 (1993), 46–65; John Bossy, *Christianity in the West, 1400–1700* (Oxford, 1985), 99.

[18] Woolfson, ed., *Reassessing Tudor Humanism*, editor's introduction, 2–9.

[19] Dominic Baker-Smith, 'Erasmus and More: A Friendship Revisited', *RH* 30 (2010), 7–25; Erika Rummel, *Erasmus and his Catholic Critics* (Nieuwkoop, 1989).

the many different variants of different Bible passages found even in the Latin manuscripts, and the way in which the Church itself used different versions of the psalms in the liturgy and the readings, arguing that educated readers needed to discern the meaning of Scripture carefully, using manuscript evidence and patristic testimony but ultimately relying on the judgement of the Church.[20]

Three points stand out here: Erasmus did not expect to find a single definitive text; he was happy (like St Augustine) to see several possible interpretations of any given biblical verse; and he expected ultimately to rely on Church tradition. This was a long way from Tyndale. When Tyndale took More to task for not criticizing Erasmus's translation of *ecclesia* by *congregatio* in his Latin New Testament, he accused More of favouritism towards his 'darling' Erasmus, given that he had attacked Tyndale himself for using the word 'congregation' in his English translation.[21] More responded: 'I have not contended wyth Erasmus my derlynge, bycause I found no suche malycyouse entent wyth Erasmus my derlynge, as I fynde wyth Tyndale'. The difference was, More argued, that 'Erasmus … ment none heresye therein'.[22] Yet there was more to it than this, because as More pointed out, Erasmus was inventing a Latin word where there had not been one before, whilst Tyndale, by contrast, had no need to employ the word 'congregation' since the English language was already supplied with the word 'church'. A Scripture translation from Greek into Latin was a completely different matter from a translation into the vernacular.

When other scholars praised Erasmus's translation of the Bible, it is important to remember that they were speaking of this translation from Greek into Latin, a translation intended solely for an educated audience. One Cambridge friend in 1516 enthused: 'Your revision of the New Testament and your notes at the same time have thrown a wonderful flood of light on Christ, and earned the gratitude of all who are devoted to it.'[23] Another told him that Cambridge men in general were 'great supporters of your edition of the New Testament; what

[20] Gergely M. Juhász, *Translating Resurrection: The Debate between William Tyndale and George Joye in its Historical and Theological Context* (Leiden, 2014), 141–2.
[21] Stewart, 'Trouble with English Humanism', 85–8.
[22] Thomas More, *The Complete Works of St Thomas More*, vol. 8, ed. L. A. Schuster, R. C. Marius and J. P. Lusardi (New Haven, CT, 1973), 1: 177.
[23] *The Correspondence of Erasmus*, 4: *Letters 446 to 593*, transl. R. A. B. Mynors and D. F. S. Thomson, ed. James K. McConica, Complete Works of Erasmus (Toronto, ON, 1977), 36 (letter 450).

a book it is! – So elegant, so clear, so delightful and so highly necessary in the opinion of all men of sound judgement.'[24] These letters, and others like them, were written not in English but in Latin. Erasmus's translation was emphatically a scholarly achievement, bringing enlightenment to the educated classes.

Yet as the name of Erasmus swiftly became one to conjure with, his sanction was claimed by a wide array of English authors with a great many different viewpoints and objectives, including King Henry VIII, who confessed to the humanist that he 'nourished an uncommon devotion' to him, and who would find his ideas a 'politically appropriate substitute for scholasticism' in the campaign for royal supremacy.[25] In particular, the association of Erasmus's name with the idea of biblical translation, based on the edition of the Greek and Latin texts in the *Novum Instrumentum* of 1516, was picked up and applied to a very different debate about the translation of the Scriptures from Latin into English. What had begun as a debate between scholars began to filter down into a broader argument about popular access to the Bible.

The first three English translations of works by Erasmus, all dating from the 1520s, demonstrate how his reputation and reform ideas could be appropriated and reapplied to the English situation. The first appeared in 1526, and was a translation of his sermon *De immensa dei misericordia*. The translator's preface to this work, as we have already seen, was lavish in its praise of Erasmus, 'whom my preyses can no more ennoble / than the son with a candel may be made clerer', and in particular singled out the work he had done explicating the Bible, explaining how the

> … clere springes of the holy scripture / that the Philistines had so troubled / so marred / and so defiled / that no man coude drynke or haue the true taste of the water … be nowe by his labour and diligence to their olde purenes and clerenes so restored that no spotte nor erthly fylthe in them remayneth …[26]

The second English translation was of Erasmus's treatise on the *Pater noster*, which again evoked the importance of Scripture, speaking of

[24] Ibid. 34 (letter 449).
[25] Pollnitz, *Princely Education*, 119; Lisa Jardine and Anthony Grafton, *From Humanism to the Humanities: Education and the Liberal Arts in Fifteenth- and Sixteenth-Century Europe* (London, 1986), 141.
[26] Erasmus, *De immensa dei misericordia* (London, 1526), sig. Aij^{v}.

spiritual hunger, and how 'we thy spirituall and goostly children / desyre and crave of our spirituall father / that spirituall and celestiall breed', namely 'thy worde full of all power / bothe the gyver and norissher of lyfe'.[27] The third was a translation of the *Paraclesis*, Erasmus's preface to the 1516 edition of the New Testament, or *Novum Instrumentum*. This was published as *An exhortation to the diligent study of scripture*, which deplored how 'at this present tyme ... with soch great diligence all mennes invencyons are studyed and commended / yet only this immortall fontayne of Christes pure philosophye / is despysed and mocked of so many'.[28]

All three of these works praised the work of biblical renewal. All three used the metaphor of living water: the *Exhortation* spoke of wisdom being gathered 'out of so small bokes as out of moste pure springes'.[29] Yet they were published by very different people with very different aims. Gentian Hervet, who translated the first of the three, was a French humanist and chaplain to Margaret Pole, countess of Salisbury, whom in his preface he praised for her 'great mynde and depe affection bothe towarde al maner of lernyng / and specially towarde that which ... concerneth the way of our salvacion'.[30] Margaret Pole was a close friend of Katherine of Aragon and tutor to the Princess Mary, well known for her conservatism in religion and mother to the Catholic reformer Cardinal Pole. She was executed by Henry VIII in 1541 for her associations with Pole in particular and Catholicism more generally.[31] The second work was translated by Margaret Roper, Thomas More's daughter, so again might be placed within the context of a reforming but staunch Catholicism.[32] The

[27] Margaret Roper, *A Devoute Treatise upon the Pater noster* (London, 1526?), sig. eiij^r.

[28] Erasmus, *An exhortation to the diligent study of scripture* (London, 1529), fol. [2^r].

[29] Erasmus, *An exhortation*, fol. [5^r].

[30] Erasmus, *De immensa*, sig. Aij^r. Hervet later joined the household of Reginald Pole in Italy where he worked on translations of the Greek fathers, and in later life became well known as a Catholic polemicist: see Elizabeth M. Nugent, ed., *The Thought and Culture of the English Renaissance: An Anthology of Tudor Prose 1481–1555*, 2 vols (The Hague, 1969), 2: 343–4.

[31] Pole had alienated Henry by his outspoken opposition to the royal supremacy in his treatise of 1536, *De Unitate*, and his mother's death was part of a vengeful attack by the king on Pole's extended family in England: see John Edwards, *Archbishop Pole* (Farnham, 2014), 39–83; Hazel Pierce, *Margaret Pole, Countess of Salisbury, 1473–1541: Loyalty, Lineage and Leadership* (Cardiff, 2003).

[32] John A. Gee, 'Margaret Roper's English Version of Erasmus' *Precatio Dominica* and the Apprenticeship behind Early Tudor Translation', *Review of English Studies* 13 (1937), 257–71; E. E. Reynolds, *Margaret Roper: Eldest Daughter of St Thomas More* (London, 1960);

third, however, was the work of William Roye, and was published in Antwerp, probably by Tyndale's publisher, and certainly using the same slightly inappropriate frontispiece of frolicking nymphs as appeared in Tyndale's *Obedience of the Christian Man* and several other works.[33] From the very first, then, Erasmus's works were being reconfigured in translation in the service of a varied array of reform objectives.

Even where the text itself resisted, appropriation could be achieved through the careful use of paratext. A slightly later translation of Erasmus's *Exposicyon of the xv psalme,* published by Wayland in 1537, was a masterly reworking of a fairly traditional text in a much more emphatically Protestant direction. The work itself emphasized 'one onely way unto salvacyon … whiche is to know god, and to obeye his comaundementes'. But the translator's preface insisted that Erasmus's eloquence accorded with 'the moost pure expositers of scripture / whome god hathe gracyouslye nowe in our tyme raysed up to the expulsyon of fylthye and grosse errours / that otherwyse be called of unpure preachers unwrytten verytes', thereby firmly anchoring the translated work within Protestant parameters. This process was continued through the text itself by glosses, such as the emphatic statement that 'they which do trust in theyr good workes (as they calle them) do nat please god'. When Erasmus reproved 'myschevous dedes, done towarde our neighbour', the gloss hastily insisted that 'Unbylefe is the rote of al myschevous dedes / lyke as faithe is the rote of charyte'; where Erasmus wrote of man's reliance on the mercy of god, the gloss optimistically endorsed the passage 'Agaynste fre wyll'. In this way, a text on charitable living was claimed for a Protestant view of justification by faith alone.[34]

In the 1530s, evangelicals of various hues were busily constructing an Erasmus who suited their purposes. Their motivations could mingle religious concerns with political aspiration. A translation of Erasmus's exposition of the Creed and the Ten Commandments published in 1534 proclaimed on its title page that it had been written 'at the requeste of the moste honorable lorde / Thomas Erle of wyltshyre: father to the moste gratious and vertuous Quene Anne'. Here

Elizabeth McCutcheon, 'Margaret More Roper', in Katharine M. Wilson, ed., *Women Writers of the Renaissance and Reformation* (Athens, GA, 1987), 449–65; John Guy, *A Daughter's Love: Thomas and Margaret More* (London, 2008).

33 Daniell, *Tyndale*, 108–11, 132–4, 142–51.

34 Erasmus, *An exposicyon of the xv psalme* (London, 1537), sigs Biii^v, Bi^v, Fv^v.

too the text was massaged by the careful deployment of glosses. Thus, in a passage about the two remedies against evil, faith and charity, Erasmus's text (faithfully translated) is a subtle elucidation of the interdependence of the two, but a gloss plucks out and reiterates the bald statement that 'Charyte is the servaunt of fayth'.[35] In the same year, Leonard Cox, the schoolmaster from Thame who had rescued John Frith from the stocks, published his translation of Erasmus's *Paraphrase* on Paul's epistle to Titus. He asked what could be a better proof of God's pleasure at the marriage of King Henry with Anne Boleyn than that it had pleased him 'to shewe abrode in this regyon, the lyght whiche afore laye manye yeres … under the bushell'.[36] At the same time he attacked those who opposed the gospel: 'To rede the new testament with them is heresy', he lamented and he commented with satisfaction on 'the angre of god evydently fallen upon the bysshop of Romes tyrannye / and his adherentes whose proude power daylye decreaseth'.[37] One particular reference was especially precise: he warned his readers 'Let here no man murmour as some do yet / that his grace is electe to be hedde of the chyrche in his realme / no forther then goddes lawes do permyt'. This was a reference to the pardon of the clergy, who in Convocation in 1531 had accepted the king's headship of the Church, but added the phrase 'so far as the law of Christ allows' as an attempt to salvage what they could of clerical authority. Cox insisted firmly that there was not 'one iote in scripture' that proved the people 'to be above kynges or temporall rulers', in words which spoke to the specific circumstances of 1534 as the supremacy was being enshrined in statute.[38]

Behind some of the translations of Erasmus we can discern the hand of Thomas Cromwell, whose ability to organize scholarly activity in support of his political aims is long attested.[39] Through the publications of Richard Taverner in particular, Erasmus was claimed for an evangelical agenda, often in ways which simultaneously aimed to bolster support for the royal supremacy. A translation of 1536, published by John Byddell, of Erasmus's colloquy on pilgrimage, had

[35] Erasmus, *A playne and godly exposition or declaration of the commune Crede … and of the x commaundementes of goddes law* (London, 1534), title page, sig. Avi^{r}.
[36] Erasmus, *The Paraphrase of Erasmus Roterodame upon the Epistle of saint Paule unto his discyple Titus* (London, 1534).
[37] Ibid., sigs Aiv^{v}, A vi^{r}.
[38] Ibid., sig. Avii^{r}.
[39] G. R. Elton, *Policy and Police*, 206–7; McConica, *English Humanists*, 150–99.

an uncompromising preface by the translator which attacked not only 'thys desperate synne of ydolatrye', but also those who had risen in rebellion 'contrary to the ordynaunce of gode, agaynst theyr kynge and liege lorde, provokynge and allurynge the symple comynaltye to theyre dampnable ypocrysye and conspyracy'.[40] The damning, if imprecise, characterization of these rebels as recognizable by 'theyr Sodomitical actes, and most horryble ypocrysy' is redolent of much of the Cromwellian anti-monastic propaganda of these years.

Yet not all the translations of the 1530s followed a Cromwellian path.[41] In 1537, even as the dissolution of the monasteries was taking hold, the Augustinian canon Thomas Paynell translated Erasmus's *Comparation of a Vyrgin and a Martyr*, dedicating it to the prior of his own community, Merton Abbey, which was the mother house of St Mary's College, Oxford, where Erasmus had stayed on his first visit to England.[42] This treatise had originally been written in 1523 for the Benedictine nuns at the Convent of the Machabees in Cologne, and gave an exalted account of the monastic life, paying careful tribute to both virgins and martyrs, and accounting their sufferings and sanctity as more or less equal. It also paid tribute to the famous relics housed in the Cologne convent.[43] Paynell was to become a prolific translator, a chaplain to Henry VIII and to all three of the king's children in turn, so he was in a sense a consummate survivor, and yet also an Erasmian who managed to balance his openness to reform with some conservative convictions.

Erasmus was not only hijacked by those of a Protestant inclination, therefore, but could also be used by those who were simultaneously evangelical and conservative. A translation of his treatise on confession, published around 1535, was an interesting example of this. In this treatise, originally written in 1524 during a difficult period in

[40] Erasmus, *A dialoge or communication of two persons … intituled ye pylgremage of pure devotyon* (London, 1536?), sigs +iij^{r}, +iiii^{v}. Usually ascribed to 1535, the reference to the Pilgrimage of Grace means it must have been published in 1536 or 1537.

[41] For a contrary claim, see J. K. Yost, 'Taverner's Use of Erasmus and the Protestantization of English Humanism', *RQ* 23 (1970), 266–76. Yost sees Taverner's use of Erasmus to steer a middle way between 'gospellers' and 'papists' as 'Protestant moderation', but his evidence for terming Taverner's views Protestant is shaky, and the works might be better viewed as more distinctively Henrician. Taverner published six translations in 1539–40.

[42] The prior, John Ramsay, would surrender his house in 1538, and later became a Protestant; he published two works in 1548, *A corosyfe to be layed hard unto the hartes of all faythfull professours of Christes gospel* and *A plaister for a galled horse.*

[43] Erasmus, *The Comparation of a Vyrgin and a Martyr*, transl. Thomas Paynell (London, 1537), sig. Cv^{v}.

Erasmus's life in Basel, he referred to the contemporary quarrels over religion, and told the reader not to look for such debates in this work. As the translation rendered it, he said 'I lyst not nowe in this unquiete worlde, and troublous state of tymes, to styrre suche botches or soores'.[44] In a skilful piece of writing, Erasmus steered between those who insisted that auricular confession had been instituted by Christ, and those who declared it unscriptural, observing that he himself was inclined more towards those who thought it was ordained by Christ, and suggesting that 'this confession is many wayes, and for many causes very profitable and holsome / yf bothe parties do theyr duetie'. A gloss in the margin noted: 'Howe the author doth esteme confession / herof thou maye iudge good reder'.[45] This was about the time that Henry VIII was canvassing opinion from his bishops on whether confession might be considered to have a scriptural basis. Erasmus's work openly acknowledged the lamentable state of many priests, but argued that this might add to the value of confession, which required of the high and mighty even more humility to 'fall downe lowly and mekely at the feete of a preest / being often tymes but a vile and an abiecte persone / and of no reputation in the syght and iudgement of the worlde'.[46] The emphasis on spiritual endeavour, disregarding all doctrinal questions, had been Erasmus's response to the antagonisms of the early 1520s; unhelpfully the English translator is unknown, but in the circumstances of the mid-1530s this publication sounded a markedly moderate note.

In 1545, a translation of another colloquy took a much more aggressive stance. *A very pleasaunt and fruitful Diologe called the Epicure* was published by Richard Grafton and translated by Philip Gerard, a member of Prince Edward's privy chamber. Here the actual translation seems to have been chiefly a hook on which to hang a lengthy preface from the translator. This was a powerful piece of writing pushing the young prince towards an unequivocally Protestant future. Rejoicing that Edward 'delecteth in nothyng more then too bee occupied in the holye Byble', Gerard laid out the blessings to be had from an evangelical commitment on the part of a prince. 'Blessed are you then if you obey unto hys word, and walke in his waies. Blessed

[44] Erasmus, *A lytle treatise of the maner and forme of confession* (London, 1535?), sig. Av^{v}.
[45] Ibid., sig. Avii^{r}.
[46] Ibid., sig. Bv^{r}.

are you, yf you supporte suche as preache Gospell'.[47] On a more practical level, he suggested some of the riches that might follow: not only the kingdom of God, but wealth and conquest on earth. 'You are promised also, too conquere great and mightie nations.'[48] He probably knew that this would go down well with a small boy who loved martial exploits.[49] More menacingly, he warned 'let your grace bee most fully perswaded in this, that ther was never Kyng nor Prince, that prospered whiche tooke parte against Goddes woord'.[50] This was the great Henrician myth, that the gospel somehow would compel obedience.[51] Gerard also wrote, with reference to reading the gospel, 'surely none but ypocrites or els devilles would go about too stoppe or allure men from suche a treasure and godly study'.[52] This reflected none too well on the king, who had two years before promoted the 'Act for the Advancement of True Religion' which so dramatically attempted to restrict Bible reading to the higher echelons of society.[53]

Erasmus during his lifetime worked hard to avoid easy categorization, and once the Reformation had begun to unfold made strenuous efforts to avoid being claimed too directly for any single confessional standpoint. He died in 1536 just as the Reformation in England was beginning to get complicated and at a time when the English translations of his works were illustrating the many shades of reformist feeling seeking expression at that time. It is impossible to know what he would have thought of the greatest work of translation from the 1540s, that of his *Paraphrases* on the New Testament, which in due course would become a foundation stone of the Edwardian Reformation, placed in all parish churches alongside the English Bible.[54] It is often not sufficiently appreciated what an extraordinary work this was, not merely in terms of scholarly endeavour, but in bringing together such an eclectic group of translators under the aegis of Queen

[47] Erasmus, *A very pleasaunt and fruitful Diologe called the Epicure*, transl. Philip Gerard (London, 1545), sigs Aiii^{v}, Aiiii^{v}.

[48] Ibid., sig. Av^{r}.

[49] Jennifer Loach, *Edward VI* (New Haven, CT, 1999), 155–8.

[50] Erasmus, *Epicure*, sig. Avi^{r}.

[51] Richard Rex, 'The Crisis of Obedience: God's Word and Henry's Reformation', *HistJ* 39 (1994), 863–94.

[52] Erasmus, *Epicure*, sig. Bi^{r}.

[53] Alec Ryrie, *The Gospel and Henry VIII* (Cambridge, 2003), 47.

[54] Catharine Davies, *A Religion of the Word: The Defence of the Reformation in the Reign of Edward VI* (Manchester, 2002), 210.

Katherine Parr.[55] It drew on the moderate humanism of Nicholas Udall and the Catholic humanism of Princess Mary, whilst the second volume of 1549 would strike a more Protestant note with the contributions of Leonard Cox and Miles Coverdale.[56]

The English translations of Erasmus, then, were conduits for the many shades of religious attitudes in these formative years of Reformation. His intellectual stature in England before the Reformation made him an authority worth appealing to long after his death. His name was invoked by Mary's Catholic Reformation as well as by the Protestant Reformation of Edward VI.[57] On the one hand this testifies to the universality of many of Erasmus's ideas. But on the other hand it demonstrates that the appropriation of Erasmus's reputation in Henry VIII's reign had given his work a veneer of political reliability. Just as all three of Henry's children would appeal indiscriminately to the memory of their father as a symbol of authority, so could churchmen and scholars appeal to the example of Erasmus as someone reliably biblical in inspiration but safely ambiguous on specifics. In Nicholas Udall's preface to the *Paraphrases*, he described Erasmus as someone 'whose doctrine the moste and best parte of all Christian Royalmes and universities hath evermore allowed and judged to be consonaunt to the trueth'.[58] In this way a figure who never straightforwardly agreed with either confessional viewpoint had been translated into a figure with whom nobody could disagree.

Translation creates a relationship between original text and translated equivalent which remains uncertain and open to manipulation. It can be seen at one level, therefore, as an exercise in deception, intended to mislead. In the 1530s, when the English Bible was for different reasons necessary to both Protestants and Catholics in England, Erasmus's authority was drawn on in support of these very different works of translation into English. This often meant ignoring much of what Erasmus had said about the vernacular, and applying sentiments which had been intended to describe the translation of

[55] McConica, *English Humanists*, 240–8.

[56] Aysha Pollnitz, 'Religion and Translation at the Court of Henry VIII: Princess Mary, Katherine Parr and the *Paraphrases* of Erasmus', in Susan Doran and Thomas S. Freeman, eds, *Mary Tudor: Old and New Perspectives* (Basingstoke, 2011), 123–37.

[57] Lucy Wooding, *Rethinking Catholicism in Reformation England* (Oxford, 2000), 114–52.

[58] Erasmus, *The first tome or volume of the paraphrase of Erasmus upon the newe testamente* (London, 1548), sigs B7^{r}–^{v}.

the Greek New Testament into Latin to translation into English.[59] Erasmus's *Paraphrases*, published in English translation in 1548, had originally been written in Latin to elucidate the revised Latin translation which Erasmus presented in the *Novum Instrumentum*.[60] In refashioning them into English, the debate about translating had itself been translated.

[59] See Naomi Tadmor, *The Social Universe of the English Bible: Scripture, Society and Culture in Early Modern England* (Cambridge, 2010), 1–9.

[60] Erasmus's famous 1519 translation of the first chapter of John using *sermo* and *oratio* was faithfully rendered by Princess Mary as 'word' and 'speech'; Pollnitz, 'Religion and Translation', 133.

'These four letters *s o l a* are not there': Language and Theology in Luther's Translation of the New Testament

Charlotte Methuen*
University of Glasgow

Luther's 1522 translation of the New Testament is one of the most significant translations in Christian history. In it, he offers a translation of Romans 3: 28 which introduces the word allein: 'So halten wir es nun, daß der Mensch gerecht werde ohne des Gesetzes Werke, allein durch den Glauben.' *As Luther himself recognized in his* Open Letter on Translating *(1530), the word 'alone' does not appear in either the Greek text of Romans or the Vulgate; nor do other contemporary vernacular translations include it. Luther asserted that the introduction of the word* allein *arose from his attention to the German language. This claim has often been regarded as specious, since the introduction of* allein *serves to underline a key aspect of Luther's theology, namely his doctrine of justification by faith. This article examines Luther's translation practice, and particularly his comments on Romans 3: 28 in his lectures on Romans, his preface to Paul's epistle to the Romans and other writings, concluding that Luther was indeed concerned to produce a fluent and coherent German translation of the biblical text, but that he wished also to produce one that was theologically unambiguous. Not only linguistic considerations, but also Luther's theological priorities, and his definition of theological unambiguity, determined his definition of a good translation.*

In 1530, Luther published his *Open Letter on Translation.*[1] In it he responded to critics of his German Bible translation, focusing in

* TRS, University of Glasgow, No. 4 The Square, Glasgow, G41 2NW.
E-mail: charlotte.methuen@glasgow.ac.uk.

[1] There is some complexity involved in writing about Luther's German Bible translation in English: German, and where appropriate Latin and Greek, will be given in the text along with English translations. Luther's preferred term, *dolmetschen*, is today generally referred to the oral process of translating known as 'interpreting'; however, I have used 'translating' here since this article explores (*inter alia*) the relationship between Luther's textual translations and his exegetical interpretation. For Luther's terminology, see Christopher Spehr, "Dem Volk aufs Maul schauen": Luther als Dolmetscher', in Margot Käßmann and Martin Rösel, eds, *Die Bibel Martin Luthers. Ein Buch und seine Geschichte* (Stuttgart and Leipzig, 2016), 76–93, at 77–9.

Studies in Church History 53 (2017) 146–163
doi: 10.1017/stc.2016.10

particular on two passages. The first was Romans 3: 28, which in his German New Testament, published in 1522 (the so-called *Septembertestament*), Luther had translated: '*So halten wir es nun, daß der Mensch gerecht werde ohne des Gesetzes Werke, allein durch den Glauben*' – 'We hold, therefore, that a man is justified without the work of the law, by faith alone'. The second was his rendering of Luke 1: 28, the angel's greeting to Mary: '*Gegrusset seystu holdselige, der herr ist mit dyr, du gebenedeyte vnter den weyben*' – 'Greetings to you, sweet Mary, the Lord is with you, you who are blessed amongst women'. In his *Open Letter*, Luther vigorously defended his choice of the adjective *holdselig*, literally 'blessed by grace' but in English probably best rendered 'gracious', 'sweet' or 'lovely', to describe Mary in preference to the Vulgate's *voll Gnaden*, 'full of grace'. He also laid out his reasons for introducing the word *allein*, 'only', into his translation of Romans 3: 28, insisting: 'I knew very well that the word *solum* is not in the Greek or Latin text; the papists did not have to teach me that. It is a fact that these four letters *s o l a* are not there.'[2] However, he assured his readers, the inclusion of *allein* reflected his desire to produce a fluent German translation, for German functioned differently from Latin. It was, Luther claimed, a matter of language rather than theology.

Is Luther's assertion to be believed? There can be no question but that his use of *allein* – *allein durch Glauben* ('by faith alone') – in translating Romans 3:28 also makes a theological point, emphasizing the doctrine of justification by faith that is fundamental to Luther's theology. Is Luther's claim in his *Open Letter on Translation* specious? This article considers this question firstly by placing Luther's translation of Romans 3: 28 in the context of other contemporary translations of other New Testament passages and secondly by comparing it to his rendering of Romans 3: 28 elsewhere. In doing so, it highlights the challenge posed by Luther's task of translating Scripture at a time when the meaning of Scripture was itself contested, and translation was not only a question of textual accuracy but also of defining orthodoxy and heresy. There can be no doubt that Luther was indeed concerned to produce a fluent and accessible German translation of the biblical text, but how did his theological priorities shape his definition of a good translation?

[2] Luther, *Sendbrief zu Dolmetschen*, *WA* 30/2, 636 (*LW* 35, 188).

The questions raised by Luther in his *Open Letter on Translation* remain pertinent to translators today.[3] All translators are faced with a challenge, as Birgit Stolt points out: 'How true to the original must one remain; how freely may one formulate things? The free, adaptive method, oriented toward the language of translation, stands over against the "alienating" method, oriented toward the original language, with its emphasis on remaining true to the words.'[4] James Arne Nestingen observes: 'Translation takes place in two dimensions. The first is a linguistic exchange, roughly equivalent language being substituted for the original. The second is cultural, the new language inevitably giving that which is being translated another hue, colored with its own specific assumptions.'[5] For Stolt, the 'truly remarkable' aspect of Luther's method of translating lies in his ability to attend both to the original text and to the language into which he was translating.[6] It is widely recognized that it was this ability to render the words of the Bible into a language which seemed familiar to those who spoke it that distinguished Luther's translations from earlier German translations of the Bible, which had generally sought to stay closer to the language of the original text, and thus had resulted in less idiomatic German.[7] Luther's linguistic aim, as Antoine Berman has pointed out, was to compose a text which was 'not Latin, not a pure dialect, but a generalized popular speech'.[8]

What, however, was the text being translated? The wider context of early modern biblical translation, and of Luther's *Open Letter* itself,

[3] Indeed, Robert Barnes believes that 'much modern debate about translation in general has arisen from debate about the principles of biblical translation': 'Translating the Sacred', in Kirsten Malmkjær and Kevin Windle, eds, *The Oxford Handbook of Translation Studies* (Oxford, 2011), 37–54; at 38.

[4] Birgit Stolt, 'Luther's Translation of the Bible', *Lutheran Quarterly* 28 (2014), 373–400, at 376; originally published in German as '"… und fühl's im Herzen …". Luthers Bibelübersetzung aus der Sicht neuerer Sprach- und Übersetzungswissenschaft', *Zeitschrift für Theologie und Kirche* 98 (2001), 186–208.

[5] James Arne Nestingen, 'Luther's Cultural Translation of the Catechism', *Lutheran Quarterly* 15 (2001), 440–52, at 440.

[6] Stolt, 'Luther's Translation', 377.

[7] Ibid. 377–81. Stolt notes, however, that Luther was also 'sensitive to the historically developed, stylistic genre of the biblical way of narration, a biblical narrative tone': ibid. 397.

[8] Antoine Berman, *The Experience of the Foreign: Culture and Translation in Romantic Germany* (Albany, NY, 1992), 25. Historians of the German language are agreed that Luther's Bible translation made a very significant contribution to the standardization of early modern high German: see, for instance, Michael Trinklein, 'Luther's Insights into the Translator's Task', *Bible Translator* 21 (1970), 80–8.

throws into stark relief the complexity of establishing what it means to '[remain] true to the original'. This is in part because the Bible presented (and continues to present) particular difficulties when it comes to establishing what is meant by 'the original'.[9] The first challenge for Luther was that of defining the source text.[10] Luther's German Bible was a new departure, not only in his efforts to produce an idiomatic German text, but also in his commitment to offering a translation (at least in theory[11]) from Greek and Hebrew rather than from the Latin of the Vulgate.[12] This decision was not value-neutral, but had far-reaching theological consequences. By the time Luther began his theological career, the humanist insistence on the importance of studying works in their original language had already generated an awareness that some aspects of medieval theology and church practice drew their rationale from passages in the Vulgate

[9] There is not space in this article to engage properly with the philosophy of translation. Suffice it to remark that structuralism tells us, with some justification, that meaning is fluid for all texts, but translators nonetheless have to proceed on the assumption that they can find a meaning in the original text that can be mediated, however imperfectly, into another language.

[10] This remains an ongoing challenge for biblical translators, as Anthony Pym observes: 'in the case of the Bible, the establishment of any "original" … depends on a multilingual collection of writings and rewritings collated over a period of centuries, some of them quite fragmentary, many of them contradictory, and more requiring interpretation in terms of non-sacred texts from the same periods': Anthony Pym, 'On the Historical Epistemologies of Bible Translating', in Philip A. Noss, ed., *A History of Bible Translation* (Rome, 2007), 195–215, at 196–7.

[11] The extent of Luther's knowledge of New Testament Greek and of Hebrew has long been the subject of debate. This article will work on the assumption that his Greek was good enough for him to be able to use Erasmus's *Novum Instrumentum* and to recognize the validity of the translation issues identified by the humanists.

[12] For discussions of Luther's Bible and its relationship to other early modern German Bible translations, see Heinz Bluhm, *Martin Luther: Creative Translator* (St Louis, MO, 1965); idem, 'Luther's German Bible', in Peter Newman Brooks, ed., *Seven-Headed Luther: Essays in Commemoration of a Quincentenary 1483–1983* (Oxford, 1983), 177–94; Andrew C. Gow, 'The Contested History of a Book: The German Bible of the Later Middle Ages and Reformation in Legend, Ideology, and Scholarship', *Journal of Hebrew Scriptures* 9 (2009), article 13 [online journal], at: <http://www.jhsonline.org>, last accessed 15 August 2016; Thomas Kaufmann, 'Vorreformatorische Laienbibel und reformatorisches Evangelium', *Zeitschrift für Theologie und Kirche* 101 (2004), 138–74; Willem Jan Kooiman, *Luther and the Bible* (Philadelphia, PA, 1961); Volker Leppin, '"Biblia, das ist die ganze Heilige Schrift deutsch". Luthers Bibelübersetzung zwischen Sakralität und Profanität', in Jan Rohls and Gunther Wenz, eds, *Protestantismus und deutsche Literatur*, Münchener Theologische Forschungen 2 (Göttingen, 2004), 13–26; Charlotte Methuen, '"novam sprach, celeste deudsch". Eine Untersuchung der theologischen Sprache von Luthers Bibelübersetzung', *Zeitschrift für Neues Testament* 13 (2010), 40–51; Heimo Reinitzer, *Biblia deutsch. Luthers Bibelübersetzung und ihre Tradition* (Wolfenbüttel and Hamburg, 1983).

which humanists had come to see as inaccurate translations of the Greek text. Lorenzo Valla, Erasmus and Jacques Lefèvre d'Étaples, amongst others, questioned the accuracy of the Vulgate's Latin translation and suggested revisions to it. Indeed, the format of Erasmus's 1516 *Novum Instrumentum* – which presented the Greek text and his own Latin translation on facing pages, followed by his annotations discussing the relationship between the two – was, as Paul Botley observes, 'largely inspired by Erasmus' decision to publish his own Latin translation of the New Testament', and his realization that this 'required an edition of the Greek text on which it was based'.[13] Luther's decision to base his own translation of the New Testament on the Greek text, which he regarded as conveying the 'true meaning' of Scripture, therefore made a theological as well as a linguistic statement. For Luther, theological authority was rooted in the principle of *sola scriptura*; and the *scriptura* which he wished to make known in German was that found in the original languages, from which, he believed, readers would learn true theology and a better understanding of what the Church should be.

For Luther, then, a translation '[remained] true to the original' when it presented the theology which he believed to be proclaimed in the Greek New Testament and Hebrew Bible. However, from 1520 that theology had been defined to be heretical. Consequently, his translation embodied and articulated precisely the theological assumptions that his opponents were seeking to suppress, and thus raised issues not just of language but of power. Lynne Long observes that 'sacred text translation' is particularly prone to 'promot[ing] contention between the users of the texts involved',[14] since, as

[13] Paul Botley, *Latin Translation in the Renaissance: The Theory and Practice of Leonardo Bruni, Giannozzo Manetti and Desiderius Erasmus* (Cambridge, 2004), 115; cf. Henk Jan de Jonge, '*Novum Testamentum a nobis versum*: The Essence of Erasmus' Edition of the New Testament', *JThS* 35 (1984), 394–413. The Basle printer, Froben, also encouraged Erasmus to produce an edition of the Greek text: see De Jonge, 'Essence of Erasmus' Edition', 401; J. K. Elliott, '"Novum Testamentum editum est": The Five-Hundredth Anniversary of Erasmus's New Testament', *Bible Translator* 67 (2016), 9–28, at 11; Bruce Metzger and Bart Ehrman, *The Text of the New Testament*, 3rd edn (New York, 2005), 142. Metzger and Ehmann assert (ibid. 145) – erroneously – that the *Novum Instrumentum* initially included not Erasmus's translation but the Vulgate translation. For the shape of the *Novum Instrumentum*, its rationale and genesis, see Erasmus von Rotterdam, *Novum Instrumentum* (Basel, 1516), facsimile edn, ed. Heinz Holeczek (Stuttgart and Bad Cannstatt, 1986), especially Holeczek's introduction, v–xxxv.

[14] Lynne Long, 'The Translation of Sacred Texts', in Carmen Millán and Francesca Bartrina, eds, *The Routledge Handbook of Translation Studies* (London, 2013), 464–74, at 467.

Lefevere asserts, 'it is not only the authority of the text that requires validation, it is also the authority of those whose power resides in the text'.[15] In the Reformation context, the challenge to authority posed by vernacular Bible translations was explosive, as Richard Duerdon highlights in relation to early modern English translations of the New Testament: 'all about and through these texts swirl the perils and promises of conviction – both kinds – and of ideology, authority, and power',[16] for 'if Tyndale is a heretic, no amount of philological ability will make the text acceptable; ideology and language form a single inter-text'.[17] David R. Glowacki argues that, for the authors of early modern English Bible prefaces, 'the economic forces, the political forces, and the effort of the translators are ultimately sanctioned by God'.[18] This was not a new phenomenon – Hermann Schüssler has shown that the scriptural authority and ecclesiology were already intimately entwined in late medieval definitions of doctrine[19] – but there can be no doubt that Luther's German New Testament, and later Bible, formed a nexus for complex processes which aimed to control both the biblical text and its interpretation.[20] Luther himself, however, makes no explicit claims to divine (or, indeed, secular) authority regarding his own translation; his stated intention was to mediate an understanding of the 'real nature of the gospel': '"gospel" [*evangelion*] is a Greek word and means in German good message, good tidings, good news, a good report, of which one sings and

[15] André Lefevere, *Translation, History, Culture: A Sourcebook* (London, 1992), 3; cited by Lynne Long, *Translating the Bible: From the 7th to the 17th century* (Aldershot, 2002), 205.

[16] Richard Duerdon, 'Equivalence or Power? Authority and Reformation Bible Translation', in: Orlaith O'Sullivan, ed., *The Bible as Book: The Reformation* (London, 2000), 9–23, at 9. For issues of power in translation in general, see Román Álvarez and M. Carmen África Vidal, eds, *Translation, Power, Subversion* (Clevedon, 1996).

[17] Duerdon, 'Equivalence or Power?', 13. For Thomas More's view of Tyndale's translation as heretical, see Morna D. Hooker, 'Tyndale's "Heretical" Translation', *Reformation* 2 (1997), 127–42.

[18] David R. Glowacki, 'To the Reader: The Structure of Power in Biblical Translation, from Tyndale to the NRSV', *Literature and Theology* 22 (2008), 195–209, at 197. Glowacki's claim is less convincing in the case of the preface to Tyndale's New Testament than it is for the Geneva Bible or the Authorized version.

[19] Hermann Schüssler, *Der Primat der Heiligen Schrift als theologisches und kanonisches Problem im Spätmittelalter* (Wiesbaden, 1977), especially 294–305.

[20] To cite just one example, Duke George of Saxony sought to suppress the *Septembertestament* by having all copies confiscated and burned: see Christoph Volkmar, 'Turning Luther's Weapons against him: The Birth of Catholic Propaganda in Saxony in the 1520s', in Malcolm Walsby and Graeme Kemp, eds, *The Book Triumphant: Print in Transition in the Sixteenth and Seventeenth Centuries* (Leiden, 2011), 115–31, at 127–8.

tells and about which one is glad'.[21] For Luther the content of this message was everything: people were to understand that 'faith in Christ overcomes sin, death, and hell, and gives life, righteousness, and salvation'.[22] But how was that faith acquired?

The theological questions raised for translators and interpreters by the return to Greek and Hebrew texts are exemplified in two texts identified by the humanists as key: Matthew 4: 17, which Luther did not discuss in his *Open Letter on Translation*, and Luke 1: 28, which he did. In the NRSV, Matthew 4: 17 is rendered into English: 'From that time Jesus began to proclaim, "Repent, for the kingdom of heaven has come near."' The key phrase is Jesus's exhortation, which in Greek reads: μετανοεῖτε, ἤγγικεν γὰρ ἡ βασιλεία τῶν οὐρανῶν. The Vulgate translation is *paenitentiam agite adpropinquavit enim regnum caelorum*, and the terminology *paenitentiam agite* ('do penance') helped to justify the practice of sacramental confession. Lorenzo Valla had recognized this as a problematic translation of the Greek term μετανοεῖτε, and Erasmus and Luther agreed.[23] In English, from the time of Wyclif, μετανοεῖτε has been translated 'repent';[24] however, neither German nor Latin has an equivalent to the English verb 'repent', and both Erasmus and Luther struggled to find a translation which did not carry the overtones of Jerome's *paenitentiam agite*. In the 1516 *Novum Instrumentum*, Erasmus opted for *poeniteat vos*; in 1519, the edition used by Luther for his 1522 *Septembertestament*, Erasmus tried *resipiscite*; in the 1522 edition he reverted to an amended version of the Vulgate: *paenitentiam agite vitae prioris*. Similarly, in 1522 Luther translated μετανοεῖτε with '*Bessert euch*' – 'improve yourselves' – but by 1534 he had opted for '*Tut Buße*' – 'do penance', returning to the reading he had offered in 1517 in the first of the Ninety-Five Theses: '*Dominus et magister noster Iesus Christus dicendo "Penitentiam agite &c." omnem vitam fidelium penitentiam esse voluit*' ('When our Lord and

[21] Luther, 'Preface to the New Testament' (1522), *WA.DB* 6, 2 (*LW* 35, 358, translation amended by Charlotte Methuen).

[22] Ibid., *WA.DB* 6, 10 (*LW* 35, 362).

[23] Jaroslav Pelikan, *The Christian Tradition*, 4: *Reformation of Church and Dogma (1300–1700)* (Chicago, IL, 1984), 308.

[24] Wycliffe has 'Do ye[e] penaunce'; see: *The Earlier Version of the Wycliffite Bible*, 7: *The Gospels, edited from MS Christ Church 145*, ed. Conrad Lindberg (Stockholm, 1994), 31; *King Henry's Bible, MS Bodley 277: The Revised Version of the Wyclif Bible*, 4: *The New Testament*, ed. Conrad Lindberg (Stockholm, 2004), 38. For the relationship between the earlier and later versions of the Wyclif translation, see Mary Dove, *The First English Bible: The Text and Context of the Wycliffite Versions* (Cambridge 2007), especially 137–88.

Master Jesus Christ said, "Do penance etc.", he willed the entire life of believers to be one of repentance').

The translation of Matthew 4: 17 demonstrates the complex interplay between theological meaning and language, but it also shows the way in which the constraints of the target language – in this case German – determine possible translations and meanings. A second problematic Vulgate translation, which Luther discussed at some length in his *Sendbrief*, was the angel's greeting to Mary at the annunciation (Luke 1: 28), which in the NRSV reads: 'And he came to her and said, "Greetings, favoured one! The Lord is with you."' Here too, it was the spoken words which presented the translation challenge. In Greek, the angel's words read: Χαῖρε, κεχαριτωμένη, ὁ κύριος μετὰ σοῦ; this was translated by the Vulgate: *Ave gratia plena Dominus tecum.* Some form of this phrase was well known to many late medieval and early modern Christians as the opening of the *Ave Maria*, one of the texts they were expected to know by heart in Latin or the vernacular, or both.[25] The problem, as humanist scholars identified it,[26] was that the Latin *gratia plena* – 'full of grace'—implied that grace was a measurable commodity, rather than describing the quality of the relationship between God and Mary, as the Greek κεχαριτωμένη seemed to do. Both Erasmus and Luther found solutions which they went on to use consistently. Erasmus in his *Novum instrumentum* translated the angel's greeting: *Ave gratiosa, dominus tecum!* Luther chose to use the term *holdselig* – 'lovely', 'sweet', 'gracious': *Gegrusset seystu holdselige, der herr ist mit dyr.*[27]

Luther's explanation for his decision centres on his view that κεχαριτωμένη expressed Mary's relationship to God:

> When does a German speak like that, 'You are full of grace'? What German understands what that is, to be 'full of grace'? He would have

[25] By the late Middle Ages, lay people were expected to know and be able to recite the *Ave Maria*, the Lord's Prayer, the Ten Commandments and the Apostles' Creed in their own language. All these texts were often chanted in the context of the liturgy and were also used in private devotions and in combination with the rosary: see Arnold Angenendt, *Geschichte der Religiosität im Mittelalter*, 2nd edn (Darmstadt, 2000), 471, 479, 545–6.

[26] Both Valla and Erasmus observed in their *Annotations* that the Greek participle meant 'accepted into grace'. See Pelikan, *Christian Tradition*, 4: 308; compare also Erika Rummel, *Erasmus' Annotations on the New Testament: From Philologist to Theologian* (Toronto, ON, 1986), 167–71.

[27] In this case, Tyndale's translation (Antwerp, 1534), apparently unconcerned about humanist objections, renders the Vulgate text into English: 'Hayle ful of grace, y[e] Lorde is with y[e]'.

> to think of a keg 'full of' beer or a purse 'full of' money. Therefore I have translated it, 'You gracious girl,' so that a German can at least think his way through to what the angel meant by this greeting. Here, however, the papists are going wild about me, because I have corrupted the angelic salutation; though I have still not hit upon the best German rendering for it. Suppose I had taken the best German, and translated the salutation thus: 'God greets you, dear Mary' – for that is what the angel wanted to say, and what he would have said, if he had wanted to greet her in German. Suppose I had done that! I believe that they would have hanged themselves out of tremendous fanaticism for the Virgin Mary, because I had thus destroyed the salutation.[28]

Beneath the polemic, which witnesses to the conflicts in which Luther and his New Testament translation had by 1530 become deeply embroiled, Luther's linguistic point was that a literal translation of the Vulgate encouraged German-speakers to misunderstand the nature of grace. However, he also held that the Vulgate had misunderstood the Greek term, which he believed to be the translation of a Hebrew phrase.[29] Luther looked for a model in angelic greetings in the Old Testament, and found one in the angel's greeting to Daniel as 'greatly beloved' (Daniel 10: 11, 19 NRSV):

> I think that the angel Gabriel spoke with Mary as he speaks with Daniel, calling him *chamudoth* and *ish chamudoth*, *vir desideriorum*, that is, 'You dear Daniel'; for that is Gabriel's way of speaking as we see in the book of Daniel. Now if I were to translate the angel's words literally, with

[28] Luther, *Sendbrief zu Dolmetschen*, *WA* 30/2, 638 (*LW* 35, 191–2, translation amended by author: the *LW* rendering 'Hello there Mary' misses the tone of Luther's rendering of the divine greeting to 'sweet Mary').

[29] Luther assumed that the spoken language of the New Testament was Hebrew, and therefore frequently considered which Hebrew term might be being translated by the Greek: Stephan Veit Frech, *Magnificat und Benedictus Deutsch: Martin Luthers bibelhumanistische Übersetzung in der Rezeption des Erasmus von Rotterdam* (Bern, 1995), 261. In this, intriguingly, Luther was following Giannozzo Manetti, whose unpublished translation of the Bible into Latin he cannot have known. Erasmus, in contrast, emphasized 'the diversity of languages which had been spoken in Roman Judaea', and argued that Christ would certainly not have spoken Latin but 'Syriac, perhaps sometimes in Chaldaic, and maybe occasionally in Greek', or maybe also Hebrew corrupted by Syriac and Chaldean: see Erasmus's annotations to Acts 10, in *Erasmus' Annotations on the New Testament: Acts – Romans – I and II Corinthians*, ed. Anne Reeve and M. A. Screech (Leiden, 1990), 299–300; cf. Botley, *Latin translation in the Renaissance*, 98, 116–17. For Manetti's translation, see also Annet den Haan, 'Giannozzo Manetti's New Testament: New Evidence on Sources, Translation Process and the Use of Valla's *Annotationes*', *Renaissance Studies* 28 (2013), 731–47.

> the skill of these asses, I should have to say this, 'Daniel, you man of desires' [*Daniel, du man der begirungen oder: Daniel, du man der lüste*]. That would be pretty German! A German would hear, of course, that *Man*, *Lueste*, and *begyrunge* are German words … . But when the words are thus put together: 'you man of desires,' no German would know what is said. He would think, perhaps, that Daniel is full of evil desires. Well, that would be fine translating! Therefore I must let the literal words go and try to learn how the German says that which the Hebrew expresses with *ish chamudoth*. I find then that the German says this, 'You dear Daniel,' 'You dear Mary,' or 'You gracious maid,' 'You lovely maiden,' 'You gentle girl,' and the like.[30]

Grace, as Luther had come to believe by 1519, is not a commodity to be bought or sold, but is manifested in 'the righteousness of Christ my God which becomes ours through faith and by the grace and mercy of God'.[31] Here too, therefore, Luther's point was not only linguistic but deeply theological.

Reflecting on the hostile reception of Erasmus's translation of the opening of John's gospel in the 1519 edition of his *Novum Testamentum* (as it was now titled), which he rendered *In principio erat sermo*, rather than *verbum*, Long comments that 'the overlay of tradition and exegesis' had 'crystallise[d] the text into an original to which any alteration was regarded with aggression and suspicion'.[32] Luther's rejection of *voll gnaden*, the German equivalent of the Vulgate's *plena gratia*, in favour of *holdselige* received a similarly negative response. And yet, when in 1523 Hieronymus Emser published a version of the German New Testament which attempted to render Luther's translation doctrinally acceptable to Catholics, he retained Luther's use of *holdselige*, even though, as he commented in a marginal note, he affirmed that Mary 'is called by the angel full of grace'.[33] Indeed, elsewhere Emser explicitly rejected Luther's interpretation:

[30] Luther, *Sendbrief zu Dolmetschen*, *WA* 30/2, 639 (*LW* 35, 192–3).

[31] Luther, *Two Types of Righteousness*, *WA* 2, 146 (*LW* 31, 299); cf. also Luther's use of a marriage metaphor for the relationship between the sinner and Christ: *The Freedom of a Christian*, *WA* 7, 54–5 (*LW* 31, 351).

[32] Long, 'Translation of Sacred Texts', 470.

[33] Hieronymus Emser, *Das naw Testament nach lawt der Christlichen kirchen bewerten Text* (Dresden, 1523), fol. 39^r. For the politics behind Emser's translation, see Volkmar, 'Turning Luther's Weapons against him'.

> Certainly the angel here was not speaking about human affection [*huld*] but about the grace of God. And Mary did not possess the honor and worthiness that she would become the mother of God from human affection but from God's grace. For this reason, we should not at this place read and pray 'You beloved one' but 'You full of grace.' For the grace that Eve forfeited, Mary regained for us, and the curse of Eve has been transformed into the blessing of Mary.[34]

Stolt argues that in the view of Emser and of others who objected to Luther's translation, 'the church had established once and for all how this passage was to be interpreted, namely, in harmony with dogma and typology, and any questioning of this reading came close to blasphemy'.[35] Emser wished to maintain this traditional theology, but his German translation nonetheless retained Luther's use of *holdselige*. A new or revised translation did not always give rise to a new theology.[36]

The Vulgate's translation of Matthew 4: 17 and of Luke 1: 28 had already been identified as problematic by humanist scholars. No such questions had been raised about Roman 3: 28, which in the Greek in Erasmus's 1516 *Novum Instrumentum* reads: λογιζόμεθα οὖν πίστει δικαιοῦσθαι ἄνθρωπον χωρὶς ἔργων νόμου.[37] This was translated in the Vulgate as *arbitramur enim iustificari hominem per fidem sine operibus legis*. Erasmus introduced minor changes which reflected the word-order of the Byzantine codex on which his edition was based, emphasizing the place of faith: *arbitramur igitur fide iustificari hominem absque operibus legis*.[38] Luther's 1522 translation, which remained un-

[34] Hieronymus Emser, *Auß was gründ und ursach Luthers dolmatschung / über das nawe testament / dem gemeinen man billich vorbotten worden sey* … (Leipzig, 1523), cited in Stolt, 'Luther's Translation', 382.

[35] Stolt, 'Luther's Translation', 382.

[36] Similarly, there are numerous discrepancies between Erasmus's Latin translation of the Greek text and the text used in his accompanying notes in the *Annotationes*.

[37] Erasmus based his rendering of the Greek text on Byzantine codices, whilst the Vulgate used an Alexandrian text, which reads: λογιζόμεθα γὰρ δικαιοῦσθαι πίστει ἄνθρωπον χωρὶς ἔργων νόμου. The latter is now regarded as closer to the original. For the manuscripts used by Erasmus in the *Novum Instrumentum*, see Patrick Andrist, 'Structure and History of the Biblical Manuscripts used by Erasmus for his 1516 Edition', and Andrew J. Brown, 'The Manuscript Sources and Textual Character of Erasmus' Greek New Testament', in Martin Wallraff, Silvana Seidel Menchi and Kaspar von Greyerz, eds, *Basel 1516: Erasmus' Edition of the New Testament* (Tübingen, 2016), 81–124, 125–44 respectively.

[38] Tyndale's English translation gives a good indication of the meaning of Erasmus's text: 'We suppose therefore that a man is iustified by fayth with out the dedes of the lawe.' I am grateful to Gergely Juhász for drawing my attention to the relationship between Erasmus's translation and the manuscript tradition.

changed in all subsequent editions, placed even stronger emphasis on the role of faith by introducing the word *allein* – 'only': *So halten wir es nun, daß der Mensch gerecht werde ohne des Gesetzes Werke, allein durch den Glauben* ('a person is justified without the works of the law, through faith alone').[39]

In his *Sendbrief*, Luther protested at the criticism being levelled at him by 'these blockheads': 'I knew very well that the word *solum* is not in the Greek or Latin text; the papists did not have to teach me that. It is a fact that these four letters *s o l a* are not there.'[40] Here too, he justified his use of *allein* on the basis of German usage:

> it is the nature of our German language that in speaking of two things, one of which is affirmed and the other denied, we use the word *solum* (*allein* – only) along with the word *nicht* [not] or *kein* [no]. For example, we say, 'The farmer brings *only* grain and *no* money'; 'No, really I now have *no* money, but *only* grain'; 'I have *only* eaten and *not* yet drunk'; 'Did you *only* write it, and *not* read it over?'[41]

The use of *allein*, he claimed, followed from his commitment to producing a German translation which was recognizably German and not Latin or Greek: 'I wanted to speak German, not Latin or Greek, since it was German I had undertaken to speak in the translation. … For the literal Latin is a great hindrance to speaking good German.'[42] Consequently, he emphasized:

> We do not have to inquire of the literal Latin, how we are to speak German, as these asses do. Rather we must inquire about this of the mother in the home, the children on the street, the common man in the marketplace. We must be guided by their language, the way they speak, and do our translating accordingly.[43]

What 'these blockheads' had failed to understand, he complained, was that his use of *allein* 'conveys the sense of the text; it belongs there if the translation is to be clear and vigorous'.[44]

[39] Heinz Bluhm has explored the relationship between Erasmus's 1519 Greek text of Romans 3: 19–31, Erasmus's 1519 translation, the Vulgate and Luther's *Septembertestament*: Heinz Bluhm, 'Bedeutung und Eigenart von Luthers Septembertestament: Eine Analyse von Römer iii. 19–31', *Luther Jahrbuch* 39 (1972), 55–79.

[40] Luther, *Sendbrief zu Dolmetschen*, *WA* 30/2, 636 (*LW* 35, 188).

[41] Ibid., *WA* 30/2, 637 (*LW* 35, 189).

[42] Ibid.

[43] Ibid.

[44] Ibid., *WA* 30/2, 637 (*LW* 35, 188).

The problem, as Waldtraut-Ingeborg Sauer-Geppert notes, is that this 'apparently simple linguistic aid' achieves 'an exclusivity which the original text can have, but which it does not have to have'.[45] Key here, therefore, is Luther's understanding of 'the sense of the text'. By 1522, he had come to emphasize that justification was by faith alone – *sola fide*. Bluhm claims that Luther uses *sola* or *allein* in 'a series' of quotations of Romans 3: 28 before the publication of the *Septembertestament*, but that none predates the 1515 lectures; however, the first direct evidence he cites is from 1518, in Luther's 'Sermon on the proper preparation for receiving the sacrament': *Apostolus … clamat omnes esse peccatores et sola iustificandos fide* – 'The apostle … proclaims that all are sinners and are justified only by faith'.[46] Bluhm is correct that the conviction that justification is received solely by grace through faith was beginning to emerge in Luther's *Lectures on Romans*. He commented on Romans 1: 17: 'Only in the Gospel is the righteousness of God revealed [*in solo evangelio revelatur Iustitia Dei*] … by faith alone [*per solam fidem*], by which the Word of God is believed.'[47] However, the *Lectures on Romans* did not yet include *sola* in the discussion of Romans 3: 28. Luther's gloss explained: '*that a man is justified*, reckoned righteous before God, whether Greek or Jew, *by faith, apart from works of the Law*, without the help and necessity of the works of the Law'.[48] In the *Schola*, he distinguished between 'works of the law' and 'works of grace':

> Thus when the apostle says that a man is justified *apart from works of the Law* (v. 28), he is not speaking about the works which are performed in order that we may seek justification. Because these are no longer the works of the Law but of grace and faith, since he who performs them does not trust in them for his justification, but he wants to be justified and he does not think that through these works he has fulfilled the Law, but he seeks its fulfillment.[49]

Luther did not refer explicitly to Romans 3 either in the 1516 disputation on the extent of human power and will without grace, or in his

[45] Waldtraut-Ingeborg Sauer-Geppert, 'Bibelübersetzungen III/1', in *Theologische Realenzyklopädie* (Berlin, 1976–2004), 6: 228–46, at 239.

[46] Luther, *Sermo de digna praeparatione cordis pro suscipiendo sacramento euchariatiae*, *WA* 1, 332; Bluhm, 'Bedeutung und Eigenart', 76.

[47] Luther, *Lectures on Romans*, *WA* 56, 171 (*LW* 25, 151); but cf. the minimal treatment in *WA* 57, 133, which does not mention faith at all.

[48] Ibid., *WA* 56, 39 (*LW* 25, 33).

[49] Ibid., *WA* 56, 264 (*LW* 25, 252).

1518 sermon on indulgences and grace.[50] Although Luther's *Lectures on Romans* show that Luther was wrestling with the relationship between justification and grace, Romans 3: 28 had not yet emerged as a foundational text for his theology.

Luther's first explicit statement of the doctrine of justification by faith alone arguably occurred in the Heidelberg Disputation, in thesis 25: 'He is not righteous who does much, but he who, without work, believes much in Christ [*non ille iustus est, qui multum operator, sed qui sine opere multum credit in Christum*].' Luther explained: 'I wish to have the words "without work" understood in the following manner: Not that the righteous person does nothing, but that his works do not make him righteous, rather that his righteousness creates works. For grace and faith are infused without our works. After they have been imparted the works follow.'[51] Here he cites Romans 3: 28 to substantiate this point, reproducing the Vulgate text (i.e. not that found in Erasmus's *Novum Instrumentum*, which he had probably not yet read): *arbitramur enim iustificari hominem per fidem sine operibus legis* – 'for we hold that man is justified by faith apart from works of law'.[52] By the time he came to dispute with Cajetan in Augsburg in autumn 1518 Luther was relating the language of *sola fide* more explicitly to justification: 'Through no attitude on your part will you become worthy, through no works will you be prepared for the sacrament, but through faith alone, for only faith in the word of Christ justifies, makes a person alive, worthy, and well prepared [*sola fides verbi Christi iustificat, vivificat, dignificat, praeparet*].'[53] Two years later, in *The Freedom of a Christian*, he similarly asserted: 'it is clear that, as the soul needs only the Word of God for its life and righteousness, so it is justified by faith alone and not any works [*ita sola fide et nullis operibus iustificantur*]'.[54] However,

[50] Luther, *Quaestio de viribus et voluntate hominis sine gratia disputa 1516*, *WA* 1, 145–51; Luther, *Sermon vom Ablaß und Gnade*, *WA* 1, 243–6. The marginal citations in Luther's writings up to 1518 (*WA* 1), suggests that he cited Romans 1[: 17] and Romans 8 quite frequently, but Romans 3 rarely, citing 3: 20 more often than 3: 28. However, some care is needed here, since in most cases the marginal references given in the *WA* represent the editors' assumptions about which passage Luther had in mind when he wrote 'St Paul says' or 'as Paul in Romans chapter 3'.

[51] Luther, *Heidelberg Disputation*, *WA* 1, 364 (*LW* 31, 56).

[52] Ibid.

[53] Luther, *Proceedings at Augsburg*, *WA* 2, 14; (*LW* 31, 271).

[54] Luther, *Freedom of a Christian*, *WA* 7, 51 (*LW* 31, 346). In the German version Luther wrote 'das der glaub allein mag frum machen': *WA* 7, 23.

Romans 3: 28 is not explicitly cited in either case, although his words in *The Freedom of a Christian* could imply that he had this verse in mind.

The first instance of the use of *allein* explicitly associated with Romans 3: 28 occurs in a sermon preached at Epiphany 1521, in which Luther affirmed 'that we do not become godly [*fromm*] through our own works, but only through faith in Christ, as Paul says to the Romans in the third and to the Galatians in the second chapter'.[55] The *Kirchen-* or *Weihnachtspostille*, completed while Luther was at the Wartburg in 1521 and published in 1522, cites Paul, presumably implying Romans 3: 28, in the same terms that Luther would use in the *Septembertestament*: 'so you see here how St Paul teaches in all places that justification does not come through works, but only from faith without any works [*das die rechtfertigung nit durch werck, ßondernn alleyn auß dem glawben ohn alle werck kome*]'.[56]

It is apparent, then, that, as Bluhm points out, 'Luther the interpreter preceded Luther the translator'.[57] By 1522 Luther had come to believe that the true meaning of Romans 3: 28 was that justification occurred not by works, but by faith alone. His inclusion of the word *allein* was intended to make this meaning – which for Luther was the true meaning of the biblical text – clear to the German reader. It was probably also intended to counterbalance the only use of the phrase 'faith alone' – in this case *fide tantum* – in the Vulgate, which occurs in James 2: 24 and inconveniently contradicts Luther's theology: '*ex operibus justificatur homo et non ex fide tantum*' ['a person is justified by works and not by faith alone'], or, in Luther's translation, '*das der mensch durch die werck gerecht wird / nicht durch den glauben alleine*'.[58] In his preface to the epistle, Luther complained that James contradicted the theology presented in Romans, which, he asserted, clearly taught 'that Abraham was justified without works, through his faith alone'.[59] Romans, he insisted, was 'the chief part of the New Testament, … truly the purest gospel',[60] and within that epistle, 3: 19–28 – or possibly 3: 23–4 – was

[55] Luther, *Sermon preached on the Day of the Holy Three Kings*, *WA* 7, 241; cf. Bluhm, 'Bedeutung und Eigenart', 76.

[56] Luther, *Kirchenpostille*, *WA* 10/1.1, 343–4; cf. Bluhm, 'Bedeutung und Eigenart', 76.

[57] Bluhm, 'Luther's German Bible', 186.

[58] James 2: 24, *WA.DB* 7, 392.

[59] Luther, 'Preface to the Letters of James and Jude' (1522), *WA.DB* 7, 384 (*LW* 35, 396).

[60] Luther, 'Preface to the Epistle of St Paul to the Romans' (1522), *WA.DB* 7, 2 (*LW* 35, 365).

> the chief part and the centre of this Epistle and the whole of Scripture, namely that all is sin which is not redeemed by the blood of Christ and made righteous in faith. Therefore, mark this text well, for here all works, services and fame is laid low, as he himself says here. Only all of God's grace and honour remain.[61]

Luther's translation of Romans 3: 28 supported – or, perhaps better, emphasized – this reading, seeking to employ the German language so as to ensure that the passage would be read with the meaning he believed it was meant to have.

By the time Luther began lecturing on Genesis in 1535, he was deeply aware that his theological position had come to be characterized by the phrase *sola fide.* Affirming, quite explicitly, that 'God wants to teach us that we are saved by grace alone or by faith alone',[62] he offered a spirited defence against the criticisms of those who 'call us "solafideists," because we attribute righteousness to faith alone' [*nos vocant solarios, propterea quod soli fidei tribuimus iustitiam*].[63] They were, he thought, wrong, and the German Bible should tell them so. As Beutel has observed, Luther's Bible translation was intended 'to renew, not the letter of Scripture, but its spirit'.[64] That is, the language of the translation was intended to claim scriptural authority for his own interpretation of Scripture. Moreover, whilst the meaning of a text expounded in a sermon was explicated by the preacher,[65] the Bible translation had to speak for itself.

Long suggests of sixteenth-century Bible translation that 'a vernacular version made the text available to the literate Christian without the intervention of the priest. The intervention of the translator was not considered to be intrusive.'[66] She is certainly right

61 *WA.DB* 7, 38. The note is positioned alongside Romans 3: 23–4, but Bluhm implies, probably correctly, that it should be taken to apply to the longer passage in the middle of which it occurs, i.e. 3: 19–28 or 19–31: Bluhm, 'Bedeutung und Eigenart', 73, 79.

62 Luther, *Lectures on Genesis* (Gen. 21: 17), *WA* 43, 178 (*LW* 4, 60).

63 Ibid. (Gen. 22: 17–18), *WA* 43, 253 (*LW* 4, 163).

64 Albrecht Beutel, *In dem Anfang war das Wort. Studien zu Luthers Sprachverständnis* (Tübingen, 1991), 28.

65 As Stolt, 'Luther's Translation', 377, observes: 'The preacher could perceive directly from the reaction of his listeners whether or not they followed what he was saying'. Cf. also Bluhm, *Martin Luther*, 77, on the difference between the *Weihnachtspostille* [WP] and the *Septembertestament* [ST]: 'In WP what matters is the sermon; the translation is but a prelude. In ST what matters is the translation itself'.

66 Long, 'Translation of Sacred Texts', 468.

that Luther's intention was to provide direct access to Scripture. He wanted, as he put it in *To the Christian Nobility of the German Nation*, to give to all people 'the power to test and judge what is right or wrong in matters of faith, … to become bold and free on the authority of all these texts, and many others, … and test all that [the Romanists] do, or leave undone, by our believing understanding of the Scriptures'.[67] However, the translator was not neutral in this process. Luther's Bible translation was intended, as Volker Leppin concludes, to offer 'not so much a popularisation, but an authoritative meaning of the Bible'.[68] Consequently, in some sense, as Alec Ryrie argues, for the reader of Luther's Bible translation, '*[s]ola fide* is logically and chronologically prior to *sola scriptura*.'[69] It was the recognition that justification came about *sola fide*, which had so profoundly informed, and fundamentally changed, his own experience of God, that Luther intended his translation to communicate to its readers.[70]

Luther's theology was, therefore, key to determining the shape of his translation of the Bible, since it defined the 'true' meaning of the text which he wished to articulate in German. Stolt argues that his theology determines his translation technique, and 'dictate[s] his decision when to remain true to the text and when to translate more freely'.[71] Luther did not believe that complete mastery of the interpretation of a text was possible, but he did think that 'the right text' would lead to a better understanding,[72] and also asserted that 'no false Christian or trouble-maker can faithfully translate [the Scriptures]'.[73] His achievement, as Berman has put it, was 'to create a work accessible to the German people, capable of providing a solid base for

[67] Luther, *To the Christian Nobility of the German Nation*, *WA* 6, 412 (*LW* 44, 135).

[68] Leppin, '"Biblia, das ist die ganze Heilige Schrift deutsch"', 17.

[69] Alec Ryrie, '"Protestantism" as a Historical Category', *TRHS* 6th ser. 26 (2016), 59–77, at 72.

[70] Cf. ibid.; and see also Hendrix's recognition that for Luther the authority of Scripture was not some kind of propositional truth: 'rather … Luther approached Scripture as we would approach a great work of art': Scott H. Hendrix, 'The Authority of Scripture at Work: Luther's Exegesis of the Psalms', in idem, *Tradition and Authority in the Reformation* (Aldershot, 1996), art. II, 144–59, at 147; first publ. in E. W. Gritsch, ed., *Encounters with Luther* (Gettysburg, PA, 1982).

[71] Stolt, 'Luther's Translation', 381.

[72] Hendrix, 'Authority of Scripture', 158, drawing on Luther's preface to the revised edition of his commentary on the penitential psalms: *WA* 18, 479 (*LW* 14, 140).

[73] Luther, *Sendbrief zu Dolmetschen*, *WA* 30/2, 640 (*LW* 35, 194, amended); cf. Pym, 'Historical Epistemologies', 203.

the religious sensibility of the Reformation'.[74] That 'religious sensibility' was significantly different to that of the late medieval Church, and Luther's translation of the New Testament both reflected and helped to define that difference. Lawrence Venuti observes that any translation 'creates values in social formations at specific historical moments'; consequently, 'retranslations reflect changes in the values and institutions of the translating culture, but they can also produce such changes by inspiring new ways of reading and appreciating the source texts'.[75] This was precisely Luther's intention. His translation – itself a retranslation – was intended to purvey a particular understanding of the central message of the gospel, with the expectation that those who read it would amend their faith, and with it their religious beliefs and their moral and ethical behaviour. To this extent, then, Long is wrong to suggest that 'the translator was not considered to be intrusive'.[76] The controversies that arose around Luther's translation – and indeed other translations of this period[77] – indicate that Luther's contemporaries were very aware that the translator was creating a text which was intended to guide its readers to, and support them in, a particular theological position. Luther's translation of the New Testament illustrates vividly the ways in which the translator was – and is – not neutral, and it shows that, and illustrates how, theology and language are intimately entwined.

[74] Berman, *Experience of the Foreign*, 24.

[75] Lawrence Venuti, *Translation Changes Everything: Theory and Practice* (London, 2013), 107.

[76] In the mid-nineteenth century, the Bible translation prepared by Luther and his team at Wittenberg came to be known as the *Lutherbibel.* The earliest use of the term I have – with the help of David Bagchi – been able to identify is in a mid-nineteenth-century edition of the 1545 Bible, the last to be published in Luther's lifetime, the erroneously named Wartburg-Bibel (Gotha, 1842), 4 n. 4, online at: <https://opacplus,bsb-muenchen.de/Vta2/bsb10223902/bsb:BV020129536>, accessed 13 February 2017. The earliest uses in book titles appear to be Gustav Baur and Johhann Friedrich Ahlfeld, *Ueber die sprachliche Revision der Lutherbibel* (Halle, 1873); Carl Ludwig Wilibald Grimm, *Die Lutherbibel und ihre Textesrevision* (Berlin, 1874). Nikolaus Schneider suggests that the terminology arose in connection with the three hundredth anniversary of the publication of the 1545 edition, and the need to agree on one authorized version: 'Luthers Arbeit an der Bibelübersetzung – Ein Beispiel reformatorischen Theologie-Treibens', address given at the conference '"Was dolmetschen für Kunst und Arbeit sei" – Die Lutherbibel und andere deutsche Bibelübersetzungen', University Church, Rostock, 17 October 2013, online at: <https://www.ekd.de/vortraege/2013/89929.html>, accessed 13 February 2017. The revised translation was published in 1883 to coincide with the four hundredth anniversary of Luther's birth. It is apparent from the titles of many works responding to it that this 1883 edition was commonly referred to as the Lutherbibel.

[77] For Tyndale's translation decisions, see Hooker, 'Tyndale's "Heretical" Translation'.

Translating Christianity in an Age of Reformations

Simon Ditchfield*
University of York

This article argues that the age of the Protestant and Catholic Reformations and the global spread of the latter brought with it the challenge that not only was it necessary to learn new languages in order to communicate the Christian message to non-European peoples encountered during the so-called 'Age of Discovery', but some kind of control had to be exercised over the new, global circulation of sacred images and relics. The latter facilitated the visual (and virtual) translation of such holy sites as Jerusalem and Rome and its specific holy treasures in the mental prayers of the faithful. It concludes that it was less Lamin Sanneh's 'triumph of [linguistic] translatability' and more the physical translatability of the sacred that made possible the emergence of Roman Catholicism as this planet's first world religion.

Andrea Pozzo's dizzying fresco, *The Worldwide Mission of the Society of Jesus*, covering the nave ceiling of S. Ignazio in Rome and carried out between 1691 and 1694, is the 'go-to' image for any publisher, author or lecturer who wants a striking icon of the making of Roman Catholicism as a world religion in the early modern period.[1] Indeed, its creator, himself a Jesuit, described it as follows:

> My idea in the painting was to represent the works of St Ignatius and of the Company of Jesus in spreading the Christian faith worldwide. In the first place, I embraced the entire vault with a building depicted in perspective. Then in the middle of this I painted the three persons of the Trinity; from the breast of one of which, that is the Human Son, issue forth rays that wound the heart of St Ignatius, and from him they issue, as a reflection spread to the four parts of the world depicted in the guise of Amazons … . These torches that you see in the two extremities of the vault represent the zeal of St Ignatius – who

* Department of History, University of York, York, YO10 5DD.
E-mail: simon.ditchfield@york.ac.uk.

[1] This well-known image may easily be found online, for example at: <https://commons.wikimedia.org/wiki/File:Triumph_St_Ignatius_Pozzo.jpg>, last accessed 27 May 2016.

Studies in Church History 53 (2017) 164–195
doi: 10.1017/stc.2016.11

in sending his companions to preach the Gospel said to them: 'Go and set the world alight (*Ite, incendite, infiammate omnia*), verifying in him Christ's words (Luke 12: 49): 'I am come to send fire on the earth; and what will I but that it be kindled?' (*Ignem veni mittere in terram, et quid volo nisi ut accendatur*).[2]

By this period in the history of the Society of Jesus, its founder had come to stand for the order as a whole, as can be seen from the frontispiece to the Jesuit Daniello Bartoli's life of Ignatius (1650), which the author, under official commission from the Jesuit father general, regarded as the first part of what became a multi-volume, though incomplete, history of the society as a truly global phenomenon. Notice here Ignatius's role as intermediary who deflects divine light so that it spreads through the whole world, represented by the four personifications of Africa, America, Europe and Asia (Fig. 1).

I

Although Roman Catholicism might have reached all four then-known continents by the time Pozzo came to paint this fresco, it had had limited impact in two of them (Asia and Africa), had been creatively reinterpreted in a third (the Americas), and expelled from significant parts of the fourth (Europe). Moreover, the fiercely defended royal monopoly over ecclesiastical appointments in the Portuguese and Spanish overseas empires – known respectively as the *padroado real* and *patronato real* – meant that the papacy was in no position to assert full jurisdiction over the missions until well into the twentieth century.[3]

2 Evonne Levy, *Propaganda and the Jesuit Baroque* (Berkeley and Los Angeles, CA, 2004), 151. Pozzo's explanation may be found in the pamphlet *Breve descrittione della pittura fatta nella volta del tempio di Sant'Ignazio scoperta l'anno MDCXCIV per la festa del medesimo santo* (Rome, 1694), which can be viewed at: <https://archive.org/stream/brevedescrittion00koma#page/2/mode/2up>, last accessed 27 May 2016; my thanks to Professor Levy for directing me to the location of this very rare pamphlet. Save for the biblical passage, which is taken from Angela M. Kinney, ed., *The Vulgate Bible*, 6: *The New Testament, Douay-Rheims Translation* (Cambridge MA, and London, 2013), 389, the translation is Levy's.

3 However, the work of Benedetta Albani is showing us that the Council of the Indies in Seville did not necessarily prevent appellants from the New World gaining access to Roman or papal justice, in the form of the Congregation of the Council: see her chapter, 'Nuova luce sulle relazioni tra la Sede Apostolica e le Americhe. La pratica della concessione del "pase regio" ai documenti pontefici destinati alle Indie', in Claudio Ferlan, ed., *Eusebio Francesco Chini e il suo tempo. Una riflessione storica* (Trent, 2012), 83–102.

Figure 1. (Colour online) Cornelis Bloemart after Jan Miel, frontispiece to Daniello Bartoli, *Della vita e dell'Istituto di S. Ignatio, fondatore della Compagnia di Gesù* (Rome, 1659). Reproduced by courtesy of the *Archivium Romanum Societatis Iesu.*

As I have noted elsewhere, if one were to make an honest appraisal of world geopolitics *c.*1500, the subsequent global spread of Roman

Catholicism would seem highly unlikely.[4] To begin with, Columbus had famously failed to find what he was looking for – a short cut to the East (which from the time of the collapse of the Roman Empire down to the mid-nineteenth century was unquestionably the wealthiest part of the globe), rather than the discovery of a 'New World'. The promise and potential of the Americas as a fertile field of Christian conversion or for economic exploitation had yet to make its impact. Save for such relatively isolated communities as the Syriac 'Thomas' Christians of south-western India, the Syriac Maronite Church of Antioch, the minority Coptic Church of Egypt and the Coptic kingdom of Ethiopia, Christendom was boxed into the western extremity of the Eurasian landmass by considerable Islamic powers, notably the Ottoman Empire to the east and the Mamluk sultanate of Egypt to the south-east. In north Africa, from Morocco to Tunis, Portuguese and Spanish influence was precarious and restricted to the coastline. Furthermore, on the coasts of Sicily and the Italian peninsula, the inhabitants were careful to locate their settlements in secure locations inland, a curious and inconvenient detail which still puzzles enterprising beach-lovers who holiday in remote parts of Sicily, Calabria and Puglia. However, this did little to protect the local population from countless raids made by Barbary corsairs, even if the numbers of those thereby cast into white slavery do not compare with the numbers of their black counterparts who would later be brutally transported across the Atlantic.[5]

In East Asia, Islam had been enjoying a wave of continuous expansion ever since the ruler of the Malay port of Melaka decided sometime between 1409 and 1436 to adopt Islam and thereby plug his economy into a flourishing trading network that stretched via Bengal and Hormuz to Cairo and Istanbul.[6] The pace of conversion was to accelerate from *c.*1500, in parallel with, and not unrelated

[4] Simon Ditchfield, 'Catholic Reformation and Renewal', in Peter Marshall, ed., *The Oxford Illustrated History of the Reformation* (Oxford, 2015), 152–85, at 162–3.

[5] Robert C. Davis, *Christian Slaves, Muslim Masters: White Slavery in the Mediteranean, the Barbary Coast and Italy* (Basingstoke, 2003). It should be noted, however, that Davis's claim that as many as one million Europeans were enslaved during this period has been vigorously contested: see, for example, Wolfgang Kaiser, *Le Commerce des captifs. Les Intermédiares dans l'échange et le rachat des prisonniers en Méditerranée, XVe–XVIIIe siècle*, Collection de l'École française de Rome 406 (Rome, 2008); Nabil Matar, *British Captives from the Mediterranean to the Atlantic, 1563–1760* (Leiden and Boston, MA, 2014).

[6] 'Indeed, so associated was Islam with Malay culture that the phrase *masuk melayu* ('to become a Malay') came to mean the adoption of Islam': see Barbara Andaya,

to, the arrival of Christianity.[7] In the Americas, the Aztec and Inca kingdoms had reached their apogee. In China, the Confucian Middle Kingdom of the Ming had admittedly abandoned its early fifteenth-century practice of sending gargantuan armadas on flag-waving voyages as far as East Africa, but this was not in response to hostile reception but because of their perceived irrelevance to China's continental concerns as Asia's most considerable power. In 1501 Shah Esmā'īl (1487–1524) seized Tabriz and inaugurated the Safavid Empire, which unified Iran and under Shah 'Abbas the Great (1587–1629) reached the climax of its power. In the territory represented by modern-day Afghanistan, Zahir ud-din Babur (1483–1530), the great-great-great-grandson of Tamerlane, was poised to invade the Indian subcontinent. He would establish what came to be known as the Mughal Empire, in which a Muslim minority ruled successfully for more than two centuries over a Hindu majority.

If the early modern period, as has been argued recently, was in global terms an 'age of empire', then the West had but a single contestant: the Habsburgs, who managed to unite their various Burgundian, Austrian and Spanish patrimonies with the title of Holy Roman Emperor for just a little under four decades (1519–56).[8] To borrow Gibbon's famous remark that, had it not been for Charles Martel's victory over the Arabs at the battle of Poitiers in 732, 'the interpretation of the Koran would now be taught in the schools of Oxford … [and her pulpits] might demonstrate to a circumcised people the sanctity and truth of the revelation of Mahomet', one might with no less justification remark that had it not been for the need for the Ottomans repeatedly to turn their attention to the Safavid threat on their south-east border, the 137-metre high steeple of Vienna Cathedral would merely have been the first such spire in the city to provide the *muezzin* with a substitute for his usual minaret from which to call the faithful to prayer.[9]

'Developments in Southeast Asia, *c.*1500–1800', in Nicholas Tarling, ed., *The Cambridge History of Southeast Asia*, 4 vols (Cambridge, 1999), 2: 164–227, at 173.

[7] 'On the basis of cultural developments in the preceding five centuries, an impartial observer in the year 1500 might well have predicted that Islam would soon become the world's dominant faith, its principal source of beliefs, values, culture and human consciousness': Jerry H. Bentley, *Old World Encounters: Cross-Cultural Contacts and Exchanges in Pre-Modern Times* (New York and Oxford, 1993), 176.

[8] John Darwin, *After Tamerlane: The Global History of Empire since 1405* (London, 2007).

[9] Edward Gibbon, *The History of the Decline and Fall of the Roman Empire*, ed. D. Womersley, 6 vols in 3 (London, 1994), 3: 336 (1st edn, 1788, vol. 5, ch. 52).

The 'triumph of the West over the Rest' would have to wait until the late nineteenth and even early twentieth centuries. Even then, it was a 'victory' expressed in terms of economic and political, and *not* religious, dominance. The Scottish explorer and missionary to Africa David Livingstone famously converted just two Africans to Christianity (one of whom subsequently apostatized). So it is perhaps not such a surprise to learn that there was not a single African in attendance at the landmark World Missionary Conference which met in Edinburgh in 1910.[10] Indeed, the 'Christian century' in Africa had not then begun and is still very much in progress. While in 1950 only about 15 per cent of the population of sub-Saharan Africa was Christian, by 2010 it had risen to over 60 per cent, and just under 24 per cent of the world's 2.2 billion Christians lived in the continent. By 2050, according to the latest figures from the Pew Research Center, this proportion will rise to 38 per cent, which will represent a sea-change in the regional distribution of Christianity in the world: as recently as 2010 there were equal numbers of Christians in Europe, Latin America and Africa, representing some 75 per cent of the world's total (at around 25 per cent each).[11] It has been speculated that by 2050 one in four Christians in Europe and North America will be from the 'Christian' South.

Historians are usually warned that we should forget the future and try to view the period we study, as far as possible, in its own terms. Hindsight is seen as a hindrance. However, it can also be a help, which, I believe, is the case here. We need to appreciate that Christianity, let alone Roman Catholicism, was not yet a world religion even by the dawn of the twentieth century. Although the nineteenth century, that third 'heroic' chapter in global missions, was more successful, numerically speaking, than either of its predecessors (i.e. the early spread of Christianity, mainly through the Roman Empire, and the early modern 'Age of Discovery'), in that the proportion of the world's population that was Christian increased from a little over a

[10] Andrew F. Walls, 'Christianity in the Non-Western World: A Study in the Serial Nature of Christian expansion', *Studies in World Christianity* 6 (1995), 1–25, at 7.

[11] Europe is the only region where the absolute number of Christians is set to decline: from 553 to 454 million. Simultaneously, the proportion of the world's Christians in Europe will plummet from 25.5 to 15.6 per cent. By comparison, Latin America's percentage remains more or less steady, with a decline only from 25.5 to 22.8 per cent. See 'Pew Research Center: Christians', online at: <http://www.pewforum.org/2015/04/02/christians/>, last accessed 13 July 2015.

fifth in 1800 to over a third in 1900 (from 22.2 to 36.6 per cent); between 300 and 500 the proportion of Christians increased from 7 to 20 per cent, while from 1500 to 1750 there was a decidedly smaller increase, from 18.5 to 21.5 per cent. It is only in our own time that the global shift south is taking place. Moreover, the proportion of Christians as a percentage of world population actually fell during the twentieth century from 33.6 to 33.3 per cent.[12] All this should help us recalibrate our understanding of what was actually achieved during the phase of extra-European mission that coincided with the so-called 'Age of Discovery'.

II

Before going any further, it is essential to move beyond the view of the communication of the Christian message simply in terms of the active broadcaster – passive receiver model. Of course, this is not to deny that the evidential record is very much weighted in favour of the broadcasters over the receivers, which encourages historians, in turn, to measure reception of the message in terms of degrees of distortion from the ideal. It is for this very reason that we need to heed the 'excursus against influence' offered by the art historian Michael Baxandall. Instead of positing a model whereby A influences B, he proposed that we invert the relationship and look at how B might act upon A. For Baxandall, 'to think in terms of influence blunts thought by impoverishing the means of differentiation'.[13] By contrast, if we make use of the richer palate of active verbs (such as: draw on, resort to, avail oneself of, appropriate from, have recourse to, adapt, misunderstand, refer to, pick up, take on, engage with, react to, quote,

[12] There was an overall increase from 200 to 500 million Christians between 1800 and 1900, including a rise in the number of Roman Catholics from 106 million to 266 million. The period from 1500 to 1750 saw a rise from 76 million to 155 million, which included an increase in the number of Catholics from 45 to 82 million. Such astonishingly precise figures are necessarily only indicative; however, they can, I think, be used to sketch, in rough terms, the overall picture. For the full dataset, see David Barrett and Todd Johnson, 'World Christian Trends across 22 Centuries AD30–AD2000', online at: <http://gordonconwell.edu/ockenga/research/documents/gd04.pdf>, last accessed 26 October 2016; my thanks to Luke Clossey for drawing my attention to this source. See also Todd M. Johnson and Brian J, Grim, *The World's Religions in Figures: An Introduction to International Religious Demography* (Oxford and Malden, MA, 2013), which provides more contextual detail.

[13] Michael Baxandall, *Patterns of Intention: On the Historical Interpretation of Pictures* (New Haven, CT, and London, 1985), 59.

differentiate oneself from, assimilate oneself to), we stand a better chance of retrieving the scope for action possessed by those – both clerics and laypeople – on the receiving end of papal and episcopal instructions or of Christian catechesis. However, this approach, which seeks to restore agency to those working on the ground – both missionaries and missionized – is not without its methodological challenges, since the weight of surviving evidence reflects, first and foremost, the view and agenda of the missionaries rather than that of their potential converts.

Another obstacle, ironically, has been the work of those pioneers, who sought, in the 1960s and early 1970s, to recover the 'visions of the Vanquished' of the missionized in the New World.[14] The emphasis such authors placed on the trauma of catastrophic destruction and disease – both physical and psychological – was not only rooted in the historical record but also framed in terms of the postcolonial polemic as forged in the white heat of anger by such authors as the Martinique-born doctor and psychiatrist Frantz Fanon, in his classic denunciation of colonialism, *The Wretched of the Earth*, written at the height of the Algerian war of independence from France and published in 1961.[15]

While such historians have undoubtedly had the beneficial effect of forcing us to modify our view of the misleadingly triumphant 'spiritual conquest' narrative of Christian missions in the Age of Discovery, I would argue that they have also had the effect of making us underestimate both the role of non-Christian rulers in the expansion of Christianity and the capacity of the latter for material as much as linguistic translation into indigenous idioms.[16] It should not be forgotten that the largest-scale conversion of indigenous peoples to Christianity, after that of the duchy of Lithuania in the late fourteenth

[14] Miguel León-Portilla, *Visión de los vencidos. Relaciones indígenas de la conquista* (Mexico City, 1959); Nathan Wachtel, *La Vision des vaincus. Les Indiens de Pérou devant la conquête espagnole, 1530–1570* (Paris, 1971).

[15] Frantz Fanon, *Les Damnès de la terre* (Paris, 1961). The English translation, by Constance Farrington, was published by Penguin in 1967 with a preface by Jean-Paul Sartre (originally composed for the French edition), following a first hardback edition of 1965. *Damnés* might more appropriately be translated 'damned'.

[16] This theme of elite conversion to monotheism across the world from 1450–1850 is currently being explored for a forthcoming monograph by Alan Strathern at the University of Oxford. I am grateful to Dr Strathern for his comments on a draft chapter of my own forthcoming book, *Papacy and Peoples*, which deals with the mission to the Kongo, and for letting me read his account of missions in Africa for the *Brill Companion to Catholic Missions* in advance of publication.

century and before those of the nineteenth, took place in the kingdom of the Kongo,[17] as a consequence of the baptism of its ruler Nzinga a Nkuwu in 1491. Taking the Christian name of João in honour of the then king of Portugal, Nzinga soon tired of his new faith, developing a particular objection to the uncompromising Christian line on polygamy. However, his son Nvemba Nzinga, who succeeded his father in 1506 and took the name Afonso, was very different; indeed, he has been called 'one of the greatest lay Christians in African Church history'.[18] At the time of Afonso's death in 1543, it is estimated that some two million people, about half the kingdom's population, had been baptized.[19] The degree of success the king had in rooting his sacral legitimacy in Roman Catholic rites and rituals was mirrored by the degree to which the noble ruling class sustained a commitment to the new religion. The centrality of ritual to the role of Roman Catholicism in Kongolese society may be best appreciated if we consider the symbolic focus offered by churches in the rebaptized town of São Salvador (formerly Mbanza Kongo). The main Christian feasts were integrated into the royal ritual cycle and the king's presence at such ceremonies was seen to enhance monarchic mystique and power. For much of the sixteenth century, there was hardly another priest in the country; São Salvador was only created a bishopric in 1596 and by that time there were still only about a dozen functioning churches in the whole kingdom, served by African or Afro-Portuguese clergy.[20] This only served to impart added significance to the actions of this Christian *nganga*, whose very title he shared with pagan priests. In the words of Adrian Hastings: 'It was a meeting between two societies and even two religions rather less different from one another than we are inclined to believe'.[21] In both Kongo and Portugal of the late fifteenth century, religion was more about ritual than doctrine; more about adoring sacred images, relics and fetishes than reading and expounding holy texts; more about the propitiation of interfering, vengeful demons or demanding spirits than the

[17] Kongo extended across what is now northern Angola, Cabinda, the Republic of the Congo, the western area of the Democratic Republic of the Congo, and the south of Gabon.

[18] Adrian Hastings, *The Church in Africa, 1450–1950* (Oxford, 1994), 81.

[19] John Thornton, 'The Development of an African Catholic Church in the Kingdom of Kongo, 1491–1750', *JAH* 25 (1984), 147–67.

[20] Anthony Disney, *A History of Portugal and the Portuguese Empire from Beginnings to 1807*, 2 vols (Cambridge, 2009), 2: 67.

[21] Hastings, *Church in Africa*, 73.

worship of a transcendent deity. In Kongo, as in so much of pre-Reformation Europe, the translatability of Christianity consisted of the repurposing of objects and rituals rather than the introduction of new texts, although the translation of the latter was itself far from being a straightforward process, as we shall now see.

The traditional Italian coupling *traduttore, traditore* ('translator, traitor') should be enough to disabuse anyone who still thinks, thanks to Paul Ricoeur, that the so-called 'hermeneutic of suspicion' was invented during the nineteenth and early twentieth centuries by the likes of Marx, Nietzsche and Freud.[22] Concern with language and meaning had been put on a new footing by humanists such as Lorenzo Valla and Desiderius Erasmus – both of whom published revised Latin translations of the gospels, with polemical intent – before the Reformation provoked a wave of new, no less polemical, vernacular translations of the entire Bible.[23] The Lutheran and Calvinist reformations, on the one hand, and the Counter-Reformation, on the other, saw unprecedented attempts at censorship of both written and oral culture by both positive and negative means. In the Roman Catholic world, this was at least partially achieved by the issue of standard 'Roman editions' of key religious texts, which included not only the so-called Sixto-Clementine Vulgate (1592) but also liturgical service books such as the breviary (1568) and the missal (1570). Revealingly, the first of these 'Roman editions' was the Roman Catechism, which was issued in 1566, soon after the official edition of the Canons and Decrees of the Council of Trent. These editions were accompanied by the publication of a series of indexes of prohibited books, not only by Rome. In the sixteenth century thirty-two editions were published, of which only six were printed in Rome, no more than the number of editions published in the space of just twelve years (1544–56) by the Sorbonne.[24] By means of these lists the authorities sought, with only qualified success, to exert control over the circulation of heterodox

[22] See Paul Ricoeur, *Freud and Philosophy: An Essay on Interpretation*, transl. D. Savage (New Haven, CT, and London, 1970).

[23] See now Euan Cameron, ed., *The New Cambridge History of the Bible*, 3: *From 1450–1750* (Cambridge, 2016), part 1, chs 1–5; and, in this volume, Charlotte Methuen, '"These four letters *s o l a* are not there": Language and Theology in Luther's translation of the New Testament', 146–63.

[24] Jesús M. de Bujanda et al., eds, *Index des livres interdits*, vols 1–9 (Québec and Geneva, 1984–94). Vols 8 and 9 are devoted to the Roman indexes of 1557, 1559, 1564, 1590, 1593 and 1596. The six indexes published by the Sorbonne in 1544, 1545, 1547, 1549, 1551 and 1556 are reproduced in vol. 1.

opinions. Rome followed up its efforts by founding a curial standing committee, the Congregation of the Index, in 1571 to supplement the Holy Office, which had been founded in 1542.[25] However, my focus in this article lies elsewhere, since I have deliberately chosen to understand 'translation' in its broadest sense: so as to include pilgrimage (both physical and virtual), conversion and the movement of relics, as well as the rendition of texts in another language from the original.

III

In his presidential address to the American Catholic Historical Association, delivered in December 1990 and published the following year in the *Catholic Historical Review*, the Jesuit historian John O'Malley memorably pointed out that, not only in his early years, Loyola's 'eyes were set on Jerusalem, not Wittenberg'.[26] O'Malley's doctoral work on the Augustinian eschatological preacher Giles of Viterbo (1472–1532) would have made him all too aware of the enduring power down to the Renaissance (and beyond) of the idea of Rome as New Jerusalem. Giles compared the Tiber to the River Jordan and saw 'Etruria' as the new Holy Land. Here the friar was simply building upon the patristic idea that Christ's baptism marked the passing from the law of the old dispensation to the new, Christian faith of redemption.[27] O'Malley calls us to avoid identifying Loyola exclusively with the 'Counter-Reformation'. Instead, we should remember, not so much Ignatius's physical pilgrimage to the Holy Land, where he so embarrassed and irritated the Franciscan Guardians of the Holy Places with his clumsy attempts to court martyrdom that they bundled him onto a ship back to Europe, but his mental evocation of the Holy Land in the *Spiritual Exercises* – unforgettably described by

[25] Gigliola Fragnito, ed., *Church, Censorship and Culture in Early Modern Italy* (Cambridge, 2001); idem, *Proibito capire. La chiesa e il volgare nella prima età moderna* (Bologna, 2005); Vittorio Frajese, *Nascita dell'Indice. La censura ecclesiastica dal Rinascimento alla Controriforma* (Brescia, 2006). Cf. the recent review article by Andreea Badea, 'Zwischen Dissimulation und Disziplinierung. Neue Literatur zur Geschichte der Buchzensur auf der italienischen Halbinsel', *Quellen und Forschungen aus italienischen Archiven und Bibliotheken* 95 (2015), 385–96; my thanks to Stefan Bauer for drawing my attention to this article.

[26] John W. O'Malley, 'Was Ignatius Loyola a Church Reformer? How to look at Early Modern Catholicism', *CathHR* 77 (1991), 177–93, at 191.

[27] John W. O'Malley, 'Giles of Viterbo: A Reformer's Thought on Renaissance Rome', *RQ* 20 (1967), 1–11; cf. Charles Stinger, *The Renaissance in Rome* (Bloomington, IN, 1985), ch. 4; Philip Jacks, *The Antiquarian and the Myth of Antiquity* (Cambridge, 1993), 67–73.

Outram Evennett as that 'shock tactic spiritual gymnastic to be undertaken and performed under guidance' (rather than simply read).[28]

As recent studies have demonstrated, this practice of 'imagined' or 'virtual' pilgrimage, whereby the devout were able to translate themselves in their imagination to the Holy Land, was still flourishing at the end of the fifteenth century.[29] It was undertaken particularly by those, such as nuns and other devout women living in the world, who had few opportunities to make the physical journey. Through works such as the *Sionpilger* by the fifteenth-century Observant Dominican Felix Fabri, who visited the Holy Land twice – once in 1480 to Jerusalem and then again in 1483–4, when he made the further pilgrimage to St Catherine's monastery in Sinai – the nuns in his spiritual charge in the German city of Ulm were encouraged to evoke in mental prayer the places where Christ walked, talked, suffered, was crucified and rose from the dead in order to intensify their apprehension of the Passion story.[30] Similar practices were also encouraged in one of the most widely disseminated texts of the pre-Gutenberg age, Thomas à Kempis's *Imitation of Christ*, which charged its readers and listeners to accompany Christ in every detail of his life.[31]

This virtual translation of the Holy Places as a way of structuring meditation had its counterpart in the physical re-creation in Western Europe and the Iberian and Lusitanian colonies of places associated with Christ's life and Passion. As Christianity is a religion built upon an avowedly historical event, it can be no surprise that such copies date back almost as far as the events they commemorate. To consider just a single western example: the origins of the building complex of S. Stefano in Bologna – referred to locally as St Jerusalem

[28] H. Outram Evennett, *The Spirit of the Counter Reformation*, ed. John Bossy (Cambridge, 1968), 45.

[29] David Morgan, *The Forge of Vision: A Visual History of Modern Christianity* (Oakland, CA, 2015), 35–41.

[30] Kathryn M. Rudy, *Virtual Pilgrimages in the Convent: Imagining Jerusalem in the Late Middle Ages* (Turnhout, 2011); Kathryne Beebe, *Pilgrim & Preacher: The Audiences and Observant Spirituality of Friar Felix Fabri (1437/8–1502)* (Oxford, 2014).

[31] This work survives in some 900 manuscript copies from the fifteenth century alone, and there were over 740 printed editions down to 1650: see John H. Van Engen, *Sisters and Brothers of the Common Life: The Devotio Moderna and the World of the Later Middle Ages* (Philadelphia, PA, 2008); Maximilian von Habsburg, *Catholic and Protestant Translations of the* Imitatio Christi*, 1425–1650: From Late Medieval Classic to Early Modern Bestseller* (Farnham, 2011).

or the Seven Churches – is dated to the fifth century CE.[32] Moreover, the Ethiopian Orthodox priests of Lalibela claim that, according to a tradition, the layout of their famous rock-hewn churches is a symbolic representation of Jerusalem, and their construction was prompted by Saladin's retaking of the Holy City in 1187.[33] However, the number of these so-called 'Passion Parks' or miniature replicas of Jerusalem (or of key buildings within it) increased markedly in the sixteenth century and later and may be found from Brazil to Bologna, and from Granada in Andalucia to Görlitz near the Polish border.[34] Perhaps the most famous manifestation of this phenomenon is the series of *sacri monti* (holy mountains) which formed a kind of confessional *cordon sanitaire* or string of watchtowers along the borders of Piedmont and Lombardy with the Reformed cantons of Switzerland. Overseen by Observant Franciscans, who also had responsibility for the Holy Places in Palestine, these included a mini-Jerusalem at Varallo (much favoured by that model Counter-Reformation prelate, San Carlo Borromeo), which was the first to be begun in 1491, and the string of fourteen chapels dedicated to the Mysteries of the Rosary at Varese dating from 1605. All were populated by numerous brightly painted full-scale figures who recreated scenes from the life, suffering and death of Christ or Mary, or (in the single exception of the Sacro Monte on Lake Orta) the life of St Francis of Assisi.

The translation of the topography of Jerusalem could also be imposed on an existing urban landscape. In 1659 the North Italian Somaschan priest Lorenzo Longo published a twenty-four-page booklet entitled *Gerusalemme piacentina*, or, to give it its full title, *The Places of Piacenza corresponding to the Holy Places of Jerusalem which may be visited by the faithful and devout Servants of God [so that they might] meditate on the*

[32] Colin Morris, 'Bringing the Holy Sepulchre to the West: S. Stefano, Bologna from the Fifth to the Twentieth Century', in R. N. Swanson, ed., *The Church Retrospective*, SCH 33 (Oxford, 1997), 31–60

[33] Jacques Mercier and Claude Lepage, *Lalibela: Wonder of Ethiopia. The Monolithic Churches and their Treasures* (London, 2012).

[34] George Kubler, 'Sacred Mountains in Europe and America', in T. Verdon and J. Henderson, eds, *Christianity and the Renaissance: Image and Religious Imagination in the Quattrocentro* (Syracuse, NY, 1990), 413–41; cf. L. Vaccaro and F. Riccardi, eds, *Sacri Monti. Devozioni, arte e cultura della Controriforma* (Milan, 1992); Rudy, *Virtual Pilgrimages*, 250–1; Annabel Wharton, *Selling Jerusalem: Relics, Replicas, Theme Parks* (Chicago, IL, 1996); F. Cardini, *Andare per le Gerusalemme d'Italia* (Bologna, 2015). The Russian Orthodox Church should not be excluded from this fashion, as can be seen from the recently restored Novoiyerusalimsky Monastery, founded in 1656, forty kilometres north-west of Moscow in the town of Istra; I am indebted to Luke Clossey for this information.

most holy Life, Passion, Death and Resurrection of our Saviour Jesus Christ with … great spiritual Profit.[35] In the preface, Longo compared his grafting of the topography of Jerusalem onto this small town, situated on the river Po some seventy kilometres south of Milan, with the presence of models of the Holy House of Loreto in the nearby cities of Alessandria and Como. He then mentioned the various places in Piacenza where there were already particular scenes from the life of Christ (overwhelmingly evocations of the Holy Crib). In order to emphasize the convenience afforded by his guide, he mentioned how the capture of the Holy Places (by the Ottomans in 1517) had made physical pilgrimage very difficult.[36] It is at this point that Longo also mentioned the Sacro Monte at Varallo, which was less than a hundred kilometres from Piacenza. Before taking the reader – or listener – through the streets of Piacenza, Longo argued that the whole of Lombardy and Piedmont – for which he used the classical Roman label *Gallia Cisalpina* – might be considered to be a kind of virtual Palestine, with Tortona standing in for Gaza, Como as Tyre, Monza as Caesarea, Milan as Jaffa and the Adda as the River Jordan. The fact that all this information was delivered in the form of a poem suggests that Longo probably intended it to be memorized by the dutiful pilgrim and recited before the local counterparts to the key sites of the Passion story. The pamphlet closed with a careful enumeration of the spiritual bounty which pilgrims would gain for their labours in the form of a list of the indulgences.

IV

This brings us to what linked all these practices. They enabled all, and not only those who journeyed all the way to the Holy Land, to benefit from the generous indulgences which such an act of piety

[35] Lorenzo Longo, *Gerusalemme piacentina, cioè chiese e luoghi di Piacenza corrispondenti a luoghi santi di Gerusalemme da visitare da fedeli e devoti servi di Dio in modo che possono meditare sulla vita santissima, passione, morte e resurrezione del nostro salvatore Jesu Cristo con gran profito spirituale …* (Piacenza, 1659).

[36] Such emphasis on the difficulties of contemporary, physical pilgrimage to the Holy Land has undoubtedly led to an underestimation of the significance of such travel during the sixteenth and seventeenth centuries, which is only now being corrected: see, for instance, Wes Williams, *Pilgrimage and Narrative in the French Renaissance: The Undiscovered Country* (Oxford, 1998); Marie-Christine Gomez-Géraud, *La Crépuscule du Grand Voyage. Les Récits des pèlerins à Jérusalem (1458–1612)*, 2 vols (Paris, 1990); F. Thomas Noonan, *The Road to Jerusalem: Pilgrimage and Travel in the Age of Discovery* (Philadelphia, PA, 2007).

brought with it. Of course indulgences have not had a very good press, particularly since 1517, but, as Elizabeth Tingle has reminded us, the triumphant revival of the cult of saints and of Catholic devotions more generally in the Counter-Reformation Church would have been inconceivable without indulgences: they were the mortar which held the whole edifice together.[37] Furthermore, they collapsed devotional distance by making possible global cults of such relics closely associated with Rome as the icon of the Blessed Virgin Mary held in the Roman basilica of S. Maria Maggiore and known sometimes as *Madonna of the Snows*, after the alleged miracle of an August snowfall which was caused by the Virgin to indicate where she wanted the basilica in her honour to be built on the Esquiline Hill, and sometimes as the *Saviour of the Roman People* (*Salus populi romani*), owing to her alleged role in bringing about the end of the plague in the city at the time of Pope Gregory the Great at the close of the sixth century.[38]

A famous print, attributed to Stefano Du Pérac, was published by the French-born adoptive Italian engraver Antonio Lafréry in time for the holy year of 1575, which with its 400,000 pilgrim visitors saw the relaunch of Rome as capital of a world religion. It depicts, in very much idealized terms, pilgrims processing between the seven major basilicas of the Eternal City (Fig. 2). As Barbara Wisch observes: 'No earlier maps of the city had ever "populated" the city in quite this way'.[39] Here Rome is not simply 'represented' but shown 'in action'. Such prints would have been bought by pilgrims to take home with them as souvenirs of their visit to the city and this one should be seen, in Wisch's words, '[as] a kind of didactic memory guide for reliving the Holy Year experience or transforming the potential pilgrim into an actual one'.[40]

Du Pérac's print also conveys Rome's claim to have become a New Jerusalem, as it was home to so many physical testimonies to the apostolic origins of Christianity. These comprised not only buildings but also bones: the relics of the early Christian martyrs, whose number was to increase exponentially only three years after the 1575

[37] Elizabeth Tingle, *Indulgences after Luther: Pardons in Counter-Reformation France, 1520–1720* (London, 2015).

[38] Gerhard Wolf, *Salus populi Romani. Die Geschichte römischer Kultbilder im Mittelalter* (Weinheim, 1990); Hans Beltung, *Likeness and Presence: A History of the Image before the Era of Art* (Chicago, IL, 1994), 311–29.

[39] Barbara Wisch, 'The Matrix: *Le Sette Chiese di Roma* of 1575 and the Image of Pilgrimage', *Memoirs of the American Academy in Rome* 56–7 (2011–12), 271–303, at 280.

[40] Ibid. 295.

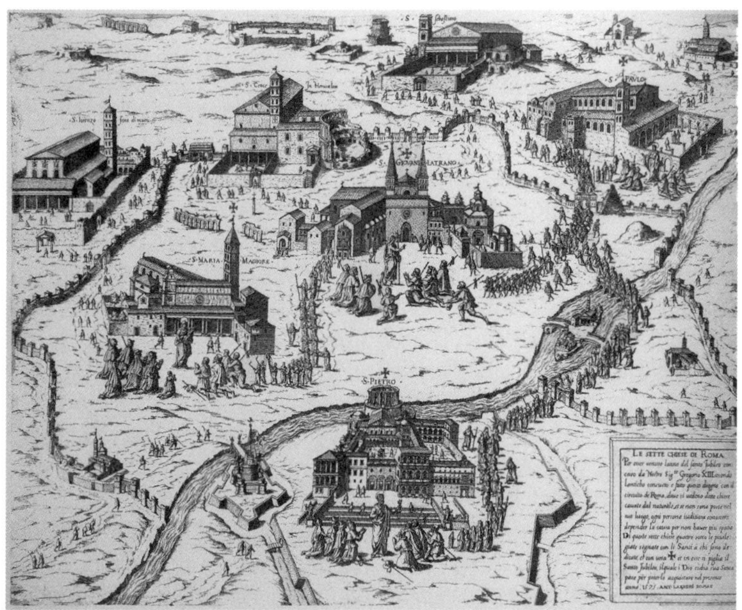

Figure 2. Stefano Du Pérac (attrib.), *Le sette chiese di Roma* (Rome, 1575), etching 39.7 x 50.9 cm. Reproduced courtesy of the Metropolitan Museum, New York, Rogers Fund, Accession number 41.72 (1.12), <http://www.metmuseum.org>.

jubilee for which Du Pérac's print was conceived. In 1578, the so-called Catacombs of Priscilla were discovered under an orchard just north east of the city walls, and a pious identification of all those buried within them as victims of Roman imperial persecution followed. This discovery of what one contemporary authority described grandiloquently as a 'subterranean city'[41] ushered in the biggest boost in relic traffic since the dramatic rise in the circulation of relics consequent on the so-called Fourth Crusade in 1204.[42] In 1635 (rather than the 1632 announced on the title page), after not inconsiderable delay owing to its extensive illustrations, the first atlas of this subterranean New World was published in Rome, *Roma sotterranea*, by the

[41] 'Mirabile dictum … eius amplitudine, multisque atque diversis eiusdem vijs, quam subterraneam civitatem': Cesare Baronio, *Annales ecclesiastici*, 12 vols (Rome, 1588–1607), 2: 59.

[42] Anne Lester discusses some of the consequences of this in her article, in this volume: 'Translation and Appropriation: Greek Relics in the Latin West in the Aftermath of the Fourth Crusade', 88–117.

Maltese Antonio Bosio.[43] As the extended title of this work makes clear, it was intended also to be a gallery displaying a visual testimony to the sufferings and martyrdom of the early Christians whose priceless relics lay beneath the soil of the Roman *campagna* outside the city walls.

The next three hundred years were to see Roman catacomb relics translated throughout the Catholic world. A recent survey has calculated that no fewer than fourteen thousand relics from this source (many of which were whole bodies) were distributed throughout the world between 1578 and 1870.[44] Unsurprisingly, they were exported particularly to frontier zones in both the Old and New Worlds. In Europe, the Upper Rhine Palatinate, which changed faith more than once during the century after the Reformation and where the Wittelsbach dukes of Bavaria replaced holy bodies destroyed during the Thirty Years' War (1618–48), was a territory particularly favoured. It is reckoned that over a thousand catacomb saints were translated from Rome into this area during the long seventeenth century (*c.*1580–*c.*1750).[45] Much less well known until very recently, however, has been the translation of such relics to the New World. Their entry into Mexico City on 2 November 1578, for example, was given a particularly magnificent treatment in the form of a pageant entitled *Triumph of the Saints*.[46] The distribution and processing of relics was a long-established Christian practice dating back at least to the time of St Augustine, who in the last book of *City of God* talked with guarded

[43] Antonio Bosio, *Roma sotterranea … nella quale si tratta de'sacri cimiterii di Roma, del sito, forma, et uso antico di essi, de cubicoli, oratorii, imagini, ieroglifici, iscrittioni et epitaffi, che vi sono … del significato delle dette imagini e ieroglifici. De riti funerali in sepellirvi i defonti de martiri in essi risposti o martirizati nelle vie circonvicine. Delle cose memorabili, sacre e profane ch'erano nelle medesime vie e d'altre notabili, che rappresentano l'imagine della primitiva chiesa. L'angustia che patì nel tempo delle persecutioni, il fervore de'primi Christiani e li veri et inestimabili tesori, che Roma tiene rinchiusi sotto le sue campagne* (Rome, 1632 [actually 1635]).

[44] Stéphane Baciocchi and Christophe Duhamelle, eds, *Reliques romaines. Invention et circulation des corps saints des catacombes à l'époque moderne* (Rome, 2016).

[45] Trevor Johnson, 'Holy Fabrications: The Catacomb Saints and the Counter-Reformation in Bavaria', *JEH* 47 (1996), 274–97; see also the lavishly illustrated photo-essay by Paul Koudounaris, *Heavenly Bodies: Cult Treasures and Spectacular Saints from the Catacombs* (London, 2013).

[46] *Tragedia del triunfo de los santos*: see Pierre-Antoine Favre, 'Reliquias romanas en México. Historia d'una migración', in Guillermo Wilde, ed., *Saberes de la Conversión. Jesuitas, Indígenas e Imperios coloniales en las fronteras de la Cristianidad* (Buenos Aires, 2012), 207–24; cf. Leandro Karnal, 'Les Reliques dans la conquête de l'Amérique luso-espagnole', in Philippe Boutry, Pierre-Antoine Fabre and Dominique Julia, eds, *Reliques modernes. Cultes et usages chrétiens des corps saints des Réformes aux revolutions*, 2 vols (Paris, 2009), 2: 731–50, at 745–50.

approval of St Stephen's wonder-working relics, which had just recently 'come on stream', as a result of the discovery of his tomb at Kafr Gamala, Palestine, in 415.[47] However, the advent of the Reformation considerably intensified the significance of the practice, since the cult of saints and the adoration of the eucharist had become the two most visible markers of Roman Catholicism.

In a letter from Québec dated 16 October 1666, the Ursuline nun Marie L'Incarnation (1599–1672) thanked her son for the 'fine present of saints' relics', which he had sent her community, and which were now venerated 'in a place set aside for the purpose', whence they were taken to be displayed on feast days in four reliquaries. Marie, who had joined the order after being widowed at a relatively young age, described an event of a magnificence that she never dared to imagine seeing in New France, 'where, since I arrived, I have seen nothing that was not uncivilized and barbarous'.[48] This was the translation of the bodies of two saints from the Roman catacombs, Flavian and Felicity, which had been given to the colony by the pope. The ceremony, which took in all four of the city's existing churches, lasted over six hours, with accompanying music, and involved no fewer than forty-seven ecclesiastics as well as the governor of New France, Daniel de Rémy de Courcelles.

However, the traffic was two-way, for Rome also imported relics, notably from the Holy Land, as exemplified in the *Sancta Sanctorum*, which had been the pope's private chapel in the old Lateran palace and was the repository of some of Rome's most sacred relics, including an *Acheiropoeton* or icon of Christ allegedly not painted by [human] hands but channelled by divine guidance through St Luke. Previously inaccessible to the public, Sixtus V had the *scala sancta* – the flight of stairs allegedly originating from Pilate's palace in Jerusalem which Christ had therefore climbed – moved from the north wing of the medieval Lateran palace, which the pope had demolished, to form a new public entrance to the *Sancta Sanctorum* facing the basilica of S. Giovanni in Laterano.[49]

[47] See Augustine, *Concerning the City of God against the Pagans*, transl. Henry Bettenson (Harmondsworth, 1972), 1041 (bk 22, ch. 8).

[48] '[Q]uand j'y suis venue je n'avois rien vue que d'inculte et de barbare': G. Oury, ed., *Marie de l'Incarnation Ursuline (1599–1672). Correspondence* (Solesmes, 1971), 767–9, at 767 (letter 223).

[49] Helge Gamrath, *Roma sancta renovata. Studi sull'urbanistica di Roma nella seconda metà del sec. XVI con particolare riferimento al pontificato di Sisto V (1585–90)* (Rome, 1987), 157–8. For

This 'connectedness' of Rome with the wider Roman Church – which may also be expressed in terms of Rome as particular place as a counterpart to Rome as universal idea – was also achieved by 'translating' the sacred topography of post-Tridentine Rome onto its heroic, early Christian prototype. It is surely no coincidence that a particularly powerful act of such spatio-temporal translation was carried out by Gregory Martin, the main translator of the Douai-Rheims Bible, the Roman Catholic translation of the Vulgate into English. Martin, who had spent eighteen months in Rome between December 1576 and June 1578, was also author of *Roma sancta*, which seemed on the surface a conventional enough pilgrim's guide to the Eternal City: its title harked back to the perennial genre of the *mirabilia urbis Romae*.[50] However, for Martin, Rome was an agent of the ultimate expression of translation in the Europe in the age of reformations: conversion. Although *Roma sancta* was to remain unpublished in its full form until 1969, extracts from it were published in English *c.*1597 – rather than the 1583 on its title page – under the title *A treatyse of Christian peregrination*.[51] Here, as in the full version, Martin liberally studded his text with quotations from the early Church fathers. One of Martin's favourite writers was the one-time archbishop of Constantinople, St John Chrysostom (*c.*347–407), whose letter to the Romans – Chrysostom here was consciously modelling himself on St Paul – Martin quoted at some length, before saying:

> As often as I read it, I am ready to melte for joye. But marke … the cause of his affection towards Rome: to wite the bodies of the Apostles lying there, and why the bodies? Because they carried the markes of the Church. This is it that causeth Pilgrimage. This consideration, for the love of Christ and the honour of him, inflamed the Godly father and all the best Christians in the Primitive Church to love sacred monuments, to be desirous to see them, to go farre and neere unto them, *to touch, to kisse, to licke them, to weep in the place*, to concieve such a lyvely imagination

a comprehensive description of the Scala Sancta and the Sancta Sanctorum, see Liliana Barroero, ed., *Guide rionali di Roma. Rione I – Monti, parte 1* (Rome, 1982), 68–77. For Sixtus V's decorative programme, see Maria Luisa Madonna, ed., *Roma di Sisto V. Le arti e la cultura* (Rome, 1993), 126–35.

[50] Gregory Martin, *Roma sancta (1581). Now first printed from the Manuscript by G. B. Parks* (Rome, 1969).

[51] *A treatyse of Chris[ti]an peregrination, w[rit]ten by M. Gregory Martin Licentiate and late reader of divinitie in the Englishe coleadge of Remes. Whereunto is adioined certen epistles written by him to sundrye his frendes* (Paris, 1583; actually *c.*1597).

> of things done there by Christ and his saynts and withall *such a sensible feeling of heavenly devotion* that it was a payne to remove from thence, a death to dwell farre of[f].[52]

Martin's *Treatyse of Christian Peregrination* was published together with several letters including one to his sisters: 'married to Protestants and themselves trained up in heresy'. In this context, I do not think it is too far-fetched to argue that the space and place of Rome – and the emotion the city evoked in the mind of the devout, orthodox Catholic – was considered by Martin to be a persuasive agent of conversion. Such a notion is reinforced by the following passage from *Roma sancta*:

> And if any where a man stand nigh to these tombes, he perceaveth his sence by and by ravished with this sayd force, for the sight of the coffin entring into the hart, pearceth it, stirreth it up, and moveth it in such a maner, as if he that lyeth there dead, did pray with us, and were visibly present to be seen.[53]

For Martin, meditation on material remains which had borne witness to the most heroic age of Christian history could transport a person with the right interior disposition to early Christian Rome itself, thus collapsing time and space.

V

But what of the 'little Romes' which emerged in the wake of the *conquistadores* from Cartagena to Cuzco, Mexico to Manila: those settlements which, by means of Roman relics and rituals, identified themselves closely with the New Jerusalem on the Tiber? One was located in the indigenous settlement of Carabuco, on the shores of Lake Titicaca, in the Spanish colony of Audiencia de Charcas, which fell within the viceroyalty of Peru (modern Bolivia). Specific interest focuses on the church's baptistery, whose fresco decorations were commissioned by the local *cacique* (native chief), Agustín Siñani, after the partial collapse of the building in 1763.[54] As a counterpart to the

52 Ibid., unfoliated (emphasis added).

53 Martin, *Roma sancta*, 27.

54 It has not been possible to secure permission to reproduce these images, and I refer the reader to H. Okada, 'Mural Painting in the Viceroyalty of Peru', in Luisa Alcalá and Jonathan Brown, eds, *Painting in Latin America, 1550–1820* (New Haven,

baptism of Christ, there is a depiction of the baptism of Agustín's ancestor, Fernando, who was the first in his line to be baptized and was shown resplendent in his Inca tunic, the *uncu*. In the foreground is a crown which rests on a cushion in front of him. This detail is picked up in the fresco the opposite wall which shows the Emperor Constantine being baptized by Pope Sylvester, who is easily identifiable wearing the papal tiara. According to Hiroshige Okada, the model for this pair of compositions was most probably an engraving of the design by Rubens for the scene of Constantine's baptism, part of a six-piece set of tapestries depicting the story of Constantine, woven in Paris 1623–7, and given by Louis XIII of France, son of Henry IV (who in the light of his conversion(s) to Catholicism was sometimes referred to by contemporaries as 'a second Constantine'), to Cardinal Francesco Barberini, nephew of Urban VIII (1623–44).[55] Both scenes are framed by spiral, corkscrew columns which not only border the scene itself but are also deployed elsewhere in the baptistery's decoration. These allude to the columns from the Temple of Solomon, a set of which, so a tradition dating from the twelfth or thirteenth centuries ran, Constantine had transported from Jerusalem to decorate the high altar and presbytery of the Old St Peter's.[56] The Solomonic column had become a prominent feature of the Latin American baroque owing, originally, to the associations made by the first wave of mendicant missionaries of the Americas with the lands of Ophir and Tarshish, where the mines of Solomon were located.[57] In the seventeenth century Bernini carefully relocated them in pairs to frame several of the basilica's most precious relics, including the Veronica and pieces from the holy lance and the cross of

CT, and London, 2014), 403–35, at 428–9 (figs 21, 22). There are also black and white reproductions as plates 2 and 3 in Hiroshige Okada, '"Golden compasses" on the Shores of Lake Titicaca: The Appropriation of European Visual Culture and the Patronage of Art by an indigenous Cacique in the colonial Andes', *Memories [sic] of the Graduate School of Letters, Osaka University* 51 (2011), 87–111, at 90, online at: <http://ir.library.osaka-u.ac.jp/dspace/handle/11094/10414>, last accessed 29 May 2016.

55 Now in the Museum of Art, Philadelphia, accession number 1958–78-4.

56 The columns were actually from Greece and arrived in two stages, in the fourth and the eighth centuries. Dale Kinney suggests that '[t]he origin of the legend probably had something to do with a widespread interest in supposedly Solomonic structures awakened by the Crusades, and with the related vogue for knotted columns': 'Spolia', in William Tronzo, ed., *St Peter's in the Vatican* (Cambridge, 2005), 16–47, at 36.

57 Jaime Lara, 'Church Interior', in Evonne Levy and Kenneth Mills, eds, *Lexicon of the Hispanic Baroque: Transatlantic Exchange and Transformation* (Austin, TX, 2013), 47–50, at 48.

Christ at the crossing of the new St Peter's. Bernini then reused the spiral column motif on a spectacular scale in the baldacchino over the tomb of St Peter, thereby dramatically reasserting the translation of the true religion from Jerusalem to Rome. Okada has argued that this pairing of Constantine with the Incan *cacique* was quite possibly inspired by the late sixteenth-century *Los comentarios reales de los Incas* (Lisbon, 1609), composed by the mestizo humanist Garcilaso de la Vega (1539–1616), son of a Spanish conquistador and an Inca princess.[58] Garcilaso had made a direct comparison of the Inca and Roman empires, referring to Cuzco as 'another Rome' and casting the Inca indigenous as 'new gentiles' (*nuevos gentiles*) whose prototype was the Romans or 'old gentiles' (*antiquos gentiles*).[59] In this way the significance of the conversion of the Inca Empire to Christianity was paired – and by implication placed on a par – with that of the Roman Empire over a thousand years earlier.[60]

However, even more important than such typological references is the evidence for the means by which Christianity was 'translated' from the Old to New Worlds offered by the tabernacle holding the host over the high altar of the small church dedicated to St James the Great in the hamlet of Coporaque, some two hundred kilometres west of Lake Titacaca in Peru. This tabernacle, placed in a church even humbler than that in Carabuco, reproduces the tabernacle from the high altar of the Duomo of Milan dating from 1561 (Figs 3a, 3b). It is immediately apparent that both high altars – albeit on very different scales – have been specifically designed to provide a secure and prominent place for the display and storage of the consecrated, transubstantiated host which, owing to its significance as, ultimately, the most important symbol of what made post-Reformation Roman Catholicism distinctive, became the signifier of embattled orthodoxy. This can be seen from Carlo Borromeo's 'Instructions for the Building and Outfitting of Churches' (1577), contained in the 1583 edition of the *Acts of the Milanese Church*, the most widely diffused 'handbook'

[58] Okada, '"Golden compasses"', 101.

[59] On Garcilaso, see D. Brading, *The First America: The Spanish Monarchy, Creole Patriots and the Liberal State, 1492–1867* (Cambridge, 1991), 255–72. There is a complete English translation by H. V. Livermore: *Royal Commentaries of the Incas, and General History of Peru*, 2 vols (Austin, TX, 1965).

[60] Okada, '"Golden compasses"', 100–1; cf. idem, 'Mural Painting', 428–30.

Figure 3a. (Colour online) Interior of Santiago Apostol Coporacque. ©Hans Roegele.

for bishops showing them how to apply the decrees and canons of the Council of Trent.[61]

Another prominent and ubiquitous visual detail to be found in even the humblest churches of the Iberian overseas empire is that of the confession box, also an emphatically Borromean innovation The centrality of both these elements of church furniture to the pastoral vision of that pre-eminent model bishop of the Counter-Reformation, Carlo Borromeo, may be seen from their prominent treatment in his handbook instructions. The *Acts of the Milanese Church*, which contained the 'Instructions', was no dry collection of synodal legislation but was designed to supply hard pressed, busy prelates with practical advice about how to govern their dioceses,

61 'Instructiones fabricae et supellectilis ecclesiasticae', in *Acta ecclesiae mediolanensis* (Milan, 1583), fols 177^{r}–211^{v}. For a complete English translation with scholarly commentary, see <http://www.evelynvoelker.com>, accessed 26 October 2016.

Figure 3b. (Colour online) High Altar Tabernacle, Duomo, Milan. ©Richard Schofield.

preach sermons, train priests and build and outfit churches. As such it should be considered the practical counterpart to the theory enshrined in the Canons and Decrees of the Council of Trent, the complete set of which had been published in 1564. Its popularity was such that Borromeo's counterparts as reforming prelates in Central and South America came to consider the archbishop of Milan as their model and prototype. Moreover, at least one near contemporary drew a direct comparison between Borromeo and Toribio de Mogrovejo, archbishop of Lima from 1581 until his death from overwork in 1606, who summoned what historians still consider to have been 'The Trent of the Americas', the Third Provincial Council of Lima of 1582–3.[62]

Just as penance was the master-key of Borromean spirituality, so for the Jesuit José de Acosta (1539/40–1600), one of the four theologians in attendance at the Council of Lima, mutual intelligibility in the confession box between the indigenous penitent and his or her confessor was of paramount importance.[63] Acosta is credited with overseeing translation into two of the pre-eminent languages of the former Inca Empire, Quechua and Aymara, of both a short catechism for lay instructors to repeat with their pupils and a longer one for more advanced converts; he also wrote a confession manual and a collection of sermons, which at the specific behest of the Third Council of Lima were to constitute an important pastoral resource in their Quechua and Aymara versions.[64]

For Acosta, as outlined in his famous missionary manual *On procuring the Salvation of the Indians* (*De procuranda indorum salute*), which was already complete by 1576 although it was not published until 1588, after his return to Spain, the *sine qua non* of the effectiveness of the missions was the capacity of the missionaries to communicate in the

[62] L. Muñoz, *Vida di S. Carlos Borromeo … puesta en nuesta lengua de la historias que del santo escrivieron el doctor Iuan Pedro Guissano [sic], don Carlos Bascapé, Iuan Baptista Possevino, Marco Aurelio Gratarola* (Madrid, 1626). For the comparison of the Third Provincial Council of Lima with Trent in importance, see Enrique Dussel, *A History of the Church in Latin America* (Grand Rapids, MI, 1981), 147; cf. A. de Leon Pinelo, *Vida del Illustrissimo i Reverendissimo D. Toribio Alfonso Mogrovejo* ([Madrid?], 1653), 77–91.

[63] W. De Boer, *The Conquest of the Soul: Confession, Discipline and Public Order in Counter-Reformation Milan* (Leiden and Boston, MA, 2001), 43–83.

[64] *Catecismo en la lengua española y quechua ordenado por autoridad del concilio de Lima en el año 1583*; *Confessionario para los curas de indios con la instrucion contra sus ritos y exhortacion para ayudar a bien morir, y summa de sus [p]rivilegios y forma de impedimentos del matrimonio. Compuesta y traduzido en las lenguas Quechua y Aymara. Para autoridad del Concilio provincial de Lima del año 1583* (Lima, 1585); *Tercero catechismo y esposicion de la doctrina christiana por sermones, para que los curas y otros ministros prediquen y enseñen a los Indios y a las demas personas, conforme a lo que e nel sancto Concilio Provincial de Lima se profeyo* (Lima, 1585). These are now all available to download at: <https://www.wdl.org/es/item/13746/>, last accessed 29 May 2016.

Indians' own languages:[65] 'For me, the priest that accepts the office of *párocco* without knowing the language of the Indians – and I have believed this for a long time and I keep on affirming it – that person is just ruining his soul.'[66]

Acosta went on to explain how this was true in the very basic sense that 'if he does not know what the Indian is confessing', a priest could not administer the sacrament of penance; 'nor will the Indian be able to understand what is commanded of him'.[67] Acosta went on to praise the Incas for their 'wisest' use of the device of a general language (*lengua general*) of Quechua which was spoken and understood, at least by the elite if not by the common people, throughout the extensive lands of their empire.[68] However, for him, the most effective way to negotiate what he referred to as the 'veritable jungle of languages' (*idiomatum tam multiplex sylva sit*) was to make cautious yet concerted use of the (at least) bilingual offspring of Spanish fathers and Indian mothers, the mestizos.[69] But such a strategy was far from foolproof.

Attempts to identify a 'general language' in which to communicate the teaching of Christian doctrine were inevitably the imperfect, artificial fruit of compromise. Nowhere can this be seen more clearly than in the case of New Granada. Unlike New Spain and Peru,

[65] 'Firstly, we must also acquire some use of the language, or, if not, preach through a faithful interpreter, if there is such a thing'. All subsequent references are to José de Acosta, *De procuranda indorum salute*, ed. and transl. G. Stewart McIntosh, 2 vols (Tayport, 1996), 1: 92 (bk 2, ch. 17); cf. ibid. 29–30 (bk 1, ch. 9): 'Fear of the difficulty of the language ought not to hinder the propagation of the gospel'.

[66] Ibid. 2: 18 (bk 4, ch. 7); cf. ibid. 2: 137–8 (bk 6, ch. 13): 'Skill in the Indian language is needed to hear confession'.

[67] Cf. Rubén Vargas Ugarte, *Concilios Limensis 1551–1772*, 3 vols (Lima, 1951–4), 1: 310 (actio 5, cap. 3).

[68] Acosta, *De procuranda*, ed. and transl. McIntosh, 2: 21 (bk 4, ch. 8). Acosta actually wrote: 'The Incas, with the wisest of laws (*consultissima lege perfici*) were able to achieve that [a general language] in all the scattered provinces of their kingdom'. For the original text, see Acosta, *De natura novi orbis libri duo et de promulgatione evangelii apud Barbaros* (Cologne, 1596), 378. For the wider picture, see now the special issue: 'Langues indiennes et empire dans l'Amérique du Sud colonial / Lenguas indígenas e imperio en la América del Sur colonial', *Mélanges de la Casa de Velázquez* n.s. 45/1 (2015), 9–151.

[69] Acosta, *De procuranda*, ed. and transl. McIntosh, 2: 21–2 (bk 4, ch. 8); cf. idem, *De natura novi orbis libri duo et de promulgatione Evangelii apud barbaros, sive de procuranda indorum salute,* (Salamanca, 1588), 379. Notwithstanding such an endorsement, the Jesuits stopped admitting mestizos as early as 1576, the very year when Acosta finished *De procuranda*, and the 1582 provincial congregation voted for a definitive ban: cf. A. Durston, *Pastoral Quechua: The History of Christian Translation in Colonial Peru, 1550–1650* (Notre Dame, IN, 2007), 83.

where the political hegemony of the Aztec and Inca empires made the adoption of Nahuatl and Quechua, respectively, practical and reasonably effective (if somewhat oversimplified) options, the absence of a correspondingly dominant indigenous power in New Granada resulted in an outcome which was singularly unsatisfactory. The only candidate for the status of 'general language' was that referred to in contemporary sources as 'Mosca' and known today by the names of 'Muisca' or 'Chibcha'. However, it was only spoken in the immediate environs of Santafé. As a solution to this fragmented linguistic landscape the city's archbishop, Zapata de Cárdenas, author of the first vernacular (Castilian) catechism for New Granada in 1576, attempted – in the words of Juan Cobo Betancourt – 'to ordain the secular church [of New Granada] out of its crisis' by creating some 124 priests to send to indigenous parishes; of these, no fewer than 22 were mestizos and 39 *criollos*.[70] Although it was to be reasonably expected that the mestizo priests would be bilingual and that their creole counterparts might have at least a basic grasp of the indigenous tongue of the community in which they had grown up, the question was 'which language'? As the archbishop himself admitted: 'in this kingdom every valley or province has a different one, and it is not like Peru and New Spain, where there are different languages but one general language, which is used throughout the land'.[71] The eventual solution, if this word is appropriate for such an untidy and contingent process, was a simple one, according to Cobo Betancourt. His painstaking examination of the remaining records from Archbishop Arias de Ugarte's marathon five-year visitation of his province (1619–24) strongly suggests that local priests were expected to translate the catechetical material which had been issued to them – that is, that approved by the Third Council of Lima, but only in Castilian – into the language of their parishioners.[72]

Acosta insisted that the Indian languages, though multiple, were not that difficult to learn when compared to, say, Hebrew, or even Latin and Greek. However, he was not blind to their qualities:

[70] Juan F. Cobo Betancourt, 'Colonialism in the Periphery: Spanish Linguistic Policy in New Granada *c.*1574–1625', *Colonial Latin American Review* 23 (2014), 118–42, at 129.
[71] Ibid. 132.
[72] Ibid. 136–7. Recent work on the Christianization of Central America emphasizes the role of indigenous scribes, authors and consumers in the creative adaptation of catechisms and confession manuals: see in particular Mark Z. Christensen, *Nahua and Maya Catholicisms: texts and Religion in Colonial Central Mexico and Yucatan* (Stanford, CA, 2013); idem, *Translated Christianities: Nahua and Maya Religious Texts* (University Park, PA, 2014).

> Yet in their uncultured barbarity they have some ways of saying things that are so beautiful and elegant, and other expressions that are so admirably concise that they say many things in one, that give us such delight, and when we wish to express in Latin or in Spanish all the power of one of these words we would have to employ many and yet we would scarcely cover all the meaning.[73]

However, when it came to spiritual or philosophical matters, the Indians' languages were found wanting, so that, in Acosta's opinion, it did not make sense to attempt to translate such key Christian concepts as 'faith, cross, angel, virginity and marriage', which should rather be left in Spanish.[74] Here Acosta might well have had in mind the initial error made just a few decades earlier by his confrère Francis Xavier in Japan where, misadvised by his guide and interpreter, the Japanese pirate Anjiro, the Jesuit missionary had first used the Japanese concept *Dainichi*, the pantheistic deity revered by the Buddhist Shingon sect, to translate 'God', before realizing his error and reverting to the use of Latin, or at least to Latinate words, slightly adapted so as to work better when spoken by the Japanese.[75]

A more difficult challenge to the efficacy of missionary work, Acosta believed, was provided by the 'most truly barbarous' pronunciation characteristic of many Indian tongues which meant that their speakers 'appeared to be gargling in their throats rather than talking'.[76] The key thing here was to overcome any sense of shame and embarrassment when attempting to deliver sermons in the Indian languages. As Acosta pithily put it: 'we have to make many mistakes

[73] 'Iam vero in illa sua veluti inculta barbarie adeo pulchros, adeo elegantes idiomatismos habet formulasque dicendi mirabili brevitate multa complexas ut delectet vehementer quorum unius vocis vim si Latinus, Hispanus exprimere velit, pluribus ipse vix possit': Acosta, *De natura novi orbis libri duo … et de procuranda indorum salute*, 382–3.

[74] Acosta, *De procuranda*, ed. and transl. McIntosh, 2: 25 (bk 4, ch. 9); cf. the challenge facing Jesuit missionaries working among the Iroquois who were trying to communicate ideas of the Christian soul and spirit, as discussed in the introduction to J. M. Steckley, ed. and transl., *De Religione: Telling the Seventeenth-Century Jesuit Story in Huron to the Iroquois* (Norman OH, 2004), in particular 24–45.

[75] Joan-Pau Rubiés, 'Real and Imaginary Dialogues in the Jesuit Mission of Sixteenth-Century Japan', *Journal of the Economic and Social History of the Orient* 55 (2012), 447–94; cf., in this volume, idem, 'Ethnography and Cultural Translation in the Early Modern Missions', 272–310, at 304. See also M. Cooper, *Rodriguez the Interpreter: An Early Jesuit in Japan and China* (New York and Tokyo, 1974), 284–5.

[76] Acosta, *De procuranda*, ed. and transl. McIntosh, 2: 24–5 (bk 4, ch. 9). The word Acosta used was *stridentes*, which might literally be translated as 'rattling': Acosta, *De natura novi orbis*, 383.

to learn not to make any mistakes'.[77] He concluded this chapter with an emphasis on the importance of simplicity and repetition, a strategy that he noted had been used with particular effectiveness by Francis Xavier with the simple fisherfolk of the Malabar coast, and with an evocation of a practice he believed to have been widespread in the primitive Church, that of reading out sermons in native tongues which had been written by others but which were accompanied by guidance so as to ensure that the correct intonation and pronunciation were employed.[78] The importance of correct pronunciation to the accurate communication of meaning was also an obsession of the Jesuit Horacio Carochi, the author of what is still the most comprehensive grammar of the Mexica language of Nahuatl, published in 1645:

> And let no one think that it matters little whether one does or does not take care with these accents and with the length of the syllables, because aside from the fact that a badly pronounced language greatly offends hearers, in this one there will be mistakes at every step and one thing will be said for another, if there is neglect with the pronunciation.[79]

VI

But what does this slow, somewhat messy and far from conclusive attempt to translate the Christian message to at least two of the four parts of the then known world during the early modern period add up to? According to the Gambia-born former Muslim, now Roman Catholic, Lamin Sanneh (b. 1942), it has been precisely the 'triumph of the translatability' of Christianity, by means of which indigenous peoples have been able to appropriate the Bible in myriad forms and

[77] 'Saepe et audacter errandum, ut aliquando non erretur': ibid. 2: 25 (bk 4, ch. 9); cf. Acosta, *De natura novi orbis libri duo … et de procuranda indorum salute*, 384.

[78] Acosta, *De procuranda*, ed. and transl. McIntosh, 2: 26 (bk 4, ch. 9); cf. a letter dated Vembar, 31 October 1548, from the Jesuit missionary and author of the first Tamil grammar, *Arte da Lingua Malabar* (1549), Henrique Henriques, to Ignatius Loyola and his companions, which explains how since he was without an interpreter he relied on a member of his Tamil congregation to repeat his sermon, which he had just attempted to deliver in the local language, so that its content was better understood: 'digo las palabras en la misma lengua Malavar, y hago que las torne a dezir otro, que es como topaz [*sic*], para que todos las entendien mejor': J. Wicki, ed., *Documenta Indica (1540–97)*, 18 vols (Rome, 1948–88), 1: 276–300, at 286–7 (letter 45).

[79] H. Carochi, *Grammar of the Mexican Language with an Explanation of its Adverbs (1645)*, ed. and transl. James Lockhart (Stanford, CA, 2001), 25 (ch. 1, section 3).

make it work for them, that has made it the world religion that we have today.[80] However, Sanneh's uplifting narrative has its origins in a distinctly nostalgic, ultimately essentialist treatment of 'African Christianity' and its indigenous agency, somehow mysteriously independent of extra-continental influence. As Joel Cabrita points out, such a model singularly fails to account for the South African (Ibandia Iama) Nazaretha Church, founded in 1910 and today with over four million members, which, deeply influenced by transnational Evangelical literary culture (with North American rather than African roots), has taken upon itself the task of writing further scriptures – a new Bible if you like – which recount the miraculous deeds of its founding prophet, Isaiah Shembe (1865?–1935).[81] Furthermore, recent work on networks of carriers of religion across the globe: whether it be the trade diaspora of Sephardic Jewish merchants, Sufi brotherhoods in South Asia or members of the Society of Jesus, has 'overturn[ed] the stereotype of a lone missionary or remote merchant carting his beliefs overseas by highlighting the role of solid but imperfect networks tied together by movement and faith'.[82] These were networks, furthermore, that were more often than not regional and unmediated by a single centre; as Luke Clossey has demonstrated in his study of the global Jesuit mission, which traces a vector of movement of missionaries from Germany to China via Mexico: here Rome was not so much a place as a state of mind.[83]

I would therefore like to close this article on the theme of translation in an age of reformations with a regrettably all too brief consideration of an object which, owing to the almost complete absence of contemporary documentation, resolutely resists being pinned down geographically. It is very small, measuring just over nine centimetres in height and little more than five in breadth. Made of (Indian or

[80] Lamin Sanneh, *Translating the Message: The Missionary Impact on Culture*, 2nd edn (Maryknoll, NY, 2009).

[81] Joel Cabrita, *Text and Authority in the South African Nazaretha Church* (Cambridge, 2015); cf., in this volume, eadem, 'Revisiting "Translatability" and African Christianity: The Case of the Christian Catholic Apostolic Church in Zion', 448–75.

[82] Karin Veléz, Sebastian Prange and Luke Clossey, 'Religious Ideas in Motion', in Douglas Northrop, ed., *A Companion to World History* (Oxford and Malden, MA, 2012), 352–64, at 357; cf. Francesca Trivellato, *The Familiarity of Strangers: The Sephardic Diaspora, Livorno, and Cross-Cultural Trade in the Early Modern Period* (New Haven, CT, and London, 2009); Carl Ernst and Bruce Lawrence, *Sufi Martyrs of Love: The Chishti Order in South Asia and beyond* (New York and Basingstoke, 2002); Luke Clossey, *Salvation and Globalization in the Early Jesuit Missions* (Cambridge, 2008).

[83] Clossey, *Salvation and Globalization*.

Figure 4. (Colour online) Plaque with St Jerome, Macao, China, 17th century, Ivory, 13.5 x 8.5 cm. Cobral Moncada Leilões, Auction 139, lot 421. Reproduced courtesy of Cobral Moncada Leilões – Art Auctioneers, Lisbon, Portugal, <http://www.cml.pt>.

African, but possibly Siamese or Cambodian) ivory, it was carved sometime in the seventeenth century, copying a lost Flemish prototype (more likely based on an engraving originating in Antwerp rather than an ivory original), probably on mainland China near Macau (although Manila is another possible candidate), by quite possibly unconverted Chinese craftsmen specifically for an overseas market.[84] Having travelled first across the Pacific on a Spanish galleon from Manila to Acapulco, where it might have been bought by a Brazil-based merchant before crossing the Atlantic at some unspecified time, it ended up being auctioned in Lisbon, where it was bought recently by a private collector. It depicts a near-naked St Jerome in the desert kneeling before and holding a cross with Christ crucified upon it. Immediately before the saint is a mound on which a skull has been prominently placed and before which sits his attribute, a tame lion. The whole scene is overseen by God the Father who blesses both the scene below and the viewer (Fig. 4). This small, exquisitely portable object of devotion is a fitting one with which to bring this selective survey of the global circulation of Roman Catholicism in the early modern period to a close, since it serves to remind us that, for all its slow, incomplete and halting nature, it was above all the portability (and tradability) of such devotional objects – in other words, its material rather than linguistic translatability – that enabled Roman Catholicism to become the first world religion.

[84] Gauvin Bailey, 'Translation and Metamorphosis in the Catholic Ivories of China, Japan and the Philippines, 1561–1800', in idem, J.-M. Massing and N. Vassallo e Silva, *Marfins no Império Português / Ivories in the Portuguese Empire* (Lisbon, 2013), 243–82; the illustration of St Jerome is on page 298.

Nella lingua di ciascuno: Church Communication between Latin and Vernacular during the Counter-Reformation

Silvia Manzi*
University of Teramo

This article investigates the reasons for the choice of vernacular language instead of Latin in the communications of bishops with clergy and laity at the end of the sixteenth century and into the first decades of the seventeenth. The spread of Lutheran doctrine, which encouraged the use of the vernacular in the Scriptures and in the mass, was confronted by a reaction: the Catholic Church denied all access to the mysteries of faith to anyone ignorant of Latin through the three Indices of prohibited books issued in the second half of the sixteenth century (1559, 1564, 1596). However, concurrently with the issuing of these prohibitions, the bishops of Italy used the Italian language to translate some papal bulls and decrees of the Council of Trent. On which issues and under what circumstances did they feel it was necessary to be understood by the non-Latinate and therefore find it necessary to supply Italian translations of official documents, such as papal constitutions and Tridentine decrees? Was the local translation of such documents faithful to the original? And if not, why not?

In recent decades Italian has become the common language of the Catholic Church and the Holy See, with the exception of some fundamental religious texts and official documents which are still written in Latin.[1] Although interest in the language of Cicero has not entirely vanished, as indicated by the weekly column in the newspaper of the Italian episcopal conference, *Avvenire*, in modern times the balance in the centuries-old relationship between Italian and Latin in Church communication has been tilted in favour of the former.

The official language of the Church and a symbol of its universality, sacredness and fixity,[2] Latin has become less and less understood as a consequence of the emergence and establishment of

* Campus di Coste Sant'Agostino, via Renato Balzarini n. 1, Località Colleparco (Teramo) 64100, Italy. E-mail: manzi.silvia@gmail.com.

[1] Leonardo Rossi, 'La Chiesa parla italiano', in Lucio Caracciolo, ed., *Lingua è potere*, Quaderni speciali di Limes 3 (Rome, 2010), 81–8.

[2] François Waquet, *Le Latin ou l'empire d'un signe. XVIe–XXe siècle* (Paris, 1998); ET *Latin or the Empire of a Sign: From the Sixteenth to the Twentieth Centuries* (London, 2002).

Studies in Church History 53 (2017) 196–209

doi: 10.1017/stc.2016.12

vernacular languages in the modern age. This applies not only to the 'simple' people attending services: clergy and nuns no longer use it with confidence either.[3] However, this process began in the early modern period, although the Catholic Church resisted it. In particular, whilst the dissemination of Lutheran doctrines encouraged the use of vernacular for the Scriptures and in the mass, the Church reacted by blocking access to the mysteries of faith for those ignorant of Latin and prohibiting the use of vernacular translations of Scripture through the three Roman Indices of prohibited books issued in 1559, 1564 and 1596. As demonstrated by Gigliola Fragnito, the ban also hit the wealth of devotional literature that had answered the need of Italians for vernacular texts since the late Middle Ages: homiletic collections, psalms, digests and summaries from the Old and New Testaments, biblical tragedies and sacred representations, writings that circulated under the title of *Natività*, *Vite*, *Passioni di Cristo* or *Lamenti della Madonna*.[4] In the 1570s sacred and profane literature were also included in this prohibition.[5] This struggle against the vernacular sought to reserve the interpretation of doctrine to clerics and to prevent what were viewed as arbitrary readings. The vernacular was used only within the narrow confines of catechesis and preaching. As shown by Rusconi, the prohibition of lay people from reading holy writ in the vernacular became the premise for a systematic indoctrination of the truths of the faith, instilled in an elementary way.[6]

[3] In the language of censors, the 'simple people' or 'idiots' were those who had not undertaken classical studies, and thus were ignorant of Latin: Marina Roggero, *L'alfabeto conquistato. Apprendere e insegnare in Italia tra Sette e Ottocento* (Bologna, 1999).

[4] Gigliola Fragnito, *La Bibbia al rogo. La censura ecclesiastica e i volgarizzamenti della Scrittura* (Bologna, 1997). On the demand for translations of the Bible in Italy before Luther, see Edoardo Barbieri, *Le Bibbie italiane del Quattrocento e del Cinquecento. Storia e bibliografia ragionata delle edizioni in lingua italiana dal 1471 al 1600*, 2 vols (Milan, 1992).

[5] Gigliola Fragnito, *Proibito Capire. La Chiesa e il volgare nella prima età moderna* (Bologna, 2005).

[6] On these themes, see Roberto Rusconi, 'Predicatori e predicazione (secoli IX–XVIII)', in Corrado Vivanti, ed., *Annali della Storia d'Italia, IV. Intellettuali e potere* (Turin, 1981), 951–1035, at 1003; Vittorio Coletti, *Parole dal pulpito. Chiesa e movimenti religiosi tra latino e volgare* (Casale Monferrato, 1993). On the rendering of the Bible text in a controlled and fragmented way, in vernacular exegetic-doctrinal and pedagogical-devotional literature between 1500 and 1600, see Danilo Zardin, 'Bibbia e apparati biblici nei conventi italiani del Cinque-Seicento. Primi appunti', in Rosa Maria Borraccini and Roberto Rusconi, eds, *Libri, biblioteche e cultura degli ordini regolari nell'Italia moderna attraverso la documentazione della Congregazione dell'Indice* (Vatican City, 2006), 63–103. On the preachers' efforts to achieve a balance between the prohibitions and the need to satisfy the desire to the Bible, see Emily Michelson, *The Pulpit and the Press in Reformation Italy* (Cambridge, MA, 2013). On

The purpose of the research presented here is to show that the Italian language was also used by bishops to translate papal bulls and Tridentine decrees. To them the Council of Trent entrusted the mission of eradicating moral and sexual transgressions, such as concubinage, common among clergy and laity.[7] This article analyses documents in order to prove that – and how – the vernacular was used by bishops as a medium for specific ends.[8] These included the defence of their own jurisdictions against the advance of the Inquisition, which in the second half of the sixteenth century, once the danger of contagion from heresy in Italy had been overcome, was applied to every field of knowledge and morality.[9] They also included the curbing of interference from civil authorities in 'mixed court' issues,[10] and the safeguarding of the reputation of the clergy and the prevention of civil unrest.

the correspondence between the declaimed sermons and rewritten sermons, see Stefano Dall'Aglio, 'Faithful to the Spoken Word: Sermons from Orality to Writing in Early Modern Italy', *The Italianist* 34 (2014), 463–77.

7 Giovanni Romeo, *Amori proibiti. I concubini tra Chiesa e Inquisizione* (Rome and Bari, 2008); Michele Mancino and Giovanni Romeo, *Clero criminale. L'onore della Chiesa e i delitti degli ecclesiastici nell'Italia della Controriforma* (Rome and Bari, 2013).

8 Archival research on these questions has focused primarily on Rome, where relevant documents, in particular the series of Bandi e Bolle pontificie del XVI secolo, are held in the Biblioteca Nazionale; the Periodici Estinti in the Casanatense Library; and the Bandi in the Archivio di Stato. In addition, and in order to trace a profile of the dynamics of communication between the centre and periphery, local diocesan archives offer precious sources: the series 'Edicta episcoporum, Decreti, Corrispondenze' with the Roman Congregations and criminal sources (such as Tribunali Ecclesiastici) retain copies of papal bulls in Italian and of edicts derived from them prepared by local bishops. The Archivio di Stato holds regulations issued by civil authorities (e.g. Gridari), including vernacular provisions issued by the ecclesiastical authorities on issues relating to both internal (the confessional) and external (the episcopal or inquisitorial court) fora.

9 On these themes, see Adriano Prosperi, *Tribunali della coscienza. Inquisitori, confessori, missionari* (Turin, 1996); Giovanni Romeo, *Ricerche su confessione dei peccati e Inquisizione nell'Italia del Cinquecento* (Naples, 1997); Elena Brambilla, *Alle origini del Sant'Uffizio. Penitenza, confessione e giustizia spirituale dal Medioevo al XVI secolo* (Bologna, 2000); Giovanni Romeo, *L'Inquisizione nell'Italia moderna* (Rome and Bari, 2002), 35–40; Roberto Rusconi, *L'ordine dei peccati. La confessione tra Medioevo ed età moderna* (Bologna, 2002).

10 'Mixed court issues' (Latin: *mixti fori*) pertain particularly to matrimonial and sexual behaviour (bigamy, rape, incest, sodomy) on which ecclesiastical and secular authorities claim exclusive jurisdiction. On these themes, see Silvana Seidel Menchi and Diego Quaglioni, eds, *Trasgessioni. Seduzione, concubinato, adulterio, bigamia (XIV–XVII secolo)* (Bologna, 2004).

Secretam denunciationem and the Autonomy of the Periphery

The constitution *Cum primum apostolatus*, issued on 1 April 1566 by Pius V,[11] denounced disrespectful attitudes in places of worship and the non-observance of feasts, as well as punishing simoniacs, blasphemers, sodomites and those who kept concubines.[12] Moreover, it sent sodomites to the secular arm for capital punishment. In order to ensure punishment of vices, it provided for the option of 'private denunciation'.[13] In addition to guaranteeing secrecy to informants, the bull also promised them a third of the fines imposed on offenders, thus providing an incentive for the misuse of secret denunciation for personal gain.[14] 'The malignity of a … foe', according to Ottavio Farnese, duke of Parma and Piacenza, could indeed lead somebody to accuse 'even falsely'.[15] The *Cum primum* provoked protests in various cities of Italy. For instance, in Benevento, the morning after its publication, the bull was torn up and burned.[16] It was named 'bolla de la Inquisitione' by the people, who protested against it, associating

[11] 'Ordinationes circa obseruantiam diuini cultus in ecclesiis, et uenerationem festiuitatum; necnon et contra simoniacos, blasphematores, sodomitas et concubinarios': L. Tomassetti et Collegi adlecti Romae virorum s. theologiae et ss. canonum peritorum, *Bullarium Romanum* [hereafter: *BR*], 24 vols (Turin, 1857–72), 7: 434–8.

[12] Rome, Biblioteca Nazionale, Bandi e bolle pontificie del XVI secolo, 68.13.E.1.76: 'Bolla della santita di N.S. Papa Pio Qvinto, nella quale si prohibisce la Simonia, la Biastema, la Sodomia, il Concubinato, il passeggiar per le Chiese: & che i poueri, & gli altri mendicanti non vi siano admessi mentre si celebrano i diuini officij, & del modo che si dee tenere nello entrare, & stare, & conuersare in Chiesa, & anchora di leuar via le Casse, & i depositi de morti, & di non lauorare il di delle feste, insieme con altre cose appertenenti al culto diuino'.

[13] 'Et ut praemissorum delictorum simoniae, blasphemiae ac stupri nefandi notitia facilius habeatur, volumus quod in singulis casibus, non solum per accusationem, sed etiam ad simplicem et secretam denunciationem procedatur per quoscumque iudices, alias tamen de iure competentes, tam ratione delicti quam personarum, ita quod inter eos locus sit praeventioni': 'Ordinationes circa obseruantiam diuini cultus in ecclesiis, et uenerationem festiuitatum; necnon et contra simoniacos, blasphematores, sodomitas et concubinarios': *BR*, 7: 434–8, at 437.

[14] Maria Anna Noto, 'Rebellio o defensio licita? La rivolta di Benevento contro la Bolla "dei Vizi" del 1566', *Nuova Rivista Storica* 93 (2009), 861–90, at 862.

[15] Parma, Archivio di Stato, Carteggio Farnesiano Interno, busta 103, fasc. 16–30 aprile 1580.

[16] Maria Anna Noto, *Viva la Chiesa, mora il Tiranno. Il sovrano, la legge, la comunità e i ribelli (Benevento 1566)* (Naples, 2010), 139.

such secret denunciations with the methods typical of the Spanish *Suprema*.[17]

Dissemination of the document took place in specific places and at defined times. In Montepulciano, Bishop Spinello Benci affixed it in Italian to the doors of the cathedral and had it read during mass on 14 July 1566.[18] Posting the document on the doors of churches, places with a deep symbolic value, ensured greater visibility, but did not always ensure the effectiveness of the provisions. Bishop Gian Ambrogio Fieschi lamented in 1570 that although the bull was 'published in this town and diocese of Savona, already translated so as to be understood by everybody', it was nonetheless 'disregarded by the people'.[19] Moreover, the document was not always translated verbatim by bishops. In some cases, for instance, the *secretam denunciationem* clause was missing.[20] Translation into the vernacular became a tool by means of which bishops mediated between the repressive

[17] 'The city of Benevento shall not be governed … with the … Inquisition, as happens in Sicily': Rome, Archivio di Stato, Tribunale Criminale del Governatore, Beneventana tumultus et conspirationis contra Bullam Sanctissimae Inquisitionis et aliorum excessum, fol. 1269ᵛ; see also Noto, 'Viva la Chiesa', 200. On the Spanish Inquisition, see Joseph Pérez, *Breve historia de la Inquisicion española* (Barcelona, 2003); Franco Cardini-Marina Montesano, *La lunga storia dell'Inquisizione. Luci e ombre della 'leggenda nera'* (Rome, 2005); Henry Kamen, *The Spanish Inquisition: A Historical Revision*, 4th edn (New Haven, CT, and London, 2014).

[18] Montepulciano, Archivio Storico Diocesano, Atti di Curia, busta 424.

[19] Savona-Noli, Archivio Storico Diocesano, Vescovi, fasc. 'Gio. Ambrogio Fieschi'.

[20] It is not included in the following examples: Modena, Archivio di Stato, Documenti di Stati e Città, busta 106, ser. XVIII, 'Sommario della Bolla del B. Pio V contro i Bestemmiatori'; Perugia, Biblioteca Comunale Augusta, ANT Misc. I.C 56 (10), 'Sommario di vna Bolla di Pio V. di fel. mem. in cui si prohibisce trà molti altri vitij la biastema', in *Sommario di alcune bolle de' sommi pontefici, et decreti de' sacri Canoni, & del Concilio di Trento. Fatti volgari per publicarsi da' parochiani ogn'anno nelle loro Chiese. Di commissione del molto illustre & reuerendissimo monsignore Giulio Cesare Salicini vescouo di Rimini* (Rimini, 1593); Piacenza, Biblioteca del Seminario Vescovile, Sala D E V 020, 'Sommario della parte della Bolla di Pio V intorno al conuersare diuotamente in Chiesa, Sommario della detta Bolla di Pio V contra li poueri, che cercano elemosina in Chiesa, nel hora delli Duini Officij, Sommario della parte della sudetta Bolla circa l'osseruanza delli giorni Festiui. Sommario della parte della predetta Bolla contro i Bestemmiatori', in *Constitutiones, et decreta condita in synodo dioecesana Placentina, sub ill.mo, et reuerendiss. D. Claudio Rangono, Dei, & Sanctae Sedis Apostolicae gratia episcopo Placentino, & comite primo habita. Sedente S.D.N. Clemente 8. pontifice opt. Maximo* (Piacenza, 1600); Rome, Biblioteca Nazionale, Misc. B. 701.15, 'Sommario di vna parte della Bolla di Pio Quinto contra i Bestemmiatori', in *Constitutiones, et decreta condita in synodo dioecesana ciuitatis Burgi Sancti Donnini prima. Quam habuit Ioannes Linatus Dei, & sanctae apostolicae sedis gratia episcopus Burgi Sancti Donnini de anno 1608. die 14. Octobris* (Parma, 1608); Rome, Biblioteca Casanatense, vol. misc. 288 1–2, 'Sommario delle Bolle di Leone X. e di Pio Quinto contro li Bestemmiatori', in *Constitutiones, et decreta synodalia promulgata in cathedrali*

requirements of the Roman Church and the local need for community harmony: a tool to restrain the activities of the Inquisition.

Protection of the Clergy and Autonomy from the Secular Authorities

Cum primum was not the only document written by Pope Pius V and dealing with sexual misdemeanours to be translated into Italian. During the synods of Vercelli (1585) and Fano (1594)[21] local bishops translated Pius V's provisions *Declaratio Concilii Tridentini, sess. XXIV cap. II et IV*[22] and *Declaratio Concilii Tridentini, sess. XXIV cap. III*, better known as *Ad Romanum spectat pontificem*.[23] However, it was the decrees on marriage promulgated at the Council of Trent (Session 24, 11 November 1563, *Doctrina de sacramento matrimoni*)[24] that were most commonly disseminated in the vernacular.

There are several testimonies which prove that the decision to translate these decrees was the free choice of the bishops. In Chiusi, Salvatore Pacino explained in an edict in 1564 that, in order to guarantee 'legitimate wedlock', he had decided to publish the *Tametsi*, specifically the first of the ten chapters on the reform of marriage, 'in *vulgar* language'.[25] The same decision was made by the bishop

---

ecclesia Fanensi à perillustri, & reuerendissimo D.D. Thoma Lapio eiusdem ecclesiae episcopo Pisauri (Pisa, 1613).

[21] Rome, Biblioteca Angelica, N.12.1\1, in *Decreta edita, et promvlgata in synodis dioecesanis Vercellensibvs III. Quas Reverendissimvs D.D. I. Franciscvs Bonhomivs, Dei, et Sedis Apostolicae gratia episcopvs S. Ecclesiae Vercellensis habuit. Additis praeterea ad extremuum edictis, constitutionibus, et decretis, uulgari sermone espressi, quae certis anni diebus, in ecclesia populo enuncianda, promulgandauè sint. Concessu Superiorum* (Milan, 1575). The bishop was Giovanni Francesco Bonòmini: *DBI*, online at: <http://www.treccani.it/enciclopedia/giovanni-francesco-bonomini>, accessed 4 August 2015. Rome, Biblioteca Nazionale, 13.15.C.3.M., in *Decreta Synodalia ecclesiae Fanensis in Synodo Dioecesana habita Fani, die XVJ. Mensis Augusti. M.D.XCIII. edita, & promulgata* (Rome, 1594). The bishop was Giulio Ottinelli: *DBI*, online at: <http://www.treccani.it/enciclopedia/tag/giulio-ottonelli/>, accessed 11 June 2015.

[22] 'Declaratio Concilii Tridentini sess. XIV, cap. II et IV, circa impedimenta cognationis spiritualis et affinitatis ex fornicatione, quoad matrimonia post confirmationem concilii contracta et de cetero contrahenda, Sequitur alia declaratio circa impedimenta cognationis spiritualis, Sequitur alia declaratio circa impedimentum affinitatis et fornicationis' (20 August, 28 November 1566), in *BR*, 7: 476–8.

[23] 'Declaratio Concilii Tridentini, sess. XIV capite tertio, super impedimento publicae honestatis, circa sponsalia uel matrimonialia' (1 July 1568), in *BR*, 7: 678–9.

[24] Giuseppe Alberigo et al., *Conciliorum Oecomenicorum Decreta*, 3rd edn (Bologna, 2013), 753–9 [hereafter: *COD*].

[25] Chiusi, Archivio Storico Diocesano, Registri dei matrimoni, busta 1.

of Camerino, Girolamo de'Buoi, in 1584.[26] The *Tametsi* was also accurately translated a few years later in many dioceses, including Venezia (1564),[27] Pisa (1565),[28] Benevento (1567),[29] Rossano (1579),[30] Venosa (1581),[31] Rimini (1593)[32] and Osimo (1594).[33] In other instances in northern and central Italy, matrimonial decrees were modified before they were translated. Two underlying aims can be identified in the changes that the bishops introduced: to safeguard the honour of the clergy and to present themselves as holding sole responsibility for disciplining misconduct in areas of life that were also of interest to the secular authorities. For instance, *Tametsi* provided for the punishment of priests if appropriate. The relevant passage runs: 'Similarly [it is] command[ed] that the Ordinary

[26] Camerino, Archivio Storico Diocesano, Diversa spiritualia, busta 1550–1606.

[27] Venice, Biblioteca Marciana, MISC 2689. 007, 'Decreto della reformatione del matrimonio contenuto nel primo capitolo della Ventesima quarta sessione', in *Parte sostantiale delli decreti del Concilio di Trento, che furono publicati nella sinodo diocesana di Venetia il dì 17. di Settembre 1564* (Venice, 1564).

[28] Pisa, Archivio Arcivescovile, Bolle, decreti, istruzioni, busta 2. The archbishop was Angelo Niccolini.

[29] Naples, Biblioteca Nazionale, V.F. 162 AOO35, 'Decreto del concilio tridentino della riforma di matrimonii fatto in uolgare', in *Constitvtiones editae in dioecesana synodo beneventana anno domini M.D.LXVII Ab Illvstrissimo Reuerendissimo D. Iacobo Sabello S.R.E. Sancte Mariae in Cosmedin. Presbytero Cardinali Archiepiscopo Beneuentano* (Rome, 1567).

[30] Rome, Biblioteca Nazionale, 68.13.C.6.1, 'Decretvm de matrimonii Reformatione – Decreto medesimo fatto volgare', in *Constitvtiones editae in synodo dioecesana Rossanensi Quam Reuerendissimus P.D. ancilots Archiepiscopus habuit Anno Domini, MDLXXIIII. Cal Iunij. Addita sunt quaedam Decreta Tridentini Concilij & Constitutiones summorum Pontificum quarum cognitio necessaria erat* (Rome, 1579).

[31] Rome, Biblioteca Nazionale, 68.13.D.29, 'Decreto del sacro Concilio di Trento, da publicarsi dalli Curati in lingua volgare almeno nel principio del'Aduento, & Quaresima per la reformatione de matrimoni, & altri tempi secondo il bisogno, per leuare molti abusi intorno ad essi', in *Constitvtiones synodales ecclesiae venvsinae editae, et promvlgatae in Synodo Dioecesana habita Venusij die XVIj. Septemb. Quae fuit Dominica tertia. Anno MDLXXXIX* (Rome, 1591).

[32] Perugia, Biblioteca Comunale, ANT Misc. I.C 56 (10), in *Decreto del Sacro Concilio di Trento fatto adi 11. Di Nouembre 1563 & da publicarsi ogn'anno da'Parochiani dentro & fuora della Città, nella Festa della Circoncisione del Signore, che è il primo dell'anno, & del mese di Genaro. Tradotto di latino in volgare per ordine di Monsignor Reuerendissimo Vescouo dal detto Concilio, nella Sess. 24. Cap. I. de refor. Matrimonio, Sommario di alcune bolle de' sommi pontefici, et decreti de' sacri Canoni, & del Concilio di Trento. Fatti volgari per publicarsi da' parochiani ogn'anno nelle loro Chiese. Di commissione del molto illustre & reuerendissimo monsignore Giulio Cesare Salicini vescouo di Rimini* (Rimini, 1593).

[33] San Sepolcro, Biblioteca Comunale, FA.G.4.272, 'Decreto del S. Concilio di Trento sulla riforma del matrimonio, nella sessione XIIII. Il capitolo primo tradotto volgare per commodità dei Parochi', in *Constitutiones et decreta aedita in synodo diaecesana Auximana. Anno post Christum natum 1593* (Perugia, 1594).

punishes severely as he sees fit a parish priest and any other minister who, with few witnesses, intercedes in such a contract [wedlock], also any witnesses doing so without a minister or other clergyman, along with the contractors themselves.'[34] However, in the memorandum of bulls in Italian addressed to Alessandria's clergy (1610), punishment was instead reserved for the couple and their witnesses, whilst priests were not mentioned: 'At the pleasure of his most reverend bishop, severe punishment shall be reserved for witnesses present at a wedding ceremony which seeks to contract a marriage contrary to the above procedure, as well as for those who have sought to enter into such a bond.'[35]

Although the Council of Trent entrusted the episcopate with the task of curbing ecclesiastical abuses, within a few years of its conclusion the need to protect the clergy's good name was being prioritized over restraining offences committed by its members. In their role as local executors of decisions taken centrally, bishops increasingly approached such offences with a degree of circumspection and confidentiality, as recommended by the popes, whose main interest lay in preserving the clergy's privilege to be tried before ecclesiastical courts only.[36]

Similarly, some translations of chapter 8 reveal changes regarding the role of the secular authorities in relation to concubinage. The original reads:

> As for those women, wed or unwed, who live openly with adulterers or in concubinage: if, upon having been thrice admonished, they do not then obey, they shall be punished severely by the Ordinaries in office at that place, even without request from another, according to their guilt, and be banished from the town or from the diocese, if this be thought fitting by the Ordinaries, who may, if need be, call upon the secular authorities for assistance.[37]

However, the edict on marriage discipline issued by the bishop of Lucca, Alessandro Guidiccioni, in which all the decrees on marriage reform are translated, omits any reference to the secular arm in the relevant section:

[34] *COD*, 756.

[35] Turin, Biblioteca Reale, C.23.38, *Libro delle bolle apostoliche. Editti, decreti, lettere pastorali, & altri ordini. Che si deuono publicare da ciascuno paroco, frà l'anno* (Alessandria, 1610).

[36] Mancino and Romeo, *Clero criminale*.

[37] *COD*, 759.

> Similarly [it is] command[ed] that measures be taken against women, whether wed or unwed, who live openly with adulterers or in concubinage. In addition to other chastisements, and having been admonished three times by the Ordinary, they shall be banished from those localities and dioceses as deemed fitting.[38]

The original document references secular authorities in three different sections: chapter 7, on vagabonds who remarry, chapter 8, and chapter 9, prohibiting secular authorities from forcing people into arranged marriages. In the edict of Bishop de'Buoi of Camerino, proclaimed on 12 December 1584, which offers a *summa* of the council's dispositions on marriage, the secular authorities simply disappear: chapters 8 and 9 are not translated at all, and in chapter 7 there is no mention of them. The original reads:

> Many there are, who wander from place to place without fixed abode. Being bad by nature, having deserted their first wife, they take another, or even many in different places, while the former still lives. The Holy Synod intends to remedy this evil and paternally admonishes all those whose duty it is not to admit this type of vagabond too easily into a bond of marriage. And it calls also upon the secular authorities to repress them with severity.[39]

The version proclaimed by Bishop de'Buoi runs:

> That neither a wedding nor even the publication of the banns for a marriage to be celebrated between foreigners from another diocese, or between vagabonds, must take place without our permission in writing. The curate shall first diligently collect information and provide it to us prior to officiating such wedding.[40]

At the Council of Trent the Church had staked its claim to exclusive power over marriages, in direct – and sometimes bitter – opposition to the civil powers. By focusing the attention of the faithful solely on ecclesiastical precepts, the Church authorities presented themselves as having sole responsibility for punishing offenders in this area, thereby removing from most people's minds any idea that the secular authorities might exercise jurisdiction.

[38] Lucca, Archivio Storico Diocesano, Atti del Clero, Sinodi, Decreti, editti episcopali Bolle per decime et altre materie, fols 40^r–42^r, 'A qualcunque persona', 9 September 1565.
[39] *COD*, 758.
[40] Camerino, Archivio Storico Diocesano, Edicta diversa, busta 1551–1559.

Confirmation of this approach is also provided by the translations of papal bulls. Following the dispositions of the Council of Trent and of his predecessor Pius V, Pope Gregory XIV in *Sicut Antiquus*, dated 1 March 1590 and published in Latin in Rome by Blado in 1591, prohibited the granting of dispensations in the first and second degrees of consanguinity or affinity. The order to translate this prohibition into the vernacular came directly from the pope:

> To ensure that our proposal be enacted, we order and command all ordinaries appointed to each province and realm throughout Christendom to publish these letters and their summaries forthwith and to expound them in sermons in the common tongue, and to affix them to the doors of their own churches, and in each cathedral and parish church of their towns and dioceses.[41]

A handwritten edition of the text was issued by Alessandro de Medici, archbishop of Florence.[42] The summary from Pienza was also in manuscript,[43] while that from Mantua was printed by the Osanna press.[44] All three summaries omit any reference to civil law. Thus, whilst the original mentions that *sacri canones, sed leges etiam civiles* ('sacred canons, but also civil laws') may cause a request for a dispensation to be rejected, in the vernacular version from Pienza the pope is presented as mentioning only 'punishments and censures prescribed by our sacred canons and councils against incestuous contractors'. In the Pienza and Mantua versions, the reference to the past concession of dispensations *principum intercessione* ('by intercession of sovereign power') is also omitted. Similarly, the vernacular translation of the bull of Sixtus V, *Ad Compescendam*. printed in Rome by

[41] Siena, Biblioteca Diocesana, vol. misc., A 044/03, 'Bulla s.mi D.N. Gregorii papae XIIII de dispensationibus Matrimonialibus, in secundo, vel in primo & secundo consanguinitatis seu affinitatis gradibus', 1 March 1590.

[42] Florence, Archivio della Curia Arcivescovile, Filze di cancelleria, busta 1589–1592, fols 274^{r}–276^{r}, 'La Bolla sopra il non concedere dispense in alcuni gradi principalmente prohibiti; et innovatione delle pene contro delli Incestuosi et abominevoli congiungimenti della Santità di N.S. Gregorio XIIII', 30 May 1591.

[43] Pienza, Archivio Diocesano, Costituzioni più necessarie alle Cure ecclesiastiche di vari Pontefici, Giubilei, Indulgenze, editti e decreti dal 1564 al 1699, busta 273\I, 'Sommario della bolla di N.Sig.re Gregorio XIIII proibente concedersi dispense nel primo e secondo grado tanto di consanguinei, quanto d'affinità', 1 March 1590.

[44] Mantua, Archivio di Stato, Archivio Gonzaga – Miscellaneo di religione e disciplina ecclesiastica, busta 3357, pezzo 25, 'Sommario della bolla di N.S. Papa Gregorio XIII sopra il non conceder le dispense nelli primo; e secondo gradi di consanguinità, & affinità, & il douer castigare gli incestuosi', 1 March 1591.

Antonio Blado in 1586,[45] which concerned the illegality of adultery and divorce and was directed to the lay inhabitants of the city of Rome, contains no reference to the fact that Roman judges had the right of appeal to the secular arm for punishment when appropriate.[46] The pivotal role of the Church in such cases was once again confirmed.

Constraining the Power of the Inquisition

A further example is offered by the bull *Effraenatam* issued by Sixtus V, promulgated on 29 October and published on 16 November 1588. This expressed a policy aimed at the control of sexuality and the promotion of the 'traditional family'.[47] Here the translation into Italian offers evidence of the episcopate's attempts to control the power of the Inquisition, as well as the desire to prevent scandal and social unrest. Unlike *Ad Compescendam*, *Effraenatam* applied to the whole Church. It reserved to the pope the right to excommunicate *ueros homicidas* ('true assassins') responsible for abortion.[48] This represented a significant change in policy: from the 1570s and 1580s bishops had sought to gain control of abortion by categorizing it amongst reserved cases.[49] Vincenzo Lavenia has argued that,

[45] Rome, Biblioteca Nazionale, Bandi e Bolle pontificie del XVI secolo, 68.13.E.2.21, 'Sommario della bolla di nostro signore Sisto Papa Qvinto Circa gl'Adulterii publici, stupri, lenocinii & separatione de Mariti, & Moglie in Roma' (Rome, 1586).

[46] 'Et nihilominus mandamus vniuersis & singulis dictae Vrbis Iudicibus ordinarijs … contra criminosos, ac delinquentes praedictos vtriusque sexus inquirant & procedant, ac in eos iuxta praemissa culpabiles repertos, praedictis poenis, vtsupra dispositum est, animaduertant: contumaces, rebelles, & inobedientes, eisq; auxilium … vel fauorem, quomodolibet praestantes, per opportuna iuris & facti remedia appellatione postposita compescendo, inuocato etiam ac adhibito, si opus fuerit, auxilio brachij secularis' ('However, we depend on the justice system of Rome for the investigation of criminals and felons of both sexes, and the conviction of culprits according to the letter of the law; we also depend on it for suitable remedies [no right of appeal], and if need be, the control of law-breakers, dissenters, rebels and their allies, by the ordinary police authorities of the secular arm'; my translation): Siena, Biblioteca Diocesana, vol. misc., FCMSS a 044/03, 'De temeraria Tori separatione, ac publicis adulteriis, stupris, et lenociniis in quibusdam casibus severius (in Alma Urbe) punienda'.

[47] *BR*, 9: 39–42.

[48] Adriano Prosperi, *Dare l'anima. Storia di un infanticidio* (Torino, 2005), 246.

[49] John Christopoulos, 'Abortion and the Confessional in Counter-Reformation Italy', *RQ* 65 (2012), 443–84, at 459. This is shown by Wietse de Boer, *The Conquest of the Soul: Confession, Discipline, and Public Order in Counter-Reformation Milan* (Leiden, 2001), 217: 'bishops or the Pope could "reserve" the absolution of select cases to themselves or to a deputy, requiring such cases to be referred to them for resolution'. On confidential

if we consider papal reserve in cases of abortion together with the other measures on mixed issues taken by the pope in order to increase the jurisdiction of the Holy Office,[50] 'the suspicion emerges that the intervention was in part intended to include the matter of abortion among those pertaining to the Inquisition'.[51] Moreover, the Latin text includes the possibility of secret denunciation, formulated in a way that frightened people because of its implicit reference to inquisitorial procedures.[52] This seems to have been an aspect that some bishops tried to mitigate through their translations.

Against the comment of Christopoulos that 'to the best of my knowledge, Contra procurantes abortum has never been translated into Italian',[53] there are at least two documented vernacular translations of the *Effrenatam*. One was published in Ancona as a broadsheet by the printer Francesco Salvioni in 1590,[54] while another manuscript translation is preserved in Pienza among the papers of Bishop Francesco Piccolomini.[55] While the Pienza version does not differ significantly from the Latin original, the Ancona translation omits the secret denunciation,[56] a measure which would have reinforced inquisitorial power and had the potential to bring to light situations that could cause scandal and social disruption. Here

---

episcopal cases, which vary from one diocese to another and of which typical examples are abortion, adultery and concubinage, see Elena Brambilla, 'Casi riservati', in Adriano Prosperi, Vincenzo Lavenia and John Tedeschi, eds, *Dizionario storico dell'Inquisizione*, 4 vols (Pisa, 2010), 1: 290–1.

[50] In this case witchcraft: Giovanni Romeo, *Inquisitori, esorcisti e streghe nell'Italia della Controriforma* (Florence, 1990), 95–6.

[51] Vincenzo Lavenia, '"D'animal fante". Teologia, medicina legale e identità umana. Secoli XVI–XVII', in Adriano Prosperi, ed., *Salvezza delle anime e disciplina dei corpi. Un seminario sulla storia del battesimo* (Pisa, 2006), 483–526, at 496 (my translation).

[52] 'Vt in his delictis quae vt plurimo in occulto perpetrantvr, contra quosqumque non solum per accusationem & declarationem, verum etiam per inquisitionem ac simplicem denunciationem procedant': *BR*, 9: 41.

[53] Christopoulos, 'Abortion', 469.

[54] Venice, Biblioteca Marciana, vol. misc., C.065C.098.029, 'Sommario di tre Bolle de Sommi Pontefici, cioè di Pio V sopra i censi, di Sisto V sopra gl' aborti, et l'altra de gli patti reprobati nelle Compagnie, che saluano il Capitale, e ìn nome di guadagno, pongono certa risposta'.

[55] Pienza, Archivio Diocesano, Editti e lettere circolari di mons. Alessandro Piccolomini dal dì 4 agosto 1564 al dì 22 maggio 1575 e di mons. Francesco Maria Piccolomini dal dì 16 ago. 1575 al dì 13 dicembre 1588, busta 26\I, fols 270^{r}–271^{r}, 'Sommario della Bolla di N.S. Sixto Quinto intorno al procurare di fare sconciare, o, sperdere le Donne grauide, o, operare che non concepischino'.

[56] 'Non solum per accusationem et declarationem, verum etiam per inquisitionem ac simplicem denunciationem procedant': *BR*, 9: 41.

too, the vernacular translation offers the opportunity to explore the contradictions 'between theological pronouncements and the socio-political realities of ecclesiastical administration', but it also shows the 'inconsistent responses among Counter-Reformation ecclesiastical authorities'.[57]

Identity between 'Centre' and 'Periphery'[58]

Regardless of the bull *Effraenatam* (indeed in direct contravention of it), many documents from bishops who desired to absolve cases of abortion can be found amongst the papers of the Congregation of Bishops and Regulars examined by Vincenzo Lavenia.[59] In the *Sedes Apostolica* (1591), Sixtus V's successor Gregory XIV revoked his predecessor's decision and returned the reserve for the sin of abortion to bishops.[60] It was not chance that the document was issued after consultation with the Congregation of Bishops and Regulars.[61] Furthermore, it was no coincidence that it was speedily translated at the bishops' behest. Thus in Bologna, in the same year as the enactment of *Sedes Apostolica*, at the time of Cardinal Archbishop Gabriele Paleotti, a translation was already circulating both as a manuscript[62] and in print.[63] Multiple copies of both editions exist, reflecting the importance that was attached to the document's dissemination.[64] That the Bologna translation does not show any significant differences from the Latin text does not come as a surprise, given the restitution

[57] Christopoulos, 'Abortion', 446.

[58] Simon Ditchfield, 'Tridentine Catholicism', in Alexandra Bamji, Geert Janssen and Mary Laven, eds, *The Ashgate Research Companion to the Counter-Reformation* (Aldershot, 2013), 15–31.

[59] Lavenia, 'D'animal fante', 497.

[60] *BR*, 9: 430–1.

[61] 'Habita super hoc eum venerabilibus fratribus nostris S.R.E. cardinalibus, super negociis et consultationibus episcoporum deputatis, matura deliberatione': ibid. 431.

[62] Rome, Archivio di Stato, Collezione di Bandi, busta 8, pezzo 31, in *Sommario della Constitutione di N. S. Papa Gregorio XIIII Moderatiua della Bolla della felice mem. di Papa Sisto V. to Contro quelli che in qual si uoglia modo danno opera al misfatto dell'Aborto* (Bologna, 1591).

[63] Bologna, Biblioteca Comunale dell'Archiginnasio, vol. misc, 16.Q.V.39, pezzo 09, in *Sommario della constitvtione di N.S. Papa Gregorio XIIII. Moderatiua della Bolla della felice mem. di Papa Sisto V. Contro quegli, che in qual si uoglia modo danno opera al misfatto dello aborto* (Bologna, 1591).

[64] Modena, Archivio di Stato, Documenti di Stati e Città, busta 106, ser. XVIII, fasc. 2, in *Sommario della constitutione di N.S. Papa Gregorio XIIII Moderatiua della Bolla della fe.mem. di Papa Sisto U contra quelli, che in qualsiuoglia modo danno opera al misfatto dell'aborto* (Bologna, 1591).

of episcopal prerogatives which resulted from the Gregorian bull. The only difference was the omission of one section in which it was argued that the severity of Sixtus's original measure *plurimorum sacrilegiorum gravissimorumque peccatorum et scelerum occasionem dedisse* ('causes many sacrileges, and serious sins and evils to happen'). This omission is probably explained by an unwillingness to criticize a pope in a text written in the vernacular.

Conclusion

The circulation of Roman directives to the localities was not only a matter of language: softened or sharpened through apparently conscious omissions; the translations altered some aspects of the Latin texts. These changes are present in both printed and manuscript versions, whose inherently 'volatile' nature suited them to this project.[65] Thus the omission of the *secretam denunciationem* from translations of the bull *Cum primum,* particularly in territories such as Modena where the Inquisition had established its own court, witnesses to attempts by the episcopate to slow the Inquisition's advance. Similarly, in the translation of the bull *Effraenatam* made for the Marches area (Ancona), secret denunciation would have helped highlight the existence of abortion, which could potentially underlie social tensions. Its absence in the translation testifies to a desire among ecclesiastical authorities to avoid fanning the flames of scandal. In translating the Council's decrees on marriage, the role of the secular authorities was omitted, indicating the clergy's desire to protect their powers over offences that could cross into civil jurisdiction. Finally, the choice made to omit from the translations of the Council decrees on marriage any mention of punishments for neglectful clergymen reveals a desire to safeguard the standing of the clergy. Analysis of the correspondence between the ordinaries and Rome, kept in diocesan archives, reveals no will at the centre to examine translations undertaken locally. Such translations thus became 'laboratories of compromise' between rules and their reception at a local level, reflecting the desire for independence of the post-Tridentine bishops.

[65] On the relationships between print and manuscript in early modern Italy, see Federico Barbierato, *Nella stanza dei circoli: Clavicula Salomonis e libri di magia a Venezia nei secoli XVII e XVIII* (Florence, 2002); Filippo de Vivo, *Information and Communication in Venice: Rethinking Early Modern Politics* (Oxford, 2007).

Transmitting and Translating the Excommunication of Elizabeth I

Aislinn Muller*
Cambridge University

In 1570 Pope Pius V issued the bull Regnans in Excelsis, *which excommunicated Queen Elizabeth I, deprived her of her right to rule, and released her subjects from obedience to her. This article attempts to trace the transmission of* Regnans in Excelsis *in the English realms during Elizabeth's reign, considering where possible the bull's publication and dispatch to different courts in Europe. It assesses efforts to distribute both publications of the excommunication, in 1570 and 1580, and what the continuity of these efforts suggests about the bull's reception amongst Elizabeth's subjects. By tracing literal translations of the bull and persistent attempts to smuggle it into the English realm, it also argues that Elizabeth's excommunication was of greater importance to her subjects than has previously been supposed.*

This article assesses physical and linguistic translations of the excommunication proclaimed against Queen Elizabeth by Pope Pius V in 1570. Although the papal bull, entitled *Regnans in Excelsis*, declared Elizabeth deposed and released her subjects from their obedience, it has received relatively little attention in histories of the English Reformation and post-Reformation English Catholicism. Until recently, many historians dismissed the bull as being of minor significance, pointing to its failure to inspire much resistance or reaction. Translations of Elizabeth's excommunication, whether physical or linguistic, have similarly received little attention.[1] Julian Lock's thesis on the origins of Queen Elizabeth's excommunication provides

* Girton College, Huntingdon Rd, Cambridge, CB3 0JG. E-mail: apm61@cam.ac.uk.

[1] No evidence appears in the works of Bossy and Haigh, for instance: Christopher Haigh, 'The Continuity of Catholicism in the English Reformation', in idem, ed., *The English Reformation Revised* (Cambridge, 1987); John Bossy, *The English Catholic Community 1570–1850* (London, 1979). Other works by Clancy, Morey and Holmes discuss the bull but similarly offer no evidence for its circulation and distribution: Thomas Clancy, *Papist Pamphleteers* (Chicago, IL, 1964); Adrian Morey, *The Catholic Subjects of Elizabeth I* (London, 1978); Peter Holmes, *Resistance and Compromise: The Political Thought of Elizabethan Catholics* (Cambridge, 1982).

Studies in Church History 53 (2017) 210–222
doi: 10.1017/stc.2016.13

valuable insight into the bull's effects on Protestant thought and writing, but offers little information on the transmission of the bull itself.[2] Stefania Tutino has demonstrated the excommunication's centrality to Nicholas Sander's resistance theories, while Thomas McCoog acknowledged the potential for the bull's renewal in 1580 to have significant implications for religious resistance.[3] Michael Questier's studies of English Catholic politics have similarly reshaped understandings of the nature of resistance during Elizabeth's reign.[4] Recent scholarship on processes of translation in English Catholicism also provides useful models for this article. Alexandra Walsham's work on the translation of continental Catholic reforms into English contexts and the engagement of post-Reformation English Catholicism with print and the vernacular shows the extent to which English Catholics engaged in both physical and linguistic translations of their faith.[5] Walsham's assessment of the importance of printing for refutation in religious disputes also highlights the potential dangers of reprinting passages of Catholic texts, and provides a framework for considering how translations of the bull in anti-Catholic polemics may have increased awareness of the queen's excommunication in unforeseen ways.[6] Further studies by Arthur Marotti, Nancy Pollard Brown and Earle Havens explore the compilation and circulation of illicit devotional and polemical literature and thus illuminate the routes by which the bull may have been physically translated across Europe and

[2] Julian Lock, '"Strange Usurped Potentates": Elizabeth I, the Papacy, and the Indian Summer of the Medieval Deposing Power' (DPhil thesis, University of Oxford, 1992).

[3] Stefania Tutino, *Law and Conscience: Catholicism in Early Modern England* (Aldershot, 2007); Thomas McCoog, *The Society of Jesus in Ireland, Scotland, and England, 1549–1588* (Leiden, 1996), 140–1.

[4] Michael Questier, 'Conformity, Catholicism, and the Law,' in Peter Lake and Michael Questier, eds, *Conformity and Orthodoxy in the English Church, 1560–1660* (Woodbridge, 2000), 237–61; idem, *Catholicism and Community in Early Modern England: Politics, Aristocratic Patronage and Religion* (Cambridge, 2006).

[5] Alexandra Walsham, 'Translating Trent? English Catholicism and the Counter Reformation', *Historical Research* 78 (2005), 288–310; eadem, '"Domme Preachers?" Post-Reformation English Catholicism and the Culture of Print', *P&P* 168 (2000), 72–123; eadem, 'Unclasping the Book? Post-Reformation English Catholicism and the Vernacular Bible', *JBS* 42 (2003), 141–66.

[6] Alexandra Walsham, '"The Spider and the Bee": The Perils of Printing for Refutation in Tudor England', in John King, ed., *Tudor Books and Readers: Materiality and the Construction of Meaning* (Cambridge, 2010), 163–90.

England, even though *Regnans in Excelsis* receives no direct attention in their analyses.[7]

This article considers endeavours to translate the excommunication physically into England and efforts to translate the bull from Latin into English. In particular, it explores the role of Jesuit and seminary priests in bringing the bull to England, especially after the renewal of Elizabeth's excommunication in 1580. Additionally, the article considers translations of the bull into English by both Catholics and Protestants. It assesses how translations appearing in anti-Catholic polemics may have opened these works to appropriation by those who were more interested in learning about the implications of the bull for Elizabeth and her subjects than they were in the refutations that accompanied it.

Pius V pronounced Elizabeth's excommunication in February 1570 after receiving word of the Northern Rebellion in England, which had begun in November 1569, hoping that the sentence would inspire more people to join the resistance.[8] Although the pope subsequently learned that the rebellion had been put down, the distribution of the bull of excommunication still proceeded.[9] Bringing copies of Elizabeth's excommunication into England required a network of co-operative rulers and agents on the continent. The pope sent printed copies of *Regnans in Excelsis* to the nuncios in the courts of Europe, who presented them to the resident rulers and governors for further propagation. Pius V took special care that coastal countries with commercial ties to England should receive some of the first copies, believing that this strategy would make it possible for news of the bull to reach England more quickly. Thus, copies were sent to the duke of Alba for distribution and reproduction in the Netherlands in

[7] Arthur Marotti, *Religious Ideology and Cultural Fantasy: Catholic and Anti-Catholic Discourses in Early Modern England* (Notre Dame, IN, 2005); Nancy Pollard Brown, 'Paper Chase: The Dissemination of Catholic Texts in Early Modern England', *English Manuscript Studies* 1 (1989), 120–43; Earle Havens, 'Notes from a Literary Underground: Recusant Catholics, Jesuit Priests, and Scribal Publication in England', *Papers of the Bibliographical Society of America* 99 (2005), 505–38.

[8] Krista Kesselring, *The Northern Rebellion of 1569: Faith, Politics, and Protest in Elizabethan England* (Basingstoke, 2007), 56–8.

[9] The rebellion in England had been subdued by crown forces by the end of December: Kesselring, *Northern Rebellion*, 88–90. News of the rebellion had been sent to Rome from early December; Pius V wrote to the duke of Alba about his concern for the rebels in early February: J. M. Hicks, ed., *Calendar of State Papers Relating to English Affairs Preserved Principally at Rome in the Vatican Archives and Library*, 1, *Elizabeth 1558–1571* [Hereafter: *CSP Rome*] (London, 1916), 315–16, 324–5.

March 1569, with instructions to circulate them particularly in those ports 'most frequented by English traders, that the news may the more readily reach England'.[10] A month later the pope sent copies to Poland, commanding that the bulls be transported to Danzig and other coastal towns that traded with English merchants, and that permission from King Sigismund II be sought to print more.[11] Advertisements announcing the excommunication were also circulated in Rome outlining the important points in *Regnans in Excelsis*: that the pope had declared Elizabeth an illegitimate heretic, released her subjects from obedience to her and granted all Christian princes permission to invade England.[12]

Nevertheless, it took time for copies to reach England; the exact point at which the bull arrived is uncertain. Mary Queen of Scots admitted to having received a copy in March 1570, though she claimed that she burned the bull after reading it.[13] The excommunication first caught the attention of the English public on 25 May 1570, when John Felton affixed a copy obtained from the Spanish ambassador Guerau de Spes to the door of the bishop of London's palace.[14] The ambassador had apparently received the bull from Roberto Ridolfi, who had brought six copies into England. Ridolfi delivered three of these copies to de Spes, the French ambassador Bertrand de Salignac Fénelon, and to John Leslie, the Scottish bishop of Ross who was in England as a supporter of Mary Queen of Scots; the fates of the other three are unknown.[15] In Ireland, the earl of Ormond blamed James Fitzgerald for posting the bull at the gates of Limerick in June 1571.[16] The bull did not appear in Scotland, however, until June 1573, when the English ambassador noted its publication by a man he called 'Andros, of Aberdeen'.[17] Back in England, 'a coppie of a bull maide

[10] Ibid. 332.

[11] Ibid. 335.

[12] Ibid. 336.

[13] Kew, TNA, State Papers (SP) 53/8, fol. 112, 'Matters wherewith the Queen of Scots may be charged', 11 June 1572.

[14] TNA, Privy Council Registers (PC) 2/10, fol. 11, meeting at Oatlands, 25 June 1570. See also *ODNB*, *s.n.* 'Felton, John (d. 1570)', online at: <http://www.oxforddnb.com/view/article/9272>, accessed 7 November 2014.

[15] Historical Manuscripts Commission, *Calendar of Manuscripts of the Most Honourable Marquis of Salisbury, preserved at Hatfield House*, part 2 (London, 1888), 555, examination of the bishop of Ross, 1571.

[16] TNA, SP 63/32, fol. 169, Thomas Butler, earl of Ormond to Sir Henry Sidney, 11 June 1571.

[17] TNA, SP 52/25, fol. 149, Sir Henry Killigrew to Sir Thomas Smith, 13 June 1573.

against hir Maiestie and the state of this Realme' was discovered in Tonbridge in April 1577.[18] Another was sent by a Monsieur Berny to Sir Amias Paulet in February 1578 during his tenure as governor of Jersey. Berny had apparently obtained the bull from a bishop (whom he did not name) and an associate named Bernaldin, who had been travelling through Spain and *plusieurs autres pais* ('many other countries') promulgating its message.[19]

The physical translation of Elizabeth's excommunication involved the efforts of agents both on the continent and within the British Isles. While the papacy used papal bulls to transmit Elizabeth's sentence across Europe, news reports and advertisements also helped to disseminate this information. Indeed, these reports may have been a more efficient means of ensuring that news of the queen's sentence reached England, because they were less conspicuous than official papal bulls and briefs and therefore less susceptible to seizure in English ports. Yet Catholics continued to transport copies of *Regnans in Excelsis* into and within England throughout the 1570s, along with other papal bulls such as the bull of jubilee proclaimed in 1575 by Gregory XIII.[20] A copy of this latter bull was confiscated from the seminary priest Cuthbert Mayne when he was arrested in 1577.[21] These processes indicate a sustained effort to promulgate news of Elizabeth's excommunication and other papal decrees to the English people, and perhaps also reveal that a demand for information from the papacy persisted in England. Little other evidence survives to indicate the extent of interest in the excommunication amongst the English people, though this does not necessarily suggest a lack of concern. The bull was a particularly dangerous item to have in one's possession, and it would be understandable if most people who came across copies of the excommunication destroyed them to avoid prosecution. If Elizabeth's subjects desired to learn about her excommunication, it would have been unwise for them to retain evidence of such a wish.

In 1580 Gregory XIII renewed the excommunication against Elizabeth and efforts to translate copies from Rome into England began

[18] Lewes, The Keep, Rye 7/47/15/15, Mayor of Rye to Lord Cobham, 23 April 1577.
[19] TNA, SP 78/2, fol. 12, letter from 'Monsieur Berny', 10 February 1578.
[20] Anthony Wright, *The Early Modern Papacy: From the Council of Trent to the French Revolution* (London, 2013), 44.
[21] See Anne Dillon, *The Construction of Martyrdom in Early Modern England, 1558–1603* (Farnham, 2002), 1–3; Richard Challoner, *Memoirs of Missionary Priests, and other Catholics of Both Sexes that have suffered Death in England on Religious Accounts from the Year 1577 to 1684*, 2 vols in 1 (Philadelphia, PA, 1839), 1: 23–7.

anew. The pope also clarified to whom the excommunication applied, explaining that the sentence of Pius V bound Elizabeth and her Protestant subjects, but that for the time being it exempted professed English Catholics.[22] The renewal also coincided with the beginning of the Jesuit mission in England. Gregory employed members of the mission to explain his amendment of the bull, instructing them that the excommunication and anathema proclaimed in the bull did not apply to English Catholics while circumstances in England made it impossible to depose Elizabeth and restore Catholicism. However, if circumstances changed to favour this enterprise, any Catholics who did not participate would also find themselves excommunicated.[23] In February 1580, Cardinal Alexander Farnese commissioned a set of copies to distribute to the ambassadors in Rome.[24] The revival of the Holy League between Spain and the papacy in 1580 reiterated 'That Queen Elizabeth be declared an usurper and incapable to reign' and required 'That the Bull of excommunication which Pius V of happy memory issued against the said Queen be published in the courts of all Christian princes'.[25] Gregory's renewal of the excommunication also coincided with the rekindling of the second Desmond Rebellion in Ireland, led by James Fitzgerald, the earl of Desmond's cousin. This rebellion assisted in the transmission of the renewed excommunication to Ireland and England: an informant in the earl of Desmond's camp in 1579 noted that John Fitzgerald, the earl's brother, 'hathe a Bull from the Pope to maintaine … excommunicacion for all that depend vpon the Queen'.[26] Desmond's declaration to the people of Ireland used the excommunication to justify his insurrection, announcing that Gregory XIII had renewed the sentence against Elizabeth, that he had sanctioned holy war in Ireland, and that he had provided the Fitzgeralds with military and financial assistance to instigate her deposition.[27] In March 1581, Elizabeth summoned the Spanish and French ambassadors to complain that copies of the excommunication had been sent into Ireland and to protest at

22 McCoog, *Society of Jesus*, 140–5.

23 Ibid. 140–1.

24 TNA, SP 78/4A, Lord Cobham to Sir Francis Walsingham, 29 February 1580.

25 Rawdon Brown and G. Cavendish Bentinck, *Calendar of State Papers Relating to English Affairs in the Archives of Venice, and in other Libraries of Northern Italy*, 7: *1558–1580* (London, 1890), 651.

26 TNA, SP 63/68, fol. 8, Mr Herbert's notes on the earl of Desmond's camp, 1579.

27 London, LPL, Carew MS 607, fol. 35, declaration of James Fitzgerald to the people of Ireland. George Carew served as an army captain in Ireland from 1579–80.

their sovereigns' possible involvement.[28] The rebellion was eventually defeated by crown forces sent into Ireland by the queen under the command of Lord Arthur Grey; however, the use of Elizabeth's excommunication by the rebellion's leaders to justify their resistance has been called an 'unprecedented ideological pitch' by Hiram Morgan in his studies of sixteenth-century Ireland.[29]

The renewal of Elizabeth's excommunication also inspired attempts to translate the decree from Latin into English.[30] James Fitzgerald brought copies of the renewed excommunication to Ireland from Rome, one of which survives at Lambeth Palace Library, the only remaining English translation of *Regnans in Excelsis* in manuscript form.[31] Its target audience is unclear: possibly Fitzgerald hoped to recruit more of the Old English in Ireland to his cause using a translation of the bull, or perhaps he hoped a few copies might be conveyed into England through Wales. Complaints about a lack of security in the western English and Welsh coastal towns occur frequently in government correspondence.[32] Smugglers ferried timber and corn between England and Ireland with impunity despite the Privy Council's efforts to enforce customs regulations, and it is plausible that copies of the excommunication could have arrived via these routes.[33] The translation of the bull into English certainly indicates a desire to inform as many people as possible about the renewed decree, and suggests that the Irish leaders hoped that there might be a demand amongst the laity for papal bulls in the vernacular, which could be more easily understood. The production of a vernacular translation after the excommunication's renewal would have ensured both wider accessibility to the bull and more effective communication of its contents.

[28] Martin A. S. Hume, ed., *Calendar of Letters and State Papers Relating to English Affairs in the Archives of Simancas, 1580–1586*, vol. 3 (London, 1896), 20.

[29] Hiram Morgan, 'Faith and Fatherland in Sixteenth-Century Ireland', *History Ireland* 3/2 (1995), 13–20, at 16. On the second Desmond Rebellion and the English response, see Anthony McCormack, 'The Social and Economic Consequences of the Desmond Rebellion of 1579–83', *Irish Historical Studies* 34 (2004), 1–15.

[30] The first publication of *Regnans in Excelsis* was not translated fully into English, although parts of it appeared in Protestant polemics.

[31] LPL, Carew MS 607, fol. 37b.

[32] TNA, PC 2/9, fol. 74, meeting at St James, 16 September 1564; TNA, SP 12/103, fol. 124, John Vaughan to Lord Burghley 6 June 1575; SP 63/112, fol. 13, Sir Richard Bingham to Sir Francis Walsingham, 14 October 1584.

[33] London, BL, Lansdowne MS 40/20, fol. 47, report of Thomas Egerton and Thomas Fenshaw on customs abuse in Chester, 1583.

Jesuits and seminary priests also participated in transporting and promulgating the excommunication in England after 1580. In January Lord Cobham, the ambassador in France, reported to Sir Francis Walsingham that:

> ther was newlie confirmed and secretlie prynted the Bull and iudgement which Pope Pius Quintus gave and pronounced against the Queenes Majestie … one Father Thomas Darbysher a Iesuite, who whas procured to seke this … came hither xx dayes paste and is presentlie hear in towne pretendinge by way of Flanders to go secretly into England.[34]

Christopher Byers, a seminary priest who arrived in England in 1580, later recalled a colleague who was at that time 'an earnest perswader' of the queen's murder, and had brought a copy of the bull into England 'to that ende'.[35] There is certainly evidence to suggest that English Catholic priests believed the excommunication to be legitimate and that resisting the queen was therefore lawful. In 1581 a priest named John Paine claimed that it would be lawful to kill the queen because 'there were divers matters from the Pope published agaynst her'.[36] In 1582 William Allen expressed relief to the rector of the English College at Rome when Henry Orton and the Jesuit James Bosgrave publicly rejected accusations that they had 'treated the bull lightly, or sought to nullify it' when they were interrogated by the Elizabethan authorities. When Robert Persons wrote to Gregory XIII and King Philip II in May 1582 about the feasibility of invading England, he emphasized that the army should bring a press to print and distribute copies of the excommunication against the queen. Persons further advised that Gregory should issue a bull of excommunication in his own name, declaring that Elizabeth was no longer fit to be queen or to be obeyed in any capacity.[37] The interrogations and martyrdom accounts of numerous priests indicate how the excommunication influenced their interactions with Elizabethan officials. When questioned about the papal bull they often refused to answer,

[34] TNA, SP 78/4A, fol. 17, Lord Cobham to Sir Francis Walsingham, 20 February 1580.

[35] TNA, SP 53/19, fol. 109, confession of Christopher Byers, 21 September 1586.

[36] BL, Lansdowne MS 33, fols 147–147a, 143a–144 respectively, letters to the earl of Leicester, 1581.

[37] Leo Hicks, ed., *Letters and Memorials of Father Robert Persons* (London, 1942), 164–5.

as was the case with Edward Shelley and Ralph Emerson in 1585.[38] Some, however, were bolder and affirmed that the queen's excommunication remained in force; this was the approach taken by the Jesuits John Hart and John Gerrard.[39] While some of this evidence indicates the missionary priests' role in physically translating *Regnans in Excelsis* into England, it also shows how Gregory XIII's instructions enabled them to translate the excommunication into the English context and explain it to Elizabeth's subjects. Thus the priests became a force for both physical and linguistic translation of the excommunication, transporting it into the kingdom and promulgating the amended sentence once there.

Efforts to translate the renewed excommunication, both physically into England and into the English language, intensified before the Spanish Armada sailed. In June 1588 William Cecil, Lord Burghley, received 'a copy of a roryng hellish Bull … prynted in Antwerp to the nombre of xiiand [12,000] the contentes wherof I do note to be … the deprivation of hir Maiesty'.[40] Cecil was referring to the *Declaration of the Sentence and Deposition of Elizabeth*, a proclamation printed in English before the armada sailed and attributed to William Allen.[41] The *Declaration* not only affirmed the excommunications pronounced by Pius V and Gregory XIII, but also announced that Sixtus V 'doth *Excommunicate, and depriue* her of all auctority and Princely dignity'.[42] As Cecil observed, thousands of these proclamations were printed in English at Antwerp, one of the main centres of printing in the Spanish Netherlands. This indicates a substantial effort to make vernacular translations of the sentence available to the English people, and suggests that translating the excommunication into and across England was considered an important part of the invasion strategy.[43]

[38] J. H. Pollen, *Unpublished Documents Relating to the English Martyrs* (London, 1908), 26–106. At least ten priests captured in the 1580s used this strategy.
[39] John Gerrard, *Autobiography of an Elizabethan*, transl. Philip Caraman (London, 1951), 98; TNA, SP 12/144, fol. 130, examination of John Hart, 1580.
[40] TNA, SP 12/211, fol. 93, Lord Burghley to Sir Francis Walsingham, 24 June 1588.
[41] A. F. Allison and D. M. Rogers, eds, *The Contemporary Printed Literature of the English Counter-Reformation Between 1558 and 1640*, 2 vols (Aldershot, 1989–94), 2: 10.
[42] *A declaration of the sentence and deposition of Elizabeth, the vsurper and pretensed quene of Englande* (Antwerp, 1588).
[43] Lock posited that many of these proclamations were destroyed after the invasion failed, but quotes no evidence for this suggestion: '"Strange Usurped Potentates"', 351–471.

While copies and translations of *Regnans in Excelsis* probably played a greater role in increasing knowledge of Elizabeth's excommunication than has previously been recognized, people also learned about this in other ways. Indeed, it could be argued that Protestant responses to the bull contributed as much, if not more, to making translations of it available to the queen's subjects. Following the bull's publication in 1570 and 1580, a number of writers produced responses to the excommunication, challenging its validity and questioning the papacy's authority. In some cases, authors included English translations of entire passages of *Regnans in Excelsis*. Alexandra Walsham has suggested that the practice of citing the text against which an author was writing, though common, could prove problematic in religious disputes, because it enabled the reader to evaluate both positions in a debate and potentially to find the author's opponent more convincing.[44] This risk became acute with formal challenges to *Regnans in Excelsis*, which circulated in a kingdom in which many remained uncertain about their religious beliefs.[45] Nonetheless, the authors of these Protestant texts seem to have believed that readers would recognize the superiority of their arguments, grounded in Scripture, when set alongside the audacious claims of the bull, and thus saw little danger in reprinting it in their works. The remainder of this article considers the extent to which translations of *Regnans in Excelsis* in Protestant polemics may have raised awareness of Elizabeth's excommunication.

Shortly after news of her excommunication reached England, leaders of the English Church sought a theologian to compose a response. At the behest of several English bishops, Heinrich Bullinger wrote the *Bullae Papisticae Refutatio*, in which he challenged the legitimacy of the excommunication and the papal deposing power.[46] His treatise was published in Latin in 1571 and translated into English by Arthur Golding in 1572 as *The Confutation of the Popes Bull*. Bullinger opened his *Confutation* with a summary of *Regnans in Excelsis*, for which he borrowed heavily from the decree's original phrasing. Golding retained this summary in his translation, describing how the bull called

[44] Walsham, 'The Spider and the Bee'.

[45] Michael Questier, *Conversion, Politics, and Religion in England, 1580–1625* (Cambridge, 1996), 1–11.

[46] Notably John Jewel, bishop of Salisbury, Richard Cox, bishop of Ely, and John Parkhurst, bishop of Norwich: Hastings Robinson, ed., *Zurich Letters; comprising the Correspondence of several English Bishops and others, with some of the Helvetian Reformers, during the Reign of Queen Elizabeth*, 2 vols (Cambridge, 1846), 1: 221–66.

Elizabeth 'an hereticke, and a fauourer of heretickes' and how 'all and singular the Queenes Nobilitie' were commanded not to obey her laws 'vnder paine of the sayd curse'.[47] The *Confutation* appears to have attracted a wide readership in England, especially in English translation. John Parkhurst, bishop of Norwich, wrote to Bullinger after the English version was published to inform him: 'Your most learned refutation of the pope's bull is in the hands of every one; for it is translated into English, and is printed at London.'[48] One can imagine how Bullinger's text might have been appropriated by those who considered the excommunication and the pope more authoritative than the author who denounced them.[49] However, concrete evidence for the acquisition of Protestant texts by English Catholics in this manner is difficult to find. This may be in part because preserving the passages of Catholic texts from Protestant polemics, either on their own or with annotations expressing disagreement with the Protestant author, might have been incriminating. The suggestion of the English bishops that the Privy Council might not want the *Confutation* published, because 'they would not have the multitude know that any such vile, railing bull had passed from that see' indicates that such appropriation was at least considered a possibility.[50] The fact that the council allowed the publication of the *Confutation* speaks of the esteem with which Bullinger was regarded in England, but it also suggests how threatened the Elizabethan regime felt by the excommunication's potential consequences.[51] For Elizabeth's

[47] Heinrich Bullinger, *A Confutation of the Popes Bull*, transl. Arthur Golding (London, 1572), 1–2.

[48] Robinson, ed., *Zurich Letters*, 1: 266.

[49] While little work has been done on such appropriation of polemical works, literature on the appropriation of devotional works provides a useful model, particularly with respect to the Jesuit Robert Southwell: Arthur Marotti, 'Southwell's Remains: Catholicism and Anti-Catholicism in Early Modern England', in Cedric Brown and Arthur Marotti, eds, *Texts and Cultural Change in Early Modern England* (Basingstoke, 1997), 37–65; Susannah Monta, 'Uncommon Prayer? Robert Southwell's *Short Rule for a Good Life* and Catholic Domestic Devotion in Post-Reformation England', in Lowell Gallagher, ed., *Redrawing the Map of Early Modern English Catholicism* (Toronto, ON, 2012), 245–71.

[50] John Strype, *Annals of the Reformation and Establishment of Religion and various other Occurrences in the Church of England during Queen Elizabeth's Reign*, 4 vols in 7 (Oxford, 1824), 1/ii: 355.

[51] A number of letters and memoranda written by and to members of the Privy Council in the 1570s and 1580s point to this: TNA, SP 12/153, fol. 147, Notes by Lord Burghley on the Bull of Pius V, 1582; SP 15/19, fol. 39, the bishop of Carlisle to the earl of Sussex, 16 October 1570; SP 52/29, fol. 36, 'Offers of Queen Elizabeth to James VI', 17 February 1581; SP 78/7, fols 38, 43, Lord Cobham to Sir Francis Walsingham 12 and 28 March

supporters, the bull was too significant a challenge to be ignored, and it was paramount that it be thoroughly refuted by a leading Reformed theologian.

English Protestants continued to translate parts of the bull in their responses to its renewal and the Jesuit mission. John Field's *Caueat for Parsons Howlet*, a response to Robert Persons's *Reasons Why Catholiques Refuse to Goe to Church*, claimed that Persons 'calleth her maiesty the pretended Queene, and sheweth howe … Elizabeth that then gouerned was an heretike, and that for that cause she was by very right fallen from all gouernment and power'.[52] In spite of Field's claims, Persons never explicitly commented on – or even mentioned – Elizabeth's excommunication. The passage quoted by Field actually came from Nicholas Sander's *De Visibili Monarchia*, a polemical treatise defending the papal supremacy, published after the first pronouncement of the excommunication.[53] Ironically, Field did more rehearsing of *Regnans in Excelsis* than the opponent he vilified, and by summarizing it succinctly in English enabled his audience to understand it clearly.

The execution of Edmund Campion and twelve other Catholic priests in 1581 prompted two further translations of *Regnans in Excelsis* into English. In 1582 the Privy Council ordered the publication of *A Particular Declaration or Testimony, of the Vndutifull and Traiterous Affection Borne Against Her Maiestie by Edmond Campion Iesuite, and Other Condemned Priestes*, which included reprinted passages of *De Visibili Monarchia* and *Regnans in Excelsis* alongside English translations of the Latin texts.[54] The Privy Council intended the *Declaration* to be seen or heard by 'all her Maiesties good and faithfull subiects', so that 'the malice of the writers may bee made knowen to the worlde'. In the same year John Garbrand published *A Viewe of a Seditious Bul sent into England, from Pius Quintus*, a transcript of a sermon preached by John Jewel at Salisbury Cathedral in 1570. Those who gathered to hear Jewel's sermon and those who read it after 1582 were treated to a full reading of *Regnans in Excelsis* and translation of the Latin text into

1582; BL, Cotton/Caligula MS C/II, fol. 125, the bishop of Ross's audience with Queen Elizabeth, 28 June 1570.

[52] John Field, *A caueat for Parsons Howlet, concerning his vntimelye flighte, and schriching in the cleare daylighte of the Gospell* (London, 1581), 87–8.

[53] Nicholas Sander, *De Visibili Monarchia* (Louvain, 1571), 730.

[54] *A Particular Declaration or Testimony, of the Vndutifull and Traiterous Affection Borne Against Her Maiestie by Edmond Campion Iesuite, and Other Condemned Priestes* (London, 1582), bii.

English. Although Jewel framed each sentence of *Regnans in Excelsis* with lengthy and vicious invective against the papacy, it is striking that he read the bull aloud and translated it in such detail for his audience.[55] However much Jewel attempted rhetorically to eviscerate the excommunication and the papacy, his sermon made the bull intelligible to everyone who listened to him, with the chance that some would be more convinced by the translated fragments of *Regnans in Excelsis* than by his criticism.[56]

In conclusion, it is apparent that the translation of Queen Elizabeth's excommunication involved both the physical movement of papal bulls across Europe into England as well as efforts to render their contents into the English language. The role of Jesuit and seminary priests in distributing copies of the excommunication after its renewal in 1580 suggests its potential importance to the English mission, and may also indicate that the renewed bull had more significant political and spiritual importance than its predecessor. Increased efforts to translate the excommunication into English after 1580, particularly before the attempted invasion of England in 1588, likewise demonstrate the significance of its renewal. This calls into question earlier historical assessments of the excommunication which have neglected the reissuing of the bull. Furthermore, Protestant publications that included translated excerpts of *Regnans in Excelsis* also played an important role in increasing awareness of the bull in England. Published polemics and sermons that included translations of the sentence provided a legitimate means of accessing information about the queen's excommunication, and these may not always have been interpreted as their authors intended them to be. The role of translation in the transmission of Elizabeth's excommunication illuminates the significance her condemnation held for her kingdom, and illustrates the continued power of excommunication by the papacy in the late sixteenth century as a political and spiritual weapon that could still provoke action.

[55] John Jewel, *Viewe of a Seditious Bul Sent into Englande, from Pius Quintus Bishop of Rome, anno. 1569*, ed. John Garbrand (London, 1582).
[56] Walsham, 'The Spider and the Bee'.

Croatian Translation of Biblical Passages in Medieval Performative Texts

Andrea Radošević*
Old Church Slavonic Institute, Zagreb

This article will examine the Croatian translations of the biblical parts of medieval Latin performative texts (sermons, dialogues) which were translated in the fifteenth and sixteenth centuries and written in Glagolitic script. The Croatian translators were acquainted with the parts of Scripture which were read during the liturgy. Their knowledge of the Bible was evident in the addition of archaisms typical for Glagolitic liturgical books written in Croatian Church Slavonic. Often the quotations from Scripture were adjusted to the narrator's (or preacher's) voice in different ways, by changing the grammar of the Latin text as well as by shortening or expanding the quotations. Research has shown that one of the main goals of the translators in changing biblical quotations was to improve the performative characteristics of translation, so that the translated text could be orally performed.

Most medieval vernacular texts were intended either to be performed or to be 'read aloud to a participative audience'.[1] They shared similar themes, such as the 'emulation of ideas of Christianity' and they were also intended to support the spread of literacy.[2] Their purpose was to persuade lay people to change their behaviour by accepting Christian teaching, and they sought to do this by quoting the *auctoritates*, mostly Scripture, and by encouraging readers or listeners to develop *compassio*. Sermons and dialogues with this performative

* Old Church Slavonic Institute, Demetrova 11, Zagreb 10000, Croatia.
E-mail: aradosevic@stin.hr.

[1] 'Every medieval literary text … was designed to be communicated aloud to the individuals who constituted its audience': Paul Zumthor, 'The Text and the Voice', *New Literary History* 16 (1984), 67–91, at 67; cf. Robert Stanton, 'The (M)other Tongue: Translation Theory and Old English', in Jeanette M. A. Beer, ed., *Translation Theory and Practice in the Middle Ages* (Kalamazoo, MI, 1997), 33–46, at 46. Vernacular theology included many kinds of texts, among them catechetical works and Passion meditations: Eliana Corbari, *Vernacular Theology: Dominican Sermons and Audience in Late Medieval Italy* (Berlin, 2013), 8.

[2] Elaine Treharne, 'The Context of Medieval Literature', in David F. Johnson and Elaine Treharne, eds, *Readings in Medieval Texts: Interpreting Old and Middle English Literature* (Oxford, 2005), 7–14, at 12; D. H. Green, 'Orality and Reading: The State of Research in Medieval Studies', *Speculum* 65 (1990), 267–80, at 275.

Studies in Church History 53 (2017) 223–241

doi: 10.1017/stc.2016.14

character can be found among Croatian translations of Latin works which were copied during the fifteenth and sixteenth centuries in Glagolitic script, a Slavic script created by St Cyril of Thessaloniki.[3] The texts considered in this article consist of a Croatian translation of the *Sermones Discipuli* by the German Dominican Johannes Herolt (d. 1468), a translation of the *Sermones de sanctis* by Peregrinus of Oppeln (1260–1333) and Pseudo-Anselm's *Dialogus beatae Mariae et Anselmo de passione Domini*.[4]

These texts are an integral part of late medieval Croatian literature, and particularly that which was copied or printed in Glagolitic script. Given the complexities of the development of Croatian literature during the fifteenth and sixteenth centuries and the fact that texts differed not only in language but also in script (the Latin, Glagolitic and Cyrillic scripts were used), it is important to begin with an overview of this literature.

In the fifteenth and sixteenth centuries, Croatian literature was being developed in two directions: the first was the continued production of medieval works and the second was the production in significant quantity of humanist and Renaissance texts. Medieval Croatian literature was largely influenced by Latin religious texts such as manuals, confessionals, hagiographic and passion texts, sermons and accounts of Marian miracles.[5] Translations from Latin had a particular purpose: they were needed to help priests to teach Christianity to a lay audience. Some of the medieval literature from this period was written in Latin, and some in a mixture of Croatian Church Slavonic and Croatian.[6]

[3] Stjepan Damjanović, *Slovo iskona* (Zagreb, 2004), 59–61. In the late medieval and early modern periods Glagolitic script was used almost entirely in Croatian countries. Slavic countries which were part of the Roman Church generally used Latin script, whilst Slavic countries which were part of the Orthodox Church used Cyrillic script. Most Glagolitic texts were intended to be read aloud: Marija-Ana Dürrigl, *Čti razumno i lipo. Ogledi o hrvatskoj srednjovjekovnoj književnosti* (Zagreb, 2007), 9, 53.

[4] Andrea Radošević, 'Pseudo-Anselmov *Dialogus beatae Mariae et Anselmi de passione Domini* u hrvatskoglagoljskom Žgombićevu zborniku iz 16. stoljeća', *Slovo* 60 (2010), 633–68.

[5] Croatian literature was also influenced by the Cyrillo-Methodian tradition, and it thus represents a bridge between Western and Eastern literature: see Ivanka Petrović, 'Hagiografsko-legendarna književnost hrvatskog srednjovjekovlja i senjski Marijini mirakuli. Izvori, žanrovske, tematske i tipološke karakteristike', *Slovo* 34 (1984), 181–201; eadem, 'Croats', in André Vauchez, ed., *Encyclopedia of the Middle Ages*, 2 vols (Cambridge, 2001), 1: 384–6, at 385.

[6] From the eleventh to the sixteenth centuries, Croatian Church Slavonic, a Croatian redaction of Old Church Slavonic, was used as a liturgical language in littoral parts of

The language in which these texts were written varied according to their intended purpose. Although Latin, Croatian and Croatian Church Slavonic were all used in the medieval and early modern periods, their roles changed. From the eleventh until the end of the fourteenth centuries, literature copied in Glagolitic script was written in Croatian Church Slavonic; literature transcribed in Latin script mainly appeared in Latin and, after the mid-fourteenth century, Croatian. Until the mid-fourteenth century, Croatian had been used mostly in legal and administrative documents. From the late fourteenth until the sixteenth century, liturgical texts were still written in Croatian Church Slavonic; practical texts were written in Croatian, while literary texts were written in both Croatian and a mixture of Croatian and Croatian Church Slavonic (the balance depended on the nature of the text). Croatian Church Slavonic texts were almost always written in Glagolitic script, whereas Croatian texts could be written in any of the three scripts. Throughout the whole period, Latin was also used for liturgy, literature and administration and was written only in Latin script. So during the Middle Ages in the Croatian lands two liturgical languages were used: Latin and Croatian Church Slavonic.

The status of these languages was rather different in the case of Croatian Renaissance and humanist texts, which were copied and printed only in Latin script, and were almost always written in Latin, Croatian (with some rare examples of Croatian Church Slavonic words which appear in religious texts) and Italian. Several factors influenced the relatively early appearance of the Renaissance and of humanism in Croatian coastal cities. These include the political and administrative connections between Croatian cities on the Adriatic coast and Venice, which led young Croatian men to study at Italian universities, and the arrival of Italian intellectuals in Croatia.[7] From the second half of the fifteenth century Croatian Renaissance and

Croatia. Mihaljević observes that it 'was never a spoken language since it was constructed in order to support the Christianization of the Slavs. For that purpose two Slavic scripts were created: Glagolitic and Cyrillic': Milan Mihaljević, '*Verba dicendi* in Croatian Church Slavonic', *Zbornik Matice srpske za filologiju i lingvistiku* 54 (2011), 63–77, at 64. In the mid-thirteenth century, Pope Innocent IV gave permission to the Benedictine monks in Omišalj, on the island of Krk, to use a vernacular liturgy and books copied in the Glagolitic script, provided that they also knew Latin. A few years earlier, Benedictines in the Senj diocese had received similar permission: Josip Bratulić, *Sjaj baštine* (Split, 1990), 98.

[7] Dunja Fališevac, 'Renesansa', in Velimir Visković, ed., *Hrvatska književna enciklopedija*, 4 vols (Zagreb, 2010–12), 3: 564–70.

humanist writers composed many works, some of which became popular across Europe. Thus Croatian Petrarchism is the oldest form to be found outside his homeland, Italy.[8] Marko Marulić's *Institutione bene vivendi per exempla sanctorum* and the *Evangelistarium* were both popular in various European countries, and the latter was even read by Henry VIII.[9]

Translators were part of the Glagolitic reading community,[10] which also included scribes, priests and those who ordered books or commissioned translations. All these individuals played a part in communicating the translated text to the lay audience, and many of them were members of the clergy or closely connected to the Church's hierarchy. As manuscript records show, many books were created on the orders of a priest or other high-ranking individual.[11] Those who commissioned books or translations were therefore important members of the Glagolitic community.[12] The production of books was very expensive; consequently, those which were ordered

[8] Tomislav Bogdan, 'Petrarkizam i ljubavna lirika', *Umjetnost riječi* 3–4 (2009), 245–78.

[9] Andrea Clarke, 'Henry VIII and Marko Marulić's *Evangelistarium*', *Colloquia Marulliana* 20 (2011), 167–74.

[10] 'Reading community' is a term developed by Sif Rikhardsdottir, deriving from Brian Stock's 'textual community': Sif Rikhardsdottir, *Medieval Translations and Cultural Discourse: The Movement of Texts in England, France and Scandinavia* (Cambridge, 2012), 11–12. According to Rikhardsdottir, Stock describes a group composed of one or more people able to read a text to a group of possibly unlettered or semi-lettered members. By contrast, '[her] use of the term "reading community" here goes beyond Stock's model in incorporating a somewhat more extended notion of the readership, which would have included the person (or persons) instigating the translation and subsequent copying of the text as well as those for whom the text was translated (or copied) and ultimately the groups of audiences who actually read and preserved those texts. It similarly comprises the translators and scribes (as they also form the readership of the texts) and hence their imagined as well as actual audience': ibid. 12, referring to Brian Stock, *The Implications of Literacy: Written Language and Models of Interpretation in the Eleventh and Twelfth Century* (Princeton, NJ, 1983).

[11] For instance, the priest Tomas Petrinić made a manuscript for the monk Matija Gašĉanin: 'ja mnogo-griš'ni pop' Tomaš' Petriniĉь … pisah počtovanomu redovniku Matiju Gašĉaninu … I bih' plaĉen' dukate .v. [= 3] ča im' bi cêna' ('I, very sinful priest Tomas, wrote for a respected monk Matthew … And I was paid 3 coins, which was their price.'): Johannes Reinhart, 'Hrvatskoglagoljski zbornik Tomaša Petrinića iz god. 1503 (Cod. Vindob. Slav. br. 78)', *Croatica* 42–4 (1996), 391–421, at 392. Broz Kolunić wrote a manucript for a vicar Levnard: 'pisahь ê Brozь … k'nige poč'tovanu mužu gospodinu Levnardu vikaru gatanskomu v nega hiži sidi za moju plaĉu' ('I, Broz, wrote "these books" for a respected vicar Levnard in his house for my salary'): Stjepan Damjanović, *Jezik hrvatskih glagoljaša* (Zagreb, 2008), 226–7.

[12] Aleksandar Stipčević, *Socijalna povijest knjige u Hrvata. Knjiga I. Srednji vijek. Od prvih početaka do glagoljskoga prvotiska iz 1483. godine* (Zagreb, 2004), 141; Andrew Butcher, 'The Functions of Script in the Speech Community of a Late Medieval Town, *c.*1300–1550',

were generally practical texts required for the proper conduct of everyday pastoral and priestly ministry in a particular context, or didactic texts.[13] The focus on a text's usefulness, together with the cost of book production, resulted in many partial translations of foreign-language works. For example, the translator of Herolt's *Sermones Discipuli* omitted the Lenten sermons because on the northern Croatian coast other *quadragesimales* were commonly used, such as the translation of Carraciolo's *Quaresimale in volgare* (Senj, 1508), printed in Glagolitic script.

In addition, it is important to describe the attitude of members of the Glagolitic 'reading community' towards Scripture. For a long time, the biblical parts of religious texts remained in Croatian Church Slavonic, mostly because knowledge of the Bible was inseparable from knowledge of liturgical texts, and, as discussed above, these were mostly written in Croatian Church Slavonic. For decades, translators and scribes showed a special attitude towards Croatian Church Slavonic, mostly by using certain archaic phrases in biblical quotations in order to render particular aspects of the text more effectively.[14] The greater prestige of Croatian Church Slavonic was a consequence of its long connection with the liturgy,[15] and the use of anachronistic Croatian Church Slavonic terms in translating biblical quotations represented a stylistic way of marking certain points or ideas in the text. At the same time, it was also an indicator of the translators' connection to the older liturgical tradition.

This article will apply the approach of Biggs, who examined the rhetorical effect of translation.[16] It will compare the performativity of Latin and Croatian texts, focusing on the rendering of biblical

---

in Julia Crick and Alexandra Walsham, eds, *The Uses of Script and Print, 1300–1700* (Cambridge, 2004), 157–90, at 170.

[13] Stipčević, *Socijalna povijest knjige*, 141, 145–6; Dürrigl, *Čti razumno i lipo*, 74; Eduard Hercigonja, *Povijest hrvatske književnosti: srednjovjekovna književnost: knj. 2* (Zagreb 1975), 202.

[14] Mihaljević, '*Verba dicendi* in Croatian Church Slavonic'; Damjanović, *Jezik hrvatskih glagoljaša*, 117.

[15] Milan Mihaljević, 'Položaj crkvenoslavenskga jezika u hrvatskoj srednjovjekovnoj kulturi', in Ilija Velev et al., eds, *Sveti Naum Ohridski i slovenskata duhovna, kulturna i pismena tradicija* (Ohrid, 2010), 229–38, at 232.

[16] Brendan Biggs, 'The Style of the first English Translation of the *Imitatio Christi*', in Roger Ellis and René Tixier, eds, *The Medieval Translator = Traduire au Moyen Âge*, vol. 5 (Turnhout, *c.*1996), 187–211, at 198. According to Biggs's exploration of the rhetorical effect of translation, a translated text can have an equal, a lower or a higher effect when compared with the original.

texts. Since these Croatian performative texts contain a large number of biblical quotations, two questions are examined.[17] First, did the intensification of the oral aspect through translation include biblical texts, and if so how? Second, how did the translators treat scriptural quotations which, as discussed above, were customarily written, at least to some extent, in Croatian Church Slavonic?

The Translators' Strategies and Goals

When translating a performative text it is important not to lose its effectiveness, and this is also – or perhaps especially – true of religious texts. A translator's efforts to preserve a text's rhetorical effect can be described with Nida's term 'dynamic equivalence'.[18] The main goal of a sermon, the most important connection between priest and congregation,[19] was to transmit a moral message which went beyond the simple communication relationship between the preacher (sender) and the congregation (receivers). Preaching is a performative genre: a sermon is intended to move its hearers to realize its moral lessons for their lives.[20] It does this by presenting reasons, offering quotations from authoritative texts and giving examples.[21]

As Kienzle observes, a sermon is 'primarily a one-sided conversation in the sense that the listener is urged to take a message [from the preacher] to heart'.[22] The communication is more complex when it comes to dialogues, in which there is either interaction between the participants, or a one-sided communication between the participants and the audience. A dialogue represents an interaction: one

[17] In sermons and other texts about key events from the gospels, the Bible is generally the most frequently cited source: Christopher Ocker, 'The Bible in the Fifteenth Century', in Miri Rubin and Walter Simons, eds, *CHC*, 4: *Christianity in Western Europe* c.*1100*–c.*1500* (Cambridge, 2009), 472–93, at 490–2; Alastair Minnis, 'Late Medieval Discussions of *compilatio* and the Role of the *compilator*', *Beiträge zur Geschichte der deutschen Sprache und Literatur* 101 (1979), 385–421, at 389.

[18] Eugene A. Nida, *Toward a Science of Translating, with Special Reference to principles and Procedures involved in Bible Translating* (Leiden, 1964); Stanton, 'The (M)other Tongue', 45.

[19] David D'Avray, *Medieval Marriage Sermons: Mass Communication in a Culture without Print* (Oxford, 2001), 30; Beverly Mayne Kienzle, 'Introduction', in eadem, ed., *The Sermon*, Typologie des sources du Moyen Âge occidental 81–3 (Turnhout, 2000), 143–74, at 154.

[20] Beverly Mayne Kienzle, 'Medieval Sermons and their Performance: Theory and Record', in Carolyn Muessig, ed., *Preacher, Sermon and Audience in the Middle Ages* (Leiden, Boston, MA, and Cologne, 2002), 89–124; Kienzle, 'Introduction', 155.

[21] Carlo Delcorno, 'Medieval Preaching in Italy (1200–1500)', in Kienzle, ed., *The Sermon*, 449–560, at 474.

[22] Kienzle, 'Introduction', 152.

participant retells the event and in doing so emotionally influences the other participant, who, however, by asking the original targeted question, had managed to penetrate into the soul of the first participant. The interaction between the participants' voices, which could be read by different readers, gives a dialogue text its particular performative characteristics.

Glagolitic texts had an audience amongst the lower clergy, especially preachers who were responsible for communicating the message of the set readings to uneducated listeners. Translations from Latin were therefore generally adjusted not only for lay people, as the final recipients, but also for priests or readers with relatively low levels of education.[23] These texts were intended to support clergy as the most important medium of the communication of meaning to their lay audience. Translators sought to produce a written text that would be as close as possible to an oral version, so that the translator, as Ellis has said, had 'an active role not just as a compiler but also as a preacher'.[24]

The fact that most of these texts were read or performed in front of an uneducated audience influenced the translation of all quotations, not just those taken from Scripture. Many of the sermons that were translated from Latin to Croatian during the medieval period were written by Dominican and Franciscan authors who used frequent citations to strengthen their argument. However, in oral communication an excess of quotations can negatively affect the audience's reception of the message, since they can make it difficult for a lay audience to follow the content. The translators recognized this, and information from authorities was often abbreviated or cut. Sometimes a scriptural quotation was signified only by phrases such as 'it is written', 'it can be read' or 'it is said'. It was clearly important to attribute these ideas to some authority, but highlighting the fact that an idea was 'written' somewhere strengthened the argument.[25] In texts with less obvious references to authorities, such as dialogues, the significance of a selected quotation was sometimes highlighted

[23] It must not be forgotten that the reader plays an important part in receiving written communication, and this is important in translation: Luis G. Kelly, *The True Interpreter: A History of Translation Theory and Practice in the West* (Oxford, 1979), 47.

[24] Roger Ellis, 'Introduction', in *The Medieval Translator: The Theory and Practice of Translation in the Middle Ages. Papers read at a Conference held 20–23 August 1987, University of Wales*, ed. Roger Ellis (Cambridge, 1989), 1–14, at 6.

[25] Marija-Ana Dürrigl, 'O čitanju, pisanju i kompiliranju u hrvatskoglagoljskom srednjovjekovlju', *Slovo* 60 (2010), 219–34, at 220.

only by using archaic forms drawn from Croatian Church Slavonic, which were closely connected to the translation of biblical readings from older liturgical books.

There are also examples in which information about the authority which in the Latin version had been given in an abbreviated form was lost. Such citation indicators were mostly highlighted by adding word such as 'here' or 'so', or *verba dicendi*, mostly in the form 'he said', 'it is to be known'. The function of this translation strategy was to facilitate a fluent oral performance by avoiding possible breaks in the preaching discourse. Frequent reference to the different authorities meant repeated transitions between citation and the 'narrative' of the text. For a lay audience that could not see the text, the inclusion of too many quotations could make it difficult to listen to and memorize the content. Moreover, reading abbreviations could pose an insurmountable problem to a poorly educated cleric.

A similarly pragmatic emphasis influenced the cutting and omission of some parts of the Latin text. For instance, the adjusting of texts for the benefit of the lay audience also affected the translation of biblical passages in sermons, especially if a particular point was buttressed by several quotations. Here the translation strategy included not only omitting the abbreviations, but also shortening quotations or converting citations into rhetorical flourishes. Sometimes translators merged two quotations into one, usually treating the second quotation as an explanation of the first and attributing it to the first authority. For example:

> [Ps. 101: 18, Ecclus. 35: 21] Ps. Respexit in orationem humilium etc. Eccle. XXXV. Oratio humiliantis se nubes penetrat.[26]
> Ps[a]lm gov[o]ri prizre na mol[i]tvu smerenih ere mol[i]tva umilenoga prohaê oblake.[27]
> The Psalm says that he [God] regards the prayer of the destitute because the prayer of the humble pierces the clouds.

> Unde etiam Cypr. Serico et purpura induti Christum induere non possunt. Unde etiam Greg. in Homil. Quid est homo pretiose ornatus, nisi sepulchrum foris dealbatum, intus autem plenum spurcitiae.[28]

[26] Johannes Herolt, *Sermones Discipuli de tempore et de sanctis cum Promptuario exemplorum et de miraculis Beatae Mariae Virginis* (Strasbourg, 1488), 32^{r}.
[27] Zagreb, Croatian Academy of Sciences and Arts, VIII 126, 'Disipul B', fol. 7c.
[28] Herolt, *Sermones Discipuli*, 32^{r}.

> Na to Ciprîên' gov[o]ri svil'na svita i purpira ne more H[rst]a oblîĉi ere ĉa e[st] č[lovê]k lipo oblečen nego k[a]ko grob' ki e[st] zvana lipo urešen a vnutri e[st] pln' smrada.[29]
> Here Cyprian said, a purple silk robe cannot be put on Christ because a well-dressed man is nothing but a tomb that is nicely decorated outside but inside is full of stench.

Some quotations were simply excluded from the translation, as can be seen from the following passage from Daniel.

> [Dan. 11: 37] Item Deus et sanctos blasphemabit. Unde Dan. XI. Adversus Deum deorum loquetur blasphemia, et omnes blasphemi sunt praecursores antichristi ...[30]
> Oĉe bude B[og]a i s[ve]te pogreval i v'si ki pogrûû B[og]a ili s[ve]te esu pos'li antih[rs]tovi ...[31]
> Also he will mock God and all the saints and all who mock God or saints are precursors of the Antichrist.

Verba dicendi

Quotations in sermons, and changes between character in dialogues were almost always announced by *verba dicendi*, often with further words added, such as 'here' or 'so'.[32] The main purpose was to facilitate oral performance. The *verba dicendi* were sometimes extended by chronological adverbs. Berardini has observed that 'another important performance indicator is represented by deictics, that is, those linguistic elements strictly connected to spatial or temporal circumstances'.[33]

[29] 'Disipul B', fol. 7c.
[30] Herolt, *Sermones Discipuli*, 36r.
[31] Zagreb, Croatian State Archives, Archdiocese of Krk, G–55 (ZM 57/16), 'Disipul A', fol. 14c.
[32] Sioned Davies, 'He was the best Teller of Tales in the World', in Evelyn Birge Vitz; Nancy Freeman Regalado and Marilyn Lawrence, eds, *Performing Medieval Narrative* (Woodbridge, 2005), 15–26, at 22.
[33] Valentina Berardini, 'Performance Indicators in Late Medieval Sermons', *Medieval Sermon Studies* 54 (2000), 75–86, at 85.

[John 19: 22] Pilatus respondit: quod scripsi scripsi.[34]
Tada odgovori Pilat ko pisah' pisah'.[35]
Then Pilate answered what I have written I have written.

Verba dicendi were sometimes added even if the Latin text already contained an expressive verb. In the translation the first verb then represents the scriptural expression ('write'), while the second begins the statement ('say'):

[Luke 23: 26] Unde et Lucas scribit. Apprehenderunt Simonem quendam Cyrenensem.[36]
Kako Luka piše govoreĉi êše Simuna Kurineiskago.[37]
And how Luke writes saying: they laid hold of one Simon of Cyrene.

[Luke 22: 67] Jesus respondit si dicero vobis.[38]
A I(su)s mu od'govori i reče Ako bih' vam' rekal'.[39]
And Jesus answers him and says: if I would tell you.

In short narratives containing few quotations, translators transformed the Gospel reading by using *verba dicendi* in order to produce continuous sentences:

[Luke 23: 43, Matt. 3: 2] … Lu. XXIII. Amen dico tibi, hodie mecum eris in paradiso, et omnibus peccatoribus dicitur a Christo, ut habetur Math. III. Paenitentiam agite, appropinquavit enim regnum caelorum …[40]
… gov[o]reći amen gov[o]rim tebi d[a]n[a]s budeši sa mnoû v rai i zato gov[o]ri se vsim grišnikom od Hrsta pokoru činite ere približit se va vas c[êsa]rstvo b[o]žie …[41]
… saying: Amen I say to you, today you shall be with me in Paradise, and that is because it is said by Christ to all sinners, repent for the kingdom of heaven has drawn near.

[34] Anselmus Cantuariensis, *Dialogus beatae Mariae et Anselmi de Passione Domini*, PL 159, cols 271–90, at 283c.
[35] Zagreb, Croatian Academy of Sciences and Arts, VII 30, 'Žgombićev zbornik', fol. 95v.
[36] PL 159, 281b.
[37] 'Žgombićev zbornik', fol. 93v.
[38] PL 159, 277a.
[39] 'Žgombićev zbornik', fol. 89v.
[40] Herolt, *Sermones Discipuli*, 31v.
[41] 'Disipul B', fol. 6d.

In dialogues, which have very few citation indicators, translators seem to have found it important to highlight at least some important quotations. Here they used phrases such as 'which goes' (*ko de*) or 'which is being said' (*ko govori*).

> [John 18: 9] Ut Scriptura impleretur quia quos dedisti mihi, non perdidi ex eis quemquam.[42]
> Da se Pismo vzbude ko govori o mne ne pogublû nih niednago.[43]
> The word might be fulfilled that says I have not lost any of them.

> [Pss 21: 17–18, 44: 11] Ita ut impleretur illud. Psalmi dinumeraverunt omnia ossa mea et tunc impleta fuit prophetia ipsius David, id est ipsius Christi, dicentis in Psalmo Audi fila et vide …[44]
> i tu se isplni rič' ka se govori v ps[a]lme: prigvozdiše rucê i nozê moi i sačtoše vse kosti moe I tada se takoe isplni pr[o]r[o]častvo Davidovo ko o H[rst]e govori v psalme: sliši d'či i vii …[45]
> And here was fulfilled the word that is said in the Psalms: they have pierced my hands and feet, they have numbered all my bones … and then was fulfilled the prophecy of David, who as Christ said in the Psalms: listen, daughter, and see.

> [Ps. 44: 11] … tunc matri potui dicere audi filia et vide.[46]
> … tada se zbist mane matere on' veras ki de Sliši hći i vii i prikloni uho tvoe.[47]
> … then my mother fulfilled that verse which goes: listen, daughter, and see, and incline your ear.

Verba dicendi changed according to the type of narration. Longer narrative sections contain announcement phrases such as 'as it is written' or 'it could be read', contrasting with 'it is said' or 'says', which are the most common elsewhere.

> Ut habetur Ioh. XX …[48]
> K[a]ko se piše po Iv[a]nu na i[= 20] …[49]
> As it is written by John in the 20th chapter …

[42] PL 159, 273c.
[43] 'Žgombićev zbornik', fol. 86v.
[44] PL 159, 282c.
[45] 'Žgombićev zbornik', fol. 95r.
[46] PL 159, 284a.
[47] 'Žgombićev zbornik', fol. 96r.
[48] Herolt, *Sermones Discipuli*, 211r.
[49] Croatian Academy of Sciences and Arts, VIa 95, 'Disipul C', fol. 51v.

Gen. XLIX …[50]
Na to se piše v [E]n[e]z[e]s na 49 k[a]p[itul] …[51]
As it is written in Genesis …

[Wisd. 5: 9] Unde dicunt damnati in inferno illud Sap. V. transierunt omnia illa tamquam umbra …[52]
Zato govore osueni v pakli k[a]ko v Mudrosti nahodi se na 5 k[a]p[itu]l proš'la su vsa ta k[a]ko sen …[53]
Therefore those sentenced to Hell say, as can be found in Wisdom in the 5th chapter, all those things have passed away like a shadow.

Grammatical Changes

Quotations from Scripture were also adjusted to the narrator's or preacher's voice by altering the grammar of the Latin text. For instance, an intensification of the narrative was produced by changing participles to the present tense, while by adding the conditional form the narrator hinted at events to come, holding his audience in suspense. In dialogues it was necessary to adjust scriptural parts to the narrator's voice, for instance when recounting events from Jesus's Passion. Participles were often paraphrased into simple sentences, generally by adding a few explanatory words.

Transforming participle:
[Luke 23: 14] Obtulistis mihi hunc hominem quasi avertentem populum …[54]
Pripelaste mi toga č[lovê]ka govoreĉe da e[st] razvratnik v lûdeh …[55]
You brought me this man telling me that he is a subverter of the people …

Addition of the conditional form:
[John 19: 31] … rogabant Pilatum ut frangerentur eorum crura, et tollerentur …[56]
… prosiše Pilata da bi im' prostil da bi prebil nih' goleni …[57]

[50] Herolt, *Sermones Discipuli*, 35^{v}.
[51] 'Disipul B', fol. 8d.
[52] Herolt, *Sermones Discipuli*, 89^{r}.
[53] 'Disipul A', fol. 52d.
[54] PL 159, 278d.
[55] 'Žgombićev zbornik', fol. 91^{v}.
[56] PL 159, 285c.
[57] 'Žgombićev zbornik', fol. 97^{v}.

… they asked Pilate that [the men's] legs might be broken and that [the bodies] might be taken down.

[Luke 22: 67] Si vobis dixero non creditis mihi.[58]
… ako bih' vam' rekal' ne veruete mi.[59]
If I were to tell you, you would not believe me.

[Matt. 26: 53] Exhibebit mihi …[60]
bih' hotel da bi mi priklonil …[61]
If I should want him to give me …

Transformation of pronouns (here from third to second person):
[Matt. 27: 42] si rex israel est descendat nunc de cruce et credemus ei …[62]
ako si c[êsa]rb iz[drai]l[e]vb slezi nine s križa i veruemo ti …[63]
If you are the King of Israel, descend from the cross and we will believe you.

Lexigraphical Changes

In some quotations the spoken words were written in Croatian Church Slavonic and the narrative part was written in Croatian. This was one of the strategies used by translators to highlight an important passage.

[Luke 22: 61–2] Et recordatus est Petrus verbi Domini quod dixerat ei: quia priusquam gallus cantet, ter me negabis.[64]
I vspomenu se Petar na onu rič' ku mu bêše rekal moi sin Isus: prvo nere peteh' zapoe trikrat otvr'žeši se mene.[65]
And Peter remembered the word of the Lord, how he had said to him, that before the rooster crows you will deny me three times.

In the narrative parts of dialogues, there are examples in which the speeches of the characters included words from Croatian Church Slavonic, such as the genitive personal pronoun (*ego*).

58 PL 159, 277a.
59 'Žgombićev zbornik', fol. 89v.
60 PL 159, 274a.
61 'Žgombićev zbornik', fol. 87r.
62 PL 159, 283d.
63 'Žgombićev zbornik', fol. 95v.
64 PL 159, 275b.
65 'Žgombićev zbornik', fol. 88r.

[Matt. 27: 25] et respondens universus populus dixit. Sanguis ejus super nos et super filios nostros ...[66]
I odgovoriše vsi i rekoše krv ego budi na nas i na čedeh' naših' ...[67]
And they all responded and said, may his blood be upon us and upon our children.

The translators' knowledge of the Bible might also manifest itself through the inclusion of quotations which were not part of the original Latin text. Sometimes one quotation was changed for another with a similar meaning. For example, one Latin sermon includes a quotation from Wisdom 11: 17 (Vulgate), but the Croatian text gives a similar quotation from Proverbs 24: 12 instead. This strategy was inherited from the older tradition of the Glagolitic scribes and translators.[68]

[Wisd. 11: 17] ... Per quae quis peccat per haec et punietur ...[69]
[Prov. 24: 12] ... ere pisano e[st] primut plaĉu po deleh svoih ...[70]
... because it is written, he shall repay a man according to his works.

The best indication that a translation is both following the tradition of the old liturgical books and adjusting quotations to make the text more performative is the use of anachronisms in the form of Croatian Church Slavonic, particularly when rendering Latin abbreviations, mostly in quotations from the gospels:

[Matt. 10: 20] Unde Math. Non enim vos estis qui loqumini etc. [sed Spiritus Patris vestri, qui loquitur in vobis] ...[71]
To se piše po Mateju. Ne ste bo vi ki govorite na duh otca vašego vzgovorit va vas ...[72]
It is written by Matthew, For it is not you who speak, but the Spirit of your Father which speaketh in you.

[Ex. 15: 17] De quo monte Exod. XV. Introduces eos et plantabis etc.[73]

[66] PL 159, 280c.
[67] 'Žgombićev zbornik', fol. 93r.
[68] Josip Leonard Tandarić, *Hrvatskoglagoljska liturgijska književnost* (Zagreb, 1993), 307–9.
[69] Herolt, *Sermones Discipuli*, 86r.
[70] 'Disipul B', fol. 71b.
[71] Peregrinus of Oppeln, *Sermones Peregrini de tempore [et] de sanctis* (Strasbourg, 1493), 'De sancto Stephano'.
[72] Croatian Academy of Sciences and Arts, IVa 99, 'Blagdanar popa Andrije', fol. 10v.
[73] Peregrinus, *Sermones*, 'De Innocentibus'.

> … od koga govori se v' knigah' od Ishoda vavedeši ih i postaviši ih v gori otočastva svoego v kripkom prebivanii …[74]
> … from which it is said in the Book of Exodus: you shall take them in and plant them, in the mountain of thine inheritance, in the firm dwelling place.

It is not unusual to find two vernacular versions of the same biblical quotation – Croatian Church Slavonic and Croatian – in the same sermon. The Croatian Church Slavonic version is often included as the *thema* (a biblical quotation at the beginning of the sermon) or at the end of the text. For example, by using the old pronoun *az* ('I' in Old Slavic), in the last sentence of the sermon for St Thomas's Day, the translator not only intensified God's message but changed the sentence into an exhortation.[75] Particular archaisms, especially those connected with the name or the words of God, give the quotation a stronger meaning.[76]

> [John 15: 5] Qui manet in me et ego in eo hic fert fructum multum …[77]
> Ki prêbivaet' va mnê i ê v' nem' ta prnest plod' mnog' …[78]
> Ki prêbivaet' va mnê i az v' nem' ta prnest plod' mnog' …[79]
> Whoever abides in me, and I in him, bears much fruit.

A similar 'strong' opening (*thema*) is found in a few sermons which begin with the old Croatian pronoun *az*:

> [John 10: 14] Ego sum pastor bonus …[80]

[74] 'Blagdanar popa Andrije', fol. 14^{r}.

[75] In fifteenth- and sixteenth-century manuscripts, *az* is most often used when God is speaking. Otherwise, most of the time, *ê* or *ja* are used: Stjepan Damjanović, *Tragom jezika hrvatskih glagoljaša* (Zagreb, 1984), 126; Eduard Hercigonja, *Nad iskonom hrvatske knjige* (Zagreb, 1983), 405. This means that, as Mihaljević observed: 'God speaks Croatian Church Slavonic, while human beings speak Croatian': 'Položaj crkvenoslavenskga jezika', 232.

[76] A parallel for this conclusion is found in Vitz's description of biblical quotation in liturgical texts and sermons: Evelyn Birge Vitz, 'Liturgical versus Biblical Citation in Medieval Vernacular Literature', in *Tribute to Jonathan J. G. Alexander: The Making and Meaning of Illuminated Medieval and Renaissance Manuscripts, Art and Architecture*, ed. Susan L'Engle and Gerlad B. Huest (London 2006), 443–9, at 447.

[77] Peregrinus, *Sermones*, 'De sancto Thoma'.

[78] 'Blagdanar popa Andrije', fol. 6^{r}.

[79] Ibid., fol. 8^{v}.

[80] Herolt, *Sermones Discipuli*, 87^{v}.

Az esam' pastir' dobri ...[81]
I am the good Shepherd.

[John 15: 1] Ego sum vitis vera ...[82]
Az' esam' trs' ...[83]
I am the true vine.

The translators' wish not only to improve a text's performability, but also to make it more memorable to listeners, can be seen in rhetorical figures, such as repetition, which were created by changing some words:

[Matt. 6: 23] Si autem oculus tuus fuerit nequam totum corpus tuum tenebrosum erit ...[84]
... ako oko tvoe tamno bude vse t[ê]lo tvoe tamno bude ...[85]
But if your eye has been darkened, your entire body will be darkened.

Shortened phrases probably demonstrate the belief that concise expression, especially when related to asking verbs, has a stronger effect than breaking up sentences by mentioning authorities, for instance, by giving information about precise Gospel references:

Omnia quaecumque orantes petitis, credite, quia accipietis [Mark 11: 24]. Item Io. sext. Petite et accipietis [John 16: 24]. Item Matt. 7. quaerite et invenietis, pulsate et aperietur vobis [Matt. 7: 7] ...[86]
M[a]rko na 11 vsa ka moleĉe se vsprosite veruite da primete [Mark 11: 24] iĉite i naidete [John 16: 24] tlcite i otvorit se v[a]m [Matt. 7: 7] ...[87]
Mark in the 11th chapter says whatever you are praying for, believe that you will receive it; ask and you shall receive, knock and it shall be opened to you.

In dialogues, Scripture quotations were adjusted to the narrator's voice so that, for instance, every moment of Christ's passion is described from Mary's point of view; all Gospel quotations are presented as her personal testimony to the events of the Passion. In order to emphasize her closeness and to intensify her motherhood,

81 'Disipul C', fol. 172r.
82 Herolt, *Sermones Discipuli*, 263v.
83 'Disipul B', fol. 139a.
84 Herolt, *Sermones Discipuli*, 49v.
85 'Disipul B', fol. 180a.
86 Herolt, *Sermones Discipuli*, 179r.
87 'Disipul B', fol. 100c.

translators often replaced the name of Jesus by the phrase 'my son Jesus' or 'my son'.[88] The testimony of Mary, a grieving mother, was believed to make more of an impact on readers than would fidelity to the Bible text.

> [John 19: 33] Ad Jesum autem cum venissent …[89]
> I ka I(su)su sinu moemu kada pridoše …[90]
> But after they had approached Jesus my son …

> [Luke 23: 26] … et imposerunt illi crucem portare post Jesum …[91]
> … i položiše mu križь na rame ponesti za sinom' moim …[92]
> … and they imposed the cross on him to carry after my son …

> [John 19: 2] … imposerunt capiti ejus …[93]
> … nabiêhu na glavu momu sinu …[94]
> … imposed it on the head of my son.

Compassio was also encouraged by the introduction of emotionally charged expressions into Mary's voice. Thus the Latin *gladius* and *gladius Simenonis* are replaced by the emotionally charged *meč boleznivi* ('sword of grief'), which is frequently repeated in Mary's description of the Passion. It functions as an allegory of Mary's pain at the suffering and death of her only son, in which prophecy from the time of Christ's childhood is connected to her present suffering. From Mary's point of view, the Passion is described as a fulfilment of Simeon's prophecy; that is, as a series of events that is going to pierce her soul. By emphasizing Mary's voice as the voice of a mother, translators seek to move the audience by causing them to feel a similar pain.

> [Luke 2: 35] Anselmus. Charissima domina, habuit adhuc finem dolor tuus? Maria. Non, Anselme, qui nondum plene prophetia Simeois impleta erat et tuam ipsius animam pertransibit gladius …[95]

[88] Amelia Fraga Fuentes, 'A Study of the Virgin Mary in the Thirteenth-and Fourteenth-Century English Crucifixion Lyrics' (Part II), *Atlantis* 3 (1981), 16–23, at 17.
[89] PL 159, 286a.
[90] 'Žgombićev zbornik', fol. 97v.
[91] PL 159, 281b.
[92] 'Žgombićev zbornik', fol. 93v.
[93] PL 159, 280a.
[94] 'Žgombićev zbornik', fol. 92v.
[95] PL 159, 285c.

An'kselam reče moê draga gospoe povei mi b[ê]še li tada ûre dosvršena žalost tvoê. Bl[a]ž[e]na Mariê reče: ne oĉe An'kselme zač ne oĉe se ne bêše plno proročastvo Semionoňo isplnilo, to e[st] reče tvoû d[u]šu proidet meč' bolez'nivi ...[96]
Anselm said, My dearest Lady, tell me, is then your sorrow complete? Blessed Mary said: Not yet Anselm, not yet, because Simeon's prophecy has not been completely fulfilled; that is, as he said, a sword of grief shall pierce your soul.

Conclusion

This article has argued that one of the main goals of the changes made by translators to Scripture quotations was to improve the performative characteristics of a translation, so that the translated text could be presented or read aloud. The translators of these religious texts sought to produce vernacular versions which would persuade lay people to change their behaviour and encourage them to develop *compassio*. However, because of the significant number of biblical quotations, translators could only preserve or intensify the oral aspects of the Latin text by making some changes. In a sermon, the aim was to produce a fluent text with very few pauses. In dialogues, the purpose of grammatical and lexigraphical changes was to highlight the emotional dimension of the text. For example, the grief of Mary, the mother of Christ, was emphasized by making Gospel quotations appear as her testimony. Translators adjusted the biblical text for reading aloud; they also used archaisms derived from Croatian Church Slavonic, which was one of the liturgical languages. In the Glagolitic reading community, knowledge of the Bible was inseparable from familiarity with relevant liturgical books. These efforts at improving the performative characteristics of the text served to fix the old language of biblical quotations in people's minds, and the use of anachronisms and archaisms generally represented a stylistic way of marking particular ideas or increasing the effectiveness of certain aspects of the text. It was also an indication of the translators' connection to the older liturgical tradition. Finally, the appearance of anachronisms was often a sign that a certain sentence derived from the Bible; sometimes the authority behind the quotation was marked only by the use of an archaism. Further examples show a combination of two different

[96] 'Žgombićev zbornik', fols 96^{v}–97^{r}.

translating strategies: the oral effect was intensified by adding *verba dicendi*, while the words of a biblical character were signified by the use of a particular sentence or even of a few words in Croatian Church Slavonic. The strategies that have been described confirm that translators sought to adjust the Latin text, not only for lay people, but also – and perhaps even primarily – for those priests or readers who had received limited education, in order to help them to preach Christian doctrine and spread Christian morality.

Translating the *Life of Antichrist* into German and Czech in the Early Modern Period

Alena A. Fidlerová*
Charles University, Prague

Based on a sociocultural and functional approach to the history of translation, this article introduces the Leben Antichristi *by the German Capuchin and famous preacher Dionysius of Luxemburg, first published in 1682 at Frankfurt am Main, as an example of the transmission of formerly elite content to a popular readership via its translation into simple vernacular prose. It then discusses possible reasons why three Czech translations of the book, created independently during the eighteenth century and preserved in manuscript, were never printed, although the German version went through twelve editions and similar works by Dionysius's fellow brother Martin of Cochem were among the most often printed books of the Czech Baroque.*

Translation, the theme of this volume, can be understood in different ways. The most obvious is the translation of a text from one language to another which, according to some recent approaches, involves not only the transition between two different language communities, but usually also that between different social and cultural milieus, and often means a functional change too.[1] This textual aspect of translation will be the primary focus of this article, which considers the translation of a late seventeenth-century German work, *Leben Antichristi* by

* Pod Pekařkou 31, 14700 Praha 4, Czech Republic. E-mail: alena.fidlerova@ff.cuni.cz.
This article was prepared with the support of the Programme for the Development of Fields of Study at Charles University, no. P12, 'History from the Interdisciplinary Perspective', sub-programme 'Society, Culture and Communication in Czech History', and of the project GA ČR P406/11/0782, 'Příprava a vydání Repertoria rukopisů 17. a 18. století z muzejních sbírek v Čechách III (P–Š)'.

[1] The so-called 'cultural turn' in translation studies during the early 1980s defined text as 'the verbalized part of a socioculture' and emphasized the sociocultural nature of translation. Any text is embedded in a socioculturally defined situation, and when transferred to the target culture through translation, it either preserves the same function as in the source culture, or it changes it to adapt to the specific needs of the target culture: Mary Snell-Hornby, *The Turns of Translation Studies: New Paradigms or Shifting Viewpoints?* (Philadelphia, PA, 2006), 50–7.

Studies in Church History 53 (2017) 242–256
doi: 10.1017/stc.2016.15

Dionysius of Luxemburg, into Czech. A second aspect of translation that will be considered is that between two different media of text dissemination which functioned in parallel during this period, namely manuscript and print.

Before considering this text, it is important to be aware of the linguistic diversity in early modern Bohemia and Moravia. Even before the incorporation of the Czech lands, the Habsburg hereditary lands represented a multiethnic and multilingual entity, in which, however, German was pre-eminent. After the inclusion of Bohemia, Moravia, Silesia, Lusatia and Hungary in 1526 and Croatia in 1527, this generally German character of the empire was permanently lost: its non-German regions were not only geographically larger, but often also more densely populated.[2] The Czech lands had effectively been bilingual since the Middle Ages: although Czech was spoken at all levels of society, including the high aristocracy, and was the language of the provincial court and diet, there was also a significant German-speaking population.[3] During the sixteenth century, however, the proportion of German-speaking families amongst the ruling classes increased, and the areas inhabited by the German-speaking population gradually expanded.[4] In response, the Czech-speaking aristocracy and bourgeoisie secured legal provisions ensuring a leading role for their language in the Czech territories. In 1615, the provincial diet proclaimed Czech the exclusive language for all legal acts in the Czech lands, and demanded that recent immigrants who had been granted citizenship must teach their children Czech and that foreigners seeking citizenship had to learn the language first.[5] However, the rebellion of non-Catholic Czech estates against Habsburg rule in 1618 and their catastrophic defeat in battle at the White Mountain in 1620 brought an end not only to confessional toleration, but also to the leading role of the Czech language in Bohemia and Moravia. Although the new provincial legal code, issued in 1627 for Bohemia and in 1628 for Moravia, recognized German and Czech equally as

[2] See Ulrike Eder, *'Auf die mehrere Ausbreitung der teutschen Sprache soll fürgedacht werden': Deutsch als Fremd- und Zweitsprache im Unterrichtssystem der Donaumonarchie zur Regierungszeit Maria Theresias und Josephs II*. (Innsbruck, 2006).

[3] Alois Míka, 'Národnostní poměry v českých zemích před třicetiletou válkou', *Československý časopis historický* 20 [70] (1972), 207–33, at 219.

[4] Ibid. 215.

[5] Antonín Pražák, *Národ se bránil, Obrany národa a jazyka českého od nejstarších dob po přítomnost* (Prague, 1945), 40–2.

the languages of government, in practice German became more significant in public life. This regulation, together with the forced re-Catholicization of the country, led to a significant reduction in Czech-speaking elites. The non-Catholic aristocracy and bourgeoisie who emigrated after 1620[6] were replaced by noble families who spoke German, Italian, Spanish or French. As a result, Czech lost its position as the language of elite culture and social intercourse. During the Thirty Years' War, the German-speaking proportion of the population increased further.[7] Thus by the mid-eighteenth century the Czech speaking population represented only a minority among the aristocracy and well-off bourgeoisie, but a majority among petty bourgeoisie and lower orders.[8]

In the post-White Mountain period, the international character of the new Catholic elites and the country's essentially bilingual (or even multilingual) character also manifested itself. It was not unusual for the same text to be published simultaneously in Czech, German and Latin; the Latin and to some extent the German versions were intended for a more educated audience. Moreover, many of the works published in Czech during this period were translations or adaptations from Latin, German, Spanish, French or Italian, although they were not always acknowledged as such. Veronika Čapská describes the early modern Czech Lands as a 'space of translation flows … shaped by the circulation of books and the movement of social actors involved in the processes of translating, publishing, reading etc'.[9] She identifies three major 'translation centres': the Jesuit circle around Jiří Plachý-Ferus and Friedrich Bridel, mostly based in Prague; the exile pietist project Collegium Biblicum Bohemicum at Halle; and the private translation activities supported by the noble families of Sporck and Sweerts-Sporck. However, these were not the only translation activities carried out in early modern Bohemia and Moravia. Dozens

[6] Alois Míka, 'K národnostním poměrům v Čechách po třicetileté válce', *Československý časopis historický* 24 [74] (1976), 535–63; for the history of non-Catholic Czech exiles in the seventeenth and eighteenth centuries, see Edita Štěříková, *Stručně o pobělohorských exulantech* (Prague, 2005), especially 7–21.

[7] See Míka, 'K národnostním poměrům'; Ludmila Fialová et al., *Dějiny obyvatelstva českých zemí* (Prague, 1996), 92–8.

[8] Míka, 'K národnostním poměrům', 559.

[9] Veronika Čapská, 'Cultural Transfers by means of Translation: Bohemian Lands as a Space of Translation Flows during the Seventeenth and Eighteenth Centuries', in eadem, Robert Antonín and Martin Čapský, eds, *Processes of Cultural Exchange in Central Europe, 1200–1800* (Opava, 2014), 77–127, at 81–2.

of translators whose names and affiliations have now been lost translated innumerable devotional works into Czech and made them accessible to their less learned compatriots. Many of these translations were rather loose (today they would be regarded as adaptations) and often did not cite the original author or title of the translated work, but others did attempt to remain faithful to the earlier text. The unknown translators of *Leben Antichristi* belonged to the latter category.

To complicate matters, it is important to note that early modern texts were not only translated from one language into another, but also circulated in two different media, script and print. Until the 1990s, scholars tended to neglect the importance of manuscript dissemination of texts in the centuries after Gutenberg.[10] However, it is now clear that, until at least the mid-nineteenth century, some types of texts circulated more often in manuscript than in print. Furthermore, for various reasons, specific groups of authors and recipients preferred manuscript as the medium of dissemination for their texts. This preference may have owed something to questions of social origin, gender or aesthetics, or may have arisen for social, economic or religious reasons. Thanks to several recent projects cataloguing early modern manuscripts in Bohemia and Moravia,[11] the outlines of manuscript culture in early modern Bohemia have become more distinct.[12]

We turn now to the Czech manuscript translation of the late seventeenth-century German printed book *Leben Antichristi* by the

[10] See Henry R. Woudhuysen, *Sir Philip Sidney and the Circulation of Manuscripts 1558–1640* (Oxford, 1996); Julia C. Crick and Alexandra Walsham, *The Uses of Script and Print, 1300–1700* (New York, 2004); Margaret J. Ezell, *Social Authorship and the Advent of Print* (Baltimore, MD, 1999); Harold Love, *The Culture and Commerce of Texts: Scribal Publication in Seventeenth-Century England* (Amherst, MA, 1998); David D. Hall, *Ways of Writing: The Practice and Politics of Text-Making in Seventeenth-Century New England* (Philadelphia, PA, 2008); Brian Richardson, *Manuscript Culture in Renaissance Italy* (Cambridge, 2009).

[11] See, for example, Marie Tošnerová et al., *Guide to Manuscript Collections in the Czech Republic* (Prague, 2011); Pavel Brodský, Jan Pařez, *Katalog iluminovaných rukopisů Strahovské knihovny* (Prague, 2008); František Hoffmann, *Soupis rukopisů knihovny Kláštera premonstrátů Teplá*, 2 vols (Prague, 1999); Jaromír Linda, *Soupis rukopisů Studijní a vědecké knihovny Plzeňského kraje*, 2 vols (Plzeň, 2004–10), Irena Zachová and Stanislav Petr, *Soupis sbírky rukopisů bývalého Františkova muzea – fondu G 11 Moravského zemského archivu v Brně* (Prague, 2010), Jaromír Linda et al., *Repertorium rukopisů 17. a 18. století z muzejních sbírek v Čechách*, 1: *A–J*, 2 parts (Prague, 2003), Alena Fidlerová et al., *Repertorium rukopisů 17. a 18. století z muzejních sbírek v Čechách*, 2: *K–O*, 2 parts (Prague, 2007).

[12] For the outline of the manuscript culture in Bohemia and its relationship to printed works, see Alena Fidlerová, 'Rukopisná kultura Čech 17. a 18. století v zrcadle muzejních sbírek', *Folia historica Bohemica* 28 (2013), 181–224.

Capuchin, Dionysius of Luxemburg. The German and Czech versions will be considered as examples of translation, not only between different language communities, but also between different media of text transmission, and thus most probably also different sociocultural groups. The aim of this discussion is to characterize the processes of these translations, and to consider why, unlike the German original, none of the three Czech versions was ever printed.

Dionysius of Luxemburg and his *Leben Antichristi*

In his study of the Antichrist legend and its history, Bernard McGinn judges the version provided by Dionysius of Luxemburg rather unfavourably, suggesting that it 'adopts a folksy and moralizing tone that seems often childish in comparison either with the evident fear found in medieval treatises or the desire for scientific completeness found in Thomas Malvenda'.[13] Other modern readers might concur, or find themselves appalled by Dionysius's vivid descriptions with scenes full of dramatic detail and his tone, partly sensationalist and partly moralizing, familiar from modern tabloids. Nonetheless, his work was undoubtedly well suited for its target audience, as can be seen from its twelve editions.

Dionysius of Luxemburg was born, probably in 1652, in Luxemburg, to a poor family. In 1669 he entered the Rhineland Capuchins, subsequently studying philosophy and theology in Bingen and Mainz under the famous preacher and writer Benignus of Lohr, and later became a famous preacher himself. He lived in a number of the Capuchin houses of the Rhineland, including Mainz, Ehrenbreitstein and Trier, and also served as guardian in Worms, Bensheim and Cochem an der Mosel, where he died in 1703. Dionysius was a contemporary of, and knew personally, the prolific Capuchin author Martin of Cochem, whose popular works were successfully published in Czech.[14] Dionysius's *Leben Antichristi* may even have been intended to complement Martin's most notable work, *Leben Christi*

[13] Bernard McGinn, *Antichrist: Two Thousand Years of the Human Fascination with Evil* (New York, 2000), 231–2.

[14] Johannes Chrysostomus Schulte, *P. Martin von Cochem. 1634–1712. Sein Leben und seine Schriften nach den Quellen dargestellt* (Freiburg im Breisgau, 1910); Leutfrid Signer, ed., *Martin von Cochem. Eine große Gestalt des rheinischen Barock. Seine literarhistorische Stellung und Bedeutung* (Wiesbaden, 1963); Konradin Roth, with Petr Scherle and Reinhold Schommers, *Pater Martin von Cochem 1634–1712 zum 350. Geburtstag des Volksschriftstellers* (Cochem, 1984); Leonhard Lehmann, 'Durch Bücher zum Beten bewegen. Zum 350. Geburtstag des

oder außführliche, andächtige und bewegliche Beschreibung des Lebens und Leydens unsers Herrn Jesu Christi (*Life of Christ, or complete, devout and inspiring Description of the Life and Suffering of our Lord Jesus Christ*), first published in 1677. Although Dionysius was quite a prolific author of devotional books, he has been largely forgotten today.[15] If he is remembered at all, it is as a popular religious writer (*religiöser Volksschriftsteller*),[16] who intentionally used a simple prose style devoid of theological or philosophical niceties and rhetorical embellishments.[17] His works were typically intended to help parish priests to prepare sermons and to be used in catechesis, but Dionysius also envisaged 'an ordinary man who hardly knows how to read' as his readership.[18]

Leben Antichristi was Dionysius's first printed work. It was first published in 1682 in Frankfurt am Main. Although it had received archiepiscopal and Capuchin approval, Dionysius seems to have been required to revise it. In 1683, a second edition appeared under a slightly altered title.[19] This revised version was the author's second

---

Volksschriftstellers Martin von Cochem (1634–1712)', *Wissenschaft und Weisheit. Zeitschrift für Augustinisch-Franziskanische Theologie und Philosophie in der Gegenwart* 48 (1985), 196–227.

[15] Bonaventura von Mehr, *Das Predigtwesen in der Kölnischen und Rhenischen Kapuzinerprovinz in 17. und 18. Jahrhundert* (Rome, 1945), 335–57; eadem, 'Dionysius von Luxemburg', in *Neue Deutsche Biographie* (Berlin, 1957), 735; eadem, 'Dionysius (auch Denis) von Luxemburg', in Bruno Berger and Heinz Rupp, eds, *Deutsches Literatur-Lexikon*, 3rd edn (Bern, 1966 onwards), 3: 297–8; Friedrich Wilhelm Bautz, 'Dionysius von Luxemburg', in idem, ed., *Biographisch-Bibliographisches Kirchenlexikon* (Hamm, 1970 onwards), 1: 1324–5; P[aul]. N[oesen]., 'P. Dionysius von Luxemburg: Ein Volksschriftsteller des 17. Jahrhunderts', *Jonghemecht* 2 (1928), 139–42; Paul Noesen, 'Luxemburger in der rheinischen Kapuzinerprovinz von 1611–1725', *Jonghemecht* 8, 3–5 (1934), 89–90; Jean Malget, 'Dionysius von Luxemburg 1652–1703: Ein Kapuziner aus Luxemburg, nicht der Geringste unter den Besten', *Hémecht. Zeitschrift für Luxemburger Geschichte – Revue d'histoire Luxembourgeoise* 57 (2005), 103–14; Roth, *Pater Martin*, 18–19.

[16] Bautz, 'Dionysius', 1324.

[17] This was in accordance with recommendations already articulated in the Capuchin order constitutions of 1535–6: Mehr, *Predigtwesen*, 398–9.

[18] Cf. the title of one of his works *Die Güldene Legend Von Christo. Das ist: Neue Beschreibung aller Hochheiten und Geheimnussen deß gantzen Lebens Christi / bestehend in dreyssig anmutigen Gesprächen oder Lobs-Versamlungen. Darin all das jenige / was in der gantzen Theologi von Christo gehandelt wird / und von dem gemeinen Mann biß dato gründlich zu wissen verlangt worden / außführlich / sinnreich und anmutig dergestalt beschrieben wird / daß der / so nur recht lesen kan / alles verstehen / vor allem aber ein wahrer inner- und eusserlicher Christ werden mag* … (Frankfurt am Main, 1698).

[19] *Leben Antichristi. Oder: Außführliche / gründliche und Historische Beschreibung Von den zukünfftigen Dingen der Welt. Allwo auß Göttlicher Schrifft / heiligen Vättern / und andern bewehrten Scribenten / die gantze Histori vom Leben / Wunderwercken und Tod Antichristi / und seines Vorläuffers erklärt und erzehlt wird. Es ist auch alhie des H. Propheten Henochs und Eliae Wandel / Marter und Himmelfahrt außführlich beschrieben / und gründlich erwiesen. Anjetzo von neuem*

most popular book, appearing in at least eleven editions by 1771.[20] The presence of copies in a number of European university and convent libraries suggests that it was read not only by its intended readership, but also by monks and other members of educated elites.[21]

The Antichrist legend had proved popular amongst Franciscans almost since the foundation of their order, so it is unsurprising that Dionysius chose this theme.[22] His *Leben Antichristi* represents a continuation of the tradition which treated the Antichrist through a form of a biography or 'reverse' hagiography.[23] It proceeds more or less chronologically, starting with the birth of Antichrist and finishing with his death. The author describes each episode in great detail,[24] discussing for instance precisely how the Antichrist and his collaborators will perform their false miracles, and supporting his argument by quotations from Scripture and the Church Fathers. Most chapters conclude with an exhortation to pious readers to consider the differences between Christ and Antichrist, to amend their lives and to beware of the ultimate enemy's deception. The entire text endeavours to be strictly Catholic and socially conservative. Dionysius rejects any conceivable connection between Rome, pope and Antichrist and urges his readers not to rebel against their superiors. He seems genuinely concerned with the danger Antichrist may pose to simple souls and wants to equip them with the means to protect themselves. To ensure that they would not neglect his warnings, he seeks to present his material in a way that will capture his readers' attention and touch their emotions.

The majority of sources which Dionysius quotes had never been translated into the vernacular. Thus his book can be considered a translation from scholarly discourse into the language of common people. The book even presents itself as a translation, providing

---

übersehen / corrigirt und verbessert; wie auch durch einen sonderbahren Zusatz vom Judischen Messia ergrössert und vermehrt: so dem begierigen Leser nützlich / und zu besserer Erkantnus dieser Histori dienlich seyn wird. Der zweyte Truck. Durch P. F. Dionysius von Lützemburg Capuciner-Ordens / der Rheinischen Provintz Prediger (Frankfurt am Main, 1683).

[20] Frankfurt am Main, 1682, 1683, 1686, 1695; Vienna, 1716, 1729, 1744, 1745, 1764, 1771; Kaufbeuren, 1742, 1750.

[21] Alena A. Fidlerová, 'Antikrist v Českých zemích raného novověku', *Acta Universitatis Carolinae, Philologica: Slavica Pragensia* 42 (2014), 133–75, at 146–9.

[22] McGinn, *Antichrist*, 152–66, 169–70, 174–6, 180–1.

[23] Ibid. 100–3.

[24] Hans Preuß, *Die Vorstellungen vom Antichrist im späteren Mittelalter, bei Luther und in der konfessionellen Polemik* (Leipzig, 1906), 253–5.

information previously inaccessible to ordinary people in a language they can understand. To support this impression, lengthy bibliographical notes in Latin are provided at the end of each chapter (these also serve to defend the work against any suspicion on the part of learned opponents), representing the respected sources, inaccessible to the non-Latin reader, but here retold in the text.

Czech Manuscript Translations of Dionysius's Book

In the collections of Czech museums and libraries, three early modern manuscript translations of *Leben Antichristi* have so far been identified.[25] None is complete, but the losses are relatively minor, at most several pages at the beginning or at the end. None bears a date or the name of the translator. The earliest version, probably dating from the first third of the eighteenth century, is preserved in Josef Hylák's Museum, in the south-west Bohemian town of Radnice.[26] Its title closely follows that of the German original.[27] Unfortunately, the name of the translator, which originally appeared in the bottom right-hand corner of the title page, has been erased by readers handling the volume. However, the language used suggests that he may have lived in south-western Bohemia.

The second manuscript is today owned by the National Library of the Czech Republic in Prague (Klementinum).[28] Most of it was probably written in the mid-eighteenth century, but the beginning and end have been copied anew by another scribe who gave the volume an abbreviated title,[29] as well as signing and dating his work 'w Knihnitzych

[25] Fidlerová, 'Antikrist'.

[26] Radnice, Muzeum Josefa Hyláka, MS H–1726.

[27] 'Ziwot Antikrysta. A Neb Weykladne, Gruntowni, a Hystorytske Rozepsani O budauczych weczech tohoto Swěta Kdežto z Pisma Swateho Swatych Otczuw, a ginssých Wznessenych Spisowateluw czela Historige o žiwotu, diwych, a Smrtj Antikrysta, též geho Přžedchudczy se wyswetluge, a powida Take tuto se dwauch Swatych Prorokuw Enocha, a Elyasse gegich obczowanj Mučedlniczstwj, y do Nebe pogitj naležite wypisuge, a gruntowne dokazuge Nynj z Nowu přžehlydnuta, a naprawena, gako y skrze obwzlasstnj Přidawek o Židowskem Mesyassy rozmnožena, Czož dobrotiwemu, a chtiwemu Čžtenaržj užitečžne k lepss[ímu Ro]zumenj teto Historie slaužitj bude Wydana w Němeczskem gazyku od P. F. Dionysa z Lützenburka Ržadu Capuczinskeho Kazatele Provincie Ržissske Nyni pak Nemeczskeho na Čžesky přželožena Od'.

[28] Prague, Národní knihovna České republiky, MS XVII E 93.

[29] 'Historické Popsání o budoucích věcech Světa, obzvláště ale, o tom Boha způstilým životu, a ukrutným přenásledováním Antikrista': ibid. v.

dne 12 Prasynce 1824. Frantz Kautny' ('in Knínice,[30] 12 December 1824. Franc Koutný').[31] The language of this text indicates that it was created in Moravia.

The third and most recent manuscript can be found in the Dr. Hostaš Museum in Klatovy,[32] also in the south-west of Bohemia. It lacks the title page but the handwriting suggests that it is an early nineteenth-century copy of an older text. A note added by one of its owners indicates that he lived in Kladno.[33] The language of this translation also suggests that it was probably written in central Bohemia.

All three manuscripts are more or less fair copies which represent faithful translations of the German original, including some of the paratexts (imprimatur, preface, index etc.) and the bibliographical notes. The Radnice manuscript also includes marginal notes added by the translator, and the translator's preface and postscript.[34] However, these do not provide much information about him or his motivation, other than commenting that he was translating into the 'Czech language' and for the sake of Czech people. The translator also included the privilege of Emperor Leopold issued to the printer of the German version of the text. This appears in the manuscript, entitled 'Privilegium Caesareum pro Spisowatele' ('Imperial Privilege for the Writer'),[35] suggesting that the text had been approved by the emperor himself and was thus beyond suspicion. The inclusion of this privilege shows that the translator used either the 1686 or the 1695 German edition, since editions printed after the emperor's death did not include it.

The scribe of the Klementinum manuscript also added his own postscripts to both parts of the book,[36] and probably also a preface to the first part which is now lost. In the postscripts, he briefly explains that he had translated the book for the sake of Moravians into the 'Moravian language' (which is quite close to standard Czech), emphasizes that he translated faithfully without adding anything of his

[30] There are several villages of this name in Moravia, but an envelope addressed to one of the owner of the book and left in it indicates that the village in question is Knínice near Boskovice.

[31] MS XVII E 93, 758.

[32] Klatovy, Muzeum Dr. Hostaše, MS RK 147.

[33] Ibid. 641.

[34] MS H–1726, [ix]–[x]; part 2, 71–2.

[35] Ibid. [v]–[viii].

[36] MS XVII E 93, 665–6, 744–5.

own, and characterizes himself as an old man close to the end of his life.

We know least about the translator of the Klatovy manuscript: not only does it lack any paratexts, but it is also a later copy and thus even the date of this translation is uncertain. One unusual feature is that its translator moved most of the Latin bibliographical notes (except those referring to the Bible which he incorporated into the text) from the end of each chapter to the very end of the book, probably so as not to trouble the ordinary reader who could be expected to be less interested in this reference material.

German vs. Czech, Print vs. Manuscript

Despite its length (almost five hundred pages in print, seven hundred or more pages in manuscript), *Leben Antichristi* was translated into Czech in its entirety at least three times during the eighteenth century, in three different places and by three different translators. All the translators made efforts to be as faithful to the original as possible and introduced only minor changes, mostly aiming to facilitate understanding by the provision of such aids as marginal notes, prefaces and postscripts. At least two of the versions bear visible traces of their readers' ongoing interest at the beginning of the nineteenth century or even later. All this shows that there was a long-term demand for Czech versions of the book, and yet for some reason it was never published. This lack of printed versions is in contrast to the major works of Dionysius's Capuchin brother Martin of Cochem. Although the style and content of Martin's works were similar to those of the *Leben Antichristi*, his works were printed in Czech from an early date and were often reissued in new editions.[37]

It is impossible to know whether any of the three translators attempted to get their work printed. Although the Radnice manuscript looks like a fair copy which could have been presented for censorship, its binding is seriously damaged; if there were ever any traces of censorship, they are now lost. In contrast, the Klementinum manuscript includes an undated Latin assessment by a censor, the chancellor of Trnava University, Ján Príleský SJ, which must have

[37] On Czech editions of his *Leben Christi*, see Miloš Sládek, 'Zrcadlo zrcadlu nastavené aneb Několik vět na okraj životů Kristových', in Martin of Cochem, *Veliký život Pána a Spasitele našeho Krista Ježíše a jeho nejsvětější a nejmilejší matky Marie Panny* … , ed. Miloš Sládek, Lucie Peisertová and Tomáš Breň (Prague, 2007), 5–45.

been written some time between 1747 and 1764.[38] It is unclear why this manuscript was sent to Trnava. As it was written in Moravia it would have been more logical for it to have been sent to Brno, from where it would have been referred to the bishop of Olomouc and then the Jesuit professors at the University of Olomouc. Possibly the translator hoped for a more favourable reception in Trnava, because the Hungarian part of the empire operated rather independently.[39] However, Príleský refused to recommend the translation for publication, citing several reasons, mostly to do with the content of the book (even though it was identical to the German version printed repeatedly in Vienna during this period), and adding: 'and finally, because the Life includes these numerous obscure and uncertain things, which I do not deem suitable to be discussed publicly in a vernacular language'.[40] This would be understandable if the original had been written in Latin, but Príleský is assessing a vernacular translation of another vernacular text. It suggests that he may have considered one language (Czech) to be 'more vernacular' than another (German). This appears to confirm the often repeated, but rarely documented, thesis that the nobility and bougeoisie were contemptuous of the Czech language.[41] The majority of Czech speakers were probably regarded as rustic, uneducated and unable to understand the message of such a difficult text correctly. Furthermore, censorship in the Habsburg Empire, organized by the state but directed by the bishops and carried out by the Jesuits, was designed to control the reading of popular classes and the so-called 'naive readers' by equipping them with printed material which would cultivate and educate them, while simultaneously protecting them against the danger of confusion or moral corruption brought about by bad reading matter. From this point of view, it is not surprising that Dionysius's text, aimed at a popular readership was regarded as dangerous, the more so when provided in a language which, in the eyes of the censors, lacked educated speakers.[42]

[38] It seems likely that Príleský was chancellor of Trnava University twice, first for four years between 1747 and 1754, and again from 1763 to 1764: Fidlerová, 'Antikrist', 160–1.
[39] Michael Wögerbauer et al., *V obeckém zájmu. Cenzura a sociální regulace literatury v moderní české kultuře 1749–2014*, 2 vols (Prague, 2015), 1: 66–7.
[40] '[D]eniqve qvia Vita haec multa admodum obscura, & incerta complectitur, qvo vel ideo populari lingva evulganda mihi non videtur': MS XVII E 93, 753.
[41] Míka, 'K národnostním poměrům', 550.
[42] In 1774, *Leben Antichristi* was included in the *Catalogus librorum a Commissione Caes. Reg. Aulica prohibitorum. editio nova* (Vienna, 1774), 175. As the translation had been censored

However, the German editions of *Leben Antichristi* seem never to have been censored in the Habsburg Empire, and they were always published with the imprimatur which originally appeared in the second, Frankfurt edition. This is rather surprising, as one of the tasks of the Austrian censors during the second half of the eighteenth century was to recensor previously censored works if the official attitude to certain types of text changed. Moreover, from 1716, the law required that each printed book include a confirmation that it had been approved.[43] That this regulation was not strictly observed can be demonstrated from the Vienna editions of *Leben Antichristi.* Similarly, the Czech translation of Martin's *Leben Christi* was published without an imprimatur, but only with a *protestatio translatoris* that his translation was faithful to the original text, which had also never been subject to censorship in the Habsburg Empire.[44] Thus there must have been ways of getting books of this nature printed without the censors' approval. Perhaps the Czech version of the life of Antichrist was too suspicious even for them, or perhaps it was simply too voluminous for the small regional presses that published such material, often with a false imprint.

An additional problem may have been that none of the translators of the *Leben Antichristi* belonged to one of the 'translation projects' identified by Čapská. On the other hand, the very existence of these manuscripts, together with the translation of Martin's *Leben Christi* by the Capuchin Edelbert Nymburský, suggests the possibility of a smaller but distinct Capuchin translation initiative. Unfortunately, the literary activities of Czech Capuchins have not so far been analysed, and the most comprehensive catalogue of Czech printed books up to 1800, *Knihopis*, does not register the affiliation of individual authors to religious orders.[45]

---

by the 1760s, language appears to have been an important factor: if the manuscript had been censored during or after the mid-1770s, it would probably not have received an imprimatur, simply because the German version was already banned. Until the 1760s, it was not banned and was freely published in German, and therefore there must have been other reasons for not allowing the Czech translations to be printed.

[43] Ibid. 96.

[44] Sládek, 'Zrcadlo', 11.

[45] Zdeněk V. Tobolka et al., *Knihopis českých a slovenských tisků od doby nejstarší až do konce XVIII. století*, 2 vols in 12 (Prague, 1925–67); Zdeněk V. Tobolka et al., *Knihopis českých a slovenských tisků od doby nejstarší až do konce XVIII. století. Dodatky* (Prague, 1994–2010), abbreviated version, accessible online at: <http://aleph.nkp.cz/F/?func=file&file_name=find-b&local_base=KPS>.

A final factor could explain the authorities' unwillingness to allow the Czech translation to be published: the region's 'heretical' past. The Hussite movement of the early fifteenth century had led to nearly two hundred years during which Catholicism was severely challenged in the Czech lands. The memory of this past was directly related to the Antichrist theme, for, according to McGinn, 'the Hussites played a key role in the history of the Antichrist legend'.[46] Although they were not the first to identify the papacy with Antichrist – that had been Wyclif, who inspired Jan Hus – McGinn suggests that 'it was among the radical Hussites that this new moment in Antichrist's story became a part of a revolutionary ideology that encouraged overthrowing the social and religious order'.[47] Moreover, and as in Germany,[48] the theme of the Antichrist had been amply represented in Czech-language Reformation polemics throughout the sixteenth century and into the seventeenth.[49] It would not be surprising if the memory of the propensity of 'notoriously heretic Czechs' to treat this theme in a heterodox way, together with the inclination of at least a part of the religious elites in the second half of the eighteenth century not to add fuel to old confessional polemics, had rung alarm bells, even over a century after the allegedly complete re-Catholicization of the rebellious land, and despite the strictly Catholic and conservative tendency of Dionysius's work.

The explanations so far suggested for the lack of Czech print editions of *Leben Antichristi* have been based on the specific historical circumstances which shaped relations between German and Czech language and literature in the Czech lands at the time when Dionysius's text was translated. However, there is also another possibility, namely to treat this text as an example of a transfer of a specific textual type between two different language communities: one larger and

[46] McGinn, *Antichrist*, 187.

[47] Ibid.

[48] Ingvild Richardsen-Friedrich, *Antichrist-Polemik in der Zeit der Reformation und der Glaubenskämpfe bis Anfang des 17. Jahrhunderts: Argumentation, Form und Funktion* (Frankfurt am Main, 2003).

[49] See, for example, Daniel Solnický, *Compendium, To gest Kratičké / Wssak těchto časů vžitečné obsaženj / některých přednėgssjch Artykulůw prawé Wijry a Náboženstwj Ržjmského Katholického, a samospasytedlného* (Prague, 1630, 2nd edn 1652, *Knihopis* K15559, K15560); *Rozmlauwánj Dwau Osob w Náboženstwj sobě odporných. O Artikuljch wjry Křestanské Czlowěka Katholjckého a Ewangeljckého. Tento gsa wyhnan z wlasti do Cyzyny wandruge; Onen pak w cestu gemu wyházy a doma geg s sebau/ pokudzby chtěl Náboženstwj geho przjgjt i / zdrzěti vsyluge* (n. pl., 1627–30; *Knihopis* K14976).

stronger and the other noticeably smaller and weaker, perceiving the language of the source community as more prestigious and socially superior than its own. It is possible that the process of double translation, between two different languages and media, as illustrated in the case of *Leben Antichristi*, may reflect a broader tendency. Such double translations seem likely to have occurred when a specific type of text (particularly one which is problematic in some respect, e. g. not entirely orthodox, or highly intellectual) migrates between such communities. This hypothesis is suggested by another translation of *Leben Antichristi*, a Slovenian manuscript translation originally produced in 1767 by a village scholar, Matija Žegar, with the title *Antichrsta Shivllenie ali Leben Antechrista.*[50] This was popular not only in Žegar's native region of Carinthia, but also in Upper and Lower Carniola, in the Pohorje Mountains and in Ljubljana. Copies of *Antichrsta Shivllenie* continued to be produced until the first half of the nineteenth century. Despite its popularity and wide circulation in manuscript (at least fourteen copies or adaptations are known so far),[51] this translation was also never printed. These two cases of unpublished double translation, Czech and Slovenian, may of course be regarded as coincidence, but it is striking that both are examples of similar processes with similar outcomes.

[50] Alfred Ogris, 'Woher stammte der Kärntner "bukovnik" Matthias Schegar/Matija Žegar?', *Carinthia I, Zeitrchrift für geschichtliche Landeskunde von Kärnten* 188 (1998), 445–63; 'Register slovenskih rokopisov 17. in 18. stoletja. Index 033. Žegar, Matija: Antikrist', online at: <http://ezb.ijs.si/fedora/get/nrss:index_index_033/VIEW/>, accessed 31 January 2016. The original manuscript is preserved in Ravne na Koroškem, Koroška osrednja knjižnica Dr Franca Sušnika, and accessible online under the title 'Življenje Antikrista (Žegarjev Antikrist)' at: <http://www.rav.sik.si/images/pdf/rokopisno_gradivo/swf/ZegarjevAntikrist.swf>. An incomplete illustrated copy of the text dating to 1823–4 and entitled 'Prerokuanie od Antichrista' is preserved in Klagenfurt, Kärtntner Landesarchiv, AT-KLA 118-A-13/43 St. Another copy from 1790 is in the same archive under the title 'Shiulenje, regie rengainu smert antikrista', AT-KLA 118-A-12/14 St. Other copies are to be found in the Ljubljana, Arhiv republike Slovenije, and in private ownership.

[51] Niko Kuret, 'Žegar, Matija', in *Slovenska biografija* (2013), online at: <http://www.slovenska-biografija.si/oseba/sbi893919/#slovenski-biografski-leksikon>, accessed 31 January 2016 (first publ. in Jože Munda et al., eds, *Slovenski biografski leksikon*, 4/15: *Zdolšek – Žvanut* [Ljubljana, 1991], 939).

Conclusion

The theme of the Antichrist and his coming at the end of time has been popular in many epochs.[52] It has been treated by many different authors, with very different aims and using different genres ranging from prophecies, theological tracts or commentaries to sacred texts, drama, poems, paintings or – today – films. In the course of history, some of these works were accessible only to educated elites, while others aimed at a more popular readership. As this article has demonstrated, the translation of some of these works into other languages sometimes encountered difficulties. This was particularly true when these texts were aimed at a popular audience. Furthermore, there was a linguistic hierarchy which meant that certain languages were perceived differently by the elites.

Dionysius of Luxemburg translated this sensitive subject from the learned languages of Latin and Greek into German and succeeded in satisfying the authorities (to the extent that they did not ban his work) and enthusing his general audience. However, the three anonymous translators of his work into Czech did not see their texts printed. Nonetheless, their translations became constituent parts of the manuscript culture of the early modern Czech lands and were preserved, read, copied and reworked by their successors.[53] Their work apparently attracted interest and was clearly appreciated, albeit by a more limited circle of readers or listeners. Although these translations were not published, they circulated in manuscript and met the needs of their intended audience. The question remains: how should we interpret and assess this simultaneous shift in language and medium? Is it an outcome of specific historical circumstances to do with the relationship between Czech and German language communities in the early modern Habsburg Empire, or is it pure historical coincidence? Or does it illustrate a general tendency, characteristic of the translation of specific texts between two language communities of uneven strength and prestige? At present this question cannot be answered with any certainty. However, these German and Czech (and Slovenian) versions of *Leben Antichristi* provide a useful starting point for further discussion and reflection on these themes.

[52] McGinn, *Antichrist.*

[53] For later additions to these manuscripts and extracts from them, see Fidlerová, 'Antikrist', 150–4.

St Pientia and the Château de la Roche-Guyon: Relic Translations and Sacred History in Seventeenth-Century France

Jennifer Hillman*
University of Chester

This article explores the connections between the translation of an early Christian relic to the Château de la Roche-Guyon in the mid-seventeenth century and the writing of local sacred histories by the priest and prior Nicolas Davanne. It finds that the translation of a finger bone of St Pientia was the culmination of efforts by a local scholar to revive the sacred history of the Vexin and to celebrate the regional liturgical traditions associated with its early Christian martyrs. In doing so, it finds support for the recent historiography on local, sacred histories which emerged during the Counter-Reformation in response to liturgical standardization. The article also discusses the unstable nature of relics as material objects and explores the ways in which relics were continually reinvested with meaning. It is shown that Pientia's relic was not only part of a defence of a local spiritual heritage in response to Trent, but also part of a claim to an early Christian spiritual heritage for a deviant and heretical movement within the Church.

Introduction: Reinventing Relics

On 29 October 1656, the archbishop of Rouen carried out an episcopal visitation at the Château de La Roche-Guyon, property of the duke and duchess of Liancourt. The purpose of the visitation of Archbishop François Harlay de Champvallon (1625–95) was to verify the authenticity of the saintly relics preserved in a silver reliquary in the Chapelle de Notre-Dame-des-Neiges.[1] Among the holy objects in the château was a relic recently translated from the monastery of Saint-Nicaise at Meulan. The relic was a finger of the third-century noble virgin martyr St Pientia (or Pience). Pientia had been converted

* Department of History & Archaeology, University of Chester, Parkgate Rd, CH1 4BJ. E-mail: j.hillman@chester.ac.uk.

[1] The word used in the document was *chasse*, an old French word for reliquary, deriving from *capsa*, Latin for 'box' or 'coffer': Robert Bartlett, *Why can the Dead do such Great Things? Saints and Worshippers from the Martyrs to the Reformation* (Princeton, NJ, 2013), 264.

Studies in Church History 53 (2017) 257–271
doi: 10.1017/stc.2016.16

to Christianity at La Roche-Guyon through the evangelizing of the missionary St Nicasius and his companions Scubiculus and Quirinus during their journeys along the Seine.[2]

La Roche-Guyon was situated on a commercial route between Paris and Rouen, on the right bank of the Seine in the Vexin, on the border of Normandy.[3] The seventeenth-century proprietors of La Roche-Guyon, the duke and duchess Roger du Plessis and Jeanne de Schomberg, were distinguished patrons of the Cistercian convent of Port-Royal, a relationship strengthened by their loyalty during the theological controversies of the middle decades of the seventeenth century, when Port-Royal was persecuted for being one of the sites at which the 'heretical' ideas of the Dutch theologian Cornelius Jansen (1585–1638) on grace, free will and salvation held sway.[4] It was largely due to the patronage and protection of families such as the Liancourts during this period that the convent eluded destruction until 29 October 1709, when it was demolished by Louis XIV's troops. The duke and duchess were also practitioners of the neo-Augustinian, penitential strand of post-Tridentine Catholicism associated with Port-Royal and the Jansenists, now often referred to as 'rigorist'.[5] The Liancourts were among the *noblesse d'épée* (sword nobility) who had purchased positions at the royal court.[6] After both experiencing conversions in the mid-seventeenth century, they became known for their staunch piety. Both also seem to have internalized the reforming agenda of the Counter-Reformation; the duke was among the noble membership of the elite *dévot* organization, the *Compagnie du Saint-Sacrement* (Company of the Holy Sacrament) and the duchess was

[2] Cergy-Pontoise, Archives départementales du Val d'Oise [hereafter: ADVO], fonds privées, 10 J, 747, 'Reliques: certificats et visites'.

[3] Vincent Gourdon and Marion Trévisi, 'Âge et migrations dans la France rural traditionnelle. Une Etude à partir de l'an VII à la Roche-Guyon', *Histoire, économie, et société* 19 (2000), 307–30, at 311. For a recent history of the château and its gardens from the late seventeenth and eighteenth centuries, see Gabriel Wick, *Un Paysage des lumières. Le Jardin Anglais du Château de La Roche-Guyon* (Paris, 2014).

[4] For a recent history of the convent and the Jansenist debate, see Daniella Kostroun, *Feminism, Absolutism and Jansenism: Louis XIV and the Port-Royal Nuns* (Cambridge, 2011).

[5] Robin Briggs, *Communities of Belief: Cultural and Social Tension in Early Modern France* (Oxford, 1989), 339; Jennifer Hillman, *Female Piety and the Catholic Reformation in France* (London, 2014), 2–3.

[6] Robert J. Kalas, 'Marriage, Clientage, Office Holding, and the Advancement of the Early Modern French Nobility: The Noailles Family of Limousin', *SCJ* 27 (1996), 365–83, at 379.

one of Vincent de Paul's most formidable *Dames de la charité* (Ladies of Charity).

The duke and duchess procured the finger of St Pientia from a larger collection of relics at the Benedictine monastery of Saint-Nicaise in Meulan, around thirty kilometres from the château. The other agent in the commissioning of the relic was Nicolas Davanne (d. 11 June 1660), superior of the institution. As well as leading a complete reform of religious life at Meulan in the early seventeenth century, Davanne also wrote prolifically. Some twenty-six years prior to the translation of Pientia's finger, he had published the first edition of his 'Life' of Nicasius and his companions, with a second edition in 1643.[7] Davanne's *vita* was alluded to in the visitation documentation of October 1656 as the 'history' serving as evidence that Pientia was 'former lady of La Roche-Guyon' and companion of Nicasius, 'the first bishop of Rouen'. Davanne was also the author of a published collection (*Recueil*) of 'acts and contracts' pertaining to the priory of Saint-Nicaise, in which he recorded the movements of the relics of Pientia and her male companions Nicasius Scubiculus and Quirinus.[8]

This article explores the connections between the translation of an early Christian relic to the Château de la Roche-Guyon in the mid-seventeenth century and the writing of these sacred histories. The first part reconstructs the broader circumstances surrounding the translation of Pientia's finger by situating it within Davanne's more recent history of movement of the early Christian relics. The second part turns its attention towards Davanne's *vitae* and the longer history of Pientia's bones that he presented, before considering the particular set of circumstances which may have motivated him to write. It finds that the translation of Pientia's finger was the culmination of efforts by a local scholar to revive the sacred history of the Vexin and celebrate the regional liturgical traditions associated with its early Christian martyrs. In doing so, it finds support for the recent

[7] Nicolas Davanne, *La vie et martyre de sainct Nigaise, premier archevesque de Roüen, S. Quirin, prestre, & S. Scuviculle Diacre ses compagnons, & de sainte Pience, jadis dame de La Rocheguyon; ensemble le recueil de la Translation de leurs sainctes reliques, et fondation du prieuré Saint Nigaise au fort de Meulent ou ils reposent* (Rouen, 1627). I have also consulted the 1643 reprint, but throughout this article, I cite the 1627 edition.

[8] Nicolas Davanne, *Recueil d'actes et contracts, faicts par M Nicolas Davanne, prestre ancien prieur du prieuré S. Nigaise au fort de Meulant; et encores par autres personnes pour fondations & Decorations audit prieuré & ailleurs; avec un breve description dudit prieuré selon son estat, en l'année 1656* (Rouen, 1656).

historiography on local, sacred histories which emerged during the Counter-Reformation in response to liturgical standardization.

In the course of this discussion, this article is also attentive to relics as objects with unstable meanings. Translation, as Robyn Malo has recently observed, was not just about the physical relocation of a holy object, but also a 'rhetorical translation', as texts and their 'relic discourse' helped generate new significance for relics.[9] Similarly, Katarzyna Rutkowski's notion of the 'textual reliquary' has helpfully illuminated how narratives help to endow relics with power.[10] Pientia's relics, it is argued here, were reinvested with meaning via different modes of commemoration. In Davanne's sacred histories, Pientia became an integral part of an articulation and defence of a local spiritual heritage in response to Trent. By her subsequent relocation to the rigorist château at La Roche-Guyon, she was also part of a claim to an early Christian spiritual heritage by the rigorist reaction within the French Church.

'Restless' Relics:[11] Pientia and Nicasius in the Vexin

The chapel, as described within an inventory taken in 1672, housed a substantial corpus of relics among which Pientia's finger was placed in December 1654. According to the inventory, the relics were contained within a silver reliquary and placed upon a small table.[12] In the château today, the life of St Pientia is depicted in reliefs on the walls of the chapel, but its relic collection has disappeared.[13]

A document dated 30 December 1654 states that Pientia's finger was translated to La Roche-Guyon from the monastery at Meulan.[14] The translation document was annotated with a sketch of the phalanx bone relic which the 'translators' claimed to have 'drawn' to

[9] Robyn Malo, *Relics and Writing in Late Medieval England* (Toronto, ON, 2013), 9.

[10] Katarzyna Rutkowski, 'Reformation of the Relic: Lydgate's and Milton's Saint Edmund', in Elizabeth Robertson and Jennifer Jahner, eds, *Medieval and Early Modern Devotional Objects in Global Perspective: Translations of the Sacred* (Basingstoke, 2010), 135–53, at 135.

[11] This is a reference to a point made excellently by Cynthia Hahn in her study of medieval reliquaries: 'What do Reliquaries do for Relics?', *Numen* 57 (2010), 284–316, at 312. Reliquaries were, she argues, like relics, 'restless' as they were 'lifted, gestured with, carried in processions, opened and closed'.

[12] ADVO, fonds privées, 10 J, 31, 'Inventaire après décès', 1672.

[13] The tourist website of the château describes the chapel: <http://www.chateaudelarocheguyon.fr/content/heading14575/content16393.html>, accessed 8 July 2015.

[14] ADVO, fonds privées, 10 J, 747.

document the relic. It is confirmed in the document that the finger came from a larger collection of bones of the virgin martyr which remained at the monastery. It is unclear exactly how the Liancourts were able to obtain this fragment from Meulan. The record describes the relic as 'granted' (*octroye*) by the monastery, taken (*tiré*) from a reliquary (*chasse*) and placed in the seigneurial chapel. The document emphasizes Pientia's status as 'former Lady of this place' (*jadis Dame dudit lieu*) and suggests that the translation was imagined as restoring Pientia to her own lands and the site of her eventual martyrdom. If at least some of the initiative for the translation lay with Davanne, it may also have been regarded as a practical move for the newly reformed monastery to reach out to potential wealthy, local patrons with such a gift. The illegibility of a portion of the document obscures some of the details, but it does also seem clear that the duke and duchess of Liancourt had actively sought out the relic with the intention of enhancing devotions and honouring God at this holy site. The seigneurial chapel was already a significant space for the veneration of saintly relics – including those of Elizabeth of Hungary; the apostles Thomas and Matthias; the martyrs Lawrence, Barbara and Catherine of Alexandria; and Marie Salomé. According to this document, the translation was a way of renewing and augmenting their devotions to these holy remains. For the Liancourts, the procurement of the relic was also related in more complex ways to their own evolving spiritual identities as rigorists.

Historically, relic translations had been subject to much regulation after initially being prohibited and condemned as 'tomb violation'.[15] Newly translated relics had to prove themselves, as Patrick Geary noted in his influential essay on sacred commodities.[16] At La Roche-Guyon, issues of veracity may have been the motivation for the episcopal visitation of the chapel in 1656. The finger of Pientia had originally belonged to another collection of truly 'restless relics'.[17]

[15] Patrick Geary, *Furta Sacra: Thefts of Relics in the Central Middle Ages* (Princeton, NJ, 1990), 110; Éric Rebillard, *The Care of the Dead in Late Antiquity*, transl. Elizabeth Trapnell Rawlings and Jeanine Routier-Pucci (Ithaca, NY, and London, 2009), 67.

[16] Patrick Geary, 'Sacred Commodities: The Circulation of Medieval Relics', in Arjun Appadurai, ed., *The Social Life of Things: Commodities in Cultural Perspective* (Cambridge, 1986), 169–94, at 181; see also Sherry L. Reames, 'Reconstructing and Interpreting a Thirteenth-Century Office for the Translation of Thomas Becket', *Speculum* 80 (2005), 118–70.

[17] Hahn, 'What do Reliquaries do for Relics?', 312. Pientia's teeth were among the relics at Avranches listed in an inventory: Samantha Kahn Herrick, *Imagining the Sacred Past: Hagiography and Power in Early Normandy* (Cambridge, MA, 2007), 149.

The body parts of the four martyrs (Nicasius, Scubiculus, Quirinus and Pientia) had been fragmented and the spoils had been circulating around local religious institutions for some time before they wound up at Davanne's priory in Meulan. It was during the eleventh century that a cult surrounding the relics of Nicasius and his companions developed in the Vexin after their translation to the monastery of Saint-Ouen at Rouen in 1032.[18] This provided occasion for the composition of the *Passio Nicasii*, the first 'life' of Nicasius and the other martyrs.[19]

During Davanne's tenure at the priory at Meulan, the relics continued in their restlessness, as recorded in his account describing their continuing movements. The translations that he recorded in the *Recueil*, along with their accompanying rituals, can be used to shed light on his aims as author. The first translation Davanne described was the movement of the relics of Pientia, Scubiculus and Quirinus to new reliquaries on 1 June 1639, the feast of the Ascension, when the relics of the martyrs were central to the local celebration of the feast.[20] Davanne explained how the relics were venerated both on the vigil and the day of their feast, as well as on the vigil and the feast day of the Ascension. Four reliquaries containing the relics of the four martyrs were displayed, according to this account, and Davanne stressed how people assembled to kiss and touch them with their rosaries, a common ritual practice surrounding relics. William Christian found similar practices in Fuencaliente, Spain, for instance, when on feast days the head of one of the legendary Eleven Thousand Virgins of Cologne was exposed to local people who were permitted to touch it 'with their heads, eyes, mouths, bowls, and other objects out of devotion'.[21] The second translation Davanne related was the relocation of Nicasius's relics on 13 May 1643, the vigil of the Feast of the

[18] Herrick, *Imagining*, 17–18.

[19] *Passio Nicasii*, in 'Appendix ad catalogum codicium hagiographicorum civitatis et academiae Leodiensis', *AnBoll* 5 (1886), 372–4; 'Appendix ad catalogum codicium hagiographicorum civitatis Namurcensis', *AnBoll* 1 (1882), 628–32, both cited in Herrick, *Imagining*, 154. See also Samantha Kahn Herrick, 'Heirs to the Apostles: Saintly Power and Ducal Authority in Hagiography of Early Normandy', in Adam J. Kosto, Alan Cooper and Robert Berkhoffer, eds, *The Experience of Power in Medieval Europe 950–1350* (Aldershot, 2005), 11–24; A. Legris, 'Les Premiers martyrs du Vexin. Saints Nicaise, Quirin, Scuvicule, Pience (11 octobre)', *Revue catholique de Normandie* (1912), 280–96.

[20] Davanne, *Recueil*, 42.

[21] William Christian, *Local Religion in Sixteenth-Century Spain* (Princeton, NJ, 1981), 127.

Ascension, to a new reliquary, at the cost of 2,400 livres.[22] This particular translation was, he noted, marked by a sermon delivered by the bishop of Chartres, and the singing of the *Te Deum* and *Veni Creator Spiritus* by the clergy and local people. (The latter is more typically used in consecrations, ordinations and coronations.) According to Davanne, this heavily ritualized translation culminated in the removal of the bones piece by piece, witnessed by the whole congregation, before they were placed in the new reliquary.[23]

In the preface, Davanne stated that his motivation for recording these and other instances of translation was the edification of the Benedictines at Meulan and the female religious at the monastery of Notre Dame de Bonnes Nouvelles in Rouen, where he was also a superior, as well as for posterity.[24] Interestingly, Davanne did not record the ceremony accompanying the conferring of Pience's finger on the chapel at La Roche-Guyon, perhaps a reflection of the more private nature of this particular translation. It seems significant that Davanne devoted more attention to carefully recording the public, liturgical ceremonies that accompanied other movements of the relics, indicating that he was probably also writing to strengthen an existing cult. This is also reflected in his commentary on the devotional traditions surrounding the relics. For instance, Davanne described how beneath the main altar in the church at Saint-Nicaise, Meulan, there was an armoire in which were kept a number of reliquaries. Among them was an ivory horn (*cor d'yvoire*) which had been formerly used both as a reliquary and to call people to mass. It was known as the 'horn of Saint Nicaise' (*cornet Saint-Nicaise*). When applied to the ears, Davanne observed, it could heal deafness.[25] This object also appears in Davanne's account of the translation ceremonies, where he again refers to its curative powers.[26]

The translation of Nicasius's bones into the costly new reliquary coincided with the publication of the second edition of Davanne's *vita*, in which he had already made a strong case for the liturgical traditions surrounding the early Christian history of La Roche-Guyon. An explanation of how the translation of Pientia's finger fitted into

22 Davanne, *Recueil*, 44–9.
23 Ibid. 46.
24 Ibid. 3.
25 Ibid. 6.
26 Ibid. 12.

these claims about the spiritual heritage of the Vexin is provided in Davanne's text.

The Spiritual Heritage of a Sacred Landscape

Davanne's life of the early Christian martyrs of the Vexin was not the first such account. The earliest reference to Nicasius was in Usuard's martyrology of 865, which simply recorded his name, status and date of martyrdom.[27] Herrick's study of the eleventh-century *Passio* has highlighted the discrepancies between Usuard's account of Nicasius as a simple priest and later hagiographies (including Davanne's) which referred to him as a bishop.[28] It seems that the abbey at Saint-Ouen had sought to elevate the cult of Nicasius as the first bishop of Rouen in the same way that the cathedral of Rouen had done for the seventh-century bishop of Rouen, St Romanus (d. 640).[29] The identity of Pientia was similarly fluid in these early hagiographies, as she oscillated between virgin and matron.[30]

The origins of Nicasius's presence in the Vexin given in the first part of Davanne's *vita* also correspond roughly to the version popularized by the eleventh-century *Passio.* Nicasius was commissioned to undertake a mission to Gaul and ordained a bishop before leaving Rome. On reaching Paris, Nicasius, accompanied by a priest Quirinus and a deacon Scubiculus, headed towards the river and chose Rouen as his bishopric.[31] Davanne pinpointed their arrival at La Roche-Guyon and identified the conversion of a local noblewoman named Pience as instrumental to their mission since it gave Nicasius the freedom to preach (*plaine liberté de prescher*) and to sow the words of the

[27] Jacques Dubois, ed., *Le Martyrologe d'Usuard. Texte et commentaire*, Subsidia Hagiographica 40 (Brussels, 1965), cited in Herrick, *Imagining*, 155.

[28] Herrick, *Imagining*, 45. The Bollandists gave a history of Nicasius and Pientia (*ActaSS*, Oct. 5: 513), but did not reproduce the *Passio Nicasii.* Herrick notes that the text of the *Passio* is accessible in part in the Bollandists' catalogues: 'Le Pouvoir du passé apostolique', in *Hagiographie, ideologie et politique au Moyen âge en Occident. Actes du colloque international du Centre d'Études supérieures de Civilisation médiévale de Poitiers, 11–14 septembre 2008*, ed. E. Bozóky (Turnhout, 2012), 129–38, at 129 n. 2. The *Livre Noir* at Saint-Ouen is also mentioned in Lucile Tran-Duc, 'Enjeux de pouvoir dans le *Livre Noir* de l'abbaye Saint-Ouen de Rouen', ibid. 199–210, at 200.

[29] Louis Violette, 'Nicaise, du martyr du Vexin au Saint Rouennais. Valorisation des reliques par l'hagiographie au XIe siècle', in Olivier Dumoulin et Françoise Thelamon, eds, *Autour des morts: mémoire et identité* (Rouen, 2001), 377–86, at 377.

[30] Herrick, *Imagining*, 149.

[31] Émile Réaux, *Histoire de Meulan* (Meulan, 1865), 40–1.

faith (*d'y semer les paroles de la Foy*). Pientia is also credited with having established oratories where converted Christians assembled to pray and celebrate the divine mysteries.[32]

The martyrdom of Pientia and her converters was, of course, central to Davanne's text. While on their knees praying to God after preaching to a congregation just outside of La Roche-Guyon, Nicasius and his priestly companions were decapitated by soldiers sent by a governor named Sifinius, following an edict of the Emperor Domitian against Christians in Gaul.[33] That night, their remains were miraculously transported to safety by angels to a site known to Davanne as the Ford of Saint Nicaise.[34] It was then that Davanne stressed the role of the 'good' Pientia, who decided to 'bury them in that same place, whose heritage belonged to [her]'. According to Davanne, the 'holy woman' then had built an oratory or chapel for their graves which later became renowned as a site of miracles.[35] Pientia's own martyrdom came shortly after, when her own father learned of her conversion to Christianity and sent troops to investigate. She declared her faith to them before they decapitated her.[36] Davanne explained that the bodies of all four martyrs withstood centuries of persecution against Christians and their tombs.[37]

The second part of Davanne's *vita* then goes on to describe the early translations of their bones and the miracles occurring surrounding these relics. These stories were, he asserts, gleaned from an inventory of 'ancient manuscripts'.[38] Davanne traced the early history of Pientia's remains to the bishop of Lisieux. He, too, was a descendant of La Roche-Guyon and translated her head, bones and some contact relics (including a belt) to the church of Saint-Cande in Rouen. In the early years of their veneration, the belt of Pientia was known to protect pregnant women and safely deliver their babies.[39] A considerable proportion of Davanne's *vita* is made up of short accounts of later miracles occurring after the relics turned up in Meulan. Some were due specifically to the intercession of Nicasius, but many others to all four martyrs; these were gleaned by Davanne from the 'ancient

32 Davanne, *Vie*, 79–80.
33 Ibid. 87–92, 94–101; their death at 102.
34 Ibid. 104–5.
35 Ibid. 106.
36 Ibid. 87–107.
37 Ibid. 50–1.
38 Ibid. 51–2.
39 Ibid. 54.

manuscripts' at his disposal. One example describes how a priest from Saint-Jacques in Meulan came to venerate the relics with a gangrenous hand, which was quickly healed after a reliquary was opened and he gazed upon the head of Pientia.[40] Similar miracles are recounted by Davanne as occurring well into the seventeenth century.[41] He also took care to identify sites which were significant for the occurrence of miracles. These included the fountain of Saint-Nicaise at Vaux-sur-Seine, where Nicasius had baptized new converts, the water from which could cure a fever.[42]

Davanne's attentiveness to the topography of the Vexin was comparable to countless other 'sacred geographies' which emerged in Europe during the early modern period. Elizabeth Tingle has, for example, identified the role of the landscape in seventeenth-century Brittany, where the *vitae* of early saints helped to reinforce a religious identity for Bretons 'strongly rooted in place'.[43] Alexandra Walsham's studies of the sacred landscape in Reformation-era Britain and Ireland have similarly revealed how topographical 'landmarks' such as springs, trees and stones played a part in the collective memory as 'signposts' of the Christian past.[44]

Davanne's writing was also part of a broader inclination to reclaim the Christian past which many historians have detected in Counter-Reformation Europe. The most recent scholarship on the writing of this sacred history has shown that the study of the early Church was not just a confessional tool used in competing Catholic and Protestant histories, but also important to intra-confessional discussions.[45] Historians such as Simon Ditchfield, Katie Harris and Howard

[40] Ibid. 89.

[41] Ibid. 92–3.

[42] Ibid. 26, 79–80. Today, a nineteenth-century construction stands on the site of the earlier chapel destroyed in the Revolution, depicting Nicasius by the side of the crucified Christ.

[43] Elizabeth Tingle, 'The Sacred Space of Julien Maunoir: The Re-Christianising of the Landscape in Seventeenth-Century Brittany', in Will Coster and Andrew Spicer, eds, *Sacred Space in Early Modern Europe* (Cambridge, 2005), 237–58, at 251. Devotion to sites such as this had been helping to create 'holy places' for centuries: R. A. Markus, 'How on Earth could Places become Holy?', *JECS* 2 (1994), 257–71, at 257.

[44] Alexandra Walsham, 'Sacred Topography and Social Memory: Religious Change and the Landscape in Early Modern Britain and Ireland', *JRH* 36 (2012), 31–51, at 31; eadem, *The Reformation of the Landscape: Religion, Identity and Memory in Early Modern Britain and Ireland* (Oxford, 2011), 223– 225, on sites of martyrdom.

[45] Simon Ditchfield, 'What was Sacred History? (Mostly Roman) Catholic Uses of the Christian Past After Trent', in Katherine Van Liere, Simon Ditchfield and Howard

Louthan have shown how such histories helped to strengthen the 'autonomy' of local religious practices in response to official attempts to regularize devotions with the revised Roman Breviary in 1568 and the creation of the Sacred Congregation of Rites in 1588.[46] Ditchfield's study of Pietro Maria Campi shows expertly how local counterparts to Cesare Baronio's *Annales Ecclesiastici* sought to 'vindicate' local devotional traditions.[47]

There are indications that Davanne was indeed working to raise the profile of the regional cults of Pientia and her companions. The timing of the two editions of Davanne's text lends further support to this hypothesis, as both followed the issuing of the Rouen breviaries of 1627 and 1642, which caused a controversy between the archbishop and the cathedral chapter.[48] François de Harlay, uncle of François de Harlay de Champvallon, was a keen reformer of the Rouen breviary: during his episcopate from 1615 to 1651, three editions were published, in 1617, 1627 and 1642, as well as an edition of the missal in 1623.[49] Reform of the breviary in France was subject to substantial regional variation but, despite some resistance, most dioceses had adopted the Roman missal and breviary of Pope Pius V by the mid-seventeenth century.[50] This preceded a wave of reforms to the French liturgy in the direction of a 'neo-Gallican' liturgy which also centred on a culling of saints' feasts, but also the addition of daily readings from the Old Testament.[51] Harlay's early reforming efforts in Rouen were undoubtedly inspired by the Tridentine spirit of standardization. In April 1627 he addressed the diocese and invited them

Louthan, eds, *Sacred History: Uses of the Christian Past in the Renaissance World* (Oxford, 2012), 72–97, at 73.

46 Simon Ditchfield, *Liturgy, Sanctity and History in Tridentine Italy: Pietro Maria Campi and the Preservation of the Particular* (Cambridge, 1995); Howard Louthan, *Converting Bohemia: Force and Persuasion in the Catholic Reformation* (Cambridge, 2009); A. Katie Harris, *From Muslim to Christian Granada: Inventing a City's Past in Early Modern Spain* (Baltimore, MD, 2007). Kirstin Noreen also presents a convincing case for the Jesuit use of early Christian martyrs: 'Ecclesiae Militantis Triumphi: Jesuit Iconography and the Counter Reformation', *SCJ* 29 (1998), 698–715.

47 Ditchfield, *Liturgy, Sanctity and History*, 10.

48 Ibid. 233–4.

49 A. Collette, *Histoire du Bréviaire de Rouen* (Rouen, 1902), 233.

50 John McManners, *Church and Society in Eighteenth-Century France: The Religion of the People and the Politics of Religion*, 2 vols (Oxford, 1998), 2: 45–50.

51 Martha Mel Stumberg Edmunds, *Piety and Politics: Imaging Divine Kingship in Louis XIV's Chapel at Versailles* (Newark, NJ, 2002), 267.

to make the transition to the new, reformed breviary.[52] The calendar of the 1627 edition confirms that the feast of Nicasius (and associated martyrs) on 11 October was retained, but perhaps it was the perceived threat to local liturgical tradition in these controversial reforms which motivated Davanne to write his first edition that year.[53]

Socially elite families had long been sequestering desirable sacred relics at their estates as part of what Peter Brown called the 'privatisation of the holy'.[54] There is less research specifically on the role played by seigneurial chapels in fostering devotions to local saints and their relics in the Counter-Reformation era, but scholars have begun to observe occasions when the European elite used relics to celebrate family lineages and spiritual heritage.[55] It was, at least in part, the mid-century renaissance of the cult of Pientia which inspired the local seigneur and his pious wife to procure the saint's finger in December 1654. We know, for example, that Davanne's mission to extol the early martyrs of the Vexin began to be endorsed by his peers by the mid-seventeenth century. The work of Cécile Davy-Rigaux on the compositions of Baroque composer Marc-Antoine Charpentier (1643–1704) has revealed his contribution towards three plainsong hymns which were dedicated to St Nicasius. These hymns were apparently composed by a Jesuit, Jean Commire (1625–1702), after a visit to the Jesuit college in Rouen in 1662.[56] As Pientia's status as 'Dame de La Roche Guyon' was emphasized by Davanne, perhaps the Liancourts sought to associate their château with this new cult. It seems that Davanne's efforts to raise the profile of the cults had begun to pay off.[57]

[52] Collette, *Histoire*, 245.

[53] This edition survives in Paris, Bibliothèque Saint Geneviève, 8BB 1194 INV 1369, 8BB 1195 INV 1370.

[54] Peter Brown, *The Cult of Saints: Its Rise and Function in Latin Christianity*, 2nd edn (London, 2015), 34; Sean Lafferty, 'Ad Sanctitatem Mortuorum: Tomb Raiders, Body Snatchers and Relic Hunters in Late Antiquity', *EME* 22 (2014), 249–79, at 266.

[55] Simon Ditchfield, 'Thinking with Saints: Sanctity and Society in the Early Modern World', *Critical Inquiry* 35 (2009), 552–84, at 555–9; Keith P. Luria, *Territories of Grace: Cultural Change in the Seventeenth-Century Diocese of Grenoble* (Berkeley, CA, 1991), 115. Scholars have also noted how the elite constructed private crypts and chapels in parish churches to participate in local devotions in the Counter-Reformation era: Elizabeth C. Tingle, *Purgatory and Piety in Brittany c.1480–1720* (Aldershot, 2012).

[56] Cécile Davy-Rigaux, 'Charpentier Plain-Chantiste', in C. Cessac, ed., *Les Manuscrits autographes de Marc-Antoine Charpentier* (Wavre, 2007), 239–50, at 239.

[57] Davanne's sketches and notes on the history of the monastery of Saint-Nicaise, now archived in Montigny-le-Bretonneux, Archives départementales des Yvelines, fonds 24H,

The decision by the duke and duchess of Liancourt to display the relic of Pientia in their family chapel has also to be interpreted as an expression of their status as rigorists and patrons of the Cistercian convent of Port-Royal, the hub of the 'Jansenist' movement. The Port-Royalists were known for the sense of identification they felt with the early Christians as 'martyrs' persecuted by their own society.[58] Patristic works were celebrated by the Port-Royalists who held up the 'apostolic purity' of the early Christian Church.[59] We know from the probate inventory taken in 1672 that in her apartment at the château de la Roche-Guyon the duchess of Liancourt was in possession of a selection of devotional books which confirms her personal interest in patristics.[60] Alongside the spiritual letters of the Port-Royalist abbot of Saint-Cyran, in her small study the duchess also kept translations of works by Athanasius and Augustine's *De libero arbitrio* ('On Free Will'), among others. Whilst readership of the Church Fathers was not uncommon in the seventeenth century, these particular titles were more unusual and, as far as we can tell from broader studies of reading practices in France, less widely read.[61] Her ownership of Augustine's *De libero arbitrio* was undoubtedly also a reflection of her engagement with the theological debates at the heart of the Jansenist controversy – the place of human free will in salvation.

These reading materials thus point to the significance of La Roche-Guyon as a site for the evocation of the Liancourts' identity as patrons of Port-Royal and (by implication) their identification with the early heritage of the Church. Importantly, this was also reflected in the material culture of the devotional spaces they used at the château. At La Roche-Guyon, Pientia's finger was 'kept company' by a substantial collections of early Christian bones which arguably had some

were drawn upon by Victor Cotron – prior of the monastery between 1669 and 1672 – whose *Chronique de saint Nicaise* was a 'preparatory work' for the *Gallia Christiana*: Madeleine Arnold Tétard, *Histoire de la vie religieuse à Meulan* (Juziers, 2009), 10.

[58] The interest of the Port-Royalists in the early Christians has been explored in Bruno Neveu, *Érudition et religion aux XVIIe et XVIIIe siècles* (Paris, 1994); Jean-Louis Quantin, *Le Rigorisme chrétien* (Paris, 2001).

[59] Brian E. Strayer, *Suffering Saints: Jansenists and Convulsionnaires in France 1640–1799* (Eastbourne, 2012), 52.

[60] ADVO, fonds privées, 10 J, 31, 'Inventaire après décès', 1672. This collection of books complemented a fuller selection in her oratory in Paris. This is explored fully in Hillman, *Female Piety*, 111–14.

[61] Henri-Jean Martin, *Livre, pouvoirs et société à Paris au XVIIe siècle 1598–1701*, 2 vols (Geneva, 1999), 1: 496, 2: 928–9.

very rigorist traits.[62] As already noted, the repository in the chapel included the relics of martyrs Thomas the 'doubting' apostle, Matthias, Lawrence, Barbara and Catherine of Alexandria. Like Pientia, these early Christian martyrs were all persecuted for their faith, which must have had a clear resonance for their rigorist custodians. Once the finger of Pientia was translated to La Roche-Guyon in 1654, her relics not only became part of the local sacred history constructed by Davanne, they were also part of a claim to a rigorist spiritual identity during the persecution of the Jansenist convent.

* * *

At first glance, the translation of Pientia's finger to the chapel at the Château de la Roche-Guyon in December 1654 might seem simply have been a way for the newly reformed monastery at Meulan to build links with pious, aristocratic patrons.[63] Read alongside the scholarship of local priest and prior Nicolas Davanne, however, a denser picture emerges. This analysis of relic translation has shown through this case study of Pientia's finger how the movement of relics was intimately connected to the writing of a local, sacred history in the face of Tridentine standardization. Davanne may have been responding directly to challenges to local devotional culture posed by the reform to the Rouen breviary; almost certainly he was also writing to celebrate the liturgical traditions associated with the monastery he had successfully reformed. Viewed in this way, the martyr in the subterranean crypts and chapel at La Roche-Guyon became an extension of the Roman catacombs.

[62] These relics are recorded in the visitation documentation and in the probate inventory of 1672. This hypothesis was first presented in Hillman, *Female Piety*, 92–3. The idea of the 'company' kept by relics shaping their meaning is from Cynthia Hahn, *Strange Beauty: Issues in the Making and Meaning of Reliquaries 400–c.1204* (Philadelphia, PA, 2012), 12. Interestingly, the Liancourts' interest in the ancient spiritual heritage of La Roche-Guyon was perpetuated by the eighteenth-century proprietors, who commissioned an 'ancient' portal to be designed on the Tour de Guy as an allusion to their family lineage; this is explored in Gabriel Wick, 'Hubert Robert (1733–1808) and the Renovation of the Tour de Guy at the Château de La Roche-Guyon', *Garden History* 41 (2013), 224–44, at 233.

[63] Edina Bozóky and Steven Vanderputten have shown how relics were symbols of authority: 'Voyages de reliques et demonstration du pouvoir au temps féodaux,' in *Voyages et voyageurs au Moyen Age*, Actes des congrès de la Société des historiens médiévistes de l'enseignement supérieur public 26 (Paris, 1996), 267–80; 'Itinerant Lordship: Relic Translations and Social Change in Eleventh and Twelfth-Century Flanders', *French History* 25 (2011), 143–63, respectively.

The case of Pientia upholds much of the recent scholarship on saints, relics and sacred history in Counter-Reformation Europe discussed in this article. Yet what also makes the case unique is the way the movement of these relics was intimately connected to their continual reinvention since the composition of the eleventh-century *Passio*. Elizabeth Robertson and Jennifer Jahner recently noted how the relocation of relics into their 'proper homes' could often be an ideological endeavour.[64] This observation seems particular apt here. The return of even a small fragment of Pientia's bones to La Roche-Guyon – the site of her conversion and martyrdom – in many ways acclaimed Davanne's scholarship and lent further support to the spiritual heritage of the Vexin, as well as being an important marker of the spiritual identity of the relic's new aristocratic hosts.

[64] Robertson and Jahner, 'Introduction', in *Medieval and Early Modern Devotional Objects*, 7.

Ethnography and Cultural Translation in the Early Modern Missions

Joan-Pau Rubiés*
ICREA and Universitat Pompeu Fabra, Barcelona

Early modern Christian missionaries often learnt about other cultures in remarkable depth, and made an extremely important contribution to the writing of ethnography and to the global circulation of knowledge. While their cultural insight was usually built upon linguistic expertise, missionary writings were of a complex nature, often combining scientific observations and historical speculations with wider rhetorical aims. In fact, issues such as accommodation to local customs became complex ideological battlegrounds. Whilst an earlier historiography may have been tempted to emphasize either the pioneering character of the Christian missionaries as proto-anthropologists, or – in a more critical fashion – their Eurocentric ideological agendas, there is growing awareness of the crucial importance of the native mediators who acted as knowledge brokers, and who also had their own personal agendas and cultural biases. However, the cultural interactions did not end here: in parallel to these complex acts of local translation, missionaries also 'translated' cultural diversity in another direction, to the European Republic of Letters, where they increasingly had to defend religious orthodoxy in the context of a rapidly changing intellectual landscape.

Missionaries as Ethnographers and as Agents of Globalization

The role of early modern Christian missionaries as ethnographers, or indeed as proto-anthropologists, has long been recognized. Often working within a consolidated colonial project, but sometimes also acting precariously in areas with limited European presence and at the mercy of local powers, missionaries were often at the forefront of the encounter with various peoples across the world, whom they generally sought to convert to their own version of the faith, while perhaps also indirectly supporting an imperialist agenda. Missionaries were not of course the only European participants in any such

* Department of Humanities, Universitat Pompeu Fabra, Ramon Trias Fargas 25–27, 08005 Barcelona, Spain. E-mail: joan-pau.rubies@upf.edu.

Studies in Church History 53 (2017) 272–310
doi: 10.1017/stc.2016.17

cross-cultural interactions, and a wide range of agents – traders, soldiers, adventurers, ambassadors and colonial officials – were involved in the process of generating knowledge about the diverse lands and peoples of the world. How often they did so, however, varied considerably depending on the circumstances. Missionaries, by contrast, beginning with the Catholic religious orders operating under the patronage of the kings of Castile, Portugal and France, often had the quasi-professional training and motivation to learn about local cultures and write about them. Assessing the historical importance of this body of sources is less a question of noting their sheer quantity than of appreciating their analytical depth, founded upon linguistic and antiquarian research.

Given the complex interconnections between commercial, political and religious aims in many of these early colonial empires, it is sometimes difficult to disentangle the strictly religious concerns of some of these missionaries from the tasks that they might also occasionally undertake as diplomatic or commercial agents. This is particularly true of those areas of Asia where the interaction was precarious and fluid: we might think of the Augustinians who first visited China from the Philippines in 1575, such as Martín de Rada; of the numerous Jesuits in late sixteenth-century Japan, with their privileged position in the port of Nagasaki and their connection to the Portuguese traders in Macao; of those Portuguese Augustinian friars who, a few years later, were allowed into the Safavid empire at the time of Shah Abbas, such as António de Gouvea, who acted as agent for the authorities in Goa, Lisbon and Madrid; or of the Jesuits who, in a parallel mission led by Jerome Xavier, spent some years at the court of Jahangir, with their close connection to the authorities in Goa, and often in rivalry with the English ambassador Sir Thomas Roe. In all these cases, missionaries were protagonists of multi-faceted exchanges and negotiations with Asian powers representing the high cultures of Persia, India, China or Japan. When assessing such mediating roles it is therefore important to distinguish the ultimate aims of missionaries and the various means – including art and science – they sometimes used to achieve them.[1] Nonetheless, it is fair to say that religious concerns were key to the ethnographic practices of the

[1] This has been noted especially of the Jesuits, but the point is also relevant for other religious orders. For an assessment of the Jesuits as cultural mediators, see Diogo Ramada Curto, 'The Jesuits and Cultural Intermediacy in the Early Modern World', *Archivium Historicum Societatis Iesu* 74 (2005), 3–22.

majority of early modern missionaries, whether Catholic or Protestant, and that such concerns account for the large proportion of ethnographic materials from this period that we owe to their pens. Even when religion was not a primary ethnographic concern, the intermediary role of the clergy was often crucial. Thus, when in the 1540s the colonial authorities of New Spain commissioned an account of the history, tributes and customs of the Mexica, they relied on a friar working with Nahua translators for the interpretation of native pictographic codices.[2] Similarly, in the following decades the Spanish historian of the Indies Francisco López de Gómara, the royal magistrate Alonso de Zorita and the naturalist Francisco Hernández would rely on the missionary writings of the Franciscans, notably Andrés de Olmos and Toribio de Benavente (or Motolinía), when describing the native history, religion and customs of New Spain.[3]

For missionaries, learning about other cultures meant first of all learning how to communicate their own message effectively. Second, it meant learning how to navigate the social codes of the host society, something especially important in areas not previously conquered. Third, it meant developing an effective missionary strategy, which often involved a degree of accommodation to local customs, and the need to distinguish those customs that could be accommodated – because they concerned matters indifferent to salvation – from those that could not be accepted by a Christian, usually because they were perceived as idolatrous (although of course 'idolatry' was a loaded term). Finally, missionaries sometimes put their ethnographic knowledge at the service of the needs of the colonial state, of the Church in Europe (for example through religious propaganda, which could at times be rather sectarian), or of the Republic of Letters more generally, intervening when necessary in debates about the rights of conquerors and conquered, natural history and ethnology, or ancient chronology and sacred history.

However, the fact that missionaries became experts on the societies they studied can lead to a misunderstanding of the nature of their work and its scientific pretensions. A case in point is

[2] This is the famous Codex Mendoza, now at the Bodleian Library in Oxford. Its authorship is discussed by H. B. Nicholson, 'The History of the *Codex Mendoza*', in *The Codex Mendoza*, ed. Frances Berdan and Patricia Rieff Anawalt, 4 vols (Berkeley, CA, 1992), 1: 2–10.

[3] On the related ethnographic works by Olmos and Benavente, see Georges Baudot, *Utopie et histoire au Mexique* (Toulouse, 1977).

the work of the French Jesuit Joseph-François Lafitau, *Moeurs des sauvages ameriquains comparées aux moeurs des premiers temps* (*Customs of the American Indians compared with the Customs of Primitive Times*, Paris, 1724). Often hailed as a precursor of scientific anthropology for his description of Huron and Iroquois customs, twentieth-century editors imbued with a positivist spirit went as far as to produce editions which were drastically abridged so as avoid presenting readers with 'outdated' antiquarian and religious speculations.[4] However, consideration of the work's title, as well as an analysis of its engraved frontispiece (with Lafitau's own explanation), immediately reveals that anyone looking here simply for an accurate description of native customs is missing the point: antiquarian comparisons were central to the Jesuit's intellectual aim, and this comparative exercise was in turn at the service of interpreting the religious history of humankind. The story of origins symbolized by the figures of Adam and Eve and their original knowledge of God was an essential inspiration to the task of the historian, providing a religious foundation for the idea of primitive humankind, and the details about native customs – few of which were the result of Lafitau's own observations – were simply the empirical materials that would prove the fundamental similarity between the customs of modern savages and those of the peoples of the ancient world, as described by Herodotus and other Greek and Roman authors. The point was to sustain a polemical argument about the unity of humankind and about the universality of its religious impulse towards a single creator God. Lafitau was indeed a missionary, but his work as ethnologist transcended his immediate aims as a preacher amongst the natives of New France. Instead, his intellectual aims were connected to Christian apologetics, an increasingly necessary task in early eighteenth-century Europe. Far from the proto-anthropologist of later editors, we have here the missionary as a participant in the crucial Enlightenment debate about religion.

The implications of exotic ethnography for sacred history were always in the background, although in a divided Europe that no longer

[4] Notably the popular pocket edition produced by Maspéro in two volumes (Paris, 1982). See also the introductory material to the otherwise excellent modern English edition: William Fenton and Elizabeth Moore, 'Introduction', in Joseph-François Lafitau, *Customs of the American Indians compared with the Customs of Primitive Times* (Toronto, ON, 1974). For a fresh assessment, see Andreas Motsch, *Lafitau et l'émergence du discours ethnographique* (Paris, 2001).

had one single authoritative source of religious orthodoxy, and in which radical ideas were gaining considerable ground, these debates became more urgent throughout the seventeenth century. By contrast, what can be considered more permanent is the fact that missionary ethnographers, whatever their confessional or theological inclinations, sought to generate knowledge that was useful for evangelization. The extent to which each missionary project was also overtly imperialist, on the other hand, varied considerably. It has often been noted that spreading the faith was frequently the counterpart for spreading European dominion, with the cross marching alongside the sword, but this is more obviously true of some areas than others. In the Spanish Americas, for example, evangelization was essential both to the justification of conquest and as an instrument of colonial rule, and friars acquired an important educational and economic role among the native communities – in some frontier areas, such as Paraguay, with remarkable levels of autonomy. However, this position was not without its contradictions, and often stood in tension with the secular concerns of the European settlers. While by implication the friars participated in the imposition of Spanish authority, they also sought to defend the Indians from abuse, and in the most extreme cases – notably the Dominican Bartolomé de Las Casas – they even questioned the legitimacy of conquest and the actual colonial order which had been created. But this was Spanish America, which saw the most massive experiment in cultural assimilation in the sixteenth century. In many other parts of the world, by contrast, the prospects for outright conquest were dubious and trading interests were paramount. Although a strict focus on commercial strategies was sometimes proclaimed as official policy – this was clearly the case of the English East India Company in the seventeenth century – the boundaries between commercial business and political pressure could be very fluid. For example, the Portuguese in Africa and Asia combined commercial negotiations with a selective use of strategic conquest when opportunity and need arose, and colonies such as Goa, Hormuz, Malacca or Macao, with varying degrees of Catholic acculturation, were the product of a marked imperial flexibility. When significant territorial conquests took place, for example in the case of Ceylon at the turn of the seventeenth century, the role of native converts to Catholicism could be highly significant, although nothing could match the thoroughness with which the Spanish imbued their conquest of the Philippines with evangelical zeal. But in many other areas, such as Japan or China, missionaries were capable of operating for many decades without any obvious prospect of conquest.

It would obviously be reductionist to assess the spread of Christianity by missionaries simply as an expression of an imperialist programme. Rather, we should think of commercial, territorial and religious strategies as largely autonomous aims that could, however, be combined in a powerful cocktail according to a variety of institutional drives and local circumstances. Missionaries acted as ethnographers and engaged in a kind of cultural dialogue in all cases: as essential participants in a colonial order, such as the Jesuits in the Philippines, or trying to distance themselves from European imperialism, like the same Jesuits in Japan, China and elsewhere; as part of a high-level diplomatic exchange, such as those Catholic missionaries active in the Safavid and Mughal courts, or on their own initiative, like the Dutch *predikant* Abraham Rogerius (1609–49), who wrote one of the most detailed accounts of Hinduism whilst employed by the Dutch East India Company in the commercial colony of Pulicat.[5] We could perhaps generalize by saying that that the most substantial missionary ethnographies were bound to two kinds of approaches: assimilating subject populations, such as in the Spanish colonies of the New World, or seducing those living under independent 'gentile' (pagan) rulers, in areas like Japan, China, South India or Siam. Two of the most insightful late sixteenth-century ethnographers, the Franciscan Bernardino de Sahagún and the Jesuit Matteo Ricci, belong to these very different kinds of context.

Beyond personal curiosity, a force never to be dismissed entirely, the point of missionary ethnographies was that one needed to know what one was fighting against: ignorance, idolatry and the Devil. In the course of learning about culturally embedded religious systems, it became necessary to identify the elements of the local culture that supported a legitimate social and political order whilst isolating those religious beliefs and practices that must be eliminated because they were considered to be superstitious or to involve idolatry. These two closely related but distinct concepts, superstition and idolatry, were essential markers, and in effect functioned to define the absolute limits of any kind of cultural accommodation; however, deciding where exactly to draw the line could be very tricky. As the Jesuits in China and South India were to discover throughout the seventeenth

[5] Abraham Rogerius, *De open-deure tot het verborgen heydendom* (Leiden, 1651).

century, being too accommodating could lead to bitter disputes between rival Catholic orders, and even within them. Nonetheless, we are talking about differences of degree. Even Protestant missionaries, despite their different attitudes on a wide range of issues (for example towards translating Scripture into vernacular languages), shared with Catholics many assumptions and strategies of accommodation: hence Bartholomäus Ziegenbalg, a pietist missionary in South India at the turn of the eighteenth century, bought manuscripts written by his Jesuit rivals, and came to adopt similar ideas about the existence of a core of doctrinal monotheism behind the multiplicity of idolatrous cults in the religion of the 'gentiles'.[6]

Rather than a single imperialist drive, what defines all the various missionary efforts, taken together, is their participation in the early modern process of globalization, understood as the development of worldwide exchanges and connections. Christian missionaries from Europe had a very prominent role in establishing those, especially in cultural terms.[7] They were often the protagonists of first encounters, and in their ethnographic practice they recorded and interpreted those very religious traditions that they sought to transform. Whether this was a friendly, dialogical process is another issue, to which we shall return.

The Religious Imagination and European Modernity

One apparent paradox that derives from this emphasis on the role of missionaries as agents of globalization is the association of religious universalism – and most clearly Roman Catholic universalism – with the emergence of modernity.[8] This seems to run counter to secularist narratives which focus on the Enlightenment critique of religious excess – clericalism, superstition, enthusiasm, intolerance and fanaticism – as the key to the emergence of modern liberal values. However, the Enlightenment critique of religion was often shaped by the intellectual strategies of Christian apologists confronting religious diversity; indeed, secular cosmopolitanism was often built upon ideas

[6] *Bibliotheca Malabarica: Bartholomaus Ziegenbalg's Tamil Library*, ed. and transl. Will Sweetman and R. Ilakkuvan (Pondicherry, 2012).

[7] This global character has been appreciated especially in relation to the Jesuits: see, for example, Luke Clossey, *Salvation and Globalization in the Early Jesuit Missions* (Cambridge, 2008).

[8] See, for example, John M. Headley, *The Europeanization of the World: On the Origins of Human Rights and Democracy* (Princeton, NJ, 2008).

of the moral unity of humankind and the universality of natural law that Christian thinkers and missionaries had been particularly keen to embrace. The apparent paradox is best resolved by considering the chronological sequence in some detail. The early modern period on the whole led to a global vision of humanity across the various parts of the world – a mental map, or a 'great map of mankind', to use Edmund Burke's felicitous phrase of 1777 – that found ample expression in both cartographic and literary genres.[9] However, between this mature vision of the late Enlightenment and the original impetus towards geographical exploration led by the Iberian monarchies at the turn of the sixteenth century, we can identify other important moments in European conceptualization of the circumnavigated world and its peoples. One such moment is the late sixteenth and early seventeenth centuries. Between 1550 and 1620, a number of historical, geographical and cosmographical works were written and published that decisively shaped a new 'modern' vision of the world. What defined 'modernity' in this context was precisely the global scope that the ancients, confined to the Mediterranean-Middle Eastern oecumene, had lacked. Hence the theme of modernity was symbolically articulated through images of trans-oceanic navigations and the increase of knowledge, combining a newly acquired global geographical reach with scientific universalism. Although the recovery of classical learning set the horizons for this notion of modernity, the new historical consciousness would eventually come to oppose newly observed facts – drawn from experience – to the authority of old books. This was not, however, in any way an anti-religious vision of modernity: rather, it was a vision primarily articulated from a religious standpoint. It was precisely because there was a providential design that all the parts and peoples of the world had a common origin and common destiny. Celebrating modernity was also celebrating the providential significance of an exceptional moment in the history of humankind, as Christian Europeans understood it (Muslims in Turkey, Persia and India, or the Chinese in the 'Middle Kingdom', might have thought about this differently). Christian humanist geographers such as Gerhard Mercator, or armchair cosmographers and travel collectors like Sebastian Münster and Giovanni Battista Ramusio, were the first to articulate this global modern vision, in the middle

[9] P. J. Marshall and Glyndwr Williams, *The Great Map of Mankind: British Perceptions of the World in the Age of Enlightenment* (London, 1982).

decades of the sixteenth century, and increasingly they came to rely on the works of missionaries in the most distant countries for their new information. In subsequent decades, missionaries, in particular those imbued with Catholic universalism, were heavily involved in articulating the new historical and geographical vision, from Peru and Mexico to Goa, Macao and Nagasaki. There was of course a distinction between the natural and civil categories of ethnographic analysis and those which concerned the 'super-natural', or religious, experience; however, for most authors at the turn of the seventeenth century this did not imply a clash between religion and secularity.[10]

It has rightly been noted that for a long time this globalized world was more a vision than a reality.[11] Indeed, while the world had been circumnavigated, interactions with distant peoples were often violent, the commercial connections tenuous and knowledge of other cultures partial and often extremely superficial. But this is precisely the point: religious idealism and propaganda helped to articulate a historical and moral vision for a united humankind out of an experience that was very fragmented and potentially bewildering. The work of the Italian cosmographer Giovanni Botero provides an example. His *Relationi universali* (*Universal Relations*; 4 parts, Rome, 1591–6) was conceived as an extended report on the situation of Christianity in the world.[12] In order to achieve this Botero developed an ambitious programme for an up-to-date description of the world, drawing on Venetian ambassadorial reports, Spanish and Portuguese accounts of the conquest of the Indies, Jesuit histories and letters – for example, the recent works of Maffei and Acosta – and travel collections, notably Ramusio's *Delle Navigationi et viaggi* (*Navigations and Travels*; 3 vols, Venice, 1553–9). He thus assembled a remarkably complete picture. The first two parts described the various countries of the

[10] To consider why and how this religious inspiration for a global vision of a reunited humankind eventually crumbled, providing the basis for a devastating critique of religious excess, would take us to another, radically different moment about one hundred years later, described by French historian Paul Hazard: *La Crise de la conscience européenne (1680–1715)* (Paris, 1935).

[11] See, in this volume, Simon Ditchfield, 'Translating Christianity in an Age of Reformations', 164–95.

[12] For a recent edition, see Giovanni Botero, *Le relazioni universali*, ed. B. A. Raviola, 2 vols (Turin, 2015). Cardinal Borromeo had asked Botero to write about 'lo stato nel quale si trova oggi la religione cristiana per il mondo'. For a discussion, see Joan-Pau Rubiés, 'Nuovo mondo e nuovi mondi. Ritorno a la questione de l'impatto culturale', in Michela Catto and Gianvittorio Signorotto, eds, *Milano, l'Ambrosiana e la conoscenza dei nuovi mondi (secoli xvii–xviii)*, Studia Borromaica 28 (Rome, 2015), 9–51.

known world geographically and politically; the third and fourth parts described the religions of the Old World and the New. Despite the growing importance of political analysis in his *oeuvre*, Botero never lost his concern with assessing the global expansion of true (that is, Catholic) religion. He was particularly emphatic about the role of European civilization in facilitating the conversion of savage barbarians, refining the distinction between different degrees of civility and barbarism proposed by the Spanish Jesuit José de Acosta. As has often been noted, Botero's descriptions were frequently rushed and error-ridden, as he copied and summarized his sources without acknowledgment and with little care for detail.[13] However, he had access to a range of materials unthinkable a few decades earlier, to a very large extent thanks to the writings of missionaries. Most decisively, he articulated a global vision of humanity imbued with Roman Catholic providentialism and not a small dose of imperialism (struggling to balance the claims of the rival dynasties of Spain with Portugal, France and the Holy Roman Empire). Although Botero's philosophical reflections about the history of the expansion of Christianity often lacked depth or cogency, his global religious vision imposed a sort of coherence onto his diverse sources, while the numerous editions and translations of the *Universal Relations* ensured that readers across Europe, whether Catholic or Protestant, would rely on a work of Catholic propaganda for their knowledge of far-flung lands and peoples.

Botero's efforts to give coherence to the political and religious diversity of the various peoples of the world were largely inspired by the more systematic thinking of José de Acosta in relation to the Spanish American Empire, both in his *Historia natural y moral de las Indias* (*Natural and Moral History of the Indies*) of 1590, and the earlier and more technical missionary treatise *De procuranda indorum salute* (*How to pursue the Salvation of the Indians*) of 1588–9. Acosta's work, the product of a high-ranking missionary who held important responsibilities in Peru and was distinguished by his exceptional training as a humanist and theologian, provided a response to decades of debate about adequate policies for the conversion of the Indians to Christianity. His key insight, that different approaches were appropriate to different kinds of

[13] As noted by Federico Chabod, 'Giovanni Botero', in idem, *Scritti sul Rinascimento* (Turin, 1967), 269–458; Aldo Albònico, *Il mondo americano di Giovanni Botero, con una selezione dalle* Epistolae *e dalle* Relationi universali (Rome, 1990).

'barbarian' according to differing degrees of rationality, or civility, was not, however, simply offered as an informed and sophisticated answer to the practical need for an effective religious and colonial policy in a mature imperial system. Instead, it was also framed by a historical reflection on the nature of the New World, as both a physical and a human reality. Hence, while part of his analysis was devoted to establishing the connection between religion and civilization (maintaining, for instance, that the most savage barbarians must be taught to become men before they could be taught to be Christians), and to a detailed analysis of the various types of idolatry, another section sought to examine the history of the American peoples, from their origins in the Old World, through a necessary migration by land in remote times, to the development of the partial civilizations of Mexico and Peru. Religious logic dictated Acosta's fundamental anthropological assumptions, in particular about the unity of humankind and the possibility of conversion of what were, in effect, rational human beings. At the same time, observations of cultural diversity amongst 'gentiles' – that is, those peoples who were not Christian, Jewish or Muslim – required a sophisticated use of analytical distinctions, and led Acosta to adopt a hierarchical model of degrees of civility which was well suited to the needs of Spanish colonialism. Acosta's model implied various historical stages of social development, culminating with the 'modern' union of reason and faith in Catholic Europe.[14] Quite clearly, Acosta was not afraid to rethink his scientific (as opposed to religious) assumptions in the light of experience, and if necessary to question Aristotle (for example in relation to the existence of a torrid zone): in the pursuit of truth, religion and science, or faith and reason, were complementary. It did not occur to Acosta that one might be used coherently to question the other.

Ethnography as Science and Ethnography as Rhetoric

Acosta's exceptional work illustrates the extent to which early modern Catholic missionaries were willing to subject rational speculations

[14] It was obviously easier to rationalize such a hierarchy in the Americas than when dealing with the Chinese and Japanese, who might be described as no less civilized than European Christians. Acosta was obliged to claim the superiority of the European alphabet as a system of writing in order to do so: José de Acosta, *Historia natural y moral de las Indias*, ed. Fermín del Pino-Díaz (Madrid, 2008), 206–8.

about the natural world and its peoples to the discipline of experience. We could emphasize Acosta's unique genius, but he was also the product of the late Renaissance eclectic cultivation of Aristotelian science, humanist historical learning and scholastic theology (in particular Aquinas). Early modern ethnography was scientific primarily in the sense that it was empirically informed and methodically organized. The concept of ethnography, the description of peoples, is of course somewhat anachronistic: early modern writers instead wrote about religions, manners and customs.[15] Despite their lack of specific academic training (until the late eighteenth century there was no such thing as a discipline called ethnography), they pursued with clarity and tenacity the production of descriptive accounts, whether simple relations and travelogues or as part of more scholarly genres such as cosmographies, histories of the missions, natural histories and comparative works. These authors assumed that new observations could correct popular opinions and the authority of earlier writers, but they also pursued the methodical exposition of distinct themes according to a notion of systematic coverage. Lafitau, for example, compared natural temperaments (that is, the character and inclinations of savage nations), religious beliefs and rituals, secular government, marriage ceremonies, education, male and female occupations, war, diplomacy, trade, hunting and fishing, medicine, languages, games and death rituals. These lists were not identical between authors, but the coverage tended to converge around similar topics. Indeed, the institutions that encouraged the continuous production of geographic and ethnographic descriptions, whether the Spanish Council of the Indies or the Jesuit order, often used questionnaires and techniques of note-taking in order to facilitate comprehensive coverage, a practice that many curious savants in Europe interested in exotic lands and peoples came to share. The scientific academies of the seventeenth century would follow suit.

While the emphasis on full and accurate descriptions was generalized across a wide range of missionary ethnographers, the step from observation to philosophical and historical, or antiquarian, speculation – what we might retrospectively define as ethnology – was less

[15] For a general discussion of early modern ethnography, see Joan-Pau Rubiés, 'Travel Writing and Ethnography', in idem, *Travellers and Cosmographers: Studies in the History of Early Modern Travel and Ethnology* (London, 2007), IV. The classic work by Margaret T. Hodgen, *Early Anthropology in the Sixteenth and Seventeenth Centuries* (Philadelphia, PA, 1964) remains valuable.

typical. Writers such as Acosta and Lafitau were clearly engaged in such theoretical speculations, and their intellectual impact was often significant. Whilst their motivations were, generally speaking, apologetic, their concerns varied, from Acosta's practical engagement with missionary policies in the Spanish New World colonies to Lafitau's desire to challenge some of the sources of religious scepticism in Europe. However, the first important impetus for a philosophical discussion of the ethnographic evidence was the debate on the legitimacy of conquest of 'barbarian gentiles' in sixteenth-century Spain. Some theologians, such as the highly influential Francisco de Vitoria, were concerned with the theory of just war in the light of natural law, but did not engage in any detailed ethnographic analysis, relying when necessary on existing relations or works of history written by laymen. Historians of the Indies of the first half of the century, such as Peter Martyr, Gonzalo Fernández de Oviedo, Francisco López de Gómara or Agustín de Zárate, were generally considered to provide reliable evidence even by those who disagreed with their usually imperialist political bias, and (as we have already mentioned in the case of Gómara) these authors in turn often depended on missionary ethnographies for some of their evidence. However, as the political debate deepened throughout the first half of the sixteenth century, Bartolomé de Las Casas, a radical thinker with an interesting transatlantic biography, responded to these polemics about imperial legitimacy and colonial policy with an ambitious effort at comparative ethnology. It was as a result of his desire to prove a number of theses about the rational capacity of the American Indians, and about the foundation of their idolatry in natural religiosity, that in his *Apologética historia* (*Apologetic History*), completed in the 1550s, he engaged in a systematic comparison of their character, religion and customs with those of the ancient gentiles – that is, those very Greeks and Romans that humanist writers so admired for their cultural achievements.

As these debates progressed, the idea that exotic gentiles could be civilized became hard to contest, even though the extent to which they were already civilized when compared to modern Europeans could still be disputed. Attempts at reinforcing hierarchies varied considerably, from a sheer assertion of the positive influence of Christianity and the evils of devilish idolatry, to a more secular emphasis on political and institutional differences (hence Botero, for example, analysed monarchical despotism in Asia), to a nuanced discussion of systems of writing (notably in the work of Acosta), and finally to some attempts to connect the capacity for full rationality to racial differences. The dubious honour of articulating this last model fell to an Italian Jesuit of aristocratic origins, Alessandro Valignano (1539–1606), who as Visitor of the Eastern Missions was also responsible for supporting a native clergy and Matteo Ricci's novel strategy of cultural accommodation in China: the Chinese and Japanese were, after all, perfectly white.[16]

By the end of the sixteenth century, while systems of cultural hierarchy proliferated, it had also become apparent that fitting the historical and religious traditions of the various newly discovered gentile nations within the unitary narrative of universal history, which was of course also that of sacred history, would pose some important challenges. The starting point was always the biblical account of human origins. While in the Americas it became imperative to be able to connect the origins of the natives to the peoples of the Old World, in Asia, especially in China, a pre-Noachian chronology posed a considerable challenge, as quickly noted by the Augustinian friar Martín de Rada in his pioneering account of the kingdom (1575) and, following him, by friar Juan González de Mendoza in his widely translated *Historia del gran reyno de la China* (*History of the great Kingdom of China*; Rome, 1585). Even before the Protestant scholar Joseph Justus Scaliger noticed the problem, writers like Jerónimo Román, also an Augustinian, had attempted to solve the conundrum by suggesting that the Chinese used lunar, rather than solar, years.[17]

While some ethnographic documents were originally produced to support the internal needs of a missionary order – for information and edification, or in order to develop more effective strategies – they were often also publicized in support of propaganda efforts. For this reason, a great deal of missionary ethnography circulated widely. Historians have often emphasized the rivalries between different orders, notably the opposition of Franciscans and Dominicans to the methods of the Jesuits, but there is ample evidence of much

[16] Alessandro Valignano, *Historia del principio y progreso de la Compañía de Jesús en las Indias Orientales 1542–1564,* ed. Josef Wicki (Rome, 1944), especially chs 4 (Oriental Indians), 17 (Japanese), 26 (Chinese). This work, completed *c.*1584, but not published during this period, was extremely influential amongst European Jesuit historians such as Maffei, Lucena and Guzmán.

[17] For a discussion, see Rubiés, 'The Concept of a Gentile Civilization in Missionary Discourse and its European Reception: Mexico, Peru and China in the *Repúblicas del Mundo* by Jerónimo Román', in Charlotte de Castelnau-L'Estoile et al., eds, *Missions d'évangélisation et circulation des savoirs XVIe–XVIIIe siècles* (Madrid, 2011), 311–50.

ethnographic material being shared, even before it was published. Some of the most important historical documents relating to the history of the natives of the valley of Mexico and their religion were based on native chronicles and oral discourses collected by the Franciscans, who were pioneers in the missions of New Spain and produced many of the best materials. The successive writings of Andrés de Olmos, Toribio de Benavente and Bernardino de Sahagún were soon read by many others in the colony: government officials such as the magistrate Alonso de Zorita, naturalists such as Philip II's scientific agent Francisco Hernández, and political activists like the Dominican Las Casas, who largely built his *Apologética historia* on their evidence (despite the fact that Toribio de Benavente and other missionaries were highly sceptical of his radical anti-colonial critique).[18] Similarly, the contents of the substantial history of the Indies by the Dominican Diego Durán, and in particular his account of the imperial history of Mexica (the Aztecs), were shared with the Jesuit Juan de Tovar, who in turn informed Acosta. Another interesting case is that of Jerónimo Román, the Augustinian with antiquarian inclinations whom we encountered in relation to the chronology of China. Active in Spain during the reign of Philip II, he had access to the manuscript of Las Casas's *Apologética historia* and offered a substantial summary in his *Repúblicas del mundo* (*Republics of the World*; Salamanca, 1575), albeit omitting its comparative arguments. In this way, an Augustinian summary of a polemical ethnological treatise by a Dominican, largely based on the ethnographic materials collected by Franciscan missionaries, came to inform the Republic of Letters in Spain about the government and customs of the *Indias Occidentales*. Román's was the only global cosmography originally written and published in Spain during its imperial century.

Linguistic expertise was the foundation of the most insightful ethnographies. It was precisely because missionaries lived close to their charges and learnt their language in order to preach to them that they had access to their oral and written cultures. Training a sufficient number of missionaries and deploying them across many

[18] Some of these men, such as Alonso Zorita and Viceroy Luis de Velasco, collaborated with the Franciscans and echoed the ideas of Las Casas because they shared a stance in favour of the rights of the Indians: see Ralph Vigil, *Alonso de Zorita: Royal Judge and Christian Humanist, 1512–85* (Norman, OK, 1987). Nevertheless, concern with the spiritual and material wellbeing of the Indians did not necessarily imply agreement with Las Casas in his radical critique of the conquest and the legitimacy of Spanish rule.

localities posed a considerable practical challenge, as not all missionaries were equally eager to learn, or capable of learning, the languages needed to work in the field, and colonial societies tended to privilege acculturation in languages such as Spanish or Portuguese. Nevertheless, the number of languages learnt by early modern missionaries, both Catholic and (to a lesser extent) Protestant, is staggering. Not only did missionaries learn to communicate, preach and hear confessions in these languages, they also wrote dictionaries, grammars and Christian literature, in some cases even printing these works. Their linguistic skill was the foundation for deeper cultural interpretation, since it allowed missionaries to go well beyond the mere observation of behaviour, and engage in an exchange of subjective information with the peoples they sought to convert. Of course many laymen, for example traders and adventurers, also learnt many of those languages, at least at the colloquial level, and a few erudite or philosophical travellers, such as Filippo Sassetti, Pietro della Valle or Jean Chardin, became expert practitioners and engaged with literary traditions. The mestizo historian of Ancient Peru, Inca Garcilaso, who took pride in his double cultural heritage, became an inspiration for many European readers in the seventeenth and eighteenth centuries, while the natural historian Engelbert Kaempfer's *History of Japan* (1727) came to replace the writings of Jesuits as a more up-to-date authority on those hard-to-access islands. Nevertheless, it was more often missionaries who wrote about the languages of America, Asia and Africa as the key to understanding native religion and customs, and who sought out the local written literatures, and even contributed to them. There were no lay equivalents of Matteo Ricci's philosophical dialogues and collections of moral maxims written in Chinese, which became classics in Mandarin literature, and it was still to the Jesuits or other missionaries – often their ideological enemies – that many philosophers of the Enlightenment such as Voltaire turned when seeking to learn more about the civilizations of China, India or ancient Mexico.

Besides their unprecedented attention to the written literatures of many gentile nations, missionaries also expressed deep appreciation for the expressive capacity of oral cultures amongst non-literate societies. The fact that some missionaries spent many years living with their converts, away from European society, and often with little prospect of returning to Europe, helped shape their attitudes. Thus the linguistic and cultural expertise of the Valencian Jesuit Francisco Ignacio Alzina, missionary in the Spanish Philippines between 1632 and 1674, was developed over many decades. As he made clear in his manuscript 'Historia de las islas e indios de Bisayas' ('History of the Bisayan Islands and Indians'; *c.*1668), the expressive capacity of the Bisayan language revealed that the key difference between the Bisayan and the Europeans was not intellectual capacity, but simply education. The cultivation of the liberal arts and sciences, which in turn depended on political organization, alone distinguished the civilized from the barbarians.[19] In this way Alzina detached the kind of cultural hierarchy that José de Acosta had brilliantly formulated from any racial or climatic explanation, by insisting that the rational capacity of human beings was ultimately linguistic.

Concern with acquiring and reporting accurate empirical information about potential converts was only one aspect of the various genres of missionary writing, what may be defined as missionary knowledge or *savoirs missionaires*.[20] In order to avoid an exaggerated emphasis on factual knowledge, I prefer to use the term 'missionary discourse', taking into consideration the full complexity of ideological and instrumental aspects that shaped the various genres of missionary writing. Ethnography could be found in many of those genres: primarily letters, relations (or memoirs) and historical works, but also other forms of apologetic and educational literature, such as catechisms, confession manuals and literary dialogues. While letters and relations were the main vehicles for reporting ethnography from the mission field (notably in the case of the Jesuit system of centralized information), the historical genre, influenced but not overly constrained by humanist models, represented the most complete, and at the same time the most complex, ethnological discourse: it combined natural and moral history, super-natural or providential history (in essence the history of the missions, often hagiographic but sometimes also polemical) and antiquarian erudition and speculation, including comparative works such as those by Las Casas and Lafitau. In this context, ethnography in the sense of organized information about peoples and their *génies* and *moeurs* was often enmeshed in, and substantially affected by, a wider narrative of religious propaganda and apologetics. Religious edification, in particular, was a central purpose of much of the published literature. While Christianity aspired

[19] Victoria Yepes, ed., *Una Etnografía de los Indios Bisayas del siglo XVII* (Madrid, 1996), 16.
[20] See, in particular, the editors' introduction in Castelnau-L'Estoile et al., eds, *Missions d'évangélisation*, 1–19.

to universalism, the actual audiences for these writings were often far more concrete, and religious propaganda could acquire a particular tinge, whether confessional, national or that of a specific religious order. With all these conditions, missionary ethnography also became, inevitably, a rhetorical exercise, quite often with elements of fictionalization.

A revealing example is the *Histoire des Isles Marianes* (*History of the Mariana Islands*) published in 1700 by the French Jesuit Charles le Gobien.[21] What interested Le Gobien about the Mariana archipelago – modern Guam – was precisely the fact that it was a Jesuit mission in a poor, remote and neglected region. The lack of resources in the islands demonstrated that the society's motivations were purely apostolic, and enhanced the contested legitimacy of its missions elsewhere in East Asia, notably in China. Diego Luis de San Vitores, who had died a martyr, was presented as the key figure: by means of his apostolic vision, he had been able to mobilize the support of lay patrons such as the governor of the Philippines and the viceroy of New Spain. The attention paid by Le Gobien to the new mission in the Marianas was therefore part of the apologetic for the society's missionary activity.

Throughout Le Gobien's *Histoire*, there is tension between two seemingly contradictory themes: on the one hand, the hagiographical construction of the role of Providence in the history of the activities of the apostle Diego Luis de San Vitores and his companions; on the other, the scientific and sometimes sympathetic tone of the descriptions of the way of life and customs of the supposedly savage islanders. The chapter devoted to describing the natives is in this respect a particularly successful example of the extent to which ethnography was a complex rhetorical construct.[22] On the one hand,

[21] Charles le Gobien, *Histoire des Isles Marianes, nouvellement converties à la religion chrestienne …* (Paris, 1700). Le Gobien's sources were primarily the writings of Spanish Jesuits, notably the life of San Vitores by the court publicist Francisco García, *Vida y martyrio del venerable padre Diego de Sanvitores, de la Compañía de Jesús, primer apóstol de las islas Marianas, y sucessos de estas islas, desde el año de mil seiscientos y sesenta y ocho asta el de mil seiscientos y ochenta y uno* (Madrid, 1683). For quotations I follow the Italian version of 1684, translated and expanded by Ambrosio Ortiz (see n. 23 below). For a recent discussion which emphasizes Le Gobien's reliance on Spanish sources, see Alexandre Coello de la Rosa, *Historia de las islas Marianas, del padre Luis de Morales, SJ & Charles le Gobien, SJ* (Madrid, 2013), with my observations in the prologue: 'Apologética y etnografía en la *Historia de las Marianas* de Luís de Morales / Charles Le Gobien': ibid. 7–20.

[22] Le Gobien, *Histoire*, 42–70. For his ethnographic chapter, Le Gobien closely followed Francisco García's account.

it depicted the Chamorro as enjoying a carefree and secure life; on the other hand, it condemned them for their ignorance. Extreme liberty (*jamais peuple n'a vescu dans une plus grande liberté, ni dans une indépendance plus absolue*) also implied lack of justice and profound ethnocentrism: the Chamorro thought of themselves the world's wisest people, or, indeed, the original stock of humankind. This was something far more complex than the simple opposition between civilization and barbarism.

This complexity was fully captured by the account of the speech 'delivered' by a native rebel leader, Hurao, and in reality mostly invented by Le Gobien according to the conventions of classical and humanist history-writing.[23] Hurao defended the traditional Chamorro lifestyle, arguing that 'we do not need their help to live happily', and opposing the natural simplicity of the natives, embodied in their nakedness, to the corruption of a 'civilizing' process that in reality created artificial needs. It was not worth while losing natural liberty in exchange for a few trinkets and the promise of a happy afterlife; in fact, the stories told by the missionaries were no less fictitious than the fables told locally.[24] Alas, the reader was not meant to agree with any of this. This was not a libertine speech, comparable to Montaigne's essay on cannibals, or the dialogues with the Canadian Huron, Adario, published in 1703 by the Baron de Lahontan; nor was it the kind of argument against the colonizing mission that others would make in the eighteenth century. The speech must be interpreted in its broad narrative context, as a dramatic counterpoint to a fundamentally apologetic and even hagiographic text. Like the stirring but futile speech of the British leader Calgacus in Tacitus's life of Agricola, an obvious model, the barbarian's eloquence was a tragic counterpoint to the triumph of civilization. This was the perspective of a civilized writer capable of feeling nostalgia (of a Stoic character) for a golden age of simplicity and innocence that was irrevocably lost. The Jesuits, ideologically more conservative than philosophers such

[23] Hurao was a historical figure who led a rebellion in 1671, but the arguments that Le Gobien puts into his mouth are very different from the account given by his probable source, García, who presents a malicious and presumptuous Hurao and offers little detail: *Istoria della conversione alla nostra santa fede dell'Isole Mariane, dette prima de'Ladroni, nella vita, predicatione, e morte gloriosa per Christo del venerabile P. Diego Luigi di Sanvitores* (Naples, 1684), 254. However, Le Gobien could have been inspired by the invented speech that García put in the mouth of Aguarín, a *Chamorri* leader of another, later, rebellion in 1676: ibid. 499.

[24] Le Gobien, *Histoire*, 139–46.

as Montaigne or Rousseau who echoed similar themes, never doubted that Christianity and civilization should go together in a project that was invariably paternalistic. Many missionaries were of course critical of the greed of many Spanish commanders and colonists, but their condemnation of the abuses of colonization did not imply a rejection of the imperial project.

Mediation, Accommodation and the Problem of Cultural Translation

These considerations make it possible to assess both the potential and the limitations of early modern missionary ethnography as a form of cultural translation. Far too often, missionaries, and especially the Jesuits cultivating experimental forms of cultural accommodation, have been hailed as pioneers of scientifically informed interpretations of cultural diversity, or even as initiators of an unprecedented cultural dialogue between religions and civilizations. On both accounts, the reality was far more complex, and we must be wary of replacing the early modern myth of the saintly apostolic missionary or martyr, such as Francis Xavier or Diego Luis de San Vitores, with the modern myth of the ethnographically sophisticated missionary devoted to a cross-cultural dialogue, whether Bernardino de Sahagún, Matteo Ricci or Roberto Nobili. Many missionaries, in particular (but not only) Jesuits, certainly excelled in linguistic competence and ethnographic research; they also believed that in order to conduct their missions successfully they had to educate natives as Christians, and when possible integrate them into the Church hierarchy, albeit in subordinate positions (there was great resistance to native clergy in positions of authority). However, their acceptance of exotic customs and cultural traditions was highly selective, and often calculating; their view of religious diversity entirely one-sided, if not deeply intolerant; and their assumptions of what constituted rational civil behaviour both hierarchical and Eurocentric. What is nevertheless true is that early modern missionaries were willing to experiment with different degrees of cultural accommodation, a consequence, paradoxically, of their deep commitment to the universal validity of their own faith.

A brief consideration of some of the most important works of missionary ethnography may help elucidate this point. The research undertaken by those such as Bernardino de Sahagún or Matteo Ricci was outstanding, not simply for its unprecedented linguistic and cultural insight, but also for its capacity for systematic synthesis. At the same time, the apologetic nature of their projects imposed important limitations. When writing his *Historia general de las cosas de Nueva España* (*General History of the Things of New Spain*; *c.*1569), the Franciscan Sahagún (*c.*1499–1590) described himself as a doctor diagnosing an illness, which in New Spain was primarily idolatry. It was because idolatry lay hidden in all kinds of everyday social practices that systematic research into all things – natural, human and divine – was necessary. Sahagún's history was divided thematically into twelve books, covering the native gods; religious festivals; beliefs and practices concerning the deceased and their afterlife; astrology; divination; moral philosophy; natural philosophy; the native lords and their customs; artisans and traders; the virtues and vices of the various native peoples and social groups, their illnesses and remedies (assuming, as was then usual, a close correlation between mental and physical health); animals, birds and fish (but not plants); and, finally, the history of the Spanish conquest from the native point of view, as remembered by those who survived it (theirs was a markedly retrospective interpretation of events, imbued with the Christian Providentialism of native converts).[25] All this amounted to a remarkably ambitious research programme, made more impressive by the rich illustrations that accompanied the text. Sahagún's method was philological, focusing on recording precise vocabularies and searching in the meanings of words for the cultural signifiers that would betray idolatry and thus help distinguish licit from illicit beliefs and practices. Thus his most important manuscript, the Florentine Codex, presents the original Mexican (Nahuatl) text alongside a Spanish translation.[26] Sahagún's originality when compared with other missionary ethnographers of his time and place was his insistence on the value of keeping a record of the original language, instead of relying on a single act of translation.

Following the precedent of Andrés de Olmos, a missionary of an earlier generation skilled in Nahuatl, Sahagún obtained information through his order's proven technique of using guided interviews with Mexican elders who remembered pre-conquest oral traditions and

[25] Bernardino de Sahagún, *Historia de las cosas de Nueva España*, ed. Juan Carlos Temprano, 2 vols (Madrid, 1990).
[26] *Florentine Codex: General History of the Things of New Spain*, ed. and transl. Arthur J. O. Anderson and Charles E. Dibble, 13 vols (Santa Fe, NM, 1950–82).

were able to interpret pre-Hispanic books of 'antiquities'.[27] These, at least from Sahagún's perspective, were often superstitious books of divination, and while they contained valuable historical detail, this was usually mixed with idolatry. The mistake of many earlier missionaries had been to burn those books, destroying the resources needed to understand what was really going on. Their zeal was in fact self-defeating: only detailed, encyclopaedic knowledge would make it possible for the friars to target effectively the twisted beliefs inspired by the Devil, their enemy in the New World, and turn the natives into good Christians. These Indians had the capacity for faith, since they were fully rational human beings and 'our brothers'; indeed, the progress of Christianity in the New World would make up for the grievous losses to heresy in northern Europe. At the same time, it was important to recognize the native capacity for *policía*, that is, their social and political organization and moral order, which before the Spanish arrived had clearly been better than afterwards (it was common to note that the Indians had picked up the worst vices from their new masters).

However, Sahagún represented a particular position within the colonial Church, that of those who believed that a deeper evangelization was possible, and who were committed to teaching Christian letters to native converts at the Franciscan school of Santa Cruz in Tlaltelolco. For critics hostile to the more adventurous friars, delving into pre-Hispanic books and keeping alive Nahuatl traditions would only help to perpetuate the very idolatry the friars sought to combat, while attempts to train a native clergy from the better qualified descendants of the native nobility were misguided: surely it was best to leave all Indians in a subordinate position, and without any knowledge of Latin, so that all religious authority would emanate from those untainted by false beliefs, that is, the Spanish? An elderly Sahagún was no doubt disappointed when in 1577 his books were recalled to Spain and their

[27] The ethnographic research by Andrés de Olmos, who was the most expert in Nahuatl language amongst the early Franciscans, had been commissioned by the president of the *Audiencia* of New Spain Sebastián Ramírez de Fuenleal in 1533 and was completed *c.*1540. It became the foundation for the work of subsequent historians of Mexican antiquities, including Toribio de Benavente, Gerónimo de Mendieta, Juan de Torquemada and Bartolomé de Las Casas. Olmos's work has only been preserved through these secondary works and some anonymous fragments. See Baudot, *Utopie*, 159–240. Sahagún, who had taught with Olmos at Tlaltelolco, followed his example, but introduced the key innovation of preserving the Nahuatl transcripts of interviews.

circulation suppressed by order of Philip II.[28] The obscurantist party had won the day and the experiment in Tlaltelolco was left in crisis. However, this was never a fight between science and religion. Rather, it was a clash of missionary strategies concerning socio-ethnic hierarchies and the proper degree of cultural accommodation, not entirely unlike the one that, a few decades later and in very different circumstances, would rock the Chinese missions.

Beyond his presentation as a model missionary who gave up family and home to pursue a religious vocation, and patiently worked for decades until he managed to penetrate the Ming Empire and reach Beijing, Matteo Ricci's lasting fame rests on his extraordinary capacity to accommodate the literary and intellectual traditions of a modern 'gentile' nation characterized by its power and civility. What made Ricci's missionary strategy truly original in comparison to that of so many other Jesuits practising accommodation in India, Japan or Tibet was his idea that, unlike Buddhism, Confucianism, if properly understood as a rational civil philosophy, was entirely compatible with Christianity, in a way analogous to ancient Stoicism. The accommodation of dress, diet, and customs, songs and poetry, as well as politics and social etiquette, had all long been practised in various mission fields; however, the idea that a non-Christian ethical tradition could be perfectly valid (albeit once purified of later Buddhist influences) was, in the early modern context, both new and radical. The move was highly controversial, and eventually spawned the rites controversy. By accepting the philosophy of Confucius in this manner, had Ricci interpreted it liberally, or reinvented it to suit his Christian agenda? It is notable the extent to which his account of an 'authentic' Confucianism, purified of atheism and idolatry, required reinterpretation of the ancient history of the religion of the gentiles, usually understood as the degeneration of a primitive natural monotheism towards idolatry. Decades later Lafitau would take a similar approach to the savage peoples of the world, looking for traces of an Adamic religion in pagan rituals and customs.

This type of intellectual accommodation had important limitations. The strategy developed by Ricci in his key work of Christian apologetics, the Chinese dialogue *Tianzhu shiyi* [*The True Meaning of*

[28] Luis Nicolau d'Olwer, *Fray Bernardino de Sahagún 1499–1590* (Salt Lake City, UT, 1987; first publ. in Spanish 1952), 65–77; cf. Baudot, *Utopie*, 475–507. Although there were deep tensions between the friars and the secular clergy, some of the criticisms faced by Sahagún arose within his own order.

the Lord of Heaven] (Beijing, 1603), required a highly creative engagement both with the Confucian tradition and against Buddhism, in a clear effort to shape the cultural landscape towards a supposedly rational alliance of Christianity and 'authentic' native culture against 'idolatry'.[29] Moreover, many of the mysteries of the faith furthest from Chinese sensibilities, including the passion of Christ, were absent from this preliminary catechism, and were introduced only gradually to converts.[30] Jesuit missionaries were also extremely selective about the image of Europe which they portrayed in China, a tactic that would come back to haunt them when they eventually lost the ability to monopolize the encounter. Nevertheless, Ricci's construction of the Confucian tradition was not entirely one-sided; nor was it a failure of translation. Rather it was developed in close collaboration with Chinese converts, whose role in shaping the processes of accommodation is only beginning to be fully appreciated.[31] Accommodation might have been very calculated and even Machiavellian in spirit – it involved manipulating discourse and image in order to achieve a further intention that was only partially declared – but it was culturally hybrid in its practical development.

All this requires a reassessment of our understanding of intercultural dialogue in general and of religious dialogue in particular. The issue is substantial (what was accommodation really about?), and it affects how we read many documents key to the process of cross-cultural negotiation. Accommodation was both translation and rhetoric.[32] It involved understanding translation – whether of philosophical and religious terms, or of rituals and customs – as a selective, dynamic process with complex political and philosophical implications; it also involved the art of persuasion, deciding the extent to which artifice and dissimulation were necessary and legitimate, and assessing whether half-truths would pave the way for full truths or could eventually backfire. Many civil customs could easily be accommodated, depending on the context, and some of the most valuable works of missionary ethnography described diversity in manners and

[29] Matteo Ricci, *The True Meaning of the Lord of Heaven (T'ien-chu Shih-i),* ed. Edward Malatesa, transl. Douglas Lancashire and Peter Zhu Guozhen (St Louis, MO, 1985).

[30] Gianni Criveller, *Preaching Christ in Late Ming China: The Jesuits' Presentation of Christ from Matteo Ricci to Giulio Aleni* (Taipei, 1997).

[31] Nicolas Standaert, *Methodology in View of Contact between Cultures: The China Case in the 17th Century*, CSRCS Occasional Paper 11 (Hong Kong, 2002).

[32] A point also made by Liam Brockey, *The Visitor: André Palmeiro and the Jesuits in Asia* (Cambridge MA, 2014), 288.

customs with a degree of relativism, without overt condemnation, indeed sometimes even with praise.

An outstanding example is the small treatise by the Portuguese Jesuit in Japan, Luís Fróis, *Tratado em que se contêm muito sucinta e abreviadamente algumas contradições e diferenças de costumes entre a gente de Europa e esta província de Japaõ* (*Treatise in which are noted very briefly and succinctly some Differences and Contradictions between the People of Europe and this Province of Japan*; *c.*1585).[33] Clearly the product of the intensive cultural analysis that informed the strategy of selective accommodation developed by the visitor of the Eastern Provinces, Alessandro Valignano, Fróis's *Tratado* proposed a series of contrasts between Japanese and European (or Portuguese) customs, including male and female dress and behaviour; ways of eating and drinking; religious institutions; books and systems of writing; medicine; streets, buildings and gardens; weapons, ships and horses; music, singing and theatre; laws and punishments; linguistic uses and gestures; and even different ways of killing flies. While Fróis expressed surprise that rational peoples could differ so much in their customs, he did not seek to draw any sceptical philosophical conclusions (as Montaigne was doing in Europe in this same period), instead highlighting the almost incredible extent to which cultural distance was possible within the parameters of 'civility, intelligence and natural knowledge'.[34] Many of the differences – for example the fact that children learnt to write before they could read, or that the Japanese did not like grapes and figs – appeared simple curiosities, but under Valignano's leadership others became the basis for missionary adaptations to local conditions, intended to lower the obstacles to the spread of the faith. Removing one's shoes when entering a house, accepting white as the Japanese colour of mourning, or taking a present for one's host were, indeed, innocuous social conventions. The crucial issue when determining which foreign customs were acceptable was that they could be considered secular, and not contrary to either faith or reason (ethical norms, as part of natural law, were assumed to be both rational and universal). Japanese raw fish and silk dress could be acceptable,

[33] See Luís Fróis, *Europa-Japão. Um diálogo civilizacional no século XVI*, ed. Raffaella D'Intino (Lisbon, 1993). There is also an annotated English translation: *The first European Description of Japan, 1585*, ed. Richard K. Darnford, Robin D. Gill and Daniel T. Reff (London and New York, 2014).

[34] Fróis, *Europa-Japão*, 52: 'que quasi parese incrivel poder aver tão opposita contradisão em gente de tanta policia, viveza de engenho e saber natural com tem'.

but a disregard for female virginity or the practices of abortion and infanticide were not.

The difficulties arose when customs with an obvious civil component, for example marriage[35] or burial ceremonies, were imbued with additional non-Christian religious connotations. Hence in China it was customary to offer condolence to recently bereaved relatives by building an altar and placing on it an image of the deceased, or a tablet with an inscription. The Propaganda Fide was willing to accept these practices as simple piety, provided they did not amount to ancestor worship; therefore, strict rules were established for the wording used in the inscriptions, in order to make clear that the soul of the dead person did not reside in the tablet. Similarly, food or paper money were not to be offered to the ancestors as a form of sacrifice or to help them in the afterlife, and a way had to be found for the expression of filial piety that did not imply that the deceased could actually accept and partake of such traditional gifts, for instance by distributing the food amongst the poor, and not burning the paper money.[36] What was crucial for Christians was to create distance from the Buddhist ideas of the afterlife, including reincarnation. Despite all these efforts, in the more experimental missions the precise boundary between civil and religious (albeit superstitious) customs created deep and lasting debates, or even divisions, among missionaries, that the Church authorities struggled to control.

The debate about the limits of accommodation led to growing awareness of what constituted an accurate translation in relation to diverse cultural connotations. The missionary faced two alternatives: he could either emphasize the different assumptions behind analogous concepts and practices in order to avoid ambiguity, and therefore the danger of contamination from idolatry, or he could embrace translation as a creative act that might transform the underlying assumptions of the converts from imperfect religiosity to perfect (Trinitarian) monotheism. The latter tendency was particularly clear in India throughout the seventeenth and early eighteenth centuries:

[35] Scholastic theology, notably Aquinas (*Summa Theologiae*, Supplementum Tertiæ Parti, q. 41), categorized marriage under natural and civil law, independently of its sacramental character: it served rational and social purposes common to all societies, namely procreation, the education of children and domestic companionship, although these universal aims were expressed through different laws and customs.

[36] Nicolas Standaert, *The Interweaving of Rituals: Funerals in the Cultural Exchange between China and Europe* (Seattle, WA, 2008), 202–41.

while a Jesuit at the Mughal court such as Roth developed a keen sense of Sanskrit grammar, his colleagues in South India, whether in Madurai, Goa or Sri Lanka, were mostly geared towards producing a 'nativized' Christian literature in many different sanskritized vernacular languages; that is, they worked towards a hybrid literature often rich in cross-cultural intertextuality that would take root in specific socio-cultural contexts, rather than towards scientific accuracy or consistency.[37] It is for this reason that, despite their common theology, Catholic missionaries adopted a variety of linguistic strategies according to a variety of audiences, and ended up with different Tamil and Sanskrit equivalents for 'God': *tampiran*, *sarvesvara* or *brahman*.

Whether missionaries sought to mark distances from underlying idolatry or to indigenize Christianity with culturally hybrid discourses, the concept of religious dialogue must be used with caution. Quite clearly, those missionaries in China who worked closely with their converts and were mindful of the concerns of Confucian literati were engaged in a process of dialogue, but for a purpose that had little to do with an open exploration of cultural differences for the sake of sheer curiosity. When Ricci and his successors sought to interpret ancient canonical writings in such a way that Confucianism could be distinguished from any Buddhist influences and made compatible with Christianity, they did not simply respond to the point-of-view of 'the other', but actively positioned themselves in the cultural landscape, seeking potential allies while defining their Buddhist rivals as enemies. Religious tolerance as a cross-cultural ideal was out of the question: Christian missionaries in Muslim or gentile countries sought tolerance only for themselves. Hence, when in the late sixteenth century some Japanese *daymios* of Kyushu converted to Christianity, the Jesuits were keen to encourage their persecution of Buddhism; similarly, in Portuguese Goa – and even more in Spanish Manila – religious tolerance was severely limited.

The rhetorical element was particularly strong in literary dialogues written for apologetic purposes. In the late 1580s Alessandro Valignano was keen to publicize the journey of four Japanese teenagers who travelled to the courts of Catholic Europe under the care of the Society of Jesus, and with the help of another Jesuit, Duarte de Sande, he composed a Latin dialogue in which the young samurai

[37] Ângela Barreto Xavier and Ines G. Županov, *Catholic Orientalism: Portuguese Empire, Indian Knowledge (16th–18th centuries)* (Oxford, 2015), 202–41.

converts recorded their admiration for Europe; however, while the young Japanese – always closely supervised – had written genuine journals, now lost, the interpretation offered in the dialogues was far from spontaneous.[38] Whose voice was being heard? Similarly, the Chinese voices of Ricci's apologetic dialogues, written with a Chinese audience in mind, were conditioned by the imperative that they would succumb to Ricci's superior arguments for Christianity, in the same way that the Socrates in Plato's dialogues was destined to convince his Greek interlocutors that their previous philosophical assumptions were wrong.[39] These voices made some plausible points (and may even have been inspired by actual personal encounters), but they cannot be taken as reliable evidence of Confucian or Buddhist views of Christianity.

This rhetorical strategy was far from unique to the Jesuit mission in Japan and China, since literary dialogues were particularly effective pedagogical tools. In seventeenth-century Siam, Louis Laneau (1637–96), apostolic vicar and member of the Parisian Missions étrangères, composed dialogues in the local language, Thai, in which Christian and Buddhist teachers competed to convince a 'seeker of wisdom' of the superiority of their ways. This approach echoes the medieval disputations between Christians and Muslims or Jews (consider the work of Ramon Llull), but was nevertheless distinctive in that the intended audience was clearly external and not yet, or not necessarily, Christian.[40] While the French Missions Étrangères were generally in conflict with the Jesuits (for instance, concerning their jurisdictions in Asia), they shared the ideal of training a native clergy, and Laneau adopted similar theses about the possible salvation of virtuous gentiles and the need for a gradual exposition of the Christian mysteries. Similarly, in the first decades of the eighteenth century the

[38] [Alessandro Valignano and Duarte de Sande], *De missione Legatorum Iaponensium ad Romanam Curiam* (Macao, 1590). For a recent English edition, see *Japanese Travellers in Sixteenth-Century Europe: A Dialogue concerning the Mission of the Japanese Ambassadors to the Roman Curia*, ed. Derek Massarella, transl. J. F. Moran, Hakluyt Society 3rd ser. 25 (Aldershot, 2012).

[39] The 'Chinese scholar' of the *True Meaning of the Lord of Heaven*, is particularly impersonal. By contrast, real characters inspired the ten dialogues published as *Jiren Shipian* [*Ten Chapters of a Paradoxical Man*] (Beijing, 1608), a subtler work of moral philosophy – in effect a Chinese exposition of Christian Stoicism – that has received less attention.

[40] Medieval religious dialogues from the Latin West, such as Ramon Llull's *Llibre del gentil e dels tres savis*, were usually written in Latin or in European vernacular languages, raising the question of whether they were really meant for Muslim or Jewish audiences.

Capuchins in India and Tibet, also sent by the Propaganda in Rome at the expense of the Portuguese-Jesuit jurisdiction over the Eastern missions, condemned Jesuit accommodation of 'superstitious' customs in South India, while claiming exclusive control of their missionary fields in the North (in 1721 even forcing Ippolito Desideri, an expert in Tibetan Buddhism, to leave Lhasa); at the same time, they followed very similar apologetic strategies, learning local languages, seeking out the religious writings of the gentiles, and (for example) composing dialogues in Hindi for the king of Bettiah which supposedly proved the superiority of Christianity over the religion of the Brahmans.[41] In the end, rivalries over jurisdiction were often more decisive than those about method.

In order to assess the real nature of any religious dialogue, 'gentile' voices in Christian apologetic sources can be compared to other documents in which the points of view of Buddhist monks, Indo-Portuguese Brahmans or Chinese converts were not overwritten by Christian missionaries for their own purposes. While sources hostile to the teachings of Christianity are abundant in Japan and China (including those written by former Christian converts returning to Buddhism, such as the famous Fukan Fabian, author of both Christian apologetic works and a refutation of Christianity), they tend to create negative stereotypes of an exclusivist foreign religion with false claims to universality. In their utter lack of sympathy, such stereotypes are like a mirror image of Christian polemical presentations of hypocritical Buddhist monks inspired by the Devil to teach idolatrous cults.[42] By contrast, materials produced by those open to Christianity can be particularly illuminating. A fascinating example is provided by the notes taken in the 1630s by a number of

[41] On Desideri's fate, see Luciano Petech, ed., *I missionari italiani nel Tibet e nel Nepal*, 7 vols (Rome, 1952–7); Michael J. Sweet, *Mission to Tibet: The Extraordinary Eighteenth-Century Account by Father Ippolito Desideri S.J.*, ed. Leonard Zwilling (Boston, MA, 2010); Trent Pomplun, *Jesuit on the Roof of the World: Ippolito Desideri's Mission to 18th-Century Tibet* (Oxford, 2010). For the dialogue in Hindi and Italian by the Capuchin Giuseppe Maria da Gargnano in 1751, see *A Dialogue between a Christian and a Hindu about Religion by Giuseppe Maria da Gargnano*, ed. and transl. David N. Lorenzen (Mexico City, 2015).

[42] On Fukan, see George Elison, *Deus Destroyed: The Image of Christianity in Early Modern Japan* (Cambridge MA, 1973). In *Myōtei Mondō* (n.pl., 1605), Fukan closely followed Alessandro Valignano's *Catechismus Christianae Fidei, in quo veritas nostrae religionis ostenditur, et sectae Japonenses confutantus* (Lisbon, 1586) to attack Buddhism, Shinto and Confucianism; in his *Ha Daiusu* (n.pl., 1620), he sought to prove his anti-Christian credentials by refuting his former arguments. For Chinese Buddhist critiques of Christianity, see Jacques Gernet, *Chine et christianisme. Action et réaction* (Paris, 1982).

Chinese converts under the care of the Jesuit Giulio Aleni, a close follower of Ricci in the province of Fujian, which were published in eight small books by the prominent convert Li Jubiao as *Kouduo richao (Diary of Oral Teachings)*.[43] Summarizing Aleni's sermons and teachings in the Chinese tradition of collections of sayings, the *Diary* recorded the Jesuit's answers to questions posed by low-level literati (*xiucai*), offering a unique glimpse of their actual concerns, and of what accommodation might have entailed in a genuine dialogical context.[44] They asked, for example, how Adam and Eve could be also the ancestors of the Chinese, since surely their own historical records were just as good as those from ancient Judea, and why God had allowed so many generations of Chinese, however virtuous, to remain in ignorance of the true teachings of Jesus, potentially condemning them to eternal damnation. Aleni's answers, often verging on the unorthodox, make it clear that missionaries struggled to avoid saying things that would not have pleased a superior ignorant of Chinese traditions such as the visitor André Palmeiro, or which might not pass muster in a pulpit in Italy, France or Mexico.[45] Thus local deities protecting cities (*chenghuang*) were not rejected as mere idols, but rather interpreted as guardian angels, and while the Incarnation or the Trinity were not ignored, the doctrinal emphasis was monotheist, insisting especially on the 'natural' doctrine of a creator God, following Ricci's selective catechism.[46] This kind of document, published by the Chinese converts rather than by the missionaries,

[43] *Kouduo richao. Li Jiubiao's Diary of Oral Admonitions: A Late Ming Christian Journal*, ed. Eric Zürcher, 2 vols, Monumenta Serica Monograph Series 16 (Sankt Augustin, 2007).

[44] Aleni widened the social penetration of the Riccian mission by extending it to the lower strata of provincial literati, without abandoning the strategic alliance with Confucianism.

[45] To counter scepticism about the universality of the biblical account, Aleni insisted on the exceptional antiquity and historical reliability of the 'chronicles of Judea', referred to the eighth-century Nestorian stele inscription in Sian, and appealed to the continuity of the first human settlers of China – savage nomads travelling eastward – with the primitive monotheism, or natural religion, of Adamic origins (*Kouduo Richao*, 550–2, 335–6 respectively); in fact, the Incarnation was implicit in the knowledge that Adam and Eve and their descendants had of God (ibid. 229–31). Truly virtuous people that lived before the Incarnation (such as Confucius) may have obtained God's grace or gone to a *limbus* to await redemption. However, this hardly satisfied converts who were also concerned about their rather more fallible immediate ancestors.

[46] For Aleni's attempt to explain how the guardian angels – legitimate figures, but subordinated to God – might have been misunderstood by the idolatrous *vulgus*, see ibid. 280.

offers unique insight into genuine native voices that, through a dialogical process, stretched the practice of accommodation.

However, even after we set aside obviously literary works of Christian apologetics, not all sources offering native voices in native languages can be accepted as genuine expressions of such native perspectives. For example some of the interventions by Chinese converts in the rites controversy, offering their linguistic and cultural expertise to clarify whether it was orthodox to venerate Confucius or to call God *Tian* and *Shangdi*, were clearly orchestrated by the Jesuit missionaries in order to support their case: consider, for instance, the letters written by a gathering of converts in Nanjing in late 1702 under the leadership of leading convert Blasius Liu Yunde Verbiest, to counter the restrictions imposed by vicar apostolic Charles Maigrot.[47] The evidence from supposedly unmediated native voices can be treacherous precisely because the fact that they were genuine was part of the rhetoric. Even such apparently local sources as the letters addressed by Tamil Brahmans to Ziegenbalg and other German Pietist missionaries based in Tranquebar (on the Coromandel Coast) between 1712 and 1714 must be treated with great caution: most seem to have been written, or at least brokered, by a local interpreter with knowledge of various European languages, named Alakappan, and his views were influenced by his considerable knowledge of the obsessive concern of the Christian missionaries who employed him with, for example, denouncing idolatry. It is true that the letters presented the Hindu Brahmans as intellectual equals of Europeans, who merited a place within a global Republic of Letters, and that the replies Ziegenbalg received from his 'heathen' correspondents informed his interpretation of Śaivism as a form of natural monotheism, certainly imperfect because bereft of Christian grace, but nevertheless essentially rational. However, the Tamil letters have only come to us through the German version sent to Europe for publication; here again, a dialogical form of religious ethnography merges with sectarian propaganda and Christian apologetics.[48]

In general, missionaries studied the religious traditions of gentiles in order to refute them. This is clearly the case for both Buddhism

[47] Nicolas Standaert, *Chinese Voices in the Rites Controversy: Travelling Books, Community Networks, Intercultural Arguments* (Rome, 2012).

[48] For a recent English translation, see *Hindu-Christian Epistolary Self-Disclosures: 'Malabarian Correspondence' between German Pietist Missionaries and South Indian Hindus (1712–1714)*, ed. and transl. Daniel Jeyaraj and Richard Fox Young (Wiesbaden, 2013).

and Hinduism. In India, many of the great Catholic treatises of the seventeenth and eighteenth centuries – from the Jesuit Jacomé Fenicio's *Livro da Seita dos Indios Orientais* (*Book about the Sect of the Oriental Indians*; written in Calicut in 1609), which was based on texts in Malayalam, to the Capuchin Marco della Tomba's *Livro in cui si descrivono diversi sistemi della religione dei gentili dell'Indostano* (*Book in which the diverse Systems of the Religion of the Gentiles of Hindustan are described*; *c.*1775), composed on the basis of translations of Hindi sources – combined the summary exposition of doctrinal and mythological texts, such as the *Ramayana*, with polemical arguments against them, often deploying scholastic distinctions that were hardly appropriate. Although it was generally believed that the Brahmans did not have properly logical philosophical arguments, they nevertheless had 'reasons', and these could only be countered by engaging with their religious literature: knowing those books therefore was 'the most necessary thing after learning their language', as Marco della Tomba declared.[49] What gradually changed was these missionaries' linguistic competence in vernacular languages or (more rarely) Sanskrit, and the range of sources to which they had access. Thus, while Rogerius, the Dutch pastor in Pulicat between 1632 and 1642, relied heavily on one single local informer, a Brahman called Padmanaba who had some knowledge of Dutch, in order to gather the materials for his *De Open-Deure tot het Verborgen Heydendom* (*The Open Door to Hidden Paganism*; Leiden, 1651), a few decades later Ziegenbalg could read a very wide range of texts directly in Tamil, as witnessed by his catalogue of sources, *Bibliotheca Malabarica*.[50] On the other hand, their interpretative tendencies – shaped by the existence of a core of monotheism hidden within idolatry – remained remarkably similar.[51]

As we have seen, the capacity of missionaries to act as ethnographers largely relied on their expertise in local languages and, when possible, local genres. However, learning languages for cultural insight also increased the potential for mistranslations and

[49] David Lorenzen, *Flagelo de la Misión. Marco della Tomba en Indostán* (Mexico, 2010), 124, paraphrasing Marco della Tomba, *Livro in cui si descrivono diversi sistemi della religione dei Gentili dell'Indostano* (ms, *c.*1775), 110–14.

[50] See *Bibliotheca Malabarica* (n. 6 above).

[51] For Rogerius's work, see n. 5 above. The theme of hidden monotheism was developed with antiquarian erudition by a certain A. W., Rogerius's anonymous editor, in the prologue. Ziegenbalg composed his own treatises on the subject: 'Malabarsiches Heidenthum' ('Malabarian Heathenism', 1711) and 'Genealogia der malabarischen Götter' ('Genealogy of the Malabarian Gods', 1713).

misunderstandings. It is important to avoid exaggerating this problem as a sign of radical cultural incommensurability. While initial errors were many, they could often be overcome with practice. What characterized missionary ethnographies was the expertise claimed by many of its practitioners, and if some found traces of the Trinity in India, or of the Flood in Peru, it was not because they were ignorant or confused about local beliefs, but rather because they were keen to interpret the evidence in a way that made sense of an assumed narrative of shared sacred history. While some foreign terms might have been culture-specific, translations are seldom about finding simple word-by-word equivalents, and historians of the New World consistently showed some awareness of the danger of false analogies, notably when describing new animals and plants (an American 'lion' was not like a lion in the Old World), but also in relation to the human world (a Mexican temple was a 'mosque' only for a while, until a local word was found: Aztecs were no Muslims). Natural and moral historians with local knowledge, like Alzina, excelled in their awareness that the uses of words were contextual. The negotiation of meanings, on the other hand, often followed non-scientific agendas, and in this respect an apparent misunderstanding might have been the result not so much of the difficulties of bridging a cultural chasm as of a motivated interpretative choice.

For missionaries, this was especially the case when dealing with theologically sensitive subjects. The ability to identify different cultural assumptions was not equivalent to a willingness to interpret them sympathetically. When the Jesuit Francis Xavier discovered that using a Buddhist analogy for the supreme deity in Japan, the *Dainichī* (cosmic principle) of the Shingon sect, carried unwanted connotations, he decided to avoid local words altogether when speaking about God, and instead simply used the Latin *Deus*.[52] In China, however, just a few decades later, Ricci adopted a very different approach, seeking to enlist the Chinese concepts of *Tian* (Heaven) and *Shangdi* (First Deity or Highest Deity, also Ruler on High), and coining *Tianzhu*

[52] *Dainichī* (*Vairocana*) was the primordial Buddha of the esoteric Shingon sect of Japan, a universal unchanging principle of wisdom inherent in all things. Although associated with solar symbols, this was not a God of creation, but rather a principle of the Buddhist mysticism of inherent (luminous) emptiness, or Buddha-nature. Anxious to avoid syncretic accommodation, in 1551 Francis Xavier sought to emphasize the distance between God and *Dainichī*, and began asking about the Trinity. The episode was reported by Luís Fróis, *Historia de Japam*, ed. José Wicki, 5 vols (Lisbon, 1976–84), 1: 40.

(Lord of Heaven) for his Christian apologetics. In both cases there was common philosophical assumption: belief in a supreme deity was essentially a natural, rational belief, and could serve as foundation for preaching Christianity. What was different was the judgement made by missionaries in the field about the potential advantages of working with local analogies against the dangers of unwanted associations with 'idolatrous' traditions. While Xavier sought no common ground with the Buddhist monks, his direct rivals, Ricci (as we have seen) hoped to find an authentic ancient version of Confucian ethical teachings that would be compatible with natural monotheism and, at a secondary stage, with a full understanding of Christianity. These different sensibilities, developed in the Jesuit missions of Japan and China in the late sixteenth century, led to disputes within the order about the limits of cultural accommodation, which preceded the full explosion of the rites controversy provoked by the attacks of Franciscans and Dominicans. Ricci undeniably developed his accommodation strategy on the basis of his growing proficiency in Mandarin Chinese, but one of the early opponents of his liberal use of Chinese terms for God was an expert in Japanese, João Rodrigues Tsuçu. Following his exile in Macao after 1610, Rodrigues objected to all the Chinese terms adopted by Ricci – who had recently died – as idolatrous.[53] He was supported by another Jesuit, Niccolò Longobardo, who was based in Beijing, had a good knowledge of Chinese, and had interviewed many Chinese converts.[54] While both Ricci and Rodrigues may be considered cultural experts in China and Japan respectively, their social and educational backgrounds and their ideological temperaments differed markedly. This was not a dispute between missionary ethnographers with knowledge of local languages and those in a distant Church who relied on European cultural prejudice, but rather between rival approaches to the deployment of cultural expertise. While *Tianzhu* eventually came to be generally accepted as distinctive of the

[53] Rodrigues was learning Chinese but his knowledge was much inferior to those he questioned. What was decisive to his uncompromising outlook was his Japanese experience: the task he had been given of writing a common catechism for the two missions had proved impossible. On Rodrigues, see Michael Cooper, *Rodrigues the Interpreter: An Early Jesuit in Japan and China* (Tokyo, 1974).

[54] A conference to resolve this issue was convened in Jiading (near Shanghai) in January 1628. At that point, *Tian* was rejected as too materialistic and thus idolatrous, but the majority accepted *Tianzhu*. Over *Shangdi* there seems to have been an impasse. For a discussion of the conference, see Liam Brockey, *Journey to the East: The Jesuit Mission to China, 1579–1724* (Cambridge, MA, 2007), 87–8.

Catholic religion, and hence not overly ambiguous, resistance to the ancient terms *Shangdi* and *Tian* as false analogies would become a recurrent theme of the Chinese rites controversy. In the end the issue opened a chasm between the Church in Rome, which in 1704 forbade the use of the terms, and the Jesuits and their converts, who sought ancient monotheistic roots for their Christian faith in China.[55] In all cases the deployment of 'local' traditional knowledge had a tactical dimension.

While one line of recent research has questioned the pseudo-liberal myth of an open cultural dialogue, emphasizing instead the ideological limitations of missionary accommodation, another has noted the importance of native converts and interpreters as mediators, both in the development of the missions – translating, preaching, participating in liturgy or even offering confession – and through the production of hybrid cultural discourses. As informants, these figures, too often invisible, were also crucial in the production of missionary ethnographies, making non-European traditions accessible to – but also interpreting them for – the missionaries; at the same time, they explained Christianity to potential converts. It is easy to underestimate the scale of this kind of mediation, both in Catholic and in Protestant missions, and its implications. For example, although several modern historians have used use the vast Nahuatl material collected by Sahagún as reliable evidence for the reconstruction of everyday life in the Mexican empire, these sources must be used with great caution, since the process of gathering this information did not take place in a cultural vacuum but implied the negotiation of meanings in a colonial setting. When in the late 1550s Sahagún, armed with a questionnaire, approached the nobility of Tepepulco and asked to interview elders who were versed in antiquities and able to interpret their pictorial books, he was supported by four 'grammarians' who had studied Latin under him in the Franciscan College of Santa Cruz in Tlaltelolco. After working with these informants for two years, he returned to Tlaltelolco, where he again interviewed the local elders, and revised his materials with the assistance of the trilingual students of the college.[56] His native informants thus represented a subaltern elite in a process of acculturation. That is, many informants

[55] Strictly speaking, the terms controversy preceded the rites controversy, but the historical development of the two was closely intertwined.

[56] Sahagún, *Historia*, 61–3 (prologue to the second book of the *Historia*). Sahagún's detailed explanation of his research methods, written many years afterwards when he edited

were also converts seeking to please, and missionary ethnographers could be their teachers, masters and protectors. Missionaries were not eager (or equipped) to question their own ideological assumptions, and while they might have been willing to dispute with other Europeans about the intellectual capacity of their charges, or about the interpretation of local rites and calendars, they questioned neither the providential meaning of their mission nor the fundamental identification of rational standards in morality and politics with European ideals. Local discourses could be only praised when they fitted these preconceptions.

What is increasingly clear is that that these mediators, as interpreters and in many cases as low-level preachers, were essential to the construction both of 'native voices' within missionary ethnography, and of the voice of Christianity in the mission fields. In the first decades of the Jesuit mission of sixteenth-century Japan, for example, no European could compete with the ability of the almost blind itinerant bard Ryosai, baptized Lorenzo, to spread the message in the local idiom.[57] Mid- and low-level converts facilitated social penetration. As recent work on Chinese and mestizo members of the Jesuit mission in Macao and China has shown, these mediators were numerically not very significant, but their impact was huge.[58] The rarer elite converts, by contrast, may have helped Christians acquire political protection, but were most important as the key to access to literary traditions. Thus, Ricci's literati collaborators were crucial to his development of accommodation in China: officials with scientific interests, such as Li Zhizao, who with Ricci translated several European works of cosmography, mathematics and astronomy into Chinese (although he was reluctant to become a Christian because he did not want to give up his concubines), or Xu Guangqi, baptized as Paul, the most prominent early convert and also a scientific collaborator, who was attracted to Ricci's powerful intellect and to an idealized image of Europe. In India, whether it was Shivadharma for Nobili, Padmanaba for Rogerius, an unnamed pandit from

---

the final manuscript, was intended to authorize the Nahuatl text as authentic history in relation to the different cultural codes of both the Spanish and the Mexicans.

[57] Lorenzo became the first Japanese Jesuit. His role is analysed by J. P. Oliveira e Costa, *O Japão e o cristianismo no século XVI* (Lisbon, 1999), 87–106.

[58] Isabel Murta Pina, 'Chinese and *Mestizo* Jesuits from the China Mission (1589–1689)', in Luís Filipo Barreto, ed., *Europe-China: Intercultural Encounters (16th–18th centuries)* (Lisbon, 2012), 117–37.

Benares for della Tomba, or Alakappan for Ziegenbalg, Brahman informers and other literate intermediaries were indispensable to the European reconstruction of the Hindu religious system, including access to Sanskrit sacred texts. It has sometimes been argued that these missionaries were 'inventing' a religion, rather than simply 'discovering' it, since they were imposing on what they found their own Christian assumptions about doctrine, theology and Scripture, not always applicable to a notoriously pluralistic and fluid religious landscape. While the extent to which Catholic or Protestant assumptions – similar but not identical – distorted, or at least shaped, the missionaries' interpretation of what they learnt about non-European cultures remains controversial, it is very clear that whatever they were doing, they did it on the basis of at least some local knowledge, and under the influence of local mediators who had their own biases and agendas.[59]

Conclusion: Missionary Ethnographies in the European Republic of Letters

Although missionary ethnographies had been a reality in the late medieval expansion of Latin Christendom – one outstanding example is John of Piano Carpini's *Ystoria Mongolorum* of 1247, remarkable for its plain empiricism and systematic organization – they became far more prominent throughout the early modern period, making an essential contribution to both a series of rival colonial ventures and the European Republic of Letters. These two kinds of contribution must be distinguished. For much of the sixteenth century, missionary knowledge and discourses about religious and cultural diversity were closely tied to the needs of local mission fields, and responded to different types of imperial and colonial contexts. However, the growth in production and circulation of missionary ethnographies – a quantitative change – soon also led to a qualitative transformation in relation to their potential impact. Throughout the late sixteenth and seventeenth centuries, the religious orders increasingly found that their access to so many non-European countries allowed them to gain authority as historians of natural and cultural diversity, and that they could use this

[59] See my 'Reassessing "the Discovery of Hinduism": Jesuit Discourse on Gentile Idolatry and the European Republic of Letters', in Anand Amaladass and Ines Županov, eds, *Intercultural Encounter and the Jesuit Mission in South Asia (16th–18th Centuries)* (Bangalore, 2014), 113–55; also Urs App, *The Birth of Orientalism* (Philadelphia, PA, 2010); Xavier and Županov, *Catholic Orientalism*.

unprecedented knowledge to support their missions with numerous publications, often mixing edification, science and propaganda. The Jesuits, with their humanist education and international organization and the vast geographical range of their fields of mission, became particularly adept at this public intervention across Europe, but many other missionaries – including some Protestant chaplains and preachers – also produced and circulated important works of religious and social ethnography. By the end of the seventeenth century, however, the intensity of philosophical debates in Europe, often informed by this evidence of cultural diversity across the world, meant that these interventions were no longer apologetic for Christianity simply in relation to other religious traditions but also in relation to the perceived threats of scepticism, libertinism and heterodoxy. By the time Lafitau wrote his great comparative work on the customs of the American Indians, his underlying theological and historical arguments were clearly more concerned with confronting freethinking and atheism in Europe than with teaching Christianity to savages.

Missionary ethnographies involved multiple acts of cultural translation. In the local fields of mission of the expanding Churches, strategies of accommodation, often controversial, were developed through an intensive interaction with local cultures, usually with the help of converts, interpreters and other mediators. Except perhaps rhetorically, this was never meant to be an open dialogue of equals. Nonetheless, it involved deep engagement with local languages, customs and literary traditions, on a scale unprecedented in European or, indeed, world history. While an earlier historiography may have been tempted to emphasize either the pioneering character of the Christian missionaries as proto-anthropologists, or – in a more critical fashion – their European Christian ideological agendas, there is growing awareness of the crucial importance of the native mediators who acted as knowledge brokers, but who also had their own personal agendas and cultural biases. This emphasis on interactions and mediations helps to challenge facile and tired dichotomies, whether Old World-New World, modern-traditional or East-West. It also challenges a simplistic relativism sustained by the idea of cultural incommensurability. Without dismissing the importance of cultural distance, the possibility of initial misunderstandings or the difficulty of accurate translations, close focus on the missionaries as ethnographers reveals their huge capacity for linguistic and cultural learning. The central importance of mastering new oral and written languages in the early modern system of missionary knowledge did not exhaust the process of cultural learning; rather, a broader kind of learning was taking place, one best encapsulated in the concept of language-games, which included the variety of cultural codes inscribed in everyday customary and ritual practices, as well as the more sophisticated conventions that regulated literary genres or even artistic traditions. The key point here is that language was only the first key to the broad range of cultural performances that missionary ethnographers sought to understand and describe.

However complex the various acts of interactive learning and interpretation that underlay the production of ethnographic knowledge in local missionary contexts, the process of translation did not end there. Instead, in the movement from efforts at evangelization, accommodation and Christian apologetics in the mission field, to the need for edification and propaganda in Europe, a different kind of translation for another kind of audience took place. This one required addressing the concerns with orthodoxy in the European metropolitan core, and intervening in the European Republic of Letters in the difficult context of a rapidly changing intellectual landscape. While the cultural distances involved in this secondary act of translation may have been much smaller, its implications for the intellectual life of Europe, increasingly beyond the control of any single Church, often challenged the Christian identities that had motivated missionaries to travel abroad; indeed, those who fought idolatry and superstition in distant countries could find themselves accused of sustaining them at home. Thus, the return movement of the missionary ethnographer towards European audiences, increasingly fascinated with the contemplation of cultural and religious diversity on a global scale, may well have been more difficult and traumatic than the translation of Nahuatl moral discourses, Japanese rules of etiquette or Chinese Confucian ethics into new forms of Christian worship.

Translating Feeling: The Bible, Affections and Protestantism in England *c.*1660–*c.*1750

Michael A. L. Smith*
University of Manchester

This article examines the way in which English Protestants of the post-Restoration period translated the affective precepts of the Bible into their own devotional practice. In so doing, it challenges persistent narratives that have understood late seventeenth- and early eighteenth-century religion as languishing under an apparent 'reaction against enthusiasm'. By examining the language used in the life-writings of English Protestants in the north-west of England c.*1660–*c.*1750, it demonstrates how biblical discourses on feeling were translated into lay and clerical accounts of their devotional practice. Drawing upon the work of Thomas Dixon and Barbara Rosenwein, the article shows the centrality of biblical injunctions to feeling within sermons and personal devotional practice. Moreover, it exhibits the manner in which affective discourses in the Book of Psalms in particular were used and translated into everyday religious experience. The Bible is shown as a text of affective instruction for the individuals discussed here.*

In his commentary on the Bible, first published between 1707 and 1712, the Presbyterian Matthew Henry (1662–1714), minister of a nonconformist congregation in Chester, argued that the Bible was not merely 'the Touchstone we are to appeal to, and try Doctrines by' but also contained the manner 'by which we must in every thing order our Affections and Conversations, and from which we must always take our Measures'.[1] Henry understood the Bible as the primary model for the control but also, and crucially, the use of feeling in everyday devotion. The roles of the Bible in shaping interpersonal relationships, and as a source of moral instruction and spiritual succour have been well explored.[2] Yet the Bible also provided a model for feeling and indeed one against which one could measure one's

* Flat 2, Village Gate, 15 Wilbraham Rd, Fallowfield, Manchester, M14 6EZ. E-mail: michaelal.smith@googlemail.com.

[1] Matthew Henry, *An Exposition of All the Books of the Old and New Testament*, 6 vols, 3rd edn (London, 1725), 1: [iii].

[2] Naomi Tadmor has explored how it was the 'Englishing' of the Bible (through various translations including Wyclif, Tyndale, Coverdale, Geneva and King James) which

Studies in Church History 53 (2017) 311–323
doi: 10.1017/stc.2016.18

feeling, a practice which was understood as a particularly important part of properly conducting devotional duties. The life-writings (biographies, diaries, letter books and notebooks) of Protestants in the north-west of England exhibited a desire to translate the affective precepts of the Bible into their own devotional exercises. As such, they demonstrated a continued commitment to a vigorous religiosity, guided by the Bible, which has often been downplayed in historiographical narratives focusing on the reaction against enthusiasm.[3] N. H. Keeble, Isabel Rivers and Dewey D. Wallace have observed the role of the heart within the religious culture that followed the Restoration of both king and Church.[4] Yet these historians, to varying extents, have identified this culture with the nonconformist minority and as one that was in decline, particularly from the turn of the eighteenth century. But in the north-west of England, Protestants, both those who conformed to the Church of England and those who did not, exhibited that affective piety observed by Wallace and Keeble in the didactic material produced by leading clerics, and the literature penned by John Bunyan and John Milton was a quotidian aspect of their devotion throughout the period. Even those in this region who

constructed, for example, the Christian, and consequently social, duty of neighbourliness: *The Social Universe of the English Bible: Scripture, Society and Culture in Early Modern England* (Cambridge, 2010), 16–26; G. F. Nuttall, *Richard Baxter and Philip Doddridge: A Study in a Tradition*, Friends of Dr Williams's Library Fifth Lecture (London, 1951), 6–7; Roger Thomas,'Parties in Nonconformity', in C. G. Bolam et al., *The English Presbyterians: From Elizabethan Puritanism to Modern Unitarianism* (London, 1968), 93–112, at 102–4; Jeremy Schildt, 'Reading the Bible in Seventeenth-Century England: A Nonconformist Case-Study', *Bunyan Studies* 15 (2011), 53–63.

[3] G. Williamson, *Seventeenth-Century Contexts* (London, 1960), ch. 9; J. D. Walsh, 'Origins of the Evangelical Revival', in *Essays in Modern English Church History, in Memory of Norman Sykes*, ed. G. V. Bennett and J. D. Walsh (London, 1966), 132–62, at 142; Bolam et al., *English Presbyterians*, 25–6; Michael R. Watts, *The Dissenters*, 1: *From the Reformation to the French Revolution* (Oxford, 1978), particularly 287–300; M. Heyd, 'The Reaction to Enthusiasm in the Seventeenth Century', *JMH* 53 (1981), 258–80; John Spurr, '"Rational Religion" in Restoration England', *JHI* 49 (1988), 563–85, at 564; Phyllis Mack, *Heart Religion in the British Enlightenment: Gender and Emotion in Early Methodism* (Cambridge, 2011), 45–6; Grant Tapsell, 'Introduction: The Later Stuart Church in Context', in idem, ed., *The Later Stuart Church, 1660–1714* (Manchester, 2012), 2.

[4] N. H. Keeble, *The Literary Culture of Nonconformity in Later Seventeenth-Century England* (Leicester, 1987), 18–24, 207–9; Isabel Rivers, *Reason, Grace and Sentiment: A Study of the Language of Religion and Ethics in England, 1660–1780*, 2 vols (Cambridge, 2000), 1: 125–46; Dewey D. Wallace Jr, *Shapers of English Calvinism, 1660–1714: Variety, Persistence, and Transformation* (New York, 2011), particularly in regard to his discussion of the works of Richard Alleine: ibid. 132–53.

only attended the Church of England continued to translate biblical injunctions to, and models of, feeling into their own writings.

The opposition between head and heart which Rivers infers from even Richard Baxter's work, and which Alec Ryrie has claimed began to be constructed in this period, was not a strong feature of the life-writings explored here.[5] By no means was all feeling understood as an unalloyed good by these lay and clerical Protestants. The concern to avoid the sectarianism and extremes of the Interregnum period, understood as product of excessive and misaligned religious enthusiasm, should not be underestimated. It is also important, however, to avoid a picture of late seventeenth- and early eighteenth-century English Protestantism that is caricatured in terms of high-church formalism, low-church moralism and dissenting rationalism, insularity and reluctance to look beyond their own congregations. The period between the Restoration and the advent of the Evangelical Revival witnessed an intensely felt religiosity, to the extent that feeling remained an important medium of devotion.

A closer understanding of the linguistic construction of feeling, which Thomas Dixon has called for, demonstrates the affective quality of devotional practice within the period 1660–1750.[6] The combination of a latitudinarian emphasis on the role of human understanding with the notion that feeling was productive of moral action (resulting in the head's dominance over the heart), which Rivers observes in Richard Baxter's work, was not a novel approach to reason.[7] Baxter's construction of the relationship between feeling and reason was consistent with well-established Christian philosophy. Dixon has observed that in Thomist thought, still dominant in the Christian tradition up to the end of the eighteenth century, the rational appetites fell within what might be constructed in the modern period as the gamut of emotional experience.[8] The passions were also understood by Aquinas as only being sinful where they were not under rational control. Aquinas included 'hope (*spes*), fear (*timor*), joy (*gaudium*) and sorrow (*tristitia*)' among the passions; when rationally controlled by the more active part of man, the intellectual appetite, they could be

[5] Rivers, *Reason*, 125–6; Alec Ryrie, *Being Protestant in Reformation Britain* (Oxford, 2013), 40–1.

[6] Thomas Dixon, *From Passion to Emotions: The Creation of a Secular Psychological Category* (Cambridge, 2006), 54, 63–81.

[7] Rivers, *Reason*, 125.

[8] Dixon, *From Passion*, 28–56.

part of a virtuous life.[9] Susan James has argued that through the seventeenth century (particularly among the Cambridge Platonists) there was in fact a greater understanding of the sensual and affective nature of knowledge.[10] This has not yet been fully brought to bear on the religious culture of the period following the Restoration. The religiosity of these north-western English Protestants thus demonstrated a continued, even enhanced, commitment to that relationship with feeling that Ryrie has observed among their Reformation forebears. The cultivation of feeling was a means of experiencing God and revelation. It was, however, to be managed and examined, lest the Christian be over-confident in the assurance of God's grace.[11]

Protestants across the region demonstrated in their life-writings engagement with this culture of cultivating and managing feeling by taking inspiration from the Bible. The lay and clerical Protestant men and women, with varying degrees of conformity to the Church of England, whom this article will consider sought to emulate biblical precedent, translating into the religious sensibilities of daily life the model of affective piety that they found in the Book of Psalms in particular. Such life-writing as a devotional practice also saw the translation of these biblical models of affectivity into their own experiences. Feeling worked alongside ritual and theology in generating a vigorous religiosity. Moreover, biblical citation was translated into injunctions to feeling where life-writings recorded the sermons they witnessed. Such texts, as Andrew Cambers has noted, are problematic as direct representations of interiority, given their composite nature.[12] Yet the influence of family members over how these Protestants presented their lives in writing, including the chronology of events as well as the inclusion of extracts from the Bible and didactic material, was not understood to prejudice the authenticity of their account. Protestant life-writers included these aspects as adding meaning to their experiences.[13] Indeed, in regard to emotions, scholars such as Barbara

[9] Ibid. 35–52, quotation at 43.

[10] Susan James, *Passion and Action: The Emotions in Seventeenth-Century Philosophy* (Oxford, 1997), 228–9.

[11] Ryrie, *Being Protestant*, 40–7.

[12] Andrew Cambers, 'Reading, the Godly, and Self-Writing in England, circa 1580–1720', *JBS* 46 (2007), 796–825, at 798–802.

[13] Roger Chartier, *Cultural History Between Practices and Representation* (Cambridge, 1988), 11; Carolyn Steedman, 'A Woman Writing a Letter', in Rebecca Earle, ed., *Epistolary Selves: Letters and Letter-Writers, 1660–1945* (Aldershot, 1999), 111–33, at 118; Patrick Coleman, Jayne Lewis and Jill Kowalik, eds, *Representations of the Self from the Renaissance to*

Rosenwein have argued that all emotions are mediated by linguistic construction and socialization, impacting upon their immediate experience and subsequent communication.[14] Given this, the use of biblical citation can be seen as a creative process, providing expression for and description of the experiences of these Protestants. They simultaneously translated biblical narratives into their own experience and their own experiences into a biblical narrative.

The Bible provided these Protestants with a model of affectivity that they could translate into their own lives and seek to emulate. Indeed, this was particularly evident in the use of the Book of Psalms. On 16 October 1687, Sarah Savage (1664–1752), daughter of the eminent ejected minister Philip Henry, noted: 'Thursd. Night in singing in ye Family Ps. 63 (barton) very affecting, I thought every line breathed divine affection thirsting & breathing after God & commun. wth. him'. Lamenting the apparent lack of zeal of her husband's family, she noted how in the '63 Ps. comes in ye 5. My soul shall bee filled', commenting: 'here's firm footing for Faith – hee has not cast me off I shall yet see his goodness in ye sanctuary bl. bee God'.[15] Savage's affective experience of God, which mirrored that of the psalmist, offered evidence that he had not abandoned her in spite of her difficult domestic situation. William Barton's text, which they sang, was:

4 Thus will I bless thee all my days,
and celebrate thy fame:
My hands I will devoutly raise,
in thy most holy Name.
5 With marrow and with fatness fill'd
my longing soul shall be:

Romanticism (Cambridge, 2000); Henk Dragstra, Sheila Ottway and Helen Wilcox, eds, *Betraying Our Selves: Forms of Self-Representation in Early Modern English Texts* (London, 2000); Ronald Bedford, Lloyd Davis and Philippa Kelly, *Early Modern English Lives: Autobiography and Self-Representation, 1500–1660* (Aldershot, 2007), 2–5, 30–5; Adam Smyth, *Autobiography in Early Modern England* (Cambridge, 2010), 2–12.

[14] Barbara H. Rosenwein, 'Problems and Methods in the History of Emotions', *Passions in Context: Journal of the History and Philosophy of the Emotions* 1 (2010), 12–24; eadem, *Emotional Communities in the Early Middle Ages* (Bristol, 2007); eadem, 'History of Emotions: Religious Emotions across the Medieval/Early Modern Divide – Barbara Rosenwein', video lecture, University of Warsaw, 20 October 2014, online at: <https://www.youtube.com/watch?v=CqeQFbjTSgw>, accessed 28 November 2014.

[15] Chester, Cheshire Archives and Local Studies, Papers relating mainly to the Henry family, DBASTEN/8, Diary of Sarah Savage, fols [22^{r}–^{v}].

My mouth shall joyn with joyful lips,
in giving praise to thee.[16]

The Psalms thus provided Savage with a text through which to guide her feeling. David's experience was translated into her own. Devotion was understood here as an inherently affective experience. Joy in the presence of God was a distinguishing characteristic of devotional practice. Barton's addition of 'longing soul', referencing the first verse of the psalm, coupled with the joyfulness of the lips (common to the King James and Geneva translations), suggested that Protestants such as Savage sought out and revelled in materials that provided a strongly affective piety to translate into their own experience.

Savage frequently aligned her own experience with that of David. On 16 September 1687 she noted that on Friday having heard 'good news from Dear Relations yt morn read in course Ps. 38 could heartily address mysf to God as ye Psalmist in ye Psalm Lord all my desire is before thee hee knows wt in my [heart] to ask before I ask it'.[17] The practice of piety here was to foster one's feeling in imitation of David. Savage translated the desire of the Psalmist, into her own experience of thanksgiving. She cited from verse 9: 'my desire is before thee; and my groaning is not hid from thee', providing a model of affectivity but also the form of expression with which to articulate this within the confines of her spiritual journal. Given her nonconformity (Savage, like her family, continued to attend Church of England services but seems to have taken communion only in dissenting congregations), this imitation of the affectivity of the psalmist might seem unsurprising, given the strong attachment to psalm-singing observed within godly culture from the sixteenth century and the established view that nonconformists were the especial heirs of this tradition.[18]

[16] Ps. 63: 4–5, in William Barton, *The book of Psalms in metre Close and proper to the Hebrew: smooth and pleasant for the metre. To be sung in usual and known tunes. Newly translated with amendments, and addition of many fresh metres. Fitted for the ready use, and understanding of all good Christians* (London, 1682), 165.

[17] Savage, Diary, fol. [20^{v}].

[18] Patrick Collinson, 'Elizabethan and Jacobean Puritanism as Forms of Popular Religious Culture', in Christopher Durston and Jacqueline Eales, eds, *The Culture of English Puritanism, 1560–1700* (Basingstoke, 1996), 32–57, at 48–9; Christopher Durston and Jacqueline Eales, 'The Puritan Ethos, 1560–1700', ibid. 1–31, at, 19; Rivers, *Reason*, 52.

Edmund Harrold (1678–1721), however, made similar pleas on a regular basis. Harrold was of broadly high-church sympathies. A wigmaker resident in Manchester, he attended the Collegiate Church most frequently and expressed support for the controversialist Henry Sacheverell. On 25 September 1713, after concluding his third marriage, he prayed: 'O Lord God who hast joined us together in holy wedlock, grant yt we may always live worthy of yt state in sobriety, chastity and love and fidelity'.[19] Prior to this marriage Harrold recorded on 18 June 1713: 'Oh my heart is sorrowful for my sin and vanity. Lord, help and direct me for ye best, not yt I heartily desire to settle, however, thy will be done.'[20] After recording the sermon he heard on 27 July 1712, he ended the entry: 'O Lord, I beseech thee, grant me peace in thee, thro' Jesus Christ our Lord amen.'[21] Harrold drew upon spiritual ejaculation, in imitation of the psalmist, in his own record. The affectivity of the Psalms was translated into his devotional practice of diary-keeping as it was for Savage. It was also true of Thomas Jolly (1629–1703), a Lancashire nonconformist minister who frequently employed these groans in his notebook. He wrote in February 1678: 'Oh! The signall providence of God as to my outward man in Manchester', having escaped unscathed after a fall from his horse.[22] These Protestants found in David a model of how to express their feeling in a godly manner and pray. This 'textual groaning' probably also served to mitigate the quietness of diary-writing, sustaining that suspicion of silent prayer which Reformation Protestants exhibited. These ejaculations, even in written form, were a means of stirring up the affections.[23] Moreover, by using biblical precedents they communicated a fervency of religiosity which avoided the extremes of sectarian enthusiasm. Biblical models thus added affective inflection, which also allowed these Protestants to straddle the divide between the fervency of Spirit-led prayer and praying with a book which John Craig has observed.[24]

[19] *The Diary of Edmund Harrold, Wigmaker of Manchester 1712–15*, ed. Craig Horner (Aldershot, 2008), 90.

[20] Ibid. 77.

[21] Ibid. 23.

[22] Henry Fishwick, ed., *The Note Book of the Rev. Thomas Jolly A.D. 1671–1693, Extracts from the Church Book of Altham and Wymondhouses A.D. and an Account of the Jolly Family of Standish, Gorton, and Altham*, Chetham Society n.s. 33 (Manchester, 1894), 33.

[23] Ryrie, *Being Protestant*, 212.

[24] John Craig, 'Bodies at Prayer in Early Modern England', in Alec Ryrie and Natalie Mears, eds, *Worship and the Parish Church in Early Modern England* (Aldershot, 2013), 173–95, at 181–2.

The Bible was also a source of direct exhortation to feeling. Sermons preached at public worship and lessons taught at family exercises drew frequently upon biblical calls to affectivity. These could take the form of rather conventional appeals to Christian charity and love. On 5 January 1687/8 Sarah Savage, noted that 'Dear Fath. came below to Fam. Prayer read. Eph. 5. Vr 25. where Husbs. are bid to love yeir wives as Xt. the church'.[25] James Parker, a layman living in Chorley, Lancashire, noted on 1 February 1740/1 that his local curate 'Mr. Ellinson' preached from 'Romans ch. 12 vss 9 part of it. Let Love be without dissimulation'.[26] These were principally moral lessons, though they required the Christian to feel as much as act. In his preaching tour of Lancashire and Cheshire in 1672, Henry Maurice (*c.*1636–82), a nonconformist minister, preached 'from John, 15.13', which asserted: 'Greater love hath no man than this, that a man lay down his life for his friends'. Maurice further reflected that he 'found ebbings & flowings in my spirit' and that of his audience who 'seemed much affected, & seemed very kind'.[27] The content of the biblical citation was, like the above, a moral lesson once more requiring the Christian to engage their affections. It was the movement of Maurice's feelings and those of the audience, however, which bore witness to his effectiveness as a preacher. While all these extracts were moral injunctions, their efficacy was predicated on that translation of God's truth from head to heart that Rivers has observed in Baxter's work.[28]

On 1 June 1712 Edmund Harrold recorded Dr Radley Aynscough preaching on Colossians 3: 2: 'Set your affection on things above, not on things on the earth'. '[I]t behoves us', Harrold recorded, 'to look on what sort of objects we place our affections on, whether earthly or heavenly'. In contrast with earthly things, 'heavenly objects never fail of satisfieing us, tho our appetites be boundless'. Indeed, he continued, there was an 'ocean of pleasures yt can never be fathomed' at God's right hand, and 'Rivers of pleasures for everyone, to wch fountain of bliss God bring us all, for Jesus sake, amen'.[29] The effusive

[25] Savage, Diary, fol. [26^{v}].
[26] Preston, Lancashire Record Office, MS Hawkshead-Talbot of Chorley, DDHK 9/1/77, Memorandum Book of James Parker, unpaginated.
[27] B. Cottle and M. J. Crossley Evans, 'A Nonconformist Missionary Journey to Lancashire and Cheshire in July 1672', *Transactions of the Historical Society of Lancashire and Cheshire* 137 (1988), 77–91, at 86.
[28] Rivers, *Reason*, 125.
[29] *Diary of Edmund Harrold*, ed. Horner, 2.

affectivity of Aynscough's sermon as recorded by Harrold showed how biblical injunctions to feeling could translate into a vigorous religiosity. Of course, as with Savage, Parker and Maurice, this required control over feeling, directing it properly in the worship of God. Such control was perfectly consistent with the Christian philosophical tradition and did not diminish the felt element, but merely redirected it. It mirrored Phyllis Mack's characterization of the 'Methodist's ability to feel correctly', a practice which meant that feeling rather than intellect was the primary medium of accessing divine truth.[30] Biblical injunctions to feeling were translated into experience by way of recording these sermons and lessons.

Harrold's diary bore witness to the didactic role of the Bible, though here too feeling played an important role in mediating teaching and practice. On 3 August 1712 he recorded a sermon preached on 1 Corinthians 12: 27, from which the preacher maintained 'yt tis a blessed thing to keep union in ye body, mysticall as well as natural, yt ye be no schism in ye body, but yt all ye members may honour and obey ye head even Christ'.[31] On 29 November 1713, Harrold recorded a sermon on Matthew 16: 27 regarding 'Christ's second Advent, when ye son of man shall come in glory, with his holy angels, and yn shall he reward every man according to his works'.[32] Although Harrold did not elaborate upon the use of this verse in 1 Corinthians, it likely served as a means to defend the established Church and perhaps to take a swipe at nonconformity. Similarly, the verse from Matthew justified the Church's greater focus on works after the Restoration, in some opposition to the focus on the power of grace that had been vaunted by the sects of the Interregnum.[33] Yet even for Harrold, teaching frequently had a strongly affective element. Preaching on 5 October 1712 from 1 Corinthians 11: 28, Aynscough asserted 'yt it is every mans duty to examin and communicate'. The dynamics of this practice of self-examination were mediated by the affections. Impediments to communicating were '1st, ignorance, 2^{ly}, self love, 3^{ly}, pride', which Harrold recorded had to be conquered if one was to 'obtain to ye end of our hopes, even ye salvation of our souls'. Here, of course, some feelings were to be restrained in

30 Mack, *Heart Religion*, 15.

31 *Diary of Edmund Harrold*, ed. Horner, 24.

32 Ibid. 96.

33 John Spurr, 'The Lay Church of England', in Tapsell, ed., *Later Stuart Church*, 101–24, at 102.

order that others, notably the hope of redemption, might be exercised. Aynscough's second sermon that day extolled the 'satisfaction in living virtuously, holily, and temperately in this world'. This was the fount of 'al[l] our comforts of long life[:] riches and honours, a good name, and peace of conscience, temprall and spirtuall etc.'[34] The focus, conventional in that religious culture which followed the Restoration, on a practical religion dominated by moral, Christian action nonetheless also involved an affective element. Much as for Baxter, the imperative of God's command to live morally was appreciated as much through feeling as the intellect. It provided satisfaction and comfort to the believer. Quiet feelings perhaps, but as Phyllis Mack has argued, these were appreciated by the Methodists later as the signs of the sanctified Christian.[35]

Biblical discourses of the heart, reflective of the emphasis that Wallace has observed in works by leading nonconformist authors, provided these Protestants with models that they could translate into their own quotidian devotional practices. The strong role played by the heart in these discourses demonstrated that pietist and Wesleyan 'heart-religion' which 'emphasised passivity and feeling' had some precedent here.[36] On 6 November 1687, after meeting God in Sunday worship, Sarah Savage noted:

> I am much comforted by yt. Promise Ps. 37. Delight thysf also in ye Ld. & hee shal give thee ye desires of thy [heart] & wt. more can I wish Dear Lord it is the desire of my [heart] yt. I may delight myself in thee thou art ye strength of my [heart] & my Portion for ever …[37]

Such affective piety, centred upon the heart, was central to Savage's devotional record. Indeed, here the translation was also significant. The King James translation, the most popular version from 1660, rendered the end of the verse 'he shall give thee the desires of thine heart', following precedents in the Geneva and Coverdale Bibles which rendered it 'hee shall giue thee thine hearts desire'.[38] The

[34] *Diary of Edmund Harrold*, ed. Horner. 38.

[35] Mack, *Heart Religion*, 35.

[36] Ibid. 13.

[37] Savage, Diary, fol. [23^r].

[38] Ps. 37: 4, Geneva Bible (1587) and Coverdale Bible (1535); Scott Mandelbrote, 'The English Bible and its Readers in the Eighteenth Century', in Isabel Rivers, ed., *Books and their Readers in Eighteenth-Century England: New Essays* (London, 2001), 35–78, at 37; Femke Molekamp has argued that there was a market for the Geneva Bible and hybrid Geneva-

second citation, Psalm 73: 26, was a popular one for Savage, who repeated it as she besought God for children on 16 November 1687.[39] Many years later, on 17 April 1737, Richard Kay (1716–51), a Presbyterian attending Bury Chapel, also besought the Lord to 'help me now to make haste, and not delay to keep thy Commandments, and ever be thou the Strength of my Heart, and my Portion forever'.[40] Here again this demonstrated a more robust affectivity than the Douai-Rheims, which read 'thou art the God of my heart, and the God that is my portion for ever'. The King James translation put a greater emphasis upon the passivity of the believer, who was dependent on God and his management of their affections. Within their own writings, these Protestants thus translated the affective norms and heart-religion of their translations of the Bible into devotional practice.

The heart-religion inherent within the Bible was also translated into the writings of those who attended and communicated at the established Church. The life of Richard Illidge (1637–1709), a farmer and an officer in the Cheshire militia, recorded him drawing upon James 5: 16 when he prayed: 'Lord, give me Wisdom from above, and teach me to pray, so that my Prayers may be acceptable to Thee, my God, that every Prayer may come warm from the Heart, may be an *effectual fervent Prayer*, which *availeth much*.'[41] Although his life was edited and written up by Matthew Henry, a family friend, Illidge owned himself 'to be a Member of the established Church of *England*, which, I think, is not exceeded by any other in Purity'.[42] The extract demonstrated how translation of one's devotional exercise into biblical narrative was perfectly compatible with allegiance to the Church of England. Illidge understood feeling as essential to prayer, effective only so far as he had a warm heart capable of fervency. This was also true of members of the congregation of Thomas Brockbank (1671–1709), then curate of Sefton, Lancashire. On 9 April 1705 two of them contacted him to request that he 'preach a funeral Sermon

King James Bibles well into the eighteenth century. She has however, also stressed the continuities between these editions in both material and expositional terms: 'The Geneva and the King James Bibles: Legacies of Reading Practices', *Bunyan Studies* 15 (2011), 11–17.

[39] Diary of Sarah Savage, [fol. 24r].

[40] *The Diary of Richard Kay, 1716–51, of Baldingstone, near Bury, a Lancashire Doctor*, ed. W. Brockbank and F. Kenworthy, Chetham Society 3rd ser. 16 (Manchester, 1968), 7.

[41] Matthew Henry, *An account of the life and death of lieutenant Illidge*, 2nd edn (London, 1720), 39.

[42] Ibid. 67.

tomorrow for Elizabeth Harrison'. One of the texts chosen by Harrison prior to her death was Psalm 38: 9–10, which declared: 'Lord, all my desire is before thee; and my groaning is not hid from thee. My heart panteth, my strength faileth me: as for the light of mine eyes, it also is gone from me.' Again, the affective nature of this citation was evident. It demonstrated a model of the good death through affective engagement with the divine. The heart was engaged, albeit with the last of its strength, and was overcome with feeling just before the expiration of the body. Such a passage was a natural choice for a funeral, yet its selection allowed the Bible's affectivity to be translated into the funeral service.

Bible passages were also cited to demonstrate the need for heartfelt conversion. On 17 August 1712 Edmund Harrold recorded hearing a sermon on Jeremiah 13: 23: 'Can the Ethiopian change his skin, or the leopard his spots? then may ye also do good, that are accustomed to do evil'. From this Harrold noted that it was indeed 'so hard … that its almost imposible as to nature, but God thro his grace can reform ye heart and thro' his grace bring good out of evill etc.'[43] This lesson suggested that the Church of England minister was determined that his congregation should translate the calls to a moral life, within biblical injunctions, into an affective exercise. Matthew Henry, reflecting on his own conversion, noted on 18 October 1675:

> it was three years ago that I began to be convinc'd, hearing a Sermon by my Father on *Psal,* li. 7. *The Sacrifices of God are a broken Spirit; a broken and a contrite heart, O God, thou wilt not despise.* I think it was then that that melted me, afterwards I began to enquire after Christ.[44]

The sermon and the words of the Bible provided for Henry a model of Christian affectivity. The psalmist's broken and contrite heart was translated into Henry's experience as a measure of his conversion. Such an account was conventional within the conversion narrative genre but it nonetheless demonstrated that conversion was a matter for the heart.[45] The translation of one's own experience into a biblical narrative ensured this.

[43] *Diary of Edmund Harrold*, ed. Horner, 28.
[44] William Tong, *An account of the life and death of Mr. Matthew Henry, minister of the gospel at Hackney, who dy'd June 22, 1714 in the 52d year of his age* (London, 1716), 12.
[45] D. Bruce Hindmarsh, *The Evangelical Conversion Narrative: Spiritual Autobiography in Early Modern England* (Oxford, 2005), 18–21, 31–2, 324.

The Bible provided models of affectivity that these north-western English Protestants in the late seventeenth and early eighteenth centuries could translate into their own devotional exercises. It provided them with forms of expression with which they could live out that heart-religion, observed by historians, inherent within the didactic material of the period. This was as true of those who attended and communicated at the Church of England, with both high- and low-church sympathies, as of nonconformists. This engagement with feeling was thus more mainstream than has necessarily been appreciated within the existing historiography. The cultivation of feeling explored here gives pause to those narratives which stress the dominance of the reaction against enthusiasm within the religious culture of the period. The strong role that feeling played in the religiosity of the Evangelical Revival has considerable precedent here. The extracts explored demonstrate a commitment by these Protestants to a vital and vigorous religiosity, guided by the affective discourses of the Bible, within an intensely felt piety. The Psalms in particular, and the commitment to adding affective inflection in imitation of David, allowed these life-writers to assimilate their affections with biblical precedents. Narratives drawn from the Bible were translated into their own experiences in personal, familial and public devotion to make sense of them. Such experiences were also translated into biblical narratives to provide structure to their witness. Feeling was not always presented by these Protestants as an unqualified good. Control, management and even repression were features of their engagement with this interiority. This was, however, consistent with Christian philosophical precedent and sought to channel affective energies in the appropriate direction, the worship of God. Feeling was thus a medium of devotion, conversion, teaching and ritual. The act of transcribing biblical citations, from sermons, family lessons and personal reading was a devotional act. It was one that translated the affectivity of the Bible into experience.

Translating Christianity and Buddhism: Catholic Missionaries in Eighteenth- and Nineteenth-Century Burma

Andrew J. Finch*
Ambleside

Catholic mission in Burma during the eighteenth and nineteenth centuries provides evidence for the importance of translation as an element of both Christian evangelism and apologetic. In Burma missionaries were faced by a varied linguistic environment, which became more complex over time. An effective mission required Burmese and the two Karen dialects. Additionally, missionaries were pastors to existing Portuguese Christian communities. British expansion during the nineteenth century added English and Tamil to these pastoral languages. English also became a language of education, Christian debate and mediation. Those wishing to understand Buddhism through its canonical texts had to acquire, or borrow from Buddhist monks, expertise in Pali. This translation and interpretation of Buddhist texts became a tool for both evangelization and Christian defence. In this latter role, the manner in which Buddhist terms were translated or employed became significant within wider European debates concerning the relationship of Christianity to Buddhism.

Christian encounter with other faiths frequently brought with it the need for interpretation and translation. Evangelization might require the translation of Christian terms and doctrinal concepts into other languages, while engagement with indigenous religious traditions often saw the process reversed. Both were complex and dynamic processes, involving multiple agents and presenting specific challenges. The interest here lies in the examination of how Catholic missionaries active in Burma (Myanmar) over a period from the early eighteenth to the late nineteenth centuries met the challenges presented firstly by a complex and evolving linguistic environment and secondly by the missionaries' desire to study Theravāda Buddhism and its texts. The

* 6 Gale Rigg House, Ambleside, Cumbria, LA22 0BA. E-mail: digital_hakase@hotmail.com. The assistance of the Scouloudi Foundation in providing a Historical Award to undertake the initial research for this article is gratefully acknowledged.

Studies in Church History 53 (2017) 324–337
doi: 10.1017/stc.2016.19

extent to which their translations of Buddhist terms may have been shaped by the needs of Christian apologetic will also be considered.

From the late seventeenth century, Christian missionaries in southeast Asia came into contact with societies in which Theravāda Buddhism had developed as the major religious tradition.[1] They were therefore some of the first Europeans to have an opportunity to study Buddhism in this form. One area of encounter was the Vicariate of Ava and Pegu, created in 1721 and corresponding to the two major political units within the area of modern Burma. The Vicariate was entrusted initially to priests of the Italian order of the Regular Clerics of St Paul (Barnabites), two of whom arrived in the following year. There were, however, Catholic communities already established in Ava (Upper Burma). These were mainly the descendants of Portuguese and Indian Christians taken captive at Syriam in 1613, and subsequently dispersed through Upper Burma, where they formed distinct communities.[2] At the time of the arrival of the Barnabites, there were two Catholic priests in Burma, one at Syriam ministering to the needs of the foreign merchant community and the other at Ava. They had been sent by the bishop of Meliapor and were either Goanese or natives of western India. Both, according to Paul Bigandet writing in the 1880s, made only infrequent visits to the dispersed Christian communities. These priests remained in Burma until at least the start of the nineteenth century and possibly into its second decade.[3] Throughout the period of their mission, the Barnabites catered in some degree to the pastoral needs of these Christian communities.[4]

By the 1820s the difficulties faced in Burma, such as the disruption caused by war and the insalubrious climate of certain areas, coupled

[1] Barbara Watson Andaya and Leonard Y. Andaya, *A History of Early Modern Southeast Asia, 1400–1830* (Cambridge, 2015), 57–8, 145–7. The title Theravāda was adopted only in 1950 by those groups previously identified as part of southern Buddhism: Kate Crosby, *Theravada Buddhism: Continuity, Diversity, and Identity* (Chichester, 2014), 1–2, 4.

[2] Andaya and Andaya, *History*, 216; Paul A. Bigandet, *An Outline of the History of the Burmese Catholic Mission from the Year 1720 to 1887* (Bangkok, 1996; first publ. 1887), 7–8, 10–11.

[3] Bigandet, *Outline*, 12–13; Vincentius Sangermano, *The Burmese Empire a Hundred Years ago as described by Father Sangermano, with an Introduction and Notes by John Jardine*, 3rd edn (London, 1893), 283. In May 1816 a 'Portuguese' priest was called to treat the infant son of the American Baptist missionaries Ann and Adoniram Judson at Rangoon: James D. Knowles, *Memoir of Mrs Ann H. Judson, Wife of the Rev. Adoniram Judson, Missionary to Burmah: Including a History of the American Baptist Mission in the Burman Empire* (Marston Gate, 2012; first publ. 1829), 123.

[4] Sangermano, *History*, xxv.

with the adverse effects of the French occupation of the Italian states, led the Barnabites to petition the *Sacra Congregatio de Propaganda Fide* to have the mission removed from their care. As a result, secular priests appointed by the Propaganda provided the mission personnel from 1829 until 1840, at which time the Society of the Oblats of the Blessed Virgin Mary of Turin took charge. However, by the 1850s, this society was, like the Barnabites before them, finding it increasingly difficult to service the mission. In 1855 a formal move was made to have the mission entrusted to the Société des Missions Étrangères de Paris (SMEP), which took control in 1856.[5]

In Burma, Theravāda Buddhism, expressed particularly through the role of the Sangha (the community of Buddhist monks and nuns), had become an integral part of the social, political and religious environment. This ensured that it could not be simply dismissed as decadent and superstitious idolatry by Christians and missionaries as was the case with, for example, Mahāyāna Buddhism in late eighteenth- and nineteenth-century Korea.[6] Missionaries seeking to evangelize effectively in Burma had therefore to engage with Theravāda Buddhist texts and practitioners in order to understand its doctrines and role within society. It was necessary, too, for them to meet the challenges presented by the linguistic diversity of Burma. Both aspects are illuminated through the publications of two missionaries active within Burma. These missionaries are Vincentius Sangermano (*fl.* 1783–1806), a Barnabite, and Paul Ambrose Bigandet (*fl.* 1856–94), the vicar apostolic of the SMEP mission. Both translated Buddhist texts and wrote on the subject of Burmese Buddhism, while Bigandet also completed a history of the Burmese mission in English that provides valuable information on the linguistic context and the missionaries' reactions to it.[7]

The works of both Bigandet and Sangermano demonstrate the challenges presented by the complex linguistic environment in Burma, and the manner in which these were met. Bigandet's studies of Buddhism, in particular, also illustrate how the fact of being a missionary and elements extrinsic to the mission could influence both the motives for studying Buddhism and the translation and interpretation of Buddhist terms. Although Bigandet sought to

[5] Ibid. 27–44.

[6] Charles Dallet, *Histoire de l'église de Corée, précédée d'une introduction sur l'histoire, les institutions, la langue, les moeurs et coutumes coréennes*, 2 vols (Seoul, 1975; first publ. 1874), cxliv–cxlvi.

[7] Bigandet, *Outline*.

follow scholarly practice and looked disparagingly on argument based upon erroneous statements, as a missionary he was, like Sangermano, studying Buddhism in order to refute it.[8] Bigandet considered engagement with Buddhist texts as the most effective way to undermine and attack this 'false creed'. This process might involve the use of scholarly conventions and produce scholarly insights, but ultimately its purpose was to reveal Buddhism as empty and unreal error, so that 'it vanishes away as a phantom and an illusion'.[9] Moreover, within Bigandet's analysis of Buddhism lies an implicit defence of Christianity in Europe. His first published account of Buddhism was in French, while his translation of a Burmese life of the Buddha was completed in English; the second expanded edition was then translated into French by a third party. Evidently, Bigandet was looking to convince a European rather than a Burmese audience.

The complex linguistic environment encountered by missionaries within Burma is made clear in Bigandet's history of the mission. The 'Portuguese' priests already resident in the country were accused of showing no interest in learning Burmese or in the evangelization of the wider population. They spoke and preached in Portuguese, or as Bigandet had it, a patois with some 'affinity' to the language, and had made this 'the distinctive characteristic of Christians'.[10] These shortcomings were not shared by the Barnabites. Sigismund Calchi, in the six years between his arrival in 1722 and his death, composed a 'small dictionary for facilitating to his Brethren … the study of the Burmese language'.[11] Giovani Percoto (*fl.* 1761–76) used the time spent on the voyage from Italy to learn Portuguese. He subsequently compiled a Latin-Burmese-Portuguese dictionary, representing the fulfilment of an ambition held by the fathers since the beginning of the mission.[12] In addition to Burmese, it was necessary to learn at least

[8] Paul A. Bigandet, *The Life or Legend of Gaudama, the Budha of the Burmese, with Annotations, Notice on the Phongies, or Budhist Religious and the Ways to Niban* (Rangoon, 1858), vi–vii. He believed that 'error is never to be combated by another error or a false supposition': ibid. 171 n. 90. Bigandet is identified as being among those 'amateur' Orientalists who made commentaries and translations into proper objects for study: Charles Hallisey, 'Roads Taken and Not Taken in the Study of Theravāda Buddhism', in Donald S. Lopez, ed., *Curators of the Buddha: The Study of Buddhism under Colonialism* (Chicago, IL, and London, 1995), 31–61, at 44.

[9] Bigandet, *Life*, vii.

[10] Bigandet, *Outline*, 12, 27.

[11] Ibid. 14.

[12] Sangermano, *History*, 285–6.

one of the two Karen dialects, depending on the area to be evangelized.[13] Those missionaries who wished to study Buddhism through its texts, required knowledge of Pali if they were to work directly with the *Tipiṭaka*, the 'Pali Canon'. However, only the Barnabite Joseph D'Amato, who served from 1783 until his death in 1832, was said to know the language well; other missionaries relied on the borrowed expertise of Buddhist monks.[14] The nineteenth century brought further linguistic challenges. A command of English became necessary in response firstly to the establishment of the American Baptist Mission in the 1810s and secondly (beginning with the annexation of Arakan and Tenesserim in 1826) to the extension of British power in Burma. The secular priest, Francis Bartelli, carried on a dispute with the Baptists during the 1830s, while the Oblat bishop, Faustino Ceretti, learnt English sufficiently well to keep up a written controversy with them, although he was never able to speak Burmese.[15] From the 1840s, the need for missionaries to cater to the spiritual needs of Catholic troops stationed in British garrisons and the introduction of English into the curricula of the mission schools made a command of the language a necessity.[16] Bishop Ceretti attempted to found a school for boys at Monhla in the mid-1840s, which taught Burmese, Latin and Italian, but this had failed within months.[17] This was probably a reflection of the increasing appeal of English as the language of the principal regional and colonizing power. Fr D'Cruz, a native Burmese priest, had studied English in Calcutta, while Bigandet's clear ability in English is likely to have been a factor in his appointment as vicar apostolic.[18] Changes brought about by

[13] Bigandet, *Outline*, 38, 48, 55, 58–60, 90–1, 93, 105. The presence of Christian Armenian merchants and priests, among whom the Barnabites sought converts to Catholicism during the eighteenth century, and Chinese Christians in Myaung-mya in the 1880s, added to this linguistic mix: ibid. 17, 141; Sangermano, *History*, 116.

[14] Bigandet, *Outline*, 26. Knowledge of Pali had also acquired a wider significance beyond that of a sacred language. Although not referred to by the Catholic missionaries, its importance as a religious language and as a marker of progress through the hierarchy of the Sangha ensured that knowledge of Pali had acquired an intellectual cachet. As Ann Judson wrote in the 1820s: '[Pali] is the learned language of the Burmans, and without a knowledge of which, a man is not considered learned': Knowles, *Memoir*, 117.

[15] Bigandet, *Outline*, 30, 33.

[16] Ibid. 34, 42, 48, 52, 67, 98, 100, 112–13.

[17] Ibid. 34.

[18] Ibid. 40. In addition to his English publications, Bigandet was involved in treaty negotiations at Mandalay in 1862 between the British and the Burmese, and in 1866 acted as an interpreter between British envoys and the Burmese Court: ibid. 62; 'Paul Bigandet

further British expansion added to the linguistic mix: by the 1870s it was necessary to speak Tamil in order to minister to congregations in Rangoon and Moulmain.[19] The murder at Moulmain in 1886 of the SMEP priest Louis Biet was therefore a significant loss, since he was 'well acquainted with the English, Burmese and Tamil languages which are necessary, to act as a Priest at that station'.[20] Finally, as Catholic priests, both Europeans and the Portuguese speakers would have known Latin. Aside from being the language of the liturgy, other aspects of the utility of Latin are perhaps easily overlooked. It still retained its importance as a *lingua franca.* In 1795 Sangermano provided the British envoy to the Burmese Court with a Latin translation of the 'most remarkable passages' from a Burmese translation of the Indian *Manu Shastra* (*Laws of Manu*).[21] It is possible, too, that Latin facilitated the acquisition of other languages, since its teaching in the seminaries provided Catholic missionaries with the experience of, and a potential model for, language learning even before they entered a mission area, as well as ensuring that they were to some degree already bilingual.

Faced with this linguistic complexity, the Barnabites began creating the tools necessary to undertake both pastorate and mission. The dictionaries of Sigismundi Calchi and Giovani Percoto have already been noted. Paolo Nerini (*fl.* 1743–56), who worked extensively among the Karen populations, produced grammars of Burmese and Karen ('Burman and Pegu languages'), as well as catechisms, dictionaries and prayer books.[22] Sections of the Bible were translated into Burmese by Percoto. These were a translation and abridgement of Genesis; the books of Tobit and Daniel, and the epistles of St Paul. The abridgement and the other two Old Testament books were put into verse under the supervision of Joseph D'Amato. In view of D'Amato's ability in Pali, this may have been a conscious mimicking of Buddhist practice since the second part of the *Tipiṭaka*, the *Sutta Piṭaka*, presents parts of the Buddha's teaching as poetry.[23] Melchior Carpani was sent to Rome in 1764 to seek the approval for these and

(1813–1894)', Archives des Missions Étrangères de Paris, online at: <http://archives.mepasie.org/notices/notices-biographiques/bigandet>, accessed 27 October 2014.

19 Bigandet, *Outline*, 89, 115.

20 Ibid. 132.

21 Sangermano, *History*, xxv.

22 Bigandet, *Outline*, 17; Sangermano, *History*, 283–4.

23 Bigandet, *Outline*, 21–2; Crosby, *Theravada Buddhism*, 288. The Barnabites also composed a life of Christ in verse: Bigandet, *Outline*, 100.

other Burmese works composed by Percoto and to have them printed at the Propaganda press. The result of this expedition is unclear, but twenty years later Caejetan Montegazza returned to Italy in the company of two Burmans, one of whom was a former Buddhist monk. They assisted Montegazza with the printing in Rome of an alphabet in Burmese characters, a small prayer book and a catechism with the Latin translation.[24] As a result, a press was established in Burma, which published Percoto's dictionary. Much later, in the 1850s, the Oblats founded a press at Moulmain, but it lacked both English and Burmese type. The former could be obtained from Calcutta, but for the latter the Oblats were at the 'mercy of the Baptist press' and this remained the case until a SMEP priest was sent to Paris and returned with the matrices and puncheons necessary 'for casting Burmese type in any quantity that might be required'.[25]

As noted above, those missionaries wishing to understand Buddhism through its canonical texts had to master Pali to some degree. The Barnabites compiled an Italian-Burmese-Pali dictionary, but they remained – as did their successors – heavily reliant upon the linguistic expertise of Buddhist monks: directly for instruction in the language or assistance in translation, and indirectly through monks' vernacular commentaries and glosses on the *Tipiṭaka* and other Pali texts or explanations of Buddhism, such as the 'Compendium of Burmese Religion' presented to Percoto by the *sayadaw* (personal instructor) of King Naungdawgyi in 1763. Percoto appears to have been the first Barnabite to have had the opportunity to engage seriously with Buddhism. He may have requested the composition of the 'Compendium', in response to which he wrote *Treatise of Christian Religion: A Dialogue between a Christian and a Theravadin Monk*. Both works were incorporated in a *vita* published in 1781.[26] Percoto was said to have translated the 'sacred books' into Italian, but it is unclear whether this was directly from the Pali or via Burmese translations, or indeed what assistance he received in making them.[27] The *sayadaw*'s 'Compendium' was later incorporated by Sangermano in his *History of the*

[24] Ibid. 21–2.

[25] Ibid. 42, 99; Barnabite Fathers USA, 'Missions in Burma 1722–1832', online at: <http://www.barnabites.com/missions-in-burma>, accessed 7 July 2015.

[26] D. M. Griffini, *Della vita di Monsignor Gio. Maria Percoto*, 3 vols (Udine, 1781). Bigandet provided the second editor of Sangermano's history with a copy of the *vita*, and he appended a summary to the edition: Sangermano, *History*, 102, 282–7.

[27] An unnamed Barnabite composed 'Dialogues between a Primitive Native and a former Theravadin Monk from Siam', but it is unclear whether this text survives. It may have been

Burmese Empire (written in Italian), together with his own description of Buddhist cosmology. Both were utilized by Dr Francis Buchanan, an East India Company surgeon, in an article published in 1799.[28] From Sangermano's explanation of the time that had elapsed since the death of the Buddha, it would appear that the *History* as a whole was completed in or after 1809, following his return to Italy.[29] Although Sangermano prepared the work for publication, this was not finally achieved until 1833 – fourteen years after his death in 1819 – and then in an English translation. The editor of what proved to be the first of three editions was the future Cardinal Wiseman.

In addition to the 'Compendium', Sangermano relied on 'abstracts of all that is worthy of notice in the three Kiam [*Piṭaka*, 'baskets'], called Vini, Padimot, and Sottan', that is to say, the *Vinaya Piṭaka* and the *Sutta Piṭaka,* which form two parts of the *Tipiṭaka*, and the *Pāṭimokka Sutta*, which lists the rules governing the behaviour of individual monks and nuns.[30] He had translated nearly the whole of these books with the help of a former monk called Ubà 'who was one of the most learned of that order in the vicinity of Narbeck, where for several years our seminary was situated'.[31] Additionally, Sangermano translated the 'Chamoazà' (*kammavācā*), a Pali 'book of ordination' for the admission of candidates to the Sangha. He considered that its ceremonies resembled those of the ordination of deacons and priests within the Catholic Church and so the book 'may, therefore, be considered as their Pontifical'.[32] He may also have read the *Jātaka* stories which relate episodes in Gotama Buddha's former lifetimes.

the 'book of religious controversy between a Christian and a Budhist [*sic*]' referred to by Bigandet, which had been composed by a Catholic priest at Ava in the eighteenth century: Bigandet, *Life*, 188 n. 97; Barnabite Fathers USA, 'Missions in Burma 1722–1832'.

[28] Elizabeth J. Harris, *Theravāda Buddhism and the British Encounter: Religious, Missionary and Colonial Experience in Nineteenth-Century Sri Lanka* (London and New York, 2006), 17–19. Sangermano described the author as 'a Zaradò or master of the Emperor': *History*, xxxviii.

[29] Sangermano, *History*, 102, 109.

[30] Ibid. xxxix. The *Vinaya Piṭaka* and *Sutta Piṭaka* contain, respectively, the rules governing the Sangha, and the teachings of the Buddha embedded in narratives about his life and former lives or in poetry. Sangermano erroneously names the *Pāṭimokka* as the second 'basket' of the *Tipiṭaka*; this is in fact the *Abidhamma Piṭaka*, an analysis of metaphysics and causality. In the English editions, the Italian phonetic spellings of Burmese and other names were retained: *History*, xxxix.

[31] Ubà taught Pali to two of Sangermano's scholars: ibid. xxxix.

[32] Ibid. 124.

In addition to these textual sources, Sangermano relied on his own observations and debates with monks.[33]

Before he was appointed vicar apostolic in 1856, Bigandet served from 1841 in the Malacca mission. He spoke Malay 'very well' (*fort bien*), and his first published work on Buddhism shows that he could at least read Burmese from early in his missionary career.[34] This 1843 article on Buddhism was based, in part, on a translation of a Burmese life of the Buddha, the fifteenth-century *Malālaṅkāvaratthu* (*The Collection* [of Stories that is] *like an Ornament of Garlands*), popular in nineteenth-century Burma.[35] This translation was subsequently published in Rangoon in 1858 with extensive annotations and appendices. An enlarged second edition appeared through the American Mission Press at Rangoon in 1866. The enlargement was accounted for by Bigandet's incorporation of portions of another Burmese biography, the *Tathāgata-udāna* (*The Praise of the Lord*). A third edition appeared in 1880 and a fourth in 1914; an edition was published as late as 1979.[36] Curiously, the second edition appeared as a French translation in 1878; the translation was not by Bigandet but by a French naval officer.[37] In addition to the life, Bigandet had read parts of the *Tipiṭaka*, the *Pāṭimokka Sutta* and 'most' of the *Jātaka*, some of which he describes as 'really beautiful, interesting, and well composed pieces of literature'.[38] Like Sangermano, he also relied on personal observations and discussions with both monks and laity.[39]

The engagement with Buddhist texts by the missionaries leads on to the second area of interest: the manner in which the motives underlying the process were shaped by factors beyond the mission and how these influenced the activities of both missionaries as translators and interpreters of Buddhism. This will be examined through their treatment of two key terms. The first is Buddha, where the interest lies in how this was translated (if at all), and whether any distinction was made between the state of the *bodhisatta* – an individual embarked on the path to enlightenment – and *buddha* – one who has entered

[33] Ibid. 110, 113–16.

[34] 'Paul Bigandet (1813–1894)'.

[35] 'Principaux points du système boudhiste', *Annales de philosophie chrétienne*, 3rd ser. 8 (1843), 85–94, 260–79; Hallisey, 'Roads Taken', 40.

[36] Hallisey, 'Roads Taken', 40, 57 n. 49.

[37] Paul Bigandet, *Vie ou légende de Gaudama le boudha des Birmans et notice sur les phongyies ou moines birmans*, transl. Victor Gauvain (Paris, 1878).

[38] Bigandet, *Life*, 4 n. 3, 289, 290–1.

[39] Ibid. 3 n. 1, 194 n. 100, 201 n. 101; Bigandet, 'Principaux points', 94, 262, 263, 277–9.

into *nibbāna*. The translation and interpretation of *nibbāna* itself, with its connotations within Buddhism of both bliss and extinction, will be the second term considered. The interest lies not in testing the accuracy of the translations per se, but rather in examining what is revealed concerning the influence of a particular mindset or agenda upon the process of translation and interpretation and its influence on the categorization of Buddhism as a religion. As observed above, in Bigandet's case, both translation and categorization seem to have been influenced by a desire to establish the superiority of Christianity over against positive views of Buddhism that were emerging within contemporary Europe.[40]

In his consideration of Buddhism's ultimate goal, *nibbāna*, Sangermano's conclusion was negative. His understanding of 'the Niban' was of 'a perfectly incorporeal and spiritual state of being, [which] deserves the name of annihilation rather than of existence'.[41] The Pali term for enlightenment has connotations of both bliss and extinction and Sangermano's conclusion that Buddhism was a nihilistic faith was an early instance of a Christian missionary emphasizing extinction over bliss when discussing *nibbāna*.[42] Nevertheless, Sangermano, through his translation of whichever Burmese or Pali word for the Buddha he encountered in the *sayadaw*'s 'Compendium' as 'G/god' (as it appears in the English translation), located Buddhism as, in some sense, a theistic system.[43] If he was translating from a Burmese text, it is likely that the term employed there was *Phra*, which was used by Burmese Christians in the nineteenth century to refer to the Christian God.[44] However, it is clear that what is being described is not a supreme being. Rather, through his use of 'G/god' Sangermano is reflecting in his translation the apotheosis of the Buddha found within Theravāda: for Sangermano, Gotama was a 'mere man' who obtained 'the privilege of divinity' at the age of thirty-five.[45]

In his 1843 article, although willing to acknowledge the moral worth of Buddhism, Bigandet likewise firmly associates the 'abyss' of *nibbāna* with annihilation of self.[46] This remains the case with the

40 Jon R. Stone, ed., *The Essential Max Müller: On Language, Mythology, and Religion* (Basingstoke, 2002), 81–2.
41 Sangermano, *History*, 32.
42 Harris, *British Encounter*, 55–6.
43 It has not been possible to consult Sangermano's original Italian manuscript.
44 Bigandet, Life, 2 n. 1.
45 Crosby, *Theravada Buddhism*, 33; Sangermano, *History*, 23, 102, 110.
46 Bigandet, 'Principaux points', 86, 90, 272–3.

1858 translation, despite his willingness to employ other terms, such as 'perfection' and 'quiescence'.[47] However, unlike Sangermano, he does not ascribe any aspect of the divine to Gotama as Buddha; in 1843 he uses the word *Phra* – by which he means a *buddha* – to describe Gotama, clearly stating that he was a mere mortal and not a creator god. Consequently, Buddhism can only be an imperfect religion as it is, in Bigandet's own metaphor, like a statue without head or legs.[48] In fact, Bigandet at this stage seemed reluctant to describe Buddhism as a religion at all. In the article as a whole, it was described as such just once and then only indirectly.[49] Otherwise it is referred to as a 'system' or a 'philosophy'. In his extensive annotation to the 1858 translation of the Burmese biography, Bigandet's treatment of Buddhism became more nuanced. He now frequently referred to it as a religion or a creed; however, Buddhism still remained imperfect. Moreover, Bigandet developed a theory (first mooted in his 1843 article) of a natural belief held by all humanity in a supreme being, that has been unnaturally suppressed and obscured by Buddhist atheism.[50] His use of terms also captured the nature of the Buddha's path to enlightenment in a way that was lacking in both his article and Sangermano's account. He was careful now to distinguish between Gotama as *bodhisatta*, for which he used either *Phra* or *Phralaong*, and Gotama as Buddha. Hence concerning the enlightenment he wrote: 'During all the while, Phra or Budha [*sic*] (let us call him now by that name) remained under that tree.'[51] While both more nuanced and accurate than Sangermano's description of the Buddha's enlightenment and changing nature, Bigandet's use of these terms, as well as *Gaudama*, the family name of the Buddha, served to reinforce his conviction that the founder of Buddhism, despite his high moral integrity and acquisition of supernatural powers, was still 'a mere man'.[52]

In conclusion, when considering the relationship between Christianity and translation, the Burmese mission is of interest in two respects. Firstly, it demonstrates the linguistic diversity that missionaries might face and the methods they employed to meet its challenges.

[47] Bigandet, *Life*, 5 n. 4, 21 n. 28, 101 n. 70 (twice), 146 n. 84, 196 n. 100.
[48] Bigandet, 'Principaux points', 86, 89–90.
[49] Ibid. 85.
[50] Ibid. 265; Bigandet, *Life*, 53 n. 49, 182.
[51] Ibid. 2 n.1, 9 n. 12, 63 n. 55, 101, 227. But in his article, he used *Phra* as equivalent to Buddha and *Phralaong* to represent the *bodhisatta* state: Bigandet, 'Principaux points', 89.
[52] Bigandet, *Life*, 2 n. 1, 286–7.

In Burma, this diversity was both complex and dynamic. Portuguese was a mark of self-definition for the earliest Christian communities and therefore a necessary pastoral tool for at least the Barnabites. As the nineteenth century progressed English and Tamil were added as pastoral languages, while English became additionally a language of interdenominational debate, education and mediation. Finally, if evangelization was to be undertaken throughout Burma, knowledge of the Karen dialects was a necessity. The challenges were met in several ways. Dictionaries, grammars, and translations were created; missionaries applied themselves to language study, receiving instruction from catechists or monks; and the physical means to publish texts in Burmese, Italian and English were obtained or borrowed.

Secondly, the mission in Burma brought the possibility of examining Buddhism through its own texts. With this came an opportunity for translation to play a role within Christian apologetic. In their engagement with Buddhist texts, the Catholic missionaries were reliant on the skills of the traditional experts, the monks of the Sangha, either indirectly through monks' vernacular translations and glosses, or directly through instruction in Pali and assistance when translating the *Tipiṭaka*. Clearly missionary translators did not act alone, whether they were translating Christian texts into one of the vernaculars, or Buddhist texts from Burmese or Pali. They were subject also to linguistic and conceptual influences from existing literary conventions. D'Amato's use of poetry may have been a conscious imitation of practice within the *Sutta Piṭaka*, while it has been noted that Bigandet's incorporation of sections from a second Burmese biography in his 1866 edition mirrors established practice among Burmese commentators.[53]

This need to translate Buddhist texts created an extra dimension within an already complex wordscape, and one in which non-linguistic influences played their part. The process of translation was neither linear nor neutral. Sangermano's use of 'G/god' to describe Gotama Buddha may well be a reflection of the apotheosis of the Buddha apparent within Theravāda. Consequently, his understanding of Buddhism as expressed through his use of language may be seen to have been more sensitive when considering the nature of buddhahood than Bigandet's. Similarly, although Bigandet is more nuanced and accurate than Sangermano in his distinction between Gotama as

[53] Hallisey, 'Roads Taken', 40.

bodhisatta and Gotama as Buddha, his view of the divine precludes him from ascribing any aspect of divinity to the Buddha. Bigandet's use of Burmese and Pali terms when discussing the progress of Gotama towards and into *nibbāna* may reflect an adherence to his own aims (to allow the sources to speak for themselves) and developing academic conventions. However, their use is underpinned by an interpretation based not on a scholarly desire to comprehend and explain but on Bigandet's role as a Christian apologist wishing to attack and refute.[54] His employment and interpretation of particular terms is designed to express his belief in the humanity of Gotama; any evidence to the contrary could be dismissed as an indication of a departure through superstition and ignorance from the 'true' Buddhism contained within the *Tipiṭaka*.[55] Despite the moral worth and supernatural abilities Gotama had acquired through his reincarnations as a *bodhisatta*, and indeed perhaps *because* of the means of their acquisition, he would never be more than human. Buddhism for Bigandet would always remain an imperfect religion stifling a natural human instinct to believe in a supreme deity.

Similarly, both Sangermano and Bigandet identified *nibbāna* with annihilation. Even though Bigandet used other terms for *nibbāna* in his translation of the Burmese life (possibly here the scholar was vying with the missionary), he still maintained that it leads only to annihilation. Both Sangermano and Bigandet matched Buddhism against a particular model of what constituted a religion and found it to be wanting. For Bigandet in particular the use of 'annihilation' – in common with Protestant missionaries in Ceylon – to translate *nibbāna* and the glossing of Buddhist terms in a way that clearly identified the Buddha as human marked Buddhism out as an incomplete religion that was closer to a system or philosophy.[56] However, although Bigandet was seeking ultimately to refute

[54] Bigandet, *Life*, vii, 285. Max Müller names Bigandet when discussing the habit among missionaries of emphasizing the 'elevated, pure and humanizing character' of Buddhism, only then to bring it low: Stone, *Essential*, 81–2.

[55] Bigandet, *Life*, 2 n. 1, 176 n. 93, 285–6, 312. Sangermano similarly relied on the classical texts rather than 'the tales and reports of the common people': *History*, xxxix.

[56] Harris, *British Encounter*, 28, 51, 104–5. Protestant writers often had their own particular model in mind, in which comparisons of Buddhism to Protestant and Catholic Christianity were 'from the perspective of a protestant representation of Catholicism as a degenerate form of Christianity': Hallisey, 'Roads Taken', 46. The American Baptist James Knowles described Buddhism as a religion in which '[t]he sacred books are sealed from the eyes of all but the learned and the priesthood, by the secrecy of a learned language;

Buddhism, his efforts were not in this case intended for a Burmese audience. Through his English and French publications, Bigandet sought to answer those Europeans who saw in Buddhism either the originator religion of Christianity or, because of its perceived rationalism and morality despite its apparent atheism, a superior alternative to theistic religion.[57]

The published works of these two Catholic missionaries demonstrate the linguistic challenges faced by missionaries within Burma. These were complex and dynamic and they were overcome through the acquisition of languages, the borrowing of the expertise of others, and the creation of practical tools, such as grammars, dictionaries and presses. These were all necessary not only to translate the Christian message, but to engage with the established religious tradition. Additionally, the manner in which both Bigandet and Sangermano engaged with Theravāda Buddhism shows the complexity and breadth of the context in which translations occurred. The works of both undertook complex linguistic journeys: from Burmese or Pali to Italian and then English in the case of Sangermano, and in Bigandet's from Burmese or Pali to (probably) French, English and then back into French. Secondly, the process of translation was not neutral, but subject to a form of 'mother-tongue interference'. In particular, Bigandet's translations show both the influence of Christian theology and soteriology, as well as his desire to advance the cause of Christianity within a wider debate. Bigandet did not acquire knowledge through translations simply to dispute more effectively with Burmese monks and laity. He sought too, by publishing in French and English, to prove to Europeans that Buddhism was both an unnatural and imperfect religion. Implicit in Bigandet's interpretation of Burmese Buddhism is a defence of Christianity in Europe. By translating and interpreting texts from other religions, missionaries hoped to further Christianity's expansion, but some might also find in their translations a means to reinforce Christianity against challenges from elsewhere.

---

and little is known of the established religion, except in popular fables, and external rites': Knowles, *Memoir*, 316. The description could equally be of Catholicism.

57 Bigandet, 'Principaux points', 86; Bigandet, *Life*, 245–6; John J. Clarke, *Oriental Enlightenment: The Encounter between Asian and Western Thought* (London and New York, 1997), 81; Sangermano, *History*, 280–1.

John Ross and Cultural Encounter: Translating Christianity in an East Asian Context

James H. Grayson*
University of Sheffield

John Ross, a late nineteenth-century missionary of the United Presbyterian Church of Scotland to Manchuria, was the effective founder of the Protestant Church in Korea through his translation of the New Testament into Korean. This article explores his work of translation by looking firstly at general issues in translating biblical texts into Korean, secondly at Ross's principles for translation, and thirdly how Ross actually conducted his translation work on a day-to-day basis. Thorough consideration will be given to the linguistic and social characteristics of the Korean language. The article concludes with an overview of the linguistic, religious and sociocultural effect of the 'Ross Translation'.

INTRODUCTION

The topic of this volume of Studies in Church History is 'Translating Christianity', a very broad but important theme. This article does not present new facts on the life and work of the Scottish missionary to China, John Ross (1842–1915), but rather reflects on his work and its importance in the development of the Christian Church in Korea.[1] Ross was unquestionably one of the key figures in late nineteenth-century missions in China, and he was effectively the father of the

* School of East Asian Studies, University of Sheffield, Sheffield S10 2TD. E-mail: j.h.grayson@sheffield.ac.uk.

[1] This article is based upon research which I conducted using Ross's regular monthly missionary reports for the *United Presbyterian Missionary Record* [hereafter: *UPMR*] (and its successors), the scant records on Ross contained in the United Presbyterian Church Archives held at the National Library of Scotland, other historical records, and interviews with older residents of Balintore and with surviving members of Ross's family. I was unable to find a diary, but the reports in *UPMR* are in many ways a better source of information about Ross and his colleagues. I have published this information in several places, notably in 羅約翰, 한국의 첫 선교사 [*Na Yohan: Han'gug-ŭi ch'ŏt sŏn'gyo-sa, John Ross: Korea's First Missionary*] (Taegu, 1982); and 'The Legacy of John Ross: A Neglected Chapter in the History of Pan-East Asian Missions', *International Bulletin of Missionary Research* 23 (1999), 167–72. *Na Yohan* was published to celebrate the centenary of the translation of the New Testament into Korean.

Studies in Church History 53 (2017) 338–358
doi: 10.1017/stc.2016.20

Protestant Church in both Manchuria and Korea. To understand his role in planting Protestant Christianity in Northeast Asia, the concept of 'translation' is a useful idea by which we can grasp how he accomplished his goals as a missionary.

The Oxford English Dictionary defines 'translation' as '[t]he action or process of turning from one language into another; also the product of this'. It goes on to state that figuratively the word could mean 'the expression of something in another medium or form'.[2] It is this figurative use which is the topic of this article: 'how can Christianity be presented in an understandable way to nations which do not have a "Christian" background?' One could say that missionary work by its very nature is a process of 'translating' the ideas, beliefs and practices of, say, Christianity into another medium or form, whether in antiquity or in more modern history. Linguistic translation, for example the translation of the Bible, is never a matter of word-for-word correspondence, but of attempting to find the best means to represent the meaning of the original text using words and concepts from the receptor culture's language, which, however, may also have resonances beyond the immediate verbal correspondence. The same could be said of the ritual practices of a religion, and the plastic and musical arts which are used to express aspects of its belief. There is no one-to-one correspondence. This article will explore as a case study how one late nineteenth- and early twentieth-century missionary attempted to translate Protestant Christianity in the context of north-east Asian culture and civilization.

To understand Ross's later work, we must understand his cultural and religious background.[3] He was born on 9 August 1842 in the village of Balintore, Easter Ross (eastern Ross-shire), near Inverness. His father is said to have been a tailor, and his mother the local schoolmistress. At that time, Easter Ross was a Gaelic-speaking area, and Ross's first language was Gaelic. He only acquired English later at school. Three important things about Ross and his approach to mission should therefore be noted. First, because the area in which he grew up was not a native English-speaking area, from a very early age John Ross was aware of the importance of knowing more than one language. Second, although the Balintore area was Gaelic-speaking, it was not remote from the world, and was comparatively

[2] *The Shorter Oxford English Dictionary on Historical Principles* (Oxford, 1977), *s.v.* 'translation'.
[3] For a more detailed discussion see Grayson, 'Legacy of John Ross'.

cosmopolitan. The village overlooked the Moray Firth and from there ships sailing to and from Inverness and eastern Europe and other parts of the world would have been a daily sight. Third, his family was 'cosmopolitan' in the sense that their work would have brought them into contact with the wider world. It is not unreasonable to suppose that as a child Ross may have dreamed of travelling and working in distant regions of the globe.

There is a fourth factor which will have moulded John Ross's view of the world: the Church to which the family belonged. The Rosses were not members of the Church of Scotland, but belonged to a group of dissenters from the established Church, the United Presbyterian Church of Scotland. The United Presbyterians, the country's third largest Protestant denomination, were a more liberal form of Scottish Presbyterianism, and were noted especially for involvement in world mission. Scottish missions in China were for many years the preserve of this denomination. Family membership in this branch of Scottish Presbyterianism meant that Ross would have been influenced by a more culturally liberal atmosphere, but also by a strong sense of the importance of world mission.[4]

Having completed his MA at the University of Glasgow, Ross trained for the ministry at the United Presbyterian Theological Hall in Edinburgh. Following completion of his studies, he was assigned to work in Gaelic-speaking churches because he was a native speaker of the language. Notwithstanding his commitment to Gaelic-language ministry, Ross had a strong sense of calling to be an overseas missionary. His chosen field was India, but the Church sent him to China instead.

Early Missionary Career

Although the subject of this article is Ross in relation to the earliest translation of the New Testament into Korean, he was first and foremost a missionary to the Chinese. Korea and the translation of Scripture into Korean was always a secondary work. At the time that Ross was sent to China, the missionary work of the United Presbyterian Church there was concentrated in the Shandong peninsula. After a three-month sea journey, on 23 August 1872 Ross and his wife arrived at Chefoo (芝罘, in pinyin Zhīfú), the principal port for the

[4] For a brief history of the United Presbyterian Church, see Hans J. Hillerbrand, ed., *The Encyclopedia of Protestantism* (New York and London, 2004), 1: 444.

area and the base of the United Presbyterian missions. However, no sooner had they had arrived than the head of the United Presbyterian mission, Alexander Williamson (1829–90), advised them to go to Yingkou (營口, in pinyin Yíngkǒu), the port at the mouth of the Liao River and the gateway to the vast area of Manchuria. He urged them to do so as quickly as possible as winter was approaching and the Bohai (渤海) Sea soon would freeze over. Consequently, the Rosses found themselves in Yingkou within a month of arriving in Shandong. Why had Williamson made such an urgent plea?

The answer to that question lies in Williamson's sense of mission and his vision for north-east Asia.[5] Williamson was not only the head of the United Presbyterian missions in China, but had also been the representative in China for the National Bible Society of Scotland since 1863. He was interested in finding new areas for missionary development, and was looking for new opportunities for the translation and distribution of Scripture. Manchuria was a wide open field for mission work. Williamson had travelled to the area on more than one occasion, and in 1867 had also visited the 'Corean Gate' (高麗門, Kaoli-men), or customs barrier between Qing (清; 1644–1912) China and Chosŏn (朝鮮; 1392–1910) Korea. He saw that there was a great opportunity for pioneer missionary work in Manchuria, and also that there was the opportunity to consider missionary work in Korea through the translation of Scripture. He urged the Rosses to go to Manchuria so that they could make an early start on pioneer work in this vast territory which had no effective Protestant missionary presence.[6]

Tragedy struck Ross immediately after the couple reached Yingkou. Mrs Ross, who had been pregnant during their journey to China, died shortly after their arrival in Yingkou while giving birth to their son Drummond.[7] Distressed, Ross appears to have buried

[5] The principal source of information about Williamson's travels and his ideas about the location and method of missionary work may be found in his book *Journeys in North China, Manchuria, and Eastern Mongolia; with some Account of Corea*, 2 vols (London, 1870).

[6] The first Protestant missionary in Manchuria was the English Presbyterian Church missionary William Chalmers Burns (1815–68). After his death in Yingkou, the Presbyterian Church of Ireland sent two missionaries to Manchuria before the arrival of the Rosses. However, the start of significant missionary work in Manchuria was undoubtedly Ross's missionary endeavours.

[7] Ross's son was cared for by a Chinese woman until Ross's sister Catherine (d. 1892) arrived in 1874 to look after him. Drummond was bilingual in English and Mandarin from his earliest years.

himself in the energetic pursuit of his work. He became convinced that the centre of missions in Manchuria had to be in the Manchurian capital, not in a Western treaty port such as Yingkou.[8] Consequently, in 1874 Ross moved to Mukden (瀋 陽, Shenyang) and made the capital the terminus of a series of projected 'mission stations' beginning at Yingkou. Using Mukden as his base, Ross began to travel widely throughout Manchuria and, not forgetting the suggestions made to him by Williamson, he too visited the 'Corean Gate' in October 1874. His visit there, at the time when the customs barrier was formally opened for an international market, was for the purpose of obtaining the services of someone who could be a Korean language tutor for him. Unsuccessful in his first visit, he returned to the 'Corean Gate' for a much longer stay during April and May 1876. This time he was successful in recruiting a tutor.[9]

His visits to the Sino-Korean customs barrier indicate that from the very earliest period of his missionary work in Manchuria, Ross had a strong interest in the translation of the Christian Scriptures into Korean. At that time, entrance into Chosŏn Korea was closed to all but Chinese diplomatic missions and other specially exempted groups. Ross conceived of beginning the evangelization of the Korean peninsula through the translation and distribution of Scripture, an idea undoubtedly reflecting Williamson's approach, but also reflecting his own bilingual childhood.

From the very beginning of his missionary work, language acquisition, translation and writing formed an important element of that work. In 1876, when he had been in China for four years, Ross published his first book, the *Mandarin Primer*. Although there is no concrete evidence to verify this, the structure and order of material in this book seem to indicate that it was based upon Ross's own programme of study of the Chinese language. The following year, he published another work, the *Corean Primer*. Although not identical to the earlier book, the *Corean Primer* follows many of the ideas of the *Mandarin Primer*, and must reflect Ross's own study of the

[8] Manchuria, although part of the Manchu Qing Empire, was the ancient homeland of the Manchus and consequently was treated as a separate administrative entity from China. There were an imperial palace, government ministries, and Confucian academies, all mirroring what was to be found in the Chinese capital at Beijing.

[9] Ross wrote two descriptions of his two visits to the Corean Gate: 'Visit to the Corean Gate', *Chinese Recorder and Missionary Journal* 5 (1875), 471–2; 'To the Corean Gate', *UPMR* 8 (1877), 355–7.

Korean language. It was published a little over a year after his second visit to the 'Corean Gate' and his acquisition of a Korean language tutor.

1876 was a critical year in the development of John Ross's missionary work. Mukden, the Manchurian capital, had become his residence and the centre of his work. He had made a successful second visit to the 'Corean Gate' and had acquired a Korean language tutor, and had made enough headway with understanding this language to be able to use his studies as the basis of a language textbook for use by missionaries when they would be able to enter the so-called 'Hermit Kingdom'. Most notably, by the end of the year, Ross had been able to gather around him and his future brother-in-law John McIntyre (1837–1905) a group of Korean herbal merchants who would form a panel for the translation of the New Testament into the Korean language. From the first he established principles of this translation work which will be discussed below.

When Ross went on his first furlough in 1879, he took with him the first draft of the Korean translation of parts of the New Testament and the manuscripts of two books: *History of Corea, Ancient and Modern with Description of Manners and Customs, Language and Geography* and *The Manchus, or the Reigning Dynasty of China*. The first book was published that same year, and the second the year after. Together, they formed a comprehensive history of north-east Asia. The *History of Corea* was the first presentation in any European language of the history of Korea, while the second was one of only a handful of works on the Manchus. The two books represented Ross's view of the indissoluble connection between the histories of the two regions. He was, perhaps, the first European to understand this.

The translation work which Ross and McIntyre undertook also saw fruition with the publication in Korean of the *Gospel according to St Luke* in 1882. This was followed by the complete translation and publication of the New Testament in 1887. By the end of his first fifteen years in East Asia, then, Ross had laid the solid foundation for the development of Chinese Protestantism in Manchuria; he had made significant contributions to supporting language acquisition by creating language-teaching resources for both Mandarin and Korean; he had overseen the earliest translation of the New Testament into Korean; and he had made pioneering contributions to the study of the history of both China and Korea. Any one of these could have been a life's work.

Ross's missionary work in all its aspects was aided by his formidable knowledge of, and appreciation of, languages. A close reading of his writings indicate that he had a working knowledge of eleven different languages: Gaelic, English, German, French, classical Latin, New Testament Greek, biblical Hebrew, classical written Chinese, contemporary spoken Mandarin Chinese, Manchu and Korean. Of these, he certainly spoke four: Gaelic, English, Mandarin and Manchu.[10]

Features of the Korean Language

Before we can look at the process of how Ross translated Scripture into Korean, we have to understand three things: the linguistic structure of the language, the ways in which it has been recorded by indigenous scripts, and the sociocultural background which influenced the way in which the language was and is used.[11]

The Korean language is a member of the broad Uralo-Altaic language family, which also includes Japanese, Manchu, Mongolian and a number of the languages of Siberia. These languages are characterized by three features: atonality, a polysyllabic word structure and agglutination. Korean possesses all three of these features, which makes it dissimilar to Chinese, but similar to Japanese.

Tonality is a key feature of Chinese, but is entirely absent in Korean which is characterized by a flat sound level throughout a sentence until the end, when rising inflection indicates a question and a falling inflection a declaration. Classical Chinese is believed to have been monosyllabic, and contemporary Chinese is not characterized by an extensive polysyllabic word structure or morphology. Korean, however, possesses a highly polysyllabic morphology.

Perhaps the most characteristic feature of the Korean language is its extensive use of agglutination, the grammatical feature in which the function of each word in a sentence is marked out by either a prefix or a suffix. Korean makes extensive use of suffix

[10] In the late 1970s, when I visited Ross's home village to learn what was still remembered about him, I was told that some time after his retirement in 1910, he and his son were conversing with some of the Gaelic-speaking villagers in Balintore. They were all looking politely blank while John Ross addressed them. His son nudged him and said: 'Dad, you're speaking Chinese!'

[11] A more thorough discussion of the Korean language may be found in my article 'Korean', in Keith Brown, ed., *The Encyclopaedia of Language and Linguistics*, 2nd edn (Oxford, 2005), 6: 236–9.

agglutination. English differentiates between an adjective and an adverb by the addition of '-ly' to indicate an adverb (thus: 'quick' and 'quickly'). However, English has very few examples of agglutination, whereas in Korean every word will have an agglutination marker indicating subject, direct object, direction of movement, intent and other aspects.

A key feature of a Korean sentence is the verb. As with other Uralo-Altaic languages, Korean has the sentence structure of subject, object, verb. The verb itself has a number of agglutinative markers attached to it, and could be a whole sentence when translated into English. The structural order of a Korean verb is verb stem + tense marker + marker for level of respect to the person spoken to + sentence type marker. Speech level (marking in speech the degree of respect towards the person addressed) represents a key feature of Korean culture as it is a mark of respect and etiquette. It is also possible in the agglutinated verb to make the sentence even more honorific (and thus to raise the speech level) by inserting an honorific marker between the verb stem and the tense marker. Additionally, there is a class of verbs which are honorific but have the same 'meaning' as a 'standard' verb. The marker placed at the end of the agglutinated verb indicates whether the verb or sentence is making a declarative statement, asking a direct question, asking a reflective question, making a command, making a suggestion or quoting someone else's sentence (also indicating whether the quoted sentence is a declarative sentence, interrogative sentence, command or suggestion). Korean does not require punctuation in the middle or at the end of sentences, because the 'punctuation' is built in with the function markers.

The subject or the object in a sentence can be removed, and the verb itself would make sense. However, no sentence could make any sense without a verb. An example of how a single verb could be a sentence in English is exemplified by the agglutinated verb *hwaganasyŏtchyo*? (화가나셨죠, 'You were angry, weren't you?') We have the verb *hwagana* + honorific marker *s* + past tense marker *yŏt* + reflexive question marker *chyo*. This description immediately indicates that a translation into English does not fully reflect the meaning of the Korean sentence as there is no way in English to indicate speech level. Removing the honorific marker in Korean subtly changes the meaning of the sentence, whereas in English there is no way to indicate speech level except through a comment or footnote explaining the type of speech level.

Speech level is important in ordinary Korean speech as it creates mood, the mood of relationship between the person speaking and the person spoken to, and in some cases the person spoken about. Two anecdotes will indicate the importance of speech levels. In the early 1970s while I was in Korean language school during the first two years of my work as an educational missionary in Korea, I made the acquaintance of a woman from Scandinavia who had learned Korean, but was horrified by the whole idea of speech levels because it offended her principles of egalitarianism. So, she decided to use the most simple form of speech, *panmal* (반 말, informal or relaxed speech, literally 'half talk'), which is used when addressing a small child. She complained to me how uncooperative her Korean co-workers were. They seemed to do everything grudgingly. Every time she spoke, she was insulting everyone but a five-year-old. If she had instead chosen the most general form of honorific speech, no one would have been offended, even if she had used it with a five-year-old child; rather they would undoubtedly have complimented her on her use of the Korean language. Mood is important.

Even Koreans get the subtleties of the language wrong, as can be appreciated from this second anecdote. One day, a Korean friend, his younger brother and I were talking together. At one point, the younger brother said: '*Hyŏng-nim* (형 님, honourable elder brother)'. His elder brother responded. The younger brother said: 'No, not you, *hyŏng* (형), I meant *hyŏng-nim*', indicating me. *Nim* (님) is an honorific marker added to nouns describing persons. Because in Korean close friends are referred as elder brothers (as I was in this case), and because the young man's relationship to me was mediated through his relationship as the younger brother of my friend, he had to indicate that there was a difference between the two of us. This is a point that at the time even my Korean friend had missed. In social relations, Korean has a high degree of complexity. There are no level relationships between people. Every relationship is hierarchical in some sense, and this must be indicated in the spoken language.

This distinction in social status must be indicated in written material translated into Korean as well as in spoken language. A simple example would be the Korean translation of the children's story *Winnie the Pooh*. In Korean, the difference between Pooh as a toy bear and Christopher Robin as his owner must be indicated. Hence, in the Korean translation Christopher Robin when speaking with Pooh uses informal speech, mentioned above, while Pooh when speaking with Christopher Robin uses a polite level of speech, as if he were talking to an adult. The broad 'meaning' of their conversations is the same, but the mood would be very different if they both spoke in the same speech level. This distinction is absolutely necessary in Korean, but it is virtually impossible to indicate it in English without making a very awkward sentence, or using a footnote.

There is one other important feature of the Korean language: its onomatopoeia. The phonology of the Korean language is very extensive, including a range of 'standard' consonants, aspirated consonants and 'tense' consonants; 'standard' vowels, vowels beginning with a 'y', monophthongs and diphthongs. Phonologically, Korean is an extraordinarily rich language. This gives it a wealth of opportunities for use in poetry and for indicating or imitating natural sounds. This feature also means that it is difficult to render Korean in any form of script other than a fully phonetic script. Discussion of this feature brings us naturally to the challenge of recording or transcribing the Korean language.

Transcribing the Korean Language

In East Asia, the classic written language was written Chinese, which used complicated monosyllabic ideographs to represent words or combinations of words. The early Korean states received the written language of China as a part of world civilization in the same way that the peoples of northern Europe received Graeco-Roman civilization. However, the Greeks and Romans used phonetic scripts. The Chinese did not. Writing for the early Korean states meant writing in a foreign language using a script appropriate for that foreign language, but which was unable to transcribe the early Korean language and its key grammatical features.[12]

Very early on, probably not later than the seventh or eighth centuries CE, the Koreans devised three different types of script to transform Chinese sentences so that they could be read as Korean sentences by putting into the Chinese sentence necessary features of the

[12] For a more thorough discussion of the various attempts to write the Korean language and its predecessors, see my article 'Korean Writing Systems', in Brown, ed., *Encyclopaedia of Language and Linguistics*, 6: 239-44. A more recent discussion of the creation of the Korean alphabet is Jaehoon Yeon, *Queries on the Origin and the Inventor of the Hunmin chŏngŭm*, SOAS-AKS Working Papers in Korean Studies 1 (London, 2008).

early Korean language in order to make the sentence comprehensible. The three scripts were called *idu* (吏讀), *kugyŏl* (口訣) and *hyangch'al* (鄕札).[13] It is not necessary here to discuss the differences between them or explain why these different scripts were created. Two points can be made. First, although the characters in these three scripts were all phonetic, the scripts were not alphabets but syllabaries. That is, each symbol represented not a single sound but a syllable. Second, each symbol was derived from a portion of a Chinese character which was felt to represent the sound of a particular Korean syllable. Modern Japanese *kana* (仮名) scripts work on this same principle, and indeed they look remarkably like one of the early Korean syllabaries.[14]

By the beginning of the fifteenth century, it was becoming obvious to many Koreans that the system of writing and transcribing was becoming increasingly awkward. The educated elite wrote in a foreign language and additionally used local derivative scripts which were not suitable for writing Korean as a whole. The issue came to a head under King Sejong (世宗; r.1418–50), who created a royal research institute known as the Chiphyŏn-jŏn (集賢殿) or Hall of Assembled Worthies. It is said that the king wanted to create a genuinely phonetic script for three reasons. First of all, he wanted a phonetic script, a genuine alphabet, to transcribe actual Korean language. There was an administrative reason for this. When a magistrate sat in court, the discussions and decisions were recorded in a foreign written language, classical written Chinese. The king wanted to know what was actually said in court, and not to read a translation of what had happened. The second reason for wanting a phonetic alphabet was to record the onomatopoetic sounds of the Korean language. Using a phonetic script meant that it would be possible to write poetry in the Korean language rather than using the script and conventions of China. The third reason for the creation of a Korean alphabet was to have a phonetic means to write the sounds of foreign languages, that is, to write foreign words phonetically so that the foreign words could be read 'properly'.

[13] Popularly, modern Koreans refer to all three scripts as *idu*, but this is not correct and blurs the distinctions between them.

[14] The most accessible and thorough description of these three early Korean writing systems is Adrian Buzo, 'Early Korean Writing Systems', *Transactions of the Royal Asiatic Society, Korea Branch* 55 (1980), 35–62. In this article, he also discusses the potential relationship between these early Korean scripts and the Japanese *kana* scripts.

Promulgated by royal edict in 1443, the phonetic Korean alphabet was based upon the sophisticated linguistic study of the phonetic structure of the Korean language by the Chiphyŏn-jŏn scholars.[15] Consisting originally of twenty-eight letters, this alphabet was first called *Hunmin chŏngŭm* (訓民正音, Teaching the People Correct Speech) which reflected the king's view that the use of the script would raise the standards of literacy and education amongst the general populace. It was immediately rejected by the literati elite. A minister of state addressed the throne and expressed his fear that as local scripts were only used by 'barbarians', use of a Korean script would separate the Koreans from East Asian civilization; it would be an embarrassment to the Koreans in front of the Chinese; and it would lead to a national moral decline because people would no longer read the Confucian classical literature.[16] Although the indigenous phonetic script was used for the next four centuries, it was considered to be the preserve of the uneducated and women. It was not until the end of the nineteenth century that the widespread popular use of the alphabet began. It would become known as *Han'gŭl* (한글), and would also become a primary symbol of Korean nationalism.

Cultural Issues in Translation

Consideration of these strictly linguistic aspects of the Korean language, taken together with the attempts over a number of centuries to create a system of writing which would adequately and simply transcribe the sounds of the language, has given some insight into the sociocultural features of the Korean language. From at least the fourth century, early Korean states absorbed world civilization, which emanated from political entities which we now identify as 'China'. Broadly speaking this flow of East Asian civilization into Korea

[15] Geoffrey Sampson, *Writing Systems: A Linguistic Introduction* (London, 1985), ch. 7, 'A Featureal System: Korean Han'gŭl', discusses the linguistic methods of research used by the Chiphyŏn-jŏn scholars and how they applied this to the creation of an alphabet which visually represented the linguistic principles which they used. A more recent collection of essays on the creation and structure of the alphabet is Young-key Kim-Renaud, *The Korean Alphabet: Its History and Structure* (Honolulu, HI, 1997).

[16] The minister of state was Ch'oe Malli (崔萬里; d. 1445), who objected strenuously to the promulgation of the indigenous script. For documents relevant to the creation of the alphabet and his criticisms of it, see Peter H. Lee, ed., *Sourcebook in Korean Civilization*, 2 vols (New York, 1993), 1: 516–20.

consisted of a script (Chinese characters), a religion (Buddhism) and a sociopolitical philosophy (Confucianism). The last proved to be the most influential of the three. Confucianism was a philosophy which addressed the questions of what makes for good government and for a good society. The whole panoply of Confucian influence led to the creation of a meritocratic, bureaucratic scholarly elite (the Confucian literati) to govern the state, a system of education to train people in Confucian philosophy so that the state could be governed appropriately, and a civil service examination system to select the governing elite on a meritocratic basis.

This system of sociopolitical philosophy dominated the political, intellectual, and social scenes in Korea for fifteen hundred years. Until the end of the fourteenth century, the influence of Confucianism was largely in the political and cultural spheres. It did not completely dominate the social sphere. Religions such as Buddhism were seen to have a place in society. The relationship between Buddhism and Confucianism changed radically with the rise of Neo-Confucianism, which when applied in Korea at the beginning of the Chosŏn dynasty at the end of the fourteenth century led to five centuries of government attempts to create a model Confucian society during which the social aspects of Confucianism were enforced by the state.[17]

Confucius's analysis of society showed that there were five role relationships in which all people participated. These were the relationship between the ruler and the governed, parent and child, spouse and spouse, sibling and sibling, and friend and friend. None of these relationships was level; they were all hierarchical. Each relationship also implied that those in a 'superior' relationship had certain duties of care and concern for those in the 'inferior' status. Each of these relationships was characterized by a set of moral values which were to be acted upon. The relationship between the ruler and governed was characterized by benevolence on the ruler's part and loyalty on the part of the governed. The relationship between parent and child was characterized by benevolence on the part of the parent and 'filial piety' on the part of the child. The hierarchical nature of social relationships in Korea was not the creation of Confucianism, but existed previously. However, Confucianism, particularly in its Neo-Confucian form, reinforced these ideas, and centuries of state policy

[17] For a survey of this period, see my *Korea: A Religious History*, rev. edn (London and New York, 2002), 205–23.

intended to create a model Confucian society reinforced these values still more. These concepts are naturally expressed in the way people speak, and how their ideas are represented in writing.[18]

In translation into Korean, therefore, two matters have to be kept in mind at all times. The focus of the Confucian analysis of society is on the propriety of social relationships. Consequently, propriety needs to be represented in the speech levels used in address and in general speech, and also in the terms of reference, the words used to describe a person including the use of honorific markers in the agglutination of nouns. The use of the suffix *nim*, discussed above, is an example of the alteration of a word to indicate propriety of social relationship.

Ross's Principles for Translation

When Ross was starting to gather together a group of men who would form a panel of translators and translate the New Testament into Korean for the first time, he established four basic principles which were to guide their work. The men whom he selected to help him were not members of the *yangban* (兩班) or aristocratic scholarly elite. Rather, his assistants were merchants of herbal medicines who bought and sold in China. They were some of the few people who could cross the border at designated times, and who participated in the international market at the 'Corean Gate' customs barrier. They were not scholarly, but they could read Chinese, and undoubtedly spoke it for commercial purposes. They would have been familiar with Confucian thought and could read the basic texts. The same translators did not participate in the group from beginning to end, nor were there the same number of translators at all times. Nonetheless, the same type of person was involved in the process of translation throughout, and the four principles established by Ross guided the work of the translation panel from start to finish. Ross and his brother-in-law McIntyre acted as supervisory editors, looking at each draft of the manuscript and making editorial decisions.[19]

[18] Ibid.

[19] In 1883, Ross wrote an extensive article about the translation of the New Testament into Korean, how it was done, the issues involved, and how they distributed the copies of the New Testament: 'Corean New Testament', *UPMR* 14 (1883), 491–7. For more detail, see his contemporary reports: *UPMR* 11 (1880), 150, 278–9; 12 (1881), 85–6, 271; 13 (1882), 33–4, 244.

What were the principles which guided Ross's work of translation? First, he had determined that the translation must be in an idiom and script which could be read by all Koreans. His concern for a non-scholarly, accurate but accessible translation derived from his own views about the various Chinese versions of the Bible, which had been a topic of major debate amongst missionaries in China for decades.[20] Ross wanted a Bible which could be read with understanding by anyone, but which would also be a literary work. The Korean alphabet was a great discovery for him because in effect it meant that anyone could read the Scriptures: because that script was alphabetic and phonetic there was no barrier to reading and understanding as there was with the ideographic, non-phonetic Chinese script.

The second principle which Ross established is what Eugene Nida and others have referred to as 'dynamic equivalence'. That is, he chose to use words which might not be the exact equivalent of the word to be translated, but which carried the same cultural sense as the original. A typical example would be early translations into Inuit (Eskimo) where 'seal' is substituted for 'lamb' as in 'Lamb of God'. At the time of the original translation, the readers of an Inuit Bible would have never seen, much less known about, an animal called a 'lamb'.[21] This principle of dynamic equivalence meant for Ross that he should seek to use an indigenous Korean word wherever possible, rather than transliterating a European term or using an established Chinese-language term. Ross's best known choice of a Korean word is the term which he chose for 'God'.

The battle over what word to use for 'God' in Chinese was at the heart of the 'Term Question', first as it was fought over amongst the Roman Catholic missionaries in China,[22] and then later amongst nineteenth-century Protestant missionaries. There are essentially three options: to use an existing term, to transliterate a Latin or Greek

[20] For a detailed discussion of the history of translation of the Bible into Chinese, and the issues around terms and terminology, see Kenneth Scott Latourette, *A History of Christian Missions in China* (London, 1929), 429–33. A more recent survey may be found in Samuel Hugh Moffett, *A History of Christianity in Asia*, 2 vols (Maryknoll, NY, 2005), 2: 286–9, and especially 301–2 (footnotes 23–30).

[21] Eugene Nida's theory of 'dynamic equivalence' is discussed in Eugene A. Nida and Charles R. Taber, *The Theory and Practice of Translation* (Leiden, 1969), 137, 140, 202.

[22] See, in this volume, Joan-Pau Rubiés, 'Ethnography and Cultural Translation in the Early Modern Missions', 272–310, at 301–2, 304.

word using Chinese characters, or to create an entirely new term.[23] In Korea, as in China, the Roman Catholic Church settled on the last of these options, which then became the standard term used formally by Roman Catholics in Korea.[24]

However, although the issue of the 'Term Question' had been settled for Korean Catholics, it was not yet settled for Korean Protestants. The same issues were raised again in the early years of Protestant missions in Korea as had arisen in China centuries before. However, the Korean Protestants' choice was different. The term chosen for 'God' was an indigenous Korean term, and not a neologism. It was the term which Ross had used from the beginning in his work of translation, *Hananim* (하나님), which literally means 'Heaven', or the 'Ruler of Heaven'. It is formed from a dialectical form of *hanŭl* (하늘), *hanal* (하날), meaning 'Heaven' or 'heavens' and the honorific suffix *nim*. Ross eschewed the use of the Chinese term *Sangje* (上帝, in Chinese *Shangdi*), which had finally been chosen by the Protestant missionaries in China, a native term rather than a neologism or transliteration. Ross's sense that an indigenous term was preferable meant that although he favoured the use of *Shangdi* in Chinese translation, in translating Korean he favoured a Korean term, despite the fact that the Chinese-character term would have been familiar to any Korean who could read the Chinese script. What mattered most, in Ross's view, was the principle that a Korean term should have preference over a non-Korean term.[25]

The third principle was to make use of the Bible in Chinese as a basis for the Korean translation when searching for and selecting technical terms such as nouns, place names or theological concepts. The translation panel used the Delegates' Version of the Bible in Chinese as the basis of their work,[26] but Ross and McIntyre also made

[23] For a more recent summary of the 'Term Question' and the related question of the acceptability of participating in Confucian ancestral rites, see Moffett, *Christianity in Asia*, 2: 220–32.

[24] The classic English discussion of this issue in Roman Catholic mission history is Latourette, *Christian Missions in China*, 131–55. A more recent, but less detailed account is found in Jacques Gernet, *China and the Christian Impact: A Conflict of Cultures* (Cambridge, 1985; first publ. in French 1982), 24–30.

[25] The best modern discussion of the 'Term Question' in Korea is Sung-deuk Oak, *The Making of Korean Christianity: Protestant Encounters with Korean Religions, 1876–1915* (Waco, TX, 2013), ch. 1, 'God, The Search for the Korean Name for God, *Hananim*'.

[26] The Delegates' Version was the standard translation of the Bible in Chinese during the latter half of the nineteenth century. The New Testament was completed in 1850. For a discussion of this translation, see Latourette, *Christian Missions in China*, 260–3, 265.

reference to the Greek New Testament and the Revised Version of the Bible in English. Because the translation panel consisted primarily of Koreans who were literate in written Chinese, the principle was that the Korean translators would work from the Chinese translation to produce a text which would be verified and emended by the Scottish editors. Understanding the Chinese terms, it would be possible for the Korean translators to suggest whether a Chinese-character term should remain or be replaced by an indigenous word.

The fourth principle was that the text must reflect social distinctions in speech. We have discussed above how important these distinctions are in Korean, at a very subtle level, in giving the correct mood and tone to the sentence. Ross's sensitivity to this issue of mood, tone and shade of meaning probably derives from the fact that he was bilingual from early childhood and that he would have been very aware of just how different Gaelic and English are.

The Process of Translation

Both Ross and McIntyre left fairly detailed descriptions of how the translation panel actually worked. There is no day-to-day description of the work, but their records offer a good account of how it proceeded. The first book of the New Testament to be translated into Korean was the Gospel of Luke. The work generated a fourfold series of drafts, the process being repeated until a satisfactory final version was felt to have been achieved. In the case of Luke, the first stage was the translation from the Delegates' Version into Korean using only *Han'gŭl* script. This initial translation then became the basis of the remaining stages of the translation process. The second draft of the manuscript took the first draft and amended it by reading through the entire text and checking it with the Greek text and with the Revised Version of the Bible in English. The third draft was based upon the second draft, and resulted from checking and rechecking the Korean with the Greek- and English-language New Testaments until a fully amended text had been achieved. In the fourth draft stage, the Scottish editors took the third draft and went through the entire text of Luke, reading it along with the Greek concordance in order to ensure consistency of terms except in the case of differences in word usage.

In translating Luke, the translators repeated this whole process four times in order to attain a text which adhered to the principles established by Ross, and which also was as faithful as possible to the original text and its meaning. The editors made use of an existing translation which would be comprehensible to the Korean translators; they undertook extensive cross-referencing with the original Greek text and with the standard English translation of their day; and they used the principal tools for translation, such as a Greek-language concordance. The process which was established by Ross and McIntyre for the translation of Luke was adhered to for all subsequent translations of each book of the New Testament. It was as thorough and accurate as possible given the fact that it was impossible at this time for Europeans to be resident in Korea.

The Ross Translation or Ross Version, as it came to be known, was the first complete translation of the Christian New Testament into the Korean language. It set a standard by which all other translations would be judged. However, it had one peculiarity to which some early Protestant missionaries objected. Because it had been translated using a phonetic script by Koreans from the north-western area of the peninsula, the translators put the translation into their dialect of Korean. Ross was well aware of this feature of the translation, but felt that it did not make the translation incomprehensible to Koreans from other regions of the country. The acceptance of a regional dialect as the basis of this translation adhered, perhaps in a curious way, to Ross's principle of using idiomatic speech, although it is also important to remember that he did not have access to translators from the capital. However, use of the dialect of the capital could have been viewed as contravening Ross's idea that a translation should not be a 'scholarly' translation.

Effect of the Ross Translation

Unquestionably, the Ross Translation was a literary, cultural and religious monument in the history of modern Korea. The translation of the New Testament had four noticeable effects. It enabled the rapid spread of Christian ideas and beliefs. Because Korea at the end of the nineteenth century was a 'closed' country, it was virtually impossible for foreign missionaries to work there. Ross conceived the idea that the Christian faith and belief could be spread through the distribution of translations of the Bible or parts of it. Here the use of the herbal merchants was important. They moved back and forth between Manchuria and the Korean peninsula, taking with them their various medicinal materials and products, now including the New Testament. Ross asked these merchants, many of whom had been part of the translation panel, to take copies of Luke's Gospel and later also other biblical books with them, and to distribute these books for free with the medicines which they dispensed. The Ross Version thus became the foundation of a self-evangelized, self-propagating Church which spread through Korea largely before the advent of foreign missionaries.[27] By the time that the first missionaries, American Methodists and Presbyterians, arrived in 1884 there were gathered groups of Christians in communities from north of the Yalu River (which was Korean territory at that time), along the north western coast of Korea as far down as the capital.[28]

The second major effect of the Ross Translation was that many of the terms which Ross and his team of translators chose to represent Christian concepts became the norm in the Korean language. Most notable among these was the choice of the term *Hananim* (하나님) for 'God'. There are some variations. The *Kongdong pŏnyŏk* (Common Translation) undertaken by a team of Korean Catholic and Protestant scholars in the early 1970s used *Hanŭnim* (하느님), from the abbreviated form *Hanŭ* (하느) for 'Heaven' and *nim*, but this has not gained widespread acceptance.[29] Moreover, although the Korean translation of the Qur'ān transcribes the Arabic term *Allah* in the Han'gŭl script, I have known Korean Muslims to refer to God as *Hananim*, even in the main mosque in Seoul.

Moreover, whenever there has been a difference of opinion about the correct – or most appropriate – term to use in the Korean Bible, even when a change has been made, in the end general usage has reverted to the term selected by Ross and his team. The most notable example of this is the choice of term for the final book of the New Testament, the Revelation of St John. The term chosen by Ross was *Muksi-rok* (默示錄), meaning a record of a dream or vision. Subsequent translations have used the term *Kyesi-rok* (啓示錄), meaning a

[27] See, in this volume, Kirsteen Kim, 'The Evangelization of Korea, *c.*1895–1910: Translation of the Gospel or Reinvention of the Church?', 359–75.

[28] For a brief history of the Korean Church, including a discussion of Bible translation, see my article 'Korea', in Hillerbrand, ed., *Encyclopedia of Protestantism*, 2: 1035–41, especially 1036.

[29] The New Testament of the Common Translation was first published in 1971, and the whole Bible in 1977: 공동번역 신약성서 [*Kongdong pŏnyŏk sinyak sŏngsŏ*, *Common Translation, New Testament*] (Seoul, 1971).

record of a prophetic statement, which could of course include a vision of what will happen. This latter term was in use in Korea in the early 1970s. However, the most recent translation of the Bible into Korean has reverted to using the term used in the Ross Translation as most clearly reflecting the content and intent of the book. Decisions such as this show that Ross's work has stood the test of time.

The third effect of the Ross Translation was the impetus which it created for the widespread use of the indigenous alphabet. Before the translation of the Bible into Korean, the *Han'gŭl* alphabet had a relatively low status. It was thought by the traditional elite, steeped in Confucian learning and the use of the Chinese script, to be suitable for use only by women and those unlearned in the Confucian classics. The ability of anyone to read the Bible in Korean meant that through the use of the alphabet anyone could read anything, and do it easily. The script rapidly became not only a means to educate people and to enable them to communicate more easily, but also a symbol of Korean nationalism. At the end of the nineteenth century, as the *Kaehwa-dang* (開化黨) or reform party strove to throw off the shackles of the past, including Confucianism, and build a modern nation, the alphabet came to be seen as a symbol of what Korea had achieved and could achieve.[30] In the final decade of the nineteenth century, the reform party's newspaper *The Independent* was a bilingual paper in English and in Korean; the latter was written entirely in the *Han'gŭl* alphabet. The two languages and scripts were seen to be emblems of modernity and progress. This connection with nationalism was not lost during the years of Japanese colonial occupation (1910–45). When the Republic of Korea was established in 1948, one of the national holidays which was created was *Han'gŭl-lal* (한글날, Korean Alphabet Day), celebrated on 9 October.[31]

A fourth effect of the Ross translation is that it preserved for the first time a provincial dialect, the dialect of P'yŏngan-do (平安道) province in the north-western part of the Korean peninsula. It was unusual, if not unique, to have whole texts written in Korean. It was certainly not common to see regional variations of Korean recorded and treated with the same dignity which would have been given to the dialect of the capital. For linguistic scholars this is especially

[30] Kim, 'Evangelization of Korea'.

[31] A thorough discussion of the role of Protestantism in the reform movement and the movement against Japanese colonial occupation is Kenneth Wells, *New God, New Nation: Protestants and Self-Reconstruction Nationalism in Korea, 1896–1937* (Honolulu, HI, 1990).

important because it helps them to see the language of this region as it was encapsulated in the native script at the end of the nineteenth century.

The work of John Ross, his brother-in-law John McIntyre, and all the named and unnamed Koreans who worked on this translation was in many respects monumental. They were all translators in every sense: scriptural, religious and cultural translators, spreading new religious ideas and beliefs, who had a cultural and social impact far beyond the religion whose spread was enabled by the translation of Christian Scripture into the national language. The Ross Translation did indeed help to spread Christianity around the Korean peninsula, but it also spread literacy, promoted a sense of nationalism in difficult times, and left an important linguistic record of a regional dialect for use as a resource for scholars. This is quite an achievement. And yet for Ross, this work of translation into Korean, however important, was secondary to his work in China.

Appendix: Books Authored by John Ross

Mandarin Primer: Being Easy Lessons for Beginners, Transliterated according to the European Mode of using Roman Letters (Shanghai, 1876).
Corean Primer: Being Lessons in Corean on all Ordinary Subjects, Transliterated on the Principles of the Mandarin Primer (Shanghai, 1877).
History of Corea, Ancient and Modern with Description of Manners and Customs, Language and Geography (Paisley, 1879).
The Manchus, or the Reigning Dynasty of China (Paisley, 1880).
Korean Speech with Grammar and Vocabulary (Shanghai, 1882).
Yesu syŏnggyo chyŏnsyŏ [*Complete Sacred Writings of Jesus* = New Testament in Korean] (Mukden, 1887).
Old Wang, the First Chinese Evangelist in Manchuria (London, 1889).
Mission Methods in Manchuria (Edinburgh and London, 1903).
The Marvellous Story of the Revival in Manchuria (Edinburgh, 1908).
The Original Religion of China (Edinburgh, 1909).
The Origin of the Chinese People (Edinburgh, 1916).

The Evangelization of Korea, *c.*1895–1910: Translation of the Gospel or Reinvention of the Church?

Kirsteen Kim*
Leeds Trinity University

Several studies of the history of Protestant Christianity in South Korea have argued that the religion's rapid growth was chiefly because of the successful translation of the gospel into Korean language and thought. While agreeing that the foundation laid in this respect by early Western missionaries and Korean Christians was a necessary prerequisite for evangelization, this article challenges the use of a translation theory, such as has been developed by Lamin Sanneh, to describe the way that Christianity took root in Korea, both on the basis of conceptual discussions in the field of mission studies and also on historical grounds. It draws on research for A History of Korean Christianity *(2014) to examine the years of initial rapid growth in Protestant churches in Korea – 1895 to 1910. Its findings suggest that rather than 'translation of the gospel' a more historically accurate description of what took place is 'reinvention of the Church'.*

It was not until the late 1870s that the first Korean Protestants were baptized, yet by the early twentieth century Protestant Christianity in Korea was noted among mission fields for its rapid growth, the believers' religious fervour, and the social transformation it was producing.[1] By 1910 Protestant numbers stood at only about 1 per cent of the population, but this proportion was significantly larger than in China or Japan in the same period and about the same as in India, which had a much longer Christian history.[2] John R. Mott, Secretary of the World's Student Christian Federation and later chairman of the World Missionary Conference at Edinburgh in 1910, visited Korea in 1907.[3] He was impressed with Koreans' commitment to

* Leeds Trinity University, Brownberrie Lane, Leeds, LS18 5HD. E-mail: k.kim@leedstrinity.ac.uk.

[1] 'Protestant' in this period of Korean history refers to Presbyterian and Methodist denominations.

[2] Kenneth Scott Latourette, *A History of the Expansion of Christianity*, 7 vols (New York, 1937–45), 6: 428–30.

[3] For the conference, see Brian Stanley, *The World Missionary Conference, Edinburgh 1910*, Studies in the History of Christian Mission (Grand Rapids, MI, 2009).

Studies in Church History 53 (2017) 359–375
doi: 10.1017/stc.2016.21

Bible study, prayer, giving and evangelism, and he reckoned that the midweek prayer meeting in P'yŏngyang (Pyongyang)[4] was 'possibly the largest meeting for united intercession which assembles anywhere in the world'.[5] At the Edinburgh conference, it was reported that '[a]lmost the whole population of Korea is now ready to listen to the Gospel'.[6] Korea was said to represent 'the most striking example of a whole nation being moved by the Holy Spirit'.[7] And it was thought that Korea – 'perhaps the most attractive and responsive field in heathenism today' – might actually achieve the 'complete evangelisation' 'within this present generation' that was the aspiration of the conference.[8]

Several studies of the history of Protestant Christianity in Korea have argued that the religion's rapid growth was chiefly because of the successful translation of the gospel into Korean language and thought in the early encounter in the 1870s and 1880s.[9] Whilst agreeing that the foundation laid in this respect by early Western missionaries and Korean Christians was a necessary prerequisite for evangelization, this article challenges the use of a translation theory, such as that developed by Lamin Sanneh,[10] to describe the way that Christianity took root in Korea, both on the basis of conceptual discussions in the field of mission studies and on historical grounds. It draws on research for *A History of Korean Christianity* (2014)[11] to examine the years of most rapid growth, roughly 1895 to 1910.[12] Its findings suggest

[4] Note on transliteration: This article uses the McCune-Reischauer system of Romanization for Korean words. Korean names will appear in East Asian order (family name first). Alternative orders and spellings will be given in brackets.

[5] John R. Mott, *The Decisive Hour of Christian Missions* (Edinburgh, 1910), 88.

[6] World Missionary Conference, *Report of Commission I* (Edinburgh, 1910), 6.

[7] Ibid. 36.

[8] Ibid. 80.

[9] Notably David Chung, *Syncretism: The Religious Context of Christian Beginnings in Korea* (Albany, NY, 2001); Sung-Deuk Oak, *The Making of Korean Christianity: Protestant Encounters with Korean Religions, 1876–1915* (Waco, TX, 2013).

[10] Lamin Sanneh, *Translating the Message: The Missionary Impact on Culture* (Maryknoll, NY, 1989).

[11] Sebastian C. H. Kim and Kirsteen Kim, *A History of Korean Christianity* (Cambridge, 2014), which offers greater detail and further indications of primary sources and secondary literature than can be given here.

[12] Although Protestant translation activities had been going on since the 1870s, it was not until about 1895 that Protestant Church growth began to accelerate rapidly; after 1910 the rate of growth slowed. For figures, see Dae Young Ryu, 'The Origin and Characteristics of Evangelical Protestantism in Korea at the Turn of the Twentieth Century', *ChH* 77 (2008), 371–98, at 397; Chung-Shin Park, *Protestantism and Politics in Korea* (Seattle, WA,

that rather than 'translation of the gospel', a more historically accurate description of what took place in these decades is 'reinvention of the Church'.[13]

The Translation Model in Mission Studies

In the study of global Christian expansion and church growth, scholars of mission history have made use of the concept of translation as a model for the process of transmission of the faith. The most prominent contemporary purveyor of this approach is Lamin Sanneh. In *Translating the Message* (1989), he argued that 'translatability' has been an inherent feature of early Christianity from Pentecost onwards.[14] In his work, translatability is a matter not only of the use of different languages to express the gospel as characteristic of Christian mission but also of the translation of the Christian faith from one cultural context into another. The paradigmatic example of translation is the transmission of Christianity from a Jewish to a Hellenistic milieu.[15] Sanneh extends this pattern through Church history.[16] His main primary research is on Protestant mission in the Niger Delta, in which Bible translation featured not only as an important foundation for missionary work but also as signalling the affirmation of local cultures as vehicles of Christian truth. Sanneh finds that the West African case confirms Christianity's translatability and therefore its inherent plurality.[17] In Sanneh's view, Christianity became an indigenous faith in West Africa by its translation into local languages and cultures through processes that characterize evangelization throughout Christian history. Its potential for re-expression in local idioms is the most important factor in its impact on culture.

Although Sanneh applied it historically, the extension of textual translation as a model for the process of evangelization had already been used by mission anthropologists in the inculturation debate of the 1970s. Louis Luzbetak drew on Eugene Nida's 'functional'

2003), 16. Cf. the outlines of Lak-geoon George Paik, *The History of Protestant Missions in Korea 1832–1910*, 2nd edn (Seoul, 1970); Allen D. Clark, *A History of the Church in Korea* (Seoul, 1971).

[13] Use of the word 'reinvention' is inspired by John Parratt, *Reinventing Christianity* (Grand Rapids, MI, 1995).

[14] Sanneh, *Translating*, 214–16.

[15] Ibid. 9–49.

[16] Ibid. 50–129.

[17] Ibid. 130–56.

or 'dynamic' equivalence model of Bible translation to analyse the relationship of church and cultures.[18] Luzbetak's early work was later developed for Protestant Evangelicals by Charles Kraft.[19] However, in discussion about the construction of 'local' or 'contextual' theologies, Stephen Bevans identified several weaknesses in the translation model. First, it presupposes that there is an essential gospel for which a dynamic equivalence must be found, and such an understanding of the gospel tends to be propositional. Second, it takes a positivist approach to culture, assuming that there are parallels between one culture and another. As a consequence, a translation approach may not treat the receptor culture on its own terms but rather subordinate it to the presumed gospel message.[20] In other words, the translation model emphasizes the message and role of the missionary who mediates it rather than the receptors' appropriation of what they see and hear.

Sanneh's historical model of translation is open to the same criticisms. He also draws on Nida's linguistic work to develop his translation model for mission, which, he believes, leads despite errors of translation and vernacularization to indigenous expression of faith. Sanneh points out that translation is most successful when it is done by the local people, emphasizes (with Nida) the importance of reception and goes on to suggest that once the message is translated, it may challenge and subvert the mission.[21] However, despite Sanneh's emphasis on the receiving end of the translation process, his interest is in the translation of a predetermined gospel and the subtitle of the book ('The Missionary Impact on Culture') makes clear that it is focused on the missionary process.

There are additional problems with Sanneh's approach. There are philosophical issues with the empiricist view that essential meaning can be separated from the words of a particular language and transferred from one language to another, and this problem is compounded when the more complex concept of culture is used. Furthermore, the translation model relies on a semiotic understanding of cultures as discrete wholes or sign systems, like languages, which condition the perceptions and behaviours of those within them. Such an approach has been challenged by postcolonial

[18] Louis J. Luzbetak, *The Church and Cultures* (Maryknoll, NY, 1988; first publ. 1963).
[19] Charles H. Kraft, *Christianity in Culture* (Maryknoll, NY, 1979).
[20] Stephen B. Bevans, *Models of Contextual Theology*, 2nd edn (Maryknoll, NY, 2002), 40–4.
[21] Sanneh, *Translating*, 192–209.

criticism that understands cultures as shaped by those within them and draws attention to cultural hybridity.[22] The assumption that the Christian gospel is in some sense new and foreign to a culture in which there is no contemporary Christian presence is also questionable, not only on the theological grounds of the *imago Dei*, the cosmic Christ or the creative presence of the Holy Spirit, but also in view of historical findings about the spread of Christianity before the modern period.[23]

There are two further concerns about Sanneh's particular use of translation as a historical model for evangelization. First, it is far from obvious from a historical perspective that translatability is an inherent feature of Christianity. Where Sanneh sees a sharp divide between the Judaic world of Jesus and the Hellenistic world of the Gentiles that necessitated translation, contemporary scholarship emphasizes the extent to which many Jews were Hellenized and the continuity between the cultures.[24] Moreover, although Catholic missionaries used vernacular languages and practised forms of what would now be called inculturation,[25] the Roman Catholic Church resisted the translation of the Bible and the liturgy in the name of orthodoxy and unity for the better part of fifteen hundred years.[26] Furthermore, Sanneh's approach is heavily influenced by two factors that are more theological than historical: by a particular reading of the New Testament that sees diversity where others have seen unity, and by the *sola scriptura* of the Reformation, which he regards as liberating the gospel from cultural accretions. Furthermore, his historical conclusions are drawn from particular West African experience of Protestant missions, whereas he concedes that Protestant mission as a whole, including in Africa, did not always use translation as its primary method and was susceptible to colonial attitudes that resisted it.[27] The second

[22] E.g. Stuart Hall, *Representation* (London, 1997).

[23] Such as the recovery of the early history of Christianity in Asia: Samuel Hugh Moffett, *A History of Christianity in Asia*, 1: *Beginnings to 1500* (Maryknoll, NY, 1988).

[24] N. T. Wright, *The New Testament and the People of God* (London, 1992), 341–5. I am indebted to Morwenna Ludlow for alerting me to this point.

[25] See, for example, William R. Burrows, 'A Seventh Paradigm? Catholics and Radical Inculturation', in Willem Saayman and Klippies Kritzinger, eds, *Mission in Bold Humility* (Maryknoll, NY, 1996), 121–38.

[26] Aylward Shorter, *Evangelization and Culture* (London, 1994), 30. Sanneh is aware of this difficulty (*Translating*, 50–87), and argues for a vernacularizing effect of Catholic missions even before the Second Vatican Council encouraged translation of the liturgy and reading of the Bible by lay people: ibid. 88–129.

[27] Sanneh, *Translating*, 88–129.

concern about Sanneh's model is the subtext that the 'translatability' of Christianity (even in its Catholic and colonial forms) results in accommodation of plurality, whereas Islam, the competing world religion in Africa, is said not to accommodate plurality, or at least not in religious matters. The Qur'ān is not translated and use of Arabic is required in worship, law and devotion.[28] Sanneh articulates a sharp division between the two faiths in this matter, which he sees as impinging closely on the theme of his book.[29] He has subsequently done further research on Islam in secular societies in Africa,[30] but it is difficult to escape the conclusion that the stress on the 'translatability' of Christianity may be driven by an agenda beyond the historical evidence.

Given the theoretical drawbacks of translation as a model and the questions about the historical foundation of Sanneh's focus on translatability, we will examine the Korean case as another particular historical example of change resulting from the introduction of Christianity that has been described as 'translation', in order to consider whether this is the best way of representing the processes involved.

Beyond Translation as a Model for Korean Evangelization

As seen above, Korea presents a notable example of the rapid and socially significant acceptance of Christianity by a particular ethnic group in modern times. Protestant mission to Korea began with Bible translation into Korean in the 1870s while the peninsula itself was closed to mission work.[31] John Ross, missionary of the (Scottish) United Presbyterian Church in Manchuria, noting that the Korean travellers and exiles he met loved books, concluded that the most effective way to reach Korea was to translate the gospels and smuggle them into the country.[32] The effectiveness of the translation work he initiated with Koreans in Shenyang (Mukden), which was

[28] Ibid. 211–38.

[29] Ibid. 212.

[30] E.g. Lamin Sanneh, *The Crown and the Turban* (Boulder, CO, 1997).

[31] Catholicism had been practised in Korea for almost a century by this date but had been largely suppressed by persecution.

[32] John Ross, *Mission Methods in Manchuria* (Edinburgh and London, 1903). On Ross, see, in this volume, James H. Grayson, 'John Ross and Cultural Encounter: Translating Christianity in an East Asian Context', 338–58.

continued later by missionaries and Korean Christians inside Korea, was enhanced by the decision to use the medium of *han'gŭl*.[33] The use of this simple script enabled the dissemination of the Christian message beyond elite males, allowing the previously illiterate and uneducated, including women, to know their culture, history and script and contributing to the growing sense of nationhood.[34] The translation work went beyond purely linguistic considerations and involved theological decisions about formulating a Christian vocabulary and identifying other affinities between the Protestant gospel and Korean religions.[35] The decision to which most attention was given was the choice of the term *Hananim* for God: this is a pure Korean word, not one of Chinese derivation. Ross claimed that this was an almost universal Korean name for God and used it in his New Testament.[36] The origins of the term are disputed by historians of Korean religions, but *Hananim* was certainly associated with the indigenous *Tonghak* teaching of Ch'oe Che-u (Choe Je-u; also known as Su-un).[37] The adoption of this indigenous term for God encouraged the inculturation of Protestantism and distinguished it from Catholicism.[38] In the P'yŏngyang Revival of 1907, which Mott observed, there was a religious outpouring similar to the holiness revivals in the Western nations in which people confessed their sins, reconciled themselves with one another, and sought to enter more deeply into their faith by reading the Bible and attending church. This event not only proved to the satisfaction of Western missionaries that Koreans had indeed become Christians,[39] but, through this 'Korean Pentecost', 'the religious experience of the people gave to the Christian [Protestant] Church in Korea a character which is its own'.[40]

[33] This was a script designed by King Sejong's scholars several hundred years before, specifically for the Korean language, but which was despised by the literati, who preferred to use Chinese characters.

[34] Martha Huntley, *Caring, Growing, Changing: A History of the Protestant Mission in Korea* (Cincinnati, OH, 1984), 28.

[35] E.g. that ancient Koreans were monotheistic: Oak, *Making*, 63–83.

[36] John Ross, *History of Corea, Ancient and Modern* (London, 1891 edn), 355.

[37] Don Baker, 'Hananim, Hanŭnim, Hanullim, and Hanŏllim', *Review of Korean Studies* 5 (2002), 105–31; Paul Bierne, *Su-un and His World of Symbols* (Farnham, 2009).

[38] Korean Catholics referred to God as 'Chŏnju', the Korean pronunciation of the Chinese term preferred by Matteo Ricci.

[39] Huntley, *Caring*, 132–8.

[40] Paik, *History*, 374.

Early studies of the growth of Korean Protestantism gave most attention to the character and activities of the missionaries.[41] While this historiographical tendency continued after the liberation of Korea in 1945,[42] the development of Korean language history since then has focused attention more on Korean reception of Christianity.[43] In a study originally completed in 1959, David Chung saw the way Korean society had long accommodated and assimilated religions of foreign origin through equation or identification with indigenous beliefs as the key to explaining the Korean case.[44] Chung's focus on 'syncretization' to explain the processes by which Christianity became established in Korea goes beyond the missionary initiative and attends to the indigenization of the faith by Koreans, although his analysis is mainly focused on the linguistic-cultural aspects of what happened, in keeping with the translation model. In the most recent (2013) example in English of this approach, Sung Deuk Oak gives an in-depth exposition of Korean-led inculturation of Protestantism and its indigenous identity as the chief way of understanding Christian growth in Korea.[45]

A few examples will indicate that once the missionaries had initiated translation and church formation, Koreans played the more significant role in spreading and defining Protestantism. First, the translation of the Bible was coupled, not only by Ross but also by later missionaries in Korea, with the use of the 'three-self' approach to mission, also known in Korea as the Nevius method.[46] Following this, Koreans studied and taught the Bible themselves and created 'self-supporting', 'self-governing' and self-propagating' churches.[47] Ross himself did not enter Korea until a short visit in 1887, but most of the first Christians, although they were baptized by the American

[41] The earliest history of Protestantism in Korea is Paik, *History*, which is a history of missions written in English and citing only English-language and missionary sources; cf. Charles Allen Clark, *The Korean Church and the Nevius Methods* (New York, 1930).

[42] Notably Clark, *History*.

[43] The leading church historians writing in Korean are Min Kyŏng-bae (Kyoung-bae Min) and Yi Man-yŏl (Mahn-yŏl Yi): see, for example, Min Kyŏng-bae, *Han'guk kidokkyo hoesa* [*A History of the Korean Church*] (Seoul, 1982); *Han'guk minjok kyohoe hyŏngsŏngsa-ron* [*The Establishment of an Indigenous Korean Church*] (Seoul, 2008); Yi Man-yŏl, *Han'guk kidok'kyo suyongsa yŏn'gu* [*Study on the Korean Reception of Christianity*] Seoul, 1998); *Han'guk kidok'kyo-wa minjok t'ongil undong* [*Korean Christianity and the National Unification Movement*] (Seoul, 2001).

[44] Chung, *Syncretism*.

[45] Oak, *Making*. Oak also included translation from Christian literature in China.

[46] John L. Nevius, *The Planting and Development of Missionary Churches* (Shanghai, 1899).

[47] Charles Allen Clark, *The Nevius Plan for Mission Work in Korea* (Seoul, 1937).

Protestant missionaries working inside Korea from 1885, were Ross's disciples and their converts. Second, Korea did not become a Western colony and was not of great strategic interest to Western missions. The initial entry of missionaries to this closed country was made possible because of invitations by progressive Koreans, one of whom – Yun Ch'i-ho (Yun Chi-Ho) – even helped to finance the mission.[48] Compared to other mission fields, missionary numbers were low and few missionaries became fluent in the Korean language. The spread of Christianity owed most to the Korean missionary 'helpers' and the labours of Korean colporteurs and bible women.[49] Third, due to lack of funds, missionaries in Korea founded relatively few institutions; it was local believers who multiplied churches, schools and hospitals around the country.[50] These examples all suggest that Koreans themselves established the Korean Church.

In view of the extent to which Koreans wanted the gospel and the effort they put into spreading it, in the final analysis the growth of the Korean Church cannot be explained without looking at it from the receptors' point of view.[51] But in order to do this we must move beyond Sanneh's translation model, which we noted above focused on the perspective of the foreign missionaries and the way in which they propagated a given Christian message in the vernacular. Taking this step may also help us to explain why many aspects of Western Christianity received in Korea were not translated into indigenous forms. When Mott held up Korea at the Edinburgh 1910 conference as an example of the transforming power of Christianity, he pointed not only to its spiritual effects but also to its social ones: in particular its contribution to modernization.[52] Korea was said to be 'vibrating with the spirit of the modern world'.[53] The rapid Christianization of Korea in terms of both church growth and modern development was described as 'one of the marvels of modern history'.[54] The delegates did not see Christianity primarily as translated into the Korean idiom

[48] Clark, *History*, 147–8; on Yun Chi-ho, see Shin Ahn, 'The International Religious Network of Yun Chi-ho (1865–1965): Mission or Dialogue?" in Jeremy Gregory and Hugh McLeod, eds, *International Religious Networks*, SCH S 14 (Woodbridge, 2012), 228–35.

[49] Paik, *History*, 295–8; Hyaeweol Choi, *Gender and Mission Encounters in Korea* (Berkeley, CA, 2009), 65–72.

[50] Paik, *History*, 419–28.

[51] Ryu, 'Origin', 398.

[52] Mott, *Decisive Hour*, 5–7.

[53] World Missionary Conference, *Report I*, 25.

[54] Ibid. 71.

but as a source and agent of the modernization that was transforming Korean society.

Moving beyond the translation model is also a shift away from an emphasis on language and culture in the study of evangelization. When in 1967 Spencer Palmer tested the hypothesis that Christianity's resonances with the religious and cultural context of Korea offered the most persuasive explanation for the early success of Protestant Christianity in Korea, he concluded that they were not the ultimate cause, which he found instead in the socio-political conditions around the turn of the twentieth century.[55] Attention to socio-political issues in Christian history also became prominent in South Korea during the labour and democratization movements of the 1970s and 1980s encouraged by the *minjung* (masses or peoples') movement.[56] In his 1985 study of the 'emplantation' of religion in Korea, the historian of Korean religions, James Grayson, emphasized the solving of conceptual and linguistic issues and the nature of Christian relations with other faiths, but in his later study, he put greater emphasis on the social instability of the period and the way Christianity was appropriated as a resource for modernization and nation-building.[57] These examples suggest that in order better to represent what happened in Korea, we should look further at both the agency and motives of Korean Christians and also the role of the Protestant churches in the socio-political context of the time.

The Reinvention of the Church in Korea

It was progressives frustrated by the gradual pace of modernization under the guidance of China who in the early 1880s encouraged the mission boards of American churches to send missionaries to Korea.[58] The first generation of missionaries generally shared the progressives' view that the dependence of Korea on China was the main reason for its 'backwardness', and aimed to liberate Korea from

[55] Spencer J. Palmer, *Korea and Christianity* (Seoul, 1967). Palmer identifies 1895–1910 as the years of most rapid growth and connects this phenomenon with the social trauma of the period: ibid. 80–1, 91–4.

[56] In Protestant historiography this was led especially by Mahn-yŏl Yi.

[57] James H. Grayson, *Early Buddhism and Christianity in Korea* (Leiden, 1985); idem, *Korea: A Religious History*, 2nd edn (Abingdon, 2002).

[58] Mahn-yŏl Yi, 'The Birth of the National Spirit of the Christians in the Late Chosŏn Period', in Chai-shin Yu, ed., *Korea and Christianity* (Seoul, 2004), 39–72, at 40–3; Kim and Kim, *History*, 62–3.

this subservient relationship.[59] Their combined attempt to promote a separate identity for Korea was one of the motives for attention to religio-cultural continuity with Korean religions. In addition, the translated gospel provided the example of a nation – Israel – with a distinct religio-cultural identity over and against threatening empires, and a nation which God promised to bless and make great.[60] This theological parallel between Korea and Israel accompanied the development of Korean self-awareness and ethnic nationalism.[61] Evidence suggesting that nationalism was the most immediate reason for the attraction of Protestantism includes the fact that the rapid growth for which the Korean Protestant churches are famed began only from about the time of Korea's Peasant Revolution (1894–5). The Revolution was inspired by *Tonghak* ('Eastern Learning') teaching, including belief in *Hananim* and the Korean people.[62] In this context, the fact that Protestants were also worshipping *Hananim* and preaching a new kingdom made their movement appear to be a nationalist one that revived traditional Korean religion.

However, Protestantism differed from *Tonghak* in that it promoted modernization. Since the *Tonghak* armies could be defeated by the government only with the help of Japan's modern forces, modernization of Korea seemed to the elite all the more necessary. The Protestant churches served the cause of modernization in several respects. The first was by the formation of the churches as modern communities. Protestant emphasis on conversion and individual conscience encouraged personal responsibility and Presbyterian polity laid foundations for Korean democracy.[63] The churches implemented social changes such as the participation of women as well as men in services, and the inclusion of butchers and other hitherto despised groups in the Christian community,[64] and they campaigned for corresponding social reforms,[65] many of which were among the modernizing reforms that were imposed on Korea by the Japanese who intervened to suppress the Revolution. These included ending the Confucian

59 Everett N. Hunt Jr, *Protestant Pioneers in Korea* (Maryknoll, NY, 1980), 90–2.

60 Wi Jo Kang, *Christ and Caesar in Modern Korea* (New York, 1997).

61 Gi-Wook Shin, *Ethnic Nationalism in Korea* (Stanford, CA, 2006), 21–57.

62 Carter J. Eckert et al., *Korea Old and New: A History* (Cambridge, MA, 1990), 214–22.

63 Kenneth M. Wells, *New God, New Nation: Protestants and Self-Reconstruction Nationalism in Korea, 1896–1937* (Honolulu, HI, 1990), 85–6.

64 Including undertakers and shamans.

65 Huntley, *Caring*, 66–80.

school and examination system for public office in favour of modern education using *Hańgŭl*, outlawing some traditional punishments, abolishing the social class system, allowing the remarriage of widows and deregulating clothing and hairstyles.[66] The defeat of China encouraged King Kojong (Gojong) to declare himself emperor in 1896, claiming Korean self-reliance and the parity of Korea with China and Japan.

A second way in which the churches promoted modernization was in their educational work. The victory of modernized Japan over Confucian society and over *Tonghak* produced a nationwide rush for Western education.[67] However, although it had dismantled the Confucian education system, the Korean government was slow to implement a replacement, so local churches and (to a lesser extent) missions largely took over the educational role which had been the foundation of Confucian power. The Bible became the new classical text; Christian theology and Western thinking, between which Koreans did not yet distinguish, provided the new philosophy; and the Church was the new moral institution.[68] Korean Christians responded enthusiastically to the need for schools; each village church established and funded an elementary school and these became feeder schools for the few secondary and tertiary institutions that had been founded by the missionaries. In addition, the wider education provided by church activities, Christian institutions and newspapers imparted Western scientific and technical knowledge and encouraged the questioning of traditional religions and the development of ideas of human freedom and social justice.[69]

At a grass-roots level, the 'three-self' method promoted initiative, self-reliance, growth and progress for national development. Following the disempowering of Confucianism, Protestantism now appeared as a contender for its place in public life. As well as practical help, protection, education and new values, Christian churches offered access to power: religious power in the form of strength to cope with what were proving to be troublesome times, the power of knowledge, legal power because of the extraterritorial powers held by the missionaries in this period, and the

66 Andrew C. Nahm, *Korea: Tradition and Transformation* (Elizabeth, NJ, 1988), 179–81.

67 Paik, *History*, 234.

68 Wells, *New God*, 30–2.

69 David Kwang-Sun Suh, 'American Missionaries and a Hundred Years of Korean Protestantism', *IRM* 74 (1986), 5–18, at 6–9.

possibility of political power.[70] From the beginning of the Peasant Rebellion in 1894 Korean men converted in significant numbers, leading to the conversion of whole households and villages.[71] Just as church communities emphasized 'three-self', progressive Christians tackled Korea's general dependence on foreign powers by espousing 'independence', in the sense of self-reliance, as their main aim. In 1896 the Protestants Sŏ Chae-p'il (Seo Jae-pil; Philip Jaisohn), Yun Ch'i-ho and others formed the Independence Club, the first modern nationalist organization in Korea.[72] Its branches were closely connected with Protestant churches[73] and its mouthpiece, *The Independent*, the first newspaper to be published entirely in *Hańgŭl*, was distinctly Christian in tone.[74] They promoted a 'self-reconstruction nationalism' which would bring about a modern nation state without recourse to violence by 'awakening' the people through free speech and education about Western values and social responsibility. This was largely the vision of Yun, who had become convinced, like the Hebrew prophets, that the problems Korea was facing lay primarily with the internal weakness of Korea itself and that Christianity offered a transcendent power to overcome evil and inculcate an innate morality and civic responsibility. He also promoted capitalism as an extension of the Christian public spirit by investment in industry and public enterprise, and other nationalist Christians like Yi Sŭng-hun (Yi Seung-hun) and Cho Man-sik (Jo Man-sik) began commercial companies to strengthen the nation.[75] Rather than Protestantism affirming – by translation – Korean culture as a vehicle of Christian truth, as Sanneh described it as doing in West Africa, Protestantism in Korea was being used by Koreans to transform Korean culture and modernize the nation. As events gradually revealed Japan to be the chief enemy of Korea, the religion of the Americans became not only less objectionable but even politically attractive. The churches came to be seen by nationalists as allies and as a means of saving the nation by raising awareness and organizing against the Japanese. Despite their avowed neutrality in politics, Protestant churches and

[70] Cf. Paik, *History*, 260–2, 356–8.
[71] Huntley, *Caring*, 125.
[72] Vipan Chandra, *Imperialism, Resistance, and Reform in Late Nineteenth-Century Korea* (Berkeley, CA, 1988).
[73] Park, *Protestantism*, 127.
[74] Wells, *New God*, 57.
[75] Ibid.

schools became vehicles of nationalism because they used the Korean vernacular and encouraged self-reliance and because they symbolized in their buildings, music and artefacts an alternative modernization.[76] The churches were motivated toward nationalism and mobilized to serve the nation.[77] Protestant churches, schools and Bible classes also offered leadership skills for activists and trained a 'new intellectual class'.[78] Despite the disciplinary measures of missionaries and Korean church leaders fearful for the future of the Church if it became a means of political insurrection, nationalist Christians made use of Christian churches and networks, not only in Korea but also in exile in Hawaii, on the US mainland and in Manchuria and Siberia. For example, Ahn Chang-ho moved to San Francisco in 1902 and founded, in addition to a church, the Sinmin-hoe (New People's Association), a secret revolutionary body that linked patriotic leaders in Korea, mostly Christians, with those in the USA.[79] Educational institutions founded by Ahn, Yun and other nationalists were accused of training resistance fighters. Not only were the churches agents of modernization, they were themselves being reinvented – contrary to missionary intentions – to serve nationalist purposes.

These socio-political arguments, which see the numerical growth and vitality of the Protestant movement resulting from its reinvention of the Church to serve Korean independence and modernization, are bolstered by the contrast with the Catholic Church in Korea, which by about 1907 was overtaken numerically by Protestant growth. Although it had been founded by Koreans as a lay community a century before the first Korean Protestant Christians were baptized, the Church was led from 1891 by Bishop Gustave-Charles-Marie Mutel and a French-dominated clergy. Furthermore, in reaction to its persecution in France by revolutionary forces, the French Catholic Church was in retreat from modernism and many aspects of the modern world. Catholic missionaries were therefore slower than Protestants to encourage modern education and Bishop Mutel rejected the idea of founding a Catholic university. Its anti-modernism is held to have hindered the growth of the Catholic Church in this period.[80]

[76] Heekuk Lim, ed., *Christianity in Korea* (Seoul, 2013), 73–84.

[77] Yi, 'Birth'.

[78] Park, *Protestantism*, 123–6.

[79] Jacqueline Pak, 'Cradle of the Covenant', in Robert E. Buswell Jr and Timothy S. Lee, eds, *Christianity in Korea* (Honolulu, HI, 2006), 116–48.

[80] Don Baker, 'Sibling Rivalry in Twentieth-Century Korea', ibid. 283–308, at 289–96.

When tensions between Japan and Russia escalated into full-scale war in 1904–5, the Japanese won and ousted the Russians from Korea. In November 1905, Korea was declared a 'protectorate' of Japan, which then occupied Korea and imposed its authority by force. When it was clear that Korea was humiliated, the institutional churches in Korea held prayer meetings for the nation. Following the example of biblical Israel, missionaries and Korean leaders such as Gil Seonju called for repentance for personal sin as the first step toward national recovery.[81] In the light of these socio-political developments, the P'yŏngyang Revival of 1907 appears not so much as a religious response to a translated gospel but much more as a cathartic opportunity to pour out the distress and panic at what had befallen the nation.[82] As well as being symbols of ethnic pride, means of modernization, mouthpieces of independence and vehicles of nationalism, the Protestant churches had become places of consolation and hope for the restoration of the nation in the context of the coming of the kingdom of God.

Whereas Chung, Oak and others, like Sanneh, have seen the translation of Christianity into the local language and culture as the chief means of its impact, in the Korean case in the period from about 1895 to 1910 it was Protestantism's discontinuity with Korean tradition that was the decisive factor in its growth and influence. Christianity was adopted because it was different from the tradition and offered salvation for the nation in a period of oppression and transition. The churches, which, due to the 'three-self' method, were organized by Koreans, could be reinvented to meet the challenges of the time. As such they became attractive to modernizers and nationalists.

Conclusion

This article has questioned the use of translation model, as presented chiefly by Lamin Sanneh, to explain the rapid growth of an indigenous Protestant Church in Korea in the period 1895–1910. It has done so both on the basis of conceptual discussions in the field of mission studies and also on historical grounds. From the point of view of mission studies, the chief weaknesses of the translation theory are that it tends to detract from the agency of the local people in

[81] Young Keun Choi, 'The Great Revival in Korea, 1903–1907', *Korean Journal of Christian Studies* 72 (2010), 129–49.
[82] Ryu, 'Origin', 394.

spreading the faith, to suggest that the gospel itself is a fixed deposit, and to focus unduly on the linguistic-cultural features of evangelization and the affirmation of local culture.

From the perspective of Korean Christian history, although the actual work of Bible translation and relating the gospel to Korean tradition had laid an important foundation, in the dire political situation of the final decade of the nineteenth century and the first decade of the twentieth, when church growth was particularly rapid, the missionary legacy of a translated gospel and its indigenization in the religio-cultural traditions of Korea were not the most important reasons for the attraction of Protestantism in Korea. On the contrary, the more modern Christianity appeared, the greater the hope it offered Koreans in their darkest hour. It could be said that Korean Christians were rather reinventing Christianity and the Church to transform their communities and country and to fulfil nationalist ends. A few months after the revival in 1907, the Presbyterian Church of Korea was formed. After Korea was finally annexed by Japan in 1910 and the state was lost, Protestant Christians saw the independent Church as continuing the nation.[83] In predominantly rural Korea, Protestant villages formed, in which the church was the social as well as the religious centre. These were self-help communities with high levels of solidarity and mutual care. They would move together into exile and they saw themselves as modelling the kingdom of God.[84] The Protestant network bound diaspora Christians with those in the peninsula and, through missionary connections, both could gain international support for the cause of Korean independence.[85]

In conclusion, the establishment of Protestantism in the years between 1895 and 1910 does not appear to be primarily a process of the translation of a persuasive Western religious tradition into Korean language and culture through missionary work. Although missionaries were involved and biblical translation did take place, a more compelling view is that what happened was that Christian forms were imported directly from the West and reconfigured to suit Korean purposes and transform Korean society. In particular, Koreans reimagined Old Testament Israel and the New Testament Church, informed

[83] Wells, *New God*.
[84] Park, *Protestantism*, 30–6.
[85] As in the independence movement of 1 March 1919: see In Soo Kim, *Protestants and the Formation of Modern Korean Nationalism, 1885–1920* (New York, 1996), 155–86.

by Western examples, to address the dire socio-political situation in which they found themselves in the decades immediately before and after 1900. The success of Christianity in Korea was less due to its translatability that affirmed the local culture and more due to its novelty and capacity for social transformation. Christianity was not so much translated into the Korean vernacular as it was reinvented to serve the need for the independence and modernization of the nation in its darkest hour.

The Nineteenth-Century Missionary-Translator: Reflecting on Translation Theory through the Work of François Coillard (1834–1904)

Esther Ruth Liu*
University of Cardiff

In the discussion of the history of Christianity, the issue of translation is inevitably present, and yet the discipline of Translation Studies too often neglects the potential for insight that this rich history of translation can bring. This article seeks to reconcile these academic fields, allowing each to enlighten the other. In particular, by presenting the example of the nineteenth-century French Protestant missionary François Coillard (1834–1904) and his translation methods, the article posits colonial missionary narratives as useful not only for considering historical translation processes but also for reconsidering some of the assumptions of contemporary translation theory. By employing sources written by Coillard as well as those written about this 'Livingstone français', it challenges the assumptions prevalent in translation theory that the translator is invisible and that he works alone.

When discussing the history of Christianity, one cannot but mention the issue of translation. The very text of the Bible is a text of translation, originally containing a combination of Hebrew, Greek and Aramaic. However, although the history of Christianity has long been associated with translation, the academic discipline of Translation Studies has been limited in its consideration of historical Christianity. Volumes such as *The Translation Studies Reader*, edited by Lawrence Venuti, include overviews of Jerome's translation theory,[1] and make reference to Wyclif, Luther and Tyndale,[2] but there is rarely an acknowledgement that Christian translation practices might be of use to

* 1 Booker St, Cardiff, CF24 1QN. E-mail: esther_j316@hotmail.com.

[1] Jerome, 'Letter to Pammachius', and Lawrence Venuti, 'Genealogies of Translation Theory: Jerome', in Lawrence Venuti, ed., *The Translation Studies Reader*, transl. Kathleen Davis, 3rd edn (London, 2012), 21–30, 483–502 respectively. See also Lawrence Venuti, 'Foundational Statements', ibid. 11–20, at 15–16.

[2] E.g. Venuti, 'Foundational Statements', 16, 20; Annie Brisset, 'The Search for a Native Language: Translation and Cultural Identity', in Venuti, ed., *Translation Studies Reader*, 281–311, at 282–3, 295; Michael Cronin, 'The Translation Age: Translation, Technology, and the New Instrumentalism', ibid. 469–82, at 473.

Studies in Church History 53 (2017) 376–388
doi: 10.1017/stc.2016.22

current translation theory. Similarly, although much of the field of Mission Studies recognizes that 'for a correct evaluation of nineteenth-century missionaries, their linguistic work is crucial',[3] scholarship is often limited to the study of translation practice amongst colonial missionaries and neglects to explore the implications of its relationship to theory. Scholars such as Derek Peterson and Jane Samson make passing references to the translation theories of Tejaswini Niranjana and Lawrence Venuti, but there is a lack of thorough engagement with Translation Studies in works on mission history.[4] This article will employ the disciplines of Mission History and Translation Studies together, using one to analyse the other. I will argue that missionary-translators from the past, such as the nineteenth-century French Protestant missionary François Coillard, are useful figures not only for the consideration of historical practices of translation, but also as we reflect on current discussions on translation.

François Coillard was born in 1834 at Asnières-lès-Bourges, in central France. After his personal conversion experience at seventeen, he trained under the direction of Eugène Casalis at the Protestant missionary society, Société des Missions Évangéliques de Paris (SMEvP).[5] In 1857, Coillard was sent to Basutoland (now Lesotho), and in 1861 he married Christina Mackintosh, daughter of a Scottish Baptist minister.[6] Coillard failed in an attempted mission to the Banyai people in Mashonaland (now in south-western Zimbabwe) in 1877, but in 1884 the Coillards, together with a group of indigenous missionaries from Basutoland, led a mission to Barotseland (now in western Zambia). Coillard remained in Barotseland after Christina's death in 1891 until his own death in 1904.[7]

[3] Adrian Hastings, *The Church in Africa: 1450–1950* (Oxford, 1994), 281.

[4] Derek Peterson, *Creative Writing: Translation, Bookkeeping, and the Work of Imagination in Colonial Kenya* (Portsmouth, 2004), 8, 9; Jane Samson, 'Translation Teams: Missionaries, Islanders, and the Reduction of Language in the Pacific', in Patricia Grimshaw and Andrew May, eds, *Missionaries, Indigenous Peoples and Cultural Exchange* (Eastbourne and Portland, OR, 2010), 96–109, at 107.

[5] Hastings, *Church in Africa*, 256.

[6] Catharine Winkworth Mackintosh, *Coillard of the Zambesi: The Lives of François and Christina Coillard, of the Paris Missionary Society, in South and Central Africa (1858–1904)* (London, 1907), 91.

[7] For the remainder of the article I will be using colonial place names.

Coillard was an active translator. He translated for local rulers and colonial administrators.[8] Furthermore, as was the case for many colonial missionaries, the interlingual translation of the Christian message was part of his daily routine. He translated the books of Psalms and Proverbs into Sesuto,[9] edited a translation of Joshua,[10] and translated psalms and 'hymns of his childhood' into Sesuto songs.[11] Many of his hymn translations are still in use today, found in the hymnbook *Lifela tsa Sione* (*Hymns of Zion*).[12] But more than this, Coillard's missionary work was itself an act of translation. The American Society of Missiology's definition of mission as 'the effort to effect passage over the boundary between faith in Jesus Christ and its absence', indicates through the 'passage over [a] boundary' that mission itself is a constant process of translation. Indeed, the etymology of the word 'translation' indicates this same idea of passage, of transferral, of carrying over or across. Just as the purpose of translation is to make accessible something previously inaccessible, by altering the language in which it is communicated, so too the purpose of mission is the rendering of previously unknown and inaccessible ideas, values and beliefs accessible. Missionaries are found constantly translating the message of Jesus into different contexts and cultures, whether or not they are carrying out formal translation work. Therefore, whilst this article engages with Coillard as a translator, it does so not only with regard to a traditional understanding of translation between

[8] Coillard translated for Lewanika during the controversial Lochner concession, whereby the British South Africa Company gained trade and mineral rights in Lewanika's territory in exchange for income and help in development (which, consequently, did not materialize), and is documented as a translator for the Basuto leader, Molapo: Gerald L. Caplan, *The Elites of Barotseland, 1878–1969: A Political History of Zambia's Western Province* (Berkeley, CA, 1970), 52; John S. Galbraith, *Crown and Charter: The Early Years of the British South Africa Company* (Berkeley, CA, 1974), 217; Edward Shillito, *François Coillard: A Wayfaring Man* (London, 1923), 86.

[9] Edouard Favre, *François Coillard. Missionnaire au Lessouto (1861–1882)* (Paris, 1912), 438; James Thayer Addison, *François Coillard* (Hartford, CT, 1929), 12–13. It is not clear whether Coillard customarily translated from Hebrew or French, although he had certainly studied Hebrew and Greek.

[10] Shillito, *Wayfaring Man*, 67.

[11] Addison, *Coillard*, 12; cf. Favre, *Lessouto*, 360, 183.

[12] Scott Rosenberg, Richard F. Weisfelder and Michelle Frisbie-Fulton, *Historical Dictionary of Lesotho* (Lanham, MD, 2004), 61. Elsewhere we read that it is 'probably the most widely used of any hymnbook across the whole of southern Africa': Morija Museum and Archives, 'Lifela Tsa Sione', 2 September 2012), online at: <http://www.morija.co.ls/museum/objects/lifela-tsa-sione/>, accessed 20 August 2015.

languages but also in this more metaphorical sense in which mission itself is an act of translation.

This article will not focus on the specific texts that Coillard translated, or the results of his intertextual translations. Rather, the ways in which Coillard is seen to translate will be used to reassess two of the dominant assumptions in current translation theory: firstly, that the translator is invisible, and secondly, that he works alone. The sources used include those written by Coillard, such as his letters and diary, which were edited, collated and published by Edouard Favre, and those written about him: newspapers, geographical society bulletins and biographies found at the Bibliothèque nationale de France's online archive, and a letter extract from the SMEvP archive in Paris.[13] Employing these texts, this article will conclude that historical missionary narratives such as that of François Coillard are useful not only for considering historical translation processes and practices but also for reconsidering the assumptions of contemporary translation theory.

Firstly, where in Translation Studies the translator is either visible or invisible in the translated text, Coillard demonstrates a translation practice whereby the translator is both visible and invisible. Lawrence Venuti, in his study *The Translator's Invisibility*, first published in 1995, challenges Norman Shapiro's assertion that '[a] good translation is like a pane of glass. You only notice that it's there when there are little imperfections … It should never call attention to itself'.[14] Instead of this self-effacing translation method, Venuti advocates a 'visible' translation practice which makes the reader aware of the translation process and the translator's presence, so as (writes Susan Bassnett) 'to ensure that readers recognise that they are reading a work that originated somewhere else'.[15] Venuti promotes translation methods that keep foreign elements in the text, such as 'Boulevard de Fleurs' and 'Monsieur Petit', rather than always finding equivalents, such as 'Flower Street' and 'Mr Small'.[16] The assumption in this debate is that translation practice promotes either visibility or invisibility, so that the

[13] Unpublished material is cited here with the permission of the Bibliothèque du DEFAP, 102 boulevard d'Arago, Paris.

[14] Norman Shapiro, cited in Lawrence Venuti, *The Translator's Invisibility: A History of Translation* (London and New York, 1995), 1.

[15] Susan Bassnett, *Reflections on Translation* (Bristol, 2011), 17.

[16] This visibility is evident in this article as I am providing my translations and the French citations.

translator is either visible or invisible. However, Coillard shows us that the missionary-translator is both.

Although to some degree simply an ordinary Frenchman, working for an obscure missionary society, Coillard was a very visible translator: he was visible in his secular and religious contemporary context, and in postcolonial critiques. In 1901 he was described in the bulletin of the Geographical Society of Lille as a 'well-known French missionary-explorer',[17] and in 1913 the *Bibliothèque universelle et revue suisse* asked: 'Who has not heard the name of François Coillard?'[18] We can assume, then, that by the time of his death he was in the public eye. From the late 1870s Coillard was visible as a missionary and explorer. On numerous occasions in the French national press he was called the 'Livingstone français' (the 'French Livingstone').[19] Moreover, he appeared in the title of the second volume of the autobiography of the imperial Portuguese explorer Serpa Pinto, his name being closely associated with that of the explorer-figure Pinto himself.[20] Coillard was portrayed as 'the man who saved me', and this image of him was perpetuated in translations of the book across Europe.[21] Coillard was thus a nineteenth-century celebrity. Of course, he was also visible in religious publications, as a hero of faith, one of the 'heroic pioneers of the gospel' and an ambassador, not for France or colonial rule, but for Christ.[22] Furthermore, following decolonization Coillard continued to be visible: his name is found in twentieth-century critiques of the European impact on indigenous culture, and his role as translator in the Lochner concession is presented by some

[17] 'Missionnaire-explorateur français bien connu': Alfred Bertrand, 'Séance du jeudi matin 23 août', *Bulletin de la Société de géographie de Lille* 35 (1901), 55.

[18] 'Qui n'a entendu le nom de François Coillard?': Maurice Millioud, 'Chronique Suisse romande', *Bibliothèque universelle et revue suisse* 72 (1913), 636–48, at 642.

[19] 'Lettre D'Allemagne', *La Justice. Journal politique du matin*, 19 July 1905, 3; Ferrari, 'Le Monde et la ville', *Le Figaro*, 17 June 1904, 2; 'Informations', *Le Figaro*, 20 November 1898, 4; Frédéric Lemoine, 'Société de géographie. Séance du 1er décembre, présidence de M. de Guerne', *Journal Officiel de la République Française*, 7 December 1905, 7087–9, at 7088.

[20] Serpa Pinto, *How I crossed Africa*, transl. Alfred Elwes, 2 vols (Hartford, CT, 1881). The second volume is subtitled 'The Coillard Family'.

[21] Ibid. iv. Pinto's book was published in Portuguese, French, English, German and Swedish in 1881, and in Spanish and Italian in 1890.

[22] '[H]éroïques pionniers de l'Évangile': 'Chronique Suisse', *Bibliothèque universelle et revue suisse* 61 (1911), 197–206, at 201; 'ambassadeur du Christ': Charles Malan, *La Mission française du sud de l'Afrique. Impressions d'un ancien soldat* (Paris, 1878), 207.

historians as manipulative and calculating[23] and by others as passive and naïve.[24] Long after his death, he continues to be visible in studies on the Zambian Church, French colonialism and mission.[25] Therefore, as he translated the Christian message into multiple contexts through his missionary work, Coillard was visible.

While in some ways this visibility was imposed on Coillard, in other instances it was something that he pursued. We know that he toured Europe twice and published his autobiography in English as *On the Threshold of Central Africa* (1897) and in French as *Sur le Haut-Zambèze* (1898), which was said to be 'an immediate best-seller in both countries'.[26] In Africa as well as in Europe, Coillard sought visibility as he translated himself into new contexts. Although he attempted to assimilate into the indigenous community to an extent, for example through acquiring the language,[27] he continued to wear European clothes.[28] Whilst living a significant proportion of his missionary life in a wagon or a tent, he erected a house reminiscent of those back home.[29] In the mission field, Coillard maintained a structure and an order to his life similar to that in Europe. A biographer of Christina Coillard writes: 'To both of them scrupulous attention to cleanliness and neatness in their dress and surroundings … were everyday requirements … If the missionary were not himself an

[23] E.g. 'Coillard … induced Lewanika … to request British protection. … with Coillard's active assistance, he [Lochner] finally persuaded Lewanika': Robert I. Rotberg, *The Rise of Nationalism in Central Africa: The Making of Malawi and Zambia, 1873–1964* (Cambridge, 1965), 15.

[24] E.g. 'Shippard's message deceived both Lewanika and Coillard. … Coillard was almost as much an innocent as Lewanika in dealing with Rhodes and his agent. … the naiveté of Coillard': John S. Galbraith, *Crown and Charter: The Early Years of the British South Africa Company* (Berkeley, CA, 1974), 213, 215, 218.

[25] E.g. Peter Bolink, *Towards Church Union in Zambia: A Study of Missionary Co-operation and Church-Union Efforts in Central Africa* (Franeker, 1967); Caplan, *Elites of Barotseland; Jean-François Zorn, Le Grand Siècle d'une mission protestante. La Mission de Paris de 1822 à 1914* (Paris, 2012).

[26] Jean-François Zorn, *The Transforming Gospel: The Mission of François Coillard and Basuto Evangelists in Barotseland*, ed. Elizabeth Visinand-Fernie, transl. Dora Atger (Geneva, 2004), 41.

[27] It is said that he 'parle leur langue comme l'un d'eux' ('speaks their language like one of them'), Auguste Glardon, 'Encore dans l'Afrique centrale', *Bibliothèque universelle et Revue suisse* 15 (1899), 545–75, at 549.

[28] For example, 'une jaquette en serge blanche, que lui avait faite Mme Coillard' ('a white serge morning coat which Madame Coillard had made for him'): Edouard Favre, *François Coillard. Missionnaire au Zambèze (1882–1904)* (Paris, 1913), 292.

[29] '[A] little cottage of dried bricks' as opposed to 'the Basuto style of building … when they move they take their houses with them': Mackintosh, *Coillard of the Zambesi*, 62, 83.

example of the graciousness of Christian life, from whom would his converts learn it?'[30] Here we see that the missionary's visibility acts as 'an example'. The missionary is visible in order to instruct, and to support that which he preaches.[31] Coillard's visibility served as a sort of propaganda whereby missionary work in general was made visible, and through it the Christian gospel. He wrote of his own fame: 'All this … did not add to our importance for ourselves. It is not us, but Africa, our Mission Society and our Protestantism that are honoured'.[32] Coillard's individual visibility served to raise awareness of Protestant missionary work more generally. This also echoes Venuti's priorities, as visibility is advocated in Translation Studies in order to inspire an awareness in the contemporary consciousness that the translation process is occurring, in order to 'promote the cause of translation', as Susan Bassnett writes.[33]

However, Coillard pursued invisibility in his work too. In a letter written to the executive committee of the SMEvP, one of Coillard's young colleagues, Frédéric Christol, wrote: 'Monsieur Coillard … told me that he only wanted a man who is completely ordinary; not especially a theologian or a linguist'.[34] In recruiting co-workers, Coillard sought ordinary, invisible people. Indeed, when writing to a young boy who wanted to be a missionary, Coillard stated that the 'first condition' for the vocation is 'that he denies himself' and 'takes up his cross', words echoing those of Christ himself.[35] Furthermore, Coillard's own motto, from John's gospel, was one of self-abnegation: '"He must increase, and I must decrease." This is what I repeat to myself every day'.[36] It seems that, according to Coillard, a missionary must make himself invisible so that the God of the Christian gospel is seen. In translation theory, this pursuit of invisibility is what

[30] Winifred Mathews, *Dauntless Women: Stories of Pioneer Wives* (London, 1947), 57.

[31] See David Maxwell, 'The Missionary Home as a Site for Mission: Perspectives from Belgian Congo', in John Doran, Charlotte Methuen and Alexandra Walsham, eds, *Religion and the Household*, SCH 50 (Woodbridge, 2014), 428–55.

[32] Zorn, *Transforming*, 12.

[33] Bassnett, *Reflections on Translation*, 17.

[34] 'Monsieur Coillard … me dit qu'il ne désirait qu'un homme tout ordinaire; pas plus spécialement théologien que linguiste': Paris, Bibliothèque du DEFAP, SMEvP archives, letter from Frédéric Christol to the 'Membres de la Commission Executives', 1883.

[35] 'Qu'il renonce à lui-même, qu'il se charge de sa croix': Favre, *Lessouto*, 508; cf. Matt. 16: 24 and parallels.

[36] '"Il faut qu'Il croisse et que je diminue." Voilà ce que je me répète chaque jour à moi-même': Favre, *Zambèze*, 483; cf. Favre, *Lessouto*, 210, 410, 453; Zorn, *Transforming*, 12. The allusion is to John 3: 30.

Lawrence Venuti calls a 'weird self-annihilation'.[37] Albert Bensoussan's invisible translator is presented as pathetic, passive and pitiful: 'The translator suffers, submits, subjugates … dispossessed of his own word. [Taking on] the word of the other, the author'.[38] But Coillard saw this 'self-annihilation' as a profoundly positive goal. Indeed, he asserted, 'the mission must not … be a personal question, the mission of M. Coillard: that would be its ruin',[39] and when discussing the controversial Anglican biblical scholar and bishop, John Colenso, Coillard declared: 'it is this gospel and not the preacher which is the power of God'.[40] Mission and the translation occurring through it, according to Coillard, ought to involve self-effacement, not self-promotion. The translator-preacher is an invisible, anonymous mouthpiece, because it is the message and the text itself which have authority. Just as Gayatri Spivak claims that in translation 'the translator must surrender to the text',[41] Coillard surrendered himself to the work and to the visibility of the 'text', the message of his mission. Following the model of Christ's own sacrifice, self-denial was therefore voluntarily and willingly undertaken.

Thus, although Coillard pursued visibility in Europe and Africa, he also desired a translation in which the translator was invisible, humble and self-sacrificial for the sake of the text. He advocated both visibility and invisibility for the missionary, a present absence. He was the example, the charisma, the visible persona. And yet he was also a preacher in the Calvinist sense of being the 'mouthpiece of God',[42] a passive, invisible instrument of the message of salvation. This historical case study thus brings to the visibility-invisibility binary a third, present-but-absent, visible-but-invisible, spectral way.

Secondly, in contrast to the singular figure of the translator that permeates Translation Studies, Coillard's process of translation is located within a context of collaboration. With a few exceptions –

[37] Venuti, *Invisibility*, 8.

[38] 'Le traducteur subit, soumis … subjugue … dépossédé de sa parole propre. Parole de l'autre, l'auteur': Albert Bensoussan, cited in Sherry Simon, *Gender in Translation: Cultural Identity and the Politics of Transmission* (London and New York, 1996), 8.

[39] 'Il ne faut pas que la mission … soit une question personnelle, la mission de M. Coillard: ce serait sa ruine': Favre, *Lessouto*, 518.

[40] '[C]'est bien cet Évangile et non le prédicateur qui est la puissance de Dieu': ibid. 147.

[41] Gayatri Chakravorty Spivak, *Outside in the Teaching Machine*, 2nd edn (Abingdon, 2009), 205.

[42] See Jon Balserak, *John Calvin as Sixteenth-Century Prophet* (Oxford, 2014), 96; cf. T. H. L. Parker, *Calvin's Preaching* (Louisville, KY, and Edinburgh, 1992).

such as Christiane Nord's assertion that translation is an 'interpersonal' process[43] and discussions of the 'fansubbing' genre[44] – 'the translator' is often discussed as an isolated being who undertakes the work of translation utterly alone. Even as Venuti writes against the 'Translator's invisibility', he renders the multitude invisible, obscuring any collaboration in his singular representation of the translator. In Mission Studies too, Derek Peterson writes: 'Translation is most often conceived as a solitary activity, carried off by scholars working in private'.[45] Admittedly, this is often for 'convenience' of argument,[46] as in this present article, but this discourse, if left unchallenged, obscures the truth of the collaboration going on in much translation practice.[47]

In a similar way, Coillard is frequently represented in secular and religious contexts as a singular hero and pioneer. Of the twenty-six biographies of Coillard that I have found, only two mention his wife or other missionaries in the title.[48] And yet Coillard's work was entirely collaborative. In the journal of the Marseilles Geographical Society, the account of Coillard's journey north into Africa includes many contributors: 'M. Coillard is accompanied by … Mme Coillard, … Mlle Coillard, missionary M. Jeanmairet, two indigenous missionary aides and their families, MM. Waddell and Middleton, … two indigenous youths … They are therefore quite a little colony … M. Coillard and his collaborators'.[49] Here, and throughout his work, Coillard is seen to work with his wife, with his niece, with other European missionaries, with indigenous missionaries, and also with supporters and

[43] Christiane Nord, *Translating as a Purposeful Activity: Functionalist Approaches explained* (Manchester, 1997), 123–8.

[44] A translation practice whereby multiple fans contribute to one translation effort, such as the translation of a manga novel into Italian.

[45] Peterson, *Creative Writing*, 8.

[46] Andrew Chesterman, 'Ethics of Translation', in *Translation as Intercultural Communication: Selected Papers from the EST Congress, Prague 1995*, ed. Mary Snell-Hornby, Zuzana Jettmarová and Klaus Kaindl (Amsterdam, 1997), 147–57, at 148.

[47] The translation of the Bible is historically undertaken in collaboration: from Jerome with his communities of women and men, through Luther and his colleagues in Wittenberg, to modern teams of Bible translators. However, in general Translation Theory focuses on the singular translator.

[48] The exceptions being Mackintosh, *Zambesi*; Zorn, *Transforming*.

[49] 'M. Coillard est accompagné de … Mme Coillard, … Mlle Coillard, de M. le missionnaire Jeanmairet, de deux aides missionnaires indigènes et de leurs familles, de MM. Waddell et Middleton, … deux jeunes indigènes … C'est donc toute une petite colonie … M. Coillard et ses collaborateurs' : Paul Armond, 'Nouvelles des voyageurs', *Bulletin de la Société de géographie de Marseille* 8 (1884), 54–88, at 66.

the mission society 'back home'. Each figure warrants much more attention, but I shall briefly consider Christina Coillard and the indigenous missionaries.

Christina Coillard, as well as undertaking her own mission work, was a vital collaborator whose presence enabled Coillard to fulfil his role. In one biography we read that when Coillard arrived in Basutoland as a bachelor, 'many … refused to regard him as sufficiently mature to teach until he had a beard and a wife. The beard he was able to produce with reasonable promptness, but for the wife, in these first years, he could only hope.'[50] The Basuto people did not trust Coillard without a wife, as he was still assumed to be dependent on his mother; he was a figure without authority. When Coillard secured a 'yes' from Christina Mackintosh after his second proposal to her, he wrote: 'I cannot believe my own happiness … Molapo, now he knows I am going to be married, considers me a man, acquaints me with his affairs, and asks my advice!'[51] Christina's acceptance, and later her presence, granted François personal happiness, but also authenticated and validated his work, facilitating both his textual translation work and the translation of his self among the people.

Christina's domestic tasks, too, can be seen as enabling the mission: 'to keep her husband and herself alive and well took up much of Christina's time'.[52] Her domestic work enabled the mission work of her husband, precisely because she kept him alive; she provided physical sustenance for him to function. Indeed, her attention to domestic details supported the whole missionary team: 'Mme Coillard was the house-mother to the whole party. She always took care to have a good stock of bottles filled with cold tea, so that the axemen and team-drivers should quench their thirst, and continue their dry work undistressed.'[53] Thus Christina, as well as performing her own missionary tasks (teaching in the school, taking sewing classes, nursing the sick, and acting as dressmaker to Queen Mokwae and her ladies in Barotseland, 'looking for opportunities of speaking to them of Christ'), enabled the mission by validating the presence of

[50] Addison, *Coillard*, 9.

[51] Ibid. 9.

[52] Mathews, *Dauntless Women*, 59.

[53] E. C. Dawson, *Heroines of Missionary Adventure; True Stories of the Intrepid Bravery and Patient Endurance of Missionaries in their Encounters with Uncivilized Man, Wild Beasts and the Forces of Nature in All Parts of the World* (Philadelphia, PA, 1909), 208.

the male missionary and by sustaining the physical wellbeing of the mission team as a whole.[54]

Secondly, Coillard worked with indigenous missionaries. They were builders and teachers, active in the mission's construction and its daily life.[55] They conducted 'translation proper' with Coillard: Nathanael Makotoko helped Coillard translate hymns and other religious material.[56] They were collaborators as they facilitated dialogue and understanding, helping with the linguistic needs of the mission.[57] But more than this, the indigenous missionaries were partners in the missionary work of the Europeans. The failed mission to the Banyai people and the successful mission to Barotseland were both initiated by a group of Basuto Christians led by 'a very intelligent catechist',[58] Asser Sehahabane, who had travelled to Mashonaland in 1875 to see if a mission would be possible. The indigenous missionaries were key partners. Indeed, referring to Aaron Mayoro, another of the Basuto evangelists from these two missions, Adrian Hastings writes: 'for ordinary Africans, encountering Christianity whether at Seleka or at Sefula, it was the Aarons not the Coillards of the Church that they encountered'.[59] These indigenous figures, often portrayed in past and present mission literature as passive recipients of colonial Christianity,[60] were in reality significant agents of the metaphorical and formal translation of the Christian message, fellow-workers with Coillard.

54 Mackintosh, *Coillard of the Zambesi*, 109–10; Mathews, *Dauntless Women*, 59, 73 (quotation); C. Rey, *Une Femme missionnaire. Souvenirs de la vie et de la mort de Christina Coillard* (Paris, 1892), 54, 62, 93; cf. François Coillard, *On the Threshold of Central Africa: A Record of Twenty Years' Pioneering among the Barotsi of the Upper Zambesi*, ed. and transl. Catharine Winkworth Mackintosh (London, 1897), 428.

55 For example, 'à Aaron revient l'honneur d'avoir fondé notre école avec ces matériaux bruts' ('Aaron had the honour of having founded our school with these raw materials'): François Coillard, *Sur le Haut-Zambèze. Voyages et travaux de missions* (Paris, 1898), 396. Aaron was also an 'instructor in reading': Addison, *Coillard*, 43.

56 J. Blanquis, 'Le Jubilé de 1908', in *Livre d'or de la Mission du Lessouto. Soixante-quinze ans de l'histoire d'une tribu sud-africaine 1833–1908* (Paris, 1912), 513–99, at 575; Rosenberg, Weisfelder and Frisbie-Fulton, *Historical Dictionary of Lesotho*, 295.

57 Favre, *Zambèze*, 195; Joseph Mujere, 'African Intermediaries: African Evangelists, the Dutch Reformed Church, and the Evangelisation of the Southern Shona in the Late 19th Century', *Studia Historiae Ecclesiasticae* 39 (2013), 133–48 at 134.

58 Catharine Winkworth Mackintosh, 'Some Pioneer Missions of Northern Rhodesia and Nyasaland', in *Occasional Papers of the Rhodes-Livingstone Museum nos 1–16* (Leiden, 1974), 249–96, at 252–3.

59 Hastings, *Church in Africa*, 439.

60 Martha McCollough makes a similar statement in her conclusion to *Three Nations, One Place* (New York and London, 2004), 111.

In Coillard's case, this collaboration was not without its conflicts. After travelling back to Basutoland, two SMEvP Basuto evangelists, Willie Mokalapa and Jacob, joined the Ethiopian church movement, a separatist movement with African leadership.[61] On their return to Barotseland they asked the ruler, Lewanika, for permission to establish a mission of their own, where English and practical skills would be taught.[62] Although Coillard was sad that his own disciples had separated from him, he was less concerned about the Ethiopian mission itself. 'Although these Ethiopians have established themselves … with hostility, they are Christians and competent men. They preach Christ in a spirit of antagonism, but they preach Christ'.[63] Coillard recognized that the opposition was to the European mission, not to mission in general or to the gospel being preached; his anxiety was that the Ethiopian mission would compete with the SMEvP mission, and not collaborate. He wrote that if the Ethiopian mission were located anywhere else, 'it would have been easy for us to support them',[64] and 'I would rejoice with all my heart because … they are working towards the realisation of a grand plan'.[65] He was concerned that 'they are coming to the very capital … to replace us',[66] and that he might have to 'fight with one of our children in the faith who has turned against us'.[67] In contrast to Coillard's desire that 'we could work in harmony and pray for each other',[68] it appeared that there would be dissonance. However, even where there was division, and difference regarding how the gospel should be translated, Coillard worked to collaborate with, and not to compete against, these potential rival translators.

The singular missionary is therefore mythical. A missionary did not work alone; we have seen that the missionary's wife and the indigenous evangelists were significant collaborators. Furthermore,

[61] Rotberg, *Rise of Nationalism*, 58.

[62] Caplan, *Elites of Barotseland*, 80.

[63] 'Bien que ces Ethiopiens se soient mis … sur un pied d'hostilité, ce sont des chrétiens et des hommes capables. Ils prêcheront le christ dans un esprit de contradiction, mais ils le prêcheront': Favre, *Zambèze*, 465.

[64] '[I]l nous eût été facile d'en prendre notre parti': ibid. 466.

[65] '[J]e m'ne réjouissais de tout mon cœur, car, après tout, ce sont nos enfants et ils travaillent à la réalisation d'une grande idée': ibid. 534.

[66] '[I]ls viennent à la capitale même … pour nous supplanter': ibid. 466.

[67] '[L]a lutte avec un de nos enfants en la foi qui s'est tourné contre nous': ibid. 535.

[68] '[N]ous pourrions travailler en bonne harmonie et prier les uns pour les autres': ibid. 536.

Coillard collaborated with other missionaries too, 'see[ing] how diverse nationalities and different denominations understand the work of the missions, and … compar[ing] the results of their systems',[69] and he worked with the mission society in Europe, unable to do much without the approval of the SMEvP committee,[70] and relying on their support and publications for his own livelihood.[71] Similarly, in translation, the translator is not isolated from the work of other translators. Peterson has claimed that '[n]o author writes in a vacuum', and I would argue that no translator translates in a vacuum.[72] Although often represented in theoretical works as working alone, in practice a translator might consult other translations, other texts, experts in a field, local language-speakers, dictionaries and databases, and works alongside publishers, proof-readers and editors. The translator is not alone in the translation process. Coillard's continual use of a team exposes the utterly collaborative nature of translation, offering a useful contrast to the singular translator assumed by much of Translation Studies.

In conclusion, the work of François Coillard is useful in the reevaluation of accepted norms of Translation Studies: those that assume the translator's visibility or invisibility, and those that assume the singularity of the translator. Where translation theory insists on a visibility-invisibility binary, Coillard is both visible and invisible, an example and a mouthpiece. Where translation theory represents the isolation of the translator, Coillard shows us that his missionary-translation work is an entirely collaborative process. The translation undertaken by historical translators – such as this missionary – not only reveals attitudes to translation in their contemporary moment, but can also impact translation theory and practice today.

[69] 'Rien de plus intéressant et de plus instructif que de voir comment diverses nationalités et différentes dénominations comprennent l'œuvre des missions, et de comparer les résultats de leurs systèmes': Favre, *Lessouto*, 140.

[70] 'The Paris Committee … gave its moral support to the undertaking': Mackintosh, *Zambesi*, 293.

[71] Zorn, *Transforming*, 41.

[72] Peterson, *Creative Writing*, xi.

Lin Shu's Translation of Shakespeare's Religious Motifs in Twentieth-Century China

Jenny Wong*
University of Glasgow

When Christian values fall into the hands of translators, how are these Christian values represented in a non-religious or areligious target culture? How do the translations reflect the conflicting ideologies of the time and of the individual translators? This article will examine Lin Shu's major translations of The Merchant of Venice *in early twentieth-century China, an important period when reform of Confucianism encountered imported Western ideals. Close textual analysis of the translation produced by Lin Shu, a Confucian literatus and a reformist, reveals that religious content in English literary works was manipulated, Christian references often being omitted or adapted. This study illustrates the translator's strategies, picking and choosing what to domesticate in the translated work to suit his ideology, and how a society's expectations and ideologies shape the translation product. The analysis offers some perspectives for understanding how the translator's linguistic and religious roles and ideologies shaped the Chinese Shakespeare, and how the religious values were re-presented in early twentieth-century China.*

Historically, the early part of the twentieth century was a critical time in China, during which two ideologies met: traditional Chinese values rooted in Confucianism competed with the importation of Western modernization. Confucian literati expended effort on asserting traditional Chinese values, whereas other intellectuals sought to abolish Confucian values, feudalism and superstition. They campaigned for the importation of Western ideas, including science, democracy, equality and freedom. Politically, this period witnessed the overthrow of the Qing Dynasty (1644–1912) and the establishment of the New Republican Era in 1911. The May Fourth cultural and political movement, which developed from protests on 4 May 1919, was led by students and intellectuals who called for a new mindset, the overthrow of Confucianism and its replacement with Western ideals of democracy and science. Ideologically, this marked a period of intense

* 9/1, 15 Kirkton Avenue, Glasgow, G13 3SF. E-mail: jenny@selbl.org.

Studies in Church History 53 (2017) 389–404

doi: 10.1017/stc.2016.23

conflict when the downfall of traditional values led to the displacement of other religious traditions. Buddhism came to be regarded as a philosophy rather than a religion, while Christian miracles were regarded as unscientific and Christianity was identified with foreign imperialism.[1] Culturally, from the beginnings of this new cultural movement the vernacular language replaced the elegant classical style as the predominant literary form. It is in this context that the political reformer and Confucian literatus, Lin Shu, translated Shakespearean religious motifs in a manner that reflected not only his own beliefs but also the prevailing ideology of the time.

This case study examines the impact of the translator's ideology on the strategies and choices made when rendering religious aspects of a text in another language. Ideology refers to 'a set of beliefs, convictions or ideas which both binds a particular group of people together and determines the actions they take'.[2] There is a particularly intense relationship between religious ideology and translation. The Belgian translation theorist André Lefevere emphasized the relationship between translation and ideology, focusing on the influence of the dominant ideology at the time of translation and the ideology of translators, and pointing out that '[t]ranslations are not made in a vacuum'.[3] This article explores how the values and ideologies of a society influenced the strategies and choices of one translator, but it also highlights the central importance of the translator's personal mission and role. The translations considered here shaped the staging of Shakespeare's work in China. Translating the Christian values that appeared in Charles and Mary Lamb's *Tales from Shakespeare*, Lin Shu sought to accommodate and reconcile Christian values with the Confucian tradition during early twentieth-century China's cultural and political transformation.

LIN SHU'S TRANSLATION OF *TALES FROM SHAKESPEARE*

Shakespeare's work was first introduced to China by Lin Zexu 林則徐 (1785–1850), governor-general of the Hubei and Hunan provinces and a key figure in halting the opium war. Shakespeare was

[1] Alexander Chow, *Theosis, Sino-Christian Theology and the Second Chinese Enlightenment* (New York, 2013), 24.
[2] Ian Buchanan, ed., *A Dictionary of Critical Theory* (Oxford, 2010), 243.
[3] André Lefevere, ed., *Translation / History / Culture: A Sourcebook* (London and New York, 1992), 14.

first cited in Lin's translation of the *Encyclopedia of Geography* (1843).[4] However, he became widely known in China when Lin Shu published the *Yinbian Yanyu* (吟邊燕語; 1904), his translation of Charles and Mary Lamb's *Tales from Shakespeare* (1807), a collection of prose adaptations of Shakespeare's plays written primarily for children. Although Lin did not speak English and did not read the original plays, he worked in collaboration with his interpreter Wei Yi (魏易) who provided an oral account of the stories. When published, Lin's translations were set out as prose texts.

Lin Shu's lack of English did not hinder him from translating Western literature; he was a prolific translator and one of the first to make many of these texts available in China.[5] Indeed, Lin has been acclaimed as the most influential twentieth-century Chinese translator, completing 184 works in total.[6] In Shakespeare's case, however, Lin did not translate directly from the original plays but from Charles and Mary Lamb's adaptations. This may be because Lin was less concerned with the original texts than with incorporating Shakespeare's heritage into the existing Confucian tradition, thus giving Shakespeare a contemporary and cross-cultural touch.

As well as being a Confucian literatus, Lin Shu was a political reformer who campaigned for change in China. During the Qing Dynasty, China faced a significant influx of Western ideologies. Reformers accused the Chinese of 'sharing a narrow world view, obstinately opposed to change, allowing her past to dominate her present, and being over-enthusiastic about gods, fairies, ghosts and demons' (識見局, 思想舊, 泥 古駭今, 好言神怪).[7] Lin Shu, however, did not share this opinion. In his preface to the *Yinbian Yanyu* (吟邊燕語), he tried to bridge the gap between Western and Chinese literature by emphasizing that both made use of the 'supernatural', introducing the 'supernatural' aspects of Shakespeare to the Chinese audience as a way of highlighting the importance of Chinese traditions, and stressing that these traditions should not be eradicated in the midst

[4] The manuscript was finished in 1839 but not published until 1843, after the Opium War, when it appeared under the title 海國圖志 (*Haiguotuzhi*).

[5] He was a leading figure in early translation history in China and regarded as on a par with another reputable early translator, Yan Fu, who translated, among other works, Thomas Huxley's *Evolution and Ethics*.

[6] Leo Chan Tak-hung, ed., *Twentieth-Century Chinese Translation Theory: Modes, Issues and Debates* (Amsterdam and Philadelphia, PA, 2004), 16.

[7] Cited in 林紓、魏易譯 [Lin Shu], 吟邊燕語 [*Yinbian Yanyu*], transl. Wei Yi (Beijing, 1981), 1–2.

of the 'wholesale importation of Western values (全盤西化)' that was taking place. Lin wrote:

> Shakespeare's sonnets and tales, which rival those of Du Fu, a renowned Chinese poet, point to supernatural forces and spirits. … it is evident that famous people in the West recite Shakespearean tales in their homes; … literati and women shed tears upon listening to these stories without dismissing them as old-fashioned, or blaming them for upholding supernatural forces. Why? Good politics and religion can influence literature. Politics and education should be beautified through literature. On the other hand, literature, however beautiful, does not benefit politics and education. Thus Westerners are busy at politics and education to empower the country and military against the invasion of enemies, while they seek pleasure through literature. Even though R[ider] Haggard's and Shakespeare's works are regarded as old-fashioned and reliant on the supernatural, civilized men do not see them as obstacles … The English seek out what is new for better government, but would never discard their Shakespeare.[8]

Here Lin offered a sociological sketch that situated the translator in the early twentieth century. While the West was regarded by some as engulfing much of the Chinese cultural scene, Confucian literati such as Lin Shu were reasserting the values of time-honoured Chinese heritage.[9] Lin's translations have been seen by scholars as a way of defending Confucian tradition and Chinese values. Robert Compton asserts that these principles were 'vibrant and alive in Lin's mind and spirit', and that Lin believed himself to bear the responsibility of 'preserving the best of what had been created in the past'.[10] In her close textual analysis of Lin's translations in the *Yinbian Yanyu*, Jean Tsui takes a similar view, arguing that *Yinbian Yanyu* is 'an expression of Lin's reformist enthusiasm in the midst of a swiftly changing political scene torn by diverse opinions and heated debates'.[11] Lin presented Shakespeare's tales as something familiar to Chinese culture, domesticating or naturalizing them as works expressing a world view

[8] Ibid. 3.

[9] Lin Shu's *Yinbian Yanyu* and his translation of other Western literature show evidence of Confucianization, giving the characters in Shakespeare a Confucian twist.

[10] Robert Compton, 'A Study of the Translations of Lin Shu' (PhD thesis, Stanford University, 1971), 99.

[11] Jean Tsui, 'Rewriting Shakespeare: A Study of Lin Shu's Translation of *Tales from Shakespeare*' (MPhil thesis, University of Hong Kong, 2009), 99.

recognizable to Chinese readers, containing stories of spirits, gods and monsters.[12] On the book's cover, he categorized these tales as stories of gods and spirits, a category which was familiar and appealing to the Chinese audience. The title of each story reflected the main plot rather than representing a literal translation of the title: thus *The Merchant of Venice* became the *Rou Quan* 肉券 (*Contract of the Flesh*), and was included as the first story in the collection.

Although Lin's translation of *The Merchant of Venice* was not his earliest, its popularity surpassed all his other translations. A. Ying (阿英) noted that although Lin's translation was not the first, it was to be preferred to others because 'it attracted the attention of many readers at the time'.[13] The popularity of Lin's translation of *The Merchant of Venice* resulted in its being reprinted as a separate text eleven times between 1905 and 1935, in addition to the three editions of the *Yinbian Yanyu*.[14] A new project launched in 2001 to render all Shakespearean plays in prose recognized Lin Shu's significant achievement.[15] In 1999, the former Chinese Premier Zhu Rongji (朱鎔基) even referred to *The Merchant of Venice* in his response to a question regarding the bankruptcy of Guangdong International Trust and Investment Company when, after the Second Plenary Session of the Ninth National People's Congress, he recalled the story of 'A Pound of Flesh' – Lin's version – which he had read in high school, and related it to the bankruptcy case.

Lin's translation was also popular with dramatists. In July 1913, the National Renewal Society (*Xin min she*; 新民社) staged *Rou Quan* (*Contract of the Flesh*), a version of *Merchant of Venice* dramatized from Lin's *Yanbian Yanyu*. The production, the first professional performance of Shakespeare in Chinese, was well received and became an immediate box office success.[16] It was followed by other

12 Lawrence Venuti sets out two translation approaches, domestication and foreignization: the former refers to adopting a fluent translation to ease readers' reception, the latter to the retention in the target text of cultural and linguistic references from the original.

13 Compton, 'The Translations of Lin Shu', 200. In 1961, Ying had reprinted a collection of translations of Western novels from the late Qing Dynasty: A. Ying (Qian Heng Cun), ed., *Wan Qing Wen Xue Cong Chao* [*Translations from Foreign Literature*], 4 vols (Shanghai, 1961).

14 Ruru Li, *Shashibiya: Staging Shakespeare in China* (Hong Kong, 2003), 16.

15 Tu An [屠岸、方平譯], *Xin Shashibiyaquanji* [新莎士比亞全集; *New Shakespeare's Works*], transl. Fang Ping (Taipei, 2000).

16 鄭振秋 [Zheng Zhenqiu], 新劇考證百齣 [*Xinju kaozheng bai chu*; *Textual Criticism on a Hundred Spoken Drama Plays*] (Shanghai, 1919), 1–29.

productions such as *Othello*, *Hamlet* and *The Taming of the Shrew*, which were staged in 1914 and 1915, also using Lin's translations.[17] The popularity of Lin's translations both in print and on stage was due to his creation of a 'fantasy world', as Cao Yu(曹禺; 1910–96) described it, or else to their exotic plots, which were just like 'fairy tales', according to Guo Moruo (郭沫若; 1892–1978).[18] A synopsis of Lin's translation of *The Merchant of Venice*, also under the title *Contract of the Flesh*, was included in an anthology of plays edited by the acclaimed director Zheng Zhenqiu (鄭振秋).[19] In the 1930s, Lin Shu's translation was exported to colonial Hong Kong and adopted by the acclaimed Cantonese opera master Ma Shizeng (馬師曾), who directed the *Yi Bang Rou* (一磅肉; *A Pound of Flesh*) as a Cantonese opera adaptation. The story was staged again as *A Pound of Flesh* in 1953, starring the Cantonese opera diva Hong Xiannu (紅線女).[20]

Lin either omitted or adapted the religious language in Shakespeare's plays, as has been noted sporadically by contemporary scholars. However, such discussions have been limited to comparing the source and target texts. Thus Alexander Huang noted the omission of Christian references from Lin Shu's translations of the Lambs' *Tales from Shakespeare* but did not elaborate further.[21] Tsui compares Lin's translations of the Christian connotations in *Romeo and Juliet* and *The Tempest*, and notes the extent of Daoist interpretation in his translations.[22] For instance, Friar Lawrence in *Romeo and Juliet* becomes a Daoist priest, residing in a monastery, who is interested in thaumaturgy. Prospero in *The Tempest*, in Lin's rendition, studies Daoist scriptures and practices such as 'Shaman's steps', a type of ritual walk or dance performed during the Daoist liturgy. This 'conventionalization' strategy of translating Christian concepts rendered Shakespeare's works familiar to Chinese readers.[23] It also helped

[17] Alexander Huang, 'Shakespeare on the Chinese Stage 1839–2004: A History of Transcultural Performance' (PhD thesis, Stanford University, 2004), 79.

[18] Ruru Li, *Shashibiya*, 16.

[19] Zheng Zhenqiu, *Xinju kaozheng bai chu*, 1.

[20] 易紅霞 [Yi Hongxia], 'Shakespeare in Guangdong', in *International Conference on Shakespeare in China – Performances and Perspectives: A Collection of Theses* (Shanghai, 2007), 197–208.

[21] See Alexander C. Y. Huang, 'Lin Shu, Invisible Translation and Politics', *Perspectives: Studies in Translatology* 14 (2006), 55–65, at 61.

[22] Tsui, 'Rewriting Shakespeare', 41–8.

[23] 'Conventionalization' is a term coined by Frederic C. Bartlett in *Remembering: A Study in Experimental and Social Psychology* (Cambridge, 1932), 280; he proposed using the term to describe a process of cultural exchange whereby 'cultural materials coming into a group

to reinforce traditional Chinese culture and values, since Shakespeare was seen employing supernatural forces in the narratives. Tsui pointed out that '[Lin's] conventionalization is more than just a cultural shift: by using Daoism to replace Christianity, still a dominant religion in the West at the time, the translator had ventured to find the native religion a place in modernity'.[24]

LIN'S DOMESTICATION OF CHRISTIAN CONTENT

Lin's domestication strategy aimed to make Shakespeare a familiar voice for a Chinese audience rather than a foreign 'other'. How did this affect the translation of the religious aspects of the plays? Lin produced a paragraph-by-paragraph translation of the Lambs' texts (which were themselves simplified versions of the plays), preserving plot and characterization but omitting what he deemed to be less important details. In the resulting translation of *The Merchant of Venice*, the complexity of the play, including the relationship between Jews and Christians and the conflicts between them, was downplayed.[25] Shylock was depicted as a cruel moneylender, while Antonio was described as 'generous'. Almost all the direct speech in the Lambs' text was translated by Lin, but the Lambs' version of the narrative removed the story line relating to Jessica's running away and the casket scenes, and Lin did so too. Some additions can be seen to conform to Chinese values and customs. Antonio was addressed as an 'elder' – a title of respect in Chinese – by his friends, including Portia. In the court scene, Portia's beauty was emphasized by Lin even more strongly than by Shakespeare, in accordance with common expectations of a beautiful female protagonist in Chinese novels: when Portia is disguised as the apprentice lawyer Balthazar, 'people at the court saw the lawyer's beauty and were stunned'.[26]

In the Lambs' version, Shylock's attack on Christians in his infamous speech had been reduced to an attack addressed to Antonio. In Lin's translation Shylock addressed Antonio as 'Roman' rather than using the pronoun 'he', as the Lambs had done.

---

from outside are gradually worked into a pattern of a relatively stable kind distinctive of that group'. The conventionalization process involves four major principles: assimilation, simplification, retention and social constructiveness.

[24] See Tsui, 'Rewriting Shakespeare', 41–8.

[25] See James S. Shapiro, *Shakespeare and the Jews* (New York, 1996), for discussion of the complexity of the play.

[26] See Lin Shu, *Yinbian Yanyu*, transl. Wei Yi, 3–4.

[The Lambs' text] On this, Shylock thought within himself: 'If I can once catch him on the hip, I will feed fat the ancient grudge I bear him. He hates our Jewish nation; he lends out money gratis; and among the merchants he rails at me and my well-earned bargains, which he calls interest. Cursed be my tribe if I forgive him!'
[Lin's translation] 歇洛克自念, 彼羅馬人視吾猶太人遺黎直狗耳,今幸見貸, 非重窘之不足洩吾憤.
[My back translation] Shylock murmured, 'That Roman sees us Jews as cut-throat dogs. Now that he needs to borrow money, I must embarrass him heavily to vent my anger.'

The hatred is here felt between Romans (personified by Antonio) and Jews. That Lin could use 'Roman' to stand in for Christian suggests that Christians were considered to be not much different from Romans, both being a foreign – potentially imperialist – 'other' to the Chinese audience. It also suggests an exotic character to Shakespeare's tales, which facilitated their reception during the early twentieth century, when the spread of Western ideologies in China prompted an interest in European and American culture. Adaptations of Antonio's identity occur not only in Lin's work, but also in the translation by Bao Tianxiao, a contemporary of Lin, who changed Antonio's nationality to British.[27] In these versions of the play, the Christian-Jewish conflicts in *The Merchant of Venice* became conflicts between Romans or Britons and Jews. Religious conflicts no longer took centre stage in the play.

Similarly, Portia's 'mercy' speech in the trial scene was reduced in Lin's translation. In Lamb's version the speech closely resembled that of the full text. The five uses of the term 'mercy' in the original play are all retained in the Lambs' text. The Christian principle of 'mercy triumphing over justice' is evident from the modified speech:

[The Lambs' text] [Portia] spoke so sweetly of the noble quality of mercy as would have softened any heart but the unfeeling Shylock's, saying that it dropped as the gentle rain from heaven upon the place beneath; and how mercy was a double blessing, it blessed him that gave and him that received it; and how it became monarchs better than their crowns, being an attribute of God Himself; and that earthly power came nearest to God's in proportion as mercy tempered justice; and she

[27] See 包天笑 [Bao Tianxiao], 女律師, ['The Lawyeress'], 女學生. [*Female Student Periodical*], 1911.

> bade Shylock remember that as we all pray for mercy, that same prayer should teach us to show mercy.
> [Lin's translation] 顧為人須尚慈愛, 君不過欲得錢耳, 即索比多金為子者, 於法亦善, 何為詪詪爭此塊肉? "反復伸理至數百次, 歇洛克屹然不為動, 堅請如約.
> [My back translation] You should be kind. What you want is just money, if you ask for more money as interest the law is still obeyed. Why do you insist so much on taking this flesh? She pleaded several hundred times to Shylock, who was unmoved and insistent that the bond must be executed.

The Christian concept of 'mercy over justice', an important theme of this play, has been reduced to a simple utilitarian emphasis on economic terms. Mercy has important Christian overtones, where divine mercy refers to the forgiveness of one's sins through Christ's sacrifice (e.g. Eph. 2: 4–5). This is a reciprocal concept: just as God is merciful to people, so believers should exercise mercy towards others: 'Be merciful, just as your Father is merciful' (Luke 6: 36 NRSV). Mercy is used to temper justice:

> Do not judge, and you will not be judged; do not condemn, and you will not be condemned. Forgive, and you will be forgiven; give, and it will be given to you. A good measure, pressed down, shaken together, running over, will be put into your lap; for the measure you give will be the measure you get back. (Luke 6: 37 NRSV)

Portia, alluding to the Lord's Prayer, asked Shylock to show mercy regarding Antonio's trespasses, in accordance with the Sermon on the Mount: 'for if you others their trespasses, your heavenly Father will also forgive you' (Matt. 6: 14 NRSV). In its secularized meaning, mercy is 'the quality of care for another, willingness to make an effort, even at great sacrifice, to ease another's pain, readiness to forgive, eagerness to help'.[28] This quality of mercy was translated as *ci ai* (慈愛) by Lin, meaning kindness and benevolence. As such, mercy was not mentioned as an attribute of God, neither was the idea of justice

[28] There are three Hebrew roots that are frequently translated 'mercy', which carry the meanings of (1) the kind of love which is mutual and dependable; (2) the 'womb's love', i.e. the love of mother for a child; and (3) 'grace' or 'favour', i.e. a free gift. The New Testament builds on the Old Testament conceptualization, and three Greek roots underlie the English translation of 'mercy': mutuality, sympathy and the major weight of the physical feeling of mercy. For fuller discussion of the theology of mercy, see J. A. Komonchak, M. Collins and D. A. Lane, eds, *New Dictionary of Theology* (Dublin, 1987), 650–2.

translated. The biblical concept of 'mercy over justice' suffered from a shift to an emphasis on kindness and a utilitarian application.

Lin's translation contains just two references to 'Christian', compared with the six times the term appears in the Lambs' version of the play. The lines where 'Christian' is still mentioned in the Chinese translation have negative connotations. It is the Christians who are suspicious, and it is a Christian whom Shylock's daughter, Jessica has married against her father's will.

> [The Lambs' text] Shylock, hearing this debate, exclaimed: 'O Father Abraham, what suspicious people these Christians are!'
> [Lin's translation] 歇洛克聞二人言, 呼曰: '阿伯拉罕乎(此猶太始祖, 猶太人動輒呼之者)! 不圖基督教中人乃亦妄測乎人至此乎?'
> [My back translation] Shylock, hearing their conversations, exclaimed: 'O Father Abraham (this is an Israelite ancestor, an expression frequently used by Jews), what suspicious people these Christians are!'

> [The Lambs' text] For Antonio knew that the Jew had an only daughter who had lately married against his consent a young Christian named Lorenzo, a friend of Antonio's …
> [Lin's translation] 安東尼曰:吾無須此。彼猶太人有女嫁基督教人, 歇洛克怒不予以奩具 …
> [My back translation] Antonio: I don't need that [Shylock's estate]. The Jew has a daughter who has lately married a Christian. Shylock was so angry that he had disinherited her.

Apart from making fewer references to 'Christian', there is also a notable change in the plot. In Shakespeare's play and in the Lambs' adaptation, Antonio required Shylock to become a Christian as a condition of reducing his financial penalty. Lin removed this requirement, and left Shylock only having to surrender his wealth, giving half to the state and entrusting Antonio with the other half, to be passed to Jessica on her father's death. As will be discussed below, the requirement that Shylock must convert was also edited out of later Chinese productions, including the immensely popular Beijing production staged between 1980 and 1986 by director Zhang Qihong.

The sanitizing of the Christian content, however, can be contrasted with the retention of the Jewish heritage in Lin's text. The foreignness of this Shakespearean tale is introduced occasionally through transliteration or change of narrative style. Lin transliterated Daniel, the Old Testament prophet, as *Dan Nier* (但尼而) but with an addition, which reads: 'Daniel, a good Jewish judge' (但尼而者，猶太良有司也). The introduction of foreign concepts through supplementation is also seen in an earlier example, where a parenthesis is added after the translation of Shylock's expression 'O Father Abraham' which reads: 'this is a Jewish ancestor, an expression frequently used by Jews'. This addition serves to remind the Chinese audience of Abraham's – and with him Shylock's – Jewishness. Jews had a long history of settlement and acclimatization in China,[29] and Shylock's Jewish identity would make him a more familiar 'other' to the Chinese audience, closer to Chinese traditions than the unfamiliar British or Roman 'other' with their negative, imperialistic connotations.

The popular reception of Lin's version and the impression of Shakespeare as recounting fantasy stories of spirits can be attributed to his narrative style. Lin was the first to introduce changes in the narrative structure of Chinese literary works to suit a revised poetics. Before him, Chinese literary narratives began each chapter with a couplet relating to the chapter content. Lin changed this style by introducing the foreign custom of prose chapter headings, which was then followed by his contemporaries. He also had a distinctive elegant literary style known as *wenyan* (文言). This was a classical style used before the vernacular movement; it was peppered with colloquial terms, which may explain its popular reception. *Wenyan* was the predominant style among literati but, when punctuated with colloquial terms, Lin's semi-classical literary style appealed to both the intellectuals and the masses, who found the pure *wenyan* form difficult to understand. His style was commended by the renowned scholar Qian Zhongshu (錢鍾書; 1910–98) as a form of '*wenyan* that is more [for the] layman, casual and flexible'.[30] A number of well-known literati and dramatists were heavily influenced by Lin's works, such as Cao Yu, who hailed him as the Shakespeare of the Orient:

> One of my favourite Western playwrights is Shakespeare, and my fondness of Shakespeare's plays started from reading Lin Shu's *Tales* when I was [a] little boy. As soon as I was able to read the original English, I was eager to get hold of a Shakespeare play, because Lin's translation of Shakespeare's fantasy world was so fresh in my young mind.[31]

[29] See Sidney Shapiro, *Jews in Old China* (New York, 1984).

[30] 錢鍾書 [Qian Zhongshu], 林紓的翻譯 [*Lin Shu de Fanyi*; *Lin Shu's Translations*] (Beijing, 1981), 36–7.

[31] Ruru Li, *Shashibiya*, 16.

Similarly, Guo Moruo, a prominent dramatist and literary figure in the twentieth century, commented: 'I was unconsciously influenced by this book [*Tales*]. I read *The Tempest* and *Romeo and Juliet* in the original when I grew up, but it seems that Lin's way of telling these stories as fairy tales was more appealing'.[32] As noted above, Lin described the *Tales* as '*shenguaixiaoshuo* (神怪小說)', stories of spirits and gods, a genre familiar to Chinese readers. The titles of the plays are translated neatly into polysyllabic terms that render them poetic. For instance, *Merchant of Venice* was translated as *Rou Quan* (*Contract of the Flesh*); *Hamlet* was rendered as *Guizhao* (*The Ghost's Command*); *Macbeth* as *Guzheng* (*Witchy Omens*). All these Chinese titles highlight the supernatural aspect of the plays.

By using a narrative that emphasized spirits and gods, and a classical literary style, Lin successfully introduced Shakespeare, the foreign 'other', under a familiar Chinese guise. In this respect Lin was reflecting the approach to translation later identified by Lefevere. According to Lefevere, one of the three factors in determining the acceptance of texts is the dominant poetics, which may include genres and the relationship between literature and the social system. As such, some literature, in this case tales of spirits and gods, will be more readily accepted because these tales are operating within a system that recognizes it.[33]

Omissions and modifications are not infrequent in Lin's other translations. He was criticized by contemporaries for distorting the text. Qian Zhongshu, for instance, judged that Lin's 'misrepresentations' were the result of a 'willful act'.[34] However, Lin was not the only literatus in that period who transformed religious themes in literary works. Translators in the late nineteenth and early twentieth

[32] The translations of the quotations of Guo and Cao are taken from Ruru Li, *Shashibiya*, 16.

[33] André Lefevere, 'Why waste our Time on Rewrites? The Trouble with Interpretation and the Role of Rewriting in an Alternative Paradigm', in T. Hermans, ed., *The Manipulation of Literature: Studies in Literary Translation* (London and Sydney, 1995), 215–43, at 227.

[34] Qian Zhongshu, 'The Translations of Lin Shu', in Chan, ed. *Twentieth-Century Chinese Translation Theory*, 112. Lin's efforts at influencing reader response are evident not only in his rendering of religious material but also in the translator's prefaces to various works. According to Martha Cheung Pui-Yiu, Lin exercised 'knowledge management' in his translation of Christian content in *Uncle Tom's Cabin*: Martha Cheung Pui-Yiu, 'The Discourse of Occidentalism? Wei Yi and Lin Shu's Treatment of Religious Material in their Translation of *Uncle Tom's Cabin*', in David Pollard, ed., *Translation and Creation: Readings of Western Literature in Early Modern China, 1840–1918* (Amsterdam and Philadelphia, PA, 1998), 127–49.

centuries were often seen as agents for social change, and rewriting of the original text was not uncommon among them. Yan Fu (嚴復; 1853–1921), who translated T. H. Huxley's *Evolution and Ethics* in 1898, added extensive commentaries on the notions of 'natural selection' and 'survival of the fittest'. His translation exerted significant influence among reformists such as Liang Qichao (梁啟超; 1873–1929) who were advocating social progress and change. Liang used classical Chinese even in the midst of the vernacular movement in China in order to address an elite audience with the aim of persuading them of the quality of Western literature.[35]

Translation as a form of rewriting was a typical approach in early twentieth-century China, where remaining faithful to the source text was not considered the most important criterion. Rather, translation was used to introduce ideas from the West in order to enrich Chinese culture. The range of literary genres was broadened as a result to include political novels, educational novels, science fiction and detective stories, all of which had hitherto been unknown. In order to facilitate reception among Chinese readers, the text was sanitized or domesticated: place names and people's names were often 'sinicized'. Lawrence Wong suggested that this was done from necessity rather than choice: owing to the lack of knowledge about the West amongst readers, the translator often could not bridge the gap between the two cultures, even when they themselves fully understood the meaning of the source text.[36]

Conclusion

As Martha Cheung points out, omissions and changes reveal as much as they conceal.[37] The religious aspects of Lin's translation of Shakespeare's tale were adapted for a Chinese audience for several reasons. Firstly, forced religious conversion is a notion foreign to the Chinese culture, deeply influenced as it is by Taoism and Confucianism, which emphasize social harmony and order. Buddhism, a major religion in China, relies on a system of rewards and punishments that is established by karma, or cause-effect relationship, an understanding which

[35] Pollard, *Translation and Creation*, 15.

[36] Lawrence Wong, 重釋 '信達雅': 二十世紀中國翻譯研究 [*Chong shi 'xin da ya': er shi shi ji Zhongguo fan yi yan jiu; Reinterpreting Fidelity, Communicability and Elegance*] (Shanghai, 1999), 222.

[37] Cheung, 'Discourse of Occidentalism?', 131.

is inimical to forced conversion.[38] Secondly, concern for the work's reception by readers may have constrained Lin's rendition to what was socially acceptable. In another of his translations, that of *Uncle Tom's Cabin*, a novel that contains a number of religious references, he asked in the translator's preface for understanding from a putative 'enlightened and educated' audience for his rendering of religious material, clearly with the aim of showing that he had not been 'won over by teachings of Christianity'.[39]

The way in which Christianity was represented in these literary texts also reflected the degree of religious freedom that existed under the pressure of the Confucian-oriented regime. In the aftermath of the First Opium War between China and Britain, foreign missionaries, under the Treaties of Tianjin and the Sino-French Convention of Beijing, were permitted to live, own property and preach in the interior of China. Lin's translation was completed in a period during which, although Christianity was protected under these treaties, hostility towards churches amongst Confucians gradually increased. They sabotaged the reputation of Christians, attacked churches and regarded religions other than Confucianism as evil. These Confucians suggested that Christians should be registered and their apartments and clothes be marked. Officials risked losing their titles if they converted to Christianity.[40] In 1905, Huang Zicai (黄梓材) argued that officials and pupils should all worship in temples. The government did not allow religious freedom, and churches and missionaries were often attacked.[41] Under such political pressure, it is possible that self-censorship took place, as translating Western religious ideas might have provoked disquiet among audiences.[42] Lin's translation of *The Merchant of Venice* highlighted the play's exoticism – the demand for a pound of human flesh, a female lawyer, the suspense in the court – rather than the story's religious dimensions, helping to ensure a favourable reception of Shakespeare among his audience.

38 Roland Robertson, *The Sociological Interpretation of Religion* (New York, 1970), 87.

39 Cheung, 'Discourse of Occidentalism?', 140.

40 J. J. M. DeGroot, *Is there Religious Liberty in China?* (Berlin, 1902), 148–50.

41 黄梓材 [Huang Zicai], 政教分權論 ['Zhengjiaofenquanlun'; 'On the Separation of Church and State'], *Wanguogongbao* 196 (May 1905), 14–15.

42 For attitudes toward Christianity in early twentieth-century China, see Paul Cohen, *China and Christianity* (Cambridge, MA, 1963), 44–5; Jane Hunter, *The Gospel of Gentility: American Women Missionaries in Turn-of-the-Century China* (New Haven, CT, 1984).

Not only did Lin's rewriting succeed in achieving mass appeal, but his strategies with regard to Christian references have left an impact on Chinese productions of *The Merchant of Venice.* From the 1910s to the 1980s, there were no Christian references in most of the stage performances of the play. Moreover, Bao Tianxiao (包天笑; 1876–1973) a popular novelist, published *Woman Lawyer* in 1911, another adaptation of *Merchant of Venice*, which also edited out the play's Christian references whilst retaining Shylock's Jewish identity. In 1914, *Rou Quan*, another adaptation based on Lin's translation, was staged in Shanghai. It followed Lin's treatment of religious materials by omitting the Christian references while retaining Shylock's Jewishness. The afterlife of Lin's de-christianized translation of *The Merchant of Venice* [*Rou Quan*] and others of the Lambs' stories was an influential one. Well-known figures including Cao Yu and Guo Moruo were profoundly inspired by this popular series of Shakespeare tales. Indeed, a parallel to such omissions can be found in the 1980 production of the play by Zhang Qihong (張奇虹; b. 1930), which she attributed to her search for conformity with the tastes of the local audience, as 'the conflicts between Christianity and Judaism that took place hundreds of years back, as well as the racial conflicts, are relatively remote for the Chinese audience'.[43]

In the past, translators of the late Qing period have often been accused of being unfaithful to the source text and making 'mistakes' owing to their ignorance of Western languages and cultures. However, when seen in the context of Lefevere's theories about translation and rewriting, it can be argued that rather than making mistakes Lin's strategy was to manipulate the responses of the readers. His translations should be 'studied in conjunction with other forms of rewriting, and not on their own'.[44] Lefevere further reminds us that such displacement of religious discourse in Chinese culture may be related to the homogeneity and ethnocentricity of the Chinese culture. He considered that any culture that does not pay attention to the 'other', including Chinese culture, 'tends to see their own way of doing things as "naturally", the only way'; and when these cultures absorb elements from outside, 'they will, once again, naturalize

[43] Zhang Qihong, 'Zai Shijian He Tansuo Zhong De Jidian Tihui: Shitan Weinisi Shangren De Daoayan Chuli [Some Points in the Process of Implementation and Exploration – Discussions on the Directorship of *The Merchant of Venice*]', in Shashibiya Yanjiuhui, ed., *ShashibiyaYanjiu* [*Shakespeare Research*] (Hangzhou, 1983), 280–7.

[44] Lefevere, "Why waste our Time?', 237.

them without too many qualms and too many restrictions. When Chinese translates texts produced by others outside its boundaries, it translates these texts in order to replace them, pure and simple. The translations take the place of the originals.'[45] By interpreting the bard's plays and characters in a Chinese manner, Lin diminished their Christian identity, but in doing so he successfully introduced Shakespeare as a familiar 'other', giving him a popularity which has lasted until the present day.[46]

[45] André Lefevere, 'Chinese and Western Thinking on Translation', in Susan Bassnett and André Lefevere, eds, *Constructing Cultures: Essays on Literary Translation* (Clevedon, 1998), 12–24, at 14.

[46] See J. Wong, 'The Translatability of the Religious Dimension in Shakespeare from Page to Stage, from West to East – with Reference to The Merchant of Venice in Mainland China, Hong Kong and Taiwan' (PhD thesis, University of Glasgow, 2015), for fuller discussion of the translatability of religious works in China from the early twentieth century to the contemporary period.

'Playwrights Are Not Evangelists': Dorothy L. Sayers on Translating the Gospels into Drama

Margaret Wiedemann Hunt*
University of Nottingham

Dorothy L. Sayers's twelve-part wartime radio life of Christ The Man Born to be King *has been judged 'an astonishing and far-reaching innovation', not only because it used colloquial speech and because Jesus was a character voiced by an actor, but also because it brought the gospels into people's lives in a way that demanded an imaginative response. In spite of this, Sayers insisted that her purpose was not evangelization. Sayers's writing on theological aesthetics asserts that a work of art will only speak to its audience if the artist 'serves the work' rather than trying to preach. This article locates her thinking in the context of William Temple's sacramentalism and Jacques Maritain's neo-Thomism, suggesting that Temple's biblical exegesis was central to her approach in dramatizing the gospels. Finally an argument is made for Sayers's influence on mid-century thinking about the arts through her association with Bishop George Bell.*

Dorothy L. Sayers was already a household name when the first play in her twelve-part BBC radio life of Christ, *The Man Born to be King*, was broadcast in December 1941.[1] She had established a literary reputation with the detective novels featuring Lord Peter Wimsey, but in the 1930s she decided to dispose of Wimsey in marriage and move on to the dramatic genre, in which she had a lifelong interest.[2] Her first full-length play, *Busman's Honeymoon*, also published as a novel,[3] was intended as the final instalment in the Wimsey saga, and this play was in rehearsal when Sayers received an invitation to write the Canterbury Festival play for 1937. The festival had been established by George Bell in 1928 when he was dean of Canterbury, and it received

* 7 Lenton Rd, The Park, Nottingham, NG7 1DP. E-mail: hunt@wiedemann.fsnet.co.uk.

[1] Dorothy L. Sayers, *The Man Born to be King* (London, 1943).

[2] Sayers was one of the scriptwriters for a local pageant in 1908 when she was fifteen, and included a short satirical verse play, 'The Mocking of Christ', in her second published work, *Catholic Tales and Christian Songs* (Oxford, 1918).

[3] Dorothy L. Sayers, *Busman's Honeymoon* (London, 1937); Dorothy L. Sayers and M. St Clare Byrne, *Busman's Honeymoon: A Detective Comedy in Three Acts* (London, 1939).

Studies in Church History 53 (2017) 405–419
doi: 10.1017/stc.2016.24

a new impetus in 1935 with Eliot's *Murder in the Cathedral*.[4] Sayers's play *The Zeal of Thy House*[5] went on tour nationally and was so well received that she was commissioned to write for the festival again two years later; her second Canterbury play was *The Devil to Pay*,[6] a version of the Faust legend. In 1938 she had written a nativity play for BBC radio, and this was followed by the major commission of *The Man Born to be King*, broadcast in instalments from December 1941. After the war she wrote two other plays for festivals[7] and published translations of Dante's *Inferno* and *Purgatorio*,[8] leaving the *Paradiso* partly completed at her death in 1957.[9]

Sayers's mid-century fame derived not only from the novels but also from her career as a lay Christian apologist: in 1938 she wrote two articles of popular theology for *The Sunday Times*,[10] and from then on she was in constant demand as a lecturer and broadcaster. In 1941, the year of *The Man Born to be King*, she published a work of theological aesthetics, *The Mind of the Maker*, in which human creativity was compared by analogy with God's work in creation.[11] The book was one of the first in a series of 'Bridgeheads' contributing to a widespread debate in the churches about the possibility of post-war reconstruction on Christian principles,[12] and with this debate in mind Sayers also drafted a proposal, which circulated among leading churchmen, for an 'Oecumenical Penguin', an accessible book-length statement of the fundamentals of Christian doctrine common to the major denominations, of the sort produced by Penguin Books.[13]

[4] T. S. Eliot, *The Complete Poems and Plays* (London, 1969), 237–82.

[5] Dorothy L. Sayers, *The Zeal of Thy House* (London, 1937).

[6] Dorothy L. Sayers, *The Devil to Pay* (London, 1939).

[7] *The Just Vengeance*, for the 1946 Lichfield Festival and *The Emperor Constantine* for the 1951 Festival of Britain in Colchester. This was followed by a London run in 1952 of a shortened version of the latter, *Christ's Emperor*, at St Thomas's, Regent Street.

[8] Dorothy L. Sayers, transl., *The Divine Comedy*, 1: *Hell* (Harmondsworth, 1949); 2: *Purgatory* (Harmondsworth, 1955).

[9] Dorothy L. Sayers and Barbara Reynolds, transl., *The Divine Comedy*, 3: *Paradise* (Harmondsworth, 1962).

[10] Published as *The Greatest Drama Ever Staged* (London, 1938).

[11] Dorothy L. Sayers, *The Mind of the Maker* (London, 1941).

[12] Other contributions to the debate included G. K. A. Bell, *Christianity and World Order* (Harmondsworth, 1940); William Temple, *Christianity and Social Order* (London, 1942). J. S. Whale's *Christian Doctrine* (Cambridge, 1941) was admired by Sayers as a benchmark.

[13] London, LPL, Bell papers 208, fols 256–64, Dorothy L. Sayers, 'Memorandum for the possible Formulation of a Statement of Oecumenical Doctrine based on the Highest Common Factor of Consent among the Christian Churches', 1942.

Although the scheme eventually foundered,[14] it is important for a discussion of *The Man Born to be King* because Sayers saw both projects in terms of translation: 'the technical vocabulary of theology has become unintelligible', she complained.[15] Her correspondence about the Oecumenical Penguin with Oliver Quick, Regius Professor of Divinity at the University of Oxford, makes it clear that she wanted a team of theologians to create a draft that she would literally translate by reworking it in accessible language, while, perhaps sensing the likelihood of interdenominational battles, the theologians envisaged that Sayers would do the initial writing.[16] Giles Watson has argued that the proposed themes of the Penguin book closely mirrored the theology Sayers was at the same time expressing dramatically in *The Man Born to be King*, 'an epic portrayal of what it meant in real terms for God to become man'.[17]

The commission to write the radio life of Christ was initially held up by disagreements with the BBC, but when Sayers finally got to work she started by making her own translation of the gospels from the Greek. This article will discuss Sayers's approach to translating the gospels into language that spoke to a mid-twentieth-century audience. This includes her justification for the use of the imagination in creating fictional dialogue and situations. We shall also consider translation in the wider sense of translating theological ideas into dramatic action. Sayers's plays should be located in the context of thinking both about religious arts in the mid-twentieth century and about the role of the Churches in post-war reconstruction, and it can be argued that Sayers was influenced by William Temple not only in her sacramental view of all creative work but also in her approach to exegesis and the nature and boundaries of translation. Indeed, Sayers's own writing on theological aesthetics may have been more influential than

[14] Between 1938 and 1947 several comparable projects were discussed by members of the theological discussion group The Moot, and in January 1939 John Baillie's comment on the draft of a pamphlet presented by its convenor, J. H. Oldham, was that 'for general distribution it would need to be rewritten by someone, like, e.g. Dorothy Sayers': Keith Clements, ed., *The Moot Papers: Faith, Freedom and Society 1938–1944* (London, 2010), 148. In the event, Sayers was not involved, and the pamphlet was published by Oldham as *The Resurrection of Christendom* (London, 1940).

[15] Sayers, 'Memorandum', fol. 257.

[16] LPL, Bell papers 208, fols 254–5.

[17] Giles Watson, 'Catholicism in Anglican Culture and Theology: Responses to Crisis in England (1937–1949)' (PhD thesis, Australian National University, 1998), 221–70, at 248; cf. idem, 'Dorothy L. Sayers and the Oecumenical Penguin', *VII: An Anglo-American Literary Review* 14 (1997), 17–32.

is often acknowledged, and that there is scope for further research on this.

A recent discussion of Sayers's debt to Temple's social ethics can be found in Christine M. Fletcher's exploration of Sayers's theology of work, and in focusing on the plays I am adding another area of investigation to Fletcher's argument that Temple's importance has been underestimated in Sayers studies.[18] Sayers has received less attention as a theologian than as a novelist but studies of her theology include Laura K. Simmons's comprehensive overview,[19] studies by John Thurmer and Michael Hampel of Sayers's Trinitarian theological aesthetics,[20] and Suzanne Bray's edition of and commentary on a collection of wartime broadcasts.[21] There are chapters on Sayers's dramatic writing in Kenneth Pickering's book on the Canterbury Festival plays,[22] in Kenneth M. Wolfe's book on the Churches and the BBC,[23] and in studies by Catherine Kenney and by David Coomes.[24] Sayers's plays are also discussed in a number of literary biographies, notably those of Barbara Reynolds[25] and James Brabazon,[26] and in the twenty-first century there has been an increased emphasis on performance and reception, and their role as contributing factors to national wartime identity:[27] for example, Crystal Downing's argument that Sayers anticipates a postmodernist sensibility[28] and Bethany Wood's

[18] Christine M. Fletcher, *The Artist and the Trinity: Dorothy L. Sayers' Theology of Work* (Eugene, OR, 2013), 56–69. Fletcher's book includes a comprehensive bibliography.

[19] Laura K. Simmons, *Creed without Chaos: Exploring Theology in the Writings of Dorothy L. Sayers* (Grand Rapids, MI, 2005).

[20] John Thurmer, *A Detection of the Trinity* (Hurstpierpoint, 2008); Michael Hampel, 'Dorothy L. Sayers: Creative Mind and the Holy Trinity' (MA dissertation, University of Durham, 2002).

[21] Suzanne Bray, ed., *Dorothy L. Sayers: The Christ of the Creeds and other Broadcast Messages to the British People during World War II* (Hurstpierpoint, 2008).

[22] Kenneth Pickering, *Drama in the Cathedral*, rev. edn (Malvern, 2001), 219–25.

[23] Kenneth M. Wolfe, *The Churches and the British Broadcasting Corporation 1922 –1956: The Politics of Broadcast Religion* (London, 1984), 218–38.

[24] Catherine Kenney, *The Remarkable Case of Dorothy L. Sayers* (Kent, OH, 1981); David Coomes, *Dorothy L. Sayers: A Careless Rage for Life* (Oxford, 1992).

[25] Barbara Reynolds, *Dorothy L. Sayers: Her Life and Soul* (London, 1993), 298–306, 317–30.

[26] James Brabazon, *Dorothy L. Sayers: A Biography* (London, 1988), 191–205.

[27] Frances Clemson's PhD thesis, 'The Theology of Dorothy L. Sayers' Dramatic Works: Dramatic Performance and the "continual showing forth of God's act in history"' (Exeter, 2012), was not available at the time of writing.

[28] Crystal Downing, *Writing Performances: The Stages of Dorothy L. Sayers* (New York, 2004).

MA thesis on *The Man Born to be King*.[29] Reynolds's study of Sayers's debt to Dante and her approach to the translations is an invaluable resource, as are the two volumes of Sayers's own lectures on Dante.[30]

Sayers was a linguist who read French at Oxford, was fluent in German and had a good knowledge of the classical languages. In 1954 she opened a lecture with the words: 'The passion for verse-translation is a kind of congenital disease. I have suffered from it all my life.'[31] While she was translating Dante she lectured and wrote in detail about the translation process, exchanging long letters with Charles Williams and after his death with C. S. Lewis, and in these discussions she was aware that in translation 'something, somewhere, is always lost, modified, to some extent travestied in passing from one language to the other'.[32] But at the same time she believed in the power of metaphor to add new and legitimate theological meaning, as her discussion of the history of atonement imagery makes clear: 'The peculiar *Angst* of our own age … has taken a new form, predominantly morbid and medical. This has most interestingly produced an entirely new set of Atonement images, of which the central symbol is Christ the Healer.'[33] That Sayers herself applied the word 'translation' to the revitalization of theological concepts through modern reformulations is apparent in her 1955 article 'Playwrights Are Not Evangelists': 'The orthodox … should welcome, and not be alarmed by, the translation of ancient and hallowed formulae into modern speech and contemporary action.'[34] The previous year, in an extended personal apologia to John Wren-Lewis, Sayers had listed the things that 'my sort can safely do': 'We can, so far as our competence goes, help to disentangle the language-trouble by translating from one jargon into another'.[35] Fletcher applies this claim to Sayers's whole

[29] Bethany Wood, 'Incorporation of the Incarnation: Dorothy L. Sayers's *The Man Born to be King* and the Wartime BBC' (MA thesis, University of Wisconsin, Madison, 2008).

[30] Barbara Reynolds, *The Passionate Intellect* (Kent, OH, 1989); Dorothy L. Sayers, *Introductory Papers on Dante* (Eugene, OR, 2006; first publ. 1954); *Further Papers on Dante* (Eugene, OR, 2006; first publ. 1957).

[31] Dorothy L. Sayers, 'The Translation of Verse', in eadem, *The Poetry of Search and the Poetry of Statement* (London, 1963), 127–53, at 127.

[32] Dorothy L. Sayers, 'On Translating the *Divina Commedia*', ibid. 91–125, at 91.

[33] Dorothy L. Sayers, 'Poetry, Language and Ambiguity', ibid. 263–86, at 283.

[34] Dorothy L. Sayers, 'Playwrights Are Not Evangelists' (1955), reprinted in *VII: An Anglo-American Literary Review* 7 (1986), 109–13, at 111.

[35] Dorothy L. Sayers, *Letters Volume Four: 1951–1957: In the Midst of Life*, ed. Barbara Reynolds (Hurstpierpoint, 2000), 141–2.

'perception of her task and method'[36] and suggests that the 'framework for understanding' opened up by the movement between old and new versions is comparable with the process of embodying theology in drama.[37]

On receiving the commission for *The Man Born to be King* in February 1940, Sayers's first and most far-reaching innovation was her request to James Welch, the BBC's Director of Religious Broadcasting, that Jesus should be a character in the drama, something forbidden on the commercial stage but legally possible on radio.[38] Most religious plays of the time observed the convention of not presenting Jesus, whether or not they were for commercial performance; Henri Ghéon's *The Way of the Cross* (1938), for instance, told the story of the crucifixion through the reactions of observers.[39] Sayers argued to Welch that 'the device of indicating Christ's presence by a "voice off", or by a shaft of light, or a shadow, or what not, tends to suggest to people that He never was a real person at all'.[40] Persuading people that Jesus 'is the only God who has a date in history'[41] was a central task both of *The Man Born to be King* and of the Oecumenical Penguin, and the presentation of Christ by an actor was essential. Sayers added to Welch: 'It would not, of course, be suitable to give to Christ any speeches which do not appear in the Scriptures, but if all the other characters "talk Bible", the realism will be lost.'[42] The answer she proposed was modern dialogue that could 'lift itself, without too much of a jolt, into the language of prophecy'.[43] Although Sayers followed the gospels fairly closely for Jesus's words, she invented dialogue using a wide linguistic register for the other characters. To Welch she pointed out that the medieval mystery plays 'let Christ say anything that seemed natural and appropriate, but we could not go so far as this without

[36] Fletcher, *Artist*, xix.

[37] Ibid. 63.

[38] Radio was not subject to the Lord Chamberlain's jurisdiction, although the scripts were submitted for his approval as a matter of courtesy. He made no objection to the inclusion of Jesus, provided that there was no studio audience and that Jesus's longer speeches were based on his words as recorded in Scripture: James Welch, Foreword to Sayers, *Man Born*, 15.

[39] Henri Ghéon, *The Way of the Cross*, transl. Frank de Jonge, 2nd edn (London, 1952).

[40] Dorothy L. Sayers, *Letters Volume Two: 1937–1943: From Novelist to Playwright*, ed. Barbara Reynolds (Hurstpierpoint, 1997), 147.

[41] Sayers, *Man Born*, 20.

[42] Sayers, *Letters 2*, ed. Reynolds, 147.

[43] Sayers, *Man Born*, 24.

arousing roars of disapproval among the pious'.[44] Roars of disapproval followed nonetheless.

Sayers believed that the widespread use of the Authorized Version, which she ironically designated the 'sacred English original',[45] made it difficult for people to engage with the content of the gospel: to churchgoers it was over-familiar, while to those outside the Churches the 'ancient and hallowed formulae' were incomprehensible. An example she discussed with Welch concerned John the Baptist's reluctance to baptize Jesus (Matt. 3: 13–15). Jesus's reply to John in the Authorized Version is: 'Suffer it to be so now: for thus it becometh us to fulfil all righteousness.' Sayers 'struggled a good deal'[46] with this and her version in the play emerged as: 'Do as I ask you now, John. It's right to begin this way, like everyone else.'[47] The problematic word was probably the multivalent Greek *dikaiosunē*, rendered in the Vulgate as *iustitia*, and Sayers decided not to expound the significance of righteousness and justice but to limit Jesus's reply to an expression of obedience to God's will, focusing on the narrative rather than the theology. Sayers's choices in translation consistently reflected her view that 'the history and the theology of Christ are one thing: His life is theology in action',[48] so that if the dramatist made the story accessible the theology would inevitably emerge. In the different context of the Beatitudes she translated *dikaiosunē* as 'holiness': 'Happy are they who long for holiness as a man longs for food, for they shall enjoy God's plenty.'[49] The familiarity of the Beatitudes was a challenge to Sayers's powers of reformulation, and in '[h]appy are they who establish peace, for they share God's very nature' her skill in translation is seen at its best: the concept of 'sharing God's nature' as a rendering of the Authorized Version's 'they shall be called the children of God' adds a wider resonance to the literal meaning.[50]

Sayers was prepared for a battle over the decision to use modern speech. Asked for a preview in a press conference of 10 December 1941, she chose to read some dialogue in which the disciple Matthew accuses his colleague Philip of being 'had for a sucker' by

[44] Sayers, *Letters 2*, ed. Reynolds, 147.
[45] Ibid. 343.
[46] Ibid. 294.
[47] Sayers, *Man Born*, 77.
[48] Ibid. 20.
[49] Matt. 5: 6; ibid. 143.
[50] Matt. 5: 9; ibid.

a market trader.[51] The following day's *Daily Mail* headline was 'BBC Life of Christ Play in U.S. Slang', and a campaign of public protest in advance of the broadcasts ensued, including a question in parliament. The furore was described by Welch in his foreword to the published plays and has been discussed in a number of later studies.[52] Not only the colloquial speech but also what the Lord's Day Observance Society called the 'impersonation' of Christ were the main targets for attack.[53] While the objection to Americanisms was short-lived, coming as it did a matter of days before the USA entered the war, anxiety about colloquial language persisted even after reactions to the first broadcasts made it clear that the series would be a popular success. In March 1942 Sayers wrote to the Chairman of the BBC's Central Religious Advisory Committee (CRAC), Cyril Garbett, the archbishop-designate of York, anticipating objections to the crucifixion scenes: 'How can it honour God to make His enemies seem less cruel, less callous, less evil than they were?'[54] Garbett, at first full of misgivings, was won over, even though, according to Sayers, Welch himself 'hadn't ever realised that the crucifixion would have sounded like that'.[55] Welch, like Sayers, chose to make a virtue of the contemporary idiom, and before the first broadcast wrote in the *Radio Times*: 'It is partly this escape from the familiar language which helps us to see Christ as a real human being.'[56] For both Sayers and Welch the materiality of the Incarnation was central to Christian doctrine and the colloquial style had a theological purpose. The realism of *The Man Born to be King* invited the listener into a collaboration with the writer and actors in the visualization of a scene based on the life of someone who had really lived.

Sayers believed that the dramatic experience was itself one in which writer, actors and audience were united in a God-given and God-like creative activity. Her Trinitarian analogy for artistic creativity in *The Mind of the Maker* had its origins in the concluding speech of *The Zeal of Thy House* and was developed further in a letter to Fr Herbert Kelly of Kelham: God the Father is represented by the Idea,

[51] Ibid. 117.

[52] Welch, Foreword, ibid. 9–16; Wolfe, *Churches and the BBC*, 218–38; Reynolds, *Life and Soul*, 317–28; Coomes, *Careless Rage*, 11–25.

[53] The broadcasts were on Sundays.

[54] Sayers, *Letters 2*, ed. Reynolds, 357.

[55] Ibid. 373.

[56] James Welch, 'The Man Born to be King', *Radio Times*, 19 December 1941, 5.

or what Sayers called 'The Book as You Think It', God the Son is the Energy, or 'The Book as You Write It', and God the Holy Spirit is the Power, or 'The Book as They and You Read It'.[57] This analogy has two important implications. Firstly, the reader or audience is involved in the creation of meaning, and in *The Man Born to be King* the audience is encouraged to engage hermeneutically with the words of Jesus in a continuing process of reception and appropriation. Secondly, Sayers believed that the Trinitarian analogy expressed something real about the way creativity operates, and this locates her within a mid-century Catholic tradition influenced by the French neo-Thomist philosopher Jacques Maritain, who wrote that '[a]rtistic creation does not copy God's creation, but continues it.'[58] Maritain's aesthetics appealed to sacramentalists such as Temple and Sayers for whom God was present in every act of creativity, as also to English Roman Catholics such as Eric Gill and David Jones.

The Trinitarian analogy enabled Sayers to claim that a divine quality was inherent in all creative work, independently of the subject matter. This is important for *The Man Born to be King* because a theology of creation in which creative activity is in itself Godlike could be used to justify the imaginative approach for which she was criticized in some quarters. In expanding the gospel stories with fictional scenes and character motivation – Sayers invented one major character – she was translating not only the words but the spirit of the original. Sayers believed that if the artistic process is a reflection of the divine, it follows that divine truth will inevitably emerge from work created with integrity. Maritain wrote that '[t]he cathedral builders had no sort of thesis in mind … Their achievement revealed God's truth, but without *doing it on purpose*, and because it was not done on purpose.'[59] Sayers had used this idea in *The Zeal of Thy House*, where the Archangel Raphael says that in spite of the cathedral architect's irregular life, his 'unsleeping arches with perpetual voice / Proclaim in Heaven, to labour is to pray.'[60] For Sayers in *The Man Born to be King*, '[i]t is the business of the dramatist not to subordinate the drama to the theology, but to approach the job of truth-telling from his own end, and trust the theology to emerge undistorted from the dramatic

[57] Sayers, *Letters 2*, ed. Reynolds, 45.

[58] Jacques Maritain, *Art and Scholasticism with other Essays*, transl. J. F. Scanlan (London, 1947 edn), 49.

[59] Ibid. 52.

[60] Dorothy L Sayers, *Four Sacred Plays* (London, 1948), 38.

presentation of the story.'[61] In *The Mind of the Maker* Sayers accepted that a dogma can be skewed by the preoccupations of the artist, but argued that this always issues in an unconvincing scenario.[62]

Sayers found further support for her imaginative approach to the gospels in William Temple's *Readings in St John's Gospel*, which emphasizes that the gospel narrative is unavoidably filtered through the mind not only of the gospel writer but also of the contemporary exegete. 'What reaches us is never a certified record but always a personal impression. Thus our concern is always with the Christ of faith, not with some supposed different Jesus of history.'[63] This had a significant consequence for the structure of Sayers's translation of the gospel into drama. A person who believes that the Bible is to be read sacramentally, that is to say, looking for the spiritual truth within a narrative, will find it less important to ask questions concerning the literal historicity of the gospels. A medievalist by training, Sayers took for granted the fourfold method of exegesis in which the literal coexists with the allegorical, moral and anagogical; paradoxically, this allowed her to present at face value passages that might strain credulity where a literal reading is prioritized. Sayers dramatized the raising of Lazarus, for instance, as it is described in the gospel, but made it an affirmation of the central importance for salvation of Jesus's material existence and a symbol of the conflict between the will to life and the will to death that characterizes the struggle between Jesus and Judas.

In pursuit of a drama that both expressed incarnational theology and invited audience engagement, Sayers built her play round the uncertainties experienced by Jesus and Judas in attempting to 'read' each other. To Welch she wrote: 'what did the man imagine he was doing? … If we can get a coherent Judas we can probably get a coherent plot.'[64] Commentators from the Church Fathers onwards have found problems in a theology which predestines Judas to damnation, and Sayers's own writing consistently emphasized the reality of free will, starting with her first detective novel in which the murderer is the author of a book entitled *The Physiological Bases of the Conscience*.[65] In the Introduction to *The Man Born to be King* Sayers rejected the idea that

61 Sayers, *Man Born*, 20.

62 Sayers, 'Scalene Trinities', in eadem, *Mind*, 120–44.

63 William Temple, *Readings in St John's Gospel (First and Second Series)* (London, 1950), xvi. The two parts of this work were first published separately in 1939 and 1940.

64 Sayers, *Letters 2*, ed. Reynolds, 172–3.

65 Dorothy L. Sayers, *Whose Body?* (London, 1968 edn), 63.

Judas's betrayal was inevitable: 'to choose an obvious crook for the purpose of letting him damn himself would be the act of a devil'.[66] Sayers's insistence on Christ's humanity meant that for most of the story Jesus believes Judas might not betray him, and he offers forgiveness even after the betrayal; one of Sayers's early poems was a ballad in which Jesus accompanies Judas to the gates of Hades.[67] More recent writers such as Nikos Kazantzakis and Stephen Adly Guirgis have fictionalized Judas as a friend of Jesus complicit in God's plan of salvation,[68] but Sayers's characterization of Judas is a natural development from her detective novels, and Judas's choice of evil within the context of a human propensity to sin mediates the emergence of a theological point about forgiveness.[69] The prevailing doctrine of human perfectibility had been revealed by two world wars to be hollow, and a popular explication of the inescapability of sin was felt by contemporary theologians to be urgently necessary. Sayers intended to address this in the Oecumenical Penguin, but her dramatization of Judas's delusional denial was perhaps more effective. A Christ-centred redemption of human 'solidarity in guilt' was subsequently central to her Lichfield play of 1946.

In the early twentieth century Judas was frequently assumed to be a disappointed revolutionary, but Sayers gave the story a twist by reversing that. Jesus's gospel of the suffering servant appeals to Judas's sado-masochistic nature, and he betrays Jesus because he believes he is going to renounce suffering and instead engage in a military coup. For Sayers there was a contemporary political resonance: in her notes to actors she compared Judas's masochism with the 'religious elements' who encouraged France's armistice with Germany in 1940.[70] Her wartime listeners would readily supply their own examples of Judas's idealistic vanity, together with instances of Herod's venality

[66] Sayers, *Man Born*, 31.

[67] Dorothy L. Sayers, 'The Gates of Paradise', in *Op. 1* (16 March 2000; first publ. 1916), online at: <http://digital.library.upenn.edu/women/sayers/opi/dls-opi.html>, accessed 11 April 2012.

[68] Nikos Kazantzakis, *The Last Temptation of Christ* (Oxford, 1960); Stephen Adly Guirgis, *The Last Days of Judas Iscariot: A Play* (London, 2006).

[69] Barbara Reynolds, in a discussion of original sin, has drawn attention to a remark by Sayers in an unpublished letter: 'The Incarnation is the answer, and the only answer, to the whole problem of free will and suffering': Barbara Reynolds, 'The Just Vengeance', in *Proceedings of the 1996 Seminar*, ed. Christine R. Simpson (Hurstpierpoint, 1997), 5–16, at 12.

[70] Sayers, *Man Born*, 137.

and the power games of Pilate and Caiaphas: Sayers compared the latter with Hitler's bishops, adding: 'we have seen something of Caiaphas lately'.[71] When Judas tells Caiaphas that 'all my hopes, all my ideals, seemed incarnate in [Jesus]',[72] he is constructing his own Jesus rather than letting Jesus transform him, with clear implications for the audience's own reception of the gospel. In the final play the audience is left with the infinite opportunities of continuing the narrative implied in the words of the gospel writer: 'And there are also many other things which Jesus did, the which, if they should be written every one, I suppose that even the world itself could not contain the books that should be written.'[73] Like the gospel, Sayers's play leaves the audience at the beginning of a different story: the history of the Church. Playwrights need not be evangelists because the tools are there for audiences to evangelize themselves.

In leaving the story in the hands of the listeners Sayers united her translation of the gospel into drama with the gospel's own appeal to its readers, putting into practice her conviction that artistic integrity demands a refusal to preach:

> It was assumed by many pious persons who approved the project that my object in writing *The Man Born to be King* was 'to do good' … But that was in fact not my object at all, though it was quite properly the object of those who commissioned the plays in the first place. My object was to tell that story to the best of my ability, within the medium at my disposal – in short, to make as good a work of art as I could.[74]

Sayers's material was the Bible and creeds and she would present them in language that people could understand and make their own. A further opportunity to engage with theology through the translation process might be found, consciously or unconsciously, in the hermeneutical challenge of comparing the old familiar version with its contemporary reformulation. At the same time, Sayers was very clear about the limitations of any one version: 'just as no translator can escape from his own personality neither can he escape from the habit of mind of his own contemporaries'.[75] *The Man Born to be King*

[71] Ibid. 23.
[72] Ibid. 230.
[73] Ibid. 343 (John 21: 25 AV).
[74] Ibid. 20.
[75] Sayers, *Search and Statement*, 130.

spoke powerfully in 1941; that it is still sometimes produced in the twenty-first century might have surprised its author.

Sayers did not subscribe fully to the agenda of any religious group of her time, but she was sympathetic to Eric Gill's craft-guild movement inspired by Maritain and to Temple's social ethics. Temple acknowledged the influence of Maritain on his social thinking, and he gave Sayers's apologetics the seal of archiepiscopal approval by inviting her to speak at his Malvern Conference in 1941, the only woman to do so. The ensuing demands on her gifts as an apologist were so great that she attempted to make a partial withdrawal from public life. Sayers was also on the fringes of the Religious Drama Society, whose president was Bell (by now bishop of Chichester) and whose executive was chaired by T. S. Eliot's director, E. Martin Browne. Browne believed that during the performance of a play the actors and audience would share an event with sacramental significance: this was close to the neo-Thomist principle that art of integrity would spontaneously reveal God. Bell was slower than Sayers and Browne to preach a theology of the arts that refused to regard them as tools for evangelization, possibly because he thought that those churchgoers for whom the arts were suspect might be won over by an evangelistic argument. In 1941 Sayers wrote in apparent exasperation: 'It's not a matter of the Church "getting hold of the Arts", as the Bishop of Chichester seems to imagine. It's a matter of (a) presenting the artist with a brand of Christianity which can inform and inspire his secular work, and (b) recognising the autonomy of the artist's vocation as such.'[76]

In 1944 Bell called a conference in Chichester on 'The Church and the Artist'. The emphasis was on painting and sculpture, and those present included Duncan Grant, Henry Moore and Thomas Monnington, who had recently abandoned a Church House commission because he felt he was under too much theological constraint. Eliot was present, but it was Sayers whom Bell invited to introduce a session on 'The Problem of Translation (Communication)'. According to Bell's memorandum, Sayers argued that familiarity with dogma was an essential background to the artist's search for an accessible contemporary language within a church context, a point reinforced by Eliot in discussion: '[theology's] main function (almost

[76] Sayers, *Letters 2*, ed. Reynolds, 334.

unconscious) was negative: it kept the writer right'.[77] Sayers wrote to Bell before the conference that she wanted in her address to ask what the artist had the right to expect from the Church,[78] and her words are echoed in Bell's article for *The Listener* published the day before the conference began: 'I do not, I hope, forget the artist's own aesthetic approach and what he has a right to expect from the Church.'[79] In 1941 Sayers believed that Bell had failed fully to grasp the importance of an artist's freedom to serve the work, but he came to accept that it was counter-productive for the Church to put constraints on artists, and I suggest that Sayers's influence can be seen in this development. In 1953 Bell wrote: 'Unless the Church is to be sterile in the fostering of creative art, it must be prepared to trust its chosen artists to begin their work and carry it through to the end as the fulfilment of a trust.'[80]

Sayers claimed throughout her life that her personal religion stemmed from the intellect. When Temple offered her a Lambeth Doctorate in 1943,[81] Sayers replied:

> I should feel better about it if I were a more convincing kind of Christian. I am never quite sure whether I really am one, or whether I have only fallen in love with an intellectual pattern. And when one is able to handle language it is sometimes hard to know how far one is under the spell of one's own words.[82]

Her friend and biographer Barbara Reynolds has challenged Sayers's self-deprecation, quoting Kay Baxter on the subject of intellect and emotion in Sayers's religious writing: 'I suspect that by reading the Testament in Greek … and slogging many hours a day at compiling the four gospels into one continuous narrative … that she actually suffered a conversion … caught up in the astounding story she had to tell.'[83] According to Sayers's own theology, it hardly mattered whether she herself was a 'convincing Christian'; the work was itself a

[77] LPL, Bell papers 151, fols 190–6, at 193.
[78] Ibid., fol. 169.
[79] George Bell, 'Church and Artist', *The Listener*, 14 September 1944, 298.
[80] Quoted in Ronald C. D. Jasper, *George Bell, Bishop of Chichester* (Oxford, 1967), 133.
[81] For a full discussion of the episode of the Lambeth doctorate, see Peter Webster, 'Archbishop Temple's Offer of a Lambeth Degree to Dorothy L. Sayers', in Melanie Barber and Stephen Taylor, with Gabriel Sewell, eds, *From the Reformation to the Permissive Society*, CERS 18 (Woodbridge, 2010), 565–82.
[82] Sayers, *Letters 2*, ed. Reynolds, 429.
[83] Barbara Reynolds, *The Passionate Intellect* (Kent, OH, 1989), 213.

God-given and God-centred activity. When the architect William of Sens realises his mortal sin in *The Zeal of Thy House*, he says: 'Let me lie deep in hell … / But let my work, all that was good in me, / All that was God, stand up and live and grow.'[84] The translation at the centre of *The Man Born to be King* was similarly something that would communicate and proliferate beyond the writer's active engagement.

Sayers believed that 'playwrights are not evangelists' and that in telling the gospel story to the best of her ability, a task that involved constant reference to the Greek original, she was creating a medium in which the theology would emerge from the action and also be manifest in the nature of the work of art as a whole. When she took on the commission for *The Man Born to be King*, her considerable experience as a translator included a published version of *Tristan in Brittany*,[85] and she brought a scrupulous attention to what the Greek actually says to the creative task of embodying theology in action. Her wide reading provided the necessary scholarly foundation. A good deal has been written on Sayers's work as a translator of Dante, not least by Sayers herself, but the role of translation in *The Man Born to be King* is a subject which would benefit from further attention, as would the relationship of her plays to contemporary aesthetic theory and culture. *The Man Born to be King* reached over two million listeners, and Sayers's influence on religious arts from then until her death in 1957 was assured. In the words of Kenneth Wolfe:

> Dorothy L. Sayers had decided from the outset that this would not be 'church' speaking to nation, but Christian tradition speaking to each fireside listener. That had not quite happened to the gospel story ever before … That it was the most astonishing and far-reaching innovation in all religious broadcasting so far is beyond dispute.[86]

[84] Sayers, *Sacred Plays*, 99.
[85] Dorothy L. Sayers, transl., *Tristan in Brittany* (London, 1929).
[86] Wolfe, *Churches and the BBC*, 237–8.

Faith in the Hearing: Gospel Recordings and the World Mission of Joy Ridderhof (1903–84)

Darin D. Lenz*
Fresno Pacific University

In the mid-1930s Joy Ridderhof, a Quaker missionary, returned from her missionary work in Honduras a physically broken woman. In the process of recovering from malaria and the other illnesses that had not allowed her to remain on the mission field she began a new project that would transform how the gospel message was disseminated around the world. Ridderhof imagined the possibilities associated with proclaiming the message of Jesus through the use of phonograph records for Spanish listeners. The benefit of making sound recordings was quickly recognized by missionaries who were trying to reach largely illiterate and, in some cases, pre-literate populations. Ridderhof was soon asked to expand from her initial foray into Spanish language records to make recordings in other North American indigenous languages and, eventually, languages from around the world. This article analyses how Ridderhof managed this endeavour while embracing new media technologies to bring the sound of the gospel to the people of the world in their native tongue.

In December 1940 an article appeared in the *Pentecostal Holiness Advocate* that announced a new approach to evangelism in world missions. It noted that '[l]ast year a new movement was launched in Latin America; it was to get the Gospel to as many as possible of the 100,000,000 persons who might not hear it in any other way; and, so, while recording hymns and Gospel messages on phonographic plates is not a new idea, the task of making thousands of them, with beautifully rendered hymns and vital Christian messages[,] is a distinctly new idea in mission projects.' The article went on to explain: 'This work was first a vision and then an answered prayer to Joy Ridderhof, Friends' missionary in Honduras; and 800 buenas nuevas (Good News) records have already been shipped to sixteen Spanish-speaking countries and to some communities in the United States.'[1]

* 917 N. Chapel Hill Avenue, Clovis, CA 93611, USA. E-mail: darin.lenz@fresno.edu.

[1] This article first appeared in *Sunday School Times* and was reprinted as '"Buenas Nuevas" Records', *Pentecostal Holiness Advocate* 24/32 (5 December 1940), 6.

Studies in Church History 53 (2017) 420–434
doi: 10.1017/stc.2016.25

Ridderhof, an unmarried missionary from Los Angeles, had launched a new project in Protestant missions that attempted to make the gospel message available through sound recordings to peoples who 'had not yet been reached by Bible translators and linguists'.[2] Although her organization would not become widely known for its translation efforts in the same way as (for instance) Wycliffe Bible Translators, the work she founded was and remains innovative in recording the living voices of people who have yet to have the Bible translated into their dialect or language. In addition to this pioneering work, the organization also provides audio recordings of Christian messages for the majority of people in the world who are 'oral learners'.[3] This article will show how Ridderhof used new media technologies combined with an emphasis on vocal performance as strategic tools for making the gospel accessible to the people of the world. Essential to Ridderhof's goal for using new media technologies was capturing the emotional power of the gospel message in a form that could be played over and over with the hope of causing a response from those who heard the recordings. This conscious use of modern audio technology brings to light a performance element in Christian translation that has been neglected by scholars simply because they have focused on textual translations. Moreover, despite Ridderhof's international network of linguistic and technological collaborators, as well as the unprecedented global reach she achieved through the recordings, Ridderhof and Gospel Recordings, Inc., the organization she founded, have been largely ignored. The exception is the work of a few North American scholars of missions who have recounted her story.[4] This neglect points to the isolated position that Ridderhof has held in an ecclesiastical culture where men and printed texts matter more than women and oral culture. Orality is the disparaged domain of women, children, pre-literate societies and illiterate

[2] Ruth Tucker, 'Female Mission Strategists: A Historical and Contemporary Perspective', *Missiology* 15 (1987), 73–89, at 86; cf. eadem and Walter L. Liefeld, *Daughters of the Church: Women and Ministry from New Testament Times to the Present* (Grand Rapids, MI, 1987), 324.

[3] Global Recordings Network describes the work today as part of 'orality missions' intended to reach 'the 70% of the world who are oral learners, and to be a catalyst for the Church to see this need for a missions movement among the non-readers of the world': 'Celebrating 75 Years of God's Faithfulness!', *Sounds* (October 2014), 1; see also Patrick Johnstone, Jason Mandryk and Robyn Johnstone, *Operation World: 21st Century Edition*, 6th edn (Carlisle, 2001), 693, 736–7.

[4] Ruth Tucker, Harold Lindsell and J. Herbert Kane have all taken Ridderhof's innovative contribution to missions seriously: see their works referenced in nn. 2, 14 and 17.

people. Orality also denotes the boundary between cultural elites and the disenfranchised in the modern world. Ridderhof and Gospel Recordings have been neglected by scholars, not because their work was insignificant, but because it occurred at the periphery of the Church and sought to reach the marginalized peoples of the world.

In 1930, under the auspices of the Friends Missionary Board, Joy Ridderhof began her missionary work in Honduras.[5] By all accounts she found it rewarding, and she expected to remain as a missionary to Latin America indefinitely.[6] However, within seven years Ridderhof returned to the United States, her health broken by malaria and amoebic dysentery. During the long period of recovery she entertained the idea of using sound recordings to reach illiterate villagers. In Honduran villages, music from gramophones drew large crowds of listeners, who responded physically and emotionally to the sounds they heard. Ridderhof recognized the potential of such technology to help evangelization efforts throughout Latin America. Gramophone records were ideal vehicles for transmitting the Christian message to illiterate Spanish listeners because the records would enable her to continue to preach the gospel even when she could not be physically present. On 31 December 1938, when Ridderhof made a short gospel recording in Spanish, 'Buenas Nuevas' or Spanish Gospel Recordings was born.[7]

The new missionary organization slowly began to grow. Ridderhof acquired a rudimentary studio in Los Angeles and an entourage of co-workers to help her with the day-to-day tasks, which included everything from recording new languages to pressing records and shipping them to faraway places.[8] The benefit of making sound recordings was quickly realized by other missionaries who were trying to reach largely illiterate populations. Ridderhof was encouraged to branch out beyond Spanish recordings, a suggestion that was feasible in the culturally diverse and multilingual region of Southern California. In 1941, she started making recordings in Navajo and other Native American

5 '"Buenas Nuevas" Records'.

6 Joy Ridderhof, *Rejoice Always* (Temecula, CA, 2009), 14; cf. Phyllis Thompson, *Capturing Voices: The Story of Joy Ridderhof* (Sydney, 1978), 46.

7 Phyllis Thompson, *Faith by Hearing: The Story of Gospel Recordings* (Los Angeles, CA, 1993), 9; see also Stuart Mill, 'How it all Began', in Allan Starling, ed., *Amazing Stories from Global Recordings Network* (Temecula, CA, 2014), 11–14, at 12.

8 Temecula, CA, Global Recordings Network, Gospel Recordings Archive [hereafter: GRA], Joy Ridderhof, 'Newsletter', Spanish Gospel Recordings, February 1942.

languages spanning areas from Mexico to Alaska.[9] With the addition of new languages, Spanish Gospel Recordings was renamed Gospel Recordings, Inc., and became a global mission organization.

Initially the records were supposed to be a device to assist missionaries in their work among the illiterate, and Ridderhof only charged a minimal fee for each record in order to cover her costs. Later she decided to distribute the records free of charge since she wanted to make them available to as many people as possible. An early piece of promotional literature for Gospel Recordings explained:

> … the results of a 3½ minute record will never be known this side of eternity. But as the records reach the many harvest fields and are faithfully used by our co-workers, the missionaries and native Christians, many are the thrilling reports of prejudice overcome, barriers surmounted, closed doors opening, and souls being saved who otherwise might never have heard.[10]

Ridderhof was convinced that the records were one of the most effective tools for presenting the Christian message to illiterate people. Indeed, sound recordings were ideal for making readings of the Bible accessible to pre-literate peoples that organizations like Wycliffe Bible Translators might not reach for decades.[11] However, after the United States entered the Second World War in December 1941, rationing and other government restrictions presented problems for obtaining supplies and funding, or for undertaking the long-distance travel needed to make new recordings.[12] In spite of these challenges the organization continued to grow throughout the 1940s and into the 1950s.

Women engaged in missionary work have seldom attracted much attention from their contemporaries for their entrepreneurial leadership. Ridderhof, however, managed to draw some attention from those studying Christian missions for her innovative use of technology in Bible translation. By the 1950s, Gospel Recordings was

[9] Allan Starling, 'Milestones: What's in a Name?' in idem, ed., *Amazing Stories from Global Recordings Network* (Temecula, CA, 2014), 15–16, at 16; see also Thompson, *Faith by Hearing*, 26.

[10] Anon., *Just 3½ Minutes: The Picture Story of a Gospel Recording's Record* (Los Angeles, CA, n.d.), 15–16.

[11] Tucker has argued that this placed Ridderhof among a select group of women who were 'at the forefront of developing new mission specializations': Tucker, 'Female Mission Strategists', 86.

[12] Ridderhof, *Rejoice Always*, 52, 55.

becoming well known for making Christianity available to peoples who did not have access to either a full-time missionary or a pastor who was fluent in their native language.[13] Harold Lindsell, in his *Missionary Principles and Practice* (1955),[14] observed: 'A new method which has been listed under literary devices is that of gospel recordings. It resembles radio in some ways and in others it is more directly related to the literary. The length of time this means has been in operation is short, but the value of the work has amply demonstrated its worth as an agency for propagating the gospel.'[15] Lindsell considered the recordings part of the literary project that had made a distinctive mark on Protestant missionary activity since William Carey, when he explained that '[t]he enterprise is one of cooperative self-sacrifice springing out of a vision which has introduced a new element [i.e. gospel recordings] into missionary methods.'[16] Lindsell was not alone in observing the tremendous potential Gospel Recordings held for evangelism. J. Herbert Kane, a former missionary with the China Inland Mission and a missiologist, also recognized the significance of what Gospel Recordings was trying to accomplish when he wrote:

> The Word of God is of value only if it can be read and understood. … But the Gospel records, together with the little portable gramophones that go with them, find their way into the most inaccessible mountainous regions, and wherever they go they excite tremendous interest among, and are understood by, the illiterate. Moreover, they have one very great advantage – they can be played over and over again until the message really takes hold of the darkened hearts of these primitive people.[17]

Gospel Recordings' focus on 'primitive people' was an objective that Evangelicals and missionary organizations supported. However,

[13] Dorothy C. Haskin, 'Kitchen Kathedral: The Unexpected Way', *Pentecostal Evangel*, 28 June 1953, 13.

[14] Harold Lindsell designated Gospel Recordings a 'lesser' agency 'engaged in missionary activity' secondary to that of 'denominational mission boards and faith mission boards': *Missionary Principles and Practice* (Westwood, NJ, 1955), 98.

[15] Ibid. 250.

[16] Lindsell went on to note: 'Since the program does involve literary problems in the preparation of the thoughts to be conveyed by the language specialists, it is closely tied into this fourth general means [i.e. literary communication] for the promotion of the gospel of Christ': ibid. 251.

[17] J. Herbert Kane, *Faith, Mighty Faith* (New York, 1956), 73.

some were troubled that the organization was only giving a superficial presentation of the Christian message in the three-and-a-half-minute recordings, without ensuring that pre-literate and illiterate people came to a more complete understanding of Christian belief and practice.[18]

Originally, Ridderhof's method for recording the Bible, a song, or a story in another language simply involved recording herself, a local speaker of the language, or another missionary who knew the language. However, this approach to making the recordings was soon abandoned when Ridderhof became aware that those who listened to records came to know them so well they could repeat the stories and songs verbatim with, as a missionary observed, an 'American accent and all'.[19] This news troubled Ridderhof. She feared that the recordings that she and the other missionaries – none of whom were native speakers – made would change the pronunciation of native languages, potentially undermining the future of these languages. Pondering the effect of the recordings on the listeners, she decided henceforth to use native language speakers as narrators and vocalists on the recordings. With this simple change Ridderhof ensured that pronunciation remained rooted in the living language of the people addressed by the recording.

Written scripts were also developed to give structure to the recordings. The scripts were malleable texts adapted to particular cultural contexts and local idioms.[20] Although a full record of the editorial changes to all of the scripts over the years does not exist, there are early examples that give insight into the process of audio production. A script entitled, 'The Lost Sheep', written in 1949, recounts the parable told by Jesus in Luke 15: 3–7. The typewritten script has numerous handwritten editing marks and cues for sound effects so that a recording can be made in Ixil, a Mayan language spoken in Guatemala.[21] The script instructs the technician to 'start [the recording] with bleating of sheep' as the initial sound effect. The English text of the script, which, as described below, formed the basis for the

[18] Ruth A. Tucker, *Guardians of the Great Commission: The Story of Women in Modern Missions* (Grand Rapids, MI, 1988), 193.
[19] Thompson, *Capturing Voices*, 52; cf. Tucker, *Guardians*, 192.
[20] Anon., *Just 3½ Minutes*, 7–8.
[21] M. Paul Lewis, Gary F. Simons and Charles D. Fennig, eds, *Ethnologue: Languages of the World*, 18th edn (Dallas, TX, 2015), online at: <http://www.ethnologue.com/language/ixl>, accessed 15 July 2015.

Ixil recording, highlights the shepherd's love and sacrifice in protecting all his one hundred sheep, especially the one lost sheep, ending with the following invitation:

> The shepherd loved his sheep so much that he was willing to give his life for even one. Jesus is our good Shepherd. He gave His life for us. God's Word says, 'All we like sheep have gone astray; we have turned every one to his own way and the Lord hath laid on Him the iniquity of us all.' Jesus says, 'Come to Me and I will save you.' Will you answer? He is calling. Won't you answer: 'Here I am Lord Jesus. I want you to save me.' He will gladly come and take you in His [arms].[22]

This invitation to embrace Jesus as Saviour remained a distinguishing attribute of Gospel Recordings and was required in some form in all the recordings produced. The script instructed the audio engineer to end the recording with the 1885 hymn, 'Bring Them In', based on Matthew 18: 12. The words of the chorus, sung in Ixil, were to be changed from 'Bring them in, bring them in, Bring the wand'ring ones to Jesus' to 'Come to Him, Come to Him, Come to Jesus the Good Shepherd'.[23] A number of familiar sounds were suggested for the recording, including: 'sheep sounds and pipe', a wolf, a leopard and storm sounds. The audio engineer was given discretion to incorporate these sounds where needed in order to produce the most compelling record possible. These additional sound effects were a crucial component of the performance aspect of the recording. The length of the recording was to be approximately 3 minutes and 45 seconds.[24] Although authorship is not stated, many of the early scripts were written by Ridderhof and other recordists in the field, based on what they could quickly glean about the culture and the language from locals, missionaries, or those with some knowledge of the region.[25] Although the effectiveness of the records among indigenous audiences cannot be determined, the goal was to use a combination

[22] GRA, 'The Lost Sheep (10–49)'.
[23] Alexcenah Thomas and W. A. Ogden, 'Bring Them In', in Elisha A. Hoffman, ed., *Best Hymns* (Chicago, IL, 1894), no. 99.
[24] The modified version of this script has been used to record a similar story in eighty-five different languages over the past sixty years. 'The Lost Sheep', GRN Scripts in English, online at: <http://globalrecordings.net/en/script/469>, accessed 14 July 2015.
[25] Sanna Morrison Barlow, *Mountains Singing: The Story of Gospel Recordings in the Philippines* (Chicago, IL, 1952), 317; cf. *Just 3½ Minutes*, 7–8.

of the local language with sounds, music and cultural references that would allow the recording to reach across the cultural divide.[26]

The process for making the recordings was slow, requiring many hours of preparation and recording time to produce a single three-and-a-half-minute story. Often the primary language of the field recordist was English, and the recordist or recording team relied on multilingual locals to pass the story along from one person to the next person until they reached the target language speaker.[27] The entire procedure was reliant on those who knew an intermediary or 'trade' language and could connect the links in the linguistic chain. The script was the anchor that kept the recording session from drifting away from the intended purpose. However, nothing, not even the script, could stand in the way of the production goal, which involved creating an entertaining and accessible story that could be easily remembered and highlighted a Bible story for listeners. To ensure that the content of the recording was accurate, the recording would be played back to someone who spoke the target language who then recounted what they had heard to another 'trade' language speaker, who in turn relayed the message back to the field recordist.[28] Although not always entirely successful, this laborious process tried to ensure that the target language speaker had properly communicated the essence of the story told to them through the chain that began with the reading of the short script.[29]

Ridderhof was aware that this process was not always reliable. In the Philippines, she had doubts about the transmission of content from one trade language speaker through the human chain to a target language. Her recording partner on the trip, Ann Sherwood, explained to friends in the United States that Joy was 'writing a small Mangyou [*sic*] vocabulary so we can more easily check whether the interpreter is getting our idea or not'.[30] The challenge of passing along an accurate interpretation was considerable and the result was constantly being scrutinized. For instance, in a letter to Gospel Recordings staff in Los Angeles, Ridderhof described how recordings were

[26] Mill, 'How it all Began', 12–13.

[27] GRA, Ann Sherwood to 'Dearly Beloved', 16 June 1950; Barlow, *Mountains Singing*, 168.

[28] The field recordist had the challenge of trying to persuade individuals who knew the target tribal language and a second language such as English, but were not necessarily Christians, to participate in the recording venture: Barlow, *Mountains Singing*, 168–71; cf. GRA, Joy Ridderhof to Muriel Hogg, 3 October 1955.

[29] Kane, *Faith, Mighty Faith*, 72–3; cf. Thompson, *Faith By Hearing*, 41.

[30] GRA, Ann Sherwood to 'My Dear, Darling Family & People', 17 June 1950.

being made in the 'Bontoc, Benguet, and Kangkanai languages' with the assistance of locals: 'the natives that are working on the records are translating the songs themselves, and some of them know how to play the guitar, and sing well. They sing solos, duets, and trios, and do so well in the speaking'.[31] Ridderhof needed indigenous language speakers to do the work that she and her recordists could not do themselves and this required trusting local contributors to communicate the message accurately.

In addition to trying to ensure the accuracy of the content, Ridderhof was deeply invested in the performance quality of the recording. In the Philippines, she noted that the locals 'put so much expression into it. Our young people just don't hold a candle to them, in the main. They are so talented, and so full of dramatic ability in expressing themselves'.[32] Her appreciation of the dramatic abilities of native speakers was extremely important to her vision of the effectiveness of sound recordings. For Ridderhof the translation process involved more than simply telling a story; translation was also entwined with the subjective qualities associated with vocal performance, which layered the recordings with educational, cultural and spiritual significance. For example, in addition to their evangelistic purpose, she was aware that the records could also have a pedagogical function. In a letter to her staff in Los Angeles, Ridderhof made clear that she wanted records intended for circulation in Alaska, Philippines, India, Jamaica and Japan to include also a minute to a minute-and-a-half recording in 'clear ABC English' of male voices for listeners to perfect their English-speaking skills. She directed her staff to make sure that they included 'very clear singing, [and a] good message. One with some pretty choruses & words in between each would be good. Or a song tapering into a chorus at the close is Excellent, gives them something to learn & a good message.'[33] What is noteworthy in Ridderhof's directions to her staff was her emphasis on performance, sound mixing and the use of male voices. She encouraged them to enlist men for solos, duos, trios and even 'mixed' quartets, but she wanted to make sure that the speakers were committed Christians who could convey the truth of their Christian faith through the sound and emotion of their voices.

[31] GRA, Joy Ridderhof to Gospel Recordings staff, January 1950 (?).
[32] Ibid.
[33] GRA, Joy Ridderhof to Gospel Recordings staff, 3 July 1950.

As a product of a North American Evangelical culture that often marginalized women, Ridderhof was mindful of the social mores in patriarchal societies that rejected the voices of women as legitimate communicators to men. Aware of this reality, she adapted to the gendered norms of particular cultural contexts in order to accomplish her mission. Her emphasis on capturing performance, whether by men or women, pushed Gospel Recordings constantly towards improving the quality of the sound recordings while remaining sensitive to cultural norms. By adapting to cultural expectations about gender in various societies, Gospel Recordings transformed the translation process from simply finding the correct words for the translation of biblical stories from one language to another into a process for seeking cultural legitimacy. Ridderhof recognized that particular voices, usually male, held authority in a given cultural context and infused the gospel message with credibility. This recognition of human authority corresponded to an awareness of divine power. Consequently, Ridderhof was not satisfied with a recording unless there was an element of spiritual vitality revealed in the recorded performance. The living gospel was more than mere words, but was a powerful truth conveyed by the voices who spoke about the life-giving message of the gospel. For her, speaking about God's work in the world, especially by Christians, should arouse a response from those who narrated the Bible stories and sang the hymns as well as from those who listened to the recordings.

Attempting to create culturally legitimate, accurate translations in emotion-provoking performances was difficult. Jane Osgood, an American Baptist missionary working in Orissa, India, was amazed by how painstaking the process was to make useable recordings:

> We remember that it took Miss [Elvie] Nicoll several days to complete a half dozen records. Over and over again the three Santali pastors, helping in this venture, sang their songs, gave their brief gospel messages, prayed, only to do it all over again when the timing wasn't exactly right, or something was recorded that shouldn't have been, or perhaps it wasn't quite clear enough for use.[34]

Ridderhof, Nicoll and her cadre of field recordists encountered endless challenges in the Philippines, Africa, India, Australia and other locations in the Asian Pacific Rim as they tried to determine not only

[34] Jane G. Osgood, 'That All Might Hear', *Tidings*, no. 3 (1962), 22.

how best to work with native language speakers,[35] but also how to get the recording equipment to work in the most challenging environments imaginable.[36] Field recordists hauled heavy recording equipment into some of the most remote villages on earth hoping to record the gospel for isolated linguistic groups, and failures with recording devices in sweltering heat or rain-soaked jungles caused constant disruption to their work.[37]

In an effort to overcome the effects of the environment on their equipment, and with the assistance of Livingston Hogg, an English electronics distributor, by the late 1950s Gospel Recordings was able to acquire the expensive but lightweight Swiss-built Nagra III reel-to-reel recorder, the cutting-edge portable sound recorder of the period.[38] These recorders were crucial for recording hundreds of languages in the most remote regions of the world.[39] Remarkably, Ridderhof and her co-workers also solved another problem associated with hearing the recordings in remote areas: what to do when there was no modern utility infrastructure to power a record player that required an electrical supply? Gospel Recordings helped to develop new media technologies, many of which involved the development of an innovative, inexpensive, hand-cranked record player 'that even a child can use without breaking it'.[40] The playback devices they developed were often improvements on the design and durability of the gramophone. In 1964 they made their most remarkable playback innovation: a cardboard hand-spun record player known as Card-Talk, which was cheap, easy to make, and worked in even the most remote parts of the earth. Gospel Recordings' ground-breaking developments in playback technology originated out of a collaborative effort of staff from around the world, and the results remain noteworthy in the history of media technology.[41]

[35] GRA, Joy Ridderhof to Muriel Hogg, 6 September 1955; cf. Thompson, *Faith By Hearing*, 57.

[36] Ridderhof's letters from recording trips in the 1950s constantly bemoan the technical problems caused in the field when the recording equipment failed to work: see, e.g., GRA, Joy Ridderhof to 'Ed, Ray, and Stuart', 20 October 1955.

[37] Barlow, *Mountains Singing*, 157.

[38] Allan Starling, 'Milestones: The Nagra Story', in idem, ed., *Amazing Stories*, 60–2.

[39] By 1959 Gospel Recordings, Inc., twenty years after its founding, could report it had recorded 1,904 languages and produced some 'two million gospel phonograph records' in its record plant: 'The Present World', *Pentecostal Evangel*, 9 August 1959, 10.

[40] Quoted in Jacob Smith, *Eco-Sonic Media* (Berkeley, CA, 2015), 149.

[41] Smith, *Eco-Sonic Media*, 145–54.

Faced with the overwhelming challenge of recording the world's living languages, in the early 1950s Gospel Recordings staff hoped that missionaries working with Wycliffe Bible Translators would assist them by collaborating in joint mission ventures. Ann Sherwood, reflecting on the constant effort by Ridderhof and other Gospel Recordings staff to woo 'Wycliffites' into recording for them, noted:

> … it will be a rare bird that will take a recorder out with him, with all we can say. And when he does, he will be as busy as the others who had hoped, and it will be years before we get a thing. That is why we want to send couples out ourselves, but that, too, is a major operation, as even we veterans will testify![42]

The challenge of recruiting field recordists observed by Sherwood reflected persistent problems faced by Gospel Recordings, affecting everything from technical and production issues to raising funds to support the work. The lack of financial resources was a constant problem.[43] Even the organization's status as a faith mission was questioned by some staff.[44] Ridderhof, however, remained resolute in her devotion to this method of missionary funding, encouraging her co-workers to embrace a piety that focused on intense, daily prayer and the expectation that God's miraculous intervention would enable them to meet their material and financial needs.[45]

Ridderhof and her co-workers (primarily women in the early years of the work)[46] represented a shift in missionary work that had taken

[42] GRA, Ann Sherwood to Jeanie Gibson, 21 May 1950.

[43] GRA, Joy Ridderhof to Muriel Hogg, undated [1950s]. Speaking at a service in the student chapel at George Fox College in Newberg, Oregon, in January 1956, Ridderhof explained how she had begun her work 'with just a vision and $15 capital', and that she was only 'supported by faith': 'Joy Ridderhof urges "Supernatural" Living,' *The Crescent* 77/7 (1 February 1965): 1; cf. Thompson, *Faith by Hearing*, 10.

[44] In one example Ridderhof described a co-worker who had returned from the field and raised issues about the lack of funds and the faith mission commitment of the organization. Ridderhof complained to Muriel Hogg: '[he] has such a negative attitude, wants to make dramatic changes in our policies against our faith principles, talks to the board and tries to influence them out of meetings.' A blue ball-point pen has been used to redact the words 'dramatic' and 'against our faith principles' from the letter. Ridderhof often scribbled handwritten notes on her typewritten letters, but there is no certainty as to who attempted to remove the words from this one: GRA, Joy Ridderhof to Muriel Hogg, 19 August 1955.

[45] Robert C. McQuilkin, Foreword to Barlow, *Mountains Singing*, 7.

[46] Thompson, *Faith by Hearing*, 19–21.

place in North America after the First World War.[47] They were part of an impulse amongst devout Evangelical women who embraced a radical piety and possessed a fervent zeal to reach the world with the gospel message. Many of these women were most interested in direct evangelism through preaching but found that reality untenable in the patriarchal hierarchies of the Church and of mission agencies.[48] However, Ridderhof also explicitly sought the assistance of men in her project, not only for their voices, but also and especially in relation to the technical issues she faced. Given the cultural expectations about gender in many societies around the world and the harsh physical realities associated with being a field recordist, Ridderhof recognized that men in certain locations were often best suited to carry out the recording work. This did not imply that men were superior

[47] Although American Evangelicals were divided in their views about the role of women in church leadership at the end of the nineteenth and the beginning of the twentieth centuries, women were encouraged to minister to women or serve overseas as missionaries. Mission historian Dana Robert notes: 'with the passage of woman's right to vote, the advent of Freudianism, and the seeming liberation of American women to social equality with men, an optimistic younger generation of women began to question gender-based thinking. The very things that had made the woman's missionary movement attractive to mothers and grandmothers – the separate women's societies, the narrow focus on woman's special obligations to work for other women, "Woman's Work for Woman" – began to seem old-fashioned': Dana L. Robert, *American Women in Mission: A Social History of their Thought and Practice* (Macon, GA, 1997), 313. Between the First World War and the 1960s the place of women in American life changed dramatically. Yet, as women gained status in American society, especially in the workplace, their place in official church leadership diminished among Evangelicals, especially after 1940. The areas where women were able to make substantial progress in leadership over the course of the twentieth century were in lay ministries with educational, medical, social and evangelistic emphases. Ridderhof's service under the auspices of the female-friendly Friends' Mission Board, her family's background in the Swedish Baptist Church, and her Bible college studies at Columbia Bible School in South Carolina reflect an immersion in the social and theological milieu of American Evangelicalism that embraced female piety and activism, though not necessarily female power over men. See, for example, Margaret Lamberts Bendroth, *Fundamentalism and Gender, 1875 to the Present* (New Haven, CT, 1993), 14–30; Letha Dawson Scanzoni and Susan Setta, 'Women in Evangelical, Holiness, and Pentecostal Traditions', in Rosemary Radford Ruether and Rosemary Skinner Keller, eds, *Women and Religion in America, 3: 1900–1968* (San Francisco, CA, 1986), 223–65, at 223–34; Rosemary Skinner Keller, 'Patterns of Laywomen's Leadership in Twentieth-Century Protestantism', ibid. 266–309, at 266–7; 'Ridderhof, N. L.', in W. Francis Gates, ed., *Who's Who in Music in California* (Los Angeles, CA, 1920), 115; Joy Ridderhof, *Rejoice Always: Devotions with Joy Ridderhof* (Temecula, CA, 2009), 15.

[48] Robert, *American Women in Mission*, 254.

to women but that they were necessary for the work she hoped to accomplish.[49]

Officially established in 1939, the year Europe plunged into war for the second time in the twentieth century, Gospel Recordings echoed a bygone era of female faith missions but went one step further and created a technological space that freed and empowered both women and men, depending on the cultural context, to play an important role in reaching the world for Christ.[50] The mission soon expanded into a global effort with offices located in nations around the world.[51] However, as important as the international expansion of the work was, Ridderhof recognized that she and her co-workers must step aside to allow the indigenous people whom they were trying to reach to retell the Christian story in culturally relevant terms using their own voices. In Lamin Sanneh's now classic work, *Translating the Message*, he argues: 'There is a radical pluralism implied in vernacular translation wherein all languages and cultures are, in principle, equal in expressing the word of God.'[52] Translating the Bible into the vernacular language of a people affirmed indigenous cultures and languages both as sacred and as equal to those in more technologically and culturally dominant Western societies. Ridderhof and her team of field recordists, technicians and production staff brought technological equality to indigenous languages through their audio recording project. Gospel Recordings consciously sought to preserve indigenous languages and cultures through the living words that preliterate and illiterate people uttered in their everyday lives. The voices they heard on the recordings were like their own, attuned to the nuances of their language and culture. The recordings also gave them a new way to understand the world through the cornucopia of sound that engaged the imagination and a Bible-based story that encouraged a response. Like the resurrected Jesus spoken about in the recorded stories, the new audio technology may have made human voices, songs and various sounds seem eternal. Later critics

[49] Thompson, *Faith by Hearing*, 24; cf. eadem, *Capturing Voices*, 110–13.

[50] Ridderhof also followed in the path of late nineteenth-century Evangelical faith missions that had proved so beneficial to women who lacked formal education, came from 'modest backgrounds', yet still desired to serve as missionaries: Robert, *American Women in Mission*, 253.

[51] J. Herbert Kane, *Understanding Christian Missions*, 4th edn (Grand Rapids, MI, 1986), 171.

[52] Lamin Sanneh, *Translating the Message: The Missionary Impact on Culture* (Maryknoll, NY, 1989), 208.

would question whether the technological exchange created by audio playback devices converted listeners to a coveting of technology as much as to Christianity. They also pointedly asked whether the use of technology for mission was not an exploitation of vulnerable people.[53] Ridderhof, however, possessed an unusually optimistic faith in the power of hearing the living word, and was confident that once a person heard gospel recordings they would want to accept Jesus as Saviour. For Ridderhof, capturing stirring, vernacular translations of the gospel in the recordings, and the use and development of new audio technologies, were strategic tools for world evangelism – the ultimate mission.

[53] Virginia Heffernan, reflecting on the role of technology in the modern world, has observed: 'I thought of the Global Recordings Network, an evangelical organization in Los Angeles with 70 years of experience introducing technology to underserved populations. In the process of recording Bible stories in every known language, Global Recordings has created a variety of hand-cranked machines, which it delivers to remote places, where Christian parables can be played without a power source. In "Tailenders", a 2005 documentary about the organization, the alien-looking contraptions can be seen making converts. But not necessarily to Christianity. Rather, people who hear the recordings come to desire, somehow, simply to share in the supernaturalism of disembodied audio. Whoever controls these animistic effects, it seems, must be worth listening to. When missionaries approach, these people are vulnerable, having just witnessed a small miracle': Virginia Heffernan, 'Children's Crusade', *New York Times Magazine*, 27 January 2008, online at: <http://www.nytimes.com/2008/01/27/magazine/27wwln-medium-t.html?pagewanted=2>, accessed 7 July 2014; cf. John L. Jackson Jr, 'The Tailenders', *Journal of Linguistic Anthropology* 17 (2007), 287–8.

Speaking to God in Australia: Donald Robinson and the Writing of *An Australian Prayer Book* (1978)

R. J. W. Shiner*
Shenton Park, Australia

Archbishop Donald Robinson (b. 1922) had a distinguished career as a New Testament scholar and senior churchman. As a New Testament scholar, he emphasized the linguistic and cultural distance between what Barth called 'the strange new world of the Bible' and our own. However, as a senior churchman, Robinson was required to traverse the distance between the Bible and twentieth-century Australians. Through his episcopal leadership, and notably through his work in producing An Australian Prayer Book *(1978), Robinson faced the challenge of speaking to Australians about God, and finding the words by which Australians might speak to God. This article will explore the ways in which a prominent scholar and churchman grappled with the linguistic and cultural challenges of speaking about God and to God in contemporary Australia, understood against the background of the crisis of (ir)relevance faced by Australian churches in the decline of the 1960s and 1970s.*

Archbishop Donald Robinson (b. 1922) had a distinguished career as a New Testament scholar and senior Australian churchman.[1] He emphasized the linguistic and cultural distance between the world of the New Testament and our own, resulting in what were often daring and original claims about the New Testament and early Christianity. He was fond of telling students he could take them to the moon (exegetically speaking), but he could not promise to bring them home again.[2] However, as a senior churchman and public figure, Robinson was required precisely to bring the Christian scriptures 'home' to contemporary Australians. Through his critical work in producing *An Australian Prayer Book* (1978) and through his leadership roles,

* 9 Rankin Rd, Shenton Park, Western Australia, Australia 6008. E-mail: rory.shiner@gmail.com.

[1] Vice-principal of Moore College 1959–72, bishop of Parramatta 1973–81, archbishop of Sydney 1982–93.

[2] D. W. B. Robinson, 'Origins and Unresolved Tensions', in R. J. Gibson, ed., *Interpreting God's Plan: Biblical Theology and the Pastor* (Adelaide, 1997), 1–17, at 6.

Studies in Church History 53 (2017) 435–447
doi: 10.1017/stc.2016.26

Robinson faced the challenge of speaking to Australians about God, and finding the words by which Australians might speak to God.

This work of translating the faith in Australia occurred during a religious crisis for the churches precipitated by rapid cultural changes across the Western world in the 1960s.[3] Christian leaders scrambled to diagnose why Australians were now disengaged with the churches and their message, and to offer solutions. Indeed, the public 'secularizing' discourse of Christian leaders in Australia, as Sam Brewitt-Taylor has argued in the British case, may itself have been a contributor to the process.[4] In Australia the crisis was augmented by a national debate on Australian identity in a context where (to use the trifecta from Hugh Chilton's recent study) 'British', 'White' and 'Christian' were increasingly abandoned as plausible sources of identity.[5]

Much of the diagnostic work of Christian leaders centred around a perceived failure to translate Christian Scripture, liturgy, thought and praxis into language contemporary Australians could understand and to which they could relate. Australian Christians, it was argued, had failed to give people a language in which they could speak authentically about God and to God, and were being punished for their failure to translate with shrinking churches.

It is easy to cast an Evangelical and conservative figure like Robinson as a non-combatant in the battle for relevance of this era. However, his leadership and liturgical work represented, in their own way, a creative response to this cultural crisis. Though Robinson's catholic

[3] See Callum G. Brown, 'What was the Religious Crisis of the 1960s?', *JRH* 34 (2010), 468–479. On the specific impact in Australia, see David Hilliard, 'The Religious Crisis of the 1960s: The Experience of the Australian Churches', *JRH* 21 (1997), 209–27. Hilliard dates the '1960s' in Australia as beginning either with the visit of the Beatles in 1964 or the committing of troops to Vietnam in 1965; Tom Frame sees a period of 'growing disinterest' in religion from 1966; Chilton talks of the 'long 1960s' extending well into the 1970s: see, respectively, Hilliard, 'Religious Crisis', 210; Tom Frame, *Losing My Religion: Unbelief in Australia* (Sydney, 2009) Kindle edn, ch. 4; Hugh Chilton, 'Evangelicals and the End of Christian Australia: Nation and Religion in the Public Square 1959–1979' (PhD thesis, University of Sydney, 2014), 84.

[4] See Sam Brewitt-Taylor, 'The Invention of a "Secular Society?" Christianity and the Sudden Appearance of Secularization Discourses in the British National Media, 1961–4', *Twentieth-Century British History* 24 (2013), 327–50. Chilton applies this analysis to Australia, arguing that the public statements by Christian leaders about 'secularization' and 'crisis' in this era were 'somewhat overstated' and 'became something of a self-fulfilling prophecy': Chilton, 'Evangelicals and the End of Christian Australia', 34.

[5] Ibid.

and urbane approach to scholarship can appear aloof from the contextual demands of the day, this article will argue that he was not a conservative looking to preserve a British identity, or a liberal seeking to reform church dogma, or even a radical seeking to translate faith into modern idiom. He was – cautiously, idiosyncratically and not always successfully – making a principled and interesting contribution to the translation and contextualization challenges of post-Christian Australia.

Responding to the Crisis

After the religiously propitious 1950s, the 1960s witnessed a sudden and dramatic decline in church attendance and Christian influence in Australia. From the perspective of the churches, it was a 'religious crisis'. Responses were varied. For liberal and progressive Christians, the crisis was an opportunity to revise traditional doctrine and practice.[6] Conservatives like Robinson's episcopal predecessor Marcus Loane (1911–2009) fought gently but persistently to see a Christian and British identity preserved in the Sydney diocese. Archbishop Loane was deeply reluctant to see his own Church of England in Australia abandon its English heritage, its Prayer Book or the King James Bible, all of which he saw as a bulwark against theological compromise as well as sources of spiritual vitality.[7]

In his recent doctoral work, Chilton has drawn attention to the creative responses of the Jesus People movement of the 1970s. It was a response at once conservative in theology and radical in practice. The Jesus People argued that the churches had failed to translate the Christian faith into idioms and language to which average Australians could relate. They longed to see 'the gospel becoming real in the Australian context'.[8] Gallant efforts were made to create evangelistic, liturgical and catechetical material able to get past the communications bottleneck. The movement occasionally spoke of a 'Gum-Leaf Theology' – a self-conscious attempt to bring Christian thought into Australian language. Uniting Church minister Bruce

[6] Hilliard, 'Religious Crisis', 211–12.

[7] On Loane, see Allan Blanch, *From Strength to Strength: A Life of Marcus Loane* (Melbourne, 2014). On his response to the religious crisis, see Chilton, 'Evangelicals and the End of Christian Australia', 223–58.

[8] Athol Gill, quoted in Chilton, 'Evangelicals and the End of Christian Australia', 272. See, for example, John Smith, *Advance Australia Where?* (Melbourne, 1989); Mal Garvin, *Us Aussies: The Fascinating History they didn't tell us at School* (Melbourne, 1992).

Prewer published his *Australian Psalms* and *Australian Prayers,* which were widely read.[9] In 1985 the biggest-selling book from the Australian Broadcasting Commission's retail outlets was *The Day the Grog Ran Out and other Stories from the Big Book*, a translation of popular Bible stories into the idiom of Australian slang.[10] The market seemed to vindicate the Jesus People's argument for, when Christian liturgy and Scripture were put into Australian vernacular, people appeared to respond favourably.

Donald Robinson

Despite holding senior office, Robinson is most remembered for his New Testament work, and not least the so-called 'Knox-Robinson' view of the Church, an interpretation of New Testament ecclesiology emphasizing the primacy of the local, gathered body of believers.[11] In the account by Moore College principal D. B. Knox (1916–94), the implication was that relationships and fellowship, rather than liturgy and polity, were at the heart of church life. Indeed, both liturgical form and denominational rules could (and, in Knox's estimation, often did) undermine authentic fellowship in churches.[12] For the generation of Sydney Anglican clergy emerging in the 1960s and 1970s, Knox's ecclesiology provided the theological vertebrae on which they could build a more accessible, less liturgical and decidedly low-church vision of ministry. They were hungry for greater freedom as they sought to evangelize a society now unsympathetic to or unfamiliar with traditional religious forms.

Robinson was also teaching and writing on ecclesiology at Moore College in the 1960s. However, despite the association of his name with the reform-conducive 'Knox-Robinson view', two aspects of his career seem difficult to reconcile with the changes his alleged

[9] Bruce Prewer, *Australian Psalms* (Adelaide, 1979); idem, *Australian Prayers* (Adelaide, 1983), both cited in Chilton, 'Evangelicals and the End of Christian Australia', 291–2.

[10] See Chilton, 'Evangelicals and the End of Christian Australia', 16.

[11] 'Knox' is a reference to D. B. Knox, principal of Moore College 1959–86. See D. B. Knox, 'De-mythologizing the Church', in Kirsten Birkett, ed., *D. Broughton Knox: Selected Works*, 2: *Church and Ministry* (Sydney, 2003), 23–34; Donald Robinson, 'The Church in the New Testament', in Peter Bolt and Mark Thompson, eds, *Donald Robinson: Selected Works*, 1: Assembling *God's People* (Sydney, 2008), 212–21.

[12] See D. B. Knox, 'The Biblical Concept of Fellowship', in Birkett, ed., *Knox: Selected Works*, 2: 57–84; idem, 'Church, the Churches and the Denominations of the Churches', ibid. 85–98.

views were helping to underwrite. Firstly, Robinson, unlike Knox, was deeply involved with liturgical work and deeply committed to the Anglican liturgical heritage. And secondly, as archbishop of Sydney in the 1980s he was locked in an increasingly unwinnable battle with many of his own clergy, who were arguing for significant change in order to meet the evangelistic challenge of the moment.[13] Many of the younger clergy were confused, perceiving that Robinson as archbishop was opposing the views he himself had taught them as his students.[14]

Marcus Loane had served as archbishop from 1966 until 1982. Widely respected and revered by his clergy, he nevertheless represented a conservative leadership over a period when the groundswell for radical change grew ever stronger. Though the first Australian-born archbishop in the Sydney see (all before him had been English), he was also an Anglophile, a loyal monarchist and a firm believer that the Anglican formularies were the best possible guardians of Evangelical orthodoxy and founts of spiritual strength. He steadfastly insisted on clerical dress, the use of the Book of Common Prayer and adherence to authorized liturgy, in a period in which both clerical dress and liturgy were seen increasingly as impediments to mission.

After sixteen years of Loane's leadership, many clergy held high hopes for change under Robinson. When, as archbishop, Robinson also proved to be deeply committed to liturgical forms, it became easy to understand him as one who had in office 'abandoned his purer teaching'.[15] Ballantine-Jones, a prominent reformist Sydney clergyman of the period, concludes: 'Robinson was a conservative in the Loane mould'.[16] It is this conclusion I wish to dispute. Robinson may have in some senses been a conservative, but he was not simply a conservative and, if the adjective 'conservative' applies, he was a

[13] On the conflicts and reforming programme in the diocese of Sydney in the 1960 through to 2013, see Bruce Albert Ballantine Jones, 'Changes in Policy and Practices in the Anglican Diocese of Sydney 1966–2013: The Political Factor' (PhD thesis, Macquarie University, 2013).

[14] Ibid. 34, 45.

[15] 'It was said by some that by accepting consecration that B[isho]p Robinson had, in practice, abandoned his purer teaching': Raymond E. Heslehurst, 'The Doctrine of the Church and the Diocesan Mission: A Preliminary Examination of the Doctrine of the Church as expressed in the Synod Addresses of Bishop D. W. B. Robinson 1982–1992' (unpublished paper presented to the Senior Common Room of the Richard Johnson College, 2004), 1; available on request from the author at: Raymond@uow.edu.au.

[16] Ballantine-Jones, 'Changes', 45.

conservative precisely *not* in the 'Loane mould'.[17] I wish to demonstrate that Robinson's apparent conservatism was not of the same genus as Loane's more nostalgic stance. Rather, it is best understood as, in its own way, a creative response to the crisis of the 1960s and should be understood alongside, rather than apart from, other contemporaneous efforts at translating the faith in the newly contested context.

AN AUSTRALIAN PRAYER BOOK

Robinson joined the Prayer Book Commission of the General Synod in 1962 with a decade of liturgical interest and scholarship behind him.[18] The commission reported back to the General Synod in 1966 with two draft liturgies.[19] In September 1966 news broke that among the submissions to the Synod was a revision of the Lord's Prayer including the line 'Our bread of the morrow give us today'. The line, based on recent linguistic and exegetical work, was Robinson's. It was widely reported, with the focus on Canon Robinson – the man 'who rewrote the Lord's Prayer' – and a tabloid-style exhortation: 'Leave the Lord's Prayer Alone: Man in the Street Doesn't Want Change'.[20]

[17] For examples of recent work stressing the continuities in Robinson's approach, see Andrew Judd, 'When Pa Met the Queen', *Anglican Historical Society Journal* 58 (2013), 32–49; idem, 'Donald Robinson and the Imperfect Unity of *An Australian Prayer Book* (1978)', *Lucas: An Evangelical History Review* 2nd ser. 6 (2013), 113–44; Heslehurst , 'Doctrine of the Church'; Rory Shiner, 'An Appreciation of D. W. B. Robinson's New Testament Theology', in Peter Bolt and Mark Thompson, eds, *Donald Robinson: Selected Works, Appreciation* (Sydney, 2008), 9–62; idem, 'D. B. Knox', in Michael Jensen, ed., *The Church of the Triune God: Understanding God's Work in his People Today* (Sydney, 2013); Michael Jensen, *Sydney Anglicans: An Apology* (Sydney, 2012), Kindle edn, ch. 6.

[18] D. W. B. Robinson, 'The Date and Significance of the Last Supper', *Evangelical Quarterly* 23 (1951), 126–33, idem, 'Apostleship and Apostolic Succession', *Reformed Theological Review* 13/2 (1954), 33–42, idem, 'The Meaning of Baptism', in Peter G. Bolt and Mark D. Thompson, eds, *Donald Robinson, Selected Works*, 2: *Preaching God's Word* (Sydney, 2007), 227–51, idem, 'The Church in the New Testament', *St Mark's Review* 17 (1959), 4–14; idem, 'A New Baptismal Service: A Criticism', in Bolt and Thompson, eds, *Robinson, Selected Works*, 2: 334–50.

[19] Judd, 'Robinson', 118.

[20] 'Leave the Lord's Prayer Alone: Man in the Street Doesn't Want Change', *The Sun*, 14 September 1966; 'Sticks Out Like Granny's Teeth: Why I Rewrote Lord's Prayer', *The Sun*, 15 September 1966; 'Anglican Lord's Prayer: Protests on New Version', *Daily Telegraph*, 15 September 1966; 'Lord's Prayer', *Daily Telegraph*, 16 September 1966; 'Lively Prayer Debate Expected', *Sydney Morning Herald*, 15 September 1966; 'Cartoon', *The Australian*, 16 September 1966; 'Why the Canon Rewrote Prayer', *The Australian*, 15 September 1966; all citations from Judd, 'Robinson', 121 n. 39.

The 1966 General Synod set up a new liturgical commission to continue the work, again including Robinson. According to Robinson, despite the diverse churchmanship of the commission, it was an easy group of people to work with, characterized by 'a remarkable degree of mutual understanding and friendliness'.[21] They were given the brief to continue drafting new liturgies, but a more ambitious cause gripped them: the writing of a whole new Prayer Book. Fellow commissioner and professor of Ancient History, Edwin Judge, explains:

> Donald suddenly actually said to us, the ten of us sitting around the table, he said something like 'we should write a whole new book.' It was his idea. It was like a bombshell. We were getting nowhere, we were sick to death of variations and revisions and floundering and so on, and inertia was settling in on the commission and really frustration as to what it was all about. And he simply said … 'We must write a book' … Nobody had thought of that. So on the one hand, it was a truly creative moment, and nobody had told us to write a book, so we were naughty in a way, we took it upon ourselves … we were going to spring a surprise on our Church![22]

Robinson at the National Evangelical Anglican Congress (1971)

In August 1971 Robinson spoke at the National Evangelical Anglican Congress (NEAC) in Melbourne. His topic was liturgy, and he began by arguing that the 'obligation to worship God is total, and is not confined to special times, places or actions'.[23] He argued that 'liturgy' is a dangerous word as it is likely to attach itself to a particular type of formal service, rather than to the totality of a life lived for God.[24] For Robinson, liturgical language in the New Testament invariably described 'the ordinary deeds and words of Christians, never rites and ceremonies'.[25]

[21] Ibid. 125; see also Donald Robinson, 'The Church of England in Australia', in Colin Buchanan, ed., *Modern Anglican Liturgies 1958–1968* (Oxford, 1968), 297–320.
[22] Judd, 'Robinson', 127.
[23] Donald Robinson, 'Liturgical Patterns of Worship', in Bolt and Thompson, eds, *Robinson: Selected Works*, 1: 318–36, at 318.
[24] Ibid.
[25] Robinson extends this to the sacraments, arguing that baptism, whilst obviously a 'symbolic' gesture, was in the New Testament a 'personal act and not part of corporate

These points raised the question of the nature and purpose of church services. Robinson believed that when studying the Book of Common Prayer, it becomes clear that the Reformers assumed a community such as a village, parish or even household whose life and network of relationship extended well beyond Sunday services and indeed for whom the Sunday services were not what primarily constituted them as a community.[26] The services of the Book of Common Prayer presupposed the same congregation (that is, the same people being present) and provided for that group of people a means of 'common prayer'. In short, it envisaged a pattern of community life differing sharply from the realities of twentieth-century suburban Australia.

Robinson's 1971 NEAC lecture demonstrated that his doctrine of church did not entail an abandonment of Anglican liturgy. Robinson was persuaded of the need for a liturgy reformed, not a liturgy abandoned. Despite an emphasis on fellowship, for him the gathering of the church is nevertheless 'to meet Christ'.[27] And the questions of engaging with, and bearing witness to, twentieth-century Australia were not questions that could be addressed simply by modernizing the Sunday service. Moreover, for Robinson, if church is primarily a meeting of the faithful, it is exactly the wrong point at which to agonize over engaging the culture. Church is not ordered so as to engage the world, but to encourage the faithful and to meet the Lord. Years later, in his 1988 synod address as archbishop, he would make his thinking explicit, calling for a 'renewal of true worship', convinced that 'as Christ exercises his kingly power in the midst of his church, we may be sure that his word will run very swiftly into the world'.[28] Within this framework, Robinson was committed to liturgical reform, but he implored his fellow Evangelicals to be patient with the national

Christian worship'. And the eucharist or Lord's Supper was not, as Dom Gregory Dix also acknowledged, a 'new rite' established by Jesus, but an existing meal to which Jesus and then the early Christians gave significance. For Robinson (again citing Dix), there was 'no need to tell men to eat bread together, or to drink wine on their festive occasions. This was their normal way of life.' Therefore the Lord's Supper was not 'liturgical' as such, but essentially a fellowship meal at which the Lord is present according to his promise: ibid. 320–1.

[26] Ibid. 321.

[27] Ibid.

[28] Donald Robinson, 'Presidential Address 1985', *Yearbook of the Diocese of Sydney* (Sydney, 1986), 211–30.

Church and 'wait for one another' (an allusion to 1 Corinthians 11: 33) in the matter of liturgical revision.[29]

On intercessions, Robinson argued that there should be less prayer for the Queen 'who is now a mere figurehead of government, and more for those in whose hand the real power rests', including trade union leaders and captains of industry.[30] This is a striking comment, unimaginable on the lips of Marcus Loane. In 1971 the monarchy still commanded enormous respect, and the Queen had had a very successful tour of Australia just the year before. Robinson's position went against this mood. He also argued against introducing extempore prayer, with an instructive aside: 'If there were evidence of a widespread gift of prayer in the churches one might be inclined to stretch the legal point'.[31] The implication was that if a widespread charisma were evident, that would be grounds to change practice. This is consistent with Robinson's 1973 address on the then-growing charismatic movement.[32] As a response to the movement it is (unsurprisingly) scholarly, but (surprisingly) irenic. Robinson approached phenomena like speaking in tongues neither with conservative cynicism nor with an aversion to supernatural phenomena characteristic of progressive Christianity.[33] He was in principle open to the supernatural claims of neo-pentecostalism, but found them wanting on specific exegetical grounds.

RECEPTION OF *AN AUSTRALIAN PRAYER BOOK*

Prayer Book revision continued throughout the 1970s, led by the two dominant figures of Donald Robinson and Anglo-Catholic

[29] Note again here a contrast with Knox, who drew the conclusion that if the local gathering is 'church' then the denomination, which never gathers, is not 'church'. Denominations in Knox's view have a fundamentally 'secular' character.

[30] Robinson, 'Liturgical Patterns', 330.

[31] Ibid. 332.

[32] Donald Robinson, 'Charismatic Christianity', in Bolt and Thompson, eds, *Robinson: Selected Works*, 2: 191–201.

[33] In the early 1950s, when students from the local girls' school asked about exorcisms, Robinson responded by inviting a missionary who had herself performed exorcism to come and address the girls. Evidently, despite a scholarly disposition, he was an unselfconscious supernaturalist: Donald Robinson, 'Some Rectors and Recollections', in Brian Fletcher and Kenneth Cable, eds, *The Parish of St Philip, Church Hill, Sydney: Three Bicentennial Lectures* (Sydney, 2003), 41–62, at 60.

liturgist Brother Gilbert Sinden.[34] By 1977 the commission was able to present a completed manuscript of *An Australian Prayer Book* to the General Synod. It was approved with only one vote against. It became available for use on 5 April 1978 and passed into wide use, apparently without controversy. Indeed, in a somewhat bad-tempered review, Australian literary figure Barry Spurr complained in 1981 that 'it has already superseded [the Book of Common Prayer] in many parishes at most services'.[35]

An Australian Prayer Book was the first prayer book in the Anglican world to replace 'thou' with 'you'.[36] More substantially, as Judd has demonstrated, it exhibited a productive and creative engagement with Scripture.[37] Whilst the 1549 Prayer Book had included prayers for the dead, the 1552 Book of Common Prayer (on which that of 1662 was largely based) had largely abandoned them, a situation twentieth-century Evangelicals celebrated and Anglo-Catholics lamented. As Judd has argued, rather than return to 1549 or simply modernize 1662, the new book drew on the New Testament doctrine of the resurrection of the dead, producing a prayer that moved beyond both 1549 and 1662:[38]

> THANKSGIVING FOR THE FAITHFUL DEPARTED
> *We give thanks for* the life and work of …
> We praise you, Lord God, for your faithful servants in every age, and we pray that we, with all who have died in the faith of Christ, may be brought into a joyful resurrection and the fulfilment of your eternal kingdom.[39]

According to Edwin Judge, the suggestion was Robinson's.[40] It allowed for the intercessor to stop short of praying for the dead whilst still affirming the congregation's fellowship with them in awaiting the resurrection together.

The book was criticized for lacking a post-British identity and for being a product of theological compromise – 'a testament to

[34] On the warm personal relations between Robinson and Sinden, see Judd, 'Robinson', 134–6.

[35] Barry Spurr, 'An Australian Prayer Book', in David Martin and Peter Mullen, eds, *No Alternative: The Prayer Book Controversy* (London, 1981), 162–74, at 162.

[36] Charles Sherlock, 'The Anglican Church of Australia', in Charles Hefling and Cynthia Shattuck, eds, *The Oxford Guide to the Book of Common Prayer* (Oxford, 2006), 324–32.

[37] Judd, 'Robinson', 137.

[38] For discussion, see ibid. 132–4.

[39] *An Australian Prayer Book* (Sydney, 1978), 141.

[40] Judd, 'Robinson', 133.

disunity'.[41] However, as Judd has argued, it stands amongst Prayer Book revisions as a testimony to precisely the opposite: it represents a product of Anglo-Catholic and Evangelical cooperation, and is grounded, not in compromise and studied ambiguity, but rather in a genuine attempt to attend to Scripture and tradition, and in so doing to 'wait for one another' until agreement, and not mere compromise, could be reached. In its own way it was a testimony to growing Australian confidence – the product of people who neither self-consciously produced 'Australianized' services, nor timidly updated the Book of Common Prayer, but who had the quiet audacity to write a Prayer Book for Australia.

Robinson on Translating Scripture

In his wider New Testament scholarship, Robinson's whole project was centred on re-introducing students to what Karl Barth described as 'the strange new world within the Bible'.[42] Like Barth, he saw his role not as translating the ancient text into modern idiom, but to bringing modern people to the ancient text, in all its strangeness and otherness. To do so required preserving the sense of distance between the Bible's world and our own.

In a 1979 review of the Good News Bible, Robinson provided some important clues to his thought.[43] He continued to hold the view that there existed within Australia a sizeable constituency of Anglicans who, despite a perhaps tenuous personal connection with the Christian faith, could be won back and who, if won, would expect the Church to which they came back to look something like the Church they had left.[44] This view contrasted sharply with that of younger clergy who believed the task was no longer to win back the lost sheep, but to gather new ones.[45] Continuity, both in liturgical reform and in Bible translation, had a pastoral imperative for Robinson.

[41] On lacking post-British identity, see citations in Judd, 'Robinson', 140 n. 115. On *An Australian Prayer Book* as a 'testament to disunity', see Spurr, 'Australian Prayer Book', 163.
[42] Karl Barth, 'The Strange New World within the Bible', in idem, *The Word of God and the Word of Man* (New York, 1957), 28–50.
[43] Donald Robinson, 'Translation of the Bible for Public Worship', in Bolt and Thompson, eds, *Robinson: Selected Works*, 2: 53–62.
[44] It is interesting to relate this to his radical revision of the Lord's Prayer suggested in the 1960s. Perhaps his views altered in the two decades of liturgical revision that followed?
[45] See Ballantine-Jones, 'Changes', 169–96.

However, it was not his purpose to make the liturgy or the Scripture sound 'normal' – either to returning 'sheep' or to as yet unbelieving Australians. His consideration of the 'dynamic equivalence' translation method employed in the Good News Bible is instructive.[46] He saw the effort to evoke in the contemporary reader the same reaction to the text which its original readers would have had as both 'impossible and misguided'. As he explained:

> … it is not possible to produce the identical reaction, since our whole presuppositional background is so different from that of the first readers. Salvation is of the Jews, and the aim of translation is to enable us to understand how that salvation appeared to a Jew, not to show how the Jew would have thought had he been an Englishman.[47]

Robinson's headline-making proposal for the Lord's Prayer is an instance of such thinking. 'Our bread of the morrow give us today' is not an effort at making the Lord's Prayer more immediate, but more strange. As such, it is an invitation to enter into a world and way of thinking not our own.

Robinson felt the evangelistic situation in Australia was confused by using church services as an evangelistic platform, and found it bemusing that, even when neutral ground was chosen for gospel proclamation (such as a showground or a public hall), Christians still had a tendency to 'dress up the proceedings to appear as much like a Christian assembly as possible'. Does this mean, he asked, 'that we really have no frontier with the genuine non-Christian today, of the kind St Paul had when he spoke at Athens?'[48]

For Robinson, it seems, evangelism in the 1970s was not too radical, but not radical enough. It failed to come to terms with the specific challenges of speaking to non-believers, rather than addressing people who were Christian but 'not Christian enough'.[49]

[46] 'Dynamic' or 'functional' equivalence translation is (very simply) the attempt to translate from one language to another in a 'thought for thought' rather than 'word for word' manner. For discussion, see D. A. Carson, 'The Limits of Functional Equivalence in Bible Translation', in Glen G. Scorgie, Mark L. Strauss and Steven M. Voth, eds, *The Challenge of Bible Translation: Communicating God's Word to the World* (Grand Rapids, MI, 2003), 65–113.

[47] Robinson, 'Translation', 55.

[48] Donald Robinson, 'The Doctrine of the Church and its Implications for Evangelism', in Bolt and Thompson, eds, *Robinson: Selected Works*, 2: 106–13, at 106.

[49] Chilton, 'Evangelicals and the End of Christian Australia', 2.

Conclusion

Donald Robinson thought deeply about the task of translating and commending the gospel to an increasingly secular and post-Christian Australia. He was not a radical. He did not promote the radical discipleship of the Jesus People, nor the house church movement of his former student, New Testament scholar Robert Banks,[50] nor even the more radical implications of his post-liturgical colleague D. B. Knox. And yet, he did (with the Jesus People) worry that insisting on 'churchly' modes of evangelism (like the Billy Graham Crusades) meant Christians had 'no frontier with the genuine non-Christian today'; he did (with Banks) agree that current patterns of church and community life could not deliver the sort of intimate community envisaged in the New Testament. Moreover, he agreed with Knox that worship embraced all of life and that fellowship, the communion of the saints, was at the heart of our purpose in being 'churched'.

If he was not a radical, neither was he (simply) a conservative. A Cambridge education made him more cosmopolitan than Anglophile.[51] He was not nostalgic for empire. He produced the first Anglican Prayer Book in the world to dispense with Elizabethan forms of address. He suggested a radical recasting of the Lord's Prayer, and encouraged a mode of evangelism in which churchly forms were set aside and evangelists were genuinely sent out, and the laity were encouraged to 'go in peace to love and serve the Lord' in their places of calling.

If Robinson's work is assessed on whether he was able to find a language to restore a principle of common prayer to Australian Anglicanism, or on whether he was able to stem the tide of Australians leaving the churches, or on whether he was able to win back disengaged Anglicans, he failed on all counts. But, since the 1960s, so has almost everyone. The purpose of this article has not been to argue that Robinson's proposals were vindicated, but merely that he should be understood, not as a conservative ('in the mould of Loane') or reactionary, but as one of those who saw the post-1960s moment, felt its significance and responded creatively, sensitively and with principle.

[50] For Banks on house churches, see Robert J. Banks and Julia Banks, *The Church comes Home* (Peabody, MA, 1998).
[51] Robinson was at Queens' College, Cambridge, from 1947–50.

Revisiting 'Translatability' and African Christianity: The Case of the Christian Catholic Apostolic Church in Zion

Joel Cabrita*
University of Cambridge

Focusing on the 'translatability' of Christianity in Africa is now commonplace. This approach stresses that African Christian practice is thoroughly inculturated and relevant to local cultural concerns. However, in exclusively emphasizing Christianity's indigeneity, an opportunity is lost to understand how Africans entered into complex relationships with North Americans to shape a common field of religious practice. To better illuminate the transnational, open-faced nature of Christianity in Africa, this article discusses the history of a twentieth-century Christian faith healing movement called Zionism, a large black Protestant group in South Africa. Eschewing usual portrayals of Zionism as an indigenous Southern African movement, the article situates its origins in nineteenth-century industrializing, immigrant Chicago, and describes how Zionism was subsequently reimagined in a South African context of territorial dispossession and racial segregation. It moves away from isolated regional histories of Christianity to focus on how African Protestantism emerged as the product of lively transatlantic exchanges in the late modern period.

The example of Christian Zionism in South Africa seems a perfect illustration of the scholarly vogue for portraying Christianity in Africa as an eminently 'translatable' religion. Zionism – not to be confused with the Jewish movement focused on the state of Israel – is the largest popular Christian movement in modern Southern Africa, to which millions in South Africa, Swaziland, Lesotho, Mozambique, Botswana, Zimbabwe and Zambia belong; by the 1960s, 21 per cent

* Faculty of Divinity, Cambridge, CB3 9BS. E-mail: jmc67@cam.ac.uk.
My thanks to the Ecclesiastical History Society for giving me the opportunity to present an earlier version of this article at their Winter 2016 meeting. I am grateful for the comments of the anonymous reviewer, and to the editorial team for their input. I would also like to acknowledge the support of the Arts and Humanities Research Council in the form of an Early Career Fellowship.

Studies in Church History 53 (2017) 448–475
doi: 10.1017/stc.2016.27

of Southern Africans were Zionist.[1] However, with now over three thousand active Zionist denominations in the Southern African region, there is no single Zionist organization. The biggest is the Zion Christian Church in northern South Africa, with six million members, while the vast majority of Zionist churches have between fifty and two hundred members.[2] Historically, adherents of this diffuse, decentralized movement have been drawn from South Africa's working classes; today, Zionists are still perceived as representative of the rank of minimally educated, economically marginalized black South Africans. And although thus vastly diverse, a unifying feature of Zionists across this region is their emphasis on health and healing. Almost uniformly, a Zionist service centres on a healing event during which congregation members receive prayer from a 'prophet' for physical, emotional or psychological ailments. Some groups still eschew both Western and African medicine in favour of exclusive reliance upon prayer.[3]

Both scholarship and popular perception have largely understood Zionism as a uniquely Southern African phenomenon, entirely indigenous to the region. The first study of Zionism was Swedish Lutheran missiologist Bengt Sundkler's 1948 *Bantu Prophets in South Africa*.[4] Sundkler's book was a pioneering effort to take Zionists seriously. Previously they had been dismissed as a superstitious corruption of Christianity; 'orthodox' Christianity was instead supposed to reside in Anglican, Methodist, Presbyterian and Roman Catholic white-led mission Churches. But, living side by side with Zionist congregations in Zululand as a missionary, Sundkler's curiosity about this popular black religiosity led him to reassess Zionists as a complex mixture of indigenous religion and Christianity. Thus while the African Christians he observed in 1940s Zululand had discarded many aspects of the old 'pagan' order, in Zionist churches he found there was still a strong emphasis on pre-Christian ritual.[5] Sundkler thus drew a now-famous chart comparing how old religious rituals – the 'surviving forms of Zulu culture' – found 'new expressions in

[1] Martin West, *Bishops and Prophets in a Black City: African Independent Churches in Soweto* (London, 1975), 2.
[2] Retief Müller, *African Pilgrimage: Ritual Travel in South Africa's Christianity of Zion* (Farnham, 2011).
[3] James Kiernan, 'The Work of Zion: An Analysis of an African Zionist Ritual', *Africa: Journal of the International African Institute* 55 (1976), 340–55.
[4] Bengt Sundkler, *Bantu Prophets in South Africa* (London, 1948).
[5] Ibid. 181.

Zionist churches'.[6] He concluded that Zionist rituals such as healing, prophecy and baptism were evidence of the old religion with merely a Christian gloss upon it, 'new wine in old wineskins'.[7] Zionism was a means for mid-twentieth-century Africans – amidst racial segregation and economic and territorial dispossession – to give 'a more honored place … to the religious and cultural heritage of the Zulus'.[8]

While Sundkler's early analysis was highly ambivalent about Zionists' orthodoxy (hc was after all a 1940s Lutheran missionary), subsequent scholarship – including a later edition of Sundkler's own *Bantu Prophets*[9] – was far more celebratory of Zionism's status as an indigenous African Christian movement. Scholars such as Jean Comaroff, amongst many others, seized upon Zionists as examples of the resilience of African religiosity against a 'foreign' European Christianity.[10] Rather than being understood in the context of an Evangelical Christian tradition long concerned with bodily healing therapies, Zionists' healing rituals were instead interpreted as remnants of indigenous cosmologies, evidence of Africans' ability to appropriate Western Christianity, to remake it in the mould of so-called traditional African religious practices and thereby to ameliorate the alienating effect of colonial capitalism.[11]

What many of these studies overlooked, however, is that the origins of Zionism in South Africa – this supposedly most 'African' of all religious movements in Southern Africa – lay far outside the region. Rather than being a genuinely local growth, Zionism, introduced to South Africa in the 1890s, was in fact the product of a white North American missionary organization known as the Christian Catholic Apostolic Church in Zion. In this respect, Sundkler's later study *Zulu Zion and some Swazi Zionists* (1976) offered an important qualification to the general trend.[12] In it, he nuanced the

[6] Ibid. 262–3.

[7] Ibid. 278.

[8] Ibid. 17.

[9] Bengt Sundkler, *Bantu Prophets in South Africa*, 2nd edn (Oxford, 1961).

[10] Terence Ranger, 'Connexions between Primary Resistance Movements and Modern Mass Nationalism', *JAH* 9 (1968), 437–53.

[11] Jean Comaroff, *Body of Power, Spirit of Resistance: The Culture and History of a South African People* (Chicago, IL, 1985); James Kiernan, 'Saltwater and Ashes: Instruments of Curing among some Zulu Zionists', *JRA* 9 (1978), 27–32; Allan Anderson, *Moya: The Holy Spirit in an African Context* (Pretoria, 1991); idem, 'The Lekganyanes and Prophecy in the Zion Christian Church', *JRA* 29 (1999), 285–312, at 308; Müller, *African Pilgrimage*.

[12] Bengt Sundkler, *Zulu Zion and Some Swazi Zionists* (Oxford, 1976).

by-then usual depiction of Zionism in Southern Africa as exclusively a black phenomenon by demonstrating the importance of local white Evangelical culture to its early history, detailing the extensive involvement of like-minded whites in propagating Zionism across the districts of the Transvaal and Orange Free State.[13] Sundkler thus showed us that the early beginnings of black Zion were not as 'exclusively African as one might like to believe. The first decade … echoes with the … relationship between White commitment and an emerging Black charismatic community.'[14]

But while Sundkler demonstrated that the earliest decade of the local movement was to a considerable degree inter-racial, he nonetheless left largely unexplored the exact character of the internationalist resources which both black and white South Africans were receiving from North America. While detailed in his analysis of why white Evangelicals in South Africa joined the movement, he spent little time situating the development of Zionism in Southern Africa as an outgrowth of a Midwestern faith healing movement. And although Sundkler showed that both blacks and whites responded with alacrity to Zionism, he did not explain why and how this worldwide Protestant phenomenon resonated so profoundly on both sides of the Atlantic. Even though within a few decades many – but not all – black and white Zionists had separated from the original North American denomination to found their own independent congregations, a large number of these autonomous groups nonetheless sustained intensive contact with the North American, white-led mother Church throughout the twentieth century. As I shall argue, the influence of turn-of-the-century Midwestern Zionism – a popular working-class religiosity focused on bodily perfection and overall self-improvement – long endured in Southern Africa, even after the departure of American missionaries. But most scholars – including Sundkler – have depicted the contribution of North Americans to African Zionism as merely a transitory phase with limited influence.[15] In this way, Zionism's origins as a phenomenon arising as the result of complex collaborations

[13] Ibid. 13–67.

[14] Ibid. 66.

[15] For two exceptions, see David Maxwell, 'Historicizing Christian Independency: The Southern African Pentecostal Movement, *c.*1908–1960', *JAH* 40 (1999), 243–64; Joel Cabrita, 'People of Adam: Divine Healing and Racial Cosmopolitanism in Transvaal, South Africa', *Comparative Studies in Society and History* 57/2 (2015), 1–36.

and alliances between blacks and white Zionists in South Africa and white Zionists in the USA, are obscured.[16]

The reasons for scholars' focus on Zionism as a nativist movement are not hard to find. Shaped by the wave of political independence sweeping the continent and the corresponding search for African identities, post-colonial scholars of the 1960s seized upon the thousands of black-led, healing-focused Zionist churches as evidence of African resistance to a 'white' Christianity, a genuinely 'African' translation of the gospel amidst politically adverse circumstances.[17] Even Sundkler in 1976 – more cognizant than most of the contribution of local whites to the movement – expressed wariness at flagging up the importance of non-African elements to Zionism at that particular historical juncture: 'it would seem unfortunate, perhaps, not to say unwise, at this time of Black Power and Black Theology to try to argue such a case, as though even this purely and gloriously Black movement of the Spirit somehow originated with a few Whites'.[18] And not only did missionaries appear to many liberal academics and observers to be profoundly implicated in the machinations of colonialism, but a growing attention to the profound demographic shift of Christianity from the North and the East to the Global South was also transforming scholarly models for the study of Christianity outside of the West. Rather than focusing on the activity of Western missionary societies in Africa, scholars were now disposed to view faith communities as unique centres of Christianity in their own right, developed with little or even no attention to traditional missionary-sending centres.

In particular, Lamin Sanneh's influential work on the 'translatable' gospel shaped how indigenous non-Western Churches such as the Zionists in South Africa were viewed. In *Translating the Message*, Sanneh described how as Christianity expanded into new environments beyond its Middle Eastern milieu it faced new challenges as a minority religion within non-Christian societies.[19] The key to Christianity's subsequent success was its 'translatability'. According to

[16] Müller, *African Pilgrimage*, 11–13.

[17] Ranger, 'Modern Mass Nationalism', 437; Harold Turner, 'A Typology for African Religious Movements', *JRA* 1 (1967), 1–32.

[18] Sundkler, *Zulu Zion*, 14. For evidence of Sundkler's own hesitations in proffering evidence of white European or American contributions to African Zion, see ibid. 57 n. 56.

[19] Lamin Sanneh, *Translating the Message: The Missionary Impact on Culture* (Maryknoll, NY, 1989).

Sanneh, this was Christianity's intrinsic, engrained capacity to not remain enshrined within a single language or cultural system, but rather to adapt to local cultural and linguistic contexts. Thus Pentecost, that singular occasion in Jerusalem when each person heard what was being spoken 'in his own tongue', reversed the disorderly confusion of Babel. Rather than humanity's different cultures resulting merely in incomprehensible fragmentation, Sanneh proposed that Christianity grafted itself onto a wide range of different cultures and languages; human cultural difference was not the seed of disorder, but rather the bearer of divine revelation.[20]

The implications of the approach of Sanneh and others for the study of Christian movements outside the Western world have been profound, predisposing scholars to focus on the local, regional characteristics of Christianity. Thus Sanneh has also argued against the term 'Global Christianity' on the grounds that it obscures the local particularity of the multiple Christianities of varying cultural contexts, wrongly foregrounding a homogenizing, European form of Christianity.[21] According to Sanneh, it is 'World Christianity', in contrast to 'Global Christianity', in which the voices of Global South Christians speak freely for themselves.[22] Guided by the particularist impulses exemplified in the scholarship of Sanneh and others, the topographical 'map' of non-Western Christianity now tends to be highly fragmented, comprised of multiple local Christianities studding the globe but rarely interacting with each other or with traditional missionary-sending centres and possessing little consciousness of belonging to a single religious community.[23] These scholars study how Christians translated a universal faith into local concerns, rather than how a universal faith knits together a range of local believers.[24] And so, in emphasizing the autonomy of local Christianities, this scholarship perhaps runs the risk of neglecting the other side of the story: that local Christians across the world have prized highly contact with Christians in the so-called Global North, as well as sustained exchanges with believers in other parts of the southern hemisphere, choosing

[20] The missionary scholar Andrew Walls made a similar argument in *The Missionary Movement in Christian History* (Edinburgh, 1996).

[21] Lamin Sanneh, *Whose Religion is Christianity? The Gospel beyond the West* (Cambridge, 2003), 35.

[22] Ibid. 22.

[23] E.g. Charles Farhardian, ed., *Introducing World Christianity* (Oxford, 2012).

[24] Dale T. Irvin, 'World Christianity: An Introduction', *Journal of World Christianity* 1 (2008), 1–2.

to stress not only their regional credentials, but also their universalist affiliations.

Furthermore, in the case of Zionism, the model of indigeneity may obscure more than it reveals. For one thing, it imbues 'Africanness' with an overly exaggerated explanatory power in accounting for the popularity of Zionism in South Africa. In seeking to emphasize local agency, exponents of this approach have placed too great an emphasis on black South Africans' reliance upon tropes of ethnicity and local culture; black South Africans, as much as any ethnic constituency in history, have also used resources far beyond their immediate cultural horizons. A rich new body of transnational history – locating South Africa within currents of global history – is pertinent in this regard.[25] Furthermore, Christianity's transformative power to cut across culture as well as be translated within culture must be accounted for. Following the recent approach of the Anthropology of Christianity school, exemplified by the work of Joel Robbins and others, it is evident that believers across the globe have chosen to stress that fidelity to Christ does not necessarily baptize their existing culture and language but rather enacts a radical break with pasts frequently characterized by converts as degenerate, corrupt and sinful.[26]

Following in this revisionary spirit, then, and building upon Sundkler's own path-breaking contribution from the 1970s, this article argues that the time is ripe for a reappraisal of Zionism as a phenomenon of transatlantic history and international Protestantism, rather than as a nativistic Christian appropriation. What follows eschews the usual portrayal of Zionism as an indigenous Southern African movement. Instead, the origins of Zionism are situated in the North American divine healing movement of the late nineteenth century, demonstrating that the Christian Catholic Apostolic Church in Zion was a unique product of the rapidly industrializing Midwestern metropolis of Chicago. It was particularly the universalist promise of the new Zion Church – its self-proclaimed aspiration to remake all humanity into a new redeemed race, characterized by healthy bodies – that appealed to a recently urbanized, working-class, largely

[25] See, for example, James T. Campbell, *Songs of Zion: The African Methodist Episcopal Church in the United State and South Africa* (Oxford, 1995); Isabel Hofmeyr, *The Portable Bunyan: A Transnational History of the Pilgrim's Progress* (Princeton, NJ, 2004); Robert Vinson, *The Americans are Coming! Dreams of African American Liberation in Segregationist South Africa* (Athens, OH, 2012).

[26] Fenella Cannell, ed., *The Anthropology of Christianity* (Durham, NC, 2006).

immigrant Northern European Chicago-based population eager to assimilate to the New World. The article then shows how the rapid transmission of these universalist beliefs to black South Africans in the farmlands of the early twentieth-century Transvaal was not, after all, so great a jump. Dispossessed by rapid industrialization and marginalized by racial segregation (these were intertwined processes), black farmers embraced Zionism's egalitarian healing techniques as a means of asserting their equality with like-minded believers across the world. Attending to this comparative element allows us to move away from isolated regional histories of Christianity in South Africa and the USA, and instead to consider Protestantism in Africa as the fruit of lively transatlantic exchanges (and conflicts) throughout the late modern period.

Zionism in the American Midwest

John Alexander Dowie was the divine healing movement's most famous figure. He was born in Edinburgh in 1847 to a tailor father. In 1860 the Dowies migrated to South Australia, part of the wave of working-class Scottish emigration of this period.[27] After returning to Edinburgh to study theology, Dowie was ordained pastor of an Australian Congregationalist church. Through periodicals and international revivalist networks, Dowie became an advocate of divine healing. This was quite a widespread phenomenon within Protestantism, reflecting both the period's Methodist-derived perfectionistic confidence (Christ could redeem the body as well as the soul) and its intense interest in bodily health against a backdrop of industrialization and urbanization, exemplified by the popularity of rival therapies such as hydrotherapy, homeopathy and magnetism. By the 1860s and 1870s, divine healing associations and groups were found in a number of European capitals and in cities along the east coast of the United States, as well as in the rapidly emerging Australian and Canadian metropolises of the 'Anglo-world'.[28] Deeply impressed by its powerful spiritual techniques, by the late 1870s, Dowie had fallen out with

[27] Eric Richards, 'Migrations: The Career of British White Australia', in Deryck M. Schreuder and Stuart Ward, eds, *Australia's Empire* (Oxford, 2008), 163–85, at 168.

[28] Heather D. Curtis, *Faith in the Great Physician: Suffering and Divine Healing in American Culture, 1860–1900* (Baltimore, MD, 2007); James Belich, *Replenishing the Earth: The Settler Revolution and the Rise of the Anglo-World, 1783–1939* (Oxford, 2009)

the Congregationalist establishment in Australia and had founded his own independent Divine Healing Association in Melbourne.[29]

From its early beginnings in Australia, Dowie's experiments with divine healing were shaped by a broader set of Protestant concerns regarding a new swathe of largely working-class city-dwellers. Melbourne, as with other major Australian cities of the period, was the site of intense anxiety on the part of Protestant activists regarding the demoralizing and enervating effects of industrialization on this new urban working class.[30] The work of many Protestant reform groups sought to 'uplift' the urban poor while leaning on an elitist rhetoric of working-class degeneracy, but other religious movements – including the newly founded Salvation Army – emerged as more populist entities. These were instances of Evangelical piety appropriated by the city's working classes for their own ends, and in ways the Protestant establishment – including Dowie's own Congregational church – often disapproved of deeply because of their exuberant public piety.[31] After resigning from the Congregationalists, Dowie worked briefly with the Salvation Army.[32] Its populist influence upon him was clear; in forming his new association, Dowie proclaimed divine healing a movement for the working people of the city, and in angry written and spoken polemic, frequently pitted it against the ineffectual interventions of the Protestant establishment. For in sharp contrast to entrenched Protestant tropes of working-class degeneracy and 'poor-shaming', his new divine healing services in Melbourne offered working men and women the promise of full and permanent bodily perfection, and proclaimed that spiritual power was available to them at merely the request of a prayer.[33] Many for whom Dowie prayed in his regular services in the working-class suburbs of Fitzroy and Collingwood told of feeling extraordinary bodily jolts during the experience of laying-on of hands, a 'shock as the Holy Spirit's power'

[29] *The Christian Alliance*, February 1888, no page number available.

[30] Graeme Davison, David Dunstan and Chris McConville, eds, *The Outcasts of Melbourne: Essays in Social History* (Sydney, 1985); A. J. C. Mayne, *Fever, Squalor and Vice: Sanitation and Social Policy in Victorian Sydney* (New York, 1982).

[31] Diana Winston, *Red Hot and Righteous: The Urban Religion of the Salvation Army* (Cambridge, MA, 1999).

[32] J. Hein, 'A Crisis of Leadership: John Alexander Dowie and the Salvation Army in South Australia', *Journal of the Historical Society of South Australia* 39 (2011), 65–77.

[33] See Joel Cabrita, *Empire of Healing: South Africa, the United States and the Transatlantic Zionist Movement* (Cambridge, MA, forthcoming).

passed through them, as one devotee recounted.[34] Some claimed that they experienced healing instantaneously, and as a consequence, found their lives transformed for the better, with resulting economic benefits; a Mrs Parker of Napier Street in Fitzroy, a tailoress who relied upon her sight for her living, recalled that Dowie prayed for a 'running cancer' in her eye, and that upon his touch it burst and 'poured' out.[35]

Following these formative years in urban Australia, Dowie and his family travelled to California where he preached and healed in missions along the Pacific Coast. By 1893, Dowie – like many others – travelled to Chicago's World Fair, holding healing meetings in a rickety wooden tabernacle on the Fair's perimeters. Riding the wave of subsequent publicity, in 1896 Dowie founded his own Chicago-based Church, the Christian Catholic Apostolic Church in Zion. In addition to divine healing, what might be called universalism was a key tenet of the Church. While the inclusion of 'Apostolic' in the Church's name reflected his preoccupation with restoring primitive Christianity (including the practice of healing through faith), 'Catholic' indicated Dowie's older commitment (discernable even in his Australian days) to an inclusivist organization that cut across secular markers of class, rank, denomination and even, as we shall see, ethnicity. In Chicago, Dowie opened several healing homes which were heavily patronized by women. He started a periodical, *Leaves of Healing*, which broadcast his healings by imitating techniques of popular broadsheets – eye-grabbing headlines, compelling testimonies and dramatic photographs. Soon, branches of the 'Zionite' Church sprung up around the Midwest and the entire country.

Chicago in the 1890s epitomized the dramatic economic and social changes catalyzed by America's industrializing economy. By 1890, Chicago was the United States' second city, subordinate only to New York in economic power and size.[36] Chicago's unique position lay in its role as broker between Eastern cities and the natural resource-

[34] John Alexander Dowie, *Record of the Fifth Annual Commemoration of the Rev. John Alexander Dowie and Mrs Dowie's Ministry of Healing through Faith in Jesus, Held in the Free Christian Tabernacle, Fitzroy, Melbourne, Lord's Day December 4th and Monday December 5th, 1887: Containing Testimonies from those Healed, and Ebenezer Address* (Melbourne, 1888), 45.

[35] Ibid. 18; W. E. Boardman, *Record of the International Conference on Divine Healing and True Holiness, held at the Agricultural Hall* [St Mary's Agricultural Hall, Islington] (London, 1885), 69.

[36] Thekla Ellen Joiner, *Sin in the City: Chicago and Revivalism, 1880–1920* (Columbia, MO, 2007), 21.

rich Midwest, as exemplified in its meat and lumber factories and steel mills, and its monopoly of railroads linking the east coast to the west.[37] The worldwide divine healing movement flourished particularly in locations such as Chicago, a premier example of the large industrializing cities of the late nineteenth-century Atlantic world. Although an occasion for self-congratulation in accounts 'boosting' the status of such cities, the rapid pace of urban social change in them also caused much anxious social commentary. Worries were voiced in terms of the poor health precipitated by industrialization and urbanization. In North American as well as Australian cities, commentators worried that industrialization undermined modern people's health, resulting in decadent manhood and poor racial health.[38] Neurasthenia was considered a principal nervous ailment linked to industrialization, draining men of their vigour and lowering the birth rate.[39] New occupational diseases abounded, including lung diseases from industrial dust and damaged spines through long hours over new machinery.[40] Housing for the new urban labouring classes was cramped and insanitary. Evangelical Protestant urban reform movements such as the YMCA and the Salvation Army focused on improving public and personal health in a swathe of these Anglo-world cities, including tightening temperance laws and advocating reform in slum housing. Stressing temperance, divine healing advocates also emphasized the intertwined importance of a sanctified soul and a healthy body, especially in environments dubbed 'unhealthy' and morally corrupting, as Chicago was imagined to be.[41]

But in Chicago Dowie also encountered a further phenomenon of urban industrialization, one he had not experienced in Melbourne, and which was unparalleled in any other American city save New York: an extraordinarily polyglot and ethnically heterogeneous working-class population. Chicago's explosive growth had largely been fuelled by migrant labour from outside the United States. By

[37] Dominic A. Pacyga, *Polish Immigrants and Industrial Chicago: Workers on the South Side, 1880–1920* (Columbus, OH, 1991), 24; William Cronon, *Nature's Metropolis: Chicago and the Great West* (New York, 1991)

[38] Clifford Putney, *Muscular Christianity: Manhood and Sports in Protestant America, 1880–1920* (Cambridge, MA, 2001), 4.

[39] Robert Fuller, *Alternative Medicine and American Religious Life* (Oxford, 1989), 63; Curtis, *Faith in the Great Physician*, 104.

[40] Bruce Haley, *The Healthy Body and Victorian Culture* (Cambridge, MA, 1978), 12; Putney, *Muscular Christianity,* 4.

[41] Curtis, *Faith in the Great Physician*, 175.

1890, 78 per cent of the city's population was of foreign, largely European, parentage, with many more immigrants arriving yearly.[42] Germans made up the largest immigrant group, with industrialization and commercialized agriculture in Germany leading to mass immigration to the New World.[43] Over two-thirds of Chicago's working-class German community engaged in traditional crafts such as furniture-making, as well as being absorbed by the city's new factories.[44] Many who flocked to Dowie's new Zion Tabernacle were drawn from precisely this newly arrived working-class constituency eager for social and economic mobility and self-improvement in the New World. Fred Trampsich, a German-born, self-professed 'low man, a drinker, a smoker, a chewer, a filthy man', was one of the thousands who by the early 1890s had heard of this 'wunder doctor at the World Fair'. He visited Zion's Tabernacle, and 'Dr Dowie laid hands on me, my disease passed away … today I can say I'm a healthy man.'[45] Another example was George Wiedeman, a second-generation German immigrant who worked his way to Chicago from New York to become a painter at the World Fair. While there, he heard Dowie preach and was so impressed that he boarded with a family near the Tabernacle so he could regularly attend services.[46] Swedes, Norwegians and Czechs were also well represented among those who attended Dowie's Tabernacle services. For example, Karin Lindquist, a Swedish-born domestic servant in Chicago, read about Zion Tabernacle in the city's newspaper *Chicago Inter Ocean* and attended Dowie's healing services. She was a sufferer from lumbago, and 'what a relief to hear that God could heal us … the first time you [Dowie] laid hands on me, the pain ceased'.[47]

What drew this group of newly industrialized, working-class immigrants to Dowie's church? Divine healing was key to its popularity in late nineteenth-century Chicago. Its rhetoric of bodily perfection undoubtedly resonated with these new urbanites, who frequently experienced their environments as deeply physically degrading. While

[42] Bessie Louise Pierce, *A History of Chicago* (New York, 1937), 22.

[43] John Bodnar, *The Transplanted: A History of Immigrants in Urban America* (Bloomington, IN, 1985), 14.

[44] Hartmut Keil and John B. Jentz, eds, *German Workers in Chicago: A Documentary History of Working-Class Culture from 1850 to World War I* (Urbana, IL, 1988), 1.

[45] *Leaves of Healing* [hereafter: *LH*] 2/45 (4 September 1896), 713.

[46] Zion City, Illinois, Zion-Benton Public Library, Manuscript Collection, *Zion Historical Society* 4th ser., 1971, 'Who's Who in Zion, 1901–1907', 8–10.

[47] *LH* 14/19 (27 February 1904), 578.

factories carried grave occupational dangers, it was estimated that half Chicago's children died before the age of five due to poor sanitation and overcrowding.[48] Dowie's promise of healing resonated with a population that – as in Melbourne – lived in the most squalid areas of the city and were simultaneously unlikely to use the expensive services of private physicians, many of whom were in any case regarded with great mistrust in this still uncertain period of medical advance. Moreover, in the context of a milieu of lively religious debate in the city, the perfectionistic underpinnings of divine healing were far from new to this immigrant constituency. Despite the fact that immigrant Lutheran and Catholic Churches were highly influential, many contemporary Midwestern religious organizations were nonetheless riven with debate over newer and still controversial forms of Evangelical spirituality.[49] This was especially true of Swedish Lutherans, who were still reverberating from the Evangelical awakenings of the 1850s, in which 'Meetingsmen' departed from the set liturgy of the Lutheran national Church of Sweden to focus on the transformative effect of a private, highly pious conversion.[50] Once transplanted to Chicago many of this Evangelical working-class group joined organizations such as the Zionist Church, whose emphasis on bodily perfectionism meshed well with their interest in personal conversion and transformation.[51]

In addition to tapping into a European-American constituency that already – among some sections – favoured an Evangelical, personal spirituality, Dowie's church was also perceived by his followers as highly sympathetic to precisely their own immigrant constituency. Dowie's marvelling appreciation of Chicago's diversity was frequently voiced in the *Leaves* editorials: repeatedly he rejoiced that 'we are living in a city where all the nations of the earth are assembled'.[52] Ethnic heterogeneity came to be interpreted via a biblical grammar that celebrated Christ's impending sovereignty over the entire world;

[48] Pierce, *History of Chicago*, 55; Stanley Buder, *Pullman: An Experiment in Industrial Order and Community Planning, 1880–1930* (Oxford, 1967), 34.
[49] Bodnar, *The Transplanted*, 144–68.
[50] Karl A. Olsson, 'Dwight L. Moody and some Chicago Swedes', in Philip J. Anderson and Dag Blanck, eds, *Swedish-American Life in Chicago: Cultural and Urban Aspects of an Immigrant People* (Uppsala, 1992), 307–26, at 323.
[51] Ibid. 307–23; Lillian Taiz, 'Applying the Devil's Works in a Holy Cause: Working Class Popular Culture and the Salvation Army in the United States, 1879–1900', *Religion and American Culture* 7 (1997), 195–223, at 199.
[52] *LH* 1/39 (5 July 1895), 620.

Dowie and his followers deeply felt the spiritual value of a pan-ethnic fellowship where 'the nations would be assembled together' in glorious foretaste of Christ's coming kingdom.[53] Dowie and this first generation of 'Zionites' saw in this cosmopolitan community a dramatic illustration of the fraternity of Christians, imperfectly realized in the present day but to be fulfilled at the end of times. A much quoted saying of Dowie's was that 'neither race, nor colour, nor education, nor position, nor wealth can be a barrier to fellowship, for our Lord said, "One is your master and all ye are Brethren." There are no aliens among Christians.'[54] Echoing the inclusivist rhetoric of his Melbourne days, Dowie was explicit in his sermons to the Chicago faithful that all were welcome in the church, regardless of ethnicity or nationality. This was especially powerful in a context where working-class immigrants often reported feeling stigmatized by the city's English-speaking Protestant establishment. The Chicago German-language newspaper *Fackel* published a satirical account of a devout working man named 'Zachary Godloving' who was refused entrance to the churches of the city's Anglophone middle and upper classes on account of his heavy accent and shabby clothing.[55] Dowie, by contrast, proclaimed his as a church for the immigrant, no matter how down-and-out, booming from the pulpit of his huge new Tabernacle on Michigan Avenue that

> … while many of us here are called 'foreigners' in this country, if you are a Christian, you are not a foreigner in the Church of God (applause). There is one place you won't be called a stranger or a foreigner, and that will be the Christian Catholic Church … we do not want to hear 'foreigner' applied to brethren or any such nonsense.[56]

In voicing such cosmopolitan sentiments, Dowie was tapping into a vein of thought already existent amongst Chicago's immigrant population. This was the aspiration to transcend ethnic and national differences by joining forces in a new common identity forged in the New World. While Old World resources were skilfully deployed in industrialized settings (language and culture could certainly be powerful identity-building resources), many within immigrant communities

[53] Ibid.

[54] *LH* 1/30 (26 April 1895), 479.

[55] E.g. 'Sunday Observations', *Fackel*, 14 September 1884, in Keil and Jentz, eds, *German Workers in Chicago*, 357.

[56] *LH* 2/17 (31 January 1896), 265.

simultaneously aspired to think of themselves in ways antithetical to narrower ethnic self-identification, seeking the elusive goal of 'Americanizing'. Trade unions of the period were important venues for such projects of ethnic cosmopolitanism; one Lithuanian packinghouse worker commented in 1904 that joining the union was 'giving me [a chance] to enjoy life like an American … it is combining all the nationalities, the night I joined the Cattle Butchers' Union, I was led into the room by a Negro member, with me were Bohemians, Germans, Poles, and the President is an Irishman who spoke to us in English'.[57] Echoing the internationalism of trade unions, the Christian Catholic Apostolic Church in Zion offered its polyglot membership a platform for pan-ethnic fellowship, while simultaneously catering to cherished ethnic and linguistic communal identities. Services were regularly translated into multiple languages, and special missions were held for different nationality groups in areas of the city where they lived.[58] *Leaves of Healing* was produced in a German version by 1895.[59] Soon editions of *Leaves* in Swedish, Norwegian, Dutch and French were appearing, translated by devout members in their own time and without charge.[60]

The church's vision of a reformed industrial society, characterized by good health, temperance and the harmonious coexistence of nationalities, culminated in the purchase in 1900 of land forty miles north of Chicago. Here Dowie and church members founded Zion City, a town envisioned by adherents as a new Jerusalem, which at its height in 1904 had six thousand residents.[61] Many Zionists – the press scathingly called them 'Dowieites' – were Northern European first- and second-generation immigrants from Chicago, while some relocated to Zion from rural states such as Colorado, Nebraska and Minnesota. All were attracted by Zion's utopian vision of an ideal environment for immigrant working people, prizing godliness, health and the promise of non-discrimination on the basis of nationality or language. To offer residents sustainable employment, Dowie imported a lace factory piece by piece from England and fifty skilled

57 James R. Barrett, *Work and Community in the Jungle: Chicago's Packinghouse Workers, 1894–1922* (Urbana, IL, 1987), 141.
58 *LH* 4/27 (30 April 1898), 522, 536.
59 *LH* 2/4 (1 November 1895), 57.
60 *LH* 4/26 (21 April 1900), 820–2.
61 *Zion Banner*, 3 May 1904, no page number available.

workers from Nottingham.[62] Unions were banned, but eight-hour working days were mandated and working conditions tightly regulated: Dowie's 'aim [was] a population of godly people who shall work together for something more than dollars'.[63] Dowie employed a civil engineer who, inspired by Ebenezer Howard's Garden City movement, located industry at Zion's periphery, ensuring a green, tranquil centre with boulevards and leafy avenues.[64] Residential lots were large, and made no discrimination in size between poorer and wealthier areas. Doctors, chemists, alcohol, tobacco and gambling were all prohibited.

Its organizers and residents made much of Zion City's cosmopolitanism, a sign of the restoration of the kingdom of God where the 'nations' mingled freely and harmoniously. Five years after the city's founding, Dowie boasted that 'Zion City, ethnologically, is a miniature representation of the world … the citizens of our city represent over 80 nationalities.'[65] The church was especially proud of the two hundred-strong community of African-Americans in Zion City, identifying blacks with the biblical 'race of Ethiopians' mentioned in Psalm 68. Zion City's incorporation of 'Ethiopians' was therefore lauded in church accounts as a foretaste of Christian triumph: 'there is victory all along the line. Prophecy is being fulfilled. Ethiopia is "hastening to stretch out her hands unto God."'[66] The view that racial difference should be subordinate to Christian unity led Dowie to controversially argue for 'miscegenation', a bio-spiritual discipline that – like divine healing – rehabilitated degenerate bodies.[67] And if Zion City was a home for the world's races, then Dowie was equally adamant that Zionist teachings should fan out across the world and draw all of humanity into its orbit. In this spirit, after 1900, the Church sent missionaries to Australia, New Zealand, China, Japan and (in 1904) the Transvaal, in the territory that would be known as South Africa, newly at peace after the devastating three-year war between Britain and the two independent Boer Republics. Politically and economically speaking, black Africans were the principal casualties of the war's after-effects, and it was precisely to this marginalized

[62] Jan Jansen, *Battle for the Garden City* (Green Bay, WI, 2011), 63.
[63] *LH* 8/13 (19 January 1901), 408.
[64] Jansen, *Garden City*, 73–5.
[65] *LH* 17/5 (24 May 1905), 262.
[66] Ibid. 263.
[67] *Zion Banner*, 1 September 1905, no page number available.

constituency that Zionism would come to speak to most powerfully in the following decades.

Zionism in South Africa

By the end of the nineteenth century, the worldwide dissemination of *Leaves of Healing* meant that Dowie's Church already had a vibrant following amongst a small community of whites – both Boers and Britons - in South Africa. In 1904, two Midwestern missionaries from Zion City – a married couple, Daniel and Emma Bryant – arrived in Johannesburg, South Africa, recently ordained evangelist and elder (the latter the highest rank a woman could hold).[68] Commissioned by Dowie to extend divine healing to the region's African population, the Bryants made contact with two local white members of Dowie's Church already engaged in missionary work with black communities: Pieter le Roux, a former Dutch Reformed cleric, and Edgar Mahon, an ex-Salvation Army captain. Le Roux was the former missionary to the Zulu for the Dutch Reformed Church in the Transvaal district of Wakkerstroom, a region dominated by stock farming, maize and tobacco production. Despite the Evangelical leanings of the Dutch Reformed Church in this period, and the fact that some in its upper echelons practised divine healing (including the highly respected theologian and minister Andrew Murray),[69] its officials had 'serious objections' to Le Roux disseminating these teachings amongst Africans.[70] They worried that divine healing would appeal primarily as an efficacious technology, rather than as part and parcel of the Christian gospel, thereby 'distracting [Africans'] attention from more essential things'.[71] But Le Roux was unable to comply with a racial demarcation of divine healing's blessings. As one who could 'personally bear witness of this 'happy tiding' he avowed he could not 'remain silent about this any longer'.[72] In 1903, Le Roux joined Dowie's Church, ordained by Dowie – via postal

[68] Zion City, Illinois, Christ Community Church Archives [hereafter: CCC], John Dowie to Daniel Bryant, 'General Instructions Given to Overseer Daniel Bryant', 5 November 1903, 12.

[69] Johann Du Plessis, *The Life of Andrew Murray in South Africa* (London, 1920), 230–1.

[70] Johannesburg, Apostolic Faith Mission Archives [hereafter: AFM], Pieter Le Roux Correspondence, Pieter Le Roux to Revs Kriel, Marais, Rossouw, Meiring and Bosman, 12 November 1898.

[71] Ibid., Andrew Murray to Pieter Le Roux, 29 November 1898.

[72] Ibid., Pieter Le Roux to Andrew Murray, 12 November 1898.

communication – as a Zion missionary to his black former Dutch Reformed congregants. Mahon was another local white figure who found that established Protestant Churches of the day would not support divine healing, particularly amongst Africans. The Irish Mahon had joined the Salvation Army in the working-class suburb of Fordsburg in early gold-rush Johannesburg, and as an adult became a Salvationist missionary.[73] During a bout of lung illness, Mahon read Dowie's literature and, greatly inspired, began to teach divine healing to the Africans to whom he was ministering. The local Salvation Army, however, opposed this (perhaps also due to a particular dislike of Dowie himself, who had since fallen out with international Army leadership),[74] leading to Mahon's resignation. Mahon became an independent missionary in the Orange Free State, where he and his family were housed upon the farms of sympathetic Evangelicals,[75] charged with preaching to Africans on the surrounding farms, as well as free to practise supplicating God through prayer for bodily healing.[76]

In South Africa, as in the United States, Zion's cosmopolitan ethos greatly appealed to both whites and blacks. Individuals such as Le Roux and Mahon were part of a group of several hundred white members of Dowie's Church in early twentieth-century South Africa. Divine healing appears to have particularly taken off during the South African War; copies of *Leaves* were disseminated amongst both Boer and British soldiers (even reaching as far as Boer POW camps in Ceylon and India), and its tenets were preached in evangelistic meetings in camps, hospitals and mess rooms.[77] While a gospel of physical uplift undoubtedly resonated during difficult war-time conditions, amidst the fierce conflict between the two white 'races', the Church's purposively internationalist message also came to the fore. Newly converted Zionists asserted that it was their duty to assert kinship with enemy combatants. John Taylor, a clerk in a law firm in Pietermaritzburg, enlisted as a military chaplain.[78] His motive: 'as Gospel messenger, Boer and British were all alike to me'.[79] Unlike Taylor,

[73] W. F. P. Burton, *When God Makes a Missionary* (London, 1936).
[74] James Opp, *Lord for the Body: Religion, Medicine and Protestant Faith Healing in Canada, 1880–1930* (London, 2005), 89.
[75] E. B. Hawkins, *The Story of Harrismith* (Harrismith, 1982), 99.
[76] Burton, *When God Makes a Missionary*, 25–6.
[77] *LH* 19/14 (6 October 1906), 432.
[78] *Kirkwell Arcadian*, 27 June 1903, no page number available.
[79] *LH* 11/20 (6 September 1902), 673–6.

most male Zionist sympathizers almost certainly fought. But even these were keen to stress, at least rhetorically, that they avoided killing Boer brethren. One soldier reported to *Leaves* that 'I had my rifle levelled at the head of a Boer, when something said to me, "If you pull the trigger, he is a dead man" … I at once cocked my rifle in the air.'[80] Another soldierly correspondent attributed his terrible injury to taking up arms against his Dutch kin: 'I [saw] that war was the Devil's work, and that God never intended me to take up arms to shoot my brother.'[81] In the aftermath of the war, 'racial' reconciliation between Boers and Britons, and the project of forging a new white South Africanism, was pursued by politicians as well as adopted by many Protestant Churches. Once again, Dowie's cosmopolitanism resonated. By 1904, the Zionist Tabernacle on Bree Street in Johannesburg was regularly packed with congregations of several hundred,[82] and one member proudly proclaimed 'our church in Johannesburg [is] one half Boer and one half Briton'.[83] Some Zionists even extended this cosmopolitan rhetoric – unusually for the day – to black congregants. The view of one Mrs Ward was that 'we love British and Boer and Kaffir alike, for we have all one Father, one Savior and one Guide'.[84]

Working alongside Le Roux and Mahon, the Bryants made rapid inroads into rural black communities in the Transvaal and the Orange Free State, baptizing thousands at open-air services. White emissaries of Zion relied heavily upon a network of talented African evangelists, including individuals such as Daniel Nkonyane and Elijah Lutango, to whom Le Roux and Mahon respectively had ministered in their former denominations, and who became the main engines of this evangelistic drive, working as interpreters as well as preaching and laying hands on converts in their own right.[85] Unusually for the period, these white and black proselytizers worked together in disseminating Zionist's divine healing teachings across farm lands. Yet the Zionists' vision of racial fraternity – discernable in church members' determination to transcend divisions between Boer and Briton as much as in this network of white and black evangelists – was a

[80] Ibid.
[81] *LH* 18/8 (18 November 1905), no page number available.
[82] *LH* 17/14 (29 July 1905), 398.
[83] *Zion City News*, 17 April 1908, no page number available
[84] *LH* 12/20 (7 March 1903), 618.
[85] Cabrita, 'People of Adam', 581.

very distant ideal in turn-of-the-century Transvaal and the Orange Free State. In previous decades, sharecropping, and its rich profits for talented African farmers, had produced an upwardly mobile class who positioned themselves as a new black elite, prizing individual landownership and their progressive Christian faith, and increasingly detached from chiefly authority.[86] Rather than seeing themselves as subjects of ethnically and linguistically determined polities, this Christian African elite appealed to the promises of the British Empire, optimistically viewing themselves members of a colour-blind worldwide federation that promised full rights and equal standing to all who embraced its progressive values and came to consider themselves civilized men.[87] Added to this heady rhetoric of imperial citizenship, the mission societies' message of Christ's redeeming death for all – regardless of race – was also appropriated by African Christians as a platform for proclaiming racial, social and economic equality.[88]

However, in the aftermath of the South African War in 1902, a shifting political and economic mood rapidly dissipated black aspirations; South Africa's non-white population was increasingly viewed merely as cheap labour for white production and agriculture. Far from ushering in the hoped for race-blind polity, imperial rule meant increased strictures upon black mobility, as Britain sought strategic compromises with disaffected Boers, leading to the creation of a new South Africa aligned with white interests.[89] The explosive growth of Johannesburg – now the gold metropolis of the world – necessitated vast amounts of labour, meaning that government policy tried to dislodge the wealthy African peasantry from farming into the mines. Independent African accumulation in the rural areas was now frowned upon as an obstacle to white industry. Denied land of their own, Africans were permitted to squat upon farmers' land. In return, they worked the farmer's land for several months annually, and paid him rent. It was a system designed to squeeze maximum labour out of black tenants for labour-hungry white farmers.

[86] Campbell, *Songs of Zion*, 161; Tim Keegan, *Facing the Storm: Portraits of Black Lives in Rural South Africa* (Johannesburg, 1988), 133.

[87] Tim Couzens, *The New African: A Study of the Life and Work of H. I. E. Dhlomo* (Johannesburg, 1985).

[88] Richard Elphick, *The Equality of Believers: Protestant Missionaries and the Racial Politics of South Africa* (Charlottesville, VA, 2012).

[89] Saul Dubow, 'Colonial Nationalism, the Milner Kindergarten and the rise of South Africanism, 1902–1910', *History Workshop Journal* 43 (1997), 53–85.

Tenants considered idle were ejected.[90] One recent Zionist convert from Wakkerstroom in the Transvaal, Muneli Ngobese, commented that 'our sorrow is that we live on land rented from the white man. We pay him rent but we have little peace.'[91] Underpinning this economic exploitation was a racial ideology that cast Africans as intrinsically inferior and best suited to manual work. African self-improvement was discouraged. Government officials and white farmers both disapproved of 'book learning' for Africans, believing industrial education of more use.[92] Finally, in the first decade of the twentieth century, both Protestant and Catholic Churches retreated from their former promise of equality for all believers. African ordinations slowed to a trickle, and missionaries increasingly echoed the racist views of politicians, industrialists and agriculturalists.[93] Many responded by breaking away from mission-led denominations and forming independent organizations under black leadership – some linked to the North American African Methodist Episcopal Church – and widely dubbed 'Ethiopian' churches for their emphasis on black autonomy from white rule.[94] The eastern Transvaal was the site of extensive Methodist activity, and thus one of the most important independent Churches of this area was a former congregant Joel Msimang's Independent Methodist Church. New Ethiopian churches such as Msimang's retreated from the former rhetoric of multi-racial fellowship, instead – in this era of dashed hopes in racial inclusivity – investing in notions of black pride and self-reliance, exemplified by the term 'Ethiopian'.[95]

But not all Christian Africans in areas such as these turned away from the older dream of cosmopolitanism; in an era of increasing restriction of African aspiration, Zion's inclusivist ethos was all the more welcomed by many blacks in the Transvaal and Orange Free State. Mahon's assistant, Elijah Lutango, observed that prior to the Christian Catholic Apostolic Church in Zion's arrival, the 'Gospel was preached and people received it, but there was no fellowship between the whites and the blacks … they were never one in the love

[90] Pretoria, South African National Archives [hereafter: SAB], LWM 30, Native Affairs Department (NAD) to Native Commissioner, Wakkerstroom, 29 August 1903.
[91] *LH* 18/11 (30 December 1905), no page number available.
[92] SAB, LWM 61, Native Commissioner SE Division to Secretary for Native Affairs, 3 May 1904.
[93] Elphick, *Equality of Believers*.
[94] Campbell, *Songs of Zion*, 66, 103.
[95] Ibid. 66.

of the Lord'.[96] But in Dowie's Zion, he found a remarkably different 'brotherly love' – this was 'the True Love which does not separate brethren because of difference in the colour of their skins'.[97] The practical implications of this cosmopolitan theology – divine healing knit humanity together – were profound; throughout the Transvaal and Orange Free State, African Zionist preachers worked in remarkably collaborative, egalitarian relationships with their white superiors. Unlike other white-led mission organizations which were increasingly dragging their foot over African ordination in this decade, the Zionist Church followed a policy that 'natives should be ordained to the office of deacon and evangelist (the highest rank outside of Zion City)'.[98] And while this was certainly an aspiration shared by the Americans Dowie and Bryant, it also seems to have been an opinion shared by local white Zionists, especially Mahon, who lamented the style of his Dutch Reformed neighbours who had 'the Bible in one hand, the whip in the other, the whip being used in preference to the Bible'. Instead, Mahon proclaimed that his own practice was to eschew 'the whip, and to actually shake hands with the natives and sit at meals with them'.[99] Evidence suggests that he did indeed fraternize with black colleagues in a manner largely unprecedented in missionary circles of the period. As late as 1915, his practice was to spend long evenings at his own home with his closest African co-workers: 'Deacons Mabula, Lutango and Ndebele called at our home and spent the evening with us. We spoke of things pertaining to the Kingdom, sang some hymns and just before parting about midnight spent a short season in prayer.'[100] A black stable boy fell ill at the Zionist headquarters outside of Harrismith run by Mahon and 'was prayed for just as earnestly and tenderly as would any of the white workers have been … for we are all one family in the Lord'.[101]

Admittedly, this cosmopolitan ethos was limited in its longevity. White South African membership fell sharply after Dowie's death in 1907 and the near-collapse of the church in Zion City. Most white Zionists migrated under the leadership of Pieter Le Roux to the

96 *LH* 18/4 (14 October 1905), 369.

97 Sundkler, *Zulu Zion*, 40.

98 'Report of Native Workers' Conference', *Zion City Independent*, 15 July 1910, no page number available.

99 *Zion City News*, 11 February 1910, no page number available.

100 *Zulu and Basutoland Missionary* 3/2 (December 1915), 7.

101 Ibid. 1/7 (May 1914), 3.

newly-formed Pentecostal Apostolic Faith Mission, which rapidly retreated from Dowie's cosmopolitan vision and had soon entrenched racial segregation into its Church life.[102] Yet there were other attractions of Zion for its African constituency. The self-improving disciplines of Zionism – forged amidst the newly industrialized cities of Melbourne and Chicago – meshed surprisingly well with this dispossessed group of African peasantry.[103] In a context in which Africans were increasingly encouraged by the white administration to view themselves as members of confined ethnic political units, the Zionist Church cut across many of the constraining solidarities the government was trying to inculcate amongst its black subjects. For example, Dowie's Church forbade the consumption of both alcohol and tobacco. But the communal brewing of beer and its consumption undergirded hierarchical relationships between chiefs and subjects, and husbands and wives, and the government was keen to uphold this, partly to enshrine cultural difference and thereby to diminish Africans' claims to equality with whites. But one woman who felt moved by Zionist teachings in this period decided to cease brewing for her husband, even though she would 'be considered to have lost love for [him]'. But the woman 'remembered the words of Jesus – "Who loveth Father and Mother more than me is not worthy of me" – and folded her hands'.[104] And if divine healing's bodily disciplines set Africans at odds with the social hierarchies of traditional society, it also engendered conflict with their white masters. Formerly employers had paid African workers in tobacco, now Zion labourers objected on the grounds of divine healing's ban on smoking: 'the master would threaten them, but "no" was the answer … [they] used to be slaves of drink and tobacco. Glory to God.'[105] Farmers increasingly objected to Zion preachers on their farms, complaining that tenants absconded from work to attend church.[106] Zion's stance on relations between the races further alienated the white settler community from the Church, leading local Harrismith farmers to treat Mahon and his family with contempt for 'lowering the prestige of the white race'.[107]

[102] Cabrita, *Empire of Healing*.
[103] *Zion City News*, 19 November 1909, no page number available.
[104] *Zion City News*, 22 October 1909, no page number available.
[105] Sundkler, *Zulu Zion*, 44.
[106] SAB, LWM 25, Native Commissioner Volksrust to Native Commissioner SE Division, 8 February 1904.
[107] Burton, *When God Makes a Missionary*, 48.

But it was the promise of healing that became the most popular aspect of Zion's work in these areas.[108] On the one hand, as much of the existing scholarship has argued, divine healing undoubtedly resonated with Nguni cosmologies in which Africans viewed sickness and health as being ultimately spiritual matters, not physiological predicaments. Popular thought held that while some illnesses stemmed from natural causes, certain bodily and societal afflictions resulted from spiritual causes.[109] The nefarious interventions of witches could precipitate these misfortunes; ancestors, too, could visit their displeasure upon the living.[110] It is hardly surprising, then, that the well-documented increasing frequency of accusations and suspicions of witchcraft in this period served as a barometer for the social and economic dislocation experienced by the region's Africans. But while Zionism's identification of sickness and health as spiritual matters clearly provided a powerful parallel, these self-consciously modernizing Africans did not prize divine healing primarily for its affirmation of indigenous healing therapies. Instead, it was understood as a technique of modernizing self-improvement, part of the broader repertoire of African progressiveness and optimism that characterized this period. For all Zion's resonance with indigenous health theories, adherents knew its bodily disciplines were strictly exclusive: all faith must be placed in the Judaeo-Christian God alone. This, therefore, was a spiritual discipline that detached Africans from local loyalties, setting them on an entirely different trajectory to one mapped out by indigenous concerns. A Zionist evangelist in the Transvaal 'gathered all the people together and explained the truths of Zion'. Immediately they 'took down all their medicine charms as a token from that day on they were going to live for God alone'.[111] Zionist evangelist Fred Luthuli preached the necessity of renouncing local therapies for divine healing's superior cures: 'a woman who had been ill for a long time was treated by the native doctor. When I came to her the woman told me that the doctor could not heal her, and we threw her medicine out.'[112] Whatever the deeply felt continuities with existing cosmologies, conversion to Zionism was cast – by both

[108] *LH* 15/25 (8 October 1904), 856, 858, 860, 861.

[109] Karen Flint, *Healing Traditions: African Medicine, Cultural Exchange and Competition in South Africa, 1820–1948* (Athens, OH, 2008), 65.

[110] Ibid. 37–66.

[111] *Zion City News*, 19 November 1909, no page number available.

[112] *LH* 18/11 (30 December 1905), no page number available.

Zionist preachers and ordinary members – as a decisive break with older religious systems.

The progressive discipline of divine healing promised working men and women uplift and self-perfection in all areas of their lives. Thus Zion also stood for education and schooling for all, cast by Dowie as an essential aspect of the self-improvement of working people, both in the Midwest amongst industrialized Europeans and amongst labouring Africans in the Transvaal and Orange Free State. And while white opinion was highly unsympathetic to education for Africans,[113] considering it supplied them with ideas above their status, Dowie instructed Bryant to 'embrace every opportunity of teaching these poor people to read and write'.[114] By 1905, there were seven Zion schools in the Transvaal, with seventy-six pupils, located on sympathetic farmers' land, founded by sharecropping families who had converted to the Church.[115] In contrast to the government's views on the desirability of manual training rather than subversive 'book learning', no industrial skills were taught by Zionist schools, which instead focused on reading, writing and arithmetic.[116] Black Zionists celebrated any prospect of progress. This was the opinion of one Zionist parent: 'we grew up in the dark … we had no school and no teaching. But we do not want our children to be the same.'[117]

Finally, in a period when African aspirations to private land ownership – a key marker of modernizing self-improvement and detachment from obligations to chiefs and other traditional leaders – were disappointed, the vision of 'Zion City' – a physical sanctuary where Zionist disciplines could be practised unmolested – resonated profoundly with black converts. Dowie had founded Zion City as a healthy haven from Chicago's urban corruption. New African converts similarly sought land to pursue their new identity as people of Zion, renouncing former societal obligations and seeking to escape racist strictures. Dowie's local representative Pieter Le Roux recognized that 'the peoples' one desire is to have a Zion City in their own

[113] *Rand Daily Mail*, 16 December 1908; Bloemfontein, Free State Provincial Archives [hereafter: VAB], ORC 332, South African Native Affairs Commission, 1903–1905, vol. 4, Evidence of Hugh Gunn (Director of Education in Orange River Colony).
[114] CCC, Dowie to Bryant, 18.
[115] *LH* 18/11 (30 December 1905), no page number available.
[116] VAB, NdAB 1, Lieutenant Commander Orange River Colony to Adviser for Native Affairs, Bloemfontein, 10 June 1905.
[117] Ibid.

country, where they can live and serve God in peace'.[118] In 1903, Le Roux leased land and applied to officials to build a church and school and settle fifty families 'for the spread of Christianity' upon it.[119] Zionist evangelist and wealthy peasant farmer Daniel Nkonyane aspired to build a Zion church and school upon his 300 acres of land.[120] There were a 'good few' Zion people living upon Nkonyane's farm, and he boasted that 'everybody in the area comes to church upon my land'.[121] In rural South Africa, as much as in the urban Midwest, working people drew upon Zionist practices in their pursuit of economic independence and social autonomy.

Conclusion

What, then, can be concluded from this brief comparative history of the origins of a Protestant divine healing movement in Illinois, and its successful transmission to the farmlands of South Africa, over a century ago? This article has sought to highlight that when the two phenomena are compared, important features emerge. Conversely, when the purely indigenous nature of Zionism is stressed – or, as is more usual, its seamless 'translation' into an African context – these aspects are invisible. This conclusion will make three brief points about the value of this comparative approach, and close by reflecting on its broader significance for scholarly histories of Christianity in sub-Saharan Africa as well as beyond.

In both the Midwest and rural South Africa, Zionism can only be understood as a product of the seismic social changes that gripped the globe in this period. Technological advances catalysed the industrialization of Chicago alongside the large-scale commercial mining of gold in Johannesburg. In both contexts, turbulent social change was triggered by these processes of mechanization and industrialization; the demand for cheap, plentiful labour produced the large immigrant European ethnic enclaves of working-class Chicago and also dislodged Africans from their territorial inheritances as gold-hungry mine owners attempted to co-opt cheap labour. Far from Zionism in South Africa being merely a unique product of local conditions – black resistance to colonialism and apartheid, for example – we see

118 *LH* 18/11 (30 December 1905), no page number available.

119 SAB, SNA 144, Le Roux to Sub-Native Commissioner, Wakkerstroom, 29 June 1903.

120 *LH* 18/11 (30 December 1905), no page number available.

121 Ibid.

instead that the transatlantic Zionist movement was a response to the economic and social changes wrought by industrialization, as well as part of the rich repertoire of responses concocted by urban residents in this period.

In both contexts, Zionism emerged in environments – North American and Southern African – in which bodily health was overlain with spiritual meaning. While South African Zionists' interest in healing is often cast as an extension of local healing therapies, in fact, industrializing communities on both sides of the Atlantic were prone to interpreting health and sickness in moral terms, notwithstanding important differences in their interpretations. In nineteenth-century Chicago, as in Melbourne, urban disorder was understood as a moral predicament that resulted in diseased and degenerate bodies; in the farmlands of Transvaal, disease was a symptom of the social, economic and political insecurity that gripped dispossessed agrarian African communities. Zionism was a way to address the social and spiritual implications of ill health that gained potency in an unusually turbulent social period across much of the world. It is necessary to historicize robustly Africans' interest in Protestant healing therapies in this period, rather than simplistically ascribing them to supposedly innate cultural predispositions on the part of African Christians to supernatural interpretations of health and sickness.

Finally, a comparative study of Zionism illuminates the popular saliency of cosmopolitan thought in South Africa. While political parties such as the African National Congress have traditionally been viewed as the main vehicles for multiracial thought, in fact, a whole swathe of cosmopolitan practices existed beneath the radar of formal political participation. Yet Zionism has largely been identified as part of a nativist, racially exclusive strand within South African social history, an insular response by besieged African communities of retreat from the broader world, and disengagement from political involvement. But a transnational lens – analysing Zionism in South Africa alongside its precursors and companions in the USA and in Australia – reveals that immigrant communities in industrializing Chicago, at the bottom of the economic ladder and socially ostracized, as well as black small-scale farmers of the Transvaal dislodged by the demands of Johannesburg, were all searching for new languages with which to assert claims as old certainties vanished. For both communities, we see the value of Zionism's cosmopolitan claim that all humanity found fraternity in a single kingdom of God. And although the local multiracialism of the movement in South African soon fractured, Zion's internationalism was carried forward in other ways. Black South Africans maintained contact via correspondence with white American Zionists throughout the twentieth century (often leaning on American brethren for strategic contacts during an era when the apartheid government was deeply suspicious of independent black churches). And in the present day, over forty missionaries commissioned by the descendent of Dowie's original church in Zion City work as theological educators amongst Zionist Churches throughout Southern Africa, offering affordable opportunities for education to black ministers hungry for the legitimacy bestowed by a diploma.[122]

In closing, then, while the above discussion has argued for the specific value of this approach for Zionism in South Africa, there are broader implications for our historical understanding of Christianity in Africa and beyond. Protestantism in Africa was not insulated from broader developments in the history of Christianity. We cannot, therefore, lean too much upon categories such as 'African', 'culture' and 'tradition' in understanding African religious change in the modern period, or at any other time. While translation is an important theme to consider, in the study of Christianity in Africa the term has often become shorthand for imprecise emphases on the 'Africanness' of Christianity as an explanatory device. The challenge now for historians of Christianity in Africa is to find better ways to describe modern Africans' experience of the modern world, as well as to account for their lively dreams of horizons far beyond their immediate environments.

[122] Cabrita, *Empire of Healing*, ch. 8.